W9-BHJ-553

Marriages and Families

Marriages and Families

Second Edition

Constance L. Shehan
The University of Florida

Boston   New York   San Francisco
Mexico City   Montreal   Toronto   London   Madrid   Munich   Paris
Hong Kong   Singapore   Tokyo   Cape Town   Sydney

Editor in Chief: Karen Hanson
Series Editor: Jeff Lasser
Senior Development Editor: Ellen Darion
Editorial Assistant: Andrea Christie
Marketing Manager: Krista Groshong
Composition Buyer: Linda Cox
Manufacturing Buyer: Megan Cochran
Editorial-Production Administrator: Karen Mason
Designer and Electronic Composition: Karen Mason
Editorial-Production Service: Colophon
Photo Researcher: Laurie Frankenthaler
Cover Administrator: Linda Knowles

For related titles and support materials, visit our online catalog at
www.ablongman.com

Copyright © 2003, 1997 by Pearson Education, Inc.

All rights reserved. No part of the material protected by this copyright notice may be
reproduced or utilized in any form or by any means, electronic or mechanical, including
photocopying, recording, or by any information storage and retrieval system, without
written permission from the copyright owner.

To obtain permission(s) to use material from this work, please submit a written request to
Allyn and Bacon, Permissions Department, 75 Arlington Street, Boston, MA 02116 or fax
your request to 617-848-7320.

Between the time Website information is gathered and then published, it is not unusual for
some sites to have closed. Also, the transcription of URLs can result in unintended typo-
graphical errors. The publisher would appreciate notification where these errors occur so
that they may be corrected in subsequent editions.

Library of Congress Cataloging-in-Publication Data
Shehan, Constance L.
     Marriages and families / Constance L. Shehan.--2nd ed.
          p. cm.
     Includes bibliographical references and index.
     ISBN 0-205-33436-9 (alk. paper)
       1. Family--United States.   2. Marriage--United States.   3. Interpersonal relations--
United States.   4. Sex role--United States.   I. Title.

HQ536 .S482 2002
306.8'0973--dc21

                                                                    2002019465

Printed in the United States of America

10 9 8 7 6 5 4 3 2 1   VHP   07 06 05 04 03 02

See photo and permissions credits on page 585, which constitutes a continuation of the
copyright page.

This book is dedicated to my father,

GEORGE E. SHEHAN (1923–2000)

Devoted son and brother,
honored war veteran,
cherished husband and father,
skilled craftsman and
successful business owner, and
generous friend.

Brief Contents

Contents

PART THREE   DYNAMICS OF INTIMATE RELATIONSHIPS

PART FOUR   PARENTS AND CHILDREN

PART FIVE   FAMILY CHALLENGES

Boxed Features

Around the World

Preface

*I*t is quite obvious, even to casual observers of contemporary life, that Americans are fascinated by intimate relationships. Family values have taken center stage in our national debates, and political pundits predict the demise of the American family. Our popular culture is filled with stories about the challenges of courtship and marriage; the intense longing many people have to be parents and the lengths to which they will go to bring children into their lives; and the devastation brought by divorce. Situation comedies revolving around family life and radio and television talk shows focusing on the steamier and seamier sides of intimate relationships are among the top-rated programs in our electronic media. Intimate relationships are, quite literally, near and dear to our hearts. Thus, it's not surprising that most of us find a great deal of interest in studying family life, in whatever form it takes.

While intimate relationships are a familiar subject to us all, there is a great deal of information about this subject that is unfamiliar or that runs counter to our common beliefs. Much of our knowledge about marriage and families is drawn from our own personal experiences, which may or may not be reflective of the majority of persons in our society. In your Marriages and Families course, you will learn about—and from—the social scientific studies conducted by sociologists, psychologists, demographers, and economists, among others. To broaden your understanding of the wide diversity of ways in which we organize our daily family lives, this book draws on the findings of hundreds of studies conducted each year. This research allows you to see the extent to which your own experiences with intimate relationships does—or does not—mirror that of the broader society.

The research highlighted in this text addresses a wide range of contemporary family issues, from teen sexuality and pregnancy, to high-tech treatments for infertility and international adoption; from dowries and bride prices to debutante balls; from interfaith marriages to same-sex couples. As you read this text, keep in mind that intimate relationships have been undergoing major transformations in form and function over the past 50 years. It is not my intention to endorse any particular life style or living arrangement. Instead, I hope to make you aware of the diversity and the vitality of American families.

This book has been inspired and informed by the work of contemporary scholars in sociology, psychology, child and family development, economics, and women's studies. One particularly lucid presentation of this perspective is found in Thorne and Yalom's 1992 edition of *Rethinking the Family.* I have tried to follow the basic beliefs about families found in that book as I conceptualized and created this book.

One basic principle of this text is that there are many different forms of intimate relationships beyond the traditional, heterosexual, two-parent family. Families include single-parent families headed by women or men; childfree unions involving heterosexual or homosexual partners; merged households of children and adults that follow divorce; and other forms of intimate relationships. Following this principle, I argue that family *form* is less important than family *function*—that is, the needs that are met by intimate relationships are more significant to individual lives than is the shape or appearance of one's household composition. I must confess, however, that when writing I often found it difficult to reconcile the conventional language used to describe living arrangements and intimate relationships with the principle that all forms of families—legal or not, heterosexual or not—should be included in this text. As an author I frequently considered whether to use the phrase *intimate relationships* or *marriages and families.* In many cases I was constrained by the research literature, which focused only on conventional marriage relationships or traditional family roles. Nonetheless, I wish to emphasize here that the term *marriages and families* encompasses for me the full range of intimate relationships and living arrangements.

I also understand that, contrary to the perspectives of many who have written similar books, marriages and families (or any intimate relationships) are not always harmonious units characterized by equality and consensus. Individuals in intimate relationships and families have different needs and interests, rights and privileges, and duties and responsibilities that derive from different experiences. Often these different experiences reflect one's sex, age, or generation, and also differ by race, ethnicity, and social class. Class, ethnicity, and skin color are, like gender, master statuses that transcend institutional boundaries and shape every aspect of a person's life. I have tried to include, whenever possible, research that describes or discusses the influences the race and class stratification systems on living arrangements and intimate relationships.

It is also my view, and this point is developed more fully in Chapter 1, that a realistic view of marriage and family life, based on sound scholarship and research, is much more valuable than a rosy, idealistic view. In my opinion, too many textbooks on marriage and families offer too much advice about what *should be,* and thereby neglect a realistic view of *what is.* Marriage, for example, *should be* based on a relationship of love, friendship, trust, open communication, and so on—and perhaps a few ideal marriages can be completely described by these traits. Most, however, cannot be. Most marriages include conflicts of interest, disagreements, power struggles, and unhappy periods when one or both partners may seriously wonder whether the marriage should continue. These aspects of marriage must be recognized and understood. Idealism is an important part of the human experience, and realism is necessary if one is to deal effectively with everyday matters.

Features of this Text

- Reflects the most **up-to-date and reliable information** and ideas available from **research studies and scholarly thinking.**

- Looks at the most **important questions** that leading marriage and family scholars and professionals are trying to answer today.

- Focuses more on **family function**—that is, the needs that are met by various forms of intimate relationships—than on the particular form a family takes, as emphasized in Chapter 5, "Making a Commitment: Legal Marriage, Heterosexual Cohabitation, and Homosexual Partnerships."

- Helps students see that **family diversity and change** are often a response to—not the cause of—wider social change.

- Examines the significant and ongoing role of **gender** in almost every aspect of marriage and family life, including dating, mate selection, sexual activity, husband–wife relations, and parenting.

NEW TO THIS EDITION

ALL NEW CHAPTER PEDAGOGY includes:

KEY QUESTIONS

The chapter opening list looks at the most important research issues that leading marriage and family scholars and professionals are trying to answer today.

Key Questions

1 Is there too much medical intervention in childbirth?

2 What are the ethical issues involved in the use of assisted reproduction?

3 Why has there been so little research into male contraception?

4 What are the long-term consequences of childlessness for couples, particularly as they reach old age?

5 Does transracial adoption harm children's development of cultural identity?

NEW INTRODUCTORY CHAPTER 1 *provides students with an engaging, high-interest look at key topics they will be covering in more detail later.*

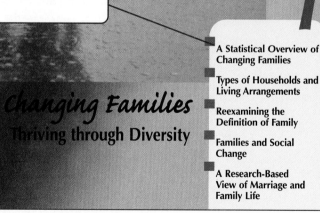

1

Changing Families
Thriving through Diversity

- A Statistical Overview of Changing Families
- Types of Households and Living Arrangements
- Reexamining the Definition of Family
- Families and Social Change
- A Research-Based View of Marriage and Family Life

A NEW DISCUSSION OF FAMILY SYSTEMS THEORY, *including the Hill and McCubbin/Patterson models of family stress, has been added to Chapter 2, "Knowledge about Marriages, Families, and Intimate Relationships."*

NEW ORGANIZATION *(based on reviewer feedback), reflects progressions and cycles across the life course.*

- Different forms of committed relationships—legal marriage, heterosexual cohabitation, and homosexual partnerships—are compared and contrasted in a single chapter, "Making a Commitment."

- The "Sexual Involvement over the Life Course" chapter now follows chapters on relationship formation and marriage.

- The chapter "Conflict, Communication, and Relationship Quality" now falls later in the book, after a variety of relationship types have been discussed.

- Three parenting chapters look at parenting tasks and challenges across the life course.

END-OF-CHAPTER MATERIAL

Every chapter ends with a Summary, Review Questions, Critical Thinking Questions, Key Terms, and Suggestions for Further Reading, all of which reinforce course content and promote active learning.

Summary

Social research that is based on scientific principles provides the best understanding of intimate relationships, including marriages and families. Research results may come from laboratory and field experiments, social surveys, and observational, demographic, and historical studies.

Social theories make social life more understandable by providing sets of ideas that explain a broad range of phenomena. **Structural-functional theory** emphasizes that every pattern of activity in society makes either positive or negative contributions. A related idea is that the institutions of a society are interrelated. Structural-functional theory can be useful for analyzing the relations between families and other institutions, but it can also be used to justify the *status quo*, which may be dysfunctional for some people in the society. Conflict theory begins with the premise that ...

Symbolic interaction theory emphasizes the importance of symbols for social groups, societies, and human behavior. Individual personalities are also shaped by symbolic interaction with significant others. **Social exchange theory** emphasizes that motivations for human behavior are most likely to be found in its costs and rewards. Social exchange theory is especially applicable when people make decisions and choices about dating, partner selection, marital relationships, and divorce. **Developmental theory** emphasizes that many families go through family life-cycle stages.

Feminist scholars have added new insights to the study of mar... families through their critiques of ... have argued persuasively that the ... amily, based on biological or legal ... that assumptions of consensus in ... They have brought many new ... research, including family vio- ... f work and family. We draw on ... points throughout this text.

Review Questions

1. What are the principal features of the scientific approach to generating and verifying knowledge? How do these features differ from other approaches to generating knowledge?

2. List and briefly discuss the sources of error that scientists encounter when studying human behavior.

3. Which types of data collection are most and least useful in stud... ...nships? Why?

4. Evaluate the ...

conducted by Kinsey, Lillian Rubin, Masters and Johnson, and Laud Humphreys. What were the strengths and weaknesses of each approach? What could the researchers have done differently to avoid these weaknesses?

5. Compare and contrast the major theoretical frameworks that were presented in this chapter. How do they differ in terms of their underlying assumptions and in the issues they are most often used to study?

Critical Thinking Questions

1. Is it really possible to study marital quality scientifically? Why or why not?

2. Is it (a) necessary and (b) desirable to quantify the emotions that occur in marriage?

3. Is it appropriate to study couples in laboratory settings, using various types of technological devices? Why or why not?

4. C... ...has no theoretical

Further Reading

Books

Boss, Pauline G., Doherty, William J., LaRossa, Ralph, Steinmetz, Suzanne, and Schumm, Walter. *Sourcebook of Family Theories and Methods: A Contextual Approach.* New York: Plenum Publishing Company, 1993. Presents the history of family theory and research methods and the interplay between the two.

DeVault, Marjorie. *Liberating Method: Feminism and Social Research.* Philadelphia: Temple University Press, 1999. Considers research methods that adequately represent marginalized groups and the social processes that organize their lives.

Ericksen, Julia A., and Steffen, Sally A. *Kiss and Tell: Surveying Sex in the Twentieth Ce...* ...MA: Harvard University Press, 199... United States over the p...

Gilgun, Jane F., and Sus... *Methodologies of Quali...* Oaks, CA: Sage, 1997... which various qualitati... of family life.

Greenstein, Theodore. M... Haworth Press, 200... methods that are fr... study families and in...

Nye, F. Ivan, and B... *Frameworks in Fami...* Essays that outline... works are included... logical study of fa...

Oakley, Ann. *Experiments in Knowing: Gender and Method in the Social Sciences.* Cambridge: Polity Press, 2000. Explores the history, ideology, and implications of methods used in the social and natural sciences.

Reinharz, Shulamit, and Davidman, Lynn. *Feminist Methods in Social Research.* Oxford: Oxford University Press, 1992. This book examines a wide range of feminist research methods, explaining the relationship between feminism and methodology.

Content*SELECT* Articles

Garcia, L. "The Certainty of the Sexual Self-Concept." *Canadian Journal of Human Sexuality* 8(4), 1999: 263–271. ...legal. Central to one's concept of self is ...information con-

Key Terms

ABC-X model of family stress (p. 47)	Field experiment (p. 34)	Quasi-experiment (p. 35)
Conflict (p. 44)	Field observation (p. 37)	Radical feminism (p. 49)
Correlational method (p. 35)	Fixed-response question (p. 35)	Random assignment (p. 34)
Cross-sectional survey (p. 35)	Function (p. 43)	Random samples (p. 37)
Deception in social research (p. 39)	Hawthorne effect (p. 32)	Reciprocity (p. 46)
Dependent variable (p. 34)	Independent variable (p. 34)	Reliability (p. 32)
Developmental task (p. 48)	Instrumental roles (p. 43)	Resources (p. 44)
Double ABC-X model of family stress (p. 47)	Key concepts (p. 42)	Self-concept (p. 45)
Dysfunctional (p. 43)	Laboratory observation (p. 37)	Significant others (p. 45)
Ethnographies (p. 40)	Liberal feminism (p. 49)	Social history (p. 40)
Experiment (p. 34)	Longitudinal research (p. 35)	Social stratification (p. 44)
Expressive roles (p. 44)	Observational studies (p. 37)	Social theory (p. 42)
Family history (p. 40)	Open-ended question (p. 35)	Socialist feminism (p. 49)
Family life-cycle stage (p. 48)	Participant observation (p. 39)	Structure (p. 43)
	Power (p. 44)	Survey research (p. 35)

THREE TYPES OF BOXES . . .

address the many new issues that emerge almost daily in marriage and family life:

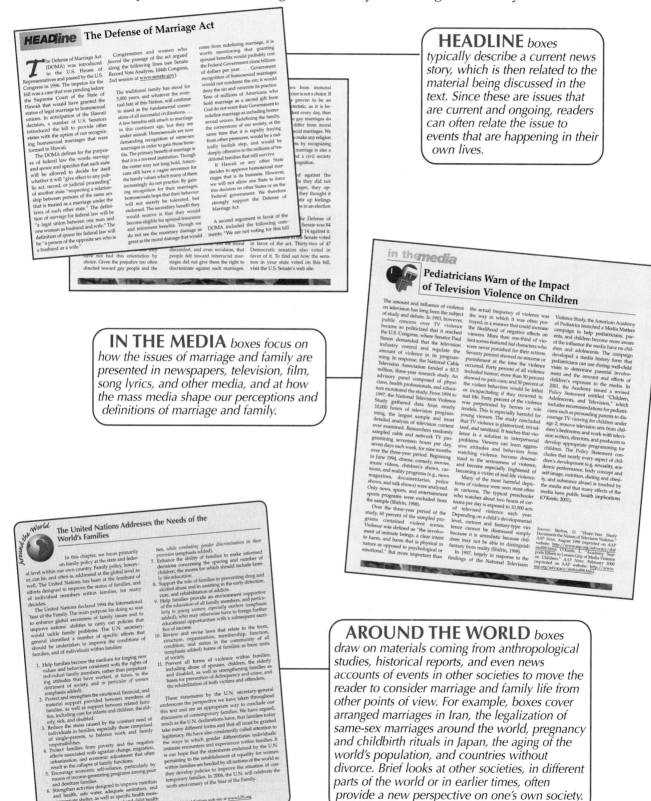

HEADLINE *boxes typically describe a current news story, which is then related to the material being discussed in the text. Since these are issues that are current and ongoing, readers can often relate the issue to events that are happening in their own lives.*

IN THE MEDIA *boxes focus on how the issues of marriage and family are presented in newspapers, television, film, song lyrics, and other media, and at how the mass media shape our perceptions and definitions of marriage and family.*

AROUND THE WORLD *boxes draw on materials coming from anthropological studies, historical reports, and even news accounts of events in other societies to move the reader to consider marriage and family life from other points of view. For example, boxes cover arranged marriages in Iran, the legalization of same-sex marriages around the world, pregnancy and childbirth rituals in Japan, the aging of the world's population, and countries without divorce. Brief looks at other societies, in different parts of the world or in earlier times, often provide a new perspective on one's own society.*

CONTENTSELECT SEARCH TERMS AND ARTICLES

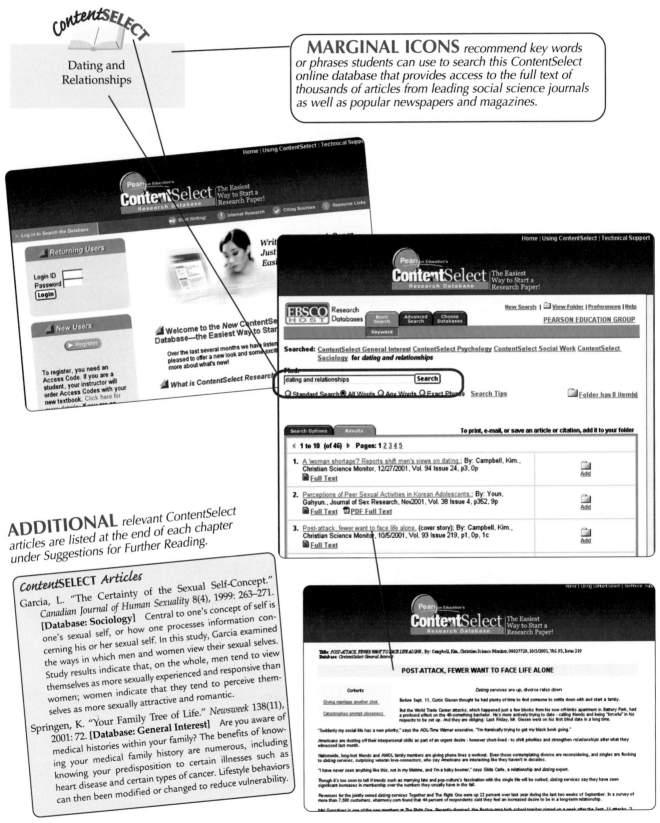

ContentSELECT

Dating and Relationships

MARGINAL ICONS *recommend key words or phrases students can use to search this ContentSelect online database that provides access to the full text of thousands of articles from leading social science journals as well as popular newspapers and magazines.*

ADDITIONAL *relevant ContentSelect articles are listed at the end of each chapter under Suggestions for Further Reading.*

ContentSELECT Articles

Garcia, L. "The Certainty of the Sexual Self-Concept." *Canadian Journal of Human Sexuality* 8(4), 1999: 263–271. **[Database: Sociology]** Central to one's concept of self is one's sexual self, or how one processes information concerning his or her sexual self. In this study, Garcia examined the ways in which men and women view their sexual selves. Study results indicate that, on the whole, men tend to view themselves as more sexually experienced and responsive than women; women indicate that they tend to perceive themselves as more sexually attractive and romantic.

Springen, K. "Your Family Tree of Life." *Newsweek* 138(11), 2001: 72. **[Database: General Interest]** Are you aware of medical histories within your family? The benefits of knowing your medical family history are numerous, including knowing your predisposition to certain illnesses such as heart disease and certain types of cancer. Lifestyle behaviors can then been modified or changed to reduce vulnerability.

Supplements

For Instructors

INSTRUCTOR'S MANUAL AND TEST BANK

By Melanie Wakeman, University of Florida

This combination manual offers a complete instructor's section and test bank to accompany each text chapter. The Test Bank includes hundreds of questions in multiple-choice, true-false, short answers, and essay formats. The Instructor's Manual includes teaching objectives, chapter outlines, key terms, class discussion questions, in-class exercises, films, and essay assignments.

TESTGEN-EQ COMPUTERIZED TESTING

The printed test bank is also available for Windows or Macintosh through our computerized testing system, TestGen-EQ, an integrated suite of testing and assessment tools. Instructors can use TestGen to create professional-looking exams in just minutes by selecting from the existing database of questions, editing those questions, or writing their own.

POWERPOINT PRESENTATION LECTURE OUTLINE

By Kelly Welch, Kansas State University

A PowerPoint presentation created for this text provides dozens of ready-to-use lecture outlines with graphics. The presentation is available on a cross-platform CD-ROM. PowerPoint software is not required to use this program; a PowerPoint Viewer is included to access the images.

MARRIAGE AND FAMILY CLASSROOM VIDEO

This exclusive video is available only from Allyn & Bacon, and records the experiences of real students. Topics include pregnancy/labor/birth, parenting, dating, cohabitation, contemplating marriage, single parenting, and divorce. The video is free to adopters upon request.

VIDEO WORKSHOP FOR MARRIAGE AND FAMILY: INSTRUCTOR GUIDE WITH CD-ROM

This combination teaching and learning system contains the same quality, course-specific footage from the Marriage and Family Classroom Video. The CD is accompanied by a guide with an overview of each segment, teaching suggestions, discussion questions, a text-specific correlation grid, and the material from the Student Guide.

TRANSPARENCIES

This package contains over 73 acetates, featuring illustrations both from the text and from other sources.

For Students

STUDENT WORKBOOK WITH LECTURE OUTLINES AND SELF-ASSESSMENTS

By Kelly Welch, Kansas State University, John Proffitt, Kansas State University, and Rifat Salam, New York University, Marymount Manhattan College

This workbook contains practice tests for every chapter, printouts of the PowerPoint lecture outlines with space for note-taking, and self-assessments students can use to explore their familiarity with and knowledge of course topics.

VIDEO WORKSHOP FOR MARRIAGE AND FAMILY: STUDENT GUIDE WITH CD-ROM

This combination Video Workshop Student Learning Guide and CD-ROM package contains all the materials students need to get started: a CD-ROM containing specially selected video clips, a text-specific correlation grid, and a student learning guide including observation questions to help students understand and visualize key concepts. The CD features 50 to 60 minutes of video footage of core topics such as pregnancy/labor/birth, parenting, dating, cohabitation, the decision to marry, single parenting, divorce, infertility, and sexuality.

MARRIAGE AND FAMILY COMPANION WEBSITE PLUS

This site includes activities on standard marriage and family topics, links to related Internet sites, and book-specific practice tests for *Marriage and Families*, Second Edition.

CONTENTSELECT RESEARCH DATABASE (ACCESS CODE REQUIRED; INCLUDED WITH EVERY NEW COPY OF THE TEXT)

www.ablongman.com/contentselect

This free research database, searchable by keyword, gives students immediate access to hundreds of scholarly journals and other popular publications from any computer with an Internet connection. *Marriages and Families*, Second Edition, includes suggested keyword search terms and recommended articles from the ContentSelect database.

RELATE ONLINE RELATIONSHIP INVENTORY

By Loyer-Carlson et al.

RELATE is an online relationship inventory developed by marriage and family professionals that enables individuals and couples to learn about themselves and what they bring to intimate relationships. Students purchase the RELATE Users Manual with access code and complete the questionnaire online at the website. Users who complete the questionnaire receive an extensive report analyzing their responses.

Acknowledgments

I have experienced many different family forms throughout my lifetime, and these experiences have greatly influenced my philosophy about intimate relationships and interpersonal commitment. This philosophy is reflected in my teaching and scholarship. I started life as the oldest daughter in a "traditional" two-parent family. Less than two years after my birth, my sister Teresa Kay, joined us, bringing me lots of joy and—at times—the minor irritations that accompany siblinghood. (I must say that my "baby" sister is now, and has long been, my dearest and closest friend.) When our mother died at age 41, Kay, my dad, and I were left to form a new family. I'm sure there were times when Dad threw up his hands in frustration at the challenges of raising two teenage daughters on his own. But most of the time, he was steady and calm—although he did occasionally drive too fast! After three years in a single-parent household, Dad married Arlene and we welcomed her and her daughters, Susie and Polly, to our home. (I won't describe the amusement Kay and I felt at watching our middle-aged father date . . .). Thus, when I teach about remarriage and stepfamilies, I often draw on the experiences of my own "step" family.

Unfortunately, while writing the second edition of this text, I experienced the lingering illness and death of my father. Thus, the revision of the chapter on families in middle and later life—particularly the discussion of grief and bereavement—has taken on a greater poignancy for me. My dad modeled for my sisters and me a strong belief in the work ethic, a generosity of spirit and curiosity about life, and a "gift of gab." He represented the best of what men have to offer their families.

For more than 15 years, I have shared a home with my life partner, Paul Mueller. Undoubtedly some of our acquaintances—and a number of family scholars—might dismiss our relationship as lacking in commitment simply because we have no marriage license. I firmly believe, however, that the conceptual tools and assumptions of family scholars—and the viewpoints of policy makers—need to expand to include the type of commitment that Paul and I demonstrate to each other every day of our lives. We have stuck by each other through major life crises (the long-term illnesses and deaths of both of our fathers), through the unrelenting challenges of combining two academic careers and providing elder care, and through the more mundane differences in personal habits that occasionally arise. Thinking about my own relationship helped me imagine a new Chapter 5: in this chapter I have grouped long-term cohabiting unions, both heterosexual and homosexual, together with legal marriage, looking at all three types of unions in the same context. While some who read this text may vehemently disagree with my affirmation of "alternative" lifestyles, most also will have had personal experiences with family diversity. Those who haven't yet experienced anything other than a "traditional" American family will undoubtedly do so in the years to come. As I said earlier, my intent is not to convert anyone to my *personal* point of view about families. But I do hope that my fair and comprehensive *academic* coverage of many types of families will help students recognize and appreciate the various ways in which family life is experienced.

In the first edition of this text, I acknowledged my intellectual roots at Penn State. I continue to feel immense good fortune at having had the opportunity to study in Penn State's Sociology, Psychology, and Human Development programs, even though I left State College more than 20 years ago. In my new academic home at the University of Florida, I've also had a number of colleagues and friends who've influenced my scholarship and teaching about families, gender, and sexualities. (In the Sociology department we refer to ourselves as the FIGS). I'd like to publicly thank the FIGS at this point: Monika Ardelt, Felix Berardo, Kendal Broad, Tanya Koropeckyj-Cox, Joe Feagin, Bill Marsiglio, Terry Mills, Milly Pena, John

Scanzoni, Gordon Streib, and Hernan Vera. Felix has been my long-term mentor and friend and has contributed in untold ways to the development of my professional career. A number of other colleagues have left us to pursue other opportunities, and I greatly miss them while I continue to be influenced by their ideas: Jay Gubrium, Gary Lee, Karen Pyke, Cynthia Rexroat, and Karen Seccombe. I would also like to acknowledge the contributions of Ken Kammeyer, my co-author on the first edition. Ken is a seasoned textbook writer and superb researcher, and his influence is still very much in evidence in this edition of the text.

All teachers know that we would be considerably less without our gifted students. And I have had more than my fair share of talented and enthusiastic students at the University of Florida. I would like to acknowledge the plentiful personal and intellectual contributions made to my life and career by the following individuals who've been my students and friends at different points over the past five years: Helena Alden, Jana Bailey, Susan Cody, Sara Crawley, Laurie Day, Doug Diekow, Susan Eichenberger, Lara Foley, Martine Gauthier, Shannon Houvaris, Leslie Houts, Kristin Joos, Elise Lyne, Erica Owens, Jesse Schultz, Brad Tripp, Laurel Tripp, and Melanie Wakeman. Each one of these people has made an indelible impact on my personal and professional lives. Many have used the first edition of the text in their own teaching and have provided me with valuable feedback that has made the second edition much better. In a number of places throughout the second edition, I have added discussions of the research conducted by many of these scholars. Elise Lyne, a 2002 UF graduate in Journalism and Communications, used her remarkable sense of "current events" to identify topics that undergraduates would find interesting. In fact, she wrote a number of boxes for the book which have been incorporated into the text itself. Her box on modern-day "swinging" appears in Chapter 6.

Nadine Gillis, my career assistant and life coach, has continued to bless me with her intelligence, loyalty, and nurturance through all my endeavors, both personal and professional. Nadine lost her husband of nearly 40 years, Walter O. Gillis, in October of 2001. Walt's warm, witty spirit buoyed us through difficult times. Diane Buehn has become a valued member of our office family and has energized us with her enthusiasm and daring spirit. She has brought us a new perspective on work and on life that has made us happier and much more productive.

One of the best changes that has happened to me since the first edition of this text was published was my sister and brother-in-law's relocation to Gainesville, my home town. Kay and Mel provide infinite amounts of instrumental and emotional support and make every day easier and happier. Their 25-year marriage is a model of commitment and superb communication. And finally, Paul Mueller, my partner of more than 15 years, has been my sounding board and main supporter. He brings out the best in me and kindly waits out my less than admirable moments. He is the exemplar of compromise and commitment.

Reviewers

The following teachers and scholars read drafts of the manuscript and I thank them for their help. For the first edition: Robert J. Alexander, Paterson Counseling Center, Inc.; Carol Deming Chenault, Calhoun Community College; Russell Craig, Ashland University; Michael C. Hoover, Missouri Western State College; Nils Hovik, Lehigh County Community College; Sharon B. Johnson, Miami-Dade Community College; Curtis Jones, Grand Valley State College; Irwin Kantor, Middlesex Community College; Gale P. Largey, Mansfield University; Harlan London, Syracuse University; Robert Walsh, Illinois State University; and Jacqueline Whitmore, Sante Fe Community College. For the second edition: Susan H. Alexander, Lycoming College;

C. Anne Broussard, Miami University; Margo Rita Capparelli, Framingham State College; John R. Henderson, Scottsdale Community College; Steven Long, North Iowa Area Community College; and CoSandra McNeal, Jackson State University.

My Thanks to Allyn & Bacon

Jeff Lasser has been my ally—in fact, my book's champion—since the day I met him. I feel privileged that he has given me and my book his attention and support. He has been enthusiastic, flexible, creative, and personable throughout this entire process. I can't thank him enough.

Ellen Darion has been remarkably patient and unceasingly tolerant of me throughout the creation of this book. I'm glad I confessed to her early on that my major coping strategy is avoidance. She came up with some humorous but gentle ways of getting around this when necessary that have been effective and painless for me! The lessons I've learned from her have paid off in other areas of my life, as well.

Karen Mason has steered me through the difficult final stages of production with grace and persistence. She and the other members of the Allyn & Bacon team seem to combine right-brain and left-brain cognitive skills in a way I've never seen anywhere else! They are at once creative and pragmatic. It's amazing!

And Peg Latham, of Colophon, has somehow found a way to keep me on track long after I wished the book was finished! Thanks, Peg!

About the Author

CONSTANCE SHEHAN is the Editor of the *Journal of Family Issues* and Director of the University of Florida's Center for Excellence in Teaching. She has served on the Board of Directors of the National Council on Family Relations, been certified by the council as a Family Life Educator, and has received court-certified training to be a family mediator and a child advocate.

At the University of Florida, she has served as President pro tempore of the Liberal Arts and Sciences Faculty, president of the Association for Women Faculty, and as director of the Center for Women's Studies. Dr. Shehan is also editor of the book *Through the Eyes of a Child: Re-Visioning Children as Active Agents of Family Life* (JAI Press, 1999).

Marriages and Families

Changing Families
Thriving through Diversity

1

The following story was written in 1999 by a professional woman named Katherine who describes the process she and her loved ones experienced as they ended one type of family and created new ones:

Key Questions

1 How does living together before marriage affect the likelihood of divorce?

2 Is nonmarital cohabitation replacing legal marriage as the preferred household living arrangement for adults?

3 What is the relationship of the increase in women's employment and economic independence to the changing divorce rate?

4 Are children of divorced parents more likely to get divorced later in their lives?

5 Is the family an agent of change in society or does it merely react to changes in the surrounding culture and society?

Nearly eight years ago, I began to understand that I was in love with another woman. At the time, I was still married to a man with whom I had lived since I was 21. After our son, Matt, was born, I knew that the way in which my husband (Ken) and I had worked out the roles and private commitments to each other as adult partners was not working. I knew that it was only a matter of time before I chose another way to live my life.

Around the same time, my relationship with TJ, the woman with whom I wanted to share my life, was intensifying. My brother, John, who has known he was gay for many years, decided it was time for him to share a residence with his partner of many years. . . . At the same time, my two best friends, who had been involved in long-term marriages, separated from their respective husbands and began to live together. These experiences opened some space for me to move toward my desire for a life with TJ. At 35, I found a new job, started a new life, and moved to Virginia with TJ and my son.

My former husband and I negotiated a careful divorce, and we remain good friends. (W)hen he and his new family come to visit in Virginia, they stay in our home. Adding to our family's diversity, Ken is now in a biracial marriage, and he and his wife have a son of their own.

Since we moved to Virginia, TJ had a child, our second son, who is now 2 years old. TJ and I are Zack's parents, but his biological father, "Papa Keith," is my brother's life partner.

My sons have complex and extensive relationships with an array of people who are related to them by biology and, as Matt says, by love. There are four sets of biological kin, given the number of parents involved. TJ is Mama and I am Tata; Ken is Dad, Keith is Papa, and my brother remains "Johnny." Sometimes, Matt calls Keith "Puncle," because he's part Papa and part uncle. Our sons have a rich language for kinship and many adults in their lives of all ages, backgrounds, orientations, and beliefs who have two things in common—these adults have *chosen* the way in which they conduct their intimate lives, and they have a fierce commitment to ensuring the well-being of these boys.

Source: Allen, Katherine. "Reflexivity in Qualitative Analysis: Toward an Understanding of Resiliency among Older Parents with Adult Gay Children." In McCubbin, H.I., Thompson, E.A., Thompson, A.I., Futrell, J.A. (eds.), *The Dynamics of Resilient Families*, pp. 71–93. Thousand Oaks, CA: Sage Publications, 1999.

*K*atherine's story is full of love, commitment, and complexity. Her life reflects many different types of family diversity that are becoming more common in our society. Some of you may also have families that don't quite fit the image of the *traditional* American family. You may have experienced the divorce of your biological parents. You may be the son or daughter of a gay or lesbian parent. Perhaps you've already formed a household or family of your own that is a **consensual union** (i.e., an intimate relationship in which partners share a home but are not legally married) rather than a legal marriage. Even if your own **family of orientation** (i.e., the family into which you were born) or **family of procreation** (i.e., the family you form in adulthood) is fairly traditional, you undoubtedly know other people whose family experiences have been more diverse.

As we emphasize throughout this book, family change and diversity have become the rule rather than the exception over the past several decades. Some people are quite concerned about the impact these changes might have on individual and societal well-being. Others recognize the challenges of living with family diversity but also find the flexibility of new family forms liberating and more fulfilling than the *traditional* forms. No matter what particular stance you take, you undoubtedly feel very strongly about families, marriages, and other types of intimate relationships.

Most of us are very curious about family changes. We often turn to the mass media for a glimpse into the family experiences of other people and to find information about perplexing family problems we're experiencing.

A vivid reflection of our continuing interest in marriage, family life, and other types of intimate relationships can be seen in the daytime television shows that feature guests who expose their intimate relationships to national audiences.

Week after week, the focus of many programs is in some way related to marriage and family life, or other types of intimate relationships. A typical week, for example, might find Montel discussing surrogate mothering, Oprah talking to twins who dislike being twins, Maury questioning children whose parents have announced they are gay or lesbian, and Ricki Lake probing the motivations of young men who marry much older women. Since the producers of these shows must come up with new topics almost daily, it is not surprising that virtually every trend, fashion, and unusual behavior associated with love, sex, intimacy, marriage, and family life have been discussed on talk shows.

In the television industry, talk shows are called "infotainment," a combination of information and entertainment. Judging by the considerable number of such shows and their high viewer ratings, there seems to be little question that they appeal to many Americans. As for providing information, there is some question about how educational it is to hear guests' personal stories, often interrupted by audience reactions and comments. When a panel includes an "expert" whose job it is to analyze the stories being told and to suggest solutions to the guests' problems, viewers may gain some insights and knowledge.

Certainly, talk shows can be informative, insofar as they discuss important and timely issues about family life and intimate relationships. Topics such as date rape, spouse abuse, and relations between stepparents and stepchildren, for example, can alert people to problems that they might not otherwise recognize or anticipate. In fact, sometimes it is through talk shows, as well as prime-time programming, that many Americans become aware of issues being studied by scholars and practitioners (sociologists, psychologists, and social workers, for example).

In this book we discuss many of the same issues related to intimate relationships and family life that appear in the mass media. Although we frequently highlight the personal stories of individuals who are experiencing particular family problems, our primary purpose in this text is to provide the most up-to-date ideas, information, and research findings about family life in general that are available from social scientific studies and scholarly thinking. In this opening chapter we consider the changes experienced by American families and the resilience they exhibit in adapting to those changes. We also discuss the expanding definition of the term *family* and explore ways in which broader societal change is reflected in changing household composition and living arrangements.

A Statistical Overview of Changing Families

*A*s you begin to read this part of the chapter, stop for a moment to think of all the changes in marriage and family-related behavior that have been occurring over the past few decades. Students who have been in my classes in previous semesters have identified many such changes, including the decreasing age at which teenagers (and preteens) are becoming sexually active; an increasing number of babies who are being born to unmarried mothers; many highly publicized incidences of marital infidelity; an apparent increase in the number of parents who leave their children at home unattended for long periods of time; and the skyrocketing number of women and children who are abused by their husbands and fathers. Many people interpret these changes as signs that the American family is in trouble.

It is true that American families have been undergoing a profound and far-reaching transformation. Dramatic changes in marriage and divorce rates and in fertility patterns have occurred. As a result, the American family today is a much different institution than it was even thirty years ago (Smith, 1999). These changes have caused many scholars to speculate about the future of the family (Teachman et al., 2000). Some have argued that the family is in decline (Popenoe, 1988, 1993; Skolnick, 1991) and that the demise of the family will have major implications for our society as a whole. Others are less worried about the *health* of the American family, believing that the changes that are occurring are not only inevitable, they may be beneficial, especially for women (Stacey, 1990, 1993).

Let's consider the evidence to support the widespread claim that the American family is in danger. One of the best ways to examine long-term changes in family patterns in our society is to examine statistical data that have been collected for over 200 years by the federal government, primarily through the U.S. Census Bureau. Many of you may have had to complete a *census* form in the spring of 2000 if you were living independently of your parents. That type of census—referred to as the **decennial census** because it is collected every ten years—provides a great deal of information about changes in household living arrangements for families as well as groups of unrelated adults. Additional data about families and living arrangements are collected from a smaller sample of the U.S. population every year in March.

No doubt you may have some healthy skepticism about the validity of statistics because you have learned how easily statistical data can be manipulated. Data provided by the U.S. Census Bureau and other federal agencies are the most comprehensive information available on the nation's population, in part, because residents of the United States are required to complete the census forms. Some people in our population are missed in every census, but the Census Bureau takes extraordinary steps to find and count every person who is living in the United States. The data obtained are used for numerous purposes, including congressional redistricting as well as identification of groups in our population and geographic areas who are in need of special forms of government assistance. Census data are available at no cost in both written and electronic forms. Throughout this text, data from the census are used to document changes in family patterns that are underway in the United States. In the next section of the chapter, we review several key trends that have occurred in marriage and the emergence of alternative forms of intimate rela-

Source: Copyright © 2000 Ashbury Park Press. Reprinted by permission of Steve Breen.

No Place for Nuclear Families on Prime-Time Television

Children Now, a national child advocacy organization that examines media messages to children, recently reported that the nuclear family is disappearing from network prime time even faster than it is in real life. Only about 11 percent of recurring prime-time characters appearing on the six broadcast networks are parents of any kind. And only 61 percent of those are still married. Television has been a barometer of change, if not exactly a mirror, reflecting demographic and cultural shifts through a lens distorted by the push for ratings. Television's portrayal of what families are or should be has changed markedly since Jim Anderson, heartland insurance agent, and his wife Margaret dispensed wisdom to their three children on *Father Knows Best*, a hit show of the 1950s.

"Was society (really) the way it was portrayed on *The Donna Reed Show* or *Father Knows Best*, or was it just an aspirational thing?" asked Larry Jones, executive vice president and general manager of TV Land, which plays reruns 24 hours a day. "People wished their families were like that; it's not how families (actually) were. As long

as families are important, you'll see that reflected on television, but how it's reflected depends on what audience is being catered to."

With the rise of cable and the subsequent fragmentation of the audience, television programmers haven't felt as compelled to represent families, nuclear or otherwise. Because families rarely watch shows together, it isn't considered necessary to try to satisfy as many generations at once. Today's prime-time television families tend to exist as mechanisms for adult characters to wrestle with their personal distress. As the definition of "family" has become more fluid and as "realistic" and "vulgar" have increasingly become synonymous, advertisers have had to adjust as well. Robert Wehling, global marketing officer for Procter & Gamble, said in a recent interview that he felt queasy when he tried watching prime-time television with his children. "Even if it was a program we really liked there would be some gratuitous sex or language that made us cringe," he said. He complained to the major networks, who listened to his complaints with sympathy (naturally,

because his company is a major sponsor), but no action was taken.

Then Mr. Wehling heard that Andrea Alstrup, marketing vice president at Johnson & Johnson, had been expressing the same concerns. The two persuaded a group of other advertisers, including IBM and General Motors, to discuss the issues. The first meeting was almost the last. "It broke down because we couldn't define family," Mr. Wehling said. "Everybody saw it differently. So I said, 'Why don't we just agree that all of us would like to see more programs that a multi-generational household would feel comfortable watching together, regardless of the makeup of the multi-generational household?'" From that meeting emerged the group of advertisers called the Family Friendly Programming Forum, whose improvement plan for television included a script development fund for "family" shows—without defining what "family" was.

Source: Copyright © 2001 by the New York Times Co. Julie Salamon, "Staticky Reception for Nuclear Families on Prime-Time TV." The *New York Times*. Reprinted by permission.

tionships, the changing circumstances of childbearing, and the incidence of divorce and remarriage. The census data reveal a complex pattern of resilience in the institution of the family in the face of profound and far-reaching change. The importance of legal marriage continues alongside increased acceptance of alternative forms of intimacy. An increased flexibility of men's and women's family roles has emerged even though on the societal level, the impact of gender stratification continues to differentially affect men's and women's everyday life experiences. An increased openness about sexuality coexists with increasing concern about the risks of early sexual involvement. And the high, but stable, divorce rate exists along with a high, but declining, rate of remarriage.

Changes in the Timing and Permanence of Marriage

A fundamental concern of many Americans is that marriage is no longer as highly valued as in the past. As evidence, they point to the many couples who are living together without being married and to the high proportion of people in their early and mid-twenties who are not married. Another ominous sign for many people is the high level of divorce among those who do marry.

Postponement of First Marriage.   Today, both women and men are marrying at a later age. The rise in age at first marriage since 1960 is dramatic. The greatest changes have occurred since 1975. Today, men are marrying at about the same age as their great-great-grandfathers did—age 26.1 in 1890, compared with 26.8 in 2000 (Fields and Casper, 2001). The trend during the first half of the twentieth century was for the age at marriage to decrease, reaching a low point in 1956, when the average age at first marriage for men was 22.5 (Smith, 1999).

Women have followed a similar pattern. Women marry today, on average, at age 25. In 1890, the average age at first marriage was about 22, but during the 1950s the age dropped to a low of just over 20 years.

Because American marriage patterns differ significantly by race and ethnicity, we'll look at the suspected rejection of, or retreat from, marriage for whites, African Americans, and Hispanics separately. In all three racial and ethnic categories, the percent of women aged 20 to 24 who are, or have been, married declined significantly over the past 25 years. The decline was greatest among African American women. By the late 1990s, only 15 percent had ever been married, compared with about 33 percent of white women in the same age group. Hispanic women are the most likely to get married by the time they reach age 20 to 24.

A similar decline has occurred among women aged 35 to 39. But once again, the decline has been most dramatic among African American women. By the late 1990s, about two-thirds of African American women in this age group had been married at least once. Because few women who haven't married by age 39 will marry in the future, it is possible that as many as one-third of all African American women

One of the most significant changes in living arrangements over the last decades of the 20th century was the increase in the number of households with only one resident.

may remain unmarried throughout their lifetimes (Teachman et al., 2000). Thus, the statistical evidence suggests that there has been a postponement of first marriage and an overall decline in marriage for African American women.

Increase in Nonmarital Cohabitation.   The trend toward later marriage has been accompanied by increased **nonmarital cohabitation** (couples who live together without being married). In 2000, there were more than 5.5 million unmarried cohabiting couples living in the United States. This was a sevenfold increase over the half million cohabiting couples in 1970 (Casper and Cohen, 2000).

The increase in cohabitation in the United States, however, is not necessarily a rejection of marriage. Only 7 percent of the total number of heterosexual couples who share a home are unmarried (Smith, 1999). Moreover, in the United States most people do not see cohabitation as a permanent substitute for marriage (Bumpass et al., 1991). Most cohabiting couples expect to marry at some point in their lifetimes, although some may not marry their cohabiting partner. For many couples, cohabitation is simply a new stage in the courtship or mate selection process. Nonmarital cohabitation is becoming the typical form that first unions take and is also increasingly common after divorce. The majority of women born between 1963 and 1974 lived with their partners before they married (Smith, 1999). African Americans are more likely than whites to be involved in a cohabiting relationship but are less likely to convert a nonmarital relationship to a legal marriage (Teachman et al., 2000).

Divorce and Remarriage.   Over the past 40 years, marriages have become less stable and the divorce rate has increased, especially in the earlier years of this period. Between 1965 and 1980, the divorce rate doubled. Since 1980, the divorce rate has declined but at a much slower pace. As a result, the divorce rate today is still twice as high as it was in 1960.

Again, the trends in divorce differ by race and ethnicity. Among whites, the proportion of women aged 40 to 44 who have ever been divorced increased from 20 percent (or one in every five women) to 35 percent (one in every three women). Among African American women, the percent who have been divorced has increased to 45 percent. Hispanic women continue to be less likely than whites and African Americans to go through a divorce (i.e., with a rate of 27 percent). Over the same period, the likelihood that divorced women would remarry has also declined, particularly among African American women. In the late 1990s, approximately 70 percent of divorced white women, compared with 45 percent of divorced African American women, were remarried (Teachman et al., 2000). As a result of high divorce rates and lower remarriage rates, women today, especially African Americans, are spending fewer years of their lives in marriage.

▲ *A substantial proportion of divorces involve dependent children who split their time between their mothers' and fathers' homes.*

Marriage is still regarded as a major source of happiness and life satisfaction among Americans. The importance that is accorded to marriage can be seen in public opinion polls, which show that Americans are reluctant to change laws in order to make divorce easier. Only 25 to 30 percent of Americans who responded to a recent University of Chicago poll said they favored a liberalization of divorce laws. Half advocated *tougher* divorce laws and another quarter favored keeping access to divorce the same as it has been for several decades (Smith, 1999).

◼ Changes in Women's Employment

One appealing feature of the idealized families of the past is that everyone had a clearly defined position and particular part to play in an ordered family life. In contrast, the roles of family members today are not as clearly segregated. In fact, to some observers, changes in male and female roles are very often considered by some to be the source of "the problems in today's family." A **role** is the behavior

Remarriage after divorce is very common, often resulting in new families that combine children from previous marriages.

generally expected of someone who occupies a particular position in a society or social group (Kammeyer, Ritzer, and Yetman, 1997). But roles can change as circumstances change, or as society changes. In families, some of the most significant changes in recent years have been associated with wives and mothers who have entered the labor force.

By the late 1990s, nearly three-quarters of women in the "prime" working ages of 25 to 64 were in the labor force. In contrast, only two out of every five in this age group were employed in 1960. Much of the growth in women's labor force participation has occurred among mothers of young children. The family form that we regard as **traditional** (with an employed husband and homemaking wife) really only existed for about 100 years, from the mid 1800s to the mid 1900s (Landry, 2000). This family form has declined in prevalence from over half of all couples in the early 1970s to about one-fifth in the late 1990s. There are some challenges associated with women's participation in the labor force. In response to all of these changes in women's behavior, a "men's movement" has developed among those who prefer the more traditional arrangement, urging men to "take back their rightful position" in their homes—as protectors, providers, and decision makers. Groups such as the Promise Keepers and the Million Man March have organized around the country with this goal in mind.

There are some challenges associated with women's participation in the labor force. Child care and inequities in the division of household responsibilities are especially burdensome for employed women. **Role overload** (having too many responsibilities to perform in a limited amount of time) is a common complaint of employed wives and mothers. But on the positive side, married women who work full time, year round, contribute substantially to the family income. In many cases, women's employment helps lift families out of poverty. Women who contribute to the economic well-being of their families may gain respect from other family members, especially husbands. In addition, when women's options in life are expanded through employment, many appear less susceptible to mental health problems (Shehan, 1984).

Those who long for the order and certainty of families of the past often overlook some of the disadvantages of traditional family roles. Women in the traditional family were clearly in subordinate positions; their voices in family decision making were often severely limited. When the television writers of the 1950s titled a show *Father Knows Best*, there was no doubt about who had authority in the family. If a father was loving, thoughtful, and intelligent, the traditional family might seem orderly and comfortable, but what if the father was cold and authoritarian, or just plain mean-tempered? Then family life was likely to be grim and stressful for the wife and children. Contemporary family life may seem less structured, and thus more confusing, but it may also be fairer for all members.

Changing Family Ties

Another major problem with contemporary American families, some say, is the lack of family ties. Sometimes this concern is expressed as a sense of loss for a way of life found in the **extended family** (three or more generations sharing a home or living in close proximity). More often the problem is seen in terms of shirking responsibilities for needy family members, especially elderly relatives. Adult children are portrayed as neglecting their elderly parents, often placing them in nursing homes where they languish while awaiting death. Although some of these concerns may have partial validity, they all require a more careful examination.

First, it must be noted that the extended family was never a form that predominated in the United States. In fact, historians of the family have concluded that since the 1600s, in Europe as well as the United States, most people have spent their lives in one- and two-generation households, not in large three-generation households (Coontz, 2000a).

The predominance of the small nuclear family household (parents and their children) in the United States has been, at least partly, a product of our particular history. Typically, immigrants who came to this country from Europe were young adults, some already married, many others not. They often left their parents and grandparents behind, so the families they started were necessarily limited to two generations. Then, as individuals and married couples moved to settle the U.S. west, relatives were again often left behind. The frontier was settled by individuals or small families rather than extended families, because the cost of moving large

Most elderly Americans who require assistance with daily life activities receive care from their daughters or daughters-in-law.

numbers of people across the large expanse of territory was prohibitive for most. Even today, when generations of a family live many miles apart they still exchange a great deal of economic aid and emotional support. The extent to which Americans socialize with their relatives who live outside their neighborhoods has changed very little over the past 30 years (Smith, 1999).

The charge that U.S. families are neglecting their responsibilities to their elderly parents and grandparents is much more myth than fact. It is true that only a small percentage of people over age 65 live with their children, but the reason is that nearly all the nation's older people live in their own homes. Most men, even at advanced ages, live with their wives, while considerably fewer women aged 65 and over live with a spouse. The elderly who are in poor health are generally cared for by family members, typically a spouse or an adult daughter or daughter-in-law (Rossi and Rossi, 1990, p. 5).

Most elderly Americans do not live in their children's homes, because they and their children mutually prefer it that way. For most elderly, it is not economically necessary to live with their children; they can continue to live independently, taking care of themselves, often until quite advanced ages.

Changing Fertility Patterns

Along with changes in marriage patterns has come a change in the circumstances of childbearing. While most people want to have children, and eventually do, the desire for large families has declined in terms of the actual level of childbearing and in terms of preferred family size. At the peak of the baby boom (in 1957), each American woman was giving birth to 3.6 children on average. Today, the average number of babies born per woman is approximately two. This is below the **replacement rate** that would be needed for our population to maintain its current size, without immigration into the country. There has also been an increase in the number of **child-free couples** (i.e., those who are biologically able to have children but who choose not to). Thus, by the late 1990s, the majority of American homes had no children under age 18 living in them (Smith, 1999).

While it is true that the birth rate is lower today than it was 200 years ago, the primary reason for the decline is positive. People typically have fewer children today because the infant mortality rate is much lower. In 1800, many children died before their first birthday. While that certainly happens today, the likelihood is much lower. Moreover while children were regarded as economic assets when the United States was primarily an agricultural economy, they are more likely to be regarded as economic liabilities today. Families often have only as many children as they feel they can afford to raise.

Child Discipline

When asked about the things they value in life, one-fourth of adults who responded to a University of Chicago survey said that having children was *one of the most important things in life*. Another two-fifths said that it was *very important* to them. Clearly, Americans do place a high value on having children. We have, however, become less traditional in terms of our childrearing values and goals. Over time there has been a shift away from emphasizing obedience and parent-centered families to valuing autonomy and independence for children. In polls conducted in the late 1990s, Americans overwhelmingly selected "thinking for oneself" as the most important trait for a child to learn. Approval for physical punishment of children also declined over the 1990s. But the emphasis placed on hard work for children increased over the 1990s. Thus, while physical discipline has given way to a more liberal approach to childrearing, hard work and other traditional American values have been gaining ground (Smith, 1999).

Changing Sexual Attitudes and Behavior

It is commonly believed that in the last generation, America underwent a sexual revolution in which attitudes and behavior became more permissive or liberal. In fact, there are statistical data that show that sex is no longer connected inextricably to marriage and childbearing. Since 1970, permissive attitudes toward premarital sex have grown notably. The proportion of adults who say that sex between unmarried men and women is always wrong dropped to less than 24 percent in the late 1990s. Accompanying these permissive attitudes has been a high level of premarital sexual activity. A majority of teenagers become sexually active before turning 20. There has also been an increase in the number of out-of-wedlock births. By the late 1990s, more than 25 percent of white births, 41 percent of Hispanic births, and 70 percent of African American births involved mothers who were not legally married (Smith, 1999; Teachman et al., 2000; Ventura et al., 2000).

Premarital sex, of course, is not a modern invention. Historical evidence from Puritan America shows fairly clearly that at least one-third of all brides were pregnant at the time they married. While premarital sexual activity is quite common today, recent evidence is showing that it is leveling off after peaking in the early 1990s. Public opinion still overwhelmingly disapproves of sex among younger teens (those aged 14 to 16). Adults prefer that teens postpone their initiation into sexual intercourse, but above all, they want young people to be well-informed about sex in general and "safe sex" in particular. Support for sex education in the schools is high (87 percent of adults favored it in the late 1990s). Birth control for teens is also strongly supported. Since the mid 1980s, about 60 percent of adults have approved of making contraception available to sexually active teens without their parents' approval. The pregnancy rate among teens actually declined in the 1990s (Smith, 1999; Ventura et al., 2000).

Approval of homosexual activity has never been high in the United States, but attitudes toward *homosexuality* became more tolerant over the 1990s. Discrimination against homosexuals in employment has also declined somewhat over this period. Thirty years ago, one-half of all adults opposed a homosexual person teaching at a college. In the late 1990s, less than one-fourth felt this way (Smith, 1999).

Disapproval of *extramarital sexuality* has always been high in this country. It actually increased over the last generation. By the end of the 1990s, about 80 percent of adults considered extramarital sex to always be wrong.

Thus, while the United States has not undergone the sweeping sexual revolution that has commonly been depicted in the media, our attitudes and practices regarding most types of sexual relationships have become more permissive over the past 30 years. The major exception is that attitudes toward extramarital sex are even more disapproving today than they were in the 1970s.

ContentSELECT

Teenage
Pregnancy

Types of Households and Living Arrangements

It should be clear that there have been many changes in family-related behavior patterns over the past several decades (see Figure 1.1 on page 14). These demographic changes have produced a variety of family forms and living arrangements that look quite different from the "traditional" American family. In order to review these changes more effectively, it is necessary to consider, first, several definitions used by the U.S. Census Bureau.

HEAD*line* The Defense of Marriage Act

The Defense of Marriage Act (DOMA) was introduced to the U.S. House of Representatives and passed by the U.S. Congress in 1996. The impetus for the bill was a case that was pending before the Supreme Court of the State of Hawaii that would have granted the status of legal marriage to homosexual unions. In anticipation of the Hawaii decision, a number of U.S. Senators introduced the bill to provide other states with the option of not recognizing homosexual marriages that were formed in Hawaii.

The DOMA defines for the purposes of federal law the words *marriage* and *spouse* and specifies that each state will be allowed to decide for itself whether it will "give effect to any public act, record, or judicial proceeding" of another state "respecting a relationship between persons of the same sex that is treated as a marriage under the laws of such other state." The definition of *marriage* for federal law will be "a legal union between one man and one woman as husband and wife." The definition of *spouse* for federal law will be "a person of the opposite sex who is a husband or a wife."

Congressmen and women who *favored* the passage of the act argued along the following lines (see Senate Record Vote Analysis, 104th Congress, 2nd session at www.senate.gov).

The traditional family has stood for 5,000 years, and whatever the eventual fate of this Nation, will continue to stand as the fundamental cornerstone of all successful civilizations. . . . A few benefits still attach to marriage in this continent age, but they are under assault. Homosexuals are now demanding recognition of same-sex marriages in order to gain those benefits. The primary benefit of marriage is that it is a revered institution. Though the center may not long hold, Americans still have a vague reverence for the family values which many of them increasingly do not practice. By gaining recognition for their marriages, homosexuals hope that their behavior will not merely be tolerated, but endorsed. The secondary benefit they would receive is that they would become eligible for spousal insurance and retirement benefits. Though we do not see the monetary damage as great as the moral damage that would

come from redefining marriage, it is worth mentioning that granting spousal benefits would probably cost the Federal Government alone billions of dollars per year. . . . Government recognition of homosexual marriages would not condemn the sin; it would deny the sin and venerate its practice. Tens of millions of Americans who hold marriage as a sacred gift from God do not want their Government to redefine marriage as including homosexual unions. Redefining the family, the cornerstone of our society, at the same time that it is rapidly fraying from other pressures, would be a radically foolish step, and would be deeply offensive to the millions of traditional families that still survive.

If Hawaii or any other State decides to approve homosexual marriages that is its business. However, we will not allow one State to force this decision on other States or on the Federal government. We therefore strongly support the Defense of Marriage Act.

A second argument in favor of the DOMA included the following comments: "We are not voting for this bill

The Census Bureau defines a **household** as a person or group of people who occupy a housing unit, whether that is an apartment, a mobile home, or a house. The **householder** is the person in whose name the housing unit is owned, being bought, or rented. Two different types of households are counted, family households and nonfamily households. For computational purposes, the Census Bureau includes as family only people who are related to the householder by birth, marriage, or adoption. Thus, a **family household** consists of a householder and one or more people living together in the same household who are related to the householder by birth, marriage, or adoption. It may also include, in addition, people who are unrelated to the householder. If the householder is married and living with his or her spouse, then the household is designated as a **married couple household.** The remaining types of family households not maintained by a married couple are designated by the sex of the householder. There are three types of family house-because we in any way favor discrimination against gays or lesbians, nor are we voting for it as a means of expressing either approval or disapproval of same-sex marriages. We support this bill solely because we favor letting the States decide the validity of same-sex marriages."

Those who *opposed* passage of the DOMA argued the following:

. . . (T)he core of this debate revolves around how we feel about intimate contact we neither understand nor feel comfortable discussing. Scientists have not yet discovered what causes homosexuals to be attracted to members of their own sex. For the vast majority of us who do not hear that particular drummer it is difficult to comprehend such an attraction. Nevertheless, homosexuality has existed throughout history. A small but significant number of our fellow human beings have always had a different sexual orientation, and the clear weight of serious scholarship has concluded that they have not had this orientation by choice. Given the prejudice too often directed toward gay people and the pressures they feel to hide the truth— their very identities—from family, friends, and employers, it is hard to imagine why anyone would actually choose to bear such a heavy burden unnecessarily.

The trend in the United States is toward acceptance of homosexuals. Older generations are still very uncomfortable and hostile to gays and lesbians, but each succeeding generation is more accepting. We are pleased by this trend. A basic respect for human dignity, which gives us the strength to reject racial, gender, and religious intolerance, dictates that in America we should also eliminate discrimination against homosexuals. We believe that ending this discrimination is the last frontier in the ultimate fight for civil and human rights.

As recently as 1967, 16 states outlawed interracial marriages because the citizenry of those states believed they were immoral. Today, nearly everyone will concede that the moral discomfort, and even revulsion, that people felt toward interracial marriages did not give them the right to discriminate against such marriages. Immorality flows from immoral choices, but skin color is not a choice. If homosexuality is proven to be an inalienable characteristic, as it is becoming more evident every day, then moral objections to gay marriages do not significantly differ from moral objections to interracial marriages. We would never vote to make any religion go against its tenets by recognizing gay marriages, but marriage is also a civil institution, and a civil society should give them recognition.

Others who voted against the DOMA said that while they did not favor same-sex marriages, they opposed the bill because they thought it was being offered to stir up feelings against gays and lesbians in an election year.

The final vote on the Defense of Marriage Act in the U.S. Senate was 84 in support of the bill and 14 against it. All 53 Republicans in the Senate voted in favor of the act. Thirty-two of 47 Democratic senators also voted in favor of it. To find out how the senators in your state voted on this bill, visit the U.S. Senate's web site.

holds: married couple households, family households headed by women, and family households headed by men.

A **nonfamily household** consists of a person living alone or a householder who shares his or her home with nonrelatives only (for example, with roommates or an unmarried partner). Unmarried partner households can be heterosexual or homosexual.

Data from the 2000 census show that the most common type of household in the United States today continues to be that headed by a married couple (see Figure 1.1). Over one-half of all U.S. households—or 54.5 million — fall into this category. The second most common type, those consisting of people living alone (numbering 27.2 million), constitute 25.8 percent of all households.

Multigenerational households numbered 3.9 million in 2000. About two-thirds of these households (2.6 million) consisted of the householder and his or her

Figure 1.1   **Households by Type: 1990 and 2000.** *Percent distribution*

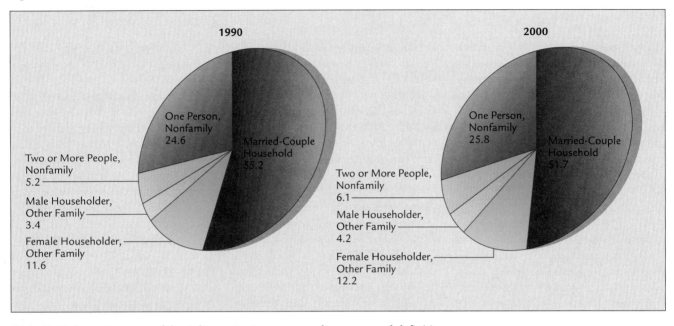

(*Note:* For information on confidentiality protection, nonsampling error, and definitions, see www.census.gov/prod/cen2000/doc/sf1.pdf)

(*Source:* U.S. Census Bureau, Census 2000 Summary File 1; 1990 Census of Population, *Summary Population and Housing Characteristics, United States* [1990 CPH-1-1].)

children and grandchildren. The remaining third (1.3 million households) consisted of the householder and his or her children and parents (or parents-in-law). Another 78,000 households (about 2 percent of all multigenerational households) consisted of four generations of family members in 2000.

Living arrangements differ greatly from one part of the country to another. Figure 1.2 shows a map of the United States color coded by the proportion of each county that consists of married couple households. The parts of the country that have the highest proportion of households headed by married couples are found in Utah and Idaho and in the west central part of the country, from west Texas northward. The lowest proportions of married couple households are found on the coastal regions of the eastern and southeastern United States, from the lower Mississippi Valley up the Atlantic seaboard to New England.

Multigenerational families are more likely to reside in areas of recent immigration, where new migrants live with their more established relatives. They are also common in areas where housing shortages or high housing costs force families to double up their living arrangements or in areas with relatively high rates of out-of-wedlock childbearing—in which case unwed mothers live with their children in their parents' homes. Hawaii, California, and Mississippi had the highest proportions of multigenerational family households.

The proportion of people living alone, a characteristic of people in different stages of life, from young adults to the elderly, was high in places as diverse as Seattle, Ft. Lauderdale, and St. Louis.

Unmarried partner households, which may or may not contain children or other relatives of the householder, numbered 5.5 million in 2000. The vast majority

Figure 1.2 Percent Married-Couple Households: 2000

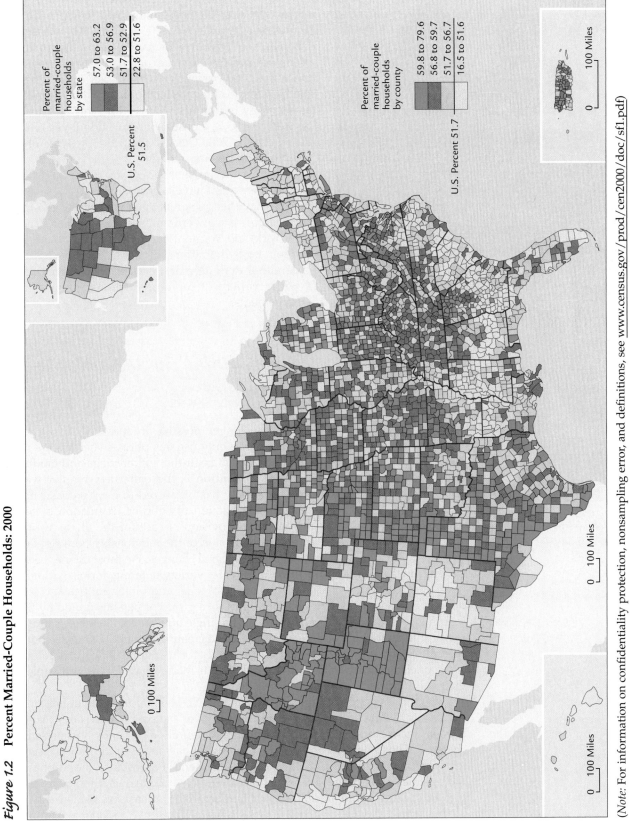

Percent of
married-couple
households
by state

57.0 to 63.2
53.0 to 56.9
51.7 to 52.9
22.8 to 51.6

U.S. Percent
51.5

Percent of
married-couple
households
by county

59.8 to 79.6
56.8 to 59.7
51.7 to 56.7
16.5 to 51.6

U.S. Percent 51.7

0   100 Miles

0   100 Miles

0 100 Miles

0   100 Miles

(*Note:* For information on confidentiality protection, nonsampling error, and definitions, see www.census.gov/prod/cen2000/doc/sf1.pdf)

(*Source:* U.S. Census Bureau, Census 2000 Summary File 1. American FactFinder at factfinder.census.gov provides census data and mapping tools.)

15

▲ *The increase in life expectancy has allowed many grandchildren to have enduring relationships with their grandparents.*

(4.9 million) consisted of heterosexual partners. Of the more than 600,000 households that were headed by homosexual couples in 2000, over 304,000 consisted of gay men and 297,000 of lesbians. The number of households headed by homosexual partners increased by more than 300 percent since 1990, yet experts believe the 2000 figures may undercount the actual number by as much as two-thirds. At the time this chapter was written, the U.S. Census Bureau hadn't yet released data from the 2000 Census about the presence of children in same-sex households.

The demographic changes in household living arrangements that have occurred over the past several decades have been so great that many city governments and several state governments (e.g., California, Hawaii, New York, and Vermont) have been forced to reconsider their legal definitions of *family*. It is necessary to expand our definition of this term to take into account a wider variety of intimate relationships and living arrangements.

Reexamining the Definition of Family

It is no longer possible to speak of *the* American family. We only use this phrase when we are referring to the social institution of marriage and family life (a **social institution** is the patterned, regular way in which a society has organized to meet its basic needs, such as socialization of children, regulation of sexual activity, and provision of care for the ill), as we do in our later discussion of the relationship between family changes and societal changes. We must define the word *family* in a way that takes into account a wider variety of family forms. Sociologists have traditionally defined family in terms of legal and biological ties and coresidence. One long-used definition of family is "a group of persons united by ties of marriage, blood, or adoption; constituting a single household; interacting and communicating in their respective social roles; and creating and maintaining a common culture" (Burgess and Locke, 1953). The family form epitomized by this definition is the **nuclear family,** which in its ideal form is made up of a married couple and their children.

The traditional definition of family may have been appropriate at one time in the past for white, middle class families, but over the past two decades there has been an increasing criticism of the traditional definition of family and pressure to change it. The traditional definition fails to encompass many of the new and emerging family forms and household living arrangements. For instance, the emphasis on the legal ties of marriage means that cohabiting heterosexual and homosexual couples are excluded from the definition of families. The emphasis on residence in a single household excludes married couples who maintain two residences (commuter marriages). It also excludes families after divorce, when the children continue to have close family relationships with both their mothers and fathers but live with

Who's Who in Your Family

We all have an idea of our own family—who belongs to it and who doesn't. We also typically believe we know what the family is, generally. We may even assume that our family is like all other families and that everyone else will immediately understand our idea of family. Read the following story to see just how much another person's idea of family can differ from our own:

A young unmarried Sami woman was pregnant and went to her local midwife in northern Norway to deliver. (The Sami are the ethnic group previously called Lapps.) Among other things, the midwife asked who the father-to-be was. The answer was, "My nephew." The midwife became upset. According to her perspective, a sexual relation between an aunt and a nephew was incest. The Sami woman noticed the confusion of the midwife, and she calmed her down by explaining that he was not really a nephew. One of her siblings was a godparent to the father-to-be and, according to Sami law, this defines a nephew. A godparent is a parent, and a sibling's male offspring is a nephew—very simple.

Source: Levin and Trost, 1992, pp. 348–351.

only one. Often in such cases the mothers and fathers also continue to interact on a regular basis. The term used to describe a postdivorce family in which there is continued interaction between mothers and fathers in the interests of their children is **binuclear family** (Ahrons, 1981; Ahrons and Rodgers, 1987).

The traditional definition of family also refers to "respective social roles." This undoubtedly means husband and wife roles, mother and father roles, and sibling roles. There is at least the suggestion that everyone's roles are neatly separate—probably with the father the *breadwinner* and mother the *homemaker*. This aspect of the definition excludes, or at least neglects, households with only one parent—quite a sizable number these days—or with two adults of the same sex.

The notion of "respective social roles," in combination with legal and biological ties, also excludes stepfamilies, for two reasons. The most obvious reason is that children are not always adopted by their parents' new spouses. The second reason is that the roles of stepparents and stepsiblings are not clearly defined. As a result, relationships between members of a **blended** or **reconstituted family** (other names for stepfamilies) may or may not be "familylike."

The last phrase of the traditional definition, "creating and maintaining a common culture," refers to family members' attempts to develop rituals and ceremonies to mark special events and occasions along with customary ways of relating to each other on a daily basis. This phrase also implies that there is absolute consensus in households, with all family members sharing identical values, agreeing on all goals, and having equal access to household resources and equal say in decision making. Feminist researchers have challenged this implication by pointing out the clinical data on family conflict and police reports of domestic violence.

The legal bond of marriage is no longer a decisive prerequisite for sexual intimacy, for parenthood, for coresidence, or economic interdependence between partners. Gay and lesbian couples cannot legally marry in the United States, and cohabiting couples choose not to enter into a legal contract, yet gays, lesbians, and domestic partners have close primary relationships, often sexually based, and they often regard their lives as interdependent. A broader definition of family is therefore required.

The meaning of *interdependence* is crucial for arriving at a broadened definition of family. Sociologically, interdependence is determined by four criteria: "diversity of exchanges, duration of exchanges, frequency of exchanges, and strength of intensity or feelings regarding the exchanges" (Scanzoni et al., 1989, p. 72). These are similar to the criteria applied by the New York Supreme Court when it sought to identify the essence of a couple relationship.

The State of New York was faced with the limitations of its legal definition of *family* in the late 1980s when the surviving partner of a long-term gay couple asked the state's Supreme Court to rule on whether a gay couple counted as a family. This case was prompted by the surviving partner's desire to continue to live in the apartment that he had shared with his lover for more than a decade under New York City's rent control laws. These laws were meant to protect tenants from being hit with major increases in rent. As long as members of the original tenants' family resided in an apartment, their rent could not be increased beyond a specified limit. Because the landlord in this case did not regard the gay tenants as family, he felt he could increase the rent after one of the partners died. In their ruling, the justices of the state supreme court recognized that New York's legal definition of family was too narrow and they offered a broader set of criteria that were to be used to determine who qualified as *family*. The determining questions included the following:

1 How long has the couple lived together?

2 Do the partners consider themselves as a family unit?

3 Do the partners present themselves as a family unit?

4 Are the partners' social lives interwoven? and

5 Are the partners financially interdependent?

The court decided that when two people have a long-standing involvement with each other, consider themselves a couple (or family), present themselves that way to the community, have interwoven social lives, and are financially interdependent, their relationship is equivalent to a legal and conventional marriage, regardless of gender or sexual orientation.

You may wonder why state governments, sociologists, and "lay" individuals care about the legal definition of *family*. Do words or labels really matter? As the rent control case demonstrated, one's status as a legitimate family member can have economic implications. Family members can enjoy the protection of rent control laws and can take time off from work to care for a sick loved one or to grieve a death. Individuals can usually be covered by the health insurance benefits of an employed family member and may have an easier time inheriting property from each other or authorizing medical care. Legal definitions can also offer protection in the event that a relationship is terminated. Thus, the definition of *family* is not simply a question of semantics. It has practical implications as well. That is one of the major reasons so many same-sex couples have fought for legal recognition as legitimate families. Another reason, of course, is the social acceptance or legitimacy that such recognition would provide.

For our purpose in this text, we define **family** as sexual or intimate relationships, or parent–child relationships, in which people live together, at least some of the time, with personal commitments to each other, who identify themselves as an intimate group and who are regarded by others as an enduring group, and are economically interdependent to some degree. With this definition we are able to include cohabiting couples, gay and lesbian couples, single-parent families (even if there has never been a marriage), blended or reconstituted families, binuclear families, and commuter marriages (spouses who live in different residences).

Families and Social Change

*T*hus far we have discussed how much marriage and family life have changed over the past several decades. The obvious question, of course, is why these changes have occurred.

One answer is that the larger society, within which the family exists, has changed. In the past, our society was primarily rural and agricultural. Today it is primarily urban, with an economy dominated by industrial production and service provision. Family members today are not likely to be working together on a farm or in a family business, but are likely to be separated for many hours a day by their employment or education.

Because both the family institution and the larger society have changed, a second interesting question emerges. Did changes in the society cause the family to change? Or did changes in the family institution lead to the broader societal changes? Although at first it may seem fairly obvious that societal changes have led to changes in the family, the alternative point of view is often heard. Since the family is viewed as the primary institution, it greatly influences the nature of the society as a whole.

The idea that the family can cause larger societal change is heard most often when societal trends are viewed as negative. When a new social problem emerges commentators very often look toward the family institution as the potential cause. For example, William Bennett, a former secretary of education and federal "drug czar," argues that drug use and its associated problems—especially among young people—are caused by a "cultural breakdown." This cultural breakdown, in turn, is caused primarily by parents' failure to teach young people the virtues of self-discipline and self-control, individual and civic responsibility. In short, Bennett is saying that families have failed to teach basic values to children and thus drug use has increased, bringing with it many other social problems. The family, from this perspective, is changing society.

Another example of the point of view that the family causes changes in the broader society, rather than the other way around, may be found in the increased numbers of children being born outside of marriage. Thirty-three percent of all births in the United States now occur outside of marriage, a percentage that has more than doubled in the last twenty years (Martin et al., 2002). Many observers argue that parents are not teaching their children the importance of morality, or responsibility. Once again, the family is seen as the cause of the problem.

But there is an alternative explanation for increases in the number of children being born out of wedlock. Perhaps the larger society has changed in some ways—illegitimacy may not be as stigmatized as it once was, changes in the economy may make many men less able to provide economic support for children, and women may have alternative means of supporting children. Any of these societal changes may have made childbearing within marriage less significant, or even less possible, than it was a few decades ago. From this perspective, a changing society may have changed or modified the family.

It is also possible, of course, that the causal connection is not one-directional but two-directional. The family is an active agent in changing the society, while at the same time the family is adapting to changes in the larger society. This is the view of family scholars who consider it unrealistic to see the family as simply a passive institution, always adapting to changes in the larger society (Hareven, 1987).

No doubt the family can have some impact on the larger society, but that impact should not be exaggerated. In fact, historical and contemporary evidence shows that the family is almost always the institution adapting to changing economic, political, and legal systems in the society, rather than vice versa. In times of

Wedlock

Working Mothers

economic downturn or depression, for example, young people often postpone marriage, not because they prefer to, but because they must. Married couples also reduce the number of children they have during bad economic times. American couples limited family size during the Great Depression of the 1930s, even though this was a time before contraception was widely available.

Present-day families also adapt to economic conditions. Over the last twenty years, the real income of couples has remained constant or declined, making it necessary for both husbands and wives to be employed in order to have the standard of living they desire. If these couples also want children, they must adapt in still other ways. Often a woman works until the birth of a child and, after a short period of time, returns to her job. Then she must find some form of child care, which may be in short supply, of questionable quality, and expensive. Instead of finding child care, a husband and wife may work on different shifts so that one of them will always be caring for the child. The impact of this arrangement on marriages can be quite negative.

Marriage, family life, and other close relationships are changed not just by economic conditions, but also by other societal changes. Changes in policies pertaining to taxation, immigration, military conscription (the draft), and abortion may all have an impact on family life. In the chapters that follow, we present many examples of how couples and families must adapt to changes in the larger society. Overall, we believe the family is more likely to be an adapting institution than it is to be the producer of basic societal changes. The direction of causality has important implications for social policy. Those who believe that it is the family institution that has caused negative societal changes advocate policies that would restore the traditional nuclear family (with husbands as breadwinners and wives as full-time homemakers) to prominence.

A Research-Based View of Marriage and Family Life

A major assumption of this book is that it is best to be as realistic and objective as possible about all aspects of courtship, dating, sex, cohabitation, marriage, and family life. We all have romantic or idealistic views about these subjects. It is not necessary to give up ideals, but there are some merits to taking a more realistic look at the subject.

What is a realistic approach? It is one that reflects, as nearly as can be determined, *the facts.* Facts, we believe, are best obtained by research conducted by scholars who are trained and committed to finding out *what is,* not *what should be.* An illustration will demonstrate what we mean.

A sexual relationship is, in the ideal world, a reflection of partners' love and caring for each other. Sexual intercourse is often described as the ultimate expression of love. At a minimum, sex is supposed to enhance or reinforce a couple's love. Not every sexual encounter meets this ideal, since there is sexual interaction based on monetary transactions, or based on coercion and force. Recognizing that sex and love are not necessarily synonymous introduces an element of realism. But a realistic view of sexual relationships goes beyond these recognitions; social research also shows that many sexual relationships are more than simply an expression of love. Sexual relationships can also be an exertion of power. **Power,** the ability to make someone else do what you want them to do, is found in most human relationships, and that includes intimate sexual relationships.

Studies of sexual relationships show that power is an inherent part of the sexual lives of many couples (Blumstein and Schwartz, 1983; Rubin, 1990). Blumstein and Schwartz found power related to the initiation of sex by one partner, and the response of the other. The very act of initiating sexual activity is, in itself, an act of power. A number of men are only comfortable when they initiate sexual activity, finding it threatening when a woman does so. Moreover, since sex between heterosexual couples is initiated more often by men than women, women have many more opportunities to reject sexual overtures. Initiation and rejection are used as ways of wielding power in sexual relationships.

In her study of sexual behavior, aptly titled *Erotic Wars,* Lillian Rubin also found a power dimension in sexual relationships. One particular focus of her discussion is on the way both men and women achieve feelings of power when engaging in oral sex. One of her female interviewees, a 25-year-old nursery school teacher, describes her feelings when she performs oral sex on her partner: "It's the ultimate power. . . . For me, it's sort of like having him tied up. . . . He's just lying there getting more and more excited . . . he's absolutely, totally vulnerable. It's the only time I'm totally in control" (Rubin, 1990, p. 122). Some of the men Rubin interviewed also recognized their feelings of power when having sex. A 32-year-old Los Angeles executive, also speaking of oral sex: "I have to admit, I get a feeling of real power, and that adds to the whole sexual thrill" (Rubin, 1990, p. 122).

These studies, and others, strongly suggest that a realistic evaluation of sexual relationships should take power into account. In Chapter 6, where we treat sexual behavior more fully, we return to the relationship between sexual behavior and power.

There are many benefits of a research-based approach to intimate relationships. Simply put, having knowledge generally results in wiser behavior and improves outcomes. In a number of areas related to marriage and family life, as we discuss later in this book, people who are the most idealistic (or unrealistic) often make poor choices and end up being the most disappointed or upset by their experiences. For example, the women who are most romantic and idealistic about pregnancy and childbirth often find the actual experience quite stressful (Oakley, 1980). The same is true of young parents who do not anticipate the stresses they will encounter during the first months of parenthood. The greatest stresses, frustrations, and disappointments come to those who have been led to believe that the first weeks and months of parenthood will be easy, perhaps even fun (Kach and McGhee, 1982; Glass, 1983; Kalmuss, Davidson, and Cushman, 1992).

A research-based approach to marriage and family matters not only reduces stress and disappointment, but in many instances also offers positive insights. Psychologist John Gottman, for example, has conducted research on arguments between husbands and wives. Taking a realistic approach by assuming that husbands and wives will have arguments, he framed his research question this way: How can husbands and wives have arguments without having them escalate to damaging quarrels? To answer this question, Gottman and his associates videotaped husbands and wives as they engaged in arguments. The couples in his study were divided into two categories: "unhappy" and "happy." A couple was classified "unhappy" if they had sought marriage counseling and if at least one partner scored below average on a marital happiness measure. A couple was classified "happy" if they responded to a newspaper advertisement recruiting couples with "good marriages" and if both partners scored above average on the marital happiness measure (Gottman and Silver, 1999).

The videotaped arguments of these unhappy and happy couples revealed a great deal about the process of husband–wife arguments (such as how the complaint of one can often lead to a countercomplaint by the other). One finding was especially informative. The happy couples actually listened to what their partners

ContentSELECT

Sex Research

in the media

Modern Realities Such as Divorce Put a New Face on the Definition of *Family,* Some Young Adults Say

Kevin Haines, 23, thinks it is to children's benefit if one parent is able to stay home, as his mother did. But he doesn't know if that will be possible for his family. "I have a traditional background, but in this day and age, and even with the career path I'm choosing, my wife and I may not be able to [afford for her to stay home]," said Haines, a criminal justice and sociology major. "I don't think of myself as being materialistic, but I don't want to have to live in a two-bedroom apartment for years, either." Haines is taking a course called Sociology of the Family at the University of North Florida. . . . Haines and his classmates . . . will form the first families of the new millennium. Some of [the students in the class] are married, some are divorced, some are single parents and about half have or plan to cohabit before marriage. During their lifetimes, most expect ever-broadening definitions of family, with a growing number of single-parent households and more dual-earner households. They also fear what happened to half of their parents' marriages: divorce. "It's not *Happy Days* out there anymore,"
said one student, Lynn Daum. "The paradigm has shifted."

Because they [were] studying the family, the *Times-Union* asked these students what they foresee for their families of the future. Here's what they said:

Proceed with Caution

Stacy MacLean, 22, a psychology major whose parents are divorced, said her peers have fears about marriage. "I think that's why there is an emphasis on education," she said. "Women want to be able to support themselves—that's a very high priority. . . . What if he just decides to leave you? You have to be able to stand on your own two feet." Another student, Ashley Hayes, 22, grew up with a dad "who is always there for me" and a mom who said staying home and raising her two children was "the most fulfilling thing she's ever done." "I would hope it's the same way, that I would be able to take off time to watch my children grow up," said Hayes, who is majoring in criminal justice. "But I would like to work, too," she said. "And the occupation I'm looking at now, I'd be on call at any time. But I don't expect a family for four or five more years anyway."

Meshun Richardson is only 24, but is a never-married single parent to sons ages 5 and 6. With help from her mother and two sisters, she is raising the boys, working full-time and going to school full-time. "It's hard," said Richardson, a sociology major. "I work seven days a week. . . . It wasn't something I decided, but it's something that happened, and I've learned to deal with it." She plans to postpone any more relationships until her children are grown, sparing them the possibility of becoming attached to someone who may not remain in their lives.

Prepping for the Test

Many of the students said they wouldn't dream of entering a marriage without first taking a trial run, living with their intended for a while before the wedding. They gave a wide range of estimates of the number of their peers who have tried or plan to try cohabitation before marriage, ranging from very few to most. Sociology

were saying during the course of the argument. Even more important, they frequently acknowledged what their partners were saying in subtle, yet significant, ways. If a wife were complaining about something her husband had done, for example, her husband might say, "Uh-huh," or simply nod his head to show he was listening. Both husbands and wives in the happy couples were likely to respond often; and these small gestures seemed to reduce the intensity of the argument. The unhappy couples were much less likely to give responses that showed major Lindsay Matheney, 22, said probably half of her peers have tried cohabitation. "I have," she said. "I would definitely live with somebody before I marry them. Because it's a whole different thing [than just dating]. It really is. I can tell you that from experience." But Jeff Walker, 22, a psychology major, said he sees his peers making commitments to remaining "sexually pure" until they are married. "I only have a couple of friends who are in a sexual relationship," said Walker, who works with a program at his church aimed at encouraging teens to abstain from sex until marriage. "Most of the friends I hang out with are also waiting until they're married."

Different Realities

"I have a husband, son and daughter, but that's my reality," said Daum, 36, a sociology major and older member of the class of mostly 20-somethings. "But I don't think there's a guarantee that other people share my reality, or have a desire to have my reality. I think with the different types of family systems, social systems, whether it's blended families, single families, divorced families, mothers who have never married, homosexual relationships, this is the forefront of our reality."

Most of the University of North Florida students believe that the definition of family will continue to be stretched. In their lifetimes, they expect more marriages that mix race or ethnicity, acceptance of gay and lesbian marriage, and more single-parent and dual-income families. "You can drive through a neighborhood now and you're going to see a majority married, but you're also going to see people living together, homosexual relationships. I think more and more things are being accepted," said Tracy Richotte, 30, a widow with a 7-year-old daughter. "There's not one definition that fits," the sociology major said. "And just because my definition is one thing, that doesn't mean it should apply to everyone else. Everybody says 'ideal family,' but there's reality. You make the best of what your life situation is."

Then Comes Marriage

For themselves, however, most of the students see not only marriage down the road, but a traditional one. They are determined not to become another divorce statistic. Richotte, who was widowed 4 and one-half years ago and hopes to remarry, said marriage "is a commitment that you make forever. But for whatever reason, people get divorced. A lot of times it's because they don't want to work at it. But you have to. Marriage is one of those things where you don't just live happily ever after."

About half of the class sees a brighter future for their families. The other half paints a more disturbing picture. Teresea Downceroux, 29 and a sociology major, came from a poor, single-parent family and said she and her four brothers were "as bad as hell," constantly in trouble despite their working mother's best efforts. So one of Downceroux's goals was to have a stable family of her own. So far, she thinks she and her husband have provided a good home for their children, ages 6 and 3. But she doesn't have as much hope for many of her peers. "I think there are a lot of naive people out there, especially young women. . . . My husband and I saved and planned for our children. It's not just having babies and hoping John is going to marry you. But I've got friends like that who have four or five kids. The man is gone, but they're stuck with another child."

Daum was more hopeful but for different reasons. "I think the idea of family is on a good road," she said. "I think everybody wants that reality [a good family] for themselves. I just think it will come in different sizes and shapes and packages. Some might just choose to be married and not have children. Some people might choose to have a baby with a sperm donor. I just don't think that we can put ourselves in a box because society no longer is in a box. And I'm not sure that it ever was. . . ."

Source: Pully, Bob. "Modern Realities such as Divorce Put a New Face on the Definition of 'Family,' Some Adults Say." *Florida Times Union,* February 22, 1999. Reprinted by permission.

they were listening, with the result that their arguments were likely to grow more heated.

In this case, then, a realistic approach—recognition that couples *have* arguments—led to a useful application in everyday life: Acknowledging that you are listening to your partner's side keeps the argument from escalating. We discuss intimate communication—including the importance of effective listening—in Chapter 7.

Summary

Marriage and family life are endlessly fascinating topics to most people. One indication of the high and universal level of interest is the amount of television time devoted to dating, love, marriage, husband–wife relationships, sex, childbearing, sibling relationships, and other such topics.

There is a widespread concern in American society about the well-being of families. Many commentators and observers say the family is in trouble. They point to the decline in marriage and the increase in cohabitation and divorce as signs of the family in trouble. Although there has been a trend toward later marriage, the available evidence shows that nearly 90 percent of Americans will marry at least once, and many will remarry after divorce. Cohabitation by about 6 percent of U.S. couples, at any one time, is not generally viewed as a substitute for marriage. Divorce, while high, has declined slightly since 1979.

The apparent turmoil and confusion within families largely reflects increasingly less rigid gender roles, which may be becoming fairer to women and children. The charge that extended family ties have weakened is largely unfounded.

A definition of family today must be broadened to include nontraditional and nonconventional arrangements. A family can be any sexual or intimate relationship, or parent–child relationship, in which people live together, at least part of the time, with personal commitments to each other, and who have a personal identity as part of an intimate group.

Although the family is often viewed as the primary institution of the society, responsible for producing societal changes, the opposite is more often true. Families are more likely to make adaptations to changes in other institutions, particularly the economic and the political.

A research-based view of marriage and family life is likely to produce more positive results than an idealistic one. A realistic view, based on scientific facts whenever possible, leads to better decisions, more favorable adjustments, and positive actions in everyday life.

Key Terms

Binuclear family (p. 17)

Blended family (p. 17)

Child-free couples (p. 10)

Consensual union (p. 2)

Decennial census (p. 4)

Extended family (p. 9)

Family (p. 18)

Family household (p. 12)

Family of orientation (p. 2)

Family of procreation (p. 2)

Household (p. 12)

Householder (p. 12)

Married couple household (p. 12)

Multigenerational household (p. 13)

Nonfamily household (p. 13)

Nonmarital cohabitation (p. 6)

Nuclear family (p. 16)

Power (p. 20)

Reconstituted family (p. 17)

Replacement rate (p. 10)

Role (p. 7)

Role overload (p. 8)

Social institution (p. 16)

Traditional family (p. 8)

Review Questions

1. List and discuss the major demographic trends that have occurred in marriage, family formation, and divorce over the past 100 years in the United States.

2. List and describe the new forms of household living arrangements and intimate relationships that have emerged in the United States over the past 50 years.

3. Identify the limitations of the traditional definition of *family*.

4. Explain the rationale behind recent corporate and municipal decisions to redefine *family* and identify the practical implications of the expanded definitions.

5. How old are American men and women when they marry for the first time? How does this compare with the average age at first marriage 100 years ago?

6. What race differences, if any, exist in the likelihood of being married?

7. How common is it for couples to live together before legally marrying? How has this changed over the past 30 years?

8. In what respects can it be said that the United States has undergone a sexual revolution?

9. How has the average age at which women begin to have children changed over the past 30 years? Among which group(s) of American women have the rates of childbearing outside of marriage increased most rapidly?

Critical Thinking Questions

1. Are there potential disadvantages associated with defining *family* too broadly? Explain your answer.

2. Do you agree with the argument that interdependence among members is a key in defining or identifying families? What do you believe are the essential elements that must be present in a group of people in order for them to be considered a family?

Is it bonds of affection? The presence of children and both parents in the home? Write your own definition of *family*.

3. How do conservatives and liberals differ in terms of their goals for American families and in their recommendations for government policies that would affect families?

Online Resources Available for This Chapter

www.ablongman.com/marriageandfamily

- **Online Study Guide with Practice Tests**
- **PowerPoint Chapter Outlines**

- **Links to Marriage and Family Websites**
- **ContentSelect Research Database**
- **Self-Assessment Activities**

Further Reading

Books

Amato, Paul R., and Booth, Alan. *A Generation at Risk: Growing Up in an Era of Family Upheaval.* Cambridge, MA: Harvard University Press, 1999. Data covering a fifteen year period from two generations are used to determine how major changes in the American family have affected children.

Cherlin, Andrew J. *Marriage, Divorce, Remarriage* (revised ed.). Cambridge, MA: Harvard University Press, 1992. A detailed discussion of demographic trends in family formation and dissolution over the twentieth century.

Coontz, Stephanie. *The Way We Really Are: Coming to Terms with America's Changing Families.* New York: Basic Books, 1997. A historical perspective on family life that gets beyond the sweeping over-generalizations about traditional as well as modern families and notes the strengths of today's families.

Goode, William J. *World Revolution and Family Patterns.* Glencoe, IL: The Free Press, 1963. A description and interpretation of the main changes in family patterns that have occurred over the past half-century in various cultures.

McAdoo, Harriette Pipes (ed.). *Black Families.* (3rd ed.). Newbury Park, CA: Sage, 1997. Twenty-one articles explore the experience of black families, includes theoretical, demographic, economic, educational, socialization, and policy.

Popenoe, David, Elshtain, Jean Bethke, and Blankenhorn, David (eds.). *Promises to Keep: Decline and Renewal of Marriage in America.* Lanham, MD: Rowman & Littlefield Publishers, 1996. A collection of thirteen articles that suggest marriage in America is in trouble and that the time has come for society to change course.

Scanzoni, John, Polonko, Karen, Teachman, Jay, and Thompson, Linda. *The Sexual Bond: Rethinking Families and Close Relationships.* Newbury Park, CA: Sage, 1989. An innovative process approach to examining close, primary, sexually based relationships that extend beyond marriage and family to characterize the reality of relationships in the United States today.

Stacey, Judith. *In the Name of the Family: Rethinking Family Values in the Post-Modern Age.* Boston: Beacon Press, 1996. A book that challenges the rhetoric and politics of family values and presents a strong case for family diversity, including legal gay marriages.

Staples, Robert, and Johnson, Leanor Boulin. *Black Families at the Crossroads: Challenges and Prospects.* San Francisco: Jossey-Bass, 1992. A picture of the black family, including its changing structures, roles of its members, and how it has been influenced by other systems.

Taylor, Robert J., Jackson, James S., and Chatters, Linda M. (eds.). *Family Life in Black America.* Thousand Oaks, CA: Sage, 1997. A view of the diversity within African American families and the forces that shape, limit, and enhance it.

Taylor, Ronald L. (ed.). *Minority Families in the United States: A Multicultural Perspective.* (2nd ed.). Upper Saddle River, NJ: Prentice-Hall, 1998. Chapters are devoted to a range of minority families in the United States, including Mexican, Puerto Rican, Cuban, Chinese, Japanese, American Indian, and others.

Zambrana, Ruth E., (ed.). *Understanding Latino Families: Scholarship, Policy, and Practice.* Thousand Oaks, CA: Sage, 1995. An integrated focus on the Hispanic/Latino family with particular attention devoted to Latino subgroups and a theoretical direction for the study of Latino families.

ContentSELECT Articles

Bianchi, S., Milkie, M., Sayer, L., and Robinson, J. "Is Anyone Doing the Housework? Trends in the Gender Division of Household Labor." *Social Forces* 79(1), 2000: 191. **[Database: Sociology]** Utilizing data gathered from husbands' and wives' time-diaries, researchers examine the basic trends in the division of household tasks to address the supposition that women are overtaxed by the demands of the *second shift*—the demands of household labor and child-rearing responsibilities after completing a career day's work. Although the results indicate some support for gender stereotypes in the division of housework tasks, time and availability to perform household labor was a stronger indicator of why or why not a household chore was performed.

Carby, C., Hutchinson, K., Jackson, A., and Mentor, R. "First Comes Love, Then Comes Marriage . . . Not Anymore." *New York Amsterdam News* 91(41), 2002, 22. **[Database: General Interest]** Controversial researcher and author David Popenoe purports potential negative effects exist for children who live in homes where the parents cohabit, rather than with parents who are married. Carby et al. disagree with Popenoe's suggestions that children in cohabiting homes are at greater risk for abuse and neglect, and that cohabiting homes are typically less stable than married homes.

Nock, S. "The Problem with Marriage." *Society* Jul/Aug(36), 2001: 20–28. **[Database: Sociology]** The ideals of individual free choice, maturity, heterosexuality, husband as the head of household, fidelity and monogamy, and parenthood are discussed as the traditional institutional foundations of marriage. The trends in U.S. society to deviate from these institutional standards frame the argument that the social establishment of marriage has failed to recognize the significance of gender in the marital relationship.

Terry, S. "Whose Family? The Revolt of the Child-Free." *Christian Science Monitor* 92(194), 2000: 1. **[Database: General Interest]** Child*less* or child*free*? Increasingly more and more married adults are opting not to bear children. Today 13 million baby boomers are childfree—and intend to stay that way. In the wake of feminism and with the ability to control fertility, the attitudinal shift towards children may mean the term *family* will take on a new definition.

Waite, L. "The Importance of Marriage Is Being Overlooked." *USA Today Magazine* 127(2644), 1999: 46–49. **[Database: General Interest]** On the whole, individuals who reside within the social institution of legal marriage appear to enjoy substantial benefits: married individuals are more apt to lead healthier lives and adopt healthier lifestyle habits; increased longevity; increased satisfaction in the physical and emotional aspects of their sex lives; increased household wealth; and enhanced children's welfare. Because marriage may be the key variable in health, longevity, and overall happiness and satisfaction, the author suggests that more support in marriage-friendly public policy should be examined and supported.

Knowledge about Marriages, Families, and Intimate Relationships

Common Sense or Science?

2

It's a surprisingly cloudless Seattle morning as newly-weds Mark and Janice Gordon sit down to breakfast. Outside the apartment's picture window, the waters of Montlake cut a deep-blue swath, while runners jog and geese waddle along the lakeside park.

Mark and Janice are enjoying the view as they munch on their French toast and share the Sunday paper. Later Mark will probably switch on the football game while Janice chats on the phone with her mom in St. Louis.

All seems ordinary enough inside this studio apartment—until you notice the three video cameras bolted to the wall, the microphones clipped talk-show style to Mark's and Janice's collars, and the Holter monitors strapped around their chests. Mark and Janice's lovely studio with a view is really not their apartment at all. It's the Family Research Laboratory at the University of Washington in Seattle, where for sixteen years psychologist John Gottman, Ph.D., has spearheaded the most extensive and innovative research ever into marriage and divorce.

As part of these studies, Mark and Janice (as well as forty-nine other randomly selected couples) volunteered to stay overnight in a fabricated apartment, affectionately known as *The Love Lab.* Their instructions were to act as naturally as possible, despite Dr. Gottman's team of scientists observing them from behind the one-way kitchen mirror, the cameras recording their every word and facial expression, and the sensors tracking bodily signs of stress or relaxation, such as how quickly their hearts pound. (To preserve basic privacy, the couples were monitored only from nine A.M. to nine P.M. and never while in the bathroom.) The Love Lab apartment comes equipped with a fold-out sofa, a working kitchen, a phone, TV, VCR, and CD player.

Key Questions

1 Can intimate behavior be studied in a laboratory setting?

2 What is the relationship between theory and empirical research?

3 Which method of constructing theories is more effective, inductive (that is, from the empirical level up to the most abstract level) or deductive (that is, from the abstract level down to the most concrete level)?

4 What are the advantages and disadvantages of using the scientific method in the study of human behavior?

5 In what ways do the personal values or beliefs of researchers affect the questions they study and the methods and theories they use?

Couples are told to bring their groceries, their newspapers, their laptops, needlepoint, hand weights, even their pets—whatever they would need to experience a typical weekend.

Dr. Gottman's goal in the Love Lab has been to uncover the truth about marriage—*to finally answer the questions that have puzzled people for so long:* Why is marriage so tough at times? Why do some lifelong relationships click, while others just tick away like a time bomb? And how can you prevent a marriage from going bad—or rescue one that already has?

*T*he questions Dr. Gottman and his research team have been attempting to answer are ones that we all care about. In fact, you will discover as you read this text that family scientists address many questions that have great personal relevance to your lives. The list that follows highlights only a few that we consider in this textbook:

1 Are *mixed* marriages (such as those between Catholics and Protestants or those between blacks and whites) doomed to divorce?

2 Does living together before marriage decrease the chance of getting a divorce later on?

3 Should parents use physical punishment to discipline their children?

4 Do children make marriages happier?

5 When is the best time (in terms of age) to marry?

6 Are husbands who earn less money than their wives more likely to be violent?

7 Why do parents physically abuse—sometimes even kill—their own children? (Why do people hurt the ones they love most?)

8 What makes people feel sexually attracted to one another—do opposites attract? Or, do birds of a feather flock together?

9 What do women—or men—really want out of their intimate relationships?

10 Can intimate relationships survive over great geographic distances?

Let's take the last question: *Can intimate relationships survive over long distances.* If you are one of the people who is involved in a *long-distance* relationship, as many college students are at one time or another, you may find yourself worrying about how this will affect your romance. Where do you turn for information or advice

Laboratory observation of couples as they communicate to complete a task or solve a problem is a valuable method of research in the family sciences.

about the likely effect of geographic separation on romantic relationships? Well, you could ask your roommate or your best friend, who are likely to turn to common sense or folk wisdom for an answer. Your roommate may ascribe to the old adage, *"out of sight, out of mind."* Or, as the lyrics of an old rock song once said, "If you can't be with the one you love, love the one you're with." This is not exactly the kind of information you want to hear when you are separated from your sweetheart. Your best friend, on the other hand, may believe another old saying—*"absence makes the heart grow fonder."* This is the advice you hope is true.

Because the answer to this question is of great consequence to you and undoubtedly may affect your future decisions, you want to have confidence that it is valid. You do not want to rely on common sense to give you an accurate picture of the social world. You may be comforted to know that family sociologists have addressed this question through the use of scientific methods. Thus, rather than having to choose between two conflicting pieces of conventional wisdom, you can turn to the research findings that have emerged. Folk wisdom or common sense differs from scientific knowledge in that it is not tested carefully. It is simply accepted as true because we trust those who have shared it with us or because it seems to "make sense." Science, on the other hand, is based on the careful testing of beliefs. It can be thought of as *a logically organized method of obtaining information through direct, systematic observation.* It relies on empirical evidence (i.e., evidence that can be directly verified through one of the five senses).

Some people, of course, are strongly opposed to the scientific study of intimate or romantic behavior. Former U.S. Senator William Proxmire (from Wisconsin), who was known for his identification of federally funded research projects that he thought were a waste of taxpayers' money, once ridiculed two researchers from the Universities of Minnesota and Wisconsin for trying to study love scientifically. Proxmire awarded the two psychologists the Golden Fleece Award and publically stated that he felt that love was one of those subjects that was best left to poets rather than social scientists.

Folk Beliefs about Marriage and Family Life among the Amish

In the past, especially before the development of the social sciences, beliefs about courtship, sex, married life, and childrearing, were often found in the folk beliefs and superstitions of traditional people. The Pennsylvania Dutch, one such traditional group, had the following superstitions and advice.

On Courtship and Marriage

Always avoid eating the last slice of bread from a loaf, because anyone who does so will not marry.

If a woman is getting pretty anxious to marry, she should feed a cat from her shoe.

A more drastic measure for someone wishing to marry is to swallow a raw chicken heart. The person one is thinking of at the time will be the person one will marry.

To have luck in married life, a newly married couple should step over a broom when entering their new home.*

On Having and Raising Children

If you feel you have had too many sons, name one Adam and the next child you have will be a girl.

Children born on Christmas Day will be brighter than others, and they will have the added advantage of being able to hear and understand cow talk.

To make a baby handsome, wash its face with its own urine. This method also works to get rid of freckles.

To prevent a child from stuttering, don't tickle it before it is a year old.

*In the nineteenth century, both English and African American culture associated marriage with jumping over a broom (Menefee, 1981). Some African Americans still use the term "jump over the broom" as a slang phrase for marriage.

Source: Aurand, 1986.

Using Science to Understand Human Behavior

Social and Behavioral Sciences versus "Natural" Sciences

Not all types of human behavior—particularly those of interest to us in this text—can be studied in a laboratory, but that doesn't mean they can't be studied scientifically. Some people assume that sociology, psychology, and anthropology are not true sciences because their subject matter (e.g., human behavior) is so familiar and because they typically do not involve the use of sophisticated equipment and tools. Because we are all involved in social relationships, research in the social sciences does not have the same kind of mystery that research in the physical and biological sciences has. In fact, studying humans is *not* quite the same as studying insects, the weather, or atomic particles. In many ways, the social sciences are not only *different from* the physical or natural sciences, they may even be *more complex.*

First, the mere fact of studying human beings may cause them to change their behavior, out of nervousness or embarrassment. This change in the behavior of persons who are being observed or studied is often referred to as the **Hawthorne effect** because it was first recognized by researchers in a study of workers' productivity in the Hawthorne Electric Plant. Such effects, of course, affect the **validity** (that is, accuracy) of the data that are obtained. Second, human behavior is not as consistent or predictable as the behavior of animals or inanimate objects. As their moods, motives, experiences, and preferences change, so does their behavior. This unpredictability or variability over time affects the **reliability** (that is, consistency) of the data that are obtained. Third, the causes of human behavior are complex and are embedded in social structures that cannot be completely controlled or easily manipulated. Sociologists, for instance, are interested in the ways in which social class affects parenting styles. Some research has found that fathers who have working-class jobs are more likely to use physical punishment, whereas fathers with middle-class jobs are more likely to try to reason with their children. However, sociologists who wish to address this question cannot manipulate (or change) a family's social class. So they must find another way to systematically investigate the impact of social class on parenting style. Fourth, ethical concerns also restrict the type of studies that can be done with human subjects. It is not acceptable, for instance, to ask parents to neglect their children or to raise their girls as boys just to examine the consequences of this type of parent–child interaction. And fifth, the social scientist is part of the population or subject matter she or he is studying. It is difficult, if not impossible, to be completely detached from one's research topics or the people you are studying.

While the view that social researchers can and should suppress their personal values and conduct **value-free research** has long been predominant in the social sciences, more researchers are questioning both the possibility and the desirability of doing so. Feminist researchers are among those who challenge the desirability of separating one's own values from the selection of research questions and the application of findings (Fox and Murry, 2000).

The subject matter of the social sciences—human behavior rather than stars, rocks, or scorpion flies—does not make these fields of study any less scientific, just more complex. As to the second challenge to the scientific status of the social sciences, it can be demonstrated easily that the type of tools or instruments that a scholarly field employs does not determine whether it is scientific. The research instruments that social scientists use to collect and record data are more likely to take the form of carefully worded questions than technological or mechanical devices. It wouldn't be effective, or appropriate for that matter, to use a telescope to study people's sexual behavior. Similarly, it wouldn't be effective or appropriate to use a telescope to measure the division of human cells or to use a microscope to study the stars and planets. One of the keys to scientific inquiry is the **systematic collection of data,** whether that involves the use of precisely calibrated tools or precisely worded questionnaires.

Cause and Effect Relationships

A basic goal of all scientific inquiry—whether it be in geology, physics, biology, or sociology—is to obtain evidence about *cause and effect relationships.* In the family sciences, we are interested in such causal questions as what causes people to fall in or out of love? What causes men to beat their wives or girlfriends? What is it about teen marriages that makes them more likely to end in divorce? There are *three basic criteria* that must be met if a cause and effect relationship is to be established. First, the researcher must observe an *association between the behaviors or outcomes* in which she or he is interested. What this means is that as one factor changes, the other does, as well. The second criterion is that the factor that is believed to be *the cause occurs before the expected outcome.* And third, the researcher must be able to *rule out any other possible explanations* for the observed association between factors.

One of the classic examples used in introductory social science classes to illustrate the criteria for establishing causality pertains to changes in the birth rate. Suppose bird watchers in upstate New York notice a substantial increase in the number of storks that are nesting on roof tops. Then, some months later, they notice a significant increase in the number of babies that are born in this same region. Would this observed association support the conclusion that the presence of storks *causes* the arrival of babies? The first criterion for causality—the observation of an association between the two facts, in this case, the number of storks and the number of babies—is met. As the number of storks increased, so did the number of babies. The second criterion—the appearance of the causal factor (that is, the storks) before the appearance of the outcome (that is, the babies)—is also met. But what about the third criterion, that is, the ability to rule out other possible causes of this observed association? In this case, it may be that a third factor, the weather, is responsible for both the number of storks nesting on rooftops near chimneys and for the number of babies born nine months later. In extremely cold temperatures, storks may build nests near chimneys to find warmth and humans may spend more time in bed, under the blankets, for the same reason. It's not the storks that are responsible for babies, but the human snuggling and sharing of body warmth that come with cold weather.

Types of Data Collection

Scientific data are collected in many different ways. Empirical observations can be made by conducting experiments, both in the laboratory and in the field, by carrying out social surveys, by making systematic observations of behavior in the field and in the laboratory, and by assembling and analyzing demographic and historical records. In the discussions that follow, we consider all these methods and offer examples of each. To demonstrate the usefulness of a wide range of different data-gathering methods, our examples focus on only one subject: sexual behavior.

Experiments

An **experiment** is a highly controlled method of attempting to demonstrate the existence of a causal relationship between two variables. Experiments take place under tightly controlled conditions, usually in a laboratory. Experimenters greatly simplify the environment so that they can more easily observe associations between the variables of interest. They manipulate the **independent variable** (the factor they believe to be the causal agent in the situation) and then watch to see if expected changes occur in the **dependent variable** (the outcome of interest). Manipulating the independent variable lets experimenters guarantee that changes in it occur before changes in the dependent variable.

Experiments also provide a way to rule out alternative causes of the observed changes in the dependent variable. Through **random assignment** participants are assigned to experimental groups randomly rather than on the basis of any of their pre-existing characteristics, such as friendliness, age, or marital status. Researchers can rule out existing differences between subjects as possible explanations for their behavior. This gives them more confidence that it was, indeed, their manipulations of the independent variable that caused the observed change in the participants' behavior. The laboratory setting and the simplification of the environment often result in artificial situations. This is the greatest disadvantage of the experimental method and one that must be accepted if researchers choose to conduct laboratory experiments.

As an alternative to laboratory experiments, some researchers—especially sociologists—carry out their work in real-life settings. Studies conducted under natural conditions are called **field experiments.**

In one ingeniously designed field experiment, two researchers demonstrated how being in a dangerous situation can increase the physiological arousal of men when they meet an attractive woman (Dutton and Aron, 1974).

Field Experiment

Just after male hikers had crossed the Capilano River (in Canada), a young woman confederate of the experimenters approached and asked them to complete a questionnaire about the impact of scenic beauty on creativity. The experimental aspect of this study was introduced by the presence of two bridges across the river. One was sturdy and not too high above the river; the other was wobbly and quite high above the water. The experimenters expected to find that men who had crossed on the high, wobbly bridge would be physiologically aroused by fear, and would label their arousal as attraction to the young woman they encountered on the bridge. Men who crossed on the lower, stable bridge would not experience the same degree of arousal and would not rate the young woman as attractive as the others had. This was, indeed, what they found.

Psychologists are more likely than sociologists to use experimental methods because the variables of greatest interest to sociologists (for example, race, age, sex, social class) cannot or should not, for ethical reasons, be manipulated. In some cases, researchers are able to examine the effects of changing conditions that occur in the real world. For instance, in Baltimore, Maryland, in the 1990s, some high schools began to offer the contraceptive Norplant to teenage girls in an effort to prevent additional teen births. Researchers could compare the teen birth rate in this school before and after the introduction of Norplant. While this offers the advantage of a real-life setting, it does not offer the same degree of confidence in the causal relationships between Norplant on the teen birth rate because so many other unforeseen factors could be operating to produce a decrease in the birth rate. This type of research would be characterized as a **quasi-experiment** rather than a true experiment, however. This is a type of research method that does not meet all of the strict standards of the true experiment because the scientist has only partial control over the research situation.

ContentSELECT

Research Ethics

Correlational Methods

Sociologists are more likely to use **correlational methods** of data collection and analysis rather than experimental methods. In this type of research, researchers do not attempt to manipulate the independent variables of interest, as they do in experimental research. They study existing relationships to describe and explain them. Two different types of correlational research are commonly used by social scientists—surveys and systematic observations.

Social Surveys.   In **survey research,** a large number of people (called *respondents*) are asked a set of questions by a researcher, either in writing (using a questionnaire that the respondent reads and answers) or orally (through interviews in which a researcher asks the respondent questions and receives a spoken response). The questions asked in survey research must be carefully designed to avoid bias and to elicit meaningful information.

Sometimes a full range of possible answers is provided to respondents who must choose the one that best describes their beliefs. These are called **fixed-response** questions and are similar to multiple choice questions on exams. The use of fixed response questions permits greater comparability across respondents but restricts the amount of detail they can provide in their answers. Other times, the questions are **open-ended,** which means the respondent is free to give an answer in his or her own words. This type of question provides "richer" data but may make comparison across respondents more time-consuming.

Most surveys collect data from respondents at only one point in time. This type of research is called **cross-sectional.** Researchers who are interested in changes in people's behavior believe that **longitudinal research** (research that follows people over a period of time, collecting information from them at different times) should be conducted.

Survey research has been used extensively in the last 60 years to study sexual behavior. One of the earliest and most influential surveys of sexual behavior was conducted by Alfred Kinsey. The Kinsey studies opened the door to surveys of sexual behavior and provided much useful information; more recent studies have improved on this research by using random sampling and contemporary questionnaire and interview procedures.

The purpose of the Kinsey studies was to obtain detailed information about the sexual histories of a large number of Americans representing different historical eras. At the conclusion of his studies, Kinsey had obtained detailed sexual information on over 17,000 individuals from a wide range of backgrounds. The interviews he conducted included over 300 questions and provided basic demographic information, physical data, information about early sexual knowledge and early sexual activity, masturbation, and number of sexual partners—both heterosexual and homosexual—along with much additional data. The findings from the Kinsey studies continued to be cited in reports well into the 1990s, even though they were criticized as not being representative of the American public, in general. Because of the sensitivity associated with studying human sexual behavior, Kinsey was forced to draw respondents from segments of the society who would be most likely to provide such personal information. His sample drew heavily from well-educated persons (such as university students and faculty and medical students and faculty), from persons with a known *liberal* bent, and from persons in institutions who were *required* to participate (prisons and mental hospitals). Thus, the responses that were provided by the people in Kinsey's studies may have exaggerated the extent of sexual activity among the population as a whole because his respondents were not representative of all American adults at the time.

Researchers from the University of Chicago conducted a more recent influential survey of American sexual behavior (Laumann et al., 1994). This study produced interviews with a sample of 3,432 adult Americans. The results of this survey have provided new and valuable information on sexual practices, sexual techniques, sexual relationships, same-sex relationships, early sexual experiences, sexual dysfunctions, risky sexual behaviors, and a variety of other topics. In Chapter 6, we describe a few of the most important findings of this study; but one example here illustrates the importance of survey research.

The University of Chicago researchers asked questions that allowed them to describe the *sexual networks* of American adults. Sexual networks are the links that people have to others through their sexual partners. In an age when sexually transmitted diseases, and especially AIDS, are very threatening, it is important to gain more knowledge about sexual networks. The extensiveness of sexual networks determines the transmission of AIDS through the general population.

The researchers found that at any given time, most adults in the United States have only one sex partner. Furthermore, most people, even those who have more than one partner, have known their sexual partners for some time before having sex with them. These facts reveal that the sexual networks of most people are quite limited.

In contrast to the large-scale and highly statistical studies conducted by Kinsey is the research conducted by Lillian Rubin (1990), who was also interested in obtaining information about people's sexual histories. Rubin conducted face-to-face, in-depth interviews with 375 people about the intimate details of their sexual histories. Her interviews consisted of a number of open-ended questions such as "Tell me about the first time you had sexual intercourse." Her method of data collection resembled a natural conversation more than a scientific investigation and as a result, they provided very detailed personal information that could not be

Sexual Partners

obtained with fixed-response questionnaires. Clearly, however, this type of data collection is very time-consuming and is not likely to allow the researcher to include as many respondents. In fact, Rubin supplemented her in-depth interviews with a 13-page self-report questionnaire that she distributed to 600 college students from eight different colleges and universities.

Information about human sexual behavior has also been obtained through *magazine surveys.* In 2000, for instance, *YM* magazine asked its readers to respond to a "super survey" about sexual activity. In fact, nearly 15,000 readers completed the questionnaire and mailed it in. The characteristics of the respondents were, as would be expected, similar to the larger readership of the magazine. While the *YM* magazine study provided interesting information on a large number of respondents, the unique characteristics of the magazine's readers made the study's findings inapplicable to the population of young women in America. Additionally, the wording of a number of the questions may have affected the way readers responded. For instance, using the euphemisms "doing the deed," "slipping between the sheets," and "doing the mattress mambo" rather than saying "having sex with someone" may have encouraged respondents to report this type of behavior.

Public opinion polls also ask Americans about their sexual behavior. Unlike the data provided by magazine readers, public opinion polls rely on **random samples** of Americans (for example, every person in the population has an equal chance of being selected for the study) and their findings can be generalized to the population at large.

Observational Studies

In **observational studies,** the researcher gathers data on the behavior of interest by observing it directly. Observational studies can take place in laboratories or in real-life settings. **Laboratory observation** has advantages and disadvantages similar to laboratory experiments. The advantage is that the researcher can have more control over the context in which the behavior occurs and thus can have greater confidence in his or her conclusions about causality. The major disadvantage is that the setting may be too artificial. **Field observation** provides a real (more

Field observation provides data about people's behaviors in "real world" settings.

in the media

PBS Documents the Everyday Lives and Private Problems of Two American Families

In 1973, PBS broadcast what might have been the first reality TV series in history. Called *An American Family,* the series followed the lives of Bill and Pat Loud and their five children: Michele, Delilah, Grant, Kevin, and Lance. The seven members of the Loud family opened up their home and their lives for seven months to the producer and film crew, who shot 300 hours of footage, only twelve of which actually made it to television screens. At the beginning of the series, the Louds, a well-to-do family in Santa Barbara, California, seemed to be living the American Dream. Their visible disintegration throughout the filming became a "national psychodrama" (Grimes, 1997). The family complained that the footage that was chosen for broadcast misrepresented their lives. "The film created a stir by documenting the troubles of one American family, bringing to hundreds of thousands of living rooms scenes of Bill and Pat Loud's crumbling marriage and Lance's evolving decision to declare openly that he was gay. The PBS show predated today's 'confessional' talk shows and camcorders. It was shocking at the time, especially its treatment of homosexuality" (Singer, 1990). Lance Loud was the first person to "come out" on national television.

Twenty-five years after PBS broadcast *An American Family,* another documentary about the private lives of a family was created. The second show, called *An American Love Story,* was based on 1,000 hours of videotape recorded over five years. The family at the center of the more recent documentary was quite different from the Louds.

Bill Sims and Karen Wilson are a biracial couple, married 18 years at the time of the final filming, who have two daughters, Cicily Wilson and Chaney Sims. They lived in Queens, the most ethnically mixed borough in New York City. The series, which was created by Jennifer Fox and Jennifer Fleming, began as a personal mission for Ms. Fox, who was motivated to create a documentary about love and race after her own interracial relationship was met with public outrage. She began to film the Wilson–Sims family in the spring of 1992. At first, she worked alone, but months later she invited Jennifer Fleming to help with the sound recording. Ms. Fleming had also been involved in an interracial relationship, so she, too, was personally interested in making the documentary.

The two filmmakers essentially lived with their subjects for extended periods of time over a 17-month period. They frequently spent nights in sleeping bags in the daughters' bedrooms, filming as much as 10 hours a day. They also followed Mr. Sims (a blues musician) on the road, accompanied the couple to Ms. Wilson's 25th high school reunion, saw Ms. Wilson through a serious illness and tagged along with Cicily on an academic road trip to Nigeria. Along the way, they recorded the myriad unremarkable incidents that make up daily life. "I kept wondering who was going to be interested in any of this," Ms. Wilson said (Grimes, 1997).

Why would a family allow two strangers to camp out in their home and film them for a year and a half? "I always thought we'd have some nice home movies," said Ms. Wilson, who speaks in an unvarnished, just-the-facts style. "A lot of times Jennifer would ask race things, and it would take me aback. To me, it's my family. I'd say many times: 'I just don't get it like that. Bill is Bill, I'm Karen, the girls are the girls, this is our life. There's nothing more to it than that.' "That's the point," Mr. Sims said. "From the beginning, I wanted to take away some of the mystery surrounding interracial relationships," he said. "I wanted the film to show that we're doing the same things as everyone else, raising our kids, paying bills, trying to make Christmas nice."

Social scientists who study families would undoubtedly love to have the opportunity to observe family interactions that take place at home. The costs involved in following one family over a five-year period, for 10 hours a day, would be prohibitive for most, if not all, academic researchers. In addition, the ethical issues associated with such an invasion of a family's private life would also have to be taken into consideration. Finally, the impact of the continual presence of the cameras and film crews on the family's behavior might be detrimental, as some people claimed happened to the Loud family. Thus, the PBS documentaries provide a rare glimpse into the lives of American families that most likely will not be duplicated by social researchers in the near future.

Sources: "Another family sits for an intimate portrait, coming to PBS," William Grimes, The *New York Times,* March 20, 1997; "The return of the Louds: WENT to air 1973 film," by Stephen Singer, originally published in *Current,* November 5, 1990.

valid) setting, but little or no control for the researcher. In some cases, the researcher participates in the behavior he or she is observing, posing as a member of the situation or group under study. This type of research is called **participant observation.** In other types of observation, the researcher maintains a distance from the people being observed. In many public settings, such as shopping malls or sports events, however, the researcher can enter without permission and the people who are being observed may not be aware of the researcher's reason for being there.

Examples of Laboratory Observation.   One of the most daring laboratory observational studies was conducted in the 1960s by William Masters and Virginia Johnson. Masters and Johnson directly observed over 10,000 episodes of sexual activity involving over 700 different individuals in their laboratory. They used sophisticated instruments to measure various physiological responses (such as blood flow, changes in vaginal chemistry, and extent of penile erection) that occur during sexual stimulation. They recruited participants for their study through newspaper ads. These participants—who were willing to be observed by researchers during this very intimate type of experience—were probably more relaxed about sexuality than the general population. Thus, they may not have been representative.

Masters and Johnson were also sex therapists, so they compiled data on more than 800 of their patients over a period of many years. When therapists collect and analyze data from their patients, their studies are referred to as *clinical research.* Although Masters and Johnson's clinical records provided in-depth and long-term data about a number of important topics such as rape, incest, and sexual abuse, they were limited in how much they could generalize about the population at large. People who seek treatment for sexual problems are undoubtedly quite different in some important ways from those who do not seek treatment.

Recently, medical researchers have been using laboratory observation techniques to better understand sexual problems in women (that is, lack of sexual desire and painful intercourse). Some researchers have begun to insert ultrasound probes that resemble electronic tampons into women's vaginas to measure blood flow. Others use female genitalia (for example, clitorises, labia, and vaginas) from cadavers, surgery patients, or animals to study body structures that are associated with sexual response. Biologists in Britain have even attached microvideo cameras to men's penises during heterosexual intercourse to study the impact of women's orgasms on their likelihood of retaining ejaculate in their bodies, thus increasing the likelihood of conception.

Examples of Field Observation.   A well-known observational study of sexual behavior was conducted in a nonlaboratory field setting by Laud Humphreys (1970) as part of his graduate work in sociology. Humphreys was interested in the extent of homosexual activity among married men. Rather than ask husbands directly about such activity, he posed as a homosexual and observed sexual interactions that occurred in public restrooms at a city park. Although he didn't participate in the sexual activities per se, he did act as a "watch queen," the person who signals the participants when "straight" people are approaching. Humphreys later traced many of the subjects through their car license plates. He visited their homes about one year later, pretending to do a market survey so that he could get more demographic information about them. This study was subsequently criticized because it violated the participants' privacy regarding a very personal and controversial issue. The use of **deception in social research** (concealing or lying about the purposes of a study) triggers ethical consideration and requires a careful consideration of the possible knowledge gained versus the potential harm done to participants.

Today, however, universities and professional associations require scientists who plan to do research that involves human subjects to submit a detailed description of their study for review by a panel of experts. The purpose of this extra step in the research process is to guarantee that people will not be harmed either physically or psychologically by participating in the research.

Ethnographies—Observational Studies of Other Cultures. Anthropologists carry out a special form of observation in which, typically, they go to another society and study the way of life of the people—their culture. Descriptions of the customs and practices of the people of other societies are called **ethnographies.** Throughout this book, we often draw on the ethnographies of anthropologists to illuminate the variety of cultural customs related to marriage, families, and sexual behavior. The boxes labeled "Around the World" are often based on anthropological ethnographies.

Studies of the customs of people in different societies can be important for our understanding of our own way of life. Such studies frequently demonstrate that marriages and families can vary greatly and still fulfill their members' needs. Thus there may not be one perfect way of organizing intimate and family relationships.

Historical Studies.   History is, of course, the study of events in earlier times, but much historical research has, until recently, dealt with elite groups in society (royalty or political and military leaders) and with major military and political events. In recent years, however, more historians have devoted their attention to the lives of ordinary people. This type of research is referred to as **social history** and often features marriage and family life of earlier times. In fact, so much of social history is devoted to the study of marriage and family life, that there is now a specialized subfield called **family history** (Coontz, 2000b).

Some family historians, like other social researchers, have devoted their attention to sexual behavior. We learn from historians that premarital sex has occurred in all periods of American history, even in the Puritan era (Smith, 1978). Social historians have discovered, through careful analysis of church records on marriage and baptism of infants, that a significant proportion of Puritan brides may have been pregnant (Ulrich, 1990). By comparing the date of baptism of a couple's first child with the date of their marriage, social historians have been able to draw this conclusion, which so sharply contrasts with modern-day beliefs about Puritan moral standards.

Research involving secondary analysis of historical or legal documents does not require the researcher to question or observe people directly.

Other social historians have analyzed diaries by people who lived in earlier historical periods. Laurel Thatcher Ulrich (1990) was able to reconstruct a fairly detailed account of women's work and family lives in colonial America through a careful analysis of the diary of Martha Ballard, a midwife who lived in Maine in the late seventeenth and early eighteenth centuries. Ballard's diary was passed down from one generation of women to another and was eventually donated to a museum in Maine. Through a painstaking examination of Ballard's diary, Ulrich discovered that women made major economic contributions to their families through their work in textile production and in professions such as midwifery.

Historian Joan Jacobs Brumberg also used diaries to understand how the meaning of sexuality for young women has changed since the Victorian era, a time span of about 150 years. Brumberg found her diaries in a number of ways—in archives and libraries, through friends and family, from students enrolled in her classes, and from people who attended her public lectures. She also advertised her project in the *New York Times* and got many diaries in response, including one from a New York City sanitation worker who found a diary in a garbage can. By comparing the comments written by young women in the late 1800s with those of more contemporary periods, Brumberg concluded that our society has changed a lot in its emphasis on virginity in women before marriage.

Marital sex has also been the subject of historical research, and at least one historian has described the sexual lives of American married women before the twentieth century in quite dismal terms (Shorter, 1982).

This discussion should illustrate that any one subject can be pursued through any number of research methods. But each method of data collection has its characteristic strengths and weaknesses. Table 2.1 summarizes the advantages and disadvantages associated with each.

A vast amount of scientific research has been done on marriage, family life, and intimate relationships. Science is not, however, the only source of information that we use to help us guide our behavior in everyday relationships, as the Around the World box on page 32 suggests. We may look to our religions, customs and laws,

TABLE 2.1

Method of Social Research: Advantages and Limitations

Method	Advantages	Limitations
Experiments	• Researcher has control over events • Provide evidence about causality	• Often artificial • May raise ethical issues
Surveys (questionnaires, interviews)	• Large sample size • Flexibility • Lower costs • Efficiency • Anonymity	• Sample selection may be biased • Poor wording may affect answers • Low response may bias results
Observational studies	• Behavior observed directly • Avoid memory distortion	• Presence of observer may bias data
Demographic studies	• Provide information on the population • Reveal relationships among family processes	• Do not reveal the motivations that influence behavior
Historical studies	• Provide a long-range perspective on human behavior	• Restricted to the data that have survived

"That's Dr. Cray conducting research."

Source: Copyright © 2001 Benita Epstein. Reprinted by permission.

myths and folk legends, and authority figures for information about developing successful relationships with spouses and children. The benefit of scientific knowledge over the various nonscientific sources, of course, is that it has "stood the test of time" and is more reliable than knowledge based on personal opinions or observations.

Social Theories

A distinguishing feature of scientific research is the systematic collection of data, but data collection can only be systematic if it is carefully organized and interpreted. Social scientists use theories as tools to aid in the organized collection and interpretation of data. A **social theory** is a set of ideas that provides explanations for a broad range of social phenomena (Ritzer, 1997). A number of theories have been used to understand marriages, families, and other types of intimate relationships. We consider five theories in this chapter: structural-functionalism, social conflict, social exchange, symbolic interactionism, and family development theory.

Although these theories have the same general objective—to better understand marriages and families—they differ in fundamental ways. For each theory we identify its (1) **unit of analysis** (that is, whether the theory attempts to explain behavior patterns on an interactional or institutional level); (2) **underlying assumptions** (what aspects of family life the theory takes for granted in order to simplify its focus); and (3) **key concepts** (specialized terms that contribute to the theory's unique vocabulary). We also highlight the topics or issues that are most fruitfully studied with each theory. Table 2.2 summarizes the features of these five theories.

Structural-Functional Theory

A basic assumption of structural-functionalism is that each social unit (whether it be a family or the society as a whole) is composed of interrelated parts

Know this

| TABLE 2.2 |

Features of Sociological Theories

Theory	Unit of Analysis	Basic Assumptions	Key Concepts
Structural-functional	Families Society	Whole is made of interrelated parts that carry out tasks for survival Equilibrium among parts	Structure Function
Social conflict	Families Society	Unequal resources Conflict is inevitable	Power Conflict
Symbolic interaction	Individuals in families	Learn meanings of symbols through interaction	Symbols Significant others
Social exchange	Individuals in close relationships	All behavior is motivated by rewards–costs ratio	Rewards Costs Reciprocity
Family development	Families	Families develop through regular stages	Family life-cycle stages Developmental tasks

that fit together and work together to carry out tasks essential for the survival of the whole. Another key assumption is that the ideal for all social units is to maintain an equilibrium or balance between its parts. When one part of the unit changes, the other parts of the unit will also change so that equilibrium can be maintained. Structural-functionalism focuses on cooperation and stability within families and societies.

The key concepts in this theory, then, are **structure** (the regular and patterned activities of a society) and **function** (the positive or negative contributions to a society).

Early structural-functionalists believed that every structure of a society had a positive function, meaning that each made a positive contribution to the continuation of the society (Malinowski, 1925, 1955). Contemporary functionalists still look for the positive functions that various institutions and structures fulfill, but they also recognize that some structures can be detrimental to the survival of the society. When institutions and social structures have a detrimental effect on society, they are said to be **dysfunctional.**

Although functional theory has proved useful, it has also received considerable criticism. Too often, earlier functionalists justified some existing structural feature of the society by claiming that it served a useful function. In effect, their arguments justified the existing arrangements—the *status quo*—and set up resistance to change. What they failed to notice was that although the existing structures or institutions benefited some parts of the society, they were detrimental or dysfunctional for others.

One of the most influential functionalist theorists was Talcott Parsons. According to Parsons, traditional female and male roles in the family produced a perfectly functioning family—a family that could relate to the other institutions of the society and carry out important societal functions. A basic premise of his theories about contemporary families is that they have only two functions, the socialization of children and the stabilization of adult personalities. He asserted that the best way to fulfill these functions is to assign spouses distinct, specialized roles. The **instrumental role** (which entails leadership and decision-making responsibilities) is best filled by the family's economic provider, which in most cases was the husband and

Gender Roles

father. The **expressive role** (which includes meeting the emotional needs of family members as well as performing domestic chores) is best assigned to wives and mothers. According to Parsons, biological differences necessitated this allocation of roles along gender lines. Much of the sociological literature on families that appeared after Parsons's influential work reflected similar assumptions. Interestingly, his perspective is quite similar to the "pro-family" rhetoric of the political right that we hear in today's political debates.

This rigid role differentiation between the sexes has been criticized on a number of grounds. First, it incorrectly speaks of the "public sphere" of work, government, and politics as separate from the "private sphere" of the home and family. In our everyday lives as workers and family members, we do not experience these two aspects of life as unconnected. Furthermore, this view denies the fact that work performed in the home is socially and economically useful and necessary. In Parsons's perspective, housework is an expression of love, part of the set of tasks that address family members' emotional needs, but is not an economically recognized type of labor. However, having the primary burden for household labor makes it difficult for women to participate in the paid labor force, which, in turn, keeps them in a position of dependence on men. In addition, portraying instrumental and expressive roles as mutually exclusive and biologically determined implies that this division of labor cannot and *should not* be changed. The traditional roles are portrayed as normal. If adults are to have normal, stable personalities, then they must be married and have children. Individuals who do not conform to this model are seen as deviant or abnormal. Finally, the structural-functional image of the home as a private, emotionally nurturing world conceals the conflict and abuse of women and children that often occur there.

◼ Conflict Theory

When structural-functional theory came under fire for being too conservative, many sociologists moved toward a theory that started with very different assumptions and led to very different conclusions. This theory, which has been applied to the family in a number of different ways, is called *conflict theory*. The basic assumption of conflict theory is that in every social group, organization, or society, the participants hold inequitable amounts of resources. Generally, the lion's share of resources go to people in certain positions in the group, and those people have more power than others. The label *conflict theory* comes from the notion that people who have greater power and resources will try to maintain their position, while those people in subordinate positions will try to gain more power and resources—thus, there is always potential for conflict (Collins, 1990; Ritzer, 1997). This is the second major assumption of the theory.

Conflict theory, like structural-functionalism, can be used on both the interactional level and the institutional level. As we show later in this text, conflict theory is useful in explaining violence within households or families. It also makes important contributions to the study of **social stratification** (the patterned ways in which privileges and rewards are distributed in a society, resulting in social classes or strata).

The central concepts of conflict theory, then, are resources, conflict, and power. **Resources** are any objects, possessions, or services that are valued by members of a society. The term **conflict** refers to the disputes or disagreements that result when two or more people are struggling for control over resources. **Power** is one person's ability to influence the behavior of others by overcoming their resistance. Each of these concepts as they apply to marriages and families is discussed in great detail in later chapters.

You may wonder how conflict theory applies to intimate relationships, because it is commonly held that families are highly cooperative social units whose members love each other. But it does apply to all marriages and families, not just to those that have overt problems or pathologies.

In our society, and in most others, two family statuses almost always have more power and control more resources: adults (compared with children) and men (compared with women). According to conflict theory, then, children, adolescents, and women will seek, by whatever means they possess, to gain more power for themselves.

A familiar example of the way family members in subordinate positions struggle to get more power is found in the relations between adolescent children and their parents. Until adolescence, the power of parents over their children is usually unquestioned by both parties. However, in our society when youngsters reach adolescence they typically strive to take a greater voice in deciding what they can and cannot do. A 16 or 17 year old is likely to want greater freedom and independence than parents are willing to give. Outright conflict sometimes results, but disobedience and subversion are more commonly the tactics of adolescents as they push for greater personal autonomy.

We give much more consideration to the issues of power and conflict in interpersonal relations in Chapter 7. Much of that discussion is based on the principles of conflict theory.

Symbolic Interaction Theory

Symbolic interaction theory deals primarily with interaction between individuals at a symbolic level. Generally, this theory focuses on individuals in families rather than with the family as a social institution in relation to the broader society (Rosenberg and Turner, 1990; Stryker, 1990; Charon, 1992). People interact and communicate with **symbols,** which can be words, gestures, facial expressions, and objects (such as flags, clothes, jewelry) that have specific meanings for people in a given society. People in the same culture generally share a common understanding of most societal symbols.

We can use one central feature of wedding ceremonies to illustrate the importance of symbols in people's lives—the traditional color of the bridal gown. White is typically worn by brides in the United States because it symbolizes purity—or, more specifically, virginity. The significance of this symbolism is strong enough that some wedding guests are disturbed if a previously married woman (or a pregnant bride) wears white, because such a bride is obviously not virginal. In fact, wedding etiquette books advise brides who are remarrying to wear off-white. In some Asian societies, in contrast, brides never wear white because that color is associated with mourning. Red is the preferred color for bridal attire in those cultures. But in the United States we rarely, if ever, see a bride wear red.

Symbolic interaction theory is built around the fact that human beings have an extraordinary capacity to learn and use verbal symbols. Children learn symbols and their meanings from those closest to them, especially their parents. People who are instrumental in the process through which we learn symbols are referred to as **significant others,** because their views have a great influence on us throughout our lives. From significant others, especially parents, children develop a **self-concept,** that is, their thoughts and feelings about themselves (Rosenberg, 1979, 1990). As a person goes through life, the circle of significant others usually expands to include people other than parents, such as friends, schoolmates, intimate partners, spouses, fellow workers, and religious and political leaders.

Symbolic interactionists stress that the symbols people learn, and the meanings they attach to them, govern their responses to all other human beings and objects. However, even within a society, individuals may attach different meanings to a symbol and those differences may influence their behavior. To illustrate this point,

Self-Perception

we again point to a word that is highly laden with meaning, but one that has varied meanings for different people. That word is *family.* To many people, family means any relationship that provides emotional, and often economic, support regardless of legal ties. Unmarried adults often form close relationships they regard as *family* with people to whom they are not related by blood or marriage. To others, family is limited to people with whom they have a legally recognized tie through biology or marriage, regardless of the emotional and economic exchanges that exist. As we saw earlier in the chapter, the definition of family has come under close scrutiny and is producing legal changes in many locales.

Symbolic interactionism has a large number of applications to marriage, families, and intimate relationships, including, among others, the gender role socialization and personality development of children, an issue we take up in Chapter 3 (on gender) and Chapter 9 (on childrearing). The significance of various expressions of love, and the confusion that results from gender differences in expressions of love can also be studied with symbolic interaction theory.

Social Exchange Theory

According to *social exchange theory* (often simply called *exchange theory*), the motivations for human behavior lie in anticipated costs and rewards. Every human action is seen as having some cost, and therefore, if carried out, it must also have some reward. Conversely, if an action is costly but unrewarded, the individual will not likely repeat it (Blau, 1964; Homans, 1973; Ekeh, 1974; Cook et al., 1990). Social exchange theory is especially useful in studying decision making about which actions to take or which relationships to start and maintain.

The usefulness of social exchange theory for studying intimate relationships is vividly illustrated by dating, because it is a more-or-less voluntary activity. When two people go on a date, each person expects some gratification from the experience. After all, a certain amount of effort is expended to go on a date, and, therefore, one expects something from it (pleasure, fun, a good meal, an interesting movie, romance, and so on). If the event does not lead to desired rewards for either partner, a second date probably won't occur. If both dating partners find the date unrewarding, it is even less likely that they will see each other again. If both get some satisfactions (rewards) from the experience, there is a good chance they will go out again. According to exchange theory, dating relationships generally continue until one or both of the partners find the experience more costly than rewarding.

Exchange theory is very useful for explaining why social relationships continue or end. Even marriage can be seen from this perspective. In societies in which divorce is possible, a marriage continues as long as both partners find the relationship rewarding or not excessively costly and if there appears to be no better alternative. When one partner finds the costs of the marriage greater than the rewards and believes another relationship promises more rewards, there is a heightened possibility of divorce. Along with dating and divorce, exchange theory is useful for understanding mate selection and the dynamics of intimate and marital relationships.

Social exchange theory may also explain, at least in part, why some women stay in violent or abusive relationships. In many cases—especially when young children are present—women depend on the economic resources provided by their male partners. Moreover, they may believe that they could not find another relationship.

A key concept of exchange theory is reciprocity. **Reciprocity** is the idea that when two people (or groups) are in a relationship, the exchanges between them must be of equal or nearly equal value. This norm of reciprocity is generally learned early in life, and for most people it endures as an important principle of social life (Gouldner, 1960). When the norm of reciprocity is violated, with one person returning less than he or she is receiving, relationships are apt to become strained.

Marital Satisfaction

Family systems theory is similar to structural-functional theory in that it regards families as social systems composed of interrelated parts. Each family member simultaneously influences and is influenced by every other member. To illustrate this idea, therapist Virginia Satir uses the analogy between a family and a mobile that hangs over a baby's crib, which maintains balance among its various components by virtue of the fixed distance between them. Families, too, make use of appropriate distances between members to maintain balance. Just as a mobile can lose its balance if a piece is bumped or moved, so can a family lose its balance when stress occurs to one of its members. Families can restore balance by changing their perceptions of the stressful events they face and by drawing on their coping resources (for example, social support from friends, family, and/or clergy, and economic assets).

In the 1950s, family sociologist Reuben Hill developed the **ABC-X model of family stress.** In this model, the letter *A* refers to a stressful life event that challenges a family system. *B* represents those skills and strategies the family possesses to cope with the event. *C* is the family's perception of the event, and *X* is the outcome of the situation, which represents the family's adaptation. In some cases, the outcome may be a crisis, in that it requires a significant shift in the family's previous way of functioning.

The ABC-X model looks at the ways in which the combination of the family's perceptions of an event, along with its coping resources, mediate the impact of the stressful event. The eventual outcome relies as much on the mediating process within the family as it does on the severity of the stressor event, itself. If the family appropriately defines the event and has sufficient coping skills, then it should not suffer a crisis as a result of encountering the stressor. On the other hand, even if the event is typically regarded as only a moderate stressor, it can trigger a major crisis within a family if the members regard it as insurmountable.

In Hill's model of family adaptation, stressful events can arise from within or outside a family. Examples of internal stresses include illness or death of a family member, job loss, or unintended pregnancy. External stressors include natural disasters, wars, or significant economic changes that affect all families, such as recessions. Stressors can also be events that occur predictably at various stages in the family life cycle (for example, the departure of young adult children from the parental home or parents' retirement). If these normative transitions occur at unusual times, they can cause severe stress.

Stressful events can also be categorized as acute or chronic. Acute stresses are random and are not likely to be repeated. Examples include robberies, beatings, and rapes. Chronic stresses refer to long-term situations such as lingering catastrophic illnesses (for example, cancer or muscular dystrophy).

An important assumption of family stress theory, then, is that it is not the stressful event in itself that determines a family's ability to maintain its balance. Instead, it is the combination of the event, the family's perception of the event, and the family's coping resources that determine the level of crisis that the event will cause in the family's life. A family that can view stressful events as challenges rather than obstacles and that can quickly and effectively marshal its resources can minimize the impact of the event. Families that do not perceive problems as solvable and/or that do not have sufficient resources may be devastated by the impact of a specific stressful event. Hamilton McCubbin and Joan Patterson (1983) expanded on Hill's model by emphasizing the fact that most families encounter a series of stressful events that can pile-up over time, impeding their ability to deal with any particular stressor. The concept of *pile-up* in the **double ABC-X model of family stress** is a useful addition to Hill's model because it recognizes that repeated challenges can drain a family's coping resources and/or dampen its optimism, thus impeding its long-term ability to cope with stressful events.

*Content*SELECT

Family System

HEADline Have Women Researchers Changed Science?

Over the past 25 years, more women have entered what were once male-dominated fields in the physical and biological sciences. Has this had an effect on the way in which science is conducted? Historian Londa Schiebinger argues that while women and men do not necessarily *conduct* science differently, they choose different questions to investigate. Their life experiences may cause them to scrutinize different aspects of nature. There are numerous examples of the ways in which the increase in the number of women scientists has changed the types of research questions that are addressed.

In marine biology in the 1950s and 1960s—when nearly all the scientists were male—research focused on *antagonism* and *competition* between organisms. By the late 1980s—after the influx of substantial numbers of female scientists into the field—more attention was being given to *cooperation.*

A similar shift in perspective occurred in the field of archeology. Many of you are undoubtedly familiar with the "man the hunter" theory of human evolution. As this theory goes, all things considered uniquely *human*—

from the development of cooperation, and the use of language and tools—emerged from the role of early human men in hunting large game animals for food. Men were the toolmakers and the *providers.* Through their expertise in hunting large animals, men enabled early human groups to survive and to evolve into thinking, talking, tool-making beings. The role of early human women was simply to bear and nurse babies. Most were confined to lives that involved squatting by the camp fire waiting for men to bring home the meat they had killed in cooperative hunts.

Feminist archeologists—both male and female—have questioned this description of early human behavior. They have suggested that women provided most of the food that was consumed by early humans through their work in gathering fruits and berries and tracking small animals. Furthermore, it was females who developed the first tools in their roles as caregivers and gatherers. Baby slings were developed by mothers to carry their infants while they gathered food. Digging sticks were used by females as the first tools. And language could just as easily have emerged from their role of caring for

infants as it did from male hunting activities. Thus, feminist anthropologists and archeologists have concluded that human evolution could have been propelled by early women. At the very least, early female humans were not the passive beings that were long accepted by the male-dominated field of archeology.

One final example of the shift in emphasis that has occurred with the increase in the number of women in science pertains to the dominant view of the role of sperm and egg in the process of conception. Until relatively recently, scientists assumed that the human egg took a passive role in the fertilization process. It sat quietly in the fallopian tubes waiting to be assaulted by a barrage of active, aggressive sperm cells. Today, it is widely accepted that the egg plays an active role in conception, sending out fingerlike microvilli to pull sperm into itself. This suggests that previous theories of human evolution and human conception mirrored the active male–passive female roles that were dominant in our society until the 1970s.

Source: Schiebinger, 1999.

◾ *Family Development Theory*

Scholars who use *family development theory* start with the basic assumption that family units, like individuals, go through a series of stages that represent growth and progression. Each stage has a set of fundamental tasks that must be accomplished before the family (or the individual) can progress to the next level. The key concept in this theory is **family life-cycle stage,** or the particular point of growth and development that is determined by the presence and age of children, and to a lesser extent, by the age of parents. Another key concept is **developmental task** (the major skills that must be learned, or basic needs that must be met in a particular stage).

The family development theory has been criticized because it is only applicable to intact families with children. It assumes that all adults marry before having children, that children are born at fairly regular intervals, and that parents stay married until they are separated by death. Thus, the theory is difficult to use in the study of single-parent and remarried families (Aldous, 1996). Nevertheless, it offers insight into understanding the challenges that children of various ages pose for their parents.

Feminist Perspectives on Families

Feminist scholars come from different academic disciplines and hold different political and philosophical views. In fact, different schools of feminist thought offer different explanations of and solutions for the lower status of women in society. **Liberal feminists** emphasize sexist ideology and ignorance as the basis for the inequality and oppression of women (Sapiro, 1990, p. 419). The key to attaining equality for women is to change people's beliefs and values. Liberal feminism is the dominant form in the United States. **Socialist feminists** question the very structure of society, arguing that social institutions are created, or at least maintained, by those in power to benefit their own interests. The key to attaining equality for women is to reshape the social institutions, including the family. **Radical feminists** argue that men use sexuality to control women; that sexual oppression is the key to women's lower status. A crucial step to improve women's status is for them to take control over their own bodies.

Regardless of their particular political or philosophical orientations, feminists who study families have emphasized some common themes, which have developed in reaction against the conventional scholarship about families, particularly the structural-functional perspective. They criticize the conventional definition of family that emphasized ties of blood, marriage, and adoption; co-residence in a single household; interaction and communication along well-defined social roles; and participation in a common culture. They single out the work of sociologist Talcott Parsons (1955) for criticism.

In the feminist critique of the structural-functional view of families, five themes have emerged (Thorne and Yalom, 1992). The first is that the nuclear family with breadwinner husband and homemaker wife and their biological offspring is not the only legitimate family form and, in fact, is not "natural" or biologically determined as structural-functionalists have claimed. The assignment of family roles into the instrumental and expressive is a social creation. It is characterized by male dominance and female dependence.

A second common theme is that families should be thought of as fluid ties or connections among people rather than as some concrete social group. If we focus on the nature of the relationships among people rather than on the composition of the household in which they reside, we get a clearer picture of intimate relationships.

A third, related theme is that peoples' experiences in families, households, and intimate relationships vary, depending on their gender, age or generation, sexual orientation, race, and social class. The prevailing ideology of the family as a "haven in a heartless world," a place where people are always offered comfort and support, is inaccurate. It ignores the unequal burdens shouldered within families, as well as the conflict and violence so frequently found in intimate relationships. Feminists have argued that traditional nuclear families offer privilege and comfort to husbands and fathers and that adults have greater power and privilege than children within homes.

The idea of the family as a "haven in a heartless world" is closely related to the view of families as separate from, and unconnected to, the larger world outside the home. Until relatively recently, social scientists ignored the many connections between workplaces and families, for instance. Feminist scholars argue that families and/or households are connected to the outside world in many ways and that what goes on inside families is shaped by the other social institutions—the economy, the government, and the educational system.

The fifth common theme addressed by feminist scholars is that women are expected to neglect their own needs in order to care for their children and male partners. The crucial, but difficult, goal is to achieve equality and freedom for women in families while maintaining the ethos of caring that has long been associated with women.

The Special Importance of Gender

Social distinctions between males and females are made in every known society, and these distinctions are used to organize social life and to influence behavior. Because these are social distinctions, they differ from one society to another, and they change over time. Nonetheless, the social definitions placed on gender are always important influences on behavior, and in no context is the influence greater than in marriage and family life (Coltrane, 1998). The significance attached to gender influences dating, courtship, mate selection, sexual activity, husband–wife relations, parenting, and all other aspects of marriage and family life.

To illustrate: In dating relationships, men have had a special power to initiate dating and to exercise considerable control over activities when they take financial responsibility. In developing sexual intimacy, men and women often attach different meanings to sex, apparently because of the way they have been taught to view it. Gender is also related to differences in views about love and romance, but contrary to prevailing stereotypes men are often more romantic than women.

There are gender differences in communication styles, in decision making, and in power processes. Many bases of power in intimate relationships and in marriage give men the advantage over women. The division of labor in households and the interplay between spouses' jobs and family responsibilities are also heavily influenced by gender.

When children are born, the impact on mothers is very different from the impact on fathers. Many couples become more traditional with the birth of children, with mothers assuming more of the nurturing responsibilities and fathers more of the teaching and economic duties.

In regard to conflict in close relationships, men and women often respond very differently. Adhering rapidly to the traditional male role may increase the likelihood of men committing violence and abusing their dating partners, lovers, or wives. Such men may expect strict obedience from female partners and may be threatened by women who act independently.

Women are less likely to be satisfied with their marriages and show a greater likelihood of considering divorce. Divorce affects women's and men's lives very differently. Most notable in this regard is that after divorce, fathers are more likely to lose contact with their children, and wives are much more likely to experience a decline in their standard of living. Even in death there are gender differences, because women are much more likely to survive their husbands than vice versa. At the end of their lives, the majority of women are unmarried, while the majority of men at the end of their lives are married.

Because gender is such a pervasive influence on all relationships, especially marriage and family, it is a primary aim of this book to be persistently sensitive to its importance. In each chapter, we call your attention to a number of prominent gender issues associated with the topics being discussed. Consistent with that perspective, we turn to the topic of gender in the next chapter. Keep in mind that the impact of gender is entangled in the effects of race and social class. Women of different races and social classes experience various aspects of family life differently, as do men of different races and social classes.

Summary

Social research that is based on scientific principles provides the best understanding of intimate relationships, including marriages and families. Research results may come from laboratory and field experiments, social surveys, and observational, demographic, and historical studies.

Social theories make social life more understandable by providing sets of ideas that explain a broad range of phenomena. **Structural-functional theory** emphasizes that every pattern of activity in society makes either positive or negative contributions. A related idea is that the institutions of a society are interrelated. Structural-functional theory can be useful for analyzing the relations between families and other institutions, but it can also be used to justify the *status quo*, which may be dysfunctional for some people in the society. **Conflict theory** begins with the premise that every social group, organization, or society has inequities in power and resources. These inequities lead to conflicts between those who have more power and resources and those who have fewer.

Symbolic interaction theory emphasizes the importance of symbols for social groups, societies, and human behavior. Individual personalities are also shaped by symbolic interaction with significant others. **Social exchange theory** emphasizes that motivations for human behavior are most likely to be found in its costs and rewards. Social exchange theory is especially applicable when people make decisions and choices about dating, partner selection, marital relationships, and divorce. **Developmental theory** emphasizes that many families go through family life-cycle stages.

Feminist scholars have added new insights to the study of marriage and families through their critiques of previous research. They have argued persuasively that the traditional definition of family, based on biological or legal ties, is too restrictive and that assumptions of consensus in families are unfounded. They have brought many new issues to the forefront of research, including family violence and the intersection of work and family. We draw on feminist scholarship at many points throughout this text.

Key Terms

ABC-X model of family stress (p. 47)

Conflict (p. 44)

Correlational method (p. 35)

Cross-sectional survey (p. 35)

Deception in social research (p. 39)

Dependent variable (p. 34)

Developmental task (p. 48)

Double ABC-X model of family stress (p. 47)

Dysfunctional (p. 43)

Ethnographies (p. 40)

Experiment (p. 34)

Expressive roles (p. 44)

Family history (p. 40)

Family life-cycle stage (p. 48)

Field experiment (p. 34)

Field observation (p. 37)

Fixed-response question (p. 35)

Function (p. 43)

Hawthorne effect (p. 32)

Independent variable (p. 34)

Instrumental roles (p. 43)

Key concepts (p. 42)

Laboratory observation (p. 37)

Liberal feminism (p. 49)

Longitudinal research (p. 35)

Observational studies (p. 37)

Open-ended question (p. 35)

Participant observation (p. 39)

Power (p. 44)

Quasi-experiment (p. 35)

Radical feminism (p. 49)

Random assignment (p. 34)

Random samples (p. 37)

Reciprocity (p. 46)

Reliability (p. 32)

Resources (p. 44)

Self-concept (p. 45)

Significant others (p. 45)

Social history (p. 40)

Social stratification (p. 44)

Social theory (p. 42)

Socialist feminism (p. 49)

Structure (p. 43)

Survey research (p. 35)

Symbols (p. 45)

Systematic collection of data (p. 33)

Underlying assumptions (p. 42)

Unit of analysis (p. 42)

Validity (p. 32)

Value-free research (p. 33)

Review Questions

1. What are the principal features of the scientific approach to generating and verifying knowledge? How do these features differ from other approaches to generating knowledge?

2. List and briefly discuss the sources of error that scientists encounter when studying human behavior.

3. Which types of data collection are most and least useful in studying intimate relationships? Why?

4. Evaluate the research on human sexuality that was conducted by Kinsey, Lillian Rubin, Masters and Johnson, and Laud Humphreys. What were the strengths and weaknesses of each approach? What could the researchers have done differently to avoid these weaknesses?

5. Compare and contrast the major theoretical frameworks that were presented in this chapter. How do they differ in terms of their underlying assumptions and in the issues they are most often used to study?

Critical Thinking Questions

1. Is it really possible to study marital quality scientifically? Why or why not?

2. Is it (a) necessary and (b) desirable to quantify the emotions that occur in marriage?

3. Is it appropriate to study couples in laboratory settings, using various types of technological devices? Why or why not?

4. Can a study be truly scientific if it has no theoretical basis?

Online Resources Available for This Chapter

www.ablongman.com/marriageandfamily

- Online Study Guide with Practice Tests
- PowerPoint Chapter Outlines
- Links to Marriage and Family Websites
- ContentSelect Research Database
- Self-Assessment Activities

Further Reading

Books

Boss, Pauline G., Doherty, William J., LaRossa, Ralph, Steinmetz, Suzanne, and Schumm, Walter. *Sourcebook of Family Theories and Methods: A Contextual Approach.* New York: Plenum Publishing Company, 1993. Presents the history of family theory and research methods and the interplay between the two.

DeVault, Marjorie. *Liberating Method: Feminism and Social Research.* Philadelphia: Temple University Press, 1999. Considers research methods that adequately represent marginalized groups and the social processes that organize their lives.

Ericksen, Julia A., and Steffen, Sally A. *Kiss and Tell: Surveying Sex in the Twentieth Century.* Cambridge, MA: Harvard University Press, 1999. A history of sex surveys in the United States over the past 100 years.

Gilgun, Jane F., and Sussman, Marvin. *The Methods and Methodologies of Qualitative Family Research.* Thousand Oaks, CA: Sage, 1997. Presents a wide range of studies in which various qualitative methods are used to study aspects of family life.

Greenstein, Theodore. *Methods of Family Research.* New York: Haworth Press, 2001. A comprehensive review of research methods that are frequently used by social scientists who study families and intimate relationships.

Nye, F. Ivan, and Berardo, Felix. *Emerging Conceptual Frameworks in Family Analysis.* New York: Praeger, 1981. Essays that outline a number of major conceptual frameworks are included. Identified as a classic work in the sociological study of families.

Oakley, Ann. *Experiments in Knowing: Gender and Method in the Social Sciences.* Cambridge: Polity Press, 2000. Explores the history, ideology, and implications of methods used in the social and natural sciences.

Reinharz, Shulamit, and Davidman, Lynn. *Feminist Methods in Social Research.* Oxford: Oxford University Press, 1992. This book examines a wide range of feminist research methods, explaining the relationship between feminism and methodology.

Content**SELECT** *Articles*

Garcia, L. "The Certainty of the Sexual Self-Concept." *Canadian Journal of Human Sexuality* 8(4), 1999: 263–271. **[Database: Sociology]**   Central to one's concept of self is one's sexual self, or how one processes information concerning his or her sexual self. In this study, Garcia examined the ways in which men and women view their sexual selves. Study results indicate that, on the whole, men tend to view themselves as more sexually experienced and responsive than women; women indicate that they tend to perceive themselves as more sexually attractive and romantic.

Springen, K. "Your Family Tree of Life." *Newsweek* 138(11), 2001: 72. **[Database: General Interest]**   Are you aware of medical histories within your family? The benefits of knowing your medical family history are numerous, including knowing your predisposition to certain illnesses such as heart disease and certain types of cancer. Lifestyle behaviors can then been modified or changed to reduce vulnerability.

The Continuing Significance of Gender

3

The national wire services released a story about a fight that broke out in the middle of a youth soccer game in Texas between the Lewisville Blaze and the Denton Solhers (Moewe, 1990).

*T*wo fathers of Denton Solhers' players, who were losing the game at the time, accused the Blaze goalie of cheating. Of course, such disputes frequently occur at children's sports events; this one made the national news because the fathers were accusing the goalie of being a boy in disguise.

This was a soccer game between two all-girl teams, and 10-year-old star goalie Natasha Dennis was playing so well that these two men could not believe she was a girl. The Blaze coach offered the men the team roster and birth certificates for each player, but they weren't satisfied. They demanded that Natasha be taken to the restroom, where she could prove that she was a girl by removing her uniform. The two fathers did not succeed in getting the "panty check," and in fact were suspended from attending any future league soccer games. Although Natasha, a 4-foot, 5-inch fourth-grader with short brown hair, acknowledges being "boyish," she did not appreciate being called a boy. She commented that the fathers "should go somewhere and check to see if they have anything between their ears" (Moewe, 1990).

Key Questions

1 Are there really only two sexes?

2 In what ways do biological and sociocultural factors interact to shape individuals' gender?

3 How do pre-existing beliefs about gender differences affect the scientific study of sex and gender?

4 What are the potential problems associated with viewing gender differences solely in terms of biology?

5 To what extent is it reasonable to draw conclusions about gender in humans from findings of research based on animals?

6 How does gender function as a dimension of social stratification?

Gender Stereotypes

*I*n the opening story, the parents of the soccer players—and Natasha herself—held a rather rigid set of expectations about how little girls are supposed to act and look. Because she played her sport aggressively and effectively, had short hair, and hated to wear dresses, Natasha violated gender role expectations and thus she and others considered her "unfeminine" and unusual. A rigidly held belief that a category of people has a particular set of personal characteristics is called a **stereotype.** Stereotypes are often applied to racial, religious, ethnic, and nationality groups, and to males and females. **Gender stereotypes** are rigidly held, categorical beliefs that associate certain personality traits with being male or female.

Studies conducted in the 1990s show that Americans still strongly associate certain personality traits, interests, and abilities with males and others with females (DeStefano and Colasanto, 1990; Ballard-Reisch and Elton, 1992; Harris, 1994). In a 1994 survey of 3,000 respondents, both men and women rated the following traits as especially desirable in males: aggressiveness, ambition, competitiveness, independence, leadership, a strong personality, and a willingness to defend their beliefs. In contrast, the most desirable personality traits in females included compassion, gentleness, sympathy, tenderness, and a love of children.

African Americans, whites, and Latinos in the survey generally concurred in their views but there were some differences between men and women. Whites were most likely to subscribe to the traditional gender stereotypes, while the Latino respondents were slightly less likely to do so. African Americans, both males and females, were the least likely to accept traditional gender stereotypes. They were more likely to consider a number of traits equally desirable in *both* males and females. For example, they said it was desirable for both females and males to be assertive, athletic, independent, self-reliant, self-sufficient, eager to soothe hurt feelings, and gentle (Harris, 1994).

In spite of the dominant stereotype that women are nurturant (that is, more willing to help or care for other people), research has found that *men,* in general, are more likely than women to help others, while women are more likely to *be* helped. There are different types of helping behaviors, some of which are more likely to be performed by women and others, by men.

The helping behaviors expected of men involve rare and risky acts of rescuing others as well as being courteous and protective of subordinates, while the helping behavior expected of women consists primarily of caring for others with whom they have close relationships. Such behaviors are encouraged by parents and reinforced by the nature of the occupations in which women and men predominate. Women are likely to be found in occupations that involve some form of personal service (such as clerical work, nursing, teaching, social work), while men are much more likely to hold jobs requiring them to jeopardize their own lives to help others (such as firefighter, law enforcement officer, soldier). Studies of gender differences in helping behavior thus need to differentiate between the various ways in which help can be provided.

One trait that is considered stereotypically masculine is aggression. Gender differences in aggression are well established in existing research. Men in all cultures for which data are available have been found to be more aggressive physically and verbally. This gender difference first appears at age 2 or $2\frac{1}{2}$ and continues through early adulthood, though to a lesser degree. Among children younger than 2 years though it is difficult to come up with a valid measure of aggression. Indicators that have been used—such as amount of movement when awake—have not reliably predicted aggressive behavior in infants (Renzetti and Curran, 1995, p. 27).

Men are slightly more likely than women to behave aggressively, but only under certain circumstances. Gender differences are greater in the laboratory than in the "field" (real-life situations) and in those situations that produce *physical* harm or pain rather than *psychological* pain (such as hurt feelings, lowered self-esteem, or damage to reputation). They are also greater when the behavior takes place in *semiprivate* rather than in a public setting, and when aggression is *required* rather than freely chosen. The presence of an audience seems to encourage people to act in stereotypical ways.

Again, these results may be explained in terms of the social roles women and men occupy. Male roles in the military, competitive sports, and certain male-dominated occupations emphasize aggressiveness and not only teach skills necessary to engage in physical aggression but also inspire men to disregard possible harm from engaging in such activity.

Gender differences in aggression are small, decrease with age, and have declined over time. The decrease may be caused by changes in socialization practices and cultural norms about maleness and femaleness, which are discussed in more detail later in this chapter.

In this chapter, we examine in more detail the female and male stereotypes in our society. We begin the chapter by defining several key concepts: sex, gender, gender roles, and gender identification and discussing the links among them. We also consider the continuing debate over nature (biology) versus nurture (environment) as the sources of gender differences. Our consideration of environmental influences on behavior focuses on the process of gender role socialization, in which parents, teachers, and the mass media bombard people with messages about appropriate behavior and characteristics for females and males in society. We close by briefly considering the impact of gender roles on health and well-being, education, and employment. Throughout the remainder of the book, we examine the ways in which our gendered society affects intimate relationships.

ContentSELECT

Aggression

Sex and Gender

*T*he question *"Is it a boy or a girl?"* is asked at each child's birth. It assumes that a baby's sex is immediately obvious on examination of its external genitalia. It also assumes that there are two and only two possibilities. Human bodies do not always fall neatly into two sex categories, however. Some bodies have both male and female parts. (Previously, individuals whose biological sex was unclear were referred to as **hermaphrodites.** Today they are generally referred to as **intersexed.**) In our culture, it is often assumed that gender flows *naturally* from one's biological sex. When bodies don't readily conform to one sex category or another, how does the person become gendered—that is, thought of as masculine or feminine?

The terms *sex* and *gender* are often used interchangeably in everyday conversation. But in the social sciences a distinction is made between the terms (Laner, 2000). **Sex** is typically defined as the biological aspects of anatomy and physiology that are associated with reproduction, whereas **gender** refers to the influence of the cultural context in creating what is regarded as male or female. **Gender roles** are defined in terms of the culturally imposed expectations for the behavior of those who are identified as female or male. The distinction between these terms has been used to emphasize the idea that behavioral differences between persons who are labeled as female/women or male/men aren't completely determined by biological factors. In this chapter, we must examine what were once considered obvious connections between bodily sex and gendered behavior.

The Influence of Biology

*I*n most respects, female and male bodies are more alike than different. But clearly, there are some visible biological differences between female and male bodies. It is tempting to use sexual and reproductive biology to explain observed gender differences in personality and behavior. And, in fact, many Americans do attribute gender differences in personality traits, interests, and abilities to chromosomes and hormones. Men are more likely than women to believe that biology is responsible for differences between the sexes.

Why should it matter whether or not gender differences in behavior are biologically based? It matters because biological explanations are frequently used inappropriately to justify the exclusion of women from certain types of occupations or to defend men's lack of involvement in child care or other family-related behaviors. For instance, some years ago an actor who portrayed the father in a large television family was discussing his real family on a talk show. When asked whether he had taken an active role in bringing up his own children, he replied that he waited until they were older because he wasn't "cut out" for taking care of babies. Diaper changing wasn't in his "makeup," while his wife had a "natural inclination" toward diaper changing. Other people have argued just as vehemently that women should not be entrusted with the important decisions associated with national security. During the cold war era, for instance, there was a widespread belief that a woman could not be president of the United States because she might push the button to activate a nuclear war during a moment of premenstrual tension. Yet another example includes criminal court cases in which women have been acquitted of murder charges because they were said to be at the mercy of their hormones.

In this section of the chapter, we consider the extent to which basic biological differences between women and men influence personality and behavior. We focus on genes and hormones, and begin by considering their influence on sexual development before birth and during puberty.

Most scientists (in the social and behavioral sciences as well as the natural sciences) now realize that the nature versus nurture debate greatly oversimplifies the processes that shape human behavior. Gendered behavior is more commonly regarded as a function of both biology (nature) and environment (nurture). The influences of biology (e.g., the brain and other components of the central nervous system and hormone secretions) and the social environment (such as family, school, and sports) operate simultaneously and reciprocally. Thoughts and behaviors, which are biologically mediated processes arising from brain activity, alter the environment that individuals experience. The environment, in turn, alters brain development and other internal processes.

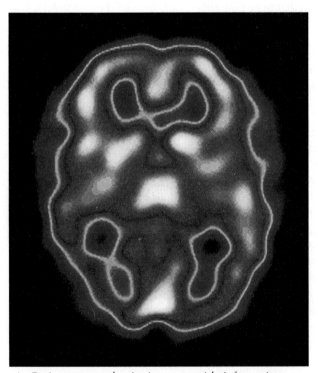

▲ *Brain scans are beginning to provide information about the links between gendered behaviors and brain structure and function.*

Life experiences change our underlying biology—they shape and reshape the brain, and the brain, in turn, influences life experiences. In addition, our thoughts, which spring from biological processes, can change our brains. We are also social organisms who are affected by environmental variables—variables that include the nutrients, pesticides, and calories in the foods we eat, the experiences to which we are exposed and the experiences that we choose for ourselves. (Halpern, 2000, p. 28)

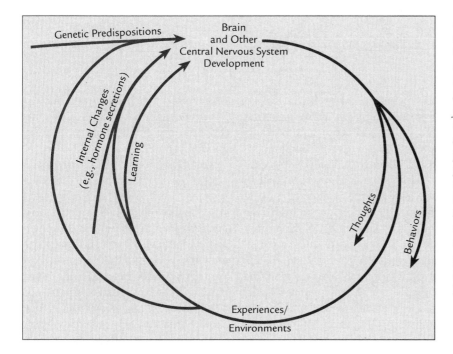

Figure 3.1 **The Interplay of Biological and Socioenvironmental Influences on Gender.** *The impact of nature and nurture on human behavior are continuous and inseparable. Thoughts and behaviors, which are biologically mediated processes arising from brain activity, alter the environment experienced by individuals, which in turn alters brain development and other internal processes (e.g., hormone secretions). Genetic potential also can be affected by some environmental stimuli (e.g., some drugs), causing changes in biological processes (e.g., signs of aging), which in turn alter the environmental experiences to which each individual is exposed.*

(*Source:* Halpern, D., 2000, *Sex Differences in Cognitive Abilities*, 3rd ed., p. 18, Mahwah, NJ: Lawrence Erlbaum Associates.)

The perspective that considers the combined effects of biology and environment on human behavior is diagrammed in Figure 3.1.

Most people are familiar with the basic part that sex chromosomes play in the physical development of male and female embryos. At conception, the genetic material in the sperm and the egg combine to begin the process of human development. Each of these sex cells contributes twenty-three chromosomes, which are responsible for various physical attributes such as height, hair color, eye color, and skin pigmentation. One of the chromosome pairs formed at conception controls the development of a fertilized egg into a boy or girl. The egg always contributes an X chromosome, and the sperm can contribute either an X or a Y. An XX combination results in a genetic female, and an XY combination results in a genetic male. (In some cases, however, the chromosomal patterns that result do not fall into these clearly differentiated categories. We discuss the implications of these cases in the next section.)

For the first six to eight weeks of prenatal development, all embryos are anatomically identical regardless of their genetic makeup. At some time in the third month of prenatal development, male and female embryos begin to differentiate. The internal sex tissues develop into either testes or ovaries and begin to secrete hormones. The testes release hormones that are collectively referred to as *androgens* (the most important of which appears to be testosterone) and the ovaries release hormones referred to collectively as *estrogens*. These sex hormones, in turn, influence the development of internal and external sex structures.

Again, though, it is important to note that the development of internal genitals doesn't always clearly differentiate a fetus by sex. Some babies are born with both ovaries and testes.

At puberty, which typically occurs between the ages of 11 and 14, sex hormone levels rise, causing the internal sex organs to mature and the secondary sex characteristics, such as the development of breasts to appear.

While we try to simplify nature by creating dichotomous categories (either male or female), neither biological sex nor sociological gender is truly dichotomous. There are many combinations of X and Y chromosomes just as there are a

HEADline   Living across Genders

JaVonn Hicks, a 17-year-old senior at Tampa Bay Vo-Tech High School, wanted to run for homecoming queen. JaVonn had all of the necessary accoutrements of beauty queens—lipstick, curling iron, and nail polish and a slinky black prom dress. But school officials refuse to allow JaVonn to run for homecoming queen because he has one characteristic that beauty queens traditionally do not have—a penis. At birth JaVonn was labeled as *male,* but s/he considers himself a girl. JaVonn says, "I'm not ashamed of who I am. I want to set a precedent and show people no matter who you are or how you dress or look, you shouldn't be discriminated against." JaVonn was given permission to compete in the homecoming pageant, but only as a candidate for King (Associated Press, 1999).

Fifteen-year-old Alex McClendon was the new kid in the Georgian Country Day School in Carrolltown, Georgia. Heads turned to gaze at her long blond hair and perfectly made-up face. Alex had a flair for style, sporting Calvin jeans and a pierced tongue. The board of trustees at the school, however, was not impressed, and they asked Alex to withdraw because she had concealed the fact that she was technically—and biologically—a he. Alex was born Matthew Alex McClendon. For two years prior to entering the private school in Carrolltown, Matthew had adopted a female persona. Most of Alex's classmates at the Georgian Country Day School didn't pay much attention to Alex after learning her biological sex identity. Dozens of students, including many boys, argued that school officials were violating Alex's rights and wore hair bows in solidarity. But parents of younger children complained that Alex was negatively influencing their children, so Alex was given the options of starting to dress like a boy or to leave the school. Alex decided to be home-schooled. S/he plans to undergo a sex change operation (Morse, 1998, p. 62).

Aurora Lipscomb, age 6, entered the first grade in her home town of Westerville, Ohio, a suburb of Columbus in September 2000. Over the summer between kindergarten and first grade, Aurora had her ears pierced, got a court's permission to change her name (from Zachary, her birth name) and announced to her neighbors that she was a girl. When an anonymous caller informed the local Children's Services agency that Aurora's parents were allowing their son, Zachary, to act and dress like a girl, the agency asked for permission to remove the child from her parents' home. A judge granted the agency temporary custody, citing that the child was suffering from an illness and was not receiving proper care.

Sherry Lipscomb, Aurora's mother, says she noticed her child wasn't a "typical" boy even before he turned two. When she took him shopping, he liked to look at sparkly dresses. He would wear his baby blanket around his head like a wig and walk on the balls of his feet as though he were wearing high heels. In spite of this "atypical" behavior, Sherry says she continued to regard her child as a boy. But after six years of insisting that he was actually a girl, Sherry and her husband decided that it was wrong for them to force their child to hide her gender in public.

Child development experts do not agree on the appropriate medical response to children and adolescents who identify themselves as persons of a gender other than the one they were assigned at birth. Some encourage parents to support their children's unconventional gender expression but warn that they may be stigmatized in the outside world. Others believe that parents should broaden their own ideas about gender. Boys and girls do not have to maintain rigid gender roles in order to remain boys and girls. Expanding the range of appropriate behavior for each gender may spare individuals the expense of undergoing sex reassignment surgery later in life. A third approach is to force children to conform to rigid gender rules. Behavior modification techniques such as rewarding "tomboys" for wearing frilly dresses or punishing "effeminate" boys for playing with Barbie dolls are the treatment of choice in this perspective. However, those who take a more accepting approach to children with gender identity disorder say that the children who undergo the coercive attempts to reinstate traditional gender behavior are often damaged for life (Cloud, 2000, pp. 90–91).

Sources: "Boy Seeks Homecoming Queen Run," *Associated Press,* October 1, 1999; "Gender Bender," by Jodie Morse, *Time,* November 9, 1998, p. 62; "His Name Is Aurora," by John Cloud, *Time,* September 25, 2000, pp. 90–91. © 2000 Time Inc. Reprinted by permission.

number of combinations of internal and external genitals within individuals. Thus, when we attempt to fit people into one sex category or the other, we must realize that there are actually four different markers for biological sex: chromosomal, hormonal, gonadal (internal sex organs), or genital (external sex organs). For most individuals these four markers are consistent with each other and with the designation of either *male* or *female*. Occasionally, these markers of biological sex are inconsistent (Fausto-Sterling, 2000).

Intersexed Individuals

Just how common is intersexuality? Biologist Anne Fausto-Sterling (2000) estimates that it occurs in about less than 2 percent of all births. While this may not sound very common, consider the fact that in a city of 300,000 people a rate of 2 percent would produce somewhere between 5,000 and 6,000 intersexed individuals. In some parts of the world—such as among certain groups of Eskimos—the incidence of intersexuality is even higher. Intersexuality appears to be on the rise because of environmental pollutants that mimic estrogen.

When doctors are faced with the birth of an intersexed baby, they typically feel compelled to "correct" the situation—to restore the baby to what they think nature intended it to be. They go through several steps to determine into which sex category the baby best fits. They look first at the baby's chromosomal makeup. If it has two X chromosomes they start with the assumption that it should be female. They next look at the baby's internal sex organs. If it has two ovaries rather than an ovary and a testis it is categorized as a genetic female and is raised as a girl. Babies who are born with an X and a Y chromosome (said to be characteristic of a genetic male) can be raised as either boys or girls, depending on the size of their external genitals. Doctors must be convinced that an infant's penis will grow large enough so that the child will be able engage in vaginal penetration during heterosexual intercourse once he reaches sexual maturity. Typically, intersexed infants with penises that are less than two centimeters in length—even if they have an X and a Y chromosome—undergo genital surgery that transforms the penis into a clitoris and vagina. Doctors then advise parents to raise their child as a girl. In the case of intersexed infants, then, social and cultural factors (such as assumptions about the necessity for boys and men to be able to urinate while standing up) are an important factor in interpreting the meaning of body parts.

Genes and sex hormones then can clearly have a dramatic effect on the physical development of girls and boys. But what about their effects on behavior?

Hormones and Human Behavior

Hormone levels fluctuate in males as well as in females, although the fluctuations of male hormones are less regular and less visible than those of female hormones. Generally, the female hormone cycle lasts twenty-eight to thirty days. Estrogen levels peak in the middle of the month-long cycle, after which they decrease somewhat for a few days, then increase slightly once more before they drop off significantly before menstruation. Another hormone, progesterone, is also involved. It peaks a few days before menstruation.

There is some evidence that anxiety and depression in women are associated with hormonal fluctuations, but it is possible that these moods are associated, at least in part, with negative attitudes toward menstruation. Most Americans believe menstruating women are emotionally unstable and difficult to live with. Many also believe menstruation affects a woman's ability to think or to function normally during their menstrual periods, that menstruating women look different, should restrict their activities while menstruating, and especially not engage in sexual intercourse (Golub, 1992; Jurgens and Powers, 1991; Markens, 1996).

Although medical researchers have been studying premenstrual syndrome (PMS) for over 70 years, they still do not clearly understand the causes or consequences of the 150 or so symptoms that are widely believed to be associated with the female hormonal cycle. Nor have they been able to estimate the number of women who suffer from PMS. In large part, this is because there is no standard, widely accepted definition of PMS.

Researchers have not been studying male hormonal cycles for as long as they have studied female cycles. Testosterone was first identified less than sixty years ago (Angier, 1995). Testosterone levels in men's blood fluctuate on a daily basis as well as in longer cycles ranging from several days to several weeks. More recent research suggests that testosterone may not cause observed aggression in men, despite popular beliefs to the contrary. In a study of fifty-four men with abnormally low testosterone, Dr. Christina Wang, of the University of California at Los Angeles, found that high levels of edginess, irritability, and anger were common. When testosterone levels in these men were raised to the normal range, their negative feelings gave way to a sense of optimism and friendliness (reported in Angier, 1995). The latest research also suggests that estrogen may somehow affect the male brain's ability to process testosterone. So perhaps estrogen, rather than testosterone, is responsible for higher levels of aggression in men.

Genetic Influences on Behavior

How do genes and chromosomes shape personality and behavior? This question has been at the center of a great deal of controversy in recent years. Some scholars believe all gender differences in personality and behavior can be attributed to biology. According to **sociobiology** (a scientific theory that draws on biological principles to explain human behavior), all human traits and tendencies, including those associated with masculinity and femininity (such as male dominance and aggression, female nurturance and the maternal instinct, and the double standard of sexual conduct) are genetically determined.

An important principle of sociobiology that is used to explain these differences is that over thousands of years, men and women have developed different mating strategies, which may explain why men are more likely than women to be promiscuous and women are more likely to be monogamous. The ideal reproductive strategy for women was to be selective about their sexual partners, choosing those who showed the most promise for staying with them to help during pregnancy and childrearing. This would increase their infants' chances of surviving. The most advantageous strategy for men, in contrast, was to have sex with as many healthy and fertile women as possible, making only limited commitments to any particular woman. In this way, men would increase their chances of passing on their genes to subsequent generations. Anthropologists and other social scientists, however, have actually found an extraordinary range of diversity in sexual behavior and are not convinced that all men are promiscuous and women, monogamous (see Laumann et al., 1994, pp. 5–8).

Sociobiologists also say that because early human men had to hunt large animals and fight off threats from other groups of humans, the evolutionary process of natural selection favored men who were stronger, faster, more aggressive, and competitive. By comparison, those women who had effective nurturing abilities might have had an advantage in the evolutionary process (Symons, 1979; Wilson, 1978, 1982).

The Influence of the Social Environment**63**

Sociobiology is gaining supporters but it is also widely criticized. One major criticism concerns the lack of direct evidence about the genetics of human behavior. Because human generations encompass so many years, it's difficult to follow them over time to examine genetic differences. In addition, ethics limit genetic experiments on humans. Thus, a related limitation of sociobiology is its dependence on animal studies, particularly of primates (monkeys and apes), for information about human behavior. Sociobiologists argue that studies of primates are valuable because they provide evidence about human behavior in its more "natural" state. That is, primate behavior resembles human behavior before it was contaminated by the artificial restraints of culture. Although there is a close genetic similarity between primates, such as chimpanzees, and humans, which may justify generalizing from their behavioral patterns to those of humans, there is little if any similarity between humans and the other animals that are frequently used in sociobiological studies. For many critics of sociobiology, using data drawn from observations of scorpionfly mating habits as a basis for explaining rape among humans (Thornhill, 1980), for instance, seems illogical (Tavris and Offir, 1984).

Even if sociobiologists restricted their observations to the animals closest to humans in genetic structure, variation among primates makes it possible to use bias in the selection of a particular species for study. Some primates exhibit behavior remarkably similar to human patterns, with male primates acting in ways thought characteristic of male humans, and female primates in ways thought characteristic of female humans. Other primate species do not show this similarity to human gender roles. Sometimes the researchers' own biases influence their choices of which primate species to observe to draw conclusions about humans. Sociobiologists have tended to select primate species in which males are dominant and aggressive and to ignore species in which females are assertive or dominant (Weisstein, 1982). Male rhesus monkeys show little interest in newborns and even act viciously if infants approach them. Thus, if we relied on sociobiological studies in which rhesus monkeys are observed, we might mistakenly conclude that male humans are by nature poor fathers. However, if we observed other primates—perhaps owl monkeys or marmosets—we would draw a different conclusion. Among these species, males often carry infants most of the day, handing them over to their mothers only for nursing (Tavris and Offir, 1984, pp. 133–134).

A similar dilemma results in regard to sexual promiscuity. In some primate species, males are indeed promiscuous, but in others both sexes are monogamous. In some, such as chimpanzees, females are promiscuous. During their period of sexual receptivity, female chimps may mate fifty times in one day. Thus, if we observed only chimpanzees, we might mistakenly conclude that females (humans as well as primates) are genetically programmed to be promiscuous and that culture has unnaturally restricted them from acting on their natural instincts (Tavris and Offir, 1984, p. 135). Although animal studies are provocative, they must be interpreted with caution, especially when they are offered as *proof* of the genetic basis of gender differences among humans.

ContentSELECT

Sociobiology

The Influence of the Social Environment

When we use the phrase *social and cultural environment*, we are referring to all the people and all the cultural products (such as music, religious writings, laws, technology, values, mass media) that directly and indirectly shape our attitudes and behaviors. From the moment of our birth onward, the social and cultural environment bombards us with intentional and unintentional messages about gender. These messages are found everywhere, from Saturday morning cartoons and car commercials on TV to religious documents and rap and rock music. In the first part of this section, we consider four different theories of gender acquisition. We then focus on methods used by agents of socialization, particularly parents and teachers, to teach children gender roles, ways of behaving that are expected for people in their sex category. In the last part of this section, we look at the considerable impact of the mass media on **gender socialization,** the social process through which individuals learn the gender-appropriate traits and behaviors expected of them.

Theories about Learning Gender

How do people learn to be female or male? A number of theories have been developed to explain this process. **Identification theory** originated in the work of Sigmund Freud. According to Freud, personality development occurs in stages. During the first two stages, oral and anal, girls and boys have very similar personalities. Both are strongly attached to their mothers (who are their primary caretakers), and their personality development is strongly influenced by this attachment. During the third stage, the phallic stage, which occurs at about age 4, differentiation between female and male personalities begins. The process occurs because children become aware of genital differences between women and men. The realization that males have penises and females don't, causes children to identify with the parent of the same sex. They model their own behavior after the same-sex parent and learn to behave in gender-appropriate ways.

Identification theory, then, attributes gender differences in personality traits and behavior to biological differences between women and men, specifically to children's awareness of differences in external genitals. This theory has been criticized for being antifemale, because it overtly states that women are inferior to men; phallocentric, because it overemphasizes awareness of genital differences; and untestable, because it rests on unconscious and thus unobservable phenomena. Evidence for the theory can only come from therapists' interpretations of their patients' memories of childhood experiences.

Other scholars have attempted to improve the theory by deleting the antifemale bias and shifting the emphasis from a biological to a social context. For instance, some theorists have argued that women experience penis envy because the penis is a symbol of male privileges and superior social status in most societies (Thompson, 1964; Lacan, 1977). Psychologist Karen Horney (1967) rejected the notion that penis envy plays a major role in females' psychosexual development. She proposed, on the contrary, that *men* are jealous of women's ability to bear children. Erik Erikson (1968) also emphasized women's reproductive capacity in explaining processes of identification. Women's reproductive role occurs in an inner space (the womb) in which they carry and nurture developing life. This causes girls and women to develop a psychological commitment to caring for other human beings. Men's reproductive organs, in contrast, are external and active, thus creating men's active and externally oriented social roles in adulthood.

Feminist sociologist Nancy Chodorow (1990) has also revised identification theory. Her revision emphasizes the social context in which children learn gender roles. Chodorow explains why females grow up to become the primary caretakers of children and why they develop closer emotional ties with children than men do. Chodorow's basic proposition is that gender is more difficult for boys to learn because fathers are so often absent from the home, due to employment commitments. As a result, boys become more emotionally detached and repressed. Girls, in contrast, do not experience a psychological separation from their mothers, who are in the home more often. Thus, mothers and daughters can maintain a close and continuous relationship. Through this relationship, girls acquire the psychological capabilities to care for children. Chodorow's theory has been criticized, however, because it applies only to white, middle-class families in the United States.

A second explanation of gender role acquisition is **social learning theory** (Bandura, 1986), which is based on behavioristic psychology. Social learning theory says that children learn gender roles the same way they learn other types of behavior—through reinforcement. Behavior that is positively reinforced is likely to be repeated, whereas negatively reinforced behavior is not likely to be repeated. Children are positively reinforced (rewarded) for engaging in what is considered gender-appropriate behavior and negatively reinforced or punished for gender-inappropriate behavior.

According to social learning theory, children also learn gender-appropriate behavior from **modeling** or **imitating** the actions of other people. Once again, they are rewarded for imitating appropriate behavior and punished for imitating inappropriate behavior. Children imitate their same-sex parent or others who are similar to themselves (same-sex siblings or teachers) if those others are engaging in gender-appropriate behavior and have the ability to reward or punish the children (Jacklin, 1989). However, the fact that children are *already* aware of what is gender-appropriate behavior suggests that the original learning of gender occurs somewhere else. This is a limitation of social learning theory. In addition, the theory depicts children as passive participants in the gender-learning process; they are born with an empty mind (or *tabula rasa*, literally translated as "a blank slate") waiting for their parents to mold and shape them. Other theories challenge this assumption.

The third explanation of gender learning, referred to as **cognitive development theory,** is based on the research of psychologists Jean Piaget and Lawrence Kohlberg. This theory proposes that children learn gender by categorizing people and objects. Children categorize by gender because it is a very visible indicator of difference (hair length, style of clothing, facial hair, etc.), which makes such categorization relatively easy for people whose level of intellectual functioning is fairly low.

Children can categorize themselves correctly as male or female as early as age 3. This occurs because they have repeatedly heard a gender label attached to themselves. Children also

Children learn gender-typed behavior, in part, by observing and imitating their same-sex parent.

begin to try to gender-label others at the same time. By age 4, they rarely mislabel other people. However, until about age 5 or 6 they don't realize that biological sex cannot be changed through a simple change of clothing or hairstyle. Once children develop a **gender identity** (a conception of themselves as male or female), they are strongly motivated to behave appropriately for a person of that gender. Conforming in this way is rewarding because it produces a feeling of competence and control over the environment.

Although cognitive development theorists argue that children begin to categorize people into male and female between the ages of 3 and 5, other theorists suggest that it happens at younger ages, perhaps as young as age 2. A second criticism is that this theory downplays the role of culture in gender role acquisition. In emphasizing children's internal motivation to use gender as a basis of categorization, this theory suggests that sex is a *natural* category rather than a *culturally imposed* one. The next theory, developed by psychologist Sandra Bem (1993), suggests that gender is used as a categorization tool because society makes it a central organizing feature of modern life.

Bem's **enculturated lens theory** of gender formation is the fourth and final theory of gender acquisition to be discussed here. The central theme of this theory is that "natives" of each culture learn to view the world in a certain way, through a common set of *lenses*. These lenses tell us how we are supposed to act, think, look, and feel; they shape our worldview. The first lens is a belief that males and females are fundamentally different and that this difference should be used as a way of organizing social life. Bem refers to this belief as **gender polarization.** The second assumption that shapes our worldview is **androcentrism,** a belief that males are superior; males have the characteristics that all "normal" people should have; women should be judged by how well they compare with men. The final lens that shapes our view of the world is **biological essentialism,** which provides the rationale for both gender polarization and androcentrism: Men are biologically superior to women; therefore, the polarization of gender is necessary.

How do these cultural lenses influence individuals? Bem identified the two key processes that must occur. First, societal institutions preprogram people's daily experiences to fit the expected pattern. Second, the culture must bombard its members with **metamessages** (implicit lessons) about what is important, what is valuable, and which differences between people are significant. It is through these processes that individuals acquire the lenses of gender.

Bem's theory incorporates several key aspects of the other theories. Like social learning theory, the enculturated lenses theory acknowledges that much gender acquisition occurs through indirect reinforcement rather than through direct rewards and punishments. As with cognitive development theory, Bem emphasizes that humans are not passive participants in the socialization or enculturation process. As adults, they readily conform to cultural expectations because they have become such an integral part of their *self*. Bem's lenses theory goes beyond cognitive development theory in that it adds the lens of androcentrism to gender polarization. In other words, children learn not only that females and males are different, but also that males are more important. Thus, as they grow to adulthood, they also become important proponents of the lens of androcentrism. These theories are summarized in Table 3.1.

We now turn to consider the specific ways in which children learn gender, focusing on the concepts of gender polarization and metamessages about gender.

Parents' Influence on Gender

The theories of gender role acquisition we have just described stress the importance of parents in teaching children the behavior expected of females and males. Research shows that parents respond in gender-specific ways to their children, starting very early in their lives. Today that may mean as early as six weeks after conception, since sonograms and amniocentesis can usually determine the sex of a fetus. Once informed, parents begin to think of their unborn babies in gender-typed terms, emphasizing very active, kicking male fetuses, for instance, as masculine (Eagly, 1987). As sociologist Judith Lorber (1993) has argued, *believing* (that certain traits are associated with maleness or femaleness) is *seeing* (those traits where you expect to see them). Many parents begin to prepare for the baby's arrival by designing a gender-appropriate nursery complete with the "proper" toys and purchasing the "correctly" colored clothing.

After birth, as before, parents continue to see the gender-appropriate behavior they expect to see. Two studies of parental behavior in a hospital nursery demonstrated this clearly (Rubin, Provenzano, and Luria, 1974; Reid, 1994). Parents of 24-hour-old babies were asked to evaluate them on a number of gender-typed characteristics. Parents of baby boys described their sons in stereotyped masculine terms (such as "strong and vigorous"), while parents of baby girls described their

TABLE 3.1		

Theories of Gender Socialization

Theory	Key People	Central Principles
Psychoanalytic theories (e.g., identification theory)	Sigmund Freud, Karen Horney, Erik Erikson, Melanie Klein, Clara Thompson, Jacques Lacan, Juliet Mitchell, Nancy Chodorow	Children pass through a series of stages in their personality development. Until around age four, these developmental experiences are similar for girls and boys. At age four, however, children unconsciously begin to model their behavior after that of their same-sex parent, thus learning how to behave in gender-appropriate ways. For boys, the motivation for identification is castration anxiety, whereas for girls, it is penis envy. Modifications of this basic argument include the notion of womb envy as well as a focus on the mother–child relationship rather than the father–son or father–daughter relationship centering around the penis. This latter revision includes the view that gender acquisition revolves around the fact that boys must psychologically separate from their mothers, while girls do not experience this separation.
Social learning theories	Albert Bandura	Children acquire gender in two ways: through reinforcement (i.e., by being rewarded for gender-appropriate behavior and punished for gender-appropriate behavior); and through modeling.
Cognitive developmental theories (e.g., gender schema theory, enculturated lens theory)	Jean Piaget, Lawrence Kohlberg, Sandra Bem	Children learn gender and gender stereotypes through their mental efforts to organize their social world. To make sense of sensory information, children develop categories or schema, which allow them to organize their observations and experiences according to patterns or regularities. Sex is one of their first schemas because it is a relatively stable, easily differentiated category with obvious physical cues attached to it. In the enculturated lens theory of gender formation, which also incorporates elements of social learning theory, children are socialized to accept their society's gender lenses (i.e., assumptions about masculinity and femininity). This enculturation occurs through institutionalized social practices as well as implicit lessons or *metamessages* about values and significant differences, which organize children's daily lives from birth.

Source: Renzetti, Claire M. & Curran, Caniel J. 1998. *Women, Men & Society*, 4E, p. 68. Reprinted by permission of Allyn and Bacon.

daughters in stereotyped feminine terms (such as "delicate"). However, when members of the hospital staff were asked to evaluate the same babies (with their sex concealed), they found no objective differences between the baby girls and boys in height, weight, or activity levels. In fact, medical evidence shows that the stereotype about boys being more robust and hardier than girls is false. Baby boys are actually more vulnerable to a variety of illnesses than are baby girls and are more likely to die in the early days of life.

Strangers usually expect parents to cue them about a baby's gender so they don't make a mistake and embarrass themselves and the parents. The assumption, of course, is that people should be able to tell a baby boy from a baby girl. In fact, however, behavioral differences between boys and girls are inconsistent or nonexistent in early infancy. Mistakes about children's gender are common in regard to

Source: Copyright © Baby Blues Partnership. Reprinted with special permission of King Features Syndicate.

2-year-old girls but rare for 2-year-old boys. Because parents are more concerned that their boys not be mistaken for girls, they are more careful to keep their hair short and to dress them in "boy" clothes.

The different perceptions that parents hold of their newborns are carried over into differential types of treatment.

Parents interact with little boys and girls differently. Because baby boys are believed to be tougher than little girls, they are played with in a rougher way and are given toys that encourage them to be active. Parents play gentle games (such as pattycake and bouncing on their knees) with their daughters, and physical activities such as wrestling and ball playing with their sons. As children get older, boys participate even more in physical play than girls.

In general, fathers are more likely to engage in physical play of any type and to increase their involvement in physical play as children get older. Mothers, in contrast, are more likely to hold and cuddle their children. Physical play, especially its rough and tumble aspects, is viewed as more masculine and more appropriate for boys than girls.

Little boys are encouraged to explore their environments and are allowed to roam farther from home than are little girls, who are given chores that keep them based in the house and protected. A study of over 500 families who visited the Sacramento Zoo illustrates this point (Burns, Mitchell, and Obradovich, 1989). Female toddlers were more likely than male toddlers to be carried by their fathers. This suggests that parents—fathers, in particular—are responsible for discouraging independence in little girls by restricting their freedom of movement. In general, dependence, passivity, cooperation, and compliance are encouraged in girls by parents and other adults such as teachers (Burns, Mitchell, and Obradovich, 1989).

One of the most interesting lines of research about parents' different treatment of girls and boys has focused on the physical environments they create for their children. Boys have more sports equipment, tools, and cars and trucks, while girls have more dolls, child-size furniture, kitchen appliances and utensils, typewriters, and telephones. Girls' and boys' clothing differ, too. Girls wear pink and multicolored clothes more often, while boys wear more blue, red, and white clothing. The colors used in little girls' rooms vary more than little boys' rooms, which are often decorated in blue. Previous studies found that boys' rooms were often decorated with animals while girls' were decorated with flowers and lace (Rheingold and Cook, 1975; Stoneman et al., 1986). "Parents and other adults still encourage sex-typed play by selecting different toys for female and male children, even before the child can express her or his own preferences" (Pomerleau et al., 1990, p. 365).

Research shows that children do express gender-typed toy preferences as early as one year of age, but their toy choices may have been inspired even earlier by parental encouragement. For example, when adults were given the opportunity to interact with a three-month-old infant dressed in a yellow jumpsuit (which is considered a gender-neutral color) they usually chose a doll as an appropriate plaything when they thought the infant was a girl. But when they thought the infant was a boy, they chose a football and a plastic ring (Fisher-Thompson et al., 1995). Parents' identification of specific toys as appropriate for one sex or the other is reinforced by toy catalogs, television commercials, pictures on toy packaging, and the arrangement of toys on shelves in toy stores (Schwartz and Markham, 1985; Shapiro, 1990).

What are the potential consequences of this different treatment by parents? Some researchers (Pomerleau et al., 1990) believe

▲ *The packaging and marketing of toys often send not-so-subtle messages to children about who is supposed to use them.*

that the toy choices parents make for children in early infancy affect their later play styles and toy choices as well as the development of different types of skills and abilities. Children who are encouraged and rewarded for playing with dolls and children's furniture learn to choose these objects because they are familiar with them and know what can be done with them. They have also learned that such objects are considered appropriate for them. When they use these objects over and over again, they are likely to develop specific skills, abilities, and behaviors. For instance, tools, cars, and sports equipment, in comparison with dolls, dollhouses, and toy kitchens, encourage more active play and contribute to the development of visual-spatial ability. Thus, young children's toy preferences and activity levels are shaped by the ways they are treated by their parents.

Toys and Books. The images of females and males in the picture books that parents give their children also contribute to the development of gender stereotypes in young children. Studies conducted in the 1970s showed that children's literature portrays males and females in a biased way. Even in award-winning books for preschool children (Weitzman et al., 1972), males were pictured much more frequently than females (in about one-third of the books there were no female characters at all) and were usually depicted as active and adventurous while females were shown as passive followers and helpers. Adult male characters were shown in a wide variety of occupational roles, but adult females were mainly shown in their homes. A follow-up study conducted in the late 1980s (Williams et al., 1987) showed a significant improvement in the visibility of female characters. Nearly all the books had female characters, and about one-third featured females as the main characters. However, some stereotyping remained. Males still outnumbered females in the titles of children's books by more than two to one (Grauerholz and Pescosolido, 1989). This pattern persists today. Kathleen Odean, a children's librarian, has reported that in the more than 4,000 children's books that are published each year, the vast majority of female characters are presented in supporting roles rather than primary roles. Very few are shown as brave, athletic, or independent. Only 600 books focus on girls who go against feminine stereotypes, take risks or

Children's books send powerful ▶
messages about gender in many
ways, including the sex/gender
of the major characters and the
activities in which boys and girls
are pictured.

face challenges without having to be rescued by a male, solve problems themselves, and learn from mistakes. There are very few books about girls' sports teams,
even though over two million girls play on various sports teams (Odean, 1997).

As a result of such findings, publishers and authors of children's literature
have attempted to eliminate sexism through gender-neutral characters. Some interesting research examining mothers' responses to these books, however, suggests
that the use of gender-neutral characters may not have the desired effect. When
mothers read aloud to their children, they refer to gender-neutral characters as
male in 95 percent of the cases (DeLoache, Cassidy, and Carpenter, 1987). Although
they may not have been intentionally omitting women from the stories they were
reading, young children assume that the characters being described by masculine
pronouns are male (Hyde, 1984).

Communication Patterns.   Parents also communicate differently with their
sons and daughters. They use a greater number and variety of words that involve
emotions with girls, particularly in regard to sadness. When parents use *emotion*
words with boys they often pertain to anger (Adams et al., 1995; Fivush, 1991;
Kuebli et al., 1995). Preschoolers whose mothers talk with them about emotions are
better able to understand other people's feelings (Denham et al., 1994). By the time
they reach the first grade, girls are better at monitoring emotions and social interactions than are boys (Davis, 1995). It seems reasonable to conclude that as a result
of interactions with their mothers in early life girls learn to pay attention to other
people's emotions and to value interpersonal relationships while boys learn that
anger is the only emotion that they are allowed to reveal. These differences are
often seen in adulthood (Erwin et al., 1992; Goleman, 1996; Schneider et al., 1994).

Can it be said that parents are just responding to biologically based sex differences in temperament when they treat their sons and daughters differently? There
are very few gender differences in the behavior of infants between the ages of three
and fourteen months. Research conducted in the late 1990s shows that girls may be
better behaved than boys simply because their mothers expect them to be. Mothers
tend to be more sensitive to their daughters' needs. Consequently, fourteen-month-
old girls seem to have a more secure attachment to their mothers than do boys of
the same age. Thus, mothers' gender-based expectations cause them to treat their
children differently (Connors, 1996).

Reinforcement of Gender Role Stereotypes in School

From the preschool grades onward, teachers also contribute to gender role socialization, although many are unaware that they are reinforcing traditional role expectations (Sadker and Sadker, 1995). Elementary teachers use various forms of sex segregation in their classrooms, for instance. They assign boys and girls different, gender-typed, classroom chores (for example, girls water plants or erase the board, while boys run errands that take them out of the classroom); they form competitive teams based on sex and pit boys against girls in spelling bees and math drills; and they seat girls and boys separately and form all-girl and all-boy lines (Sadker and Sadker, 1995; Thorne and Luria, 1986). The problem with gender segregation in elementary classrooms is that it denies young children an opportunity to learn to interact cooperatively with people of the other sex. It may cause children to feel most comfortable with persons of the same sex and make later life interactions with persons of the opposite sex more difficult. It may also perpetuate stereotypes about females' and males' abilities and interests (Lockheed, 1986; Sadker and Sadker, 1995).

There are other ways in which elementary teachers treat girls and boys differently in terms of the frequency and content of their interactions. They respond more frequently to boys than to girls, not only in positive ways but in negative ways. They reinforce dependence among little girls but encourage independence among little boys. Teachers take more steps to ensure that boys learn to perform tasks on their own. They give boys detailed instructions about how to complete a task and help them correct mistakes. When girls have problems with an assignment, teachers simply do the assignment for them (Sadker and Sadker, 1995). Interestingly, teachers typically deny that they treat girls differently from boys. Even when they are shown a film of a classroom discussion and asked whether the boys or the girls were talking more, they say girls were. In reality, boys are out-talking girls by a three-to-one margin. Even feminist teachers can be greatly influenced by gender stereotypes of "gossipy women" so that they fail to notice the sex bias in their own actions.

Much teacher–student interaction in the early years is focused on behavior management. Teachers encourage aggressive behavior among boys and passivity among girls (Serbin et al., 1973). Thus, girls learn they can get rewards from their teachers by being well-behaved while boys learn that being smart is more important than being well-behaved.

The gender messages that teachers send to elementary students are reinforced by textbooks and other educational materials. Regardless of the subject, females and minorities are underrepresented in textbooks. One analysis of history books found that less than 1 percent of the pages were devoted to women (Davis, 1995). There is evidence that children's literature has improved significantly in respect to the use of gender-neutral language and the inclusion of females. But imbalances continue in favor of males in regard to the rate of portrayal and the types of roles assigned to

Research has suggested that among children who are in mixed-gender classrooms, boys are reinforced by teachers for taking dominant roles in activities.

males and females in the stories (e.g., girls must be rescued by boys) (Odean, 1997). This may cause students to believe that boys' lives are more interesting and important than girls' lives.

Gender-typed treatment of students continues throughout the school years. High school teachers tend to offer their male students more encouragement, publicly praise their scholastic abilities, and act in a friendlier manner toward them than toward female students (Orenstein, 1994). Curriculum materials often send girls the message that they are unlikely to fulfill their ambitions. High school texts reflect gender biases, including gender stereotypes and language bias, omission of women and a focus on "great men," and failure to include the scholarship of women (Davis, 1995).

Women in college often find themselves encountering subtle forms of sex discrimination that single them out, ignore them, or discount them and their work simply on the basis of gender (referred to as **micro-inequities**). Female students are called on less frequently and interrupted more often when speaking in classes; professors use sex-stereotyped examples when discussing careers and occupations; women are referred to as "girls" or "gals" while male students are referred to as "men"; irrelevant comments are made about women's physical attributes or appearance when they are discussing academic ideas; and comments are made that disparage women's intellectual abilities and academic commitment. Although these behaviors may seem trivial, over an extended period of time they have a cumulative negative impact on women's ambition, on their class participation, and on their self-confidence.

Gender Messages in the Mass Media

We have seen the many ways in which parents and teachers create and maintain gender differences. It is also important to consider the influence of the mass media (such as television, radio, and magazines) in the process of gender role socialization.

Television.   Television is a major agent of socialization in American society. Its influence on gender development is largely because of the amount of time people spend watching it. By the time they graduate, students between the ages of 5 and 18 will have spent more time in front of a television set than in the classroom. For people in their mid 20s, television viewing is the third greatest time consumer, after working and sleeping (Davis, 1990).

Many studies have examined the role of television in gender role socialization. These studies consistently reveal that women and men on television have been portrayed in traditional and stereotypical ways (Signorielli and Bacue, 1999). In the 1950s and 1960s, men outnumbered women on television by a ratio of two to one, even though over 50 percent of the U.S. population was female. In addition, women were portrayed as overly emotional, dependent, dominated by men, and less intelligent. In the 1970s, new shows appeared that featured female leads in roles other than homemakers (such as *Mary Tyler Moore, Phyllis, Rhoda, Policewoman,* and *Charlie's Angels*). The image of women in these shows was still stereotyped, however. For instance, in *Charlie's Angels*, the three lead female characters, who were private detectives, were shown investigating situations that required them to wear provocative clothing and to run toward the camera (and audience) with their breasts jiggling.

A number of recent studies that have examined the portrayal of women and men on television show that the gender differences continue today. One study, which compared dramas that were aired over a 30-year period—from the late 1960s to the late 1990s—showed that women received less air time than men. While programs broadcast in the late 1990s had more women than those broadcast in the late 1960s and early 1970s, women still were not shown in proportion to their numbers in the population. The study also revealed, however, that the more recent dramas seemed to give women more respect than their counterparts 30 years earlier. Women in television dramas still tend to be younger than their male counterparts, but they are more likely to be shown employed outside their homes. Furthermore, the jobs television women hold are more prestigious today than in the past. In the 1970s, for instance, one out of every four employed women in television dramas held traditional female jobs in teaching or nursing. This changed in the 1980s and 1990s. Today, women in these shows are more likely to be shown in "male" jobs or in gender-neutral jobs (Signorielli and Bacue, 1999). Still, one of the most popular female characters on prime-time television—Ally McBeal (an Ivy League graduate who practices law in Boston)—spends most of her time fantasizing about her ex-boyfriend. She is presented as a childlike person rather than an adult.

Gender and
the Media

When children watch television shows, they draw on their stereotyped beliefs and expectations about women's and men's roles. Their stereotypes are particularly strong in regard to male roles. When asked to indicate who would be likely to perform various occupational roles, children's stereotypes come into play. Children's preconceived expectations about gender roles help them make sense of the gender information they see on television (Durkin and Nugent, 1998).

Even animated characters who represent products are more likely to be male than female. The use of male spokes-characters reinforces the stereotyped notion that men are more important than women. In fact, the impact of animated characters may be even more influential than other aspects of advertising because of their memorability and popularity (Peirce and McBride, 1999).

Women's appearance is also emphasized more than men's in television programs. Thin women are overrepresented in situation comedies. The more a female character weighs, the more negative comments are made *about* her—and sometimes *to* her—by male characters. These derogatory remarks are typically accompanied by audience laughter. The emphasis on extreme thinness combined with the laugh track presented in situation comedies may contribute to viewers' acceptance of gender and weight stereotypes that can seriously harm the health of female adolescents (Fouts and Burggraf, 2000).

Gender stereotyping in televised sports coverage also continues to reinforce divisions along gender lines and to reproduce traditional expectations regarding femininity and masculinity. The representation and portrayal of athletes in televised sports programs continue to be biased by gender in terms of the quantity and type of coverage. Less than 10 percent of the total sports news time in the late 1990s covered female athletes and less than 2 percent was devoted to covering women athletes in *male-dominated* sports. These patterns can influence viewers' beliefs about gender-appropriate sports behavior (Koivula, 1999).

Advertisements.   The average American is exposed to at least 3,000 ads every day and spends at least three years of his or her life watching television commercials (Kilbourne, 1999, pp. 58–59). Advertising sells a great deal more than products—it sells values, images, and concepts of love and sexuality, romance, success, and *normalcy*. It tells us who we are and who we should be as men and women, boys and girls. There has never been a propaganda effort to match that of advertising in the twentieth century. More thought, more effort, and more money go into advertising than has gone into any other campaign to change social consciousness (Kilbourne, 1999, pp. 74–75).

in the media

Disney Heroines

Kathi Maio, a feminist journalist in Boston, Massachusetts, looks at the way Disney's animated movies present women, race, and other cultures. Maio doesn't think Disney's heroines have changed very much since the days of Snow White: They are all happy housewives. She thinks this does not give a good message to young girls today. Maio is worried about some of the racial and cultural messages in Disney's movies, too.

Snow White

Snow White was the heroine of the first full-length animated film, *Snow White and the Seven Dwarfs*, in 1937. Snow White is young, pretty, virginal, sweet-natured, and obedient. She doesn't mind housework because she is sure that a rich young man will soon come and take her away.

When Snow White is afraid, she runs away and falls down in tears. When she finds shelter in a dirty little house in the woods, she immediately cleans it from top to bottom. When she lives there, she continues to do the housework: The group of (small) working males who live in the house clearly need a "mother" to clean for them, so this is Snow White's natural role.

Snow White's only enemy is her wicked and powerful stepmother. (Another typical Disney character is the evil older woman, who has a lot of power. She is always destroyed.)

Snow White's wicked stepmother tricks Snow White into eating a poisoned apple and she falls into a coma. The dwarfs cannot help her. Snow White must wait until she is rescued by the kiss of a handsome prince, and then she rides off happily with her new love.

This is typical of Disney's movies. Young women are naturally happy homemakers; they wait (like Snow White in her coma) until a man comes along to give them life.

After *Snow White*, Disney used other fairy tales for his movies, for example, *Cinderella* (1950) and *Sleeping Beauty* (1959). The heroines and their stories were very similar to *Snow White*.

Then, in 1966, Walt Disney died and the Disney Company did not produce any good animated films for a long time. Then, in 1989, the company produced a new, and very successful, cartoon feature film, *The Little Mermaid*.

The Little Mermaid

Ariel, the mermaid, is the heroine of the movie. It seems that Disney did not pay much attention to the Women's Movement: Ariel is the same as the earlier Disney heroines, except that she is somewhat sexy and wears a bikini made from shells. And the answer to all her dreams is to get her man. Ariel will do anything to make the prince fall in love with her. She even gives up her voice so that she can have legs.

But Disney movies have happy endings, and so Ariel gets her voice back and she keeps her prince. On the other hand, she loses everything else. When she becomes human and marries the prince, she must leave behind her underwater home, her father, and her friends. She gives up everything in her life for romance. That's OK for a fairy tale, but it is not a good idea for young girls in real life.

Many women complained to Disney about *The Little Mermaid*, and Disney promised to think more carefully about women's roles in the future. They hired a female screenwriter for their next movie, *Beauty and the Beast* (1991). Disney's publicity people promised that Belle, the heroine,

How does advertising influence us? Companies spend over $200 billion dollars each year on advertising. They can spend as much as $250,000 to produce one television commercial and another $250,000 to air it. The immediate impact on people's behavior can often be measured. For instance, during the 1999 Super Bowl, over one million people went to the Victoria's Secret Web site shortly after its 30-second commercial appeared on TV. Because the audience for the Super Bowl and other popular television events (e.g., the Academy Awards) is very large, advertisers often spend as much as $1 million on a commercial that lasts only seconds.

would be "modern," "active," and even "feminist."

Beauty and the Beast

The press thought Disney had done a good job, but the only real improvement is that Belle likes reading!

However, the most important problem in this movie is not the Disney company's idea of an independent woman. The problem is how Disney changed the hero, and the message of the story.

In the original story, the Beast looks terrible and frightening, but he is really kind and gentle. The message of the story is that you should not judge someone by what they look like. An ugly outside can hide a loving heart.

Disney changed this. The company decided to create a Beast with a "very serious problem." Disney's Beast terrifies his household and frightens Belle, his prisoner. The Beast does not attack Belle, but the threat of physical violence is present.

In the Disney movie, Belle changes the character of the Beast. Her beauty and her sweet nature change him from a beast into a prince, from someone who is cruel, into someone who is kind. So the movie's message is very different from the message of the fairy tale.

The movie says, if a young woman is pretty and sweet-natured, she can change an abusive man into a kind and gentle man. In other words, it is a woman's fault if her man abuses her. This is another dangerous message for young girls because it is not true: If Belle lived in the real world, she would almost certainly become a battered wife.

Pocahontas

After *The Lion King*, Disney became interested in the idea of "multiculturalism" and made *Pocahontas* in 1995. This movie mixes Disney's favourite story of the princess-in-love with a real story from Native American history. That is a problem because Pocahontas was a real woman, and she was very different from the Pocahontas that Disney invented. To give only one example: In real life, Pocahontas was a child when she first met the "hero" John Smith and there was no romance between them. When Pocahontas met Smith again years later, she called him "father."

But there are even more serious problems with the Disney version of *Pocahontas* and the video follow-up, *Pocahontas II*. The movies ignore the real fate of both Pocahontas and her people. The first movie ends cheerfully with peace between the colonists and natives; in fact, many, many of the Powhatan Nation (Pocahontas' people) were later killed.

As for the real Pocahontas, she was kidnapped and held hostage. She was forced to become a Christian and behave like a "civilized" white woman. She was married to a colonist who believed that the civilization she grew up in was evil. Later, Pocahontas was taken to England, to help advertise the colony of Virginia. In England, she was homesick. She became ill and died before she could return to her homeland.

None of this is in Disney's movie. And that is very worrying, because many people believed that they were learning about history when they watched *Pocahontas*.

Mulan

Disney has done a similar thing with *Mulan* (1998), the story of a Chinese hero. The real Hua Mu-Lan lived so long ago that her story has become a Chinese legend—a legend that Disney has reinvented so that it fits the pattern of a young woman in love.

Disney created Shang, a male hero for Mulan. He is her commanding officer. In the movie, Mulan is wounded in battle and everyone finds out that she is a woman. Her punishment is death but Shang cannot kill her, so he sends her away. After the war he comes to find her and marry her.

Disney has done it again. Brave, kick-boxing Mulan does not look like Snow White but, in fact, the life of a Disney heroine has not changed very much. Men still have power over them (Shang quite literally decides whether Mulan will live or die); and the best thing that can happen to them is to marry the hero and live "happily ever after."

Source: Adapted from "Disney's Dolls" by Kathi Maio, December 1998, *New Internationalist.* Reprinted by permission.

Advertising is the most important aspect of the mass media. It supports more than 60 percent of magazine and newspaper production and almost 100 percent of the electronic media. Magazines are essentially catalogs for goods—less than one-half of their pages are routinely devoted to content (Kilbourne, 1999, p. 36).

Popular consumer culture is both producer and product of social inequality (Coltrane and Messineo, 2000). In their study of nearly 1,700 television commercials that were aired in the 1990s, sociologists Scott Coltrane and Melinda Messineo discovered that characters in television commercials have more prominence and

ContentSELECT

Gender and Advertising

exercise more authority if they are white or male. Additionally, they discovered that images of romantic and domestic fulfillment also differ by race and gender. In commercials, white men were portrayed as powerful, white women as sex objects, black men as aggressive, and black women as inconsequential. These commercial images contribute to the perpetuation of subtle prejudice against African Americans by exaggerating cultural differences and denying positive emotions.

In the late 1990s, men were still less likely than women to be shown cooking, cleaning, washing dishes, or shopping in commercials. They were rarely shown taking care of a child (e.g., feeding, bathing, or diapering) but were often shown teaching, reading, talking to, eating with, and playing with children. To the extent that men in commercials are shown involved in family life, they still tend to depend largely on knowledge and activities that are stereotypically male (Kaufman, 1999).

Other researchers have shown that gender-role stereotyping in television commercials is not restricted to the United States. It is also found in Australia, Denmark, France, Hong Kong, Indonesia, Kenya, and Mexico, among many other countries (Furnham and Mak, 1999).

What then is the *impact* of the stereotyped gender messages that pervade television programs and commercials? Many studies have sought to answer this question. Children who spend a great deal of time watching television are more likely to think of occupations in stereotyped ways and give sexist responses to questions about the "nature" of women and men. Television cultivates such stereotyped notions as "women are happiest at home raising children" and "men are born with more ambition than women." One of the most interesting studies on this topic compared children from three communities in Canada (Kimball, 1986). One community had no television, another had only one channel, and the third had four channels. Children in the communities with television had more stereotyped attitudes about gender than those who had no television. Even more interesting, when television was introduced into the community that had not had television at the start of the study, children's attitudes became more stereotyped.

Magazines and Newspapers.   Television is by no means the only mass medium that presents gender messages. Magazines are just as stereotypical as television broadcasts. For instance, dominant messages in teen magazines are that a girl should care most about her appearance, finding a man to take care of her, and learning to take care of a house. Magazines are only one source of the many gender messages that young people are bombarded with every day, but they do contribute to the cumulative effect of all such messages, which is that appearance is central in a teenage girl's life. These messages may help to explain why teenage girls tend to become very dependent on their boyfriends, less interested in school, and less ambitious.

Finally, even cartoons reflect traditional stereotypes about women and men. The nagging and gossiping housewife, the inept woman driver, and the helpless-in-the-kitchen husband are exaggerated to enhance humor. In newspaper comic strips, women appear in traditional roles more often than is true in real life. Women are more often depicted as the victims of sexual coercion, as sexually naive and childlike, and as having more attractive bodies than their male companions.

The Impact of Gender on Everyday Life

As you conclude this chapter, stop for a moment to consider the ways in which your life is affected by the fact that you were labeled as female or male at birth. You'll find it quite difficult to identify any aspect of your life—from simple

Around the World

Gender Apartheid in Afghanistan

In September 1996, the Taliban (an extremist militia comprised of boys and young men of Afghan descent who were raised in refugee camps and trained in ultraconservative religious schools in Pakistan), took control of Kabul, the capital of Afghanistan, and violently enforced a state of **gender apartheid** (a system of gender-based segregation and stratification) in which women and girls were stripped of their basic human rights. On seizing power, the Taliban essentially put Afghan women into a state of virtual house arrest. Taliban policies banished women from the work force; closed schools to girls and expelled women from universities; prohibited women from leaving their homes unless accompanied by a *mahram* (the legally mandated male relative who acts as chaperone); ordered the windows of women's houses painted black so that women wouldn't be visible from outside their homes; and forced women to wear burqa (or chadari), which completely shroud the body, leaving only a small mesh-covered opening through which to see. The Taliban also prohibited women and girls from being examined by *male* physicians, while at the same time prohibiting most *female* doctors and nurses from working. Women who were found in the company of an unrelated male could be branded as adulterers and could be stoned to death.

Women who violated the Taliban decrees have been brutally beaten, flogged, and even killed. For instance, one woman who dared to defy the decree by running a home school for girls was shot and killed in front of her husband, daughter, and students. An elderly woman was brutally beaten with a metal cable until her leg was broken because her ankle was accidentally showing underneath her burqa. Many women who were forced to stay in their homes attempted suicide by swallowing household cleaners rather than continue to live under these circumstances. Nearly all of the women surveyed by Physicians for Human Rights showed signs of severe depression. Before the Afghan civil war and the takeover by the Taliban, women were educated and employed: 50 percent of the students and 60 percent of the teachers at Kabul University were women, and 70 percent of school teachers, 50 percent of civilian government workers, and 40 percent of doctors in Kabul were women. The Taliban claimed that their policies were based on a pure, fundamentalist Islamic ideology, but the oppression they perpetrated against women has no basis in Islam, which says that both women and men should be educated, that women can work, and that men and women should be treated equally. Other Islamic organizations—such as the Organization of Islamic Conference and the Muslim Brotherhood in Egypt—denounced the Taliban's decrees. The United Nations called the Taliban the most misogynistic regime in the world. Former President Clinton said that Afghanistan is "perhaps the most difficult place in the world for women."

Source: The Feminist Majority Foundation Online (www. femajority@feminist.org). Amnesty International Report-ASA (November 1999); Afghanistan. Women in Afghanistan: Pawns in Men's Power Struggles; Goodwin, J. *Glamour,* March 2000, pp. 287–300.

things such as the side on which your clothes button to more consequential things such as the major you are studying in college, the type of part-time job you hold, and your aspirations for the future—that aren't in some way affected by your biological sex and your socially constructed gender. Women and men in contemporary industrialized societies and in most, perhaps all, other places around the world can expect to live qualitatively different lives based solely on whether they are socially defined as male or female (Halpern, 2000, p. 7).

Throughout this text we consider the impact of gender on various aspects of close relationships. We close this chapter with a brief discussion of some of the major ways in which your life experiences are influenced by the fact that you are regarded as male or female. In our society, women and men are not only different; our lives are, in many respects, unequal. Such fundamental aspects of life as physical health, susceptibility to disease, and life expectancy are influenced by an individual's biological sex and gender roles.

Health, Illness, and Life Expectancy

Although we tend to think of men as stronger than women, **vital statistics** (information about birth, death, illness, marriage, divorce, and other major life events) show us this is not true. Throughout the twentieth century in the United States and all other industrialized nations, women have had a longer **life expectancy** (the average number of years a person can expect to live from a given age or from birth) than men. In fact, the gap is larger today than it was in 1900.

Life expectancy also varies by race and social class. Black men have the lowest average life expectancy while white women have the highest (67 vs. 79, respectively). White men and black women can expect to live to about age 74, on average. The gender differences in life expectancy result in an unbalanced *sex ratio* (the number of men in the population for every 100 women). In the United States, there are only 95 men for every 100 women. More boys than girls are *conceived* (some biologists estimate that as many as 130 male fetuses are conceived for every 100 female fetuses) and more baby boys are *born* (105 for every 100 baby girls). Genetic abnormalities that plague boys more often than girls result in a greater spontaneous abortion rate among unborn boys and also cause earlier death after birth. The presence of two X chromosomes in girls helps protect them against diseases such as muscular dystrophy (Stillion, 1995).

Behavioral differences between women and men also contribute to sex differences in health and illness. There seems to be an association between life expectancy and traditional gender role stereotypes. A large part of the difference in the death rate between women and men can be accounted for by men's greater susceptibility to heart disease, stroke, arteriosclerosis, and related problems (Waldron, 1995). One of the major reasons that men are more likely to have these problems is cigarette smoking. Men are not only more likely than women to smoke, but they also begin smoking at earlier ages, inhale more deeply, and smoke more of each cigarette they light (Waldron, 1995). Women's rate of smoking has increased significantly over the past decade; so this gender difference may soon disappear. However, even among nonsmokers the death rate from coronary heart disease for men exceeds that for women. Clearly, other factors play a role. One such factor is that men are more likely to exhibit what medical professionals refer to as the *coronary-prone behavior pattern* (also called type A personality by laypeople). The characteristics of this type of personality or behavior pattern resemble those considered masculine in our society: competitive, impatient, ambitious, and aggressive (Hegelson, 1995).

Another major health difference between women and men is that men's death rate due to cancer, particularly respiratory cancer, is considerably higher than women's. Again, differences in smoking habits are largely responsible. Unfortunately, the number of women smokers has been increasing, and as a result their death rate from lung cancer has increased dramatically (Thun et al., 1995). Differences in the types of jobs men and women hold also contribute to the gender difference in mortality rates due to cancer of the respiratory system. Men are more likely to hold jobs in which they inhale dust and toxic fumes, such as asbestos, arsenic, benzene, coal soot, lead, and vinyl chloride, all known or suspected carcinogens, or cancer-causing agents (Waldron, 1995).

Gender differences in alcohol consumption are also related to mortality. Chronic liver disease and cirrhosis of the liver are caused by excessive alcohol consumption. Men are considerably more likely to drink excessively and are twice as likely to die from these diseases. Men's substance use also contributes to their rate of accidental deaths, including auto accidents (Waldron, 1995). Alcohol consumption appears to be compatible with stereotyped masculinity. Traditional masculinity, which encourages risk taking, independence, aggressiveness, and even violence, has also been linked with higher death rates from accidents, homicide, and suicide among males (Staples, 1995; Stillion, 1995).

ContentSELECT

Gender and Health

Despite the fact that women have longer life expectancy and lower mortality rates than men, they have higher **morbidity** (illness) rates. For instance, women report more symptoms than men and are somewhat more likely to report that their health is only fair or poor (Waldron, 1995). They also report more days of restricted activity, including bed rest, than men. Women also visit doctors and hospitals more often than men. Once in the hospital, though, men tend to stay longer than do women.

These gender differences in susceptibility to various illnesses and in medical treatment may be attributed, in large part, to old age and to pregnancy and childbirth. Older people are more likely to suffer from chronic illnesses that restrict their activities. Elderly women are also more likely to be poor, which affects their health. We discuss aging in more detail in Chapter 11, which focuses on families in later life. Another explanation may be that women are less likely to ignore symptoms and more likely to use preventive health measures than are men (Waldron, 1995).

The traditional female roles of housewife and mother may also have negative consequences for women's *mental* health. Studies have shown that married women are more susceptible to depression than are men. *Depression* is defined clinically as feelings of discontent or displeasure accompanied by four of the following symptoms: poor appetite or weight loss, insomnia or increased sleep, psychomotor agitation or retardation, loss of interest in usual activities, loss of energy or fatigue, feelings of worthlessness, diminished concentration, and thoughts of suicide. These symptoms must be experienced on a daily basis for a minimum period of two weeks for the problem to be defined as depression.

Two explanations of married women's greater susceptibility to depression have focused on traditional roles. The first theory, which refers to the idea of **learned helplessness,** says that when women are confronted with a stressful life event they become depressed rather than take action, whereas men attempt to deal with the situation in an active way. The theory ignores the fact that women may not be able to take effective action because social conditions deprive them of problem-solving resources. The **social status hypothesis,** in contrast, explains married women's greater likelihood of being depressed in terms of the limited sources of satisfaction in the roles of homemaker and mother. Housework can be boring, repetitive, unchallenging, and isolating; so housewives may find themselves bored, isolated, and depressed. Employment can be more challenging, more variable, and a source of social interaction, which helps to account for the lower rates of psychological distress found among women who are employed in high-status, high-income jobs. Married men have the lowest incidence of depression because they not only have two sources of satisfaction—home and family, and job, but also can rely on their wives for social support (Hegelson, 1995).

Education and Employment

Today, American women and men have similar levels of education. Although this might suggest that full equality has been achieved in education, some notable differences remain. First, the highest levels of education (such as Ph.D.s) are dominated by men. Second, fields of study in higher education are gender labeled, and female and male students are segregated by major. Women cluster in the humanities, health sciences, and education, while men cluster in the physical sciences. Third, the highest levels within a field tend to be male dominated. For instance, while men were awarded 49 percent of the bachelor's degrees in international relations, they received 79 percent of the doctoral degrees in that field. A similar pattern holds for mathematics. The fields of study chosen by women seem to reflect stereotyped ideas about women's and men's interests and abilities; that is, women are nurturant and emotional and more highly skilled in verbal areas, whereas men are rational, independent, and more highly skilled in mathematics. Research shows that such differences are quite small, and not always in the expected direction.

Similar patterns of gender labeling and gender segregation occur in employment. Jobs are labeled as *male* or *female,* and workers are segregated by sex. One major consequence of this pattern is a persistent gender gap in pay and in women's greater likelihood of living in poverty, particularly after divorce. These issues are discussed in more detail in Chapter 12 (on families and work) and in Chapter 13 (on divorce).

Summary

Gender stereotypes are rigidly held, categorical beliefs that certain personality traits are associated with being of the male or female gender. Many Americans still closely follow gender stereotypes, believing women and men have very different abilities, interests, and personality traits. Men are seen as having the characteristics necessary for achievement and leadership in the outside world, while women are described as having the traits and interests necessary for caring for others and for maintaining close relationships.

Even though there may be some small differences in women's and men's *average* abilities, they still overlap greatly. Generally, the differences are too small to justify treating women and men along gender-stereotyped lines.

Biology may influence sexual development and possibly behavior in three basic ways: chromosomal differences, genetic dispositions, and hormonal differences. The differences in male and female sex chromosomes do produce physical differences, most notably the secondary sex characteristics. Hormonal differences between men and women exist, but no clear scientific evidence shows that hormones differentiate between their behavior.

Sociobiology is a theory of human behavior based on the idea that genetically inherited traits shape behavior. Because during prehistoric evolutionary processes men and women may have had distinctly different reproductive strategies, sociobiologists argue that the two sexes are genetically predisposed to behave differently. Critics of sociobiology point to the lack of evidence about the lives of prehistoric humans and note that genes related to specific kinds of behavior have not been identified. Other critics point out that even if there are some biological tendencies and proclivities, the cultural environment is a stronger influence on human behavior.

Gender differences in cognitive abilities, according to the available research, are not great and seem to be diminishing. In some cases, gender differences are the opposite of common beliefs.

Social and cultural influences that operate through the process of socialization are likely to shape gender behavior as much as, if not more than, biological factors. Four theories help to explain the way gender roles are learned, especially by young children. *Social learning theory* posits that rewards for acting in gender-appropriate ways and punishments for acting in gender-inappropriate ways produce the behavior expected of girls and women and boys and men in our society. Modeling and imitation are also part of the social learning process. *Cognitive development theory* stresses how children learn to categorize their world according to gender. This theory makes children active participants in the development of gender identities. *Enculturated lens theory* emphasizes that our worldview is shaped by a series of fundamental assumptions about the ways things are. The key lenses are polarization, androcentrism, and biological superiority of males.

Gender socialization occurs because boys and girls are treated differently by parents and other family members. Empirical evidence shows how parents, both intentionally and unintentionally, see girls and boys differently and respond to them accordingly. Parental socialization efforts are influenced by gender-typed advertising for children's products. The school system also contributes to gender role socialization; teachers often unknowingly reinforce traditional gender roles in their classrooms. The mass media, especially television, but also radio and the print media, continue to portray women and men in stereotyped ways.

Gender has an impact on nearly all aspects of life, beginning with life and death issues. Throughout this text, we examine the ways in which gender affects people's lives and especially their close relationships—dating, cohabitation, marriage, parenthood, divorce, remarriage, and widowhood.

Key Terms

- Androcentrism (p. 66)
- Biological essentialism (p. 66)
- Cognitive development theory (p. 65)
- Enculturated lens theory (p. 66)
- Gender (p. 57)
- Gender apartheid (p. 77)
- Gender identity (p. 65)
- Gender polarization (p. 66)
- Gender role (p. 57)
- Gender socialization (p. 64)
- Gender stereotype (p. 56)
- Hermaphrodites (p. 57)
- Identification theory (p. 64)
- Intersexed individuals (intersexuals) (p. 57)
- Learned helplessness (p. 79)
- Life expectancy (p. 78)
- Metamessages (p. 66)
- Micro-inequities (p. 72)
- Modeling (imitating) (p. 65)
- Morbidity (p. 79)
- Sex (p. 57)
- Social learning theory (p. 65)
- Social status hypothesis (p. 79)
- Sociobiology (p. 62)
- Stereotype (p. 56)
- Vital statistics (p. 78)

Review Questions

1. Discuss the differences between sex and gender as characteristics of humans.

2. Discuss the role various biological factors play in shaping sex-based differences in behavior.

3. Define gender role socialization.

4. Discuss the ways in which parents, peers, the public school system, and the mass media influence our ideas about "masculinity" and "femininity."

5. Outline the broad ways in which the simple fact of being born female or male affects an individual's rights, responsibilities, and opportunities in our society.

Critical Thinking Questions

1. Should parents try to raise their children in a gender-neutral way? What problems would they encounter if they tried to raise their children in this way?

2. How are women and men portrayed in the mass media? In what ways do portrayals of women and men vary by race, age, and social class?

3. Do the mass media create gender stereotypes or do they simply reflect stereotypes that already exist in our society?

4. What areas beside gender roles have been subject to controversies over nature versus nurture? How does this impact society's responses toward the participants? What would be some potential outcomes if a decision were made that gender differences are the result of socialization? What if they are the result of biology?

5. How has recent media portrayal of transgendered persons and behaviors changed?

Online Resources Available for This Chapter

www.ablongman.com/marriageandfamily

- Online Study Guide with Practice Tests
- PowerPoint Chapter Outlines

- Links to Marriage and Family Websites
- ContentSelect Research Database
- Self-Assessment Activities

Further Reading

Books

Bem, Sandra. *The Lenses of Gender: Transforming the Debate on Sexual Inequality*. New Haven: Yale University Press, 1978. A leading theorist on sex and gender discusses how hidden assumptions embedded in our cultural discourses, social institutions, and individual psyches perpetuate male power and oppress women and sexual minorities.

Chodorow, Nancy. *The Reproduction of Mothering: Psychoanalysis and the Sociology of Gender*. Berkeley: University of California Press, 1978. One of the most influential books of the past 25 years. Chodorow links psyche and culture, psychoanalysis and sociology.

Coltrane, Scott. *Gender and Families*. Thousand Oaks, CA: Pine Forge Press, 1997. Coltrane uses images from pop culture and events from everyday lives to explore how families and gender are mutually produced and inseparably linked.

Fausto-Sterling, Anne. *Myths of Gender: Biological Theories about Women and Men*. New York: Basic Books, 1992. A careful examination of the biological, genetic, evolutionary, and psychological evidence pertaining to assumptions of biologically based sex differences.

Fausto-Sterling, Anne. *Sexing the Body: Gender Politics and the Construction of Sexuality*. New York: Basic Books, 1990. Using real-life cases and an analysis of centuries of scientific research, Fausto-Sterling demonstrates how scientists have politicized the body. The book goes beyond the nature–nurture debate to offer an alternative framework for understanding sex and sexuality.

Gilligan, Carol. *In a Different Voice: Psychological Theory and Women's Development*. Cambridge, MA: Harvard University Press, 1993. Arguing that developmental theories have been built exclusively on observations of men's lives, Gilligan attempts to correct psychological misperceptions of women's personalities.

Halpern, Diane. *Sex Differences in Cognitive Abilities*. Mahwah, NJ: Lawrence Erlbaum Associates, 2000. Halpern reviews hundreds of studies that have attempted to uncover sex differences in various cognitive abilities and

offers a theoretical framework for understanding the influence of biology and socio-cultural environment on sex and gender.

Kilbourne, Jean. *Deadly Persuasion: Why Women and Girls Must Fight the Addictive Power of Advertising*. Glencoe, IL: Free Press, 1999. Kilbourne details the ways in which images of women in advertising contribute to a number of serious social problems.

Pipher, Mary. *Reviving Ophelia: Saving the Lives of Adolescent Girls*. New York: Ballantine Books, 1995. Pipher examines the far-ranging negative consequences of our appearance-obsessed culture on adolescent girls today.

Sadker, Myra, and Sadker, David. *Failing at Fairness: How Our Schools Cheat Girls*. New York: Touchstone (Simon & Schuster), 1995. A comprehensive review of the ways in which textbooks, teaching methods, tests, and teacher behavior contribute to a bias against girls in our educational system.

Tavris, Carol. *The Mismeasure of Woman*. New York: Touchstone (Simon & Schuster), 1992. Tavris unmasks the widespread custom in the social sciences, medicine, law, and history of treating men as the normal standard and women as deviating from that standard.

Thorne, Barrie. *Gender Play: Boys and Girls at School*. New Brunswick, NJ: Rutgers University Press, 1993. Thorne draws on her daily observations of elementary school children in classrooms and on playgrounds to show how children construct and experience gender at school.

ContentSELECT Articles

Carpenter, L. "The Ambiguity of 'Having Sex': The Subjective Experience of Virginity Loss in the United States." *Journal of Sex Research* 38(2), 2001: 127–140. **[Database: Sociology]** During the 1998 independent council investigation of President Bill Clinton, few could come to agreement in classifying certain intimate acts as *sex*. Because of the heightened ambiguity in society in terms of what sex is and what it is not, Carpenter explores the meanings and definitions of virginity loss as defined by 18- to 35-year-old respondents. While there was complete agreement that virginity loss occurs with penile-vaginal intercourse, few were in agreement when other intimate acts were considered.

Chang, Y. "Hollywood's Latest Cause." *Newsweek* 134(23), 1999: 42. **[Database: General Interest]** Unable to attend school, learn to read, or leave the house without male supervision, Afghanistan women and girls are receiving the attention of Hollywood. The Taliban's regime and its subjugation and suppression of women's rights in Afghanistan have led a number of television and motion picture celebrities to support the movement to end gender apartheid and improve conditions for these women and girls.

Matthews, B., and Beaujot, R. "Gender Orientations and Family Strategies." *Canadian Review of Sociology and Anthropology* 34(4), 1997: 414–429. **[Database: Sociology]** Women's traditional gender role orientations were compared with women who held more egalitarian role orientations. While both groups clearly preferred marriage and children, each group reported differences in the strategies of marriage timing and childbearing timing. Overall, traditional women plan their lives around their fertility, while egalitarian women plan their fertility around their careers.

Miller, S. "When Sexual Development Goes Awry." *World & I*, 15(9), 2000: 148–156. **[Database: General Interest]** Sexual differentiation, or the development of the internal and external sexual organs and reproductive systems, begins at about the sixth week of pregnancy and is a process that requires a delicate balance of the masculinizing and feminizing sex hormones. Providing a detailed explanation of sexual differentiation, the author examines the many aspects of ambiguous and/or mixed genitalia.

Quindlen, A. "Uncle Sam and Aunt Samantha." *Newsweek* 128(76), 2001: 76. **[Database: General Interest]** Is the military draft system in the United States fair to both genders? Currently, the U.S. Selective Service requires registration for the draft of all males ages 18 to 25, yet women, to date, are not required to register. The author argues that military service is a responsibility for *all*, not only men.

The Search for Love
Dating and Relationship Formation

The following letter was posted on the Love Letters page of <u>match.com</u>, an online dating service:

Darrell answered my ad and I liked what he had to say about himself and what he was looking for in a mate, so I asked if he wanted to meet. He had mentioned that he liked kayaking and that he lived only a few minutes from a nice spot to paddle. So without reading his ad or seeing a picture of him, I asked if he'd like to take me kayaking. He agreed.

At the time I lived an hour away from him, so the evening of our first date, I hopped on my motorcycle and raced over to his house. I figured that if the date didn't go well, at least I would have a nice ride and this would give me a way out if things got weird (to say that I needed to leave before dark, which I didn't have to do). Riding is also a big part of who I am and I wanted this to be clear. I am not a stay at home, do nothing kind of gal. The right man would have to know and accept this.

I showed up (at) the island where he lives right on time, but realized that I had forgotten his address and phone number. I rode around aimlessly for almost an hour thinking the whole time that he thought that I had stood him up. I felt so bad until he finally called me to see if things were okay. I quickly explained what had happened and met him a few minutes later at his house where he had the kayak all ready to go. Wow was he cute, too! I remember thinking how lucky I was. How could a guy sound so good in his emails and be so good looking?

We spent about two hours paddling around Lake Washington, picking blackberries, and getting to know each other. It was so nice! He really seemed like a man who could treat me "like one of the boys" while at play, but who also knew

Key Questions

1 Is contemporary dating adequate preparation for marriage?

2 What factors lead dating couples to increasing levels of commitment?

3 In what ways do dating partners "do gender" as a means of attracting and keeping mates?

4 In what ways are societal changes, such as those associated with modernization and urbanization, reflected in the ways in which intimate partners are selected?

5 To what extent can dating and mate selection processes in contemporary western societies be adequately described in *market* or economic terms?

85

how to treat me like a lady. After kayaking, we went out for sushi and then back to his house where we talked until 11:00 P.M. Wow, what a great evening!

I can't believe that I really did meet the man of my dreams from an online dating site! Now that I have him, it really does seem the best, safest, most efficient way to meet a man. It only took two months to find him here, and I had been looking for three years. Thank you, match.com.

_____

Signed: *Susan* (posted on May 7, 2001).

*S*tories similar to Susan and Darrell's are occurring every day in our society. Those who wish to have an intimate relationship must take the initiative to find a compatible and attractive partner. Although they may meet potential mates through family, friends, and co-workers, the work of determining compatibility or suitability still rests on their own shoulders. Often, though, those who are searching for a partner turn to the use of technological matchmakers (e.g., the internet and personal ads in newspapers). They put themselves on the mate market, so to speak. Sometimes the search takes a lot longer than they would like. And it doesn't always have a happy ending like Susan and Darrell's (who married within a few months of meeting each other online.)

In this chapter, we consider the methods people use to find intimate partners in different types of societies. In agricultural societies that use some type of arranged marriage systems, adults have primary responsibility for finding suitable spouses for their children. We next consider the traditional courtship model in which adults also have an important role to play in monitoring interactions between the courting couple. In this type of mate selection system, however, young adults do have the opportunity to get to know each other before making a commitment to marry.

The chapter focuses primarily on contemporary dating, which is still the most common way in which people in our society meet and get to know potential partners. We use the term *dating,* while recognizing the fact that the word now has a wide range of meanings for people who are in various stages of relationship formation. We begin with a discussion of the various definitions the term *dating* has today.

What Is Dating?

*C*ouples often experience a great deal of difficulty defining and negotiating the status of their relationship. In the arena of dating the language is often contradictory or inadequate to express the type of relationship or emotional attachment the couple experiences. The same labels can be used to describe very different types of relationships or degrees of commitment and exclusivity, which can lead to confusion, not only in the partners themselves but in their wider social circle (Brackett, 1996, p. 113). For Charles and Vanessa, who live in the same apartment complex and participate in many dating activities with a close friendship group, dating is a casual interaction or activity that has little claim to commitment or permanence on the part of either partner. Following is part of an interview that sociologist Kim Brackett conducted with Charles and Vanessa in her study of new dating relationships (p. 114):

KIM: Do you call it *dating* or something else?

VANESSA: Dating. I do.

CHARLES: Yeah, I just say dating too.

KIM: Do people understand what you mean?

VANESSA: I think most people do.

CHARLES: A lot of my friends don't. Well, I've always been . . . we just got out of real serious relationships and so they, my friends, have always seen me in a relationship, a steady relationship, you know. And I say we're just dating, you know, and they find that hard to believe. One of my roommates goes, "well, you're not dating anybody else." And I'm like, "yeah, but you can still date this one person. You don't have to be like dating."

For Dana and Ben, another couple in Brackett's study who had been seeing each other for seven months, *dating* was the term they used to describe their relationship, but the connotation of the term was more serious than it had been for Vanessa and Charles. Dana and Ben used the term in conjunction with boyfriend–girlfriend status (pp. 114–115):

KIM: Do you call it *dating* or something else?

BEN: I don't know. I've never really paid that much attention to how I talked about it.

DANA: I mean, I call him my boyfriend, but even that is weird for me because I haven't dated a lot. But I don't think I started calling him that until like two months ago.

BEN: Yeah, about then.

KIM: (To Ben) How do you introduce her to people that she doesn't know?

BEN: As my girlfriend. As Dana.

KIM: When you were describing how you met, you used the term "seeing each other."

DANA: It seems like . . . it seems like a lighter sense of the word. I would consider the first month like seeing each other. Since then, I guess, dating. It just sounds funny, old fashioned, to say dating. It is really not talked about a lot. It is just . . . it's kind of, it's almost a given now. Maybe call it a '90s thing, but if you talk about it a lot and you are using strong terms, like dating and seeing, a lot of people are uncomfortable with it because they are scared of commitment nowadays. They are like, oh, they get skittish about it. But that's just . . . there really isn't the terminology. It's almost dropped. It's just becoming a given.

ContentSELECT

Dating and Relationships

Since it seems unlikely that society will develop a language for dating that all couples will understand and use consistently, the work of creating a discourse of dating falls squarely on the shoulders of the partners. They must decide what language they will use with each other as well as with "outsiders." The construction of this shared image of the social arena of dating, the roles of the partners, and the nature of the association is among the primary work that those who consider themselves to be dating are engaged in (Brackett, 1996, pp. 115–116).

In this chapter, we consider the ways in which today's singles meet partners, including "high-tech" matchmaking services such as those offered in newspaper personals sections, 900 phone numbers, and the Internet.

We describe the actual processes in which potential partners are weeded out until only those who are deemed most compatible and most desirable remain. The importance of physical attractiveness in this process is given special consideration.

Although we tend to think of dating as innocent, carefree, and pleasurable, it is often filled with stress and anxiety. Dating can become a high-stakes game in which both partners are out to maximize their own pleasures while minimizing their own efforts and commitments. In this chapter we take a realistic view of dating, showing that even in its more routine forms, it often reflects power struggles that may result in the exploitation of one partner. In the extreme, women may experience sexual coercion and violence in heterosexual dating relationships. We look at different problems that are associated with dating, including practical issues such as what to do and how to pay, to more serious concerns such as jealousy, power struggles, courtship violence, and date rape.

After discussing the ways in which people meet partners, and the problems dating couples face, we then examine in detail the process of falling in love, giving attention to various theories that have been offered to explain this experience. We consider a claim that love in our society has become "feminized," or defined in feminine terms, and the implications that can have for heterosexual relationships.

The final section of the chapter examines the process of ending intimate relationships, including reasons for breaking up, strategies used to inform a partner about an impending breakup, and types of relationships that end before marriage. We conclude with a brief discussion of adults who remain unpartnered.

Changing Models of Partner Selection

Scientific studies of dating, which we refer to in this chapter, illustrate the impact of societal change on individual lives and help us to see the extent to which human behavior is patterned and predictable. These issues are of great interest to social scientists. To illustrate the impact of societal change on intimate relationships, we examine three different ways in which partners are selected: the traditional agrarian model, the courtship model, and the contemporary dating model (McCall, 1966).

The Traditional Agrarian Model

In many cultures, dating as we know it in the United States and Canada is not the dominant method of finding partners. In such diverse places as China, India, and much of South America and Africa, dating is rare. It is forbidden in most Muslim countries, including Egypt, Iraq, Iran, and Saudi Arabia. It is only in westernized countries such as Canada, the United States, Great Britain, and Australia that dating is the most common way individuals select partners.

In traditional **agrarian** (agricultural) **societies,** parents or other kin members select marriage mates for children when they reach the appropriate age. The criteria used in choosing a potential mate include primarily economic considerations (such as social status or wealth) and often the potential for political alliance between the families. The bride and groom have little or no personal contact with each other before their marriage. Love between bride and groom is not expected.

Many agricultural societies have used the traditional type of mate selection processes. Ireland in the last half of the nineteenth century is a good illustration. Marriage was closely tied to inheritance of a family farm. The son who was designated as the family heir could not marry until his parents were willing to turn over their farm to him. Irish parents were usually not eager to give up their farm, so the son's marriage could easily be postponed until he was in his thirties or even forties. When the death or disability of one of the parents made it necessary for them to turn over control of the farm to the son, they would set out to find him a wife. Often a matchmaker or go-between would be used to bring the families of the potential bride and groom together. Sometimes a friend of the family or even a family member would make the first contact to arrange a meeting.

One Irish man describes how the procedure worked:

> If I wanted to give my farm over to my son and I would be worth, say, two hundred pounds, I would know a fellow up the hill, for instance, that would be worth three hundred pounds. I would send up a neighbor fellow to him and ask him if he would like to join my family in marriage. If the fellow would send back word he would and the girl would say she was willing, then on a day they agreed on I and the fellow would meet in (the local market town) and talk over the whole thing as to terms, maybe sitting on it the whole day. (Arensberg and Kimball, 1940, p. 109)

The two families would work out a tentative financial arrangement. It was customary for the groom's family to provide the newlyweds with a farm while the bride's family would contribute a **dowry** consisting of furniture and other household goods, jewelry, or livestock. By the end of the nineteenth century, the dowry typically consisted of money the bride's family had saved to make sure she could marry. Lengthy negotiations between the fathers of the potential bride and groom were necessary to determine whether the monetary value of the dowry was equal to that of the farm. The matchmaking process was a hard-headed economic negotiation rather than an emotional consideration. Once again, an Irish man describes the bargaining that went on:

ContentSELECT

History of Marriage

> The (matchmaker) goes with the young man and his father . . . and they meet the father of the girl and his friends. . . . The first drink is called by the young man, the second by the young lady's father. The young lady's father asks the (matchmaker) what (dowry) do he want. He asks him of the place how many cows, sheep, and horses it is. He asks what makings of a garden are in it; is there plenty of water or spring wells? Is it far from the road or on it? What kind of house is in it, slate or thatch? If it is too far from the road, he won't take it. Backward places don't grow big fortunes. And he asks too is it near a chapel and the school or near town? If it is a nice place, near the road and the place of eight cows, they are sure to ask three hundred and fifty pounds fortune. Then the young lady's father offers two hundred and fifty pounds. Then maybe the boy's father throws off fifty pounds. If the young lady's father still has two hundred and fifty pounds on it, the (matchmaker) divides the fifty pounds between them, so now it's two hundred and seventy-five. Then the young male says he is not willing to marry without three hundred pounds—but if she's a nice girl and a good housekeeper, he'll think of it. (Arensberg and Kimball, 1940, p. 111)

Often it wasn't until after a tentative arrangement was reached by their fathers that the prospective bride and groom would get a chance to have their say in the decision. The woman would bring her friends, her brothers, and perhaps even her parents. The man would also bring his friends. Among this group of people, the future bride and groom would evaluate each other. If at that point one or the other decided they could not go through with the marriage, the arrangement could be called off. If they found each other acceptable, however, the agreement was finalized and a wedding would quickly follow.

This is a general description of the way the Irish mate selection system worked, especially in the last part of the nineteenth and early part of the twentieth centuries. Selection of a partner was largely controlled by the parents. The decision to marry was based on the success of the bargaining about the economic aspects of the

Around the World

The Emergence of Dating in Iran

Marriage in Iran has traditionally been regarded as a union between the families of the bride and groom. In the past, tribes used marriage as a way to increase the number of people in their community and to help strengthen their defense against enemies. Today, families often encourage young people to marry their second cousins as a way to strengthen family ties and reduce the likelihood of divorce. Marrying a second cousin gives the bride and groom's families an assurance that they will be marrying into a reputable group.

In arranged marriages in Iran, the prospective wife and husband are introduced in a **khasegarien** (a business meeting in which a potential marriage is discussed). The man who is looking for a wife usually asks his mother or close acquaintance to set up the meeting. Once the families are together, information about the man's profession, background, and family reputation is presented to the bride's family. After the meeting, the woman and her family must think about the offer of marriage. She is allowed to refuse, but she is usually pressured by her family and friends to accept. Because the Islamic Civil Code requires a male guardian to give final consent for a woman's marriage, a marriage contract made by a male relative after the girl reaches puberty is valid. If a father or grandfather believes that his family would benefit from a young girl's marriage he can take her out of school and sell her. Illiteracy among young girls in Iran is currently running at 82 percent.

Traditionally, Iranian girls married at age 13 and boys at 15. The legal age of marriage was lowered to age 9 for girls during the Iranian Revolution, which began in 1979. In urban areas, however, where young women may plan to attend a university and enter professional careers, the average age at marriage is closer to 25. Poor economic conditions in Iran today often mean that young people are dependent on their families and can't afford to marry until later ages. In rural areas, families adhere more closely to tradition and encourage their children to marry at a young age. Islamic law forbids women to be seen in public with a man other than her husband or close relative. This makes public dating difficult. Social outlets for mingling with people of the other sex are limited to family gatherings and school functions. Public areas such as trains and buses are segregated by sex. Even at the beach, men and women are separated. Men must swim in the morning and women in the afternoon. The lifeguard (who is always a man) spends the afternoon on the street waiting to be summoned in case of an emergency. Even in large social gatherings such as weddings and birthday parties, it is illegal to seat men and women in the same room. This is often ignored, however.

Source: Filabi, Azish. "Holding Hands in Public: The Emergence of Dating in Iran: Dating Customs Changing Slowly." *World and I,* 15 (12), 2000: 192.

match. The Irish way of selecting partners almost totally lacked any elements of courtship or love.

Not every Irish marriage at the time followed this model exactly. Young people sometimes became attracted to one another, perhaps fell in love, and then on their own, without parental blessing, dowry, or farm, ran off to get married. Sometimes these *runaway marriages* (elopements) would eventually gain the acceptance of parents; at other times, not.

Arranged marriages are still common in many parts of the world today. In India, for example, most marriages are arranged by parents. But with increasing numbers of Indians who are migrating from small villages to cities or other countries in search of economic opportunities, families who enter into marriage arrangements are less likely to have known each other personally. Increasingly, arranged marriages occur through brokers, classified ads, or Internet services. Brides and their families often feel compelled to buy their way into a marriage by providing a dowry (that is, gifts of cash, jewels, and various consumer goods) to their prospective in-laws. The value of the gifts increases in proportion to the groom's apparent economic prospects. A groom who works for the government, for instance, may be able to command a dowry of $100,000 or more. Men who are not satisfied with the value of the dowry they receive from their wives' family often murder their wives as a way of resolving dowry disputes. Widowed husbands can then receive another dowry upon remarriage. Indian journalists estimate that as many as 6,000 to 15,000 women are murdered or driven to suicide in India each year as a result of disputes over dowries (Mandelbaum, 1999).

In many parts of Africa today, marriages are also arranged through economic negotiations between families. In Uganda, for instance, a man who wishes to marry assembles a group of male friends and relatives to visit the home of a prospective bride where they will bargain with her male relatives to reach an agreement that will allow the marriage to occur. In Uganda, however, it is the family of the groom who must pay the family of the bride. The **bride price** often consists of cows, goats, and money that are given to the bride's family to persuade them to give a young woman in marriage. Sometimes the groom borrows part of the bride price from his father and other male relatives,

▲ *Fifty years ago, dating activities took place in homes under the close supervision of parents.*

who may then feel they "own" a part of the bride. Should the husband die before his wife, she may be "inherited" by one of the male relatives who contributed to the price that was paid when she married (WIN News, 2000). The bride price is a major source of income for African fathers, who may force their daughters as young as age 10 to marry elderly men who can pay a high price. This custom of arranged marriages in which men pay for brides has the effect of keeping girls from getting an education. It has also been associated with the death of large numbers of young girls in child birth (WIN News, 1999). In marriage negotiations involving the dowry and the bride price, brides are not consulted and are often the victims of male violence. The government of Uganda, however, prohibits any customs or traditions that work against the dignity, welfare, or interest of women or that undermine their status. Thus, the practice of paying a bride price, while common, is against the law in that nation (WIN News, 2000).

As surprising as it may seem to us, many of the young people who live in cultures in which arranged marriage is practiced say they prefer having adults select their mates rather than having to choose one for themselves. Adults may make wiser choices, they say. But also, arranged marriages free them from the unpleasantness of dating and ensure that they will not be rejected as a mate based on physical appearance or other personal characteristics (Schwartz and Scott, 2000, p. 113).

We turn next to a second way in which intimate partners are selected, the courtship model. This method was actually more common in the United States in earlier periods than the traditional agrarian model.

The Courtship Model

Even though the United States started as a rural, agricultural society, the traditional agrarian model was never the most common way partners were selected (Furstenberg, 1966; Demos, 1970). The courtship model, in which young people are given much independence in their choice of partners, was typically followed. In the United States, young men and women have always been given a great deal of freedom to be together and enjoy each other's company. In fact, many European visitors in the eighteenth and nineteenth centuries believed that American young people, especially women, were given *too much* freedom (Furstenberg, 1966). From our earliest history, marriages have been based primarily on romantic attachments and love. The courtship model of partner selection, then, has the following characteristics:

1 Young people have substantial control over mate selection, although at some crucial points the parents have considerable impact on their choice.

2 There are steps in the process that serve to narrow the **field of eligibles** (the people available to be chosen as a partner).

3 Among the field of eligibles, a number of individuals are considered as possible mates.

4 Over a period of time, those who prove to be the poorest bargains are dropped from consideration.

5 The narrowing of the field of eligibles continues until only one person is left, based on mutual feelings of love.

6 The two people in the couple become, at this point, committed to each other. They reach a *private* understanding, which will soon be followed by a *public* announcement of plans to marry.

7 A period of engagement is followed by marriage, a permanent contract meant to last a lifetime. *contract is between you, spouse, + state in which you marry in,*

In the early colonial period of our history (during the 1700s), marriage was considered essential not only for individuals' economic survival but for social stability. As a result, much of a village's attention was focused on finding spouses for unmarried individuals. A number of community activities or events provided opportunities for single people to get to know each other under the watchful eyes of other village residents. Explicit rules governed the courting process. Parents were not allowed, by law, to choose a partner for their children, but they did exercise considerable influence over the partner selection process. Daughters were strictly supervised. If a young man wanted to court a young woman he had to meet her parents and get their permission to court or "call on" her. Laws of the time required a suitor to get permission from a young woman's father before beginning the courting process. After a formal introduction, the young people were allowed to spend time together but usually not alone. Chaperones (who were typically older women) were a common feature of the courting process.

One interesting aspect of this type of courtship is that women and their parents were in control. A young man was not allowed to go to a young woman's home to call on her unless he had been explicitly invited to do so by her mother. If the woman was not at home when the young man stopped by—or if she did not wish to see him—he was asked to leave his calling card to let her know that he had been there. At the calling stage of a relationship, men and women were allowed to visit with more than one person. One way a young woman could indicate to a particular suitor that she did not wish to pursue a relationship with him was to repeatedly have her mother tell him she was not available when he visited her home (Whyte, 1995).

When a more serious relationship developed between a couple, their relationship went from being known as "going calling" to "keeping company." Keeping company was a formal and morally above-board relationship. In some ways, "keeping company" was the precursor for "going steady," a term that emerged in the twentieth century. Couples who were "keeping company" were expected to be monogamous (Whyte, 1995).

Living conditions in America were very different in the eighteenth century than they are today. There was no central heat or lighting in homes and transportation typically took the form of horseback (or horse and buggy). If a young man traveled a long distance to "keep company" with a woman he was courting, it was often impossible for him to return to his home on the same day. One custom that developed in Holland and the British Isles and spread to New England at this time was called **bundling.** This was a practice in which engaged or courting couples slept together, fully clothed, in the same bed but did not engage in any sexual activities. Sexual contact was allegedly prevented in many ways, most often by placing a board down the length of the bed to separate the woman and man. Sometimes the young woman was placed in a bundling sack that covered her body from toes to neck. The film *The Patriot* (which starred Mel Gibson) includes a scene in which the eldest son gets sown into a large burlap bag so that he can spend the night in bed with the young woman he is courting. Bundling had the advantage of giving the young couple some privacy so they could get to know one another, but it supposedly prevented premarital sex. There is not much evidence to indicate whether the bundling boards and sacks actually prevented sexual contact before marriage, however. The practice was generally abandoned in the early 1800s because of widespread social disapproval (*Columbia Encyclopedia*, 2001).

Teens today have many opportunities to interact with persons of the other gender.

The "coming out" party or debutante ball provides a contemporary illustration of the way the courtship model works. The coming-out party is the official recognition by some social groups that a young woman is ready to be seriously courted, that she is ready to begin the process of narrowing the field of eligible men until at last only one is left, whom she will marry. The debutante ball also shows how a young woman's social class influences her choice of suitors. Only the elite families in our society can send their daughters and sons to a debutante ball.

One of the most famous, the International Debutante Ball, began in New York City in 1954. It is typically held at the Waldorf Astoria where the teenage daughters of rich and famous Americans and Europeans mingle at what has become a rite of passage for affluent young women. The event is expensive and full of tradition. Every debutante's family hosts a table or two at the ball. Each table costs approximately $5,000. The debutantes are typically escorted by young men from military academies who are dressed in their uniforms or white tuxedoes. At the stroke of midnight, the young women are announced in alphabetical order, by state. As each is introduced she must curtsy. This is the moment at which she makes the formal transition from girl to marriageable woman (Schappell, 1998).

Families who are not as well off have less control over the suitors of their daughters, but their social class also affects the field of eligibles because it determines the neighborhoods they live in and the schools to which they send their children. Of course, parents can simply prohibit their children from seeing others who are of the wrong social class, religion, or race.

Even though parents play a part in the selection of mates in the courtship model, the major burden for finding eligible partners still falls on the young people themselves. They must meet and date a wide range of possible mates before making a final commitment to any one.

In the courtship model of mate selection, bargaining between potential brides and grooms is going on, just as it does in the traditional agrarian model, but the emphasis is placed on their personal qualities. Economic aspects are not irrelevant, but they compete with appearance, style, manners, and most of all, love. Once the person with the best combination of personal qualities has been found, a permanent commitment is made and is formalized through an engagement.

Shortly before the engagement, however, the young people visit each other's parents. This is serious business, for now the parents know that the relationship may lead to marriage. If the parents are going to try to stop the marriage for some reason, they must do so at this point. In the courtship model, it is customary for the man to ask the woman's father for permission to marry.

If both families agree to a wedding, the engagement period begins. It lasts long enough for the young people to be certain they are "meant for each other." Only then do they marry. Ideally, their marriage will last a lifetime.

When and why did this youth-controlled courtship process emerge as the primary method through which life partners are chosen? Although young people in the United States have always had considerable freedom in mate selection, during the early decades of the twentieth century, when the United States was being transformed from a rural, agrarian society to an urban, industrialized society, the courtship model began to flourish. Large numbers of families moved to cities where young people came into close contact with others of the opposite sex in their neighborhoods and workplaces. The development of coeducational schools also provided situations in which girls and boys had the opportunity for regular, casual interaction.

The invention of the automobile and telephone made it possible for young people to talk to each other without formal introductions and to get away from their parents' watchful eyes to spend time in private places. Another important event of this time was the passage of the Nineteenth Amendment in 1920, which gave women the right to vote. This was associated with a change in U.S. attitudes about women: specifically, that young women as well as young men deserved more freedom from parental control.

The courtship model was widely accepted for many years in the United States. Some elements of this ideal still exist, though not to the same extent as they did sixty or seventy years ago. There is still the notion of "playing the field": meeting and dating a wide range of potential mates, and waiting until one falls "truly in love" to marry. Parents still place their children in neighborhoods, churches, and colleges that greatly influence their selection of intimate partners. But young people today are more likely to announce their plans to their parents *after* they become engaged, rather than to ask for their permission to marry. To get a more complete picture of mate selection processes today, we need to consider a third model, contemporary dating.

The Contemporary Dating Model

In the contemporary model, the selection of a partner is almost totally in the hands of young people themselves. There is evidence, however, that parental support is often important for dating relationships to succeed (Lewis, 1973; Parks, Stan, and Eggert, 1983). Because young people are aware of the crucial role their parents can play in making or breaking their relationships, they consciously attempt to manipulate their parents' opinions of their dating partners (Leslie, Huston, and Johnson, 1986). They emphasize their partner's "good points" and ask their parents to trust their decisions concerning their dates. They also set up "spontaneous" meetings between their dates and their parents. They are usually successful in winning their parents' support (Leslie, Huston, and Johnson, 1986).

Parents show their approval by asking about the partner, saying they like him or her, being nice to the partner, giving the young couple privacy to be alone, lending a car for dates, and planning joint activities with the couple. When they want to show their disapproval, they give the partner nasty nicknames, ask what their

 **Reviving Traditional Courtship: No Kissing—or Anything Else— until Marriage**

An increasing number of Christian parents in the United States are deciding that contemporary dating—with its emphasis on superficial characteristics and early sexual involvement—is not right for their teenage children. One of the most prominent parents who is speaking out in favor of a return to courtship is Jim Ryun, a three-time Olympic athlete and, more recently, a representative from Kansas. Ryun and his wife Anne run a family ministry in Kansas. A central aspect of their religious philosophy is the belief that dating should be replaced by traditional, parent-controlled courtship. A prospective suitor must ask a young woman's father for permission to court his daughter. Before approaching a father, however, the young man is expected to pray for guidance and consult with his own parents. Only men who are willing to seriously consider marriage are given permission to begin the courtship process. But before the young cou-

ple can begin courting, the young man must get to know the girl's father by spending time with him alone. Further information about the prospective suitor is also obtained from people who know him well. Once the young woman's father is satisfied that the young man is an appropriate and well-intentioned suitor he asks his daughter if she is interested in pursuing a relationship with the young man. If she agrees, they begin to spend time together in closely chaperoned situations. Absolutely no physical contact between the young couple is permitted before marriage. Those who advocate this form of courtship over dating argue that it helps couples determine whether they are right for each other without the biasing influence of sexual involvement. Those who decide to marry after courting for a while are better able to establish a stable and committed relationship. The enforced abstinence before marriage is said to in-

crease romance because it builds anticipation and mutual respect.

Some conservative families have also resurrected the custom of **dowries** (that is, the bride's family gives the future husband's family land, money, or even a house) so that the young couple doesn't have to go into debt early in the marriage. It has also been suggested that prospective grooms be required to pay the bride's family any price her father demands to ensure that the groom not take his future wife for granted. Critics of these practices argue that they treat women as property and rob them of significant input into decisions that are made about their marriages.

Sources: Goodstein, Laura. "New Christian Take on the Old Dating Ritual." The *New York Times,* September 9, 2001; Hart, Marybeth. "An Old-Fashioned Practice Gains Some New Adherents." *The Washington Times,* March 12, 1999; Ryun, Jim, and Ryun, Anne. "Courtship Makes a Comeback: Dating in the Nineties." *Focus on the Family Magazine,* November, 1995.

child sees in the person, suggest other potential dating partners, and even refuse to speak to the date (Leslie, Huston, and Johnson, 1986). Because their social class determines the types of people their children encounter in the course of their daily lives (in school, in their neighborhood, and in church), parents are generally inclined to accept the dating choices of their children.

The contemporary dating model differs from the courtship model in some important ways. Courtship was viewed as a pathway to marriage. Thus, it was much less spontaneous than today's dating. Activities were planned far in advance and were governed by an elaborate system of rules and regulations. The amount of sexual contact considered appropriate at each stage of a developing relationship was clearly spelled out. Today there is more variation in the pace of sexual activity and in the types of commitments that dating couples make. As the Headlines box shows, there is a growing movement—among fundamentalist Christian families and others who are tired of the the contemporary dating scenario—to resurrect traditional courtship.

Hooking Up

In recent years, the phenomenon of *hooking up* has become more prominent in the social scene. Hooking up goes beyond simply meeting someone or getting together with friends, a common usage of the term among older generations. Dr. Paul C. Reisser, a family physician in California and a member of the Physicians' Resource Council of the Focus on the Family (a conservative Christian organization), defines **hooking up** as "a spontaneous non-conversational, usually emotionless, apparently meaningless and definitely commitment-less physical encounter, typically at a social gathering where alcohol or other intoxicants serve as catalysts" (Reisser, 2001).

Hooking up became the subject of considerable media attention in the summer of 2001 when a study conducted by the Institute of American Values (a conservative think tank) reported that 40 percent of the 1,000 undergraduate students who were surveyed about dating and courtship said they had hooked up at least once, and 10 percent said they had done so six or more times. A great deal of ambivalence about hooking up was revealed in the study. Sixty percent of the women who said that hooking up made them feel *desirable* also said it made them feel *awkward* as well. In-depth interviews that were conducted with 62 of the women in the study (from 11 different colleges and universities) suggested that women often wonder what will happen after they hook up; that is, whether the encounter will lead to an ongoing relationship. They also report feelings of vulnerability, regret, and hurt feelings. The researchers who conducted the study argue that college women really want the love and security that comes from a marriage commitment (Glenn, 2001).

Meeting possible partners and initiating relationships are two of the most difficult and stressful aspects of dating today. We turn next to these topics.

Meeting Partners Today

There are many ways to meet dating partners, some of which can be quite romantic. Most often, though, couples meet under fairly ordinary circumstances. Surveys of young people often ask how they met their current or most recent dating partner. For example, in the spring of 2001, nearly 1,500 single men and women were surveyed by an online market research firm for *American Demographics* magazine. In Table 4.1, responses to the survey are summarized. Participants were asked where they go to look for dating partners. The most common way they found partners was through friends, co-workers, or family. Roughly two-thirds used this approach. Other common places to meet dates included at work, school, on the internet, and at bars or coffee shops. Less common ways to meet were at church, in line at a grocery store, at libraries or bookstores, or at the gym. Singles from various sociodemographic groups have somewhat different ways of meeting dating partners. Black singles are significantly more likely than whites to meet someone at church, waiting in lines, and at the gym. Those who have previously been married are twice as likely as never married singles to go on line to find potential partners.

TABLE 4.1	
How Do You Usually Meet Your Dating Partner? (*N* = 1,500)*	
Through friends, co-workers, family	65%
In class/at school	27%
At work	36%
At a bar or coffee shop	26%
At church or religious service	20%
Online	26%
In line at grocery stores	<20%
In libraries, bookstores	<20%

*Percentages do not add up to 100 because multiple responses were given by many respondents.

Source: Adapted from data provided in *American Demographics*, 10 (April 1, 2001), p. 10.

▌ *The Mass Media as Matchmaker*

Changes in U.S. society associated with industrialization, modernization, and urbanization have altered the ways in which individuals meet intimate partners. Life in urban areas may mean that individuals date people who were not previously known to their families or their friends. The mass media, however, have stepped in to fill the matchmaker gap. Today, many people try to find partners by placing personal ads in newspapers or magazines, paying for "high-tech" matchmaking services, and/or going online.

Personal Ads in Newspapers and Magazines.   Personal ads provide a unique way to seek prospective dates. It allows advertisers to present themselves in the best possible light and to make it clear what qualities in a dating partner they value most highly. For some busy people, using personal ads is preferable to more traditional methods because ads don't require as much *face time* in the preliminary sorting through of potential dates (Bartholome, Tewksbury, and Bruzzone, 2000).

To respond to adults' needs for assistance in finding dates, many newspapers have "personals" sections in which advertisers pay a minimal charge for several lines of text in which they describe themselves and the partner of their dreams. Ads often run for a week to ten days. Readers who wish to reply to personal ads write to the box number listed in the ad or call a 900 phone number.

"(Personal ads) are no longer considered the province of the 'sad' and viewed negatively as indicative of individual 'failure.' In modern life circumstances which are mass-mediated, time pressured, and work centered, (personal) ads are now deemed to be a relationally 'efficient' and 'natural' response to modern life circumstances" (Coupland, 1996). Even the *New York Times* began to publish personal ads in 2001.

A variety of other dating services have developed in conjunction with personal ads. One issue of *New York Magazine,* for instance, featured an ad for "Check-a-Mate," an investigation service offering discreet background checks, which uses the slogan "Is he or she everything they [sic] claim to be?" Highly specialized dating services geared toward specific demographic groups in the population are also advertised, including "Class Dating"—which specializes in matching "men of stature" with pretty women; "Catholic Singles," which features a special program for professionals; and "Classical Music Lovers Exchange," for unattached music lovers.

Some publications that run personal ads have rules that regulate the content and language that are used by the advertisers. They may restrict the service to unmarried individuals who are looking for monogamous relationships. Often those who place ads must be 18 or older. Some publishers claim the right to edit or to refuse to print ads that are harmful to its public image or unsuitable for readers. In this way, community moral standards still enter contemporary dating, just as they did in the traditional agrarian and courtship models.

Online Dating.   Since the early 1990s, people have been looking to the Internet as a place to find dating partners. An online research firm, Media Metrix, has estimated that the number of people who regularly use online matchmaking sites such as matchmaker.com, socialnet.com, and blinddate.excite.com reached 5 million by early 2001 (*Newsweek*, 2001). Users who sign up with many of the online dating services are matched by computers on the basis of their responses to questions about their personal history, hobbies, and preferences in a mate. Some of the services give subscribers the option of adding a photograph to their files. Highly specialized online services that target specific demographic groups (e.g., jdate.com, for Jewish singles; and Altmatch.com for gay and lesbian singles) are springing up all over the country. Adult singles (that is, those who are no longer in school) may find these online services especially useful because their access to more traditional ways of meeting partners is limited by time constraints and geographic challenges. Gays and lesbians in small towns, for instance, may worry about *outing* themselves if they are seen perusing alternative newspapers or magazines. Single parents may be isolated in their homes because of childcare responsibilities. And elderly women, who greatly outnumber men of the same age, may find the number of eligible people in the local area limited.

▲ *Increasing numbers of adults are turning to the Internet to find potential dating partners.*

In some respects, online dating is similar to old-fashioned courtship (*Time*, 2000). The dating sites serve the same functions as nineteenth century parlors in young women's homes, where couples sat in chairs and talked but had no physical contact. The computer serves as a *chaperone* of sorts, guaranteeing that no one gets too physical early on and encourages or enables dating partners to get more information about each other before they become sexually involved. Online dating also puts a premium on verbal fluency, another bygone romantic skill. Online suitors can pay attention to their feelings, ideas, and words without worrying about how they look when they're saying it.

The Choice of Partners and the Development of Relationships

A number of family scholars have proposed that interpersonal relationships develop in a series of stages of increasing involvement and commitment, starting with early meetings between partners (Kerckhoff and Davis, 1962; Murstein, 1970; Lewis, 1972). Scholars who describe the partner selection process in developmental terms focus on the **filtering process** or weeding out of ineligibles or incompatibles until only one person remains. As people spend more time together and learn more about each other's values, needs, and behavior patterns, they are better able to determine whether they wish to develop even greater levels of intimacy and to become committed to the relationship. We offer a brief overview of the various stages through which relationships develop, focusing on the various factors that become important along the way. It is important to recognize that the order of these stages may vary from one couple to another.

First, we start with the idea that there is a large field of eligible dating partners for most individuals. High-tech dating services may make the number of eligible partners even larger. With so many to choose from, how do people begin to reduce the number of potential dates to a more manageable size? One of the first, and most important, *filters* is referred to as **propinquity** (or geographic closeness). Many of the people we end up dating are those with whom we come into frequent contact in our neighborhoods, schools, places of worship, workplaces, clubhouses, or "playgrounds."

Although the propinquity filter reduces the number of potential dates quite a bit, people must reduce the pool of eligibles even further. One of the major factors that influences early decisions is physical appearance. People are most likely to bring another person into their small circle of dating partners if they find that person physically appealing. All other factors are relatively unimportant, at least until later in the selection process. Typically, a potential date's interests and values are evaluated only after age and appearance. Sometimes, however, individuals aren't able to evaluate a potential date's attractiveness directly; they must rely on information provided by their friends or, in the case of personal advertisements, through the person's own description and photograph. In their descriptions, women are more likely to provide information about their weight and to seek men who are of a specific height. Men are more likely to provide information about their height and to seek women of specific weight. Men who describe themselves as tall and women who describe themselves as slim receive more responses to their personal ads (Koestner and Wheeler, 1988).

If potential partners are mutually attracted, they may choose to pursue the relationship by spending time together. Some people, however, may not act on their attraction because the other person differs from themselves in terms of major social characteristics such as age, race, religious affiliation, educational attainment levels, or family background, and, as a result, consider him or her an inappropriate or ineligible partner. The tendency for people to mate with others who are similar to themselves is referred to as **homogamy.**

Those who decide to act on their attraction by spending time together begin another stage in the process of partner selection. Through their interactions and conversations, they begin to discover similarities or dissimilarities in values, particularly in the important areas of religious beliefs, political views, philosophies of life, gender role beliefs, and attitudes toward diversity, among others. Through their observations of each other's behavior, they also assess the extent to which they are compatible in terms of personal habits, temperament, lifestyle preferences, and sexual and emotional needs. At this point, another decision about the continuation of the relationship occurs. Many attractive people may be weeded out of one's pool of eligibles for "serious" relationships because they are dissimilar in these important areas. Those who remain "in the running" may move on to increasing levels of commitment, often involving nonmarital cohabitation or legal marriage.

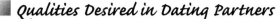

Qualities Desired in Dating Partners

In a number of studies conducted over the years, researchers have asked participants some version of the following question: "What qualities or characteristics are important to you in a person you date?" The most recent data come from the 2001 *American Demographics* survey discussed earlier in this chapter. Male and female respondents gave nearly identical responses to the question about the traits they valued most highly in dates. The number one adjective on both their lists was "intelligent" (identified by 79 percent of respondents). This was followed by "funny" (70 percent), "attractive" (34 percent), "athletic" (12 percent), and "wealthy" (6 percent). This ordering of qualities was not only comparable across men and women, it was consistent across age, income, level of education, race, and ethnicity. The similarity found between women and men today differs from patterns found in earlier decades, when women tended to emphasize a man's earning potential because they were typically dependent on men economically. Today, employed women may be better able to afford—literally and figuratively—to emphasize other qualities in their dates.

When people are actually searching for dates or mates rather than simply describing in the abstract the qualities they desire, however, they may emphasize different traits than those listed previously. For instance, a study of personal ads conducted in Scotland and England found that some women still emphasized traditional *feminine* traits when describing themselves to potential partners. Over half of the women in the study mentioned their nurturing ability, personal warmth, listening abilities, and physical attractiveness (Jagger, 2001). They made frequent references to themselves as slim or petite, with none describing themselves as overweight (Jagger, 2001).

Studies of personal ads also continue to reveal some gender differences in the qualities that are sought in partners. Men still tend to emphasize physical attractiveness and sexual availability while women stress financial security in their ads (Smith, Waldorf, and Trembath, 1990; Gonzales and Meyers, 1993; Fischer and Heesacker, 1995; Kenwick et al., 1995). This pattern has emerged in several nations. A cross-cultural study conducted in the United States, Japan, and Russia found that men gave greater preference to physical attractiveness while women emphasized

"I asked for someone who was loyal, a good listener, and likes long walks on the beach. You fixed me up with a dog."

(*Source:* Copyright Art Bouthillier. Reprinted by permission.)

intelligence, ambition, money, status, and potential for success in male partners (Hatfield and Sprecher, 1995).

American men generally find relatively thin women most sexually desirable (Harris, Walters, and Washull, 1991). Heavier women are often stigmatized (Crandall, 1994; Miller et al., 1995), especially with regard to issues of sexuality and courtship (Regan, 1996; Sobol, Nicolopoulus, and Lee, 1995), and may have decreased opportunities for heterosexual dating. Overweight women are perceived as having less dating and sexual experience and as being cold and asexual, compared with their female peers of average weight (Regan, 1996).

Facial attractiveness is also an important determinant of men's romantic and sexual interest in particular women (Gangestad, 1993; Symons, 1995). A study of 200 college women was conducted to examine the relationship between women's heterosexual dating experiences and their *objective* (that is, as rated by observers) and self-rated facial attractiveness (Wiederman and Hurst, 1998). Women in the study who were relatively heavier (with a higher body mass index) and had less attractive facial features were also the ones who were less likely to be involved in a steady dating relationship. The researchers asked whether these differences were due to a lack of opportunity, different attitudes about sex, or inhibition due to self-consciousness on the part of larger women. Although they had no data in their study that would allow them to examine this question directly, they believed that it was a lack of opportunity to date because of less interest by potential male partners that explained why heavier women had less dating and sexual experience. It is important to keep in mind, though, that the sample included in this study may not be representative of the larger population, particularly those who are older than twenty-two (Wiederman and Hurst, 1998).

Some evidence suggests that changing gender roles are starting to be reflected in qualities that are sought in mates in personal ads. Personality characteristics of potential mates (e.g., kindness, honesty, sense of humor, warmth, intelligence) are extremely important to both men and women. In one study of personal ads, personality traits were mentioned more often than attractiveness or professional and educational characteristics by both men and women. However, men did rank "good looks" second in importance in their search for a desirable female partner. They also mentioned professional characteristics as one of the top five qualities they valued. Women ranked financial, educational, and professional characteristics as the second or third most important after various personality traits (Lance, 1998).

Among gay men, physical appearance may be of even greater importance than it is among heterosexual men (Hatala and Predhodka, 1996). A study of personal ads placed in a Canadian newspaper by gay men showed that the dominant theme was age and physical appearance, including stature and size. Over 80 percent of the advertisers described themselves and/or their ideal date. Three-quarters of the ads included information about height. Almost as many included some description of weight. Less than half mentioned hair color or length, eye color, and muscular build.

ContentSELECT

Gender Differences in
Relationships

Social Exchange Theory and the Selection of Dating Partners

Modern matchmaking services vividly illustrate the dating and mate selection process that takes place in the larger population. For example, it is clear that people who read personal ads or go online to choose partners are looking for someone who has attractive qualities. These are expected to be comparable with their own best qualities. In general, we all select people who have the most desirable characteristics we think we can attract with our own personal attributes. The sociological theory that supports this view of selecting dating partners is called **social exchange theory** (see Chapter 2).

Social exchange theory has long been used to explain the dating and mate selection process (Sabatelli and Shehan, 1993). A person entering a dating relationship feels that he or she is offering something of value (looks, charm, intelligence, money, and so on) and therefore should receive something of equal or comparable value in return.

The exchanges that are specified clearly in personal ads are very likely the same kinds of exchanges that are going on in the more informal ways of meeting dating partners; they are simply more explicit.

The exchange of rewards between dating partners also determines whether their relationships will continue. Two people will date each other as long as each is getting adequate rewards from the relationship. When one person feels that there are more costs than rewards coming from the relationship and believes there is another, more attractive alternative available, the relationship will probably end. At the end of the chapter, we discuss further the process of breaking up.

We have seen how traditional ideas about gender influence the selection of dating partners. Now let's look in more detail at the ways in which these traditional expectations operate in dating relationships. They are not just amusing remnants of the past—they have real consequences for today's dating couples.

Gender Roles and Dating Rituals

One approach to enhancing our understanding of dating and courtship is through script theory (Laner and Ventrone, 2000). **Scripts** are cognitive schemes that are used to organize our experiences and are usually composed of a set of stereotypical actions. Scripts allow us to predict the actions of others and serve as guides for our decisions about how to act. Thus, in many ways, people who use social scripts in their interpersonal interactions are doing much the same as actors who follow scripts in plays and films. Research conducted over the 1990s showed that contemporary heterosexual dating scripts are explicit, formal, and are not very different from those of the 1950s, even though today's students claim to adhere to egalitarian beliefs about gender roles (Rose and Frieze, 1993; Laner and Ventrone, 1998, 2000). First-date behavior, in particular, is extremely predictable. The dominant heterosexual dating script tells women to be subordinate, sexual objects who facilitate men's plans, and tells men to be dominant, to plan events, pay for them, and initiate sexual activity. This script doesn't allow dating couples to be very spontaneous or natural, but it may reduce the awkwardness they feel as they attempt to impress each other (Laner and Ventrone, 1998).

A list of over forty different behaviors that typically happen on first dates has been compiled by several different research teams using information received from college students (Laner and Ventrone, 1998, 2000). When students are presented with the list of behaviors, in approximately the same order in which they happen on actual dates, they consistently identify certain acts as being most appropriate for men and others as most appropriate for women (Laner and Ventrone, 2000, p. 494). Table 4.2 reveals the gender labels that are attached to these acts. Considerable agreement exists about who typically does what on a first (heterosexual) date. Students' responses indicate that men are usually responsible for asking women out; for making the plans about when, where, and what will happen on the date; for preparing their cars for the date; buying flowers; driving to and from the women's residence; opening doors; and paying. Men are also likely to be the first to make any affectionate and/or sexual moves. Women's general role on first dates is to react to men's actions. They wait to be asked for a date; buy new clothes so they can look "attractive"; wait for their dates to pick them up; introduce them to

TABLE 4.2

Identification of First Date Behaviors as Male or Female Responsibilities (N = 103 men, 103 women)

Behavior	MEN'S RESPONSES (%)			WOMEN'S RESPONSES (%)		
	Man	Woman	Either or Both	Man	Woman	Either or Both
1. Ask someone for a date	83	2	16	68	1	29
2. Wait to be asked for a date	4	86	10	2	87	8
3. Decide on plans by yourself	71	3	17	52	9	26
4. Discuss plans with date	43	16	38	17	26	54
5. Talk to friends about date	11	29	60	1	53	44
6. Buy new clothes for date	3	69	22	0	80	17
7. Select/prepare clothes for date	7	31	61	1	41	57
8. Groom for date (shave or put on makeup)	6	9	84	1	4	94
9. Take extra time to prepare	5	45	48	2	53	43
10. Call date on day of date	53	10	22	47	15	23
11. Prepare car (get gas, etc.)	83	1	13	69	8	18
12. Prepare house/apartment	24	18	56	7	44	47
13. Get money; collect keys	63	5	30	44	1	52
14. Get flowers to bring to date	83	7	8	79	4	2
15. Wait for date to arrive	13	82	5	11	76	11
16. Pick up your date	84	7	8	81	4	14
17. Greet/introduce date to family	16	50	33	5	58	35
18. Go to dinner	13	10	75	6	5	87
19. Eat light	5	78	16	0	87	5
20. Make small talk	31	13	54	15	20	60
21. Pay the bill	91	0	8	77	0	21
22. Open doors for date	88	5	4	89	1	3
23. Go somewhere else (e.g., movie)	22	4	71	11	1	86
24. Pay the bill	88	6	5	67	6	22
25. Go to bathroom to primp	4	76	17	2	73	17
26. Go somewhere else (e.g., drinks)	21	11	59	10	12	73
27. Have a deeper conversation	16	43	37	3	50	38
28. Pay the bill	82	3	15	67	4	23
29. Make affectionate move (e.g., hug)	60	6	30	52	7	39
30. Make sexual move	75	2	12	67	2	15
31. Take date home/walk to door	90	2	7	88	0	7
32. Discuss possible second date	59	5	34	38	5	53
33. Thank date for a good time	9	18	72	4	30	65
34. Call a friend to discuss date	9	54	36	0	67	31
Equalitarianism scores:		Men = 31.85			Women = 35.85	

Note: Both authors scored each of the response groups (men and women) separately, achieving an interrater reliability of 95 percent or greater for all but three items. These were rescored and then reached agreement. Among men, fewer than 10 percent answered "neither" on all items except 3, 10, and 30. Among women, fewer than 10 percent answered "neither" on all items except 3, 10, 14, and 30.

Source: Laner, M., Ventrone, N.A. "Dating Scripts Revisited." *Journal of Family Issues* 21(4), 2000: 488–500. Thousand Oaks, CA: Sage Publications. Reprinted by permission.

their roommates; primp in the bathroom during the evening; and try to initiate meaningful conversation (Laner and Ventrone, 2000).

While these rigidly scripted behaviors may take the awkwardness out of first dates, they do little if anything to help dating partners learn anything genuine about each other. When subsequent dates proceed along the same traditional scripts, little progress is made toward establishing a successful relationship. "Traditional couples 'sacrifice the elemental goals of intimacy, deep friendship, and mutual respect'" (Schwartz, 1994, p. 3, cited in Laner and Ventrone, 2000). True "intimacy is only possible between equals—two people who have both the emotional development and the verbal skills to share their inner life with each other" (Rubin, 1983, p. 140, cited in Laner and Ventrone, 2000).

Sociologist Kim Brackett interviewed twenty college-aged heterosexual couples in depth to examine the extent to which they followed traditional scripts in getting to know each other (Brackett, 1996). Generally speaking, traditional gender roles are relatively easy for heterosexual couples to follow because they are familiar with the expectations for women and men in dating relationships. However, many dating couples follow only part of the gender prescriptions. They may see traditional roles as too limiting or old-fashioned, or they simply may not find them comfortable. Whether or not couples follow or reject traditional dating scripts, they usually provide some type of justification for their behavior. One important factor that allows couples to follow less traditional dating roles is simply surviving the initial stages of the relationship. Having known each other for a long enough time, either as friends or as dating partners, frees them from having to follow rigid gender roles.

The experiences of one of the couples in Brackett's study, Veronica and Paul (both pseudonyms), illustrate how the issue of traditional versus nontraditional dates was a constant theme (Brackett, 1996, pp. 83–87). Veronica, an 18-year-old freshman, had known Paul, a 22-year-old senior, for three years. They had been close friends and decided to start dating eight months before they were interviewed. Both came from financially stable, Catholic families. The following are excerpts from Dr. Brackett's interviews with Veronica and Paul.

> KIM: Who generally drives and pays when you go out?
>
> VERONICA: He does.
>
> PAUL: That would be me.
>
> KIM: (To Paul) How do you feel about that?
>
> PAUL: I like it. . . . I'm an only child and I was taught that's what you're supposed to do. At this point . . . we've been dating and friends long enough that it's . . . not much of a big deal if she pays for something. Whereas in the beginning, you know, that would have never been the case. I don't think I would have felt comfortable letting her pay for something. And I know eight months isn't really long, but I think when you look at the length of the relationship, the friendship, I mean, it is.
>
> VERONICA: Yeah, it made it easy 'cause it could be one of those awkward transitions, but . . . I already know so much about him. . . .

In their separate interviews, Paul again mentioned that he is not comfortable having a woman pay on dates:

> KIM: How do you feel about women paying?
>
> PAUL: I've never been in a relationship where I've felt comfortable with a girl paying.
>
> KIM: Why?
>
> PAUL: I just think that there are some things that, I don't want to sound incredibly chauvinistic here, but there are some things that a man is responsible for.

And I know that sounds just as chauvinistic . . . not in the fact that I think I'm superior or any other (thing), you know. I just think that she shouldn't, you know. I'm taking her on a date, I'm taking. That answer doesn't surprise me as much as I want it to, but . . . I couldn't tell you. I think it is just one of those things that was really drilled into me as a kid and is one of those things that has stayed there and has gone unquestioned.

In her individual interview with Dr. Brackett, Veronica acknowledged Paul's greater financial contribution to their relationship but added that she tried to contribute, as well. Occasionally, her parents would give her steaks that she would then cook for Paul, or gift certificates to local restaurants that she would use to take Paul out to dinner. When Dr. Brackett asked if she was comfortable with the general situation in her relationship with Paul, Veronica responded "Yeah, (I'm) very traditional; I know that's probably horrible and just not at all like the '90s thing but it's definitely a reason I'm glad I'm a girl."

Brackett concluded that all areas of gender-specific behavior on dates are influenced by the degree of closeness of the couple and the length of their relationship. The introduction of more egalitarian gender roles occurs after the couple has become comfortable filling more traditional roles. In regard to taking on financial responsibilities, for instance, women's accepted contribution level increases the longer they are involved in the relationship. Traditional expectations provide a *jumping off* point for partners to illustrate how their behavior is different from the expectations. They are able then to show their individual selves and the unique qualities of their relationship. The couples in Brackett's study overwhelmingly supported the idea of interchangeable gender roles, but many women in the study said they could not bring themselves to initiate dates and many men did not want to relinquish the responsibility for covering date expenses. Dating behaviors—and the interpretations of them—changed throughout the association of the couples, suggesting that the successful establishment of the expected way to interact leads partners to be more free to negotiate roles and responsibilities that meet their unique needs and preferences (Brackett, 1996).

The persistence of traditional gender roles in dating, while providing some comfort, can cause problems for the people involved. We consider dating problems, those related to gender and those that are not, in the next section.

Dating Problems and Perils

Some dating problems pertain to practical, everyday concerns, like the cost of dating and indecision about dating activities. These are real problems; but in the larger scheme of things, they are minor. Dating can also involve sexual and emotional exploitation, jealousy, threats, and violence.

Practical Problems of Dating

Nearly 40 percent of the male college students in a study conducted at the University of Florida reported that their major dating problem was not having enough money to spend on dates. Only half as many women reported lack of funds as a dating concern. The second most frequently mentioned problem among both men and women was deciding where to go. Communication problems—specifically, knowing what to talk about on dates—were also mentioned frequently (Shehan and Asmussen, 1992).

Although there was a great deal of similarity in the dating problems mentioned by women and men, important gender differences emerged in the study. Both men and women described difficulty in fulfilling traditional gender roles and responsibilities in dating. The emphasis on appearance for women showed up in their worry about what to wear on dates. They were four times more likely to say this was a problem. And although roughly one in seven men said that *encouraging* sexual intimacy was a major dating problem, nearly one in five women said that *discouraging* sexual intimacy was a problem. We discuss sexual aspects of dating later in this chapter.

Power Struggles

Generally, social scientists think of **interpersonal power** as one person's ability to get another person to do what you want the person to do. Interpersonal power can be observed in a number of ways. Most often, it has been viewed in terms of decision making and dominance. For purposes of illustration, we'll first look at the power dynamics in dating in terms of the decision making that occurs from the early stages of the relationship through the later stages. We've already talked about the ways in which first dates among heterosexuals continue to be shaped by gender expectations. Men still, by and large, initiate dates; that is, they decide who they wish to spend time with and then invite the person to go out. Even in traditional gender-based scripts, however, women have decision-making power in that they can decide if they wish to accept or decline an invitation to go out. Other decisions that are made frequently in the early dating encounters include what to do, where to go, how much money to spend, and who should pay. As we saw earlier in the chapter, traditional gender expectations often influence these decisions.

As a relationship develops, new decisions emerge. How fast should the relationship develop? That is, what label should the couple use to describe the relationship to themselves and to other people? Should the individuals be free to date other people? How do the partners expect each other to demonstrate their love and commitment? How do other people (e.g., friends and family) fit into—or compete with—the couple's time together? Decisions surrounding sexuality also develop. When should a couple become sexually involved? What types of sexual behavior are acceptable? Will the couple use some type of contraceptive? And if so, what will it be and who will pay for it? What will the couple do in the case of an unplanned pregnancy?

All of the decisions mentioned previously are common in the development of romantic relationships. Each has the potential to be contested. When a particular decision is contested, that is, when the partners have different ideas about what should occur, power comes into play. Whose wishes takes precedence? Who "wins"? Sometimes one partner may defer to the other simply because the issue isn't of great importance to him or her. Couples may develop mutually acceptable ways to resolve contested issues. They may develop rules that help them make sure both partners' wishes are given consideration. If they have different hobbies, for instance, they may agree that they will participate in both as a couple. If she likes playing basketball and he likes going to boat shows, for instance, they may decide to do both. If one likes sushi and the other likes pasta, they may develop a pattern where one night they go to a Japanese restaurant and the next time they go to an Italian restaurant.

In some cases, however, couples are unable to develop effective strategies for working out differences of opinion. Sometimes, gender-based beliefs may swing the decision to one partner or another. Alternatively, one partner may get his or her way through the use of unfair tactics, such as those that involve threats of violence or actual use of physical force. In Chapter 7 we discuss the dynamics of intimate relationships, including the determinants and outcomes of interpersonal power, more completely. In a later section of this chapter, we look at those dating situations in which contested decisions or conflicts of interest result in violence.

When dating partners follow traditional gender roles, there is unequal power in the relationship. Traditional gender roles automatically give men the final word in decision making if there is a conflict of interest. "Sometimes boys dictate whom their girlfriends see, where they go, what they do" (Ingrassia, 1993, p. 67). In a *Newsweek* article on dating violence, several examples of boys' attempts to control their girlfriends were presented. One couple, 18-year-olds Carmen and John, represent a typical situation. When Carmen met John, they both were "swept away." But after two months of dating, he accused her, falsely, of cheating on him when she was on vacation. So, he began to control her activities to prevent her from seeing anyone else. He "guards her closely and insists that she bring home a daily class schedule signed by each teacher" (Ingrassia, 1993, p. 67).

Jealousy

Jealousy is the emotional reaction individuals experience when they believe a relationship of value is being threatened in some way (Knox et al., 1999). The effects of jealousy include feelings of rejection, insecurity, and suspicion (Peretti and Pudowski, 1997). As might be expected, jealousy is a rather common emotion. One national study conducted in the 1990s reported that one-third of all couples seen by marriage therapists had problems with jealousy (Pines, 1992). Jealousy can also be a problem in dating couples. When 185 students who were enrolled at East Carolina State University were asked to indicate the degree to which they had experienced feelings of jealousy in their current or most recent relationship, on a scale of 1 to 10 (with 1 being the lowest levels and 10 the highest), their responses indicated that, on average, they had experienced a moderate level of jealousy—a score of 5.3. Those who had been dating their partners for a year or less reported significantly higher levels of jealousy than those who had more established relationships. The actions or events of their partners that caused them to feel jealous were "actually talking *to* a previous partner" (reported by 34 percent) or "talking *about* a previous partner" (19 percent). No significant differences between women's and men's feelings of jealousy were reported (Knox et al., 1999).

In another study conducted at the same university, over two-thirds of more than 600 students were asked about their experiences with infidelity (Table 4.3). The majority of the participants in the study said they would end a relationship with someone who cheated on them. Men and women were equally likely to predict that they would react to infidelity in this way (Knox et al., 2000). Forty-five percent had *actually* ended a relationship because of infidelity. The specific nature of the partner's cheating may affect men and women differently, however. Some studies show that women are more troubled by *emotional* infidelity, whereas men are more troubled by *sexual* infidelity. Students who had been abused, either physically or emotionally, by their partners were most likely to end their relationships if the partner also cheated on them (Knox et al., 2000).

Courtship Violence and Date Rape

Courtship violence and date rape have received a great deal of attention over the past decade (Cate and Lloyd, 1992; Lloyd, 2000). **Courtship violence** is the use or threat of force or restraint carried out with the intent of causing pain or injury to a dating partner. The most common types of violent behavior experienced by dating couples are pushing and shoving, slapping, hitting with a fist or an object, and

ContentSELECT

Jealousy

		MEN		WOMEN	
		Percentage	Number	Percentage	Number
A.	**Percent who have ever engaged in extradyadic sexual activity**				
	Romantic kissing	68.2	264	61.0[b]	354
	Kissing and fondling	64.8	264	49.4[b]	354
	Performing oral sex	47.2	214	29.3[b]	283
	Receiving oral sex	53.4	238	30.6[b]	291
	Sexual intercourse	49.1	230	30.8[b]	273
B.	**Percent who have ever engaged in each activity more than once**				
	Romantic kissing	81.1	180	63.0[b]	216
	Kissing and fondling	83.0	171	64.0[b]	185
	Performing oral sex	85.1	101	68.7[c]	83
	Receiving oral sex	78.0	127	69.7	89
	Sexual intercourse	85.8	113	61.9[b]	84

TABLE 4.3

Individuals Who Have Engaged in Sexual Activities with Someone Other than Their Romantic Partner (Percent)[a]

[a] All respondents have been in at least one serious relationship. At the time of the study, 46 percent were involved in a serious relationship (1.2 percent were married). Twenty-two percent were casually dating, and 32 percent were not dating anymore.

[b] $p < .001$. P figures indicate that the differences between men and women are statistically significant. In all cases, women are less likely than men to have engaged in the particular extradyadic sexual activity.

[c] $p < .01$.

Source: Laner, M., Ventrone, N.A. "Dating Scripts Revisited." *Journal of Family Issues* 21(4), 2000: 488–500. Thousand Oaks, CA: Sage Publications. Reprinted by permission.

kicking and biting. But it may also include more severe acts such as beating up, threatening with a weapon, and actually using a weapon against a partner.

Using data collected by the Centers for Disease Control and Prevention, Ann Coker analyzed the experiences of 5,500 high school students in South Carolina. Twelve percent of the students in her analysis reported that they had been involved in severe dating violence—hitting, kicking, throwing someone down—in the past year. Half were victims, half were perpetrators (Coker, 2000). The data Coker analyzed were part of the Centers for Disease Control and Prevention's Youth Risk Behavior Surveillance System, which monitors six categories of health priorities among youth and young adults, including use of tobacco, alcohol, and other illegal drugs; sexual behaviors that contribute to unintended pregnancies and sexually transmitted infections; unhealthy dietary behaviors; and physical activity. The data provided by this surveillance system include a national school-based survey as well as state, territory, and local school-based surveys conducted by education and health agencies. During the 12 months preceding the survey, 8.8 percent of students nationwide were hit, slapped, or physically hurt on purpose by their boyfriend or girlfriend. Overall, black students were significantly more likely than white students to report dating violence (12.4 percent versus 7.4 percent, respectively).

Estimates of the prevalence of dating violence ranged from 7.1 to 13.1 percent across state surveys and from 6.5 to 15.9 percent across local surveys. Female victims and male perpetrators of dating violence are more likely to report poor mental and physical health and suicide attempts than peers who haven't been involved in dating violence. Adolescents in mutually violent relationships have been found to receive and perpetrate significantly more abuse as compared with adolescents in one-sided violent relationships (Gray and Foshee, 1997).

Courtship violence is usually reciprocated; that is, both partners in an abusive relationship use violent behavior against each other (Cate and Lloyd, 1992). Men are more likely to use more severe types of violence (such as striking their partners with an object or beating them up), and women are injured more often, both physically and emotionally, than men (Makepeace, 1986; Cate and Lloyd, 1992).

Rape is defined as any type of sexual activity that is performed against another person's will, through the use of physical force, threats of force, continual arguments or verbal pressure,

▲ *Colleges and universities are increasingly being called on to lead workshops and seminars, like the one shown here at an eastern college, to educate their students about date rape.*

use of alcohol and/or drugs, or holding a position of authority over the victim. Half to three-quarters of female college students may have experienced some type of sexual aggression in a dating relationship (Cate and Lloyd, 1992, p. 99). In most of those cases, the victims knew the perpetrators. Date rape is often accompanied by physical violence. In the majority of date rape situations, the female victims have bruises, black eyes, cuts, or internal injuries.

What causes courtship violence and date rape? Factors associated with date rape and courtship violence can involve the individual victim or attacker's characteristics, their social networks, characteristics of their relationship, and circumstantial factors (Cate and Lloyd, 1992; Lloyd, 2000). Men who sexually abuse women tend to hold traditional beliefs about women, view dating relationships as adversarial, display hostility toward women, and believe in rape-supportive myths. They may use sex as a way of expressing anger or dominance and are more accepting of physical violence, in general. They are also quite sexually active, reporting a greater number of sexual partners, greater use of exploitative sexual techniques, and a wider search for sexual experiences. Female victims of sexual abuse, however, do not differ significantly in self-esteem, assertiveness, or belief in feminism from women who have not been victimized (Cate and Lloyd, 1992; Lloyd, 2000).

Many factors associated with the dating relationship, itself, can cause violence and rape to emerge (Laner, 1983):

1 *Emotions* (such as jealousy, guilt, insecurity about the relationship),

2 *Problem-solving dilemmas* (including misunderstandings and arguments between partners),

3 *Temperament* (anger and irritation at the partner),

4 *Reflexive response* (feeling deceived, attacked, or insulted),

5 *Misjudgment* (such as teasing or fooling around that turns serious),

6 *Personality* (characteristics such as being stubborn, selfish, or inconsiderate),

7 *Feelings of rejection* (such as breaking up, loss of interest in the relationship),

8 *Power struggles* (such as dependence, dominance, sexual denial), and

9 *Use of alcohol and drugs.*

Women are most likely to mention temperament and power struggles as causes and men mention problem-solving dilemmas, retaliation, and rejection as the cause of the violence or sexual aggression in their relationships.

Social networks (such as friendship groups and organizations to which individuals belong) can also play an important role in the perpetuation of courtship violence and sexual aggression if approval for this type of behavior is demonstrated (Cate and Lloyd, 1992). Men who have sexually aggressive peer groups, such as members of some fraternities, are significantly more likely to be physically and sexually aggressive (Gwartney-Gibbs and Stockard, 1989; Martin and Hummer, 1989; Boeringer, Shehan, and Akers, 1991).

Various circumstances surrounding a date can also lead to physical and sexual aggression. The use of alcohol, for instance, increases the likelihood that a person will be an attacker or a victim. Among attackers, alcohol use may act as an inhibitor of or as an excuse for aggressive behavior. Among victims, alcohol use may decrease the ability to resist aggression and may encourage others to blame women for their victimization. Male initiation of dates, along with responsibility for paying and driving may also be associated with a greater likelihood of physical and sexual aggression.

Violence does not always lead to the end of a dating relationship. In fact, in one report of high school students who had encountered violence at the hands of a dating partner, one-fourth felt that such behavior had led to an *improvement* in their relationship, and another third said that it had produced no change. Sixteen-year-old Erica, from a suburb of Los Angeles, said that the violence in her dating relationship began as "play fights." But one day during an argument, her boyfriend slapped her across the face. The abuse continued after that. At one point he even held a knife to her throat. Despite the seriousness of the abuse, Erica stayed with her boyfriend, even though her mother forbade her to. Erica's explanation for her refusal to leave the relationship: "I loved him so much he could have had me do anything and I would have done it" (quoted in Ingrassia, 1993, p. 67).

Why do people continue to date partners who have used violence against them? Perhaps they do not regard this type of behavior as unusual and may even interpret it as a sign of love. They may believe that when situational factors (such as school stress, family pressure, or wedding planning problems) improve, the violence will end (Lloyd, 1991, 2000). Some victims may think that they are responsible for the violence and that if they change *themselves* the violence will stop. Others expect the violence to be conquered by "true love." Unfortunately, those who experience violence in dating relationships are likely to experience it in marriage as well. Dating may be a training ground for marital violence.

Falling in Love

Thus far in this chapter we have discussed many aspects of dating, but we have said little about one objective of the dating process—the search for love. Usually, it is only when we have found "true love" that we consider making a long-term commitment, especially one that involves marriage. As we discussed earlier in the chapter, not all cultures place so much importance on love in the selection of

HEADline   When Scientists Fall in Love

Mileva Maric was 21 years old when she entered the Swiss Federal Institute of Technology in Zurich (the European equivalent of MIT). Her dream was to become a physicist. While she was a student at the institute, Mileva met—and fell in love with—17-year-old Albert Einstein. They became lovers and eventually married, but not until after their first child, a daughter, was born in 1902.

In 1905, Einstein published three papers that were highly regarded, including his famous theory of relativity. He became increasingly famous, while Mileva cared for their children. In 1914, Albert and Mileva separated. As part of their divorce settlement, Albert promised to share any future Nobel Prize money he would receive as a result of his pioneering work. He soon made good on his promise.

Eventually Albert remarried and moved to America. Mileva and their children stayed behind. She died in 1948, never having published any scientific papers in her own name. Her dream of being a physicist apparently went unfulfilled.

Recently, however, information regarding Mileva's achievements as a scientist has surfaced. One important source of information regarding Mileva's scientific work is Einstein's love letters to her, written in the early years of the twentieth century when they were students and young lovers. There are references in Einstein's letters to the work on relativity they engaged in jointly, as partners. Additional support for her contributions to the theory of relativity comes from a biography of Mileva in which a Russian physicist claims to have seen the original papers from 1905 that were signed Einstein-Maric. Although it may never be known exactly what role Mileva played in the work on relativity, we can be fairly certain that Einstein produced his greatest work when he was in love with Mileva and living with her and their children.

Source: Overbye, 2000.

marital partners. But there is almost total agreement that what we call *love* is a universal human emotion. Many ancient and historical documents describe intense feelings of attraction between two people. Studies of virtually every culture report the existence of these same feelings. Despite this, however, there is little, if any, consensus about what love is.

Components of Love

Although it is acceptable for poets and novelists to hold unique and abstract definitions of love, social scientists need a more concrete statement of the types of behaviors and emotions that indicate the phenomenon of love if they are to study it empirically. We draw on the work of social scientist Robert Sternberg, who has attempted to develop more specific ideas about the dimensions or components of love.

Sternberg has developed the **triangular theory of love,** which identifies three components of love, and several different types of love based on particular combinations of the three components. The three central components of love, according to Sternberg, are intimacy, passion, and commitment. The term **intimacy** "refers to [the] close, connected, and bonded feelings [that exist] in a loving relationship." Happiness and warmth, intimate communication, sharing of possessions, and the exchange of emotional support are all included in this component of love. **Passion** includes the psychological and physiological "drives that lead to romance, physical attraction, and sexual consummation" in a loving relationship. And the **commitment** component of the relationship refers to decisions that lovers make about the current and future nature of their relationship (Sternberg, 1986, pp. 120–121).

▲ *Principal components of love in our society include intimacy, passion, and commitment.*

Sternberg recognizes that there are many different types of love, not all of which include the three basic components of intimacy, passion, and commitment. The type of love that does include all three—**consummate love**—is what most of us hope to find with a romantic partner. Needless to say, it is very difficult to find and maintain this type of complete love.

True consummate love develops slowly over time; the three components grow and develop at different rates. Passion develops first and fades quickest but must always be maintained at some level if the relationship is to continue. Intimacy develops at a slower rate and becomes increasingly important as the relationship endures. And commitment is the factor most closely related to happiness in relationships (Sternberg, 1988). Because of the different rates of growth in these three important aspects of love, close relationships are always changing.

▮ *Love Styles* - know this.

Psychoanalyst Erich Fromm (1956) popularized the idea that romantic love is only one of many different types of love. Other forms include brotherly love, maternal and paternal love, infantile, immature, and mature love. According to Fromm, there are four essential aspects of love: knowledge, respect, responsibility, and care. These can be described as

1 Being aware of another person's needs, values, goals, and feelings;

2 Accepting that person for what he or she is;

3 Attempting to be sensitive to and responsive to his or her needs; and

4 Wanting only the best for him or her.

When two people experience all four of these dimensions of love they become a couple. As Fromm acknowledged, finding a person with whom all of these aspects of love are present is difficult. And once a partner has been located, individuals must learn to adapt to the everyday realities of life together.

One of the reasons that finding a compatible partner is difficult is because individuals have different styles of loving. Nearly thirty years ago, sociologist John Alan Lee (1974) developed a **typology** (that is, a set of types) of love styles that was based on 4,000 published accounts of love and 112 personal interviews. All of the people in Lee's study were young (under age 35), white, and heterosexual. Roughly half were women and the other half were men. Based on his study, Lee identified three primary styles of love and three styles that were based on combinations of the primary styles. Lee's work remains of interest and importance today.

Lee's three primary love styles are referred to as eros, ludus, and storge. **Eros** (or romantic love) is characterized by overwhelming feelings of physical attraction combined with intense desire to engage in sexual relations with the partner and to do anything to please him or her. This is the type of love that figures in romance novels and television soap operas. It is the type of love that led Romeo and Juliet to commit suicide because of their fears that they had lost each other. **Ludus** (or game-playing love) lacks the single-minded preoccupation and seriousness of eros. Ludus love is casual and carefree. Sexuality does not carry the same connotations of deep emotional attachment that it does in eros love. It is simply another enjoyable activity in which consenting adults can engage. Because commitment is not part of the ludic love style, marriage is not regarded as the ultimate expression of the emotion the lovers feel for each other. **Storge** (or best friend's love) emphasizes close friendship above everything else. The sexual element of the relationship develops late in the relationship, if at all. To others, this type of love may appear to be unexciting. But to those who approach love from this perspective, romance blooms out of friendship and a relationship continues even if the sexual component ends. Couples who have known each other since childhood often follow this type of love pattern.

The three styles of love that develop from the combinations of the primary styles are referred to as mania, pragma, and agape. **Mania** (possessive love) results from the combination of eros and ludus. It is characterized by obsession and possessiveness. Those who follow this type of love style tend to be jealous and to demand constant demonstrations of the partner's love and devotion. Manic love is so stressful that it rarely, if ever, leads to a long-lasting relationship. Individuals who require frequent proof of a partner's love often suffer from low self-esteem and can never be persuaded that they are worthy of love. **Pragma** (practical love), on the other hand, is based on a logical calculation of one's needs and a partner's ability to adequately meet these needs. Thus, compatibility between partners is the primary concern to pragmatic lovers. The final type of love that has been identified by Lee is **agape** (altruistic love). Agapic lovers are concerned, first and foremost, with meeting the needs of the other person. They give to others with little or no thought of getting anything in return. Sexual abstinence is expected in agapic love. Agape is the love style of saints. John Lee found no agapic lovers in his study.

Individuals typically prefer one love style over another, but they often express more than one style in their actual relationships. As relationships develop over time or different partners are found, an individual may shift between styles. In order to maintain a mutually satisfying relationship, partners must, at the very least, understand each other's preferred style of approaching love. If they actually share preferred love styles their chances of developing a satisfying long-term relationship may be better, according to Lee.

The Development of Love

Social psychologists have concluded that being in love is largely a state of mind (Walster and Walster, 1978). For a person to decide she or he is in love, two necessary conditions must be present. First, there must be some type of physiological arousal, and second, it must be reasonable to label this arousal as love (Berscheid and Walster, 1974). To fall in love, a person has to define the physiological arousal that occurs in the presence of another person as love.

Romantic relationships go through a series of stages that start with the very first meeting between the partners. Various scholars have labeled and described these stages. In the following discussion, we combine the stages identified by Reiss (1960) and Weiner (1980). Figure 4.1 shows the stages of love and the turning points that may occur along the way.

Rapport. First, there is the initial attraction and the sense of **rapport** (Reiss, 1960). When two individuals feel at ease with each other the first time they meet and enjoy each other's company, they will choose to spend more time together to get to know each other better. In the early days of the relationship, the partner's good qualities are emphasized, perhaps even exaggerated. Similarities between oneself and the loved one are discovered and cherished. Annoying habits or characteristics

Figure 4.1 **The Wheel of Love**

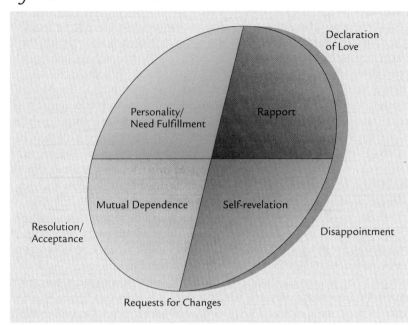

(*Sources:* Adapted from Reiss, 1960; Weiner, 1980.)

are ignored. People in love put on their best behavior, carefully manage their physical appearance, and attempt to hide their bad qualities. They have high hopes for the future of their relationship, believing it will fulfill all their dreams. It is at this point that couples declare that they are falling in love (Weiner, 1980).

Self-Revelation.   As lovers begin to spend more time together they gradually share more and more information about themselves. The actual speed of **self-revelation** (providing information about themselves) and the type of information that is shared depend on many things, such as gender and self-esteem. Some information about ourselves (e.g., our middle name or political party affiliation) we're willing to share with just about anyone. Providing this type of information to another person typically isn't very threatening. As we get to deeper and deeper layers of our self, we reach increasingly private information, and the number of people we're willing to share it with decreases (Altman and Haythorn, 1965). Usually the amount of private information that is shared by one partner is matched by the other.

As partners learn more about each other through the process of self-revelation (Reiss, 1960) they inevitably experience some *disappointment* (Weiner, 1980). They discover that their earlier image of their lover is not quite accurate. As the lovers see each other in a variety of situations, perhaps including those in which it's impossible to control their appearance and behavior, they get a more realistic sense of what the person would be like in a long-term relationship. At this point, couples must decide whether they are willing to stay in the relationship. Some may become so disillusioned or even disgusted with their partner that they end the relationship. Others may feel that the relationship would be worth pursuing if the partner would change.

In this stage of *requesting changes* (Weiner, 1980), partners "work on" each other to fit them into their ideal, or they keep their disappointments to themselves, thinking that a change in the status of the relationship will magically transform the partner. People may say, "He (or she) will be different when we get married."

As partners talk about their disappointment with each other and attempt to make changes in the relationship, they may experience a great deal of conflict. Their ability to learn to handle conflict effectively determines the future of their relationship.

Mutual Dependence.   As partners spend more time together and learn more about each other, their daily lives become more intertwined. They develop joint routines and consider each other's needs when they make decisions about their own lives. This is what Reiss refers to as **mutual dependence.**

The amount of dependence in a relationship is an important factor. **Dependence** can be thought of as relying on another person for continuous support or assistance for fulfillment of basic needs. Depending heavily on a partner can make a person relatively powerless. Independence, in contrast, involves extreme self-reliance and enables people to live in isolation from others. The ideal situation for couples is to strike a balance between extreme self-sufficiency and extreme reliance on each other.

John Crosby (1985, p. 49) has described three types of intimate relationships that differ in terms of the amount of dependence that is exhibited by partners. The **A-frame** relationship is characterized by extreme dependence of partners on the relationship (and on each other). The partners have very weak self-identity. Each always thinks of him- or herself as half of a couple, as do their friends and family. They lean on each other in a way that is symbolized by the letter A. They cannot stand alone. If one partner leaves the relationship, the other one falls. The story of one student's grandparents illustrates the A-frame relationship quite well. The couple had been happily married for over fifty years. They had a very traditional division of labor, with the grandfather taking charge of finances and automobiles and the grandmother running the home and taking care of children and grandchildren. When the grandfather died, the grandmother found herself in a difficult situation because she had never learned to drive or to use a checking account. She had depended on her husband to do these things and found it difficult to stand alone after her husband's death. Had she been the one to die first, her husband might have found himself equally distressed by his inability to perform the tasks she had performed for the fifty years of their marriage.

In the opposite type of relationship, the **H-frame** (independent), the partners have very strong individual identities but are so independent of each other that they are barely connected. They share few interests and spend little time together. They make major life decisions without taking the other person's needs into account. They do not share information about themselves and may fail to provide the type of support the other needs. They have no identity as a couple. They do not have a very strong influence on each other; others may ask why they bother to have a relationship. Should the relationship end, their lives would continue with little interruption. This type of relationship does not appear to offer the kind of personality need fulfillment (Reiss, 1960) that we typically think of as love. An illustration of the H-frame relationship would be the couple who marry for "appearances," because one has a traditional employer who believes that only married employees are stable enough to be promoted to the highest levels of management. The other needs a source of income and a nice place to live. They present themselves as a couple to the outside world when necessary, but they rarely spend time with each other. They maintain their own separate lives, much as they would if they hadn't married.

In the third type of relationship, the **M-frame,** each person has high self-esteem and a strong individual identity. Each is quite capable of standing alone but values the connection to the partner. In this type of relationship, there is mutual influence

ContentSELECT

Dependence in
Relationships

and support. Neither partner is needier than the other. Neither is more powerful. If the relationship ends, both partners feel a profound sense of loss but are able to recover and go on with their individual lives. The balanced mutual dependence represented by the M-frame is a goal that all couples can strive for, but not every couple can achieve.

Personality Need Fulfillment.   The final stage in the development of love relationships occurs when partners find that they've succeeded in changing each other or, more likely, have learned to understand and accept what had been disappointing earlier in the relationship. It is during this resolution/acceptance stage that couples can learn effective conflict resolution techniques and develop increasing trust in each other. As they develop a stable and enriching pattern of emotional exchange and mutual support, they are better able to meet their basic human needs. Reiss (1960) refers to this as **personality need fulfillment.**

Clearly, the balance that should be sought in healthy love relationships is a combination of high self-esteem and self-sufficiency combined with a mature concern for the partner's well-being and a genuine enjoyment of time spent together. In many relationships, however, the partners don't have positive feelings about themselves and look to each other for proof of their worth as individuals. Partners may have come to their current relationship with a history of unsuccessful relationships in which their needs for acceptance, understanding, and support were not met. They look to their new partner to make up for the problems of the past. Receiving emotional support, companionship, and sexuality is used as evidence of their worth.

Individuals with low self-esteem are afraid to present themselves fully and openly to their partners out of a fear of rejection. Some hesitate to voice their needs to their partners because they believe those needs are not legitimate, or that they do not deserve to have their needs fulfilled. They believe the only way to maintain a relationship is to devote all their energy and resources to fulfilling their partner's needs. Although this may sound like a positive strategy, it can eventually lead to resentment when the self-sacrificing partner gets tired of the inequalities in the relationship. An opposite, but equally undesirable pattern of maintaining a relationship is to expect your partner to provide constant demonstrations of love and commitment. Once again, this type of dependence can make one partner relatively powerless.

Individuals with high self-esteem, in contrast, know they're worthy of being loved and realize they have a right to expect support, acceptance, and understanding from a partner. They also feel they have something of value to give another person and get pleasure and satisfaction from openly and honestly sharing themselves with their loved one. Mature love is characterized by partners' unconditional acceptance and understanding.

Are There Gender Differences in Love and Loving?

There is a contradictory answer to this question: Research suggests that men are more romantic (Rubin, 1973) but that women are better at love. Studies show that men are more likely than women to have "crushes" and to fall in love with someone who doesn't love them in return (Rubin, 1973; Rubenstein, 1986). In fact, men fall in love more quickly and earlier in their relationships than women do (Kanin, Davidson, and Scheck, 1970). They stay in love longer than women, are more resistant to breaking up (Hill, Rubin, and Peplau, 1976), and have a harder time recovering after a breakup (Hill, 1989). Men are also more likely to idealize their partners, to see them as the love of their lives, and to use love as their major criterion for selecting a spouse.

Women are more practical or pragmatic about love (Lester, 1985). They are more likely to evaluate a man's potential earning ability, whereas men assess women in terms of more spontaneous reactions regardless of social character (Rubin, 1973). This pattern gets at what some people refer to as the "women as sex objects, men as success objects" standard. These gender differences are not as strong as they once were. For women who believe they will determine their own social status, a man's earning capacity and occupational status may no longer be a primary consideration in selecting a mate.

Sociologist Arlie Hochschild (1983) found that if a woman determines a man would be a "good husband"—that is, a good provider—she works hard to develop strong feelings for him. If, however, she has strong feelings for a man who doesn't appear to be acceptable, she works hard at falling out of love. This tendency was demonstrated in an interesting study conducted in the late 1960s. College men and women were asked, "If a man or woman had all of the other qualities you desire, would you marry the person if you weren't in love with him or her?" Two-thirds of the men, but only one-fourth of the women, said they would *not* marry the person (Kephart, 1967, p. 473). Three-quarters of the women were undecided. One of the undecided women said "It's rather hard to give a 'yes' or 'no' to this question. If a boy had all the other qualities I desired, and I was not in love with him—well, I think I could talk myself into falling in love" (Kephart, 1967, p. 473).

Hochschild refers to this process of evaluation and emotional control as **emotion work.** It involves intense thinking about the relationship as well as discussing and analyzing it with one's friends. Women are made to feel primarily responsible for the success and stability of a love relationship. When there are problems, women are more likely to suggest discussing them. Men may fear these discussions because they don't feel skilled in emotional expressions. If they withdraw from the conversation, that may make their female partners angry and resentful. Both partners may end up feeling manipulated and powerless (Cancian, 1985).

Women's tendency to discuss relationships and to express feelings of love and affection may have given rise to the popular impression that women are more concerned with love. Francesca Cancian has argued that our society defines love in a feminized way, that is, in terms of nurturance, sensitivity, and verbal expressions of emotions (Cancian, 1987). She traces this **feminization of love** to the split in the public and private worlds that occurred as our country became industrialized. At that time, economic activity moved out of the home and became attached to the male role (which was conceived of as an instrumental role), while home and family work became more closely associated with the female or expressive role (see Chapter 3, on gender). Masculine ways of showing love, such as providing practical assistance, sharing activities, and spending time together, have been underemphasized or even unrecognized in our society. A new, androgynous approach to love is emerging, however, according to Cancian. In this approach, love is considered the responsibility of women *and* men and includes feminine types of emotional support and masculine types of practical help and sexuality. This is a positive development, in Cancian's opinion, because the overspecialization in gender roles has damaging effects on both men and women and makes us unaware of our true needs:

> When they are unhappy, women usually think they need more love, but the objective evidence suggests that they need more independence. Men typically are too independent and too focused on achievement at work. They think they need more success, but studies of illness and death rates indicate that they need more close relationships. (Cancian, 1987, p. 81)

Breaking Up

*C*ourtship is regarded by many people who are involved in *serious* relationships as a period in which they test their compatibility for an eventual marriage. Some couples decide, after examining their similarities and their ability to communicate, that they should terminate their relationship rather than allow it to develop any further. Three general categories of factors may lead to breakups (Cate and Lloyd, 1992, pp. 84–85). The first, **social incompatibility,** includes discrepancies in age, educational aspirations, or religious orientations. **Low relationship quality,** reflected in low levels of love and communication, is a second major source of problems leading to breakup. And **social network influences,** most notably parental disapproval of the relationship, constitutes the third major factor.

■ Reasons for Ending a Relationship

People give any number of reasons for ending a relationship. The most commonly mentioned reason is desire for greater independence. Other common reasons include feeling a lack of commonality with one's partner, a partner's failure to listen and/or to support the person, a lack of openness in the relationship, infidelity, physical separation, an absence of equity between partners, and an absence of romance. Men are more likely to report that an absence of romance caused them to end an intimate relationship. Women are more likely to mention a desire for more autonomy, a lack of openness, and an absence of equity (Baxter, 1986).

▲ *When two people begin the process of breaking up, they tend to distance themselves from each other emotionally, and even physically. Distancing emphasizes their differences and downplays their similarities.*

■ Strategies for Ending a Relationship

Once the decision has been made to end a relationship, how do people inform their partners? A number of strategies for breaking up have been identified. The **fait accompli** involves one person announcing to the other that the relationship is over, with no hope of repair or compromise. Other people break the news in the middle of a **state-of-the-relationship talk** in which they discuss their perceptions of the problems with the relationship. A third strategy, called the **attribution conflict,** involves an intense argument between partners that becomes the alleged reason for the breakup. In a **negotiated farewell,** both partners recognize the problems with the relationship and mutually agree to end it (Baxter, 1986).

There are indirect strategies, as well. Some individuals who are afraid to tell their partners outright that they want to end the relationship attempt to make their intentions clear by spending less and less time together or by avoiding contact altogether. This is referred to as **relationship withdrawal.** In other cases, one or both partners state that they want the relationship to be less close or intense, when they actually want the relationship to end. This strategy is known as **pseudo-deescalation.** People who take the

cost escalation approach try to get the partner to be the one to initiate the breakup by making the relationship unrewarding to them. Finally, in the case of **fading away,** both partners know the relationship has ended, but they don't talk about it (Baxter, 1986).

Recovering from a Broken Heart

It is quite common for college students to have been in a dating relationship that ended. In one study conducted at a college in North Carolina, 87 percent of the students who were surveyed reported that they had experienced a romantic breakup. Women were more likely to have initiated the breakup, and men experienced more difficulty recovering from the breakup (Knox et al., 2000). A significant proportion of the students in the study said they remained friends with their former boyfriends or girlfriends. Only a small percentage said they and their former partners didn't like each other. The most effective ways of recovering from a breakup seem to be just "waiting it out" and finding another boyfriend or girlfriend. Men were slightly more likely than women to use the latter strategy to get over a broken heart (Knox et al., 2000).

After the Breakup: Just Friends?

"Our language describing former romantic relationships is very final. We 'breakup,' our relationship 'fails,' and we have an ex-spouse or an 'ex-lover.' These terms leave little room for change and redefinition. . . . When a romantic relationship no longer fulfills the romantic needs of one or both partners, it can either be endured, terminated, or redefined" (Foley and Fraser, 1998). In a study of individuals who chose to redefine rather than completely sever their ties with former romantic partners, Lara Foley and James Fraser looked at the ways in which people negotiated new definitions of their relationships after the romance faded. They asked the participants in their study to tell the story of their relationship, from the predating stages, through the dating and postdating phases. They also asked them about societal guidelines they may have drawn on to work out the thorny challenges of learning to relate to a former romantic partner in a different way.

Most of the individuals in Foley and Fraser's study felt they had no choice but to figure out a new way of relating to their former boyfriends or girlfriends because they either worked with them or saw them regularly because they were part of the same social circle. Some simply did not want to lose contact with the person because they cared about him or her so much and would miss their friendship. This was especially true of couples who had been friends before becoming romantically involved. One of the persons in the study made the following comment when asked who initiated contact after the official breakup:

> Nobody really initiated it, it was just sort of a given. We never even thought about not being friends, because we were friends for so long. I mean, I think had I said well, ya know, I can't deal with being your friend now that we've been sleeping together for such a long time, I think he would have looked at me like I was crazy; what do you mean you can't deal with it?

The participants in the study also acknowledged that it was often very difficult to redefine themselves as friends with former boyfriends or girlfriends and to learn to interact with them in a new way. Many felt extremely awkward when they interacted with former romantic partners immediately after the breakup. This seems to be a result of the fact that there are no social scripts to rely on for advice on how to treat a former partner. One respondent described it in the following way:

> When you date a person you can hug and kiss them. And when you stop dating and you see them you think in your mind that if we were together now I would go up and hug him, but we're not so I can't. You feel awkward and you don't know what to say to each other.

One of the most confusing aspects of postdating relationships is the sexual dimension. Three-quarters of the individuals had been sexually involved when they considered themselves a couple. But after the breakup, physical or sexual intimacy was limited to hugging for about 40 percent of the former partners. About 13 percent actually continued to engage in sexual intercourse with their former partners, and another 22 percent said they would like to but apparently hadn't yet figured out a way to negotiate that aspect of their postdating relationships. Most had figured out, however, that they should avoid talking about their past romantic relationship, the reasons for their breakup, and any new romantic relationships they had. Safe topics included work and mutual friends (Foley and Fraser, 1998).

Still Single: Unmarried and Unpartnered

*F*or many people, dating is simply a way to have fun and meet new friends. For others, it is viewed primarily as a way to find a life partner. When one dating relationship ends, most people go through a period in which they are *single*, meaning that they are unmarried and without a partner. Individuals regard their unpartnered state in various ways, as we will see in the following discussion.

Voluntary versus Involuntary and Temporary versus Permanent Singlehood

Unmarried adults can be categorized on two dimensions, whether their situation is voluntary or involuntary, temporary or lifelong (Stein, 1981). The four types of unmarried adults that result from combining these two dimensions can be identified as ambivalent, wishful, resigned, and resolved (Shostak, 1987).

Ambivalent singles are those for whom singlehood is both voluntary and temporary. That is, they are not actively seeking mates but are open to the idea of marriage. This group includes many younger women and men who are postponing marriage to finish their educations or establish themselves in careers. It also includes some cohabiting couples who are testing their relationships to determine if they want to marry. People in this category may discover they enjoy the freedoms of singlehood and decide they do not wish to marry after all. Their singlehood would then become voluntary and stable.

Wishful singles hope to marry in the near future and are actively trying to find a suitable mate. At some point, if they continue to have difficulty finding a partner, they may become **resigned singles.** This group includes people who want to be married but accept that they will probably never be because they have not been able to find a partner.

Figure 4.2   **Types of *Singles* Based on Whether Their Unmarried/Unpartnered State Is Permanent or Temporary and Voluntary or Involuntary**

Know this

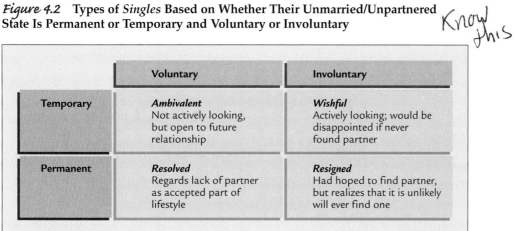

	Voluntary	Involuntary
Temporary	***Ambivalent*** Not actively looking, but open to future relationship	***Wishful*** Actively looking; would be disappointed if never found partner
Permanent	***Resolved*** Regards lack of partner as accepted part of lifestyle	***Resigned*** Had hoped to find partner, but realizes that it is unlikely will ever find one

In some populations, the difficulty of finding a partner may be tied to an imbalanced **sex ratio** (the number of men per 100 women in the population). In the United States, the overall ratio of men to women is .96, which means that there are .96 men for every 100 women in the population. This number is only an average, however. The actual ratio varies by age. At younger ages, unmarried men outnumber women. This reverses at about age 40 and among those 65 and over, the sex ratio is highly imbalanced in the other direction (.71). The fact that most elderly people are women means that the majority cannot remarry after a divorce or the death of their husbands because there aren't enough men available. Among African American women, the sex ratio at *younger* ages is also highly unbalanced. The number of available men is much lower than the number of available women, in part because of high rates of homicide and incarceration.

The fourth type of single is referred to as **resolved** because their unmarried state is both stable and voluntary. Having weighed the positives and negatives of the single and married lifestyles, they have concluded that being married has less to offer than remaining single. Some of these people have been previously married and have had an opportunity to explore both lifestyles at first hand. Figure 4.2 summarizes the four types of singles that result from the categorization along the dimensions of temporary/permanent and voluntary/involuntary.

Never-Married Adults

We typically think of singles as young, never-married people who have not yet found a partner or established an intimate relationship. But as we discuss, adult singles can be of any age, with a wide range of social and demographic characteristics, and live in a variety of household arrangements. Some have been married and are currently divorced or widowed. Some are involved in an intimate relationship other than legal marriage. All share the characteristic of being legally unmarried. We discuss homosexual and cohabiting heterosexual couples in the next chapter.

Most young, never-married people believe that there is a *soul mate* for everyone and that they will find their own when they are ready to marry (Gallup, 2001). Some people, though, remain unmarried—and unpartnered—for life.

Figure 4.3   **Factors Influencing the Decision to Remain Single**

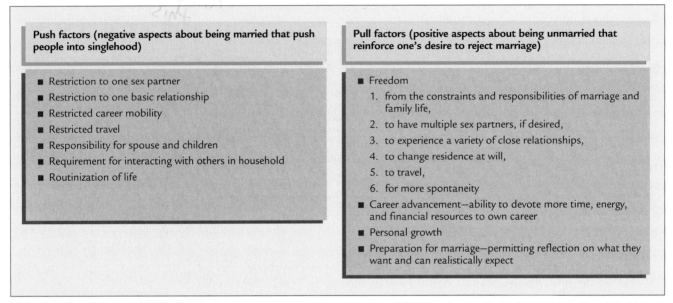

Push factors (negative aspects about being married that push people into singlehood)

- Restriction to one sex partner
- Restriction to one basic relationship
- Restricted career mobility
- Restricted travel
- Responsibility for spouse and children
- Requirement for interacting with others in household
- Routinization of life

Pull factors (positive aspects about being unmarried that reinforce one's desire to reject marriage)

- Freedom
  1. from the constraints and responsibilities of marriage and family life,
  2. to have multiple sex partners, if desired,
  3. to experience a variety of close relationships,
  4. to change residence at will,
  5. to travel,
  6. for more spontaneity
- Career advancement—ability to devote more time, energy, and financial resources to own career
- Personal growth
- Preparation for marriage—permitting reflection on what they want and can realistically expect

(*Source:* Adapted from Stein, 1975, "Singlehood: An Alternative to Marriage." *The Family Coordinator* 24, 489–503. Reprinted by permission of Peter J. Stein.)

One way of viewing the decision to stay single is in terms of pushes and pulls. **Push factors** are negative aspects of being married that cause an individual to reject it in favor of singlehood. **Pull factors** are positive aspects of being unmarried that attract individuals to singlehood. Figure 4.3 summarizes major push and pull factors for singlehood.

Summary

Historically, dating goes back a long way, but in the past, dating was done in the context of family and community life. Over the course of the twentieth century, dating has moved from a somewhat formal and ritualized activity to a more informal and spontaneous form of interaction. The formal date reflected, and often exaggerated, traditional gender roles, and was a recognized stage of courtship that would lead to marriage.

Parents still exert some influence on their children's dating relationships. Generally, parents are more involved in their daughters' dating relationships than in their sons'.

The most common way for college students to meet dating partners is through friends, parties, and classes. However, today, since marriage is often postponed beyond the college years, people are more likely to use unconventional ways of meeting dates, including placing personal ads in newspapers and magazines and going online.

Physical attractiveness plays an important part in the choice of dating partners, even though most people claim to rank personality and character traits higher. We assume that physically attractive people are also more intelligent, have better characters, and more pleasant personalities. Experimental studies and analyses of personal ads show that physical attractiveness is a more important criterion for men in selecting dating partners.

Social exchange theory highlights how dating and partner selection is a process of two people exchanging valued qualities and characteristics. The things that are valued may differ for men and women, often by traditional gender role expectations. Gender roles are also deeply embedded in the rituals of dating—men are still more likely to initiate, pay for, and control dating activities.

Dating problems range from practical, everyday matters to jealousy, struggles for power, abuse, and violence.

Almost 9 percent of American high school students report having experienced some physical violence on dates. Violence has been found to be related to individual characteristics of dating partners, to their social networks, and the circumstances surrounding dates.

Love is almost certainly a universal human emotion, but in various historical periods and cultures it is assigned different significance and importance. At a social psychological level, love is best described as a state of mind. Love involves a series of stages, including rapport, self-revelation, mutual dependence, and personality need fulfillment. At various points in the process of a developing love relationship, there can also be disappointment and requests for changes.

Mutual dependence in relationships can be described in terms of three structures: The A-frame is characterized by extreme dependence of both partners on each other; the H-frame is typified by partners who are linked but are extremely independent; the M-frame characterizes relationships in which the two people are interdependent but each can stand alone if necessary.

The major gender difference in love and loving is that men are more romantic (quick to fall in love and more likely to remain in love), while women are more practical about love. Women are more in touch with their emotions and are more able to exert active control of their emotional states (including love).

Love in American culture became *feminized* in the sense that it became associated with nurturance, sensitivity, and verbal expressions of love. This association is closely connected with the traditional expressive role assigned to women. Men, following the traditional instrumental role, show love through economic support and assistance. There may be some contemporary convergence between the genders and their expression of love.

A relationship may break up due to social incompatibility, low relationship quality, or social network influences. The actual method of breaking up can be by blunt announcement, announcements made in a state-of-the-relationship talk, a conflict-induced breakup, or a negotiated farewell. Many singles decide to spend time with friends instead of—or while they are—dating.

Key Terms

A-frame relationship (p. 115)
Agape (p. 113)
Agrarian societies (p. 88)
Ambivalent singles (p. 120)
Attribution conflict (p. 118)
Bride price (p. 91)
Bundling (p. 93)
Commitment (p. 111)
Consummate love (p. 112)
Cost escalation (p. 119)
Courtship violence (p. 107)
Dependence (p. 115)
Dowry (p. 89)
Emotion work (p. 117)
Eros (p. 112)
Fading away (p. 119)
Fait accompli strategy (p. 118)
Feminization of love (p. 117)
Field of eligibles (p. 92)

Filtering process (p. 99)
H-frame relationship (p. 115)
Homogamy (p. 99)
Hooking up (p. 96)
Interpersonal power (p. 106)
Intimacy (p. 111)
Jealousy (p. 107)
Khasegarien (p. 90)
Low relationship quality (p. 118)
Ludus (p. 112)
Mania (p. 113)
M-frame relationship (p. 115)
Mutual dependence (p. 115)
Negotiated farewell (p. 118)
Passion (p. 111)
Personality need fulfillment (p. 116)
Pragma (p. 113)
Propinquity (p. 99)
Pseudo-deescalation (p. 118)

Pull factors (p. 122)
Push factors (p. 122)
Rape (p. 109)
Rapport (p. 113)
Relationship withdrawal (p. 118)
Resigned singles (p. 120)
Resolved (p. 121)
Scripts (p. 102)
Self-revelation (p. 114)
Sex ratio (p. 121)
Social exchange theory (p. 101)
Social incompatibility (p. 118)
Social network influences (p. 118)
State-of-the-relationship talk (p. 118)
Storge (p. 113)
Triangular theory of love (p. 111)
Typology (p. 112)
Wishful singles (p. 120)

Review Questions

1. Compare and contrast the ways in which intimate partners are selected in different types of societies.

2. When did dating emerge in the United States? What societal conditions gave rise to this type of partner selection process?

3. How are possible partners *filtered out* by individuals? What factors play important roles in narrowing one's field of eligible partners?

4. What are the qualities that today's daters identify as most desirable in partners? What do studies of personal ads reveal about traditional gender expectations?

5. In what ways does interpersonal power become an issue in dating relationships?

6. How prevalent is date rape and dating violence? Where do social scientists obtain information about violence?

7. Summarize the wheel theory of love.

8. What are the six primary and secondary love styles, as identified by John Lee?

9. In what respects can it be said that love in our society has become *feminized*?

10. What difficulties do former partners face in adjusting to a breakup?

11. Along what two dimensions can unmarried people be categorized?

Critical Thinking Questions

1. Does romantic love exist in all societies? Why or why not?

2. What does the prevalence of arranged marriages around the world suggest about the importance of love in mate selection? If love is not the primary criterion for selecting a partner in a particular society, what else might be?

3. In what respects might it be appropriate to view the selection of intimate partners as a dating or marriage market?

4. What are the most prevalent myths about rape? How have these myths changed over the past several decades?

Online Resources Available for This Chapter

www.ablongman.com/marriageandfamily

- Online Study Guide with Practice Tests
- PowerPoint Chapter Outlines

- Links to Marriage and Family Websites
- ContentSelect Research Database
- Self-Assessment Activities

Further Reading

Books

Bailey, Beth. *From Front Porch to Back Seat: Courtship in Twentieth Century America.* Baltimore: Johns Hopkins University Press, 1988. An historical discussion of changes in courtship among middle class Americans between the 1920s and the 1960s.

Cancian, Francesca. *Love in America: Gender and Self-Development.* Oxford: Cambridge University Press, 1987. Compares traditional forms of marriage with newer forms of close relationships, showing that images of love in America have shifted from polarized gender roles toward more flexible roles and interdependence.

Cate, Rodney, and Lloyd, Sally A. *Courtship.* Newbury Park, CA: Sage Publications, 1992.

Discusses the factors that discriminate between stable and unstable premarital relationships and reveals the processes involved in the dissolution phase of premarital relationships.

Lloyd, Sally A., and Emery, Beth. *The Dark Side of Courtship: Physical and Sexual Aggression.* Thousand Oaks, CA: Sage Publications, 2000. Examines the negative interactions that take place between dating and courting partners, most notably physical aggression and sexual exploitation, emphasizing the importance of power dynamics, verbal aggression, and issues of control.

Overbye, Dennis. *Einstein in Love: A Scientific Romance.* New York: Penguin Books, 2001. An account of Einstein's scientific work in the first two decades of the twentieth century, including his marriage to fellow student Mileva Maric.

Swidler, Ann. *Talk of Love: How Culture Matters.* Chicago: University of Chicago Press, 2001. Uses interviews with 88 white, middle class, middle-aged Americans to show how cultural ideas influence people's experiences.

Whyte, Martin King. *Dating, Mating, and Marriage.* New York: Aldine de Gruyter, 1990. A comparative analysis of the dating and marital experiences of three cohorts of American women who married between 1925 and 1984.

ContentSELECT Articles

Cere, D. "Courtship Today: The View from Academia." *Public Interest* 143, 2001: 53–72. **[Database: General Interest]**   Courtship practices and rituals in the postmodern era are addressed by means of a thorough literature review of mate selection, love, and sociobiology theoretical approaches. The ideologies of courtship practices are also discussed.

Ducharme, J., and Koverola, C. *Journal of Interpersonal Violence* 12(4), 1997: 590–600. **[Database: Sociology]**   Ranging in ages from 18 to 24 years, 276 university students completed self-assessment instruments to assess intimacy development following childhood physical abuse. As expected, those students who were not physically abused as children reported statistically significant higher intimacy levels than those students who were physically abused during childhood. Because the ability to form healthy interpersonal relationships is a key developmental milestone, those who experience abuse as children may have difficulty in this realm.

Lavoie, F. "Teen Dating Relationships and Aggression." *Violence Against Women* 6(1), 2000: 6–37. **[Database: Sociology]**   Teenagers ages 14 to 19 years discuss aggression in teen dating relationships. Controlling through jealousy, physical abuse, death threats, sexual abuse, psychological abuse, denigration and insults, and damaging reputations/harassment are the areas of violence addressed in this qualitative study. Of great concern is that violence exists in several forms among very young adolescent relationships. As noted by one teen respondent, "He knows you too well, you see, so he knows exactly how to hurt you . . . it's very subtle."

Nichols, M., and Rohrbaugh, M. "Why Do Women Demand and Men Withdraw? The Role of Outside Career and Family Involvements." *Family Journal* 5(2), 1997: 111–120. **[Database: Psychology]**   Why do women want and desire more closeness and intimacy in the couple relationship while men want and desire more independence and distance? Nichols and Rohrbaugh examine the polarizing demand/pursuing role of women and the withdrawing/distancing role of men in relationship to career involvement. Results of this study suggest that the demanding–withdrawing magnitude is greater when one partner is more involved in career endeavors than the other partner; however, pursuing-distancing is also strongly related to overall dissatisfaction with the couple relationship.

Paul, E., McManus, B., and Hayes, A. "'Hookups': Characteristics and Correlations of College Students' Spontaneous and Anonymous Sexual Experiences." *Journal of Sex Research* 37(1), 2000: 76-89. **[Database: Sociology]**   Analyzing self-report data from 555 undergraduate college students, Paul et al. identify and explore a common, risky sexual behavior pattern typically demonstrated among university students: hooking up. Hooking up is a brief (usually one night), casual sexual encounter with a relative stranger and may or may not involve sexual intercourse. Alcohol intoxication by both partners appears to be a powerful predictor in whether coitus occurs during hook ups.

Making a Commitment
Legal Marriage, Heterosexual Cohabitation, and Homosexual Partnerships

5

■ **The Continuing Significance of Legal Marriage**

■ **Commitment and Nonmarital Heterosexual Cohabitation**

■ **Commitment among Gay and Lesbian Couples**

When Dana Morosini met Christopher Reeve in 1987, she was an aspiring actor, dancer, and singer, and he had already achieved world-wide fame and fortune as Superman in several films.

Tall, handsome, and athletic, Chris participated actively in a number of sports, including skiing, scuba diving, sailing, and horseback riding, and had a pilot's license. When he and Dana married in 1992, their future looked bright and full of promise. When Chris and Dana recited the marriage vow to love and cherish each other through sickness and health, they undoubtedly never anticipated the personal and family tragedy that would befall them in just a few short years. On May 27, 1995, Chris was participating in an equestrian competition when his horse, Buck, refused a jump, throwing Chris, who landed on his head and fractured his upper vertebrae. Chris was instantly paralyzed and unable to breathe on his own. He was 43 years old. Dana was 33. And their son was only three.

At one point in his hospital room, after doctors informed Chris and Dana about the full implications of his injuries, Chris suggested to Dana that "maybe we should just let me go." Dana started to cry and told Chris that the decision was his but that she was with him for the long haul, no matter what. "You're still you. And I love you." Chris responded by saying, "This is way beyond the marriage vows—in sickness and in health." Chris later said that Dana's response to his suggestion that he be allowed to die "meant more to me than just a personal declaration of faith and commitment. In a sense it was an affirmation that marriage and family stood at the center of everything, and if both were intact, so was your universe" (Reeve, 1998, p. 54).

Key Questions

1 How does nonmarital cohabitation affect subsequent marital stability?

2 Are marriage preparation courses effective?

3 Why are teen marriages less stable than marriages of people in their 20s? How is age related to readiness for marriage?

4 What impacts might the legalization of homosexual marriages have?

5 Are rates of *mixed* marriages changing? If so, why? What are the consequences for marital satisfaction and stability?

Dana and Chris Reeve honor the commitment they made to each other in their wedding vows.

In the book he wrote to describe their life since the accident, Chris also said that "a crisis like my accident doesn't change a marriage; it brings out what is truly there. It intensifies but does not transform it. We had become a family. . . . We made a bargain for life. I got the better part of the deal" (p. 94).

After his initial surgeries and recovery, Chris spent six months in a rehabilitation program to prepare him for life as a quadriplegic and Dana had their home renovated to accommodate his wheelchair and the other equipment that is needed to sustain his life. Dana and Chris have both returned to their careers and continue to raise their son Will and Chris's two older children. Chris has had many frightening medical episodes over the years since his accident but through it all, Dana has been at his side. Both work tirelessly for the foundation they created to generate funding for spinal cord research. And Dana speaks frequently to other caregivers about the challenges and rewards of living with a family member who has had a life-changing accident.

_____

Source: Reeve, Christopher. *Still Me.* New York: Random House, 1998.

*C*hris and Dana Reeve have demonstrated a remarkable degree of courage and commitment to each other and to their relationship in the years following Chris's accident. Not only have they stayed together through one of the most stressful situations that could face any couple, they have also devoted considerable time to provide the support each other needs to become the best people they can be. The majority of American couples, like Dana and Chris, demonstrate their desires and intentions to stay together for the rest of their lives, no matter what, by getting legally married and having some type of public wedding ceremony. Many, of course, do not follow through on their public declarations of love and commitment. They do not stay together until death parts them. Or, if they do stay married they don't devote their energies toward being the best partner they can be. They fail, for whatever reason, to provide the support their spouse needs from them. While these couples could be said to be *committed* in the broadest legal sense of being married, they might not exhibit the more nuanced, more private aspects of interpersonal commitment.

A growing number of intimate partners are deciding not to formalize their commitments to each other and to their relationships through marriage licenses or expensive weddings. They focus instead on the day-by-day challenges and rewards they experience in their lives together, continually trying to honor their commitments privately. Some American couples do not even have the legal right to publicly demonstrate their commitment through marriage. Yet in the deepest sense of the idea of commitment, they may be as likely to maintain meaningful, mutually enriching relationships as legally married couples. It is the theme of this chapter that intimate commitments can take many forms. Not all involve legal marriage. As the In the Media box for this chapter argues, there continues to be a pervasive idea in our society, primarily perpetuated through the mass media, that legal marriage is the only *real* or acceptable form of intimate commitment. As we discuss, *commitment* is a difficult term to define or measure.

While we often speak about commitment, we rarely explain what we mean by it. Social scientists have not consistently defined or measured it. Typically, both lay people and social scientists alike think of commitment in terms of behavior in the broadest terms. Those who get—and stay—legally married to their partners are committed. Those who get divorced aren't committed. Similarly, heterosexuals who could legally marry but choose to live together instead aren't committed in this particular view of commitment. The limitations of thinking of commitment simply in terms of choosing to legally marry or not are clearly illustrated in the case of homosexual couples who can't legally marry even if they wish to, but stand by each other through good times and bad (Adams and Jones, 1997). In this text we define **commitment** as the pledge individuals make to devote the time, energy, and other resources to maintain the relationship, regardless of the form it takes.

Researchers who have studied commitment in the context of marriage have begun to explore its various dimensions. We believe these ideas are relevant to cohabiting heterosexual couples and to homosexual couples, as well as to legally married couples. Sets of questions that can be used to measure commitment have been developed. These include the following:

1. *Quality of alternatives* (e.g., "I have to stay with my spouse because I couldn't find anyone better.");

2. *Investments* (e.g., "I invest so much of my time and energy into my marriage that I feel forced to keep it going.");

3. *Relational identity* (e.g., "I identify more strongly with my marriage than I do with myself as an individual.");

4. *Personal dedication* (e.g., "I'm dedicated to making my marriage as fulfilling as it can be.");

5. *Moral constraints* (e.g., "I could never leave my spouse because it would go against everything I believe in.");

6. *Social constraints* (e.g., "A divorce would ruin my reputation.");

7. *Family constraints* (e.g., "I have to stay married to my spouse or else my family will think badly of me.");

8. *Financial constraints* (e.g., "It would be very financially difficult for me to leave my spouse.");

in the media

"Wishin' and Hopin' and Thinkin' and Prayin', Plannin' and Dreamin' . . ."

In several television situation comedies the importance of the wedding gown and the dream of a white wedding are dominant themes for female characters. Revealed in these episodes are patterns pertaining to the naturalization of weddings as integral to being a woman. As Sally in *Third Rock from the Sun* says in response to Dick's query about why she agreed to get married, Sally explains, "I'm a woman and he asked me. That's what women are supposed to do." Even an alien from another galaxy can see the significance of the wedding and marriage to a woman's identity. Sally also realizes what cultural capital weddings provide when, upon agreeing to marry a man in need of a green card, she proclaims, "Finally, I have something I can lord over other women!" It's not simply a matter of feminine duty, it is also a measure of a woman's worth in patriarchal heterosexual culture and shows her allegiance to patriarchal priorities.

Everyone Loves Raymond is a situation comedy about the issues a lower middle class couple with three young children face with their family, Ray's parents, and his single brother. In two

episodes of *Raymond,* Ray and his wife, Debra, reminisce about their wedding. When Raymond proposed marriage to Debra, several mishaps occurred. To make sure Debra really said yes, Raymond went to her apartment, presented her with a diamond, and asked her all over again if she would marry him. She grabbed the ring, began screaming, and jumped up and down for joy, spinning around the room. Ray still was not convinced that Debra was saying yes to him. He pulled the diamond away from her and asked her again. Finally, she said yes in a way he thought he could believe. When he gave her back the diamond, she began squealing all over again, giving Ray the impression that what she was saying yes to was the ring. Once she calmed down, Debra called Ray to the couch to show him her plans. "I've got to show you all my plans . . . I've been planning this since I was twelve." It turns out Debra has a box full of wedding-planning materials she's been saving for years. Ray remarks that they've only known each other for three months and wonders how she could have been planning this wedding since she was

twelve. At that moment, there's a knock on the door, and Debra's parents come in. They've confirmed the country club for the reception. Even though she tells Raymond she wants to have a small wedding, it quickly becomes clear that small for Debra is 200 to 250 people, affirming the average (natural) expenditure for $19,000 on a white wedding. As Debra and her mother share dream plans for the wedding, Raymond wonders if he even needs to come. Debra exclaims: "It's the happiest day of our lives!" Once again, the commodification of the wedding and the heterosexual imaginary are secured. How can anyone refuse to participate in the happiest day a woman has been planning since she was a small child? For women, the message is clear. Anything women do or achieve pales in comparison to the moment of the wedding. Happiness, contingent upon such an event in her life, is the ultimate goal.

Source: From *White Weddings: Romancing Heterosexuality in Popular Culture,* by Chrys Ingraham (1999). New York: Routledge, pages 154–155. Reproduced by permission of Routledge, Inc., part of the Taylor & Francis Group.

9 *Commitment to the marital relationship* (e.g., "The marriage relationship is extremely valuable in and of itself.");

10 *Promise* (e.g., "I've promised my spouse that I would never leave him or her.");

11 *Fringe benefits* (e.g., "Marrying my spouse raised my social standing.").

These eleven items can be reduced to three major dimensions of commitment: *commitment to spouse* (that is, commitment to the marital partner based on devotion and personal dedication); *commitment to marriage* (that is, commitment to marriage as a sacred institution based on a sense of moral obligation) or to the relationship, regardless of its form; and *feelings of entrapment* (that is, an appraisal of the external factors that would make leaving a relationship difficult, such as family disapproval or financial hardship).

In this chapter, we consider the various ways in which committed couples organize their intimate relationships. We look at legal marriage, nonmarital heterosexual cohabitation, and homosexual partnerships. We provide recent statistics concerning the prevalence of these three primary forms of committed intimate relationships. Much of our attention is given to the impact of the law on demonstrations of commitment. We look first at the federal and state statutes that influence marriage decisions, including those that restrict age at marriage and choice of partner, contrasting American patterns with other cultures. We review statistics about the incidence of *mixed* marriages (that is, those involving partners from different social categories such as race and ethnicity). We also examine the legal rights and responsibilities that are bestowed on legal marriages as well as legislation that might offer some of these benefits to unmarried partners, homosexual as well as heterosexual. We look at the legal marriage contract that includes somewhat hidden assumptions about the roles and responsibilities of women and men in marriage.

Before moving on to consider committed couples who choose to live together without the legal benefits of marriage, we consider research and scholarship that has identified factors that affect readiness to marry. We argue that the same types of maturity that are studied in regard to readiness for legal marriage are also relevant to any couple's decisions to form a committed partnership. We consider the emerging *marriage movement* and the resulting efforts by churches and state governments to increase couples' readiness for marriage by involving them in marriage preparation classes. After considering demographic and legal aspects of nonmarital and homosexual cohabitation, we end with a discussion of legislative efforts to define more clearly the boundaries of legal marriage.

The Continuing Significance of Legal Marriage

*I*n the United States, it has traditionally been very important for both men and women to be married. In the past, not having a spouse greatly limited what a person could do; women's lives, in particular, were very restricted if they did not marry. Most unmarried women remained in their parents' homes to care for them until they died.

Historically, people who remained unmarried were labeled *bachelors* or *spinsters,* terms that carry negative connotations and a certain amount of stigma. For women especially, the "old maid" stereotype implies that they are too unattractive or unappealing to attract a husband. Men who remain bachelors for life are often suspected of being "odd" or thought to be homosexual (Davis and Strong, 1977; Simenauer and Carroll, 1982).

In colonial America, the stigma attached to singlehood was quite severe. Social and economic sanctions were often used to push people into marriage. Older single women were ridiculed, despised, and regarded as failures. They were forced to do all the unpaid drudge work for their parents and for their married siblings. Even in American literature at the time, single women were depicted as neurotic busybodies, who had sour dispositions and were prim and proper. Bachelors were also mocked and treated with disdain and disapproval.

During this early period of American history, unmarried people were not allowed to live alone; the courts decided their place of residence, and licensed families supervised them. Unmarried people were penalized financially. Bachelor taxes were levied against single men, and women who inherited property had to marry within seven years or turn over their land to other relatives.

Today some Americans still disapprove of lifelong singles. In the Senate confirmation hearings for David Souter's nomination to the U.S. Supreme Court, for example, there was much public speculation about whether a never-married man such as Souter could fill such an important position. An editorial in the *New York Times* asked whether "his bachelor life isolate(s) him from routine human problems" (cited in Goodman, 1990, p. 8A). Even some of Judge Souter's friends wondered "whether a solitary man has the understanding of real life, of real family life, real female life to certify the humanity behind his judgments" (Goodman, 1990, p. 8A).

Today unmarried women and men have many more options and considerable freedom to choose from a variety of living arrangements and may be in no hurry to marry. They enjoy their freedom and often have satisfying intimate relationships without being married.

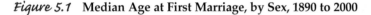 ## *The Timing of Marriage*

In Chapter 1 we noted that the average age at marriage has been increasing. In the mid 1950s, women were over 20 years old, on the average, when they married (20.2 years), and men were just about two years older (22.5). By 2000, the average age for young women had increased to 25.1 and for men, to 26.8. Clearly, Americans are marrying later today than in the 1950s. In fact, over the entire twentieth century, it was in the mid 1950s that Americans married at the youngest ages (Figure 5.1). At the beginning of the twentieth century, men married at about the same age as today (26), while women were younger (about 22).

Figure 5.1 **Median Age at First Marriage, by Sex, 1890 to 2000**

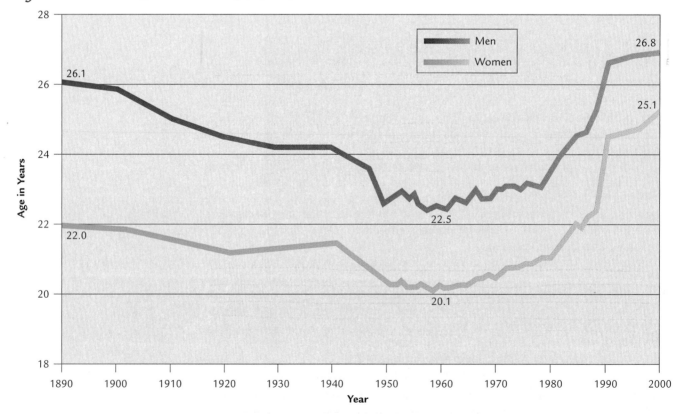

(*Source:* Saulter, 1989, Figure 1, p. 1.)

Figure 5.2   **POSSLQ and Adjusted POSSLQ, 1977 to 1997**

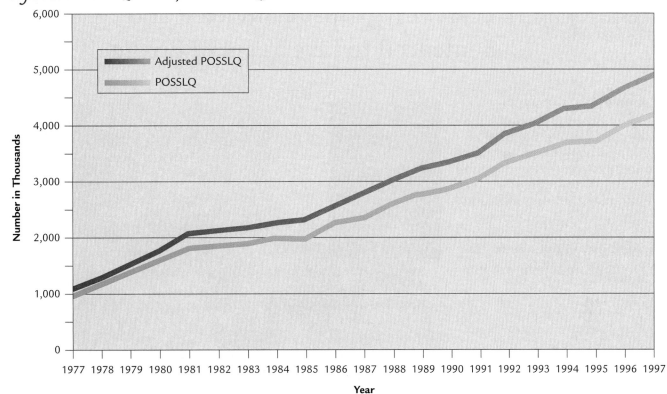

(*Source:* Adapted from Casper and Cohen, 2000. "How Does POSSLQ Measure Up? Historical Estimates of Cohabitation," Figure 1, p. 241. *Demography* 37: 237–245. Population Association of America. Reprinted by permission.)

As the average age at first marriage increased, the proportion of unmarried men and women in their twenties and early thirties also increased (Figure 5.2). In 1960, 28 percent of women and 53 percent of men aged 20 to 24 had not yet married. By 2000, these figures had increased to nearly 73 percent and 84 percent, respectively. As people reach their thirties, however, they are increasingly likely to marry. In 2000, about 22 percent of women and 30 percent of men between the ages of 30 and 34 had never married. These percentages are considerably higher than they were back in 1960, when only about 7 percent of women and 12 percent of men between 30 and 34 years had never married (Saluter, 1991; Fields and Casper, 2001).

■ Legal Restrictions on Marital Partners

Marriage is usually considered a very important aspect of life in every society and is therefore not left to chance. There are laws, rules, and norms that govern who marries whom and when they are allowed to marry. In the United States, there are laws in every state that specify the minimum age at which people may marry; these laws are often supported by social norms. In some societies, marriage is expected shortly after the age of puberty (or even before), while in others people are not expected to marry until their mid-twenties or later.

The society in which a person lives influences not only the time of marriage but also expectations about appropriate mates and how marriage partners are to be selected. In the following pages, we consider the formal and informal restrictions on the number of spouses a person may have and who a person may marry.

HEADine Utah Polygamist Convicted and Sentenced to Five Years in Prison

Tom Green (age 53), a resident of Snake Valley, Utah, was convicted on four counts of **bigamy** (having two spouses at one time). Green had five wives and thirty children when he went to trial. He was sentenced to five years in prison and ordered to repay $78,000 to the state of Utah for welfare checks that he fraudulently collected for his family. Green is thought to be the first major polygamist to be convicted since 1953. The legal investigation into Green's marital situation began after he appeared on a number of television shows such as *Dateline* and the *Jerry Springer Show* to discuss his lifestyle (CNN.com, 2001).

Polygamy was outlawed in the United States in 1870. Utah's state constitution also specifically outlaws plural marriage and the Mormon Church excommunicates those who commit polygamy. Yet there are an estimated 30,000 polygamists in the United States today, about half of whom live in Utah, the birthplace of the Church of Jesus Christ of Latter-Day Saints (also known as the Mormon Church), to which Green belongs. Joseph Smith, the founder of the Mormon Church, reportedly had twenty-seven wives at the time he died. Smith preached that God had

▲ *Tom Green, pictured with three of his wives and three of his 25 children, was convicted of bigamy in Provo, Utah.*

commanded him to see that his people reproduced and in so doing help the world flourish. Polygamy was a way through which God's will could be obeyed. Some contemporary practitioners of polygamy, like Tom Green, claim that men who have more than one wife are not tempted to have sexual relationships outside their marriages. Thus, polygamy—actually in this case, polygyny—is a way to end adultery.

Plural marriages (another term for polygamy) often resemble arranged marriages. Girls are married off as early as fifteen and expected to start having children within the year. Men may claim any unmarried women they desire as wives. But their first wives are often asked to give their consent before they are allowed to bring another wife into the family. Women often share a husband with a sister, cousin, aunt, or other close relative.

The United States, and all European societies, allow only one marriage partner at a time, a pattern referred to as **monogamy.** Many societies allow more than one spouse at a time, which is called **polygamy.** Polygamy takes two forms: **polygyny** where men can have more than one wife and **polyandry** where women can have more than one husband.

Many societies allow men to have two or more wives, but very few societies allow women to have two or more husbands. Only three or four documented societies have practiced, or still practice, polyandry. In most of the world's largest and most economically developed countries both men and women are limited to one spouse at a time. Even when monogamy is the rule, it is possible, because of death or divorce, for a person to have more than one spouse—one after another—during a lifetime. In the United States and other societies, because divorce rates are high and remarriage is frequent, people sometimes use the term **serial monogamy.**

Polygyny has been found in the majority of the world's societies. One widely accepted explanation for the widespread existence of polygyny is that men, especially the wealthiest ones, benefit from it. They benefit from the work and services provided by their many wives and children. Another advantage of polygyny for men is the greater sexual variety provided by multiple sex partners. Their wives, however, are generally restricted to having sex with their one shared husband. Thus, polygyny is found more frequently because men, with their greater power, have established this form of marriage to give themselves more economic and sexual advantages.

Every society also has rules about who is and who is not eligible as a marriage partner. Even in the United States, where people like to believe that they are totally free to marry whomever they please, choices are restricted by laws and by social norms. In the not-too-distant past, for instance, there were legal restrictions on marriages between members of different races (see the Headlines box). Rules about appropriate mates are referred to as exogamy and endogamy.

The term **exogamy** refers to any rules, norms, social customs, or laws that require a person to marry someone who is not a member of his or her own social group. In the United States, for instance, it is not legal to marry someone who is of the same gender as oneself. Thus, according to the laws, we must marry *outside* of our gender category or group—an exogamous law. The fact that various political jurisdictions in the United States are now recognizing *de facto* marriages among gay and lesbian couples suggests that this rule of exogamy is not as strong as it once was.

Another exogamous rule is the prohibition against marrying members of one's family. Every known contemporary society has rules that prohibit marriage between siblings and between parents and children. With regard to other relatives, however, the rules prohibiting marriage have historically been much less consistent. That inconsistency is still evident today, with rules and laws differing from one society to another, or differing from one region to another within a single society. An interesting example of this inconsistency is found in the rules and laws about marrying first cousins.

Many societies allow first cousins to marry. In fact, there are a number of societies in which the *preference* is for first cousins to marry. In these societies, the cousins who marry are typically **cross cousins,** which means that while two of the parents of the bride and groom are siblings, they are of different genders. For example, a woman who marries the son of her father's sister is marrying her cross cousin. Marrying the son of her father's brother would be a **parallel cousin** marriage.

In contemporary Europe, every country allows first-cousin marriages (both cross cousin and parallel cousin), although in the past that was not the case. In the United States, twenty states permit first-cousin marriages, while thirty prohibit such marriages. Before the middle of the nineteenth century, only a few states prohibited cousin marriages, but at the same time many prohibited marriages between people who were related only by marriage. Relatives related by marriage are called **affinal relatives,** as for example, one's father-in-law or one's wife's sister.

The term **endogamy** refers to rules, norms, social customs, and laws that call for a person to marry someone who is also a member of a group to which he or she belongs. The most common endogamous rules are associated with race, social class, nationality, and religion.

Religious groups often have rules that make it impossible, or at least difficult, for their members to marry people of a different religion. Sometimes the rules of religious endogamy are enforced by threatening to expel a person from the faith if he or she marries an outsider. At other times, the rules of a religion may require that certain procedures be followed (perhaps religious instruction or conversion) if a partner outside the faith is to be married. Rules of religious endogamy can also be enforced by the actions of families who prohibit their children from marrying someone of a different religion. Newly established religions are especially likely to have prohibitions against marrying outsiders and often impose strict procedures to ensure endogamous marriages.

In addition to religious rules of endogamy, many nationality groups, ethnic groups, and racial groups favor marriage within their groups. In the United States today, it is possible to marry outside one's group, but there is still a strong tendency for people to marry people like themselves.

The social rules of endogamy produce marriages in which brides and grooms have similar social characteristics. The term **homogamy** is used to describe married couples in which the husband and wife have similar characteristics; they belong to the same race, religion, ethnic group, or social class. Couples are also generally of similar ages, although husbands are typically two or three years older than their wives. The contrasting term, **heterogamy,** refers to married couples in which husband and wife belong to different social groups and categories (or are of significantly different ages).

It should not be surprising that the majority of marriages are homogamous, because the social pressures (familial, religious, economic, and even political) tend to push individuals in that direction. In many cases even impersonal factors, such as where one lives, can lead to homogamous marriages. Research has shown that generally people date and fall in love with those who live relatively close to where they live. This is referred to as the influence of *residential propinquity* (closeness). By extension, people tend to marry those who attend the same schools and colleges, work in the same occupations, and belong to the same social organizations. To the extent that neighborhoods, communities, schools, and colleges are homogeneous, the potential partners likely to be encountered in these settings will be similar. All these factors, in conjunction with the social norms of families, religions, races, and ethnic groups, produce homogamous marriages.

We can gain some understanding of the degree of homogamy in U.S. society by examining the opposite side of the coin, the amount of heterogamy, often called **intermarriage,** between major race and ethnic groups.

Intermarriage

One convenient way to examine intermarriage is to consider the number and percentage of each race or ethnic category that marries someone of another category. The number of married couples who are of different ethnic or racial backgrounds has doubled since 1980. Today, more than 3 million couples (or 5 percent of all marriages) involve spouses from different racial or ethnic groups. In 1980, only 3 percent of all marriages fell into this category (Suro, 1999). If cohabiting couples are added to the count, the percentage would be even higher. A *Washington Post* survey conducted in 2001 found that four out of every ten Americans had dated someone from a racial or ethnic group other than their own. Nearly three of every ten said it had been a serious relationship (Russo, 2001).

Intermarriage rates vary by race and ethnicity, gender, age, and social class. Hispanics are most likely to marry a person from another racial or ethnic background. Asians are next most likely. African Americans and whites are least likely to intermarry on racial or ethnic lines. The lower incidence of marriages involving black and white Americans is partly a function of the fact that there are more whites and African Americans in the population so it is easier for people from these groups to find same-race partners. Today, less than half a million marriages involve African Americans married to whites. There are, on the other hand, two million couples that include Hispanic Americans and whites and 700,000 involving Asian Americans and whites (Russo, 2001).

Interracial or interethnic marriages are geographically concentrated in states that have disproportionately high Hispanic and Asian populations (e.g., California,

Texas, Florida, and New York). This pattern is related to the availability of potential partners from various groups. Asian Americans have higher rates of mixed marriage when they live in states that have had low rates of immigration (Suro, 1999).

In the 2001 survey conducted by the *Washington Post,* the Kaiser Family Foundation, and Harvard University, 72 percent of respondents who were involved in biracial relationships said their families had accepted their relationships immediately. Acceptance was less likely among families of black–white couples, two-thirds of whom objected to their relationships at first (Russo, 2001).

African American Intermarriage.   African Americans are the least likely of all racial and ethnic groups in the United States to marry someone of another race. The current rate of interracial marriage among blacks is 5 percent. African American women are less likely than African American men to marry someone of another race. Some demographers estimate that 10 percent of all black men in the United States have spouses of another race (Suro, 1999). In this regard African Americans differ from other minority groups, since it is usually the women of minority groups who have the higher rates of intermarriage (Tucker and Mitchell-Kernan, 1990). The higher rate of intermarriage for black men, compared with black women, has prevailed for many years, but as yet there is no accepted explanation for why this is so. The rates of intermarriage among African Americans are higher among young people. Eleven percent of all married African Americans under age 24 are in interracial marriages.

Asian American Intermarriage.   Compared with other racial and ethnic groups in the United States, Asian Americans have fairly high rates of intermarriage. Fifty percent of married Asian Americans under age 35 are in mixed-race marriages.

The younger generations of Asian Americans and those born in the United States generally have higher rates of intermarriage than the older and foreign born. Although there are some exceptions, there is a general tendency for those Asian Americans who intermarry to be more educated and to have higher status occupations (Suro, 1999). The intermarriage patterns of Asian Americans probably reflect their economic and educational attainments and their level of social assimilation in American society (Lee and Yamanaka, 1990).

Assuming that Asians who marry other Asians are in homogamous marriages, however, is incorrect. There is great cultural variation across Asian countries. Using the broad category *Asian American* can conceal a large number of heterogamous marriages. Roughly one in every six Asian Americans is married to an Asian of a different ethnic background (Clemetson, 2000).

Latino Intermarriage.   The Latino population in the United States is composed of several major national groups, the largest of which are Mexican, Puerto Rican, and Cuban. One-third of all married Hispanics under 35 is involved in a mixed race or ethnic marriage. Among college-educated Hispanics, the rate of intermarriage is even higher. Two-thirds of Hispanic Americans who have completed at least some college are married to people from a different ethnic group (Suro, 1999).

▲ *Interracial marriage was illegal in many states until the Supreme Court ruled otherwise in 1967.*

Love, Commitment, and the Law

Marriage is not only a *personal* commitment between two individuals, it is also a *legal* commitment. The legal commitment is embodied in the laws passed by gov-

HEADline When "Loving" Overcame the Laws Prohibiting Interracial Marriage

*I*n 1967, only a generation ago, the U.S. Supreme Court struck down state laws that prohibited interracial marriage. At the twenty-fifth anniversary of the decision, in 1992, many newspaper writers revisited the case (Duke, 1992; Nash, 1992).

The court case that stopped states from prohibiting interracial marriage was ironically titled *Loving* v. *Virginia*. Mr. and Mrs. Loving prevailed over the Commonwealth of Virginia, although in the process they paid a high price for their interracial marriage.

The story of Richard and Mildred Loving began in Caroline County, Virginia, in the early 1950s, when Richard, then only a teenager, occasionally visited the home of a black male friend who shared an interest in cars and country music. At the time, Richard Loving might not have paid much attention to the young sister of his friend, but by 1958 Mildred Jeter was 18 years old. Soon Richard (then 24) and Mildred fell in love and decided to marry. However, he was of English and Irish background and she was African American and Cherokee, and by the definitions of the culture of the era she was "colored" and he was white. According to Virginia law, they could not marry. The punishment for

violating this law was "confinement in the penitentiary for not less than one nor more than five years" (Nash, 1992, p. C5).

In 1958 there were still seventeen states, including Virginia, that had laws prohibiting interracial marriage. Less than two decades earlier, nearly two-thirds of the states had had such laws. The Virginia law did not, in fact, prohibit *all* interracial marriages, but only marriages between whites and other races. The law did not, for example, prohibit marriage between African Americans and Asians; it was clearly a law aimed at keeping whites from marrying members of other races. The pejorative term of that era was *race mixing.*

Richard Loving and Mildred Jeter were married in neighboring Washington, D.C., in 1958, but after the marriage they returned to live in their home community in Virginia. In the middle of the night on a Sunday in July, the Caroline County sheriff came to the Lovings' home and arrested them for violating the law against interracial marriage. They were handcuffed and taken to jail. Richard, because he was white, was released on bail the next night. Mildred, because she was "colored," had to remain in jail for five days, until a hearing could be held. Ultimately they were

convicted and sentenced by the presiding judge to one year in jail. However, the judge suspended the sentence with the provision that the Lovings leave the state and not return for twenty-five years. The judge added to his opinion as he pronounced his sentence: "Almighty God created the races white, black, yellow, malay and red, and he placed them on separate continents. . . . The fact that he separated the races shows that he did not intend for the races to mix" (Nash, 1992, p. C5).

The Lovings lived in exile in Washington, D.C., until the early 1960s, when with the help of the American Civil Liberties Union (ACLU) they appealed their conviction. Although the Virginia Supreme Court in 1966 upheld the conviction, in June 1967 the U.S. Supreme Court declared the Virginia law, and all others like it, unconstitutional.

After the Supreme Court decision, the Lovings did return to Virginia with their three children. Richard Loving died in an automobile accident in 1975, but Mildred, today, lives quietly in her community, surrounded by her friends, family, and church.

Sources: Duke, 1992, p. A3; Nash, 1992, p. C5.

ernments—local, state, and federal. For example, federal statutes relating to taxes or inheritance may be very different for married and unmarried people. In the United States, individual states also have laws that only apply to married people. In a very real sense, governments create a **hidden marriage contract** through their laws, administrative rulings, and court decisions. The contract defines the rights, responsibilities, and obligations of married people. Any person who marries is agreeing to conform to any and all conditions of these governmental actions (Stetson, 1991).

The Traditional Marriage Contract. Imagine yourself going into a lawyer's office and signing a legally binding contract but not being allowed to see the terms of that contract. You sign the contract, but only later will you learn what your rights and responsibilities are. Any competent lawyer would advise you not to sign such an agreement. Yet when people marry, most are entering into a contract about which they know very little.

The hidden contract people enter at the time of marriage is likely to be based on traditional assumptions about the roles of husbands and wives. And when they marry, regardless of personal beliefs or values, they are bound by the laws that are based on these assumptions.

The major assumptions found in the marriage laws of the United States regarding marriage grew out of English common law and have been perpetuated in the American legislative and judicial system:

1 The husband is the head of the household.

2 The husband is responsible for the economic support of his wife and children.

3 The wife is responsible for domestic services and child care.

In the legal system, as well as in the practices of many nongovernmental organizations, it is still often assumed that husbands are the heads of their households. Under common law tradition, husbands had the right to decide where they and their family would live and wives had to live where their husbands chose. A woman who married a man from a state other than the one where she was a resident risked losing her residence rights in her home state. However, the assumption that men are always the heads of households has been challenged in recent years, as have the other traditional assumptions.

When husbands were considered the family's primary economic providers, they were also given control of the family's economic resources. Historically, under English common law, a husband acquired ownership and control over his wife's property and possessions at the time of their marriage. When a woman was employed under these conditions, her husband was also entitled to her wages. As recently as 1978, in Louisiana, a woman lost a home that she had purchased with her own earnings because of this feature of the law. Her husband, without her permission, was able to borrow money on the home she had purchased. When he failed to repay the loan, the mortgage holder foreclosed. The Louisiana courts ruled the husband had the right to use his wife's property, and the U.S. Supreme Court refused to hear the case. Since that time, Louisiana has given wives the right to control community property equally with their husbands (Weitzman, 1981).

ContentSELECT

Marriage and
Roles

That wives were responsible for domestic duties and child care was a third major assumption of the traditional marriage contract. The legal term for all these services is **consortium.** It has been the tradition under common law that a husband could sue for "loss of consortium" if his wife's services, including sexual services, became unavailable to him as a result of the negligence or actions of a third party.

When wives were obligated by the marriage contract to perform domestic services for their husbands, there were certain legal ramifications. First, a married woman was deprived of the legal right to her own labor; it was not hers if she "owed" it to her husband. Second, domestic labor done by the wife was not considered to be a contribution to the family's wealth and property. This was often an important issue in divorce cases where the wife's domestic work was not counted as having contributed to the wealth and property of the family. Third, when a woman owed services to her husband she could not receive wages for her work. Court decisions repeatedly denied requests by wives, especially in divorce cases, to be compensated for the years of "wifely service" they rendered.

This brief consideration of state-produced marriage contracts underscores the fact that marriage laws are based on assumptions that may be very different from our personal values and preferences. Often the laws and court rulings are based on older traditions and outdated assumptions relating to married life. Second, in the

United States, if we move from one state to another, our marital rights, obligations, and duties may change because of differences in state laws (Stetson, 1991).

Rights and Benefits Conferred by Marriage. Marriage also entails many rights and benefits that are not available to homosexual couples and heterosexual couples who are living together outside of marriage. Laws regulating marriage and family life vary from one state to another, but in most states, spouses are accorded the following rights (nolo.com):

1 To file joint income tax returns with the Internal Revenue Service and state taxing authorities;

2 To create a "family partnership" under federal tax laws, which allows people to divide business income among family members, which often lowers the total tax on the income;

3 Create a marital life estate trust;

4 Receive a wide range of financial benefits, including Social Security disability, unemployment, veterans, pension plans, and public assistance, should something happen to your spouse;

5 Receive a share of your deceased spouse's estate under intestate succession laws;

6 Claim an estate tax marital deduction;

7 Sue a third person for wrongful death of your spouse and loss of consortium;

8 Sue a third person for committing offenses that interfere with the success of your marriage, such as alienation of affection and criminal conversation (only in selected states);

9 Pay family rates for insurance;

10 Avoid the deportation of a noncitizen spouse;

11 Enter hospital intensive care units, jails, and other places where visitors are restricted to immediate family members;

12 Live in neighborhoods zoned for "families only";

13 Make medical decisions about your spouse in the event of disability;

14 Claim the marital communications privilege, which means a court can't force you to testify against your spouse.

Some countries (see the Around the World box) have laws that extend many of these benefits to same-sex couples and cohabiting heterosexual couples.

Readiness to Marry

Once individuals have found a partner and fallen in love, the next step in the development of the relationship is often the decision to marry or to live together outside of marriage. How do couples decide if they are ready to make this type of legal commitment to each other? Readiness for marriage can be thought of as the perceived ability of an individual to perform marital roles.

Maturity and Marital Readiness. Whether an individual is ready and able to make the kind of commitment to a partner and a relationship depends on his or her degree of maturity. Four different dimensions of maturity come into play (Knox,

Around the World

Same-Sex Marriage around the Globe

Americans aren't the only ones wrestling with the issue of providing legal rights for same-sex couples. A number of European countries now provide recognition of gay and lesbian couples.

- *Belgium:* A nationwide law gives same-sex couples inheritance rights.
- *Canada:* The Canadian Supreme Court has ruled that where protections are offered to "spouses" they must also be offered to same-sex couples. While the right to marry was left undecided, a poll taken after the decision showed that the majority of Canadians support the right of same-sex couples to have legally recognized marriages.
- *Denmark:* Denmark was the first country, in 1989, to allow same-sex couples to form "registered partnerships," giving them a status and benefits similar to marriage. Registered couples in Denmark are not permitted to adopt children, however.
- *Finland:* In 2001, Finland passed a same-sex partnership law similar to Denmark's.
- *France:* Registered partnerships are available, including tax benefits, public insurance and pension benefits, inheritance and lease protections, and even the right to demand concurrent vacation schedules. In addition, property acquired together is considered jointly owned unless an agreement states otherwise.
- *Germany:* Gay and lesbian couples may register same-sex partnerships. Registered partners have the same inheritance rights as married couples, and may adopt the same last name, but they do not have the same tax advantages and rights to adopt that married couples have.
- *Greenland:* The Danish law extends to same-sex couples in Greenland. (Greenland is a territory of Denmark.)

- *Hungary:* Same-sex couples are covered by the nation's common-law marriage rules, which carry some of the same rights—particularly regarding inheritance rights. Same-sex couples do not, however, have the right to register under Hungary's marriage law.
- *Iceland:* Iceland's law is similar to Denmark's, allowing same-sex couples to register their partnerships in order to receive many of the rights of marriage, but registered couples cannot adopt children.
- *Italy:* Pisa and Florence allow same-sex couples to register as domestic partners.
- *Netherlands:* The Netherlands has become the first and only country to offer full legal marriage to same-sex couples. Under a law that went into effect in 2001, couples who registered as domestic partners under Dutch law have the option to convert that partnership into a marriage, and are subject to the same laws that govern straight married couples. The law applies only to citizens and legal residents of the Netherlands.
- *Norway:* Registered partnerships similar to those in Denmark are available to same-sex couples.
- *Spain:* Many cities allow same-sex couples to register as domestic partners. Also, a nationwide law allows a widowed partner to remain in rental housing when only the deceased signed the lease.
- *Sweden:* Sweden's law is similar to Denmark's, allowing same-sex couples to register their partnerships in order to receive many of the rights of marriage, but registered couples cannot adopt children.

Source: Reprinted with permission from *A Legal Guide for Lesbian & Gay Couples,* 11th Edition, by Denis Clifford, publisher, Nolo, Copyright 2002, http://www.nolo.com.

1975). **Emotional maturity** refers to an individual's ability to respond appropriately to a full range of situations. When conflict arises in a relationship, the emotionally mature person attempts to find a solution and indicates a sincere willingness to compromise, rather than becoming defensive or threatening to leave the relationship. **Value maturity** involves an individual's awareness of and confidence in the goals and ideas he or she holds in highest priority. Individuals who have this type of maturity ground their important life decisions and behavior in their core beliefs. **Economic maturity** refers to an individual's ability to support him- or herself and a partner, if necessary. Finally, **relationship maturity** refers to an individual's ability to communicate clearly and effectively with a partner. This involves the ability to state one's own values clearly and to stand up for them in a fair and evenhanded manner. It also involves being able to listen to and appreciate another person's point of view even if it differs greatly from one's own.

Some years ago, *People* magazine published the diary of a young woman written in the months leading up to her marriage (Desimone, 1987). The bride-to-be, Angie, was 20 and her fiancee, Mark, was 25 at the time the diary was written. They met when Angie was 16 and Mark, 20. Angie was employed as an administrative assistant in her father's tile business, and Mark was employed as an air-conditioning mechanic. Neither had lived on their own before marriage. Both still lived at home with their parents. When Mark and Angie first started dating, her parents opposed the relationship and forbid her from continuing the relationship. When she didn't obey, they sent her to Italy for four months to keep them apart.

In terms of their chronological age, Angie and Mark were below the average age at which women and men marry in the United States today. Angie, at 20, was five years younger than the typical bride. To what extent, if any, were their chronological ages correlated with their maturity levels? Without knowing the couple, it is difficult to say, of course. But the entries in Angie's diary may provide some clues.

Let's look first at *emotional maturity*. How effectively did Angie and Mark respond to the inevitable stress and disagreements that can arise in the planning of a large wedding? One of the first difficulties that Angie encountered involved the reluctance of several of her ten bridesmaids to pay for their dresses. At $225 per dress, the cost was fairly steep, especially for young women who did not have college educations and were most likely to be working in clerical positions. The cost of the dress could easily have been equal to a week's salary. Angie, though, had difficulty understanding why her bridesmaids weren't coming through with the money, viewing their reluctance as self-centeredness. "It's like they are so wrapped up in their own lives they don't have time to think about me and my wedding" (March 15).

Another problem Angie had early in the wedding planning involved the invitations. Mark's mother ordered them without consulting Angie, who reported in her diary that she was upset and nearly in tears. In spite of her anger, she "bit her tongue" and told her future mother-in-law that it was OK with her.

Angie and Mark also began to fight a lot. Angie wrote that "little things Mark does are starting to drive me crazy. The way he eats and smacks his lips irks me. Little by little things are starting to change. Six months ago if I had on my tennis shoes, he would take them off and start rubbing my feet. But now he says, 'Take a shower first.'" (February 28). In an entry about two weeks later, Angie described a fight they had at McDonalds when they were going through the drive-in and the bag of food fell apart in the car. Mark, according to Angie, "went crazy. We are both off the wall, arguing about stupid little things. He told me that he thinks we are under so much stress that we are taking it out on each other" (March 13). Finally, a week before her wedding, Angie wrote that she was "mad at the world. I'm rude to my parents and barely talking to Mark. Today I burst into tears because there was no Coke in the fridge" (June 21).

It is difficult to determine, of course, to what extent Angie's emotional reactions were due simply to the stresses of planning her wedding or to low levels of emotional maturity. The important issue is whether she would be able to respond to the stresses of everyday married life with confidence and equanimity. In some of the stressful situations she faced, Angie responded appropriately. But in others, her behavior did not approach the level of maturity that would enable her to meet the challenges of marriage and adult life.

We can also look to Angie's diary to get an idea about her *value maturity*. The diary provides only a glimpse into Angie's heart and mind, of course, and is slanted toward the wedding planning. As a result, Angie's comments tend to focus on the material aspects of the wedding rather than married life after the wedding ceremony. Many of the entries in the diary suggest that she may not yet have formed a clear idea about what her role will be in marriage. On April 21, for instance, she described a premarital counseling session she and Mark had with the priest who was going to marry them. One of the tasks Angie and Mark were given was to list their priorities. Angie's top priority was to be a good wife and homemaker and to live her life as she had been accustomed to. Two months later, she wrote in her diary: "I'm still nervous about being married, working full-time and then going home and fixing dinner and cleaning up. I'm not used to that stuff. Mom has dinner ready, irons my clothes, washes my underwear. I don't remember the last time I made my own bed." But just a few lines later, in the same entry, she continued: "I think I will be a wonderful wife. I used to think, 'Do I really want this?' I probably won't have the 450SL Mercedes convertible I've been dreaming of. But I prefer Mark over a car and a billion dollars. The only bad part is I'll have to change the way I dress. I like minis and tight jeans but Mark doesn't think they're appropriate once you're married." A month before, on March 14, the issue had also come up. Angie wrote "Sometimes I worry that Mark's expectations are too high. He's used to being taken care of. His mother keeps her spices in alphabetical order."

Evaluating Angie and Mark's *economic maturity* level is impossible to determine with only the information that is provided in the diary. But it is evident from a number of the entries Angie wrote that she had very high—and perhaps unrealistic—aspirations for her marital standard of living. When they signed a contract for a town house, Angie expressed some disappointment that it didn't have a Jacuzzi or fireplace in the master bedroom. At mortgage payments of nearly $1,000 a month, however, the town house they bought threatened to strain their budget. But Angie reported on May 11 that Mark had calculated their combined monthly income and felt that the payments wouldn't "totally rip us." Working out a budget and sticking to it are two indicators of economic maturity. So on this dimension, Mark and Angie get "high marks."

What can be gleaned from the diary entries about Angie and Mark's *relationship maturity?* Many of the comments provided previously suggest that they were able to work through the stresses of the wedding planning by stepping back and talking about the impact it was taking on their relationship. The diary, of course, only gives a glimpse into Angie's reactions to the stresses. It would have been interesting and insightful to have had Mark's perspective as well. From Angie's perspective, it seems that both she and Mark had a great deal of affection for each other and attempted to work out their differences through discussion. This suggests that they had one of the key ingredients for having a successful relationship—open communication.

As this extended case study illustrates, a number of different types of factors—those related to the individuals involved, to the quality of their relationship factors, aspects of their social networks, and demographic factors such as age—influence marital readiness. When a person is older, financially and educationally "settled," has the support from family and friends for the chosen partner, and a highly satisfying relationship, he or she typically feels ready and has the requisite maturity to get married (Holman and Li, 1997).

Preparation for Marriage

Most, if not all, couples go into their own marriage expecting it to last forever. Few anticipate the likelihood that they will divorce. Nevertheless, many marriages do end in divorce. As we discuss in Chapter 13, the divorce rate has remained at high levels for the past 20 years. The high costs of marital failure have led many political and religious leaders, media spokespersons, and public policy advocates to argue that something must be done on a national basis to reduce or prevent divorce. As a result, a *marriage movement* has been gaining momentum in the United States (Stanley, 2001). Various

Source: JEFF STAHLER reprinted by permission of Newspaper Enterprise Association, Inc.

private organizations have become active in sounding the alarm about marital breakdown (e.g., Smart Marriages, Smart Families; the Association for Couples in Marriage Enrichment; the Institute for American Values; and the Family Life Education initiative of the National Council on Family Relations).

One of the actions that is being advocated by these various organizations is for premarital education. Such education has typically taken place within religious organizations. But there have also been efforts within various state governments to prevent marital distress and divorce. Some states (e.g., Louisiana and Arizona) have attempted to establish covenant marriage. Others have passed legislation to encourage couples to undergo premarital education (e.g., Florida and Texas). Florida, for example, passed the Marriage Preparation and Preservation Act in 1999, which reduces the marriage license fee for couples who complete four hours of premarital education before applying for their license. It also requires high school students to take marriage and family life education courses.

The expected benefits of premarital education are fourfold. It can (1) slow the pace of the relationship so that couples deliberate more carefully before marrying; (2) send couples a message that marriage is important; (3) help couples learn about support if they later run into trouble; and (4) lower the risk of subsequent marital distress or divorce. We consider each of these benefits in more detail.

Premarital education or preparation delays marriage. The delay gives a couple more time to think about their relationship so that they might discover any weaknesses or problems. This is especially important for couples who haven't known each other for sufficient time and/or who haven't had many discussions about their relationship or their expectations for each other once married. Marriage preparation courses may lead some couples to reevaluate their relationship and decide not to marry. It's difficult to determine what the optimal amount of time might be for couples to deliberate about their impending marriage. Many Catholic churches require couples to notify them at least six months in advance of a wedding for the purpose of premarital training.

The Catholic marriage preparation program is a three-step program that typically takes four to six months. The first step—the *discernment phase*—allows couples to confirm their intention to marry and includes an initial interview with a priest or deacon. Couples complete a premarital inventory and have follow-up sessions to discuss their responses with the priest. This is also the stage in which the legal documents required for marriage are gathered. The second stage of the program—the *educational phase*—is a scriptural-based time of reflection on the spiritual basis of marriage. It also includes instruction in conflict management, communication skills, financial responsibilities, child development and parental responsibilities, and potential problem areas in marriage. In Florida, training in these areas is required by the Marriage Preparation and Preservation Act. The final step of the program involves *planning for the wedding ceremony* (The Florida Catholic Conference, 1998).

Premarital education can convey to engaged couples that marriage has long-term consequences and should be taken seriously. Psychologist Scott Stanley, a leading scholar in the area of premarital education, believes many couples today do not give enough weight to the decision to marry, seeing it instead as a revocable decision that can be reversed if the marriage isn't satisfactory. He cites the television show *Who Wants to Marry a Millionaire* as a portrayal of marriage as a trivial, marketed commodity (Stanley, 2001). Stanley also believes that Americans are increasingly seeing marriage as a private matter between two partners, not as something of value to the community. Premarital education can show couples just how important stable marriages are to a society. Such programs can also help couples realize that the quality of a marriage isn't just a matter of fate or luck but the result of careful decisions they make jointly.

During the course of a marriage preparation course couples learn that there are professionals in several different fields who can help them if they have marital difficulties in the future. The simple fact of having been involved in premarital preparation may reduce couples' resistance to getting professional help in the future.

Research about the effectiveness of premarital preparation courses has found that couples who complete such training can learn to communicate more positively and less negatively; are less likely to break up or divorce within a five-year period; experience higher levels of relationship satisfaction in the years following the program; and experience a smaller chance of relationship aggression (Stanley, 2001).

Commitment and Nonmarital Heterosexual Cohabitation

*R*arely has a social or cultural change occurred as rapidly as the appearance and acceptance of nonmarital cohabitation in the United States (Seltzer, 2000; Smock, 2000). In the late 1960s, very few couples cohabited, and those who did were commonly described as "living in sin" or "shacking up." Even well into the 1970s, cohabiting couples were often stigmatized. Traditionally, if an unmarried couple lived together for an extended period of time (usually seven years) most states declared them a *de facto* **marriage,** also called a **common law marriage.** A common law marriage, however, was viewed as something done only by the more disreputable elements of the society. Today cohabitation is widely—if not universally—accepted, and many people see it as one stage in the development of an intimate relationship; others regard it as a long-term alternative to marriage.

The Increasing Number of Cohabitors

One sign of our society's increased acceptance of cohabitation is that the federal government now collects and reports data on cohabitation as part of its monthly Current Population Survey. For many years the government collected information on the number of households where two unrelated and unmarried people of the opposite sex shared living quarters. The resulting statistic was referred to as **POSSLQ**—persons of opposite sex who are sharing living quarters. This provided an estimate of the number of cohabiting couples, but it also included people who might simply have been living as roommates, and it did not count intimate partners who lived together, but had other roommates in their homes.

In the 1990 census, however, the federal government specifically asked about the nature of the relationship between adults living together. For the first time, two unmarried people of the opposite sex sharing a household could be classified as a cohabiting couple. (Similarly, if two people of the same sex described themselves as an unmarried couple, they were classified as a gay or lesbian couple.)

Both the old and improved methods of counting cohabiting couples show that the number has increased substantially over the past few decades, from less than 1 million in 1970 to over 5 million couples today (Casper and Cohen, 2000). Figure 5.2 plots this increase. Unmarried heterosexual cohabitation has become so prevalent that the majority of marriages and remarriages now begin as cohabiting relationships, and most younger men and women cohabit at some point in their lives (Smock, 2000; see also Casper and Cohen, 2000). The percentage of marriages preceded by cohabitation rose from about 10 percent for those who married between 1965 and 1974 to over 50 percent for those who married between 1990 and 1994 (Bumpass and Lu, 1999). Divorced individuals who remarry are even more likely than first-married persons to cohabit before getting married. The proportion of all first unions that began as nonmarital cohabitation rose from 46 percent (between 1980 and 1984) to nearly 60 percent (between 1990 and 1999). The percentage of women in their late thirties who have cohabitated at least once rose from 30 percent in 1987 to 48 percent in 1995 (Bumpass and Lu, 1999, cited in Smock, 2000).

Part of the apparent increase in the number of couples who share a residence without being married may simply reflect more honest reporting of living arrangements. Because there is less negative stigma associated with living together today, cohabitors may be more willing to reveal that they are living as unmarried partners. But the actual behavior of Americans has also undoubtedly changed; as cohabitation has become more accepted than it once was, more people are cohabiting (Seltzer, 2000; Smock, 2000).

Even though young Americans are postponing marriage, they are not willing to live without emotional and sexual intimacy. In other words, the increase in unmarried young adults in the population in recent years does not mean a corresponding increase in the number of unattached or uninvolved individuals. Young people are forming intimate households today at roughly the same age as they did in the previous generations. The legal status of those unions, however, is different. By substituting cohabitation for marriage, at least for a temporary period, young people can fulfill their sexual and emotional needs at the same time they are meeting their occupational and economic goals.

Scholars who attempt to explain why nonmarital cohabitation has increased so dramatically over the past three decades generally agree that its rise is just one aspect of the profound changes that have taken place in families in the United States and Europe (that is, declining fertility levels, rising marital disruption rates, and a growing proportion of children being born outside of marriage). These broader societal changes are both *cultural* (including an increased emphasis on individual goals and a decline in the importance of religion in everyday life) and *economic* (changes in women's labor market participation and shifts in attitudes and values about men's and women's roles). Other factors include a decreased stigma on sexual relations outside of marriage and an increased awareness of the impermanence of legal marriage (Smock, 2000).

Characteristics of Cohabitors

Cohabiting couples can be found at virtually all ages and educational levels, and in all racial and ethnic groups. But some patterns and variations are worth noting. Figure 5.3 summarizes characteristics of cohabiting partners.

Age and Marital Status.   In the late 1990s, well over three-quarters of cohabiting heterosexual men and women were under age 45. Over one-third were between the ages of 25 and 34, while one-fifth of the total fell into the next older age category (35 to 44). Over half of all cohabiting individuals had not been mar-

Unmarried
Couples

Figure 5.3 Characteristics of Cohabiting Couples and Their Households: Estimates from Traditional and Adjusted POSSLQ Measures (1997)

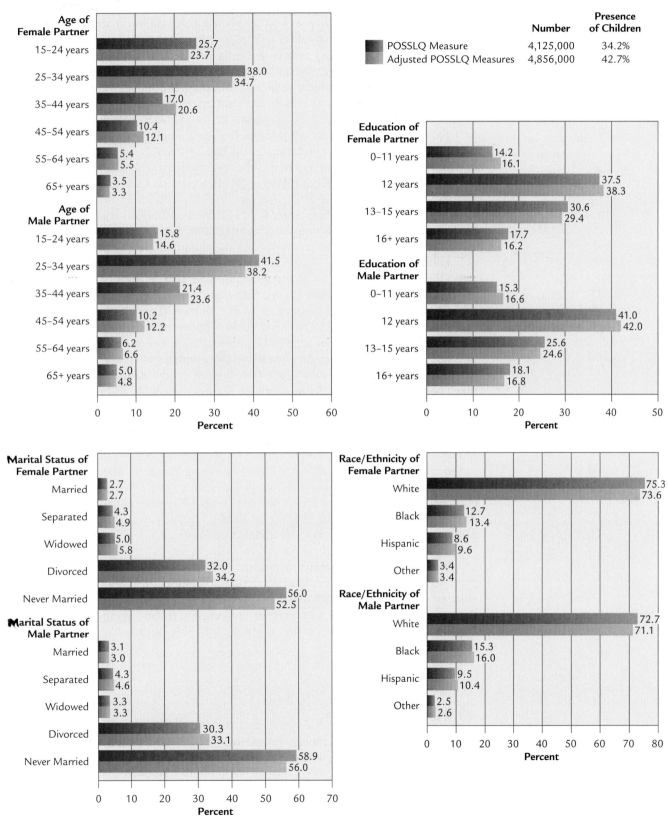

(*Source:* Adapted from Casper and Cohen, 2000. "How Does POSSLQ Measure Up? Historical Estimates of Cohabitation," Table 4, p. 242. *Demography* 37: 237–245. Population Association of America. Reprinted with permission.)

ried before moving in with their cohabiting partner. Another 40 percent of the cohabitors were divorced or separated from a previous partner.

Education.   Contrary to a widely held belief, cohabitation is not greater among college students than among other groups in the population. In fact, it never has been most common among college students. In the late 1960s and early 1970s, cohabitation among college students attracted the attention of the media and university researchers, giving the impression that college students invented this type of living arrangement. In actuality, they were simply imitating a lifestyle that already existed among other groups in the population (Bumpass, Sweet, and Cherlin, 1991, p. 917). At that time, the highest rates were found among the least educated segments of the young adult population. In the late 1990s, over half of the heterosexual women and close to 60 percent of the heterosexual men who were cohabiting with a partner had a high school education or less (Casper and Cohen, 2000).

Race and Ethnicity.   Two decades ago, African American women were more likely than white women to be in cohabiting relationships (Espenshade, 1985). More recent studies show little difference among racial and ethnic groups (Smock, 2000).

Although Latinas, in general, have relatively low rates of cohabitation, considerable differences exist within the Latina population. For example, Puerto Rican women living in the mainland United States are much more likely to cohabit than other Latina women and non-Latina white women (Landale and Forste, 1991; Landale and Fennelly, 1992). The explanation is partly cultural. **Consensual unions** (sexually based primary relationships between women and men who have not gone through religious or civil ceremonies) have been common in certain Latin American countries for hundreds of years. These unions often produce children and are recognized both socially and legally as a form of marriage (Landale and Fennelly, 1992).

In Puerto Rico, consensual unions began in the sixteenth century with Spanish colonizers who wanted a way to legitimize their sexual relationships with native women and slaves. By the end of the nineteenth century, approximately one-third of all heterosexual unions were informal rather than legal. Since then, consensual union rates have declined in Puerto Rico, yet among Puerto Rican women who live on the mainland United States rates have significantly increased over the past several decades. It may be that economic conditions—low rates of labor force participation, high unemployment, low earnings, and high poverty—discourage the formation of stable, legal marriages (Landale and Forste, 1991).

Parental Status.   Contrary to popular belief, cohabitation is not a childless state. About one-half of previously married cohabitors and 35 percent of never-married cohabitors have children living in their homes. In most cases (70 percent) these are children of only one partner, making the arrangement somewhat like stepfamilies. The remainder of the children are the biological offspring of the couple (Smock, 2000).

Types of Cohabitors

People enter into cohabiting relationships at different times in their lives and with very different motivations. Some of the relationships are primarily sexual in nature and relatively short-lived. Others are more marriage-like insofar as the partners are connected in many ways other than sexually.

At the most minimal level, a cohabiting couple can be in a **part-time** or **limited relationship.** This type of relationship usually develops without much conscious deliberation or discussion between the partners. These couples often drift into cohabitation, but the relationship may last for only a short time.

The part-time, limited relationship often begins with the individuals maintaining separate residences but spending two, three, or four or more nights together each week. After a while, they decide to live together full-time, but the decision is not very explicit.

Since their cohabitation starts without a clear-cut decision, part-time and limited cohabitors may also fail to make decisions about other important issues. They may not have established the degree to which the relationship is sexually exclusive, or worked out the economic details (such as who will pay for rent, groceries, utilities, phone, and entertainment). They may also not discuss how their relationship is related to marriage.

A second type of living-together arrangement can be described as **premarital cohabitation.** In this relationship, two people who plan to marry decide to live together until the wedding date arrives. This seems to be the most common pattern for many couples today. These relationships are often called **trial marriages,** because couples are trying to decide whether marriage is an appropriate step to take.

The final type of cohabiting relationship can be thought of as a long-term alternative to marriage. Sometimes it is called **substitute marriage.** These couples do not plan to marry but do intend to maintain a lifelong relationship with each other. Their commitment to each other may result in their having children together as well as pooling their finances and making major purchases together. We have no firm statistics about the incidence of this type of cohabiting relationship.

Some couples who regard cohabitation as a long-term substitute for legal marriage have commitment ceremonies and/or obtain domestic partner certificates when they are available in their cities. A number of the cohabiting couples in a study conducted by Marion Willetts (1997) demonstrated the commitment they felt for each other and for their relationship by obtaining **domestic partnership certificates** (that is, legal recognition of a cohabiting couple that bestows some legal rights but still maintains the distinction between married and unmarried couples) and by having public ceremonies in front of their families and friends. Teresa and

Lynn Goyette (left) *and Eileen Blackwood were among the first to apply for a domestic partner certificate in Vermont.*

Donald, for instance, had lived together for a year before getting their partnership certificate. Teresa was in her late twenties and Donald was in his mid-thirties when they went to the courthouse for their certificate. While Teresa told Dr. Willets that she and Donald did not feel that they needed a religious seal of approval on their relationship, they did want to have a commitment ceremony. Theirs was held in a park with nine people present, but there was no government or church official to conduct the ceremony. Afterward, 100 people attended their reception. The purpose of the ceremony and reception was to allow Donald and Teresa to affirm their commitment to each other and to the other people who were important in their lives. Teresa says, "It was just that we do think that there's power to declaring your commitment in front of people that you love, and doing it openly, so that saying the words as witnessed sort of conveys or reaffirms the power of the commitment itself" (Willetts, 1997).

The Meaning of Nonmarital Cohabitation

Researchers have suggested that nonmarital cohabitation can be either a stage in the courtship process (that is, an extension of dating and sexual relationships and for many couples, a form of engagement that culminates in marriage) or a longer term substitute for marriage (that is, the couples involved in this type of relationship do not intend to legally marry). A large proportion of cohabiting couples go on to marry, providing support for the idea that cohabitation functions as a type of engagement (Smock, 2000). Little research has been done on cohabiting couples who reject legal marriage, though studies based on small nonrandom samples suggest that these are not very common in the United States. These couples may not consciously reject marriage; they simply don't see it as necessary to define their commitment to each other in this way (Seltzer, 2000).

> The meaning of cohabitation outside of marriage . . . depends on the social context in which (it) occurs. As cohabitation . . . becomes more common, individuals are less likely to think of [it] as deviant behavior. In the United States, individuals are marrying and forming nonmarital families in a changing social context. Marriage, as an institution, is increasingly defined as a short-term relationship. Divorce is more acceptable now than in the past. . . . Laws no longer assume that marriage is forever . . . and celebrations of marriage are less likely to emphasize its permanence. The meaning of cohabitation is shifting, in part because the meaning of marriage has shifted. Marriage offers fewer benefits relative to cohabitation now than in the past. Most young people expect to marry and believe that it is important to have a good marriage and family life, but most do not believe that they *must* [emphasis added] marry (in order) to live a good life." (Seltzer, 2000, pp. 1248–1249)

Entering a cohabiting relationship may be carefully thought out and discussed between the partners, but many couples simply drift into the arrangement. In this situation, cohabitation can lead to disappointment or even exploitation. When one partner enters a cohabiting relationship thinking it is one step closer to marriage, while the other regards it simply as a convenient living arrangement and has no intention of marrying, the situation is ripe for confusion and conflict. The late 1980s film "About Last Night," featuring Demi Moore and Rob Lowe, illustrates this quite vividly. Couples who are thinking about living together might discuss their reasons for doing so, to make clear what their expectations are. Couples who are contemplating cohabitation—or who have already made the step to move in with each other—are often advised by attorneys to consider writing a contract in which their rights, responsibilities, and expectations relative to each other are spelled out. A number of legal information sites on the Internet provide guidelines for writing such a contract.

▪ *Why Don't Cohabiting Couples Marry?*

In a recent study, women and men who had rejected legal marriage and chose to cohabit with their partners outside of marriage were interviewed (Elizabeth, 2000). None of the people in the study had been previously married, but quite a few had had other significant relationships. The length of their current relationships ranged from four to eleven years. Study participants ranged in age from early twenties through late thirties.

Many of the cohabiting individuals in the study felt that legal marriage greatly constrained spouses, forcing them into rigid roles and limiting their freedom. Nonmarital cohabitation was an alternative form of heterosexual intimacy and commitment that allowed partners the freedom to organize their finances independently of each other if they wished, to determine their household division of labor without having it dictated by traditional gender roles, and to retain their distinct identities without simply being considered as an extension of their partners. Those who lived with their intimate partners outside of marriage regarded their choice as a way to develop a more authentic bond that was not encumbered by rigid gender roles. Any expectations that cohabiting partners faced in the conduct of their relationships were those they freely negotiated with each other.

The author of this study on cohabitants who reject legal marriage, Vivienne Elizabeth, offers the following analogy to describe the difference between legal marriage and nonmarital cohabitation (p. 95):

> Marriage [is like] a house that has already been built—all one has to do is occupy it. Cohabitation, on the other hand, requires those who wish to dwell within its walls to build the shelter first. As a consequence, the house may incorporate some of the materials used to build the marital house but, nevertheless, be designed to fit the unique needs and desires of individual cohabitants.

From the perspective of these long-term cohabiting individuals, marriage operates to trap people at a fixed point in their personal histories. It pins married individuals to choices they made at some stage in their past. They conceptualize legal marriage as a threat to their freedom to organize their relationships according to their current rather than their past needs, wants, and desires. This perspective is illustrated by the following comment from a woman in her mid-twenties who is living with her partner rather than marrying him (p. 96):

> One thing I have against marriage is that you are locking yourself into something. And you are saying, "I am not going to change. We are not going to change. We are always going to be the same as we are on this day." And you have got to give yourself room to grow and change.

Commitment to one's partner in cohabiting relationships is the result of personal choice not from the government-imposed obstacles that make it difficult to leave a legal spouse. The degree of commitment cohabiting partners feel for each other is not, in their eyes, any less than that proclaimed by legal spouses. In fact, they believe, it may be even greater than that experienced by people who are legally married because it's based on personal choice and devotion, rather than the external constraints imposed on marriages by the government and the church.

Many people do not share the sentiments expressed by the cohabitors in this study. The *majority* view seems to be that legal marriage is the superior form of heterosexual relationship and that nonmarital cohabitation is inferior. Partners in cohabiting relationships, especially female partners, are often questioned about their intentions to marry. They often feel the need to pass as married under certain circumstances. And they often use the term *partner* rather than boyfriend or girlfriend to give their relationship more status or legitimacy. One of the women in Elizabeth's study (2000, p. 105) described her own experiences in this regard:

ContentSELECT

Cohabitation

On most occasions where I think it is more expedient to appear to be married I will just pretend, or wear a wedding ring, or act as if I am married. . . . I don't have any scruples about it. I mean it is not a matter of principle for me. I don't insist on everybody knowing my true marital status. It doesn't bother me at all how they perceive it. And mostly I prefer to ignore that I am not. . . . [People describe me as Matthew's wife] quite often.

Legal and Financial Aspects of Nonmarital Cohabitation

Despite the dramatic increase in the number of cohabiting couples over the past thirty years, the legal implications of cohabitation are unclear. The law is much clearer about marital relationships than about cohabiting relationships. Cohabiting partners are at a disadvantage with regard to inheritance and survivors' benefits, insurance, and division of property and assets if their relationship ends with either death or separation. For instance, when a legal spouse dies without a will, most state laws transfer the ownership of property to the surviving spouse. The same holds for Social Security benefits: Surviving spouses get an income as well as a lump sum payment on the other's death. When a cohabiting partner dies, however, property goes to the nearest relative unless a will specifies that it is to be given to the surviving partner. Cohabiting individuals have no automatic legal right to survivors' income or to any other economic benefits on the death of their partners.

When cohabiting partners separate, they have almost no legal protection for their property or assets. Attorneys advise cohabiting couples to buy few items jointly and to keep records and receipts for everything acquired individually during the relationship. They are also advised against opening joint bank accounts or obtaining joint credit cards, because doing so means that each partner is fully responsible for debts incurred by the other.

Unmarried couples can reduce the legal ambiguity of their relationship by drawing up a written agreement stating their intentions and obligations to each other. For cohabiting couples with few major assets, contracts can be simple. Many books on living together provide fill-in-the-blank forms that can be used for this purpose. But for couples with substantial assets and incomes, a contract might require the assistance of an attorney.

Contracts describe the financial obligations partners have to each other, if any, including plans for support should one partner become ill or lose a job. They detail how jointly acquired property is to be disposed of, if the relationship ends. Writing up a contract of this nature requires couples to consider not only financial matters, but also their degree of commitment to each other.

Experts say financial agreements should be written early in the relationship, when partners are feeling positive about each other. However, this is also the time romantically involved couples are most reluctant to be practical, and even agreements written in the early, happy days of a relationship may be disputed when a couple splits up.

Cohabitation and Common Law Marriages

Contrary to popular belief, two people who live together do not automatically become a common law marriage after a specific period of time. A common law marriage can only occur under the following conditions:

1 A heterosexual couple lives together in a state that recognizes common law marriages (e.g., Alabama, Colorado, District of Columbia, Iowa, Kansas, Montana, New Hampshire [for inheritance purposes only], Oklahoma, Pennsylvania, Rhode Island, South Carolina, Texas, and Utah)

2 for a significant period of time (which is not actually defined in any state)

3 holding themselves out as a married couple (typically this means using the same last name, referring to the other as "my husband" or "my wife" and filing a joint tax return), and

4 intending to be married.

Unless all four of the conditions are met, there is no common law marriage. When a common law marriage exists, the couple must go through a formal divorce to end the relationship (nolo.com, 2001).

Commitment among Gay and Lesbian Couples

Number of Gay and Lesbian Couples

It has been difficult to obtain accurate statistics about the size of the gay and lesbian population. Few national surveys of the U.S. population contain information about sexual orientation. Many of the studies that did provide information about gays and lesbians used convenience sampling (e.g., readers of gay publications or people who frequented gay and lesbian bars and clubs). Obviously, trying to generalize from these limited and undoubtedly unique samples to the entire population of gays and lesbians would lead to inaccurate estimates and distorted descriptions of their characteristics. More recently, however, social science researchers have begun to use information obtained in large national surveys (e.g., the U.S. Census, the General Social Survey conducted by the National Opinion Research Center at the University of Chicago, and the National Health and Social Life Survey) to obtain more accurate data about the gay and lesbian population. This is an important step forward in social science research because it can provide data that are useful to public policy questions concerning, for instance, the need to extend domestic partnership benefits to gay and lesbian couples (Black et al., 2000).

Clearly, in order to count the number of gays and lesbians accurately, it is essential to have a clear idea of what constitutes a homosexual. Should homosexuality be defined in terms of *actual behavior?* If so, should it be restricted to those who only engage in sexual activities with persons of the same sex? Is there some specific number of sexual acts with a person of the same sex that determines when a person is or becomes a homosexual? Should homosexuality be extended to include sexual *preferences* rather than just behavior? These are important questions, which are discussed in more detail in the next chapter. For present purposes, we draw on a report that compares statistics based on several alternative methods of defining homosexuality to get estimates of the proportion of the gay and lesbian

Same-sex couples are denied the right to have civil marriage ceremonies, but many churches are allowing ministers to perform weddings for them.

population that is currently involved in an ongoing partnership with a person of the same sex and of the proportion of homosexual households that includes children. (For information about the various definitions that were used in the report on which we based this discussion, see Black et al., 2000).

Using the narrow definition of homosexuals as individuals who have engaged exclusively in same-sex sexual activities over the previous year, approximately 2.5 percent of men are gay and 1.4 percent of women are lesbians. Partnership rates

TABLE 5.1

Twenty Cities with the Largest Gay/Lesbian-Couple Populations

	Cities Ordered by Number of Gay Couples	Cities Ordered by Number of Lesbian Couples
1	Los Angeles, CA	New York, NY
2	New York, NY	Los Angeles, CA
3	San Francisco, CA	San Francisco, CA
4	Washington, DC	Minneapolis, MN
5	Chicago, IL	Washington, DC
6	Atlanta, GA	Seattle, WA
7	San Diego, CA	Boston, MA
8	Oakland, CA	Chicago, IL
9	Boston, MA	Oakland, CA
10	Seattle, WA	Philadelphia, PA
11	Dallas, TX	Sacramento, CA
12	Houston, TX	Atlanta, GA
13	Philadelphia, PA	San Diego, CA
14	Anaheim, CA	Baltimore, MD
15	Minneapolis, MN	Tampa, FL
16	Fort Lauderdale, FL	Portland, OR
17	Tampa, FL	Houston, TX
18	Phoenix, AZ	Phoenix, AZ
19	Denver, CO	Denver, CO
20	Sacramento, CA	San Jose, CA

Source: Adapted from Black, Gates, Sanders, and Taylor (2000). "Demographics of the Gay and Lesbian Population in the United States." *Demography* 37(2): 139–154, Table 4, p. 148. Population Association of America. Reprinted by permission.

among these two groups are 28.4 percent and 44.1 percent, respectively. To place these numbers into broader perspective, less than 1 percent of adult men and women in the United States are believed to be living in homosexual partnered households. However, these are simply estimates and they are subject to numerous reporting errors.

One of the factors that greatly determines the ability of a homosexual individual to meet an intimate partner and form a household with him or her is the number of available partners. Table 5.1 presents a list of the twenty cities in the United States that have the largest estimated gay and lesbian populations. The twenty cities with the largest number of gay couples account for approximately 60 percent of the entire gay population in the nation, but only 26 percent of the entire U.S. population. Clearly, gay men are concentrated in a selected number of urban areas. Lesbian women are somewhat less geographically concentrated (Black et al., 2000). The majority of the smaller cities with high concentrations of gay men and lesbian women (which do not show up in Table 5.1) contain a major university (i.e., Madison, Wisconsin, is home to the University of Wisconsin and Ann Arbor, Michigan, is home to the University of Michigan).

A substantial number of same-sex couples, especially lesbian couples, currently have children present in their home. About 22 percent of partnered lesbians and

TABLE 5.2			
Presence of Children in Households by Relationship Status of Adults (Percentages)			
	Partnered Gay/Lesbian	Partnered Heterosexual	Married	Not Partnered
Men				
No children	94.8	63.8	40.8	95.2
1 child	3.0	18.1	22.4	2.9
2 children	1.2	11.0	23.0	1.4
≥ 3 children	1.1	7.1	13.8	0.5
Women				
No children	78.3	63.8	40.8	77.9
1 child	12.6	18.1	22.4	10.1
2 children	5.0	11.0	23.0	7.6
≥ 3 children	4.1	7.1	13.8	4.5

Source: Adapted from Black, Gates, Sanders, and Taylor (2000). "Demographics of the Gay and Lesbian Population in the United States." *Demography* 37(2): 139–154, Tables 6 and 7, pages 150–151. Population Association of America. Reprinted by permission.

slightly over 5 percent of partnered gay men are living in households with children. Most of the children in these homes are relatively young. Three-quarters are under age 18. Many of the children in gay and lesbian households were most likely born in previous marriages, since nearly 20 percent of men in gay partnerships and 30 percent of women in lesbian partnerships were previously married (Black et al., 2000). Table 5.2 presents estimates of the number of gay and lesbian households that contain children, and Table 5.3 summarizes the current marital status of gay men and lesbian women who are currently involved in homosexual partnerships.

TABLE 5.3	
Current and Past Marital Status for Partnered Gays and Lesbians (Percentages)	
Marital Status	**Partnered Gay/Lesbian**
Men (Sample size = 7,567)	
Currently married	1.3
Widowed, separated, or divorced, and not currently married	17.2
Never married	81.4
Women (Sample size = 6,081)	
Currently married	1.2
Widowed, separated, or divorced, and not currently married	28.7
Never married	70.1

Source: Adapted from Black, Gates, Sanders, and Taylor (2000). "Demographics of the Gay and Lesbian Population in the United States." *Demography* 37(2): 139–154, Tables 6 and 7, pages 150–151. Population Association of America. Reprinted by permission.

Legalization of Same-Sex Relationships

In the early 1970s, lesbian and gay couples began to apply for marriage licenses, ask courts to allow them to adopt each other, and take other steps to get legal recognition for their relationships. Most of their efforts failed. By the mid 1980s, the emphasis of gay rights activists shifted to an attempt to earn domestic partner recognition. This effort continues today with increasing intensity. The desire to legally marry has also emerged again among some parts of the gay and lesbian community. Some couples are applying for marriage licenses and suing their state governments when their requests are denied. Many gay and lesbian couples are participating in their own commitment ceremonies supported by their friends, families, and churches (nolo.com, 2001).

It is important to keep in mind that not all members of the homosexual community support efforts to win the right to legally marry. Some argue that regardless of their own desire to legally marry, all gay men and lesbians should support efforts to achieve legal recognition of gay and lesbian relationships. Others condemn marriage as a sexist and patriarchal institution that should be rejected at all costs. And still others are of high enough socioeconomic status that they aren't constrained by the fact that their relationships are not recognized by state and federal governments.

Same Sex Marriage

The Vermont Civil Union Law.   Marriage was declared a fundamental right by the U.S. Supreme Court in 1978, yet no state recognizes same-sex marriage. But changes may come soon. In December 1999, the Vermont Supreme Court ordered the state's legislature (in *Baker* v. *State of Vermont*) to come up with a system that would provide same-sex couples with traditional marriage benefits and protections. In response, the legislature passed the **Vermont Civil Union Law,** which went into effect on July 1, 2000. While the law doesn't legalize gay and lesbian couples, it does provide them with many of the same advantages, including the following: use of family laws such as annulment, divorce, child custody and child support, alimony, domestic violence, adoption, and property division; the right to sue for wrongful death, loss of consortium, and any other law related to spousal relationships; medical rights such as hospital visitation, notification, and durable power of attorney; family leave benefits; joint state tax filing; and property inheritance without a will. The Vermont Civil Union Law only applies to couples who reside in Vermont. But even Vermont residents cannot take advantage of federal rights and benefits awarded to legally married couples. Couples outside Vermont can go to the state to be joined in civil union, but other states undoubtedly will refuse to recognize their unions as legal.

Prior to the ruling in Vermont, rights of lesbian and gay partners to receive the same benefits as married couples rested on a case that was pending in the Supreme Court in the state of Hawaii (*Baehr* v. *Miike*, 1999). The case was deliberated for over nine years. The plaintiff in the case argued that Hawaii's marriage license rules were discriminatory. The case became the subject of a national debate and actually led to a barrage of state and federal legislation that was designed to counteract the possibility that other states would be forced to recognize Hawaii's decision, should it legalize same-sex marriage. In fact, in 1996, the U.S. Congress passed the **Defense of Marriage Act,** which stipulated that no state could be forced to recognize a same-sex marriage that was formed in another state. The case was finally dismissed, however, because the Hawaii legislature passed a prohibition against same-sex marriages before the state Supreme Court could reach a decision that would have recognized such unions as legal. (For more information about the history of same-sex marriage laws in the United States visit the web site nolo.com.)

The Federal Marriage Amendment.   In July 2001, a group called Alliance for Marriage, which is a coalition of religious and family policy experts, proposed an amendment to the United States Constitution which they labeled the Federal Marriage Amendment. This amendment would add the following two sentences to the Constitution: "Marriage in the United States shall consist only of the union of a man and a woman. Neither this Constitution or the constitution of any state, nor state or federal law, shall be construed to require that marital status or the legal incidents thereof be conferred upon unmarried couples or groups." The amendment was apparently prompted by concerns that the state of Vermont's civil union law, which grants marriage-like rights to same-sex couples, will lead to numerous lawsuits from gay couples across the nation. If the amendment passes, not only would Vermont's law lose its constitutional support, so would workplace benefits given to gay couples by private and government employers in a number of states. Granting legal recognition and rights to same-sex couples has been controversial for quite some time. Legislation to ban same-sex marriage has sprung up all over the country in recent years. In March 2000, the state of California passed Proposition 22, which declares that only a marriage between a man and a woman can be legally binding. Thirty-three other states have passed laws that state that they will not recognize same-sex unions. In some states where such legislation is pending, same-sex couples are challenging them.

Summary

Recent increases in the unmarried population are largely the result of two factors: delayed marriage and divorce. The unmarried population can be divided into those who have never married, those who have been divorced and have not remarried, cohabitors, and same-sex couples.

Most single, never-married Americans are relatively young, although some men and women remain single for life. Historically, and still today, lifelong singleness is somewhat stigmatized. Divorced singles are more likely to be women than men, primarily because of the shortage of available men at the older ages. The popular image of a single's lifestyle is misleading, because there are significant differences among singles. Singleness can be voluntary or involuntary and temporary or permanent, and these factors in combination produce different types of singles. Remaining single may be seen as the product of a set of pushes (negative factors about marriage) and pulls (positive aspects of being unmarried). Most Americans still believe it is better to be married than single.

The social and cultural acceptance of cohabitation in the United States has become widespread in the past thirty years, but is not universal. Sample surveys and preliminary results from the 2000 census both show rapid growth in the number of cohabiting couples, recorded at more than five million in the late 1990s. The increase in cohabitors reflects the greater social acceptance of living together. Young people are forming intimate relationships at roughly the same ages as in previous generations, they are just not marrying as soon.

Cohabitors are generally young—40 percent between 25 and 34. Over half have not been married, and 40 percent have been divorced or separated. Cohabitation is found more often among the less educated than the most educated. African American, Latina, and white women have very nearly the same levels of cohabitation today. Among Latinas, Puerto Rican women have the highest rates of cohabitation. The number of cohabiting households with children is increasing.

Cohabiting relationships can be part-time or limited, premarital, or a permanent alternative to marriage. The most common reason for cohabiting is to determine compatibility for marriage. Sharing expenses is a second major reason. Most cohabitors, but not all, expect to marry the person with whom they are living. Most cohabitors do not believe marriage will change their relationship; when they do feel a change will occur, they usually expect it to be positive.

Legal aspects of cohabitation are still unclear. Legal ambiguities can be reduced by producing written agreements early in the relationship.

The total number and the characteristics of same-sex couples are not firmly established because of a lack of research, although recent research is focusing more attention on the nonsexual aspects of same-sex couples.

Key Terms

Affinal relatives (p. 135)

Bigamy (p. 134)

Commitment (p. 129)

Common law marriage
(p. 145)

Consensual union (p. 148)

Consortium (p. 139)

Cross-cousin marriage (p. 135)

De facto marriage (p. 145)

Defense of Marriage Act (p. 156)

Domestic partnership certificate
(p. 149)

Economic maturity (p. 141)

Emotional maturity (p. 141)

Endogamy (p. 135)

Exogamy (p. 135)

Heterogamy (p. 136)

Hidden marriage contract
(p. 139)

Homogamy (p. 136)

Intermarriage (p. 136)

Monogamy (p. 134)

Parallel cousin marriage (p. 135)

Part-time/limited cohabiting
relationship (p. 148)

Plural marriage (p. 134)

Polyandry (p. 134)

Polygamy (p. 134)

Polygyny (p. 134)

POSSLQ (p. 145)

Premarital cohabitation (p. 149)

Relationship maturity (p. 141)

Serial monogamy (p. 135)

Substitute marriage (p. 149)

Trial marriage (p. 149)

Value maturity (p. 141)

Vermont Civil Union Law (p. 156)

Review Questions

1. What are the three dimensions of commitment? What kinds of questions are included in each dimension?

2. What is the average age at first marriage today for women and men? What proportion of adults between the ages of 20 and 24 are unmarried? Between the ages of 30 and 34?

3. What does it mean to say that there is a hidden marriage contract? What are the major assumptions about the rights and obligations of spouses in American marriage laws?

4. What are the implications of the legal assumption that wives are obligated to provide domestic services for their husbands?

5. What are the legal rights and privileges that are given to married couples but not to committed gay couples or to cohabiting heterosexual couples?

6. How has the number of cohabiting heterosexual couples increased since 1970? Why has it changed in this way? What are the difficulties associated with counting the number of cohabiting couples? What are the limits of the POSSLQ count?

7. To what does the term *domestic partner* refer? What types of benefits are being extended to domestic partners in various locales around the United States? What opposition has arise against domestic partnership laws or policies?

8. What are the difficulties involved in counting the number of gay and lesbian couples? How has the U.S. Census Bureau changed its method of counting these couples?

Critical Thinking Questions

1. Discuss ways in which *singles* might be discriminated against.

2. What are the advantages and disadvantages of being unmarried and unpartnered throughout your lifetime?

3. While often linked together under the label *homosex-ual*, gay men and lesbians may have quite different experiences of being homosexual. Discuss the ways in which homosexual men and women might differ. How might any differences be linked to gender?

4. Is marriage less necessary today than in previous generations?

Online Resources Available for This Chapter

www.ablongman.com/marriageandfamily

▪ Online Study Guide with Practice Tests

▪ PowerPoint Chapter Outlines

▪ Links to Marriage and Family Websites

▪ ContentSelect Research Database

▪ Self-Assessment Activities

Further Reading

Books

Altman, Irwin, and Ginat, Joseph. *Polygamous Families in Contemporary Society.* Cambridge: Cambridge University Press, 1996. Examines marital relationships in contemporary Morman polygamous families.

Blood, Robert O. Jr., and Wolfe, Donald. *Husbands and Wives: The Dynamics of Married Living.* Glencoe, IL: Free Press, 1960. One of the first and most comprehensive examinations of power and decision making in marriage.

Blumstein, Philip, and Schwartz, Pepper. *American Couples: Money, Work, and Sex.* New York: William Morrow and Company, 1985. A groundbreaking national study of couples in three types of relationships: legal marriage, heterosexual cohabitation, and homosexual commitment.

Corral, Jill, and Miya-Jervis, Lisa (eds.). *Young Wives' Tales: New Adventures in Love and Partnership.* Seattle, WA: Seal Press, 2001. Examines the wide range of committed partnerships experienced by young women today.

Dryden, Caroline. *Being Married, Doing Gender: A Critical Analysis of Gender Relations in Marriage.* London: Routledge, 1999. Explores marital and personal identity, gender relations, and emotional experiences in the lives of heterosexual couples.

Nock, Steven L. *Marriage in Men's Lives.* New York: Oxford University Press, 1998. Nock examines the beneficial effects of marriage for men, and marriage as a means for developing and sustaining masculinity.

Patterson, Charlotte. "Family Relationships of Lesbians and Gay Men." *Journal of Marriage and the Family, 62,* 2000: 1052–1069. A comprehensive review of research on this topic conducted over the 1990s.

Seltzer, Judith. "Families Formed Outside of Marriage." *Journal of Marriage and the Family,* 62 (2000): 1247–1268. A comprehensive review of research conducted on this topic over the 1990s.

Waite, Linda, and Gallagher, Maggie. *A Case for Marriage: Why Married People are Happier, Healthier, and Better Off Financially.* New York: Doubleday, 2000. A review of research that argues legal marriage is superior to other forms of intimate commitment.

Weiss, Jessica. *To Have and to Hold: Marriage, the Baby Boom, and Social Change.* Chicago: University of Chicago Press, 2000. Studies the lives of people who married in the 1950s, gave birth to the baby boom, and set the stage for the profound social change that occurred in the 1970s.

ContentSELECT Articles

Cohen, D., and Bruce, K. "Sex and Mortality: Real Risk and Perceived Vulnerability." *Journal of Sex Research* 34(3), 1997: 279–292. **[Database: Sociology]** Serial monogamy is viewed as a monogamous sexual relationship with one or two partners that lasts in duration for about nine months. The authors attempted to determine real sexual practices risk versus perceived sexual practices risk among those who engaged in extended relationships, serial monogamy, or casual sexual encounters. Study participants involved in serial monogamy reported higher discussion of sexual history and lower rate of STD infection as compared to those engaged in casual relationships. Additionally, serial monogamy participants had a lower risk of HIV infection.

Epstein, H. "Ironies." *Humanist* 59(2), 1999: 46–48. **[Database: Social Work]** The early 1970s ushered in the bra-burning epoch of freedom for women . . . freedom from mundane suburbanite existence as well as mundane sexuality. Epstein provides a personal account of her reaction to and the impact of feminism and the sexual revolution.

Salkever, A. "Republican Tide in U.S. Politics Doesn't Reach Hawaii's Shores." *Christian Science Monitor* 89(242), 1997: 3. **[Database: General Interest]** In 1997 Hawaii (the first state to do so) mandated that health benefits were to be made available to domestic partners who could not legally marry. Salkever discusses Hawaii's multiethnic and historical political environment that led to the decision to allow benefits to unmarried domestic partners.

Searight, H. R. "Therapy with Unmarried Heterosexual Couples: Clinical and Ethical Issues." *Family Journal* 6(3), 1998: 295–303. **[Database: Psychology]** Increasingly, more and more heterosexual couples are opting to cohabit rather than to marry, giving rise to cohabiting-specific couple issues. Case studies are presented to illustrate the difficulties of parenting and also the ambiguity of "cohabitation." Because widely varying degrees of commitment exist between cohabiting couples, options for treatment are discussed.

Sexual Involvement
over the Life Course

6

Yvonne Blue, a student at the University of Chicago, lived a sheltered life.

She had only started to date the previous year and was still living in her parents' home. At age 19, Yvonne was not ready for sexual intercourse but she did enjoy "necking" and "petting." In her diary, she described her sexual interactions with her boyfriend Peter, using euphemisms for various types of sexual behavior (e.g., getting "worked up" and only "going so far") rather than giving explicit descriptions of her behavior. Most of her sexual encounters involved the consumption of alcoholic beverages, even though it was the Prohibition Era and the encounters took place in Peter's car. Yvonne worried about protecting her reputation and felt compelled to tell her diary that she was "still a good girl." After one date she wrote, "I was frightfully ashamed of myself . . . for letting him go so far, but I enjoyed myself." Yvonne was still a virgin at age 20, though she came close to having intercourse on a date with an older man she met at a party. Yvonne was "coming of age" during America's first great sexual revolution of the 1920s.

1 What is the relationship between sexual frequency and relationship satisfaction?

2 To what extent is sexual orientation influenced by biological factors?

3 Why do individuals continue to engage in sexual risk-taking behaviors?

4 In what ways does the frequency of sexual intercourse change over the life cycle and how is this change related to physical health?

5 To what extent does the double standard of sexual behavior still exist in western cultures today?

Laura Ramirez, a high school sophomore (class of 1971), lived with her mother, step-father, and older sister in a middle-class neighborhood in Melbourne, Florida.

Laura was a good student who, in spite of the era, was not a hippie, a rebel, or an anti-war activist. She attended Sunday school regularly and loved Richard Nixon (who was president at the time). Despite her mainstream conservative attitudes, Laura did not place a high value on virginity. She was, in fact, quite sexually adventurous. In her diary she graphically described her ongoing sexual relationships with her boyfriend Mike. One entry included the following: "He did what I guess you could call finger coitus for about twenty-five minutes and neither of us said anything during the whole time. It was fantastic and I enjoyed it immensely." After school one day in 1970, Laura and Mike pledged to "commit coitus" in the summer of 1975. But they broke up before they had a chance to honor their pledge.

Deborah Perry was 14 in 1982, just before the nation became aware of AIDS.

Even before she had her first date, Deborah considered the possibility of intercourse, which was a major topic of conversation among her friends. In the summer after her freshman year in high school, Deborah told her diary that she had spent three hours making love with a boy named Pete, although their attempts to have intercourse failed and she was still a virgin. Within a month, Deborah went to her mother's gynecologist to get fitted for a diaphragm and eagerly awaited her chance to try it out with Pete. "I can't wait! Gotta get some mileage on my diagrahm [sic]." But because they couldn't find enough time to be alone together, Deborah and Pete never consummated their relationship. Six months later, Deborah met another boy she liked a lot. She started to wear her diaphragm continuously so that she would be ready to have sex whenever the opportunity arose. By the time she was 16, Deborah had had sexual encounters with several different partners.

Source: Brumberg, Joan Jacobs, *The Body Project.* 1997, pp. 154–155, 166–167, 183–184. Copyright 1997 by Joan Jacobs Brumberg. Reprinted by permission of Random House.

The three stories that open this chapter vividly illustrate the profound changes in sexual scripts that have occurred in western societies over the course of the past 100 years. Yvonne Blue came of age during America's first sexual revolution in the 1920s. Laura Ramirez became sexually active during the second sexual revolution in the late 1960s. And Deborah Perry began to experiment with her sexuality just as AIDS was being "discovered" in the medical community. All three of these women enjoyed sexual interactions, taking an active role in initiating sexual behavior with male partners. But sexual enjoyment was often associated with guilt and shame for women of the earlier periods (as revealed in Yvonne's diary.) As the twentieth century wore on, the age at first intercourse declined. Yvonne was still a virgin at age 20, whereas Laura was approximately 16 and Deborah 14 when they had sexual intercourse for the first time. Young women became more open about sexual issues (as reflected in the increasingly explicit language used to describe encounters) and apparently more knowledgeable about contraception. Then as now, cars and the consumption of alcohol played an important role in sexual encounters.

In this chapter, we take a close look at the history of the sexual revolution in America, focusing on the ways in which young women's sexual attitudes and behavior have changed to become more similar to men's. Using information provided from detailed analyses of diaries as well as national surveys, we examine changes in the sexual behavior of American teens and young, unmarried adults. We consider the role that sexuality plays in marriage and other long-term relationships, particularly its association with the quality of such relationships. We look at results of studies that describe changes in the frequency of sexual intercourse over time, particularly in later life, and try to understand the reasons—physical, emotional, and relational—for these changes. We also examine the new treatments that are being developed to help men and women who have impaired sexual functioning.

We look at results of scientific research that address the issue of marital infidelity, to get an idea of how common it is for women and men to engage in sexual relations with someone other than their spouse or partner and to understand Americans' attitudes toward infidelity. Finally, we consider homosexuality, focusing on the incidence of individuals whose sexual orientation is primarily toward others of the same gender. It is important to note here that homosexual individuals and couples should not be reduced to the sexual dimension alone. Throughout this text we discuss various characteristics and dynamics of same-sex couples.

The Sexual Revolution

What do we mean when we say there has been a **sexual revolution?** There are several major societal changes that have occurred that, taken together, constitute the sexual revolution. First, sexuality has been increasingly disassociated from marriage and childbearing. Unmarried persons are sexually active and many sexually active—married or unmarried—persons attempt to avoid pregnancy. Sexuality is often engaged in for pleasure rather than for procreation. Second, childbearing is increasingly disassociated from marriage. The fertility rate among married couples has been declining while the rate among unmarried persons has been increasing. Third, the average age at first sexual experience dropped for a generation or two, but has remained stable over the past two decades. Fourth, the average number of sexual partners over the lifetime appears to be increasing. Fifth, women's sexual behavior is becoming more similar to men's. There is still a gender gap in terms of the average age at first sexual intercourse, the number of partners, and in the social significance assigned to sexual activity, but the gap seems to be decreasing somewhat. Finally, there is considerably more openness about sexual matters today.

An Historical Perspective on the Sexual Revolution

Although most of us tend to think of the 1960s as the decade of the sexual revolution, the changes that are associated with this revolution started long before and have continued to the present. In fact, sexual historians have identified significant events in every decade of the twentieth century that have contributed to the sexual revolution in one way or another.

1900 to 1920.   The first two decades of the twentieth century marked the transition away from the sexual conservatism of the Victorian age. During the earlier period, virginity for young women was a moral issue. The **hymen** (the thin mucous membrane at the juncture of the **vulva** and the **vagina**) was revered as an anatomical marker of sexual purity. A bride without an intact hymen was viewed as "damaged goods." Thus, doctors were called on to prove or disprove a woman's virginity. Even though doctors realized that the hymen was not a reliable indicator of virginity they got involved in diagnosing chastity anyway. They were careful not to rupture or stretch the hymen when doing examinations. In fact, they promoted rectal examinations rather than vaginal examinations. They didn't want to shock girls' sensibilities or to focus their thoughts on their genitals. When anesthesia became available in 1870, it was used to knock out women so they wouldn't have to endure the embarrassment of pelvic examinations (Brumberg, 1997).

1920 to 1929.   The 1920s have been identified as the decade of the first sexual revolution in the United States because of the marked changes in the social and sexual behavior of American women. The decade began with the passage of the nineteenth amendment to the U.S. Constitution that gave American women the right to vote. This was the era of the flapper, when young women shocked society by wearing short skirts, *bobbing* their hair (that is, cutting it short), smoking cigarettes, and drinking alcohol. Cheek-to-cheek dancing became popular—giving unmarried persons an unaccustomed amount of body contact—and dating appeared as a new stage in courtship and mate selection. It was also during this decade that some European physicians began to advocate foreplay and sexual variety—including oral sex—for married couples.

Girls began to talk more openly about their bodies and their sexuality. This new openness reduced their reluctance to go to gynecologists for examinations and treatment. Virginity had lost some of its moral importance. Petting became a common part of dating. In the 1920s and 1930s, a new view of marriage emerged in which sexual pleasure was an important component. Physicians began to perform **hymenotomies,** a procedure in which the hymens of virginal women were enlarged to make sexual intercourse less painful for them. Before doctors would perform these operations, however, they asked the unmarried woman's future husband for permission (Brumberg, 1997).

It was also during this time period that Sigmund Freud presented a theory of personality development that gave sexuality a central place. The first nude calendar and the first commercially produced pornographic film were also distributed. Margaret Sanger opened the first birth control clinic in the United States, and Dr. Paul Erlich discovered a treatment for syphilis.

1930 to 1939.   The Great Depression dominated the decade of the 1930s with its high level of unemployment. Married couples relied on careful use of condoms and diaphragms to prevent additional pregnancies, and the U.S. birth rate dropped dramatically. The first college course on human sexuality to be taught in the United States was offered by Alfred Kinsey at Indiana University.

The first commercially produced tampons were introduced in 1936. They were well received by American women because they offered greater freedom of move-

ContentSELECT

Sexual
Revolution

ment. However, tampons were considered a threat to virginity and parents often needed medical assurance that tampon use wasn't dangerous or immoral before they would allow their daughters to use them. Using tampons allowed and/or required girls and women to become more familiar with their genitals and may have made it emotionally easier for them to have intercourse as well as internal pelvic examinations. Even into the 1960s, though, some unease about the use of tampons remained (Brumberg, 1997).

1940 to 1950. The years between 1941 and 1945 were consumed by World War II. As millions of American men went to fight the war in Europe and the Pacific, women entered the labor force to take on the jobs men had left behind. Because women's labor was so essential to the war economy—particularly in the ammunition factories—the government launched a major propaganda campaign to convince the public that it was acceptable—even desirable—for wives and mothers to work outside their homes. Even though these women were encouraged to give up their jobs at the end of the war to men who were returning from fighting, the participation of married women in the labor force had a profound effect on gender roles that reemerged later in the century.

From the end of the war in 1945 to the end of the decade and beyond, Americans directed their energies at resuming *normal* family life that had been forced aside during the 1930s by the Great Depression and postponed by World War II. Marriage and fertility rates began an upward climb, producing the infamous *baby boom,* drawing women's energies into childcare and homemaking. Suburbs bloomed around major cities, and factories that were once occupied by war production produced durable goods for households (e.g., refrigerators, stoves, and washing machines) and so-called labor-saving devices took center stage in American homes. The film industry in Hollywood began to censor itself, resulting in such practices such as having married couples shown sleeping in separate beds.

1950 to 1959. Family togetherness continued to be the theme of the 1950s as the baby boom hit its peak. In spite of this, a number of significant events in the sexual revolution occurred. The first sex-change operation occurred in Denmark (in 1952). The first *Playboy* magazine appeared the next year. Elvis Presley appeared on the Ed Sullivan show (probably the most popular variety show of the era), but the camera could not film below his waist because his gyrating hips were considered too sexual to be seen by the viewers in the television audience. The Supreme Court ruled that certain sexually explicit materials (e.g., *Lady Chatterly's Lover* by D. H. Lawrence) could be distributed in the United States. The decade closed with the introduction of the bikini bathing suit.

1960 to 1969. The 1960s, with its social and political protest and experimentation with sex and drugs, marked the beginning of the second sexual revolution in the United States. The decade opened with the approval of the birth control pill by the Food and Drug Administration in 1960. This drug gave women unprecedented control over reproduction. However, it was only available to married women. *Hippies* (also referred to as the *counter-culture*) protested the war in Vietnam, urging young people to "make love, not war." Men grew their hair long and wore flowing beards; mini-skirts and love beads were popular with young women and "flower power" was in. In spite of these superficial changes, however, the age at first marriage was still quite young, and respectable middle-class folks did not live together without being married. Premarital pregnancies typically led to *shotgun* marriages.

1970 to 1979. Many of the beliefs and practices of the 1960s continued into the early 1970s. Premarital chastity was becoming the exception rather than the rule. Physicians began to adopt a nonjudgmental attitude and neutral language when dealing with sexually active unmarried women. Parents, too, became less controlling over their unmarried daughters' sexuality. There were few constraints on girls' sexual activity as long as they used contraceptives reliably. Sexual expression was considered a fundamental right for girls and women as well as boys and men. This shift in the stance of parents and physicians toward young girls' sexuality had negative as well as positive consequences, however. While it represented a lessening of repressive control over girls' bodies, it made them more accessible and vulnerable to sexual pressures. So in some ways, girls were both the beneficiaries and the victims of the sexual revolution (Brumberg, 1997).

Throughout the 1970s, there continued to be increased openness about sexuality. The U.S. Supreme Court ruled in 1971 that adults should not be prevented from obtaining sexually explicit materials. In 1973, the Court ruled in *Roe* v. *Wade* that states could not prohibit women from terminating their pregnancies during the first trimester. Courses in sexuality became common at American colleges and universities. Books that offered tips on how to improve one's sex life became best sellers, and X-rated movies became popular forms of entertainment. Public concern about sexually transmitted infections grew as herpes cases increased.

Public awareness of homosexuality also continued to increase over the decade. In 1969, gay men fought against police harassment at the Stonewall Bar in New York City. Five years later, members of the American Psychological Association and the American Psychiatric Association voted to no longer regard homosexuality as a psychological disorder. By the end of the decade, however, an organization called Save Our Children convinced voters in Dade County, Florida, to repeal existing laws that safeguarded the civil rights of homosexuals.

1980 to 1989.   The beginning of this conservative backlash gained momentum in the 1980s. This was a decade of increased political and religious conservatism and also the time when AIDS was discovered. The first AIDS cases were diagnosed in 1980. Public support for sex education in the schools increased in response to concerns about AIDS and the high teen pregnancy rate. Open discussion about homosexual activity, including anal sex, and the proper use of condoms became commonplace. In mid decade, the U.S. Supreme Court declared that Georgia could outlaw homosexual sodomy. By the decade's end, the Court had given individual states the right to restrict access to abortion somewhat. However, in 1989, the New York Supreme Court ruled that the traditional legal definition of *family* should be expanded to include committed homosexual couples.

1990 to Present.   During the 1990s, sex became a major topic of discussion in the mass media. In 1991, a nationally televised congressional hearing involving Clarence Thomas (a nominee and eventual appointee to the U.S. Supreme Court) and Anita Hill (a law professor who had worked with Thomas at the Equal Employment Opportunity Commission), who had accused him of sexual harassment, brought a discussion of sexual harassment in the workplace into the public consciousness, along with a discussion of the genitalia of male stars in pornographic films (e.g., Long Dong Silver). Later in the decade, media coverage of the sexual activities between then-President Clinton and Monica Lewinsky, brought discussions about oral sex into everyday conversations. When Viagra, a drug

▲ *Since the 1960s, sexual activity among adolescents has increased greatly.*

for erectile dysfunction (another term for male impotence) was introduced, numerous anecdotes circulated about elderly men going crazy with newfound sexual vigor after taking the drug.

In the 1990s an explosion of more explicit sexuality was seen on television. Prime-time shows on the major networks featured partial nudity (e.g., *NYPD Blue*) as well as the first title character who was a lesbian (*Ellen*). The Internet became a primary avenue for the distribution of pornographic material, exposing children and teens to inappropriate material, which led to the passage of the Child Online Protection Act (in 1998). In spite of the increased emphasis on sexuality in the media, the proportion of high school students who had had sex declined over the decade (Leland, 1998).

Is the Sexual Revolution Over?

We can look at the findings of several surveys of sexual behavior in the 1990s to address this question. In 1993, the Alan Guttmacher Institute surveyed 3,321 American men in their twenties and thirties. Some journalists regarded the findings of this study as quite dull. For instance, the average (median) number of sexual partners these men had had over their sexual lifetimes up to that point was 7.3. This means that half of the 3,321 men had seven or fewer sexual partners and the other half had had eight or more. One-quarter of the men had had three or fewer partners; but an equal number had had twenty or more. The average age at which white men had lost their virginity was 17.2, while the age for African American men was somewhat lower—15. And most of the men reported having sex about once per week.

In the next section of the chapter, we take a closer look at the changing association between sexual behavior and marriage.

The Changing Association between Sex and Marriage

*I*n American society, sex has traditionally been associated with marriage. The cultural ideal has been to refrain from sexual intercourse until marriage, especially for women. The evidence indicates that this ideal is not widely practiced in the United States today. In fact, historical data show that from the earliest days of American history premarital chastity has been far from universal.

The Puritan period of American history is noted for its religious strictness and the close community scrutiny of all citizens' personal lives. Yet even during that period many couples had sex before marriage. Approximately one-third of Puritan brides confessed to their ministers that they had had sex before marriage. Most were forced to confess because they were already pregnant and wished to have their babies baptized. Other brides, who might have had sexual intercourse, but were not pregnant, may not have felt as compelled to confess.

Other historical evidence also shows that premarital sexual intercourse occurred at significant levels early in American history (Smith, 1978). Church records of marriages and baptisms from the eighteenth and nineteenth centuries reveal that many first-born children were probably conceived before marriage. The highest percentages of premarital conceptions came in the late 1700s, when slightly over one-third of the births were most likely conceived before marriage. Data suggest that in the seventeenth and eighteenth centuries in America about one in five first births were conceived before marriage (Smith, 1978; see also D'Emilio and Freedman, 1988, pp. 22–23).

Again, these figures only reflect premarital pregnancies, not premarital sexual intercourse. Some women who became pregnant while unmarried might have intentionally aborted their pregnancies, had spontaneous miscarriages, or had children without marrying. These cases would not be reflected in the births occurring within nine months of marriage. Other couples might have had sexual intercourse while unmarried but did not conceive a child. This could have been the result of sterility on the part of either the man or the woman, the use of some elementary form of birth control (such as withdrawal before ejaculation), or having intercourse at a time when conception was not possible. If all these considerations are taken into account, it is possible to estimate from these data that at least one-fourth, and perhaps as many as 40 percent, of young American women had sexual intercourse before they were married. The percentages for young men were probably higher, because they were generally given more sexual liberty.

Sexual Activity among Adolescents and Young Adults

A number of surveys of sexual behavior among adolescents and young adults have shown that premarital sexual intercourse, especially among young women, increased greatly over the twentieth century. The most rapid early increases occurred in the 1970s, but the rates peaked in the early 1990s and then started to decline slightly. By the time they reach age 20, more than two-thirds of women and three-quarters of men report having had sexual intercourse.

Adolescents and Sex

In the fall of 1997, the Kaiser Family Foundation, in conjunction with *YM*, a leading teen magazine, conducted a national study of 650 randomly selected American teens between the ages of 13 and 18. Just under one-third of the teens (31 percent) had already had sexual intercourse. Teens today, even those as young as 13 and 14, struggle with complex sexual situations, involving (peer) pressure, drinking and drug use, or relationships that are moving too fast, for which they are often unprepared. They also worry a lot about pregnancy, HIV/AIDS and other sexually transmitted infections (also referred to as STIs). More than one-third of all teens in the study (and close to one-half of those who had been in an intimate situation) said they had done something sexual, or *felt pressured* to do something sexual, that they were not ready to do. One in two had been in a situation when they *could* have had sexual intercourse with someone they liked but decided not to at the time. A majority of the teens who were sexually experienced reported that they did not use contraceptives every time they had sex. More than one-third had never talked with a sexual partner about pregnancy prevention or disease. And about one in five of those who did talk about pregnancy or STIs with a partner did so only *after* having sex (Kaiser Family Foundation, 1998).

In spite of the fact that sexuality was so prevalent in their social environment, most teens were quite supportive when their friends decided to wait to become sexually involved. Three-quarters considered it a "good thing to make a conscious decision to not have sex until some later time," and the same proportion said they knew someone who had made that decision (Kaiser Family Foundation, 1998). Common reasons teens give for waiting to have sex included fear of pregnancy and STIs; belief that sexuality should be reserved for marriage; and a desire to have sex for the first time with someone they loved (Sprecher and Regan, 1996). Some young men were also hesitant to become sexually involved because they felt sexually inadequate.

Factors Associated with Sexual Experience among Adolescents.   *Race* is one of the most important factors associated with the beginning of sexual activity. African

American adolescents, especially males, start having sex much earlier than whites and Hispanics. They are three times more likely than white and Hispanic males to have sex before age 15. African American females also begin to have sex earlier than white and Hispanic females, but the differences are much less than for males.

African Americans also accumulate a greater number of sexual partners over their lifetimes, on average, including those who are casual partners (that is, outside the context of an ongoing relationship). These patterns of sexual behavior put African Americans at greater risk of contracting AIDS and other STIs (Smith, 1998; Quadagno et al., 1998).

Coming from lower socioeconomic status is also related to starting sex early (Furstenberg et al., 1987; Kahn et al., 1988), as is dropping out of high school (Mott and Haurin, 1988). Adolescents who have higher academic performance and educational aspirations are less likely to have sexual intercourse early.

Teenagers who are more religious are also less likely to have sex. Those who attend religious services are less likely to become sexually active, to have casual sex, and to have multiple partners (Hogan, Sun, and Cornwell, 1998; Brewster et al., 1998).

First Sexual Intercourse. Although surveys of sexual behavior can tell us when, how many, and which adolescents have sex, they do not tell us much about how the young people themselves define and interpret the experience. What motivates them to have sex? What is the first sexual experience like for most adolescents? Research evidence consistently shows that at the time of first sexual intercourse, the *relationship* with one's partner is very different for young men and women. A national survey of adults conducted in the 1990s asked about the nature of the respondent's relationship with his or her first sex partner and found that 75 percent of women were married to or in love with their first sexual partner. Only 41 percent of the men said they were married to or in love with their first sexual partner (Laumann et al., 1994). This is consistent with studies of teenagers and college students, which have found that women are much more likely than men to say that their first sexual partners were persons with whom they had a serious or committed relationship.

▲ *Because of the danger of AIDS, condom use has increased in the United States, but some of the people at greatest risk still engage in unprotected sex.*

These differences in the relationships of young men and women with their first sexual partners are likely a product of the different meanings that sex has for adolescent males and females. Women are more likely to associate sex with feelings of love and affection for their partners. Young men, in contrast, are much more likely to focus on sex as a physical activity. For boys, the objective is often simply to experience sex. Sex for them is an achievement, and they may care very little about who their partner is.

When adult men recall their first sexual experience, they often use terms that show how important it was for their masculinity. In the words of one researcher: "They characterized the experience as an 'important accomplishment' a 'landmark achievement.' For them, it was a rite of passage, a crucial step on the road to manhood—a step in which they exulted" (Rubin, 1990, p. 43). For young men, then, the first sexual experience is usually a measure of achievement, but for young women it is more likely to be an expression of love.

in the*media*

Condom Commercials on Television

Until the early 1990s, no television network would air a paid condom commercial. Today, three of the six major networks allow condom companies to advertise on their airwaves, with some limitations on topic, tone, and time of day. Fox began accepting condom ads in 1991, CBS in 1998, and NBC in 1999. ABC, UPN, and The WB continue to prohibit paid condom ads. ABC airs ads for prescription birth control pills, and The WB says it would consider ads for the pill as well. Several cable companies have allowed condom advertising for years, and some broadcasters that restrict paid condom ads accept public service ads referencing condoms or safer sex.

Studies released by the Kaiser Family Foundation show that condom advertising, banned for many years on network television, is acceptable to most Americans today. Figure 6.1 highlights some of the findings from the studies.

The survey of 1,142 adults found that 71 percent of Americans favor allowing condom ads on TV, with 37 percent saying such ads should be allowed to air at any time, and 34 percent saying only at certain times, such as after 10 P.M. One in four adults (25 percent) say condom ads should not be allowed on TV at all. Americans aged 18 to 49 are significantly more likely than those 50 and older to support condom advertising. Among adults under age 50, 82 percent say condom ads should be allowed, compared with 60 percent of those 50 and older. According to the survey, more people oppose beer advertising on TV (34 percent) than condom advertising (25 percent).

A "dial test" conducted by the Foundation—similar to those used by networks to try out new TV shows—finds that most viewers do not object to seeing a condom ad in regular TV pro-

gramming. Using a scale of 0 (very negative reaction) to 100 (very positive), viewers gave an ad for Trojan condoms an average score of 52, similar to other ads viewed in the experiment: Allegra (allergy drug), 50; Victoria's secret, 51; Toyota Camry, 52; Juno (Internet service), 52; Sears, 51; and Honda Civic, 55. This research also indicates that condom ads have no negative impact on viewers' assessments of the show or network on which they air, or of the products advertised after a condom ad.

Sources: Changing Standards: Condom Advertising on American Television (Publication 3139); *Condom Ads on Television: Unwrapping the Controversy* (Publication 3125); and *A Survey Snapshot: Condom Advertising on Television* (Publication 3127), Henry J. Kaiser Family Foundation, www.kff.org. Released in June 2001.

Although young men might be pleased by the accomplishment of their first sexual experience, they do not necessarily enjoy it. The overwhelming majority of both sexes look back on their first sexual intercourse as a neutral or negative experience. The most common words used to describe the experience were "'overrated,' 'disappointing,' 'a waste,' 'awful,' 'boring,' 'stupid,' 'empty,' 'ridiculous,' 'awkward,' 'miserable,' [and] 'unmemorable'" (Rubin, 1990, p. 43).

Once again, however, the disappointments that the young men may have had with the actual experience were overshadowed by their "exhilaration of achievement" (Rubin, 1990, p. 44). The young women had more complicated reactions, often tied to ambivalence about what was acceptable sexual behavior for them. It is noteworthy that women who had the most positive reactions to their first sexual experience were the ones who had sex with men they had known for a long time and cared deeply about.

Figure 6.1 **Attitudes toward Condom Advertising on Television**

Percent of adults who say TV advertising should not be allowed for . . .

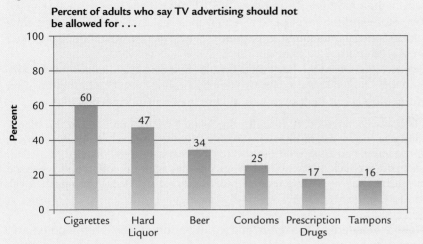

Percent of adults who say TV advertising for condoms should not be allowed, by age.

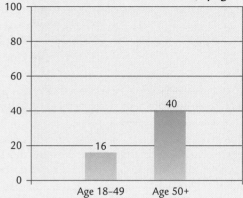

Survey Question:

Now I'm going to name some different products and ask whether you think there should be any restrictions on television advertising for each product. First, what about. . .? Should advertising for this product be allowed on TV at any time of day, OR should the ads be restricted to certain times, like after 10 o'clock at night, OR should TV advertising for this product not be allowed at all?

	Allowed at Any Time	Allowed but Restricted to Certain Times	Total Allowed	Not Allowed at All	DK/Ref[*]
a. Beer	23	41	64	34	2
b. Hard Liquor	15	36	51	47	2
c. Cigarettes	14	24	38	60	2
d. Condoms	37	34	71	25	3
e. Prescription Drugs	57	20	77	17	5
f. Personal Products such as Tampons	54	26	80	16	4

Percent of adults who say TV advertising for condoms should be . . .

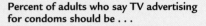
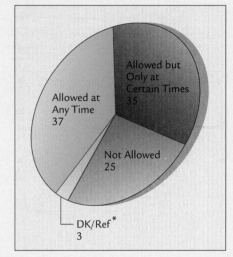

[*] DK/Ref = Don't know/Refused to answer

(*Source:* Henry J. Kaiser Family Foundation, 2001.)

Stories about first sexual intercourse experiences have two different themes: The first, which is reported by a large number of young women, emphasizes how the experience was one of physical pain, discomfort, or general unpleasantness; the second describes the pleasure and excitement.

Not only do many young women describe their first sexual experience negatively, but often they are also unsure about what actually happened. They tell of not knowing what was going to happen until it was over.

Many young women describe to their friends the fear and pain they experienced when they first had sexual intercourse. But some recount the experience with a kind of bravado to show their "superiority over other girls who don't have what it takes to be women" (Thompson, 1990). One girl bragged, "I really didn't feel nothing special. Most girls say, 'Oh, God, it really hurt,' and like that. It was nothing to me" (Thompson, 1990, p. 348).

But another set of young women describe their first sexual experience positively, which may stem from the positive way in which they learned about sex, especially from their mothers (Thompson, 1990). Unlike the young women who tell the negative stories, these girls have a sexual memory that goes back to a time before their first sexual intercourse experience. They describe how they had looked forward to sex, often for a long time.

Adolescent women who had pleasurable first-sex experiences frequently describe how they talked openly with their mothers about sex. Their mothers often shared information about their own sexual lives, in a natural and positive way:

> Mom had always talked very casually about sex. I mean, I have sat at the dinner table and discussed with mom what contraceptive she used when she was, uh uh, you know, having an affair with my dad for the year before she married him. And, uhm, actually we have discussed what sex was like with my father and what she did in—in the way of fooling around before she got married. (Thompson, 1990, p. 354)

The Double Standard. Teenagers and young adults today, both women and men, undoubtedly have greater freedom and fewer constraints in their sexual lives than the same age groups did only a few decades ago. But there is still the question of whether young women (or women in general) have the same freedom as men. Not so many years ago, the **double standard** of sexual behavior was nearly universally accepted: one set of rules for women and another, less restrictive set, for men. The traditional double standard would have included the following:

- Young men may have sexual intercourse before marriage; young women should not.
- Young men may have sexual intercourse with women even when there is no emotional feeling or commitment; young women should only have sexual intercourse when they are in love, or are in a committed relationship.
- Young men may have multiple sexual partners; young women should not.

Because of the undeniable liberalization of U.S. sexual norms over the last several decades, some of these traditional standards are not as rigidly upheld as they once were. But the double standard has not disappeared; researchers continue to uncover evidence that it is still with us (Milhausen and Herold, 1999).

The persistence of the double standard can be found in the different labels applied to men and women who are especially sexually active. Men are given a great latitude in their sexual behavior before they are criticized. There are few negative expressions applied to sexually active men; the most common label is *womanizer*, along with the statement that a man "can't keep it in his pants," neither of which has the same dampening effect on men's behavior that the labels given to sexually active women can have. Sexually active men are more likely to be commended for their actions and labeled as studs, players, lovers, or bounders. Sexually active women, on the other hand, are subjected to over two dozen negative labels, including slut, whore, tramp, ho, pig, skank, and sleaze (Tanenbaum, 2000).

One of the primary ways in which girls' sexual behavior is controlled is by their peers, who stigmatize and ostracize them. Teens may be having sex, but they often look down on others, especially girls, who are sexually active. Despite the sexual revolution, despite three decades of feminism, despite the pill, and despite legalized abortion, teenage girls today continue to be defined by their sexuality. The sexual double standard—and the division between *good* girls and sluts—is alive and well. Some of the rules have changed, but the playing field is startlingly similar to that of the 1950s (Tanenbaum, 2000, p. 4). For instance, in 1998, two high school girls in Kentucky were denied membership in the National Honor Society

The double standard of sexual behavior still persists today and allows men to judge the behavior of women—often negatively.

because they were pregnant, even though boys who engaged in premarital sex faced no such exclusion (Tanenbaum, 2000, p. 4).

Even today, a common way to damage a woman's credibility is to call her a slut. Teenage girls who are labeled in this way are caught between the conflicting pressures to have sex and to maintain a good reputation. Boys and girls are encouraged to have sex by their friends, the magazines they read, and the lyrics of their favorite songs and music videos, but only boys can "get away with it." Girls have been told they can and should do anything boys do. But they discover that sexual equality has not arrived. Certain things—sex, in particular—continue to be the privilege of men alone (Tanenbaum, 2000).

A girl may be called a slut for any number of reasons, including not fitting in in some way, developing breasts earlier than her friends, being a rape victim, and doing something that offends her friends. Many of the girls who are called sluts have no more sexual experience than their peers; some have no sexual experience at all. One type of girl is picked on because she appears to flaunt a casual attitude toward sexuality—she is either sexually active or is perceived to be. Some girls who are not at all sexually active are presumed to be because of their bodily development. A girl with well-developed breasts, for instance, becomes sexualized because she possesses a constant physical reminder of her sexual potential. Leora Tanenbaum, a journalist who interviewed numerous girls and women who had been labeled sluts, recounts the story of 18-year-old Paula, from Wisconsin, who started to menstruate in the fifth grade and was wearing a size 36C bra by the seventh grade. She was insulted daily by her classmates. In eighth grade, she was being called a hooker and a slut, even though she was still a virgin. Julie, a girl who was raped after passing out at a party, was labeled a slut because no one believed that she had been forced to have sex against her will. Typically, girls who are labeled sluts fail to conform to a very narrow range of feminine behavior.

The double standard, to the extent that it prevails, is a way that men have of controlling the sexual lives of women. Historically, in the United States, and in many other societies, the double standard has been enforced by men (often broth-

Protect Your Virginity or Die

While premarital sex is common in the United States, in other parts of the world it is not only rare but extremely dangerous. In Jordan in 1993, a 16-year-old girl who had been raped by her older brother was killed by her family because they believed she had seduced him into sleeping with her. In Afghanistan, where, at times, women have been required to remain covered from head to toe in shrouds that are called *burqas*, a federal bureau responsible for preserving virtue and preventing vice beat women for wearing white socks or plastic sandals with no socks because this type of attire is believed to provoke impure thoughts among Afghani men. In Turkey, girls are often forced to undergo virginity examinations. An unmarried woman who is discovered to be a nonvirgin risks being beaten or killed. Thus, girls often attempt suicide to avoid these virginity examinations. In 1998, five girls ate rat poison in their efforts to escape the virginity tests. Most of the girls survived the rat poison but were forced to undergo the virginity examinations while recovering in their hospital beds. Even the girl who succeeded in killing herself was examined posthumously, upon her father's request (Golden, 1998; Edut, 1998; Burns, 1997; Couturier, 1998).

In many Arab cultures a woman's virginity is closely monitored because it is viewed as the key to her family's honor. The need to guard that honor is so great that it has led to the brutal practice of *honor killings* across the Middle East and in Pakistan. Honor killings—the execution of women *suspected* of sexual improprieties—are often carried out by close family members in order to restore the honor tarnished by inappropriate behavior, which can consist of anything from being raped to allegedly committing adultery or even having just minimal contact with unrelated men. A woman's guilt is always assumed and her punishment carried out on the basis of suspicion alone. Official statistics show that twenty-five women, the majority of whom are teenagers, are killed in Jordan each year as a result of honor crimes. Most of these girls and women are buried in unmarked graves. Honor killings accounted for one-third of the murders of women committed in Jordan in 1999.

A group of male and female activists have launched a nationwide campaign in Jordan to stop crimes of honor. They have been supported by numerous writers and columnists. A primary target of the reform is the Jordanian penal code. Two articles of the code have been targeted. Article 340 stipulates that "he who discovers his wife or one of his female relatives committing adultery (with a man) and kills, wounds, or injures one or both of them, is exempted from any penalty." Article 98 states that "He who commits a crime in a fit of fury caused by an unlawful and dangerous act on the part of the victim benefits from a reduction in penalty." While the royal family of Jordan has supported these reforms, influential Bedouin tribesmen insist that the current law is necessary to prevent decadence and fornication. "Women adulterers cause a great threat to our society because they are the main reason that such acts take place. If men do not find women with whom to commit adultery, then they will become good on their own," argued Deputy Mohammad Kharabsheh, a strong opponent of efforts to revise Jordan's penal code (Halaby, 2000). Contrary to popular assumption, honor killings are not mandated by Islam, which is very strict about killing. The only time murder is allowed as a justifiable punishment for adultery is when one spouse is unfaithful and there are four eyewitnesses to the act.

One specific case involved 62-year-old Mohammad Abdul Karim, who killed his 55-year-old wife in 1999 after 14 years of marriage. He claimed that as he was approaching his house he saw a strange man walking out of the home and when he entered, he found his wife wearing only a bra. When he asked her to identify the man, she refused, saying it was none of his business. This prompted him to shoot her once in the back, killing her instantly. Karim received only a one-year sentence for his crime. The court justified the light sentence because the victim had allegedly committed an act that tarnished her husband's honor, causing him to become temporarily insane.

Source: Rana Husseini, ummahnews.com, April 27, 2001.

ers, fathers, and uncles) to control women family members. In some Islamic societies, as just one example, male family members may beat or even kill a woman of their family who has brought dishonor on the reputation of the family through some real or alleged sexual indiscretion.

In most instances, the double standard of sexual behavior is a system that works to the advantage of men and the disadvantage of women. It is men who evaluate and judge whether a woman is acceptable as a girlfriend, or as a wife. Furthermore, the double standard goes beyond the social world of dating partners and mate selection. The courts often still declare women unfit to have custody of their children, simply because of their sexual behavior. Courts rarely, if ever, declare a father unfit as a parent because he is having sex with a woman (or women).

The Importance of Sex in Marriage

Sexual activity in marriage not only has obvious implications for fertility, it also has an impact on the quality of the marital relationship. Yet until recently, sexuality within the context of marriage has not received much attention from social scientists (Christopher and Sprecher, 2000).

Two people who are married for twenty-five or thirty years will probably have sexual intercourse more than 3,000 times if their weekly average is close to the averages reported by American couples. In light of this statistic alone, it is safe to say that sex is an important part of married life. Some people would say that sex is *the* most important aspect of marriage. For particular married couples that might be true, because for some people sex can be the cornerstone of their marriage. At the opposite extreme, there are couples for whom sex is inconsequential. Most couples fall somewhere in between.

Frequency of Sexual Intercourse in Marriage

Adults have sexual intercourse sixty-one times each year, or about once each week, on average (Smith, 1998). The frequency of sexual intercourse varies with age, however. Those aged 18 to 29 have sexual intercourse an average of eighty-three times per year; the frequency drops after age 29. Adults in their forties report having sex sixty-four times per year; by age 70 and older, the frequency drops to just under ten times per year. Sexual frequency also varies by marital status. Married couples engage in sexual intercourse more often, but the decline with age is even more pronounced. Married couples under age 30 have sexual intercourse 112 times per year, on average, while those aged 70 and over have sex just ten times over the same period (Smith, 1998). Table 6.1 summarizes these statistics.

The most common explanation for the decline in sexual activity over time is that it reflects biological changes that come with age (Call, Sprecher, and Schwartz, 1995; Christopher and Sprecher, 2000). There is no doubt that some declines in physical ability and sexual interest may accompany the aging process and, of course, physical illness and disability are associated with less sexual activity. However, aging does not eliminate sexual desires or sexual activity.

A second explanation for the decline in sexual activity among couples is **habituation**—which means that couples become accustomed to each other and their sexual activity loses some of its early excitement. Support for the habituation explanation comes from the fact that after the honeymoon year there is a precipitous decline in sex followed by a steady decline thereafter (Call, Sprecher, and Schwartz, 1995, p. 649).

TABLE 6.1

Frequency of Sexual Intercourse by Age and Marital Status: Average Number of Events per Year

Age	Total	Married	Unmarried
18–29	82.6	111.6	69.1
30–39	78.6	85.7	65.6
40–49	63.6	69.2	49.8
50–59	47.4	53.8	31.2
60–69	27.4	32.5	15.7
70+	9.8	16.2	2.6
Average (across ages)	61.0		

Source: Adapted from Smith, Tom (1998). American Sexual Behavior: Trends, Socio-Demographic Differences, and Risk Behavior. University of Chicago: National Opinion Research Center, *GSS Topical Report* no. 25, December 1998. Table 10, pp. 55, 57. Reprinted by permission.

Sexual Satisfaction

Most studies of sexuality in marriage have found that couples are very satisfied with their sexual relationships (Christopher and Sprecher, 2000). When asked how they feel after having sex with their spouses, most individuals say they feel loved, excited, or even thrilled. Only a small proportion of married couples report any negative feelings about their sexual relationship. In fact, of all sexually active individuals, those who are married and faithful to their spouses have the highest levels of sexual satisfaction. And although the frequency of sexual intercourse declines over time, little evidence exists that sexual satisfaction declines over the course of marriage (Christopher and Sprecher, 2000).

How important is the frequency of sexual intercourse in determining the overall quality of marriage? Couples who have sex more often tend to be more satisfied with their marriages overall. But frequency alone is not the most important factor. Couples who are satisfied with the sexual dimension of their relationship have even greater levels of marital satisfaction. It is difficult to determine which is the causal factor. Do the more happily married couples have sex more often? Or, does frequent sex make couples happier? These factors are difficult to untangle (Christopher and Sprecher, 2000).

When couples are dissatisfied with their marriage, they have sex less often. Possibly a decline in sex makes the marriage unsatisfactory, but researchers have usually seen the relationship working in the opposite direction. "Other problems come into the bedroom and make it less likely that the couple will want to have sex together" (Blumstein and Schwartz, 1983, p. 201). In one study about one-fourth of the couples acknowledged that trouble in some other part of their marriage led to a decrease in sexual interest (Rubin, 1990). Sometimes partners punish each other by withholding sex, either for limited periods of time or permanently. A study of blue-collar men revealed a number of couples who had not had sex for years. One man, a mechanic, who quarreled frequently with his wife and had not had sex with her in four years,

▲ *Many married couples have so many everyday responsibilities that their sexual lives are diminished.*

HEADline Viagra: Miracle Cure for Impotence?

*I*n December 1994, Lorne had just turned 40 and life was good. He was married and had two young children, a house near Vancouver, and a job he enjoyed. Then disaster struck: As he changed a tire on his car along the road, another car hit him. Though Lorne could walk and was able to go back to work after a period of recuperation, the accident damaged his spinal nerves and left him with enduring problems. He experienced numbness in some parts of his body and distressing limits on his sex life due to difficulties having and maintaining erections. Doctors suggested remedies involving penile pumps and injections, but Lorne was not interested in trying them. Then, he had the opportunity to take part in clinical trials for a then unknown drug called Viagra that was designed to deal with problems like his. In December 1996, Lorne began taking the sky-blue tablet whenever he and his wife wanted to have sex. Once again, his life was transformed. "Sex is as good as it used to be—maybe even a little better," he says. "This medication is just fantastic" (MacLeans, 1998).

Viagra was developed when researchers who were testing a drug for angina (that is, chest pain) found that it caused erections in men. Now, it seems destined to replace existing treatments that, though effective, cause many men a lot of pain and discomfort. The most commonly used method requires a man who expects to have sex to use a needle to inject a drug that produces an erection into the side of his penis. Another involves attaching a vacuum pump to the penis to draw blood into it, creating an erection. Rubber bands are then placed around the base of the penis to keep it erect. Some older treatment methods could leave men with erections that lasted for hours if sex didn't occur. But Viagra only becomes effective when a man is sexually aroused. Some men report that the drug can remain effective for up to twenty-four hours, which means that if they begin to think about sexual activities throughout the day they may feel a physical response (MacLean's, 1998).

For some older men, sexual problems may respond as well to more traditional marital counseling methods than they do to Viagra. In one experimental study that involved the use of Viagra and traditional sex therapy, two-thirds of couples who received "talk" therapy without Viagra were able to resume satisfactory sexual relations after eight weeks. These couples were taught how to talk to their partners about their sexual needs and desires. This therapeutic approach recognized that aging men have sexual needs that are different from those they had in earlier life. They need more emotional connection and more caressing (Russo, 2001).

Since Viagra hit the market in 1998, many insurance companies have been trying to decide whether they should pay to cover the costs of using it to treat erectile dysfunction. While Viagra has been very effective in treating erectile dysfunction (70 to 80 percent of the impotent men who have taken it report that they got very good results) it is very expensive, running more than $10 per pill. In spite of this, physicians are writing 120,000 prescriptions for the drug every week. Insurance companies are caught in a bind. To limit their costs, health plans usually cover only medical necessities and reject treatments that are seen as experimental or purely cosmetic. Erectile dysfunction, which can impair the quality of a man's life, is regarded as a medical disorder. Many other treatments for impotence are even more expensive than Viagra.

The question, then, is whether health care plans must guarantee their subscribers sexual pleasure. How much sexual pleasure is enough? Some large health care providers have decided to limit their coverage of Viagra to six pills per month, based on the results of studies of the average sexual frequency of married couples.

said, "I honestly don't give a s___ any more [about the marriage]. My wife won't give me sex anymore" (Halle, 1984, p. 66).

But lower marital satisfaction and marital problems cannot account for the more general decline in sex after marriage among all couples. Couples who continue to love each other and have good relationships nonetheless often acknowledge that they have less sex and the sex they do have lacks intensity and passion (Rubin, 1990). When asked why their sexual activity has declined, most couples

HEADline The Revival of Swinging

Lawyers, teachers, doctors, police officers, and business owners: Sounds like a group of professionals, right? Possibly. But it could also be a list of the members of the local swinging club. **Swinging,** a slang term referring to consensual and mutual extramarital sexual relations with persons other than one's spouse, used to be called *wife-swapping,* in the days before the second wave of feminism. There are now over 300 clubs affiliated with the North American Swing Club Association. Commonly thought to have disappeared along with the AIDS epidemic, currently thousands of unaffiliated clubs exist, according to investigative reporter Terry Gould (author of *The Lifestyle: A Look at the Erotic Rites of Swingers*). Annual conventions—with themes such as Swing Fling Campout, Swingtock, and XXX-Tasy—draw crowds from all over the nation. In fact, the amount of traveling related to swinging events has led to the development of at least one travel agency (Lifestyles Tours and Travel) that specializes in serving swingers.

The number of swingers in the United States and Canada is now estimated at 3 million. Those involved in "the lifestyle" feel that they are portrayed negatively in the media, much as gays were in the 1960s and 1970s. Couples become swingers for a number of reasons. Some do it purely for fun and excitement; others do it to become closer to their spouse; and of course others do it to fulfill some ultimate sexual fantasy.

Those on the *outside* often condemn swingers as immoral, uncivilized, and even revolting, but careful studies of the population do not support these stereotypes. Not only are swingers no more *deviant* than the average American, they do not consume more liquor or partake of more illegal drugs. Swingers defend their honor by emphasizing that they always follow "the rules," including always being completely honest with their spouses and other members of their clubs and not coercing anyone—including their spouses—to engage in unwanted sexual activities. Swinging is, in fact, regarded by participants as a "couple activity." In fact, at many of the conventions there are couple's sessions that give spouses a chance to evaluate their own relationships.

A police raid on a swingers club in Fort Lauderdale (in July 2000), brought the legal aspect of swinging into the public eye. Sexual activities that occur in private with mutually consenting adults are usually legal, but police raids continue to occur, exposing the identity of participants. Many swingers lead double lives in fear of what would happen to them professionally and personally if their activities were known. The raid on the Fort Lauderdale club forced many members to confess to their friends and families, though many (such as the principal of an elementary school and one mother of three) chose to keep their private lives out of the public domain.

Source: Written by Elise Lyne. From *The Lifestyle: A Look at the Erotic Rites of Swingers,* by Terry Gould (2000). Buffalo, NY: Firefly Books Ltd.

Related web sites: www.nasca.com, www.swingstream.com, and www.trapezeclub.com

point to problems of time and pressure. Couples who may have had passionate sex lives before marriage complain that their lives are now too rushed and the pressures too great for the same kind of sex.

Often sex gets lost in everyday activities—work, shopping, cooking, cleaning, paying the bills, and so on. Declines in sexual activity do not mean that couples have lost interest in sex or each other. As evidence of this, many couples report that when they take vacations their sexual activity increases dramatically (Rubin, 1990).

Many married couples accept the declines in their sexual lives as a normal and natural part of a maturing relationship, but at the same time they admit that they miss the excitement, the adventure, the passion that was often part of their sexual lives before marriage. Both husbands and wives will admit to an interviewer that they are bothered by the lowered passion and intensity of their sexual lives, but many say they find it difficult to speak openly about these concerns with their spouses (Rubin, 1990).

Sexuality in Middle and Later Life

In 1999, the American Association of Retired Persons (AARP) and *Modern Maturity* magazine commissioned a study of the sexual attitudes and practices of 1,384 Americans aged 45 and older. This was the first national study to examine sexuality from mid-life to old age (Jacoby, 1999). As we discuss later, today's generations of elders may experience their sexuality differently than the people who will become the next generation of elders.

The AARP/*Modern Maturity* study found that while sexual frequency does drop with age, it may be as much a function of a simple lack of partner than biological problems. Elderly women are much more likely than their male counterparts to be without a spouse. At age 75 and above, more than four out of five women, but only one out of five men, are widowed. The loss of a spouse means the end of sex for many elderly people. Seventy-five percent of the women aged 75 or older had gone at last six months without sexual intercourse or any type of sexual touching or caressing. Two-thirds of the women this age had also been deprived of sensual kisses and hugs (Jacoby, 1999).

More than 70 percent of the men and women in the survey who *had regular partners*, on the other hand, had intercourse at least once or twice a month. Only a small proportion of the middle-aged and elderly men, less than 6 percent, were trying the new treatments for impotency. The majority of those who had tried Viagra said it had increased their enjoyment of sex. While those aged 60 and older believed that better health would do more than anything else to enhance their sexual lives, few said that poor health impaired their sexuality. The majority of the study participants were extremely or very satisfied with their physical relationships.

There are a number of indicators that the next generation of elders (the baby boomers who are middle aged today) will experience their sexuality differently, and perhaps more actively, than today's elders (the parents of the baby boomers). Women aged 45 to 49 are much more likely than those aged 60 and over to approve of sex between unmarried partners, to engage in oral sex and masturbation, and perhaps more importantly, less likely to think that sex is only for younger people. Older men also have more conservative sexual views than younger men, but the gap is much smaller (Jacoby, 1999).

Sexual Infidelity in Marriage

There are probably more scientifically worthless facts on **infidelity** (e.g, extramarital relations) than on any other facet of human behavior. Popular magazines, advice columnists, and "pop" sexologists have contributed to the national discussion on this issue. Nonscientific reports (those that are based on nonrandom samples) typically find extremely high levels of extramarital sexual activity, claiming that the behavior has become much more common over time. But nationally representative scientific surveys of extramarital sexuality indicate that this type of sexual activity is much lower than commonly believed. The best estimates are that about 3 to 4 percent of currently married people have a sexual partner besides their spouse in any given year; and about 15 to 17 percent of people who have ever been married have had a sexual partner other than their spouse while married. Levels

ContentSELECT

Adultery

TABLE 6.2

Trends in Extramarital Sexual Relations by Gender*

Year	Total	Men	Women
1988	3.9	5.0	2.8
1989	3.6	5.8	1.7
1990	3.8	5.3	2.3
1991	4.4	5.4	3.4
1993	2.9	4.1	1.9
1994	2.4	3.6	1.3
1996	3.8	5.2	2.5
1998	3.6	4.9	2.5

*Percent having sexual relations with a person other than their spouse during the previous 12 months.

Source: Adapted from Smith, Tom (1998). American Sexual Behavior: Trends, Socio-Demographic Differences, and Risk Behavior. University of Chicago: National Opinion Research Center, *GSS Topical Report* no. 25, December 1998. Table 6, p. 44. Reprinted by permission.

of extramarital sexual activity have not changed since the late 1980s (Smith, 1998). Table 6.2 summarizes these statistics.

Extramarital affairs are more common among younger adults. This is largely a function of the fact that younger persons have been married a shorter period of time and may have difficulty adjusting from a premarital pattern of multiple sexual partners to monogamy expected in marriage. The rates of extramarital sexual relations are also higher among men. Husbands are twice as likely as wives to report that they've had sexual relationships with someone other than their spouses. Extramarital relations are also more common among blacks, those with lower incomes, those who attend church less frequently, those who are unhappy with their marriage, and those who have been separated or divorced previously (Smith, 1998).

Americans have never been very accepting of extramarital sexual relationships, but the rates of disapproval have actually increased over the past twenty years. Eighty-five percent of the respondents in a national opinion poll conducted by *Time* magazine and CNN in August 1998 said they believe adultery is *morally wrong*. In 1977, when a similar poll was conducted, only 76 percent said they believed adultery was wrong. Respondents in the 1998 poll were also asked if they believed infidelity is unavoidable in today's society. The overwhelming majority said they didn't think it was unavoidable, but they knew someone who had been adulterous. The last figure is somewhat surprising, in light of findings from a 1994 survey of Americans' sexual behavior that showed only 25 percent of husbands and 15 percent of wives admitted to having had extramarital relationships.

The *Time* magazine survey also asked Americans what behaviors they would regard as infidelity. Nearly all (95 percent) said they believed that when a married man had sex with a prostitute he was committing adultery. Slightly more than two-thirds thought that having a sexually explicit conversation on the telephone or Internet with someone other than one's spouse could be considered infidelity. Two other behaviors—holding hands with someone else or casually flirting with someone else—were considered unfaithful behaviors by less than half of the respondents (44 percent and 35 percent, respectively) (Handy, 1998).

Sex, Consent, and Desire

Many social historians believe that marital sex was very different in the United States one or two centuries ago, largely because of the male domination of most marriages and because men were believed to have different sexual natures. Men dominated sex, just as they dominated most other aspects of family life, and therefore simply dictated when they would have sexual intercourse with their wives.

Husbands often abused their sexual power, showing little regard for either the emotional feelings or the physical health of their wives. As one social historian wrote, "[I]ntercourse in the traditional family was brief and brutal, and there is little evidence that women derived much pleasure from it" (Shorter, 1982, p. 9). Evidence reveals that many husbands did not abstain from having sex with their wives either during pregnancy or immediately after the birth of a child (Shorter, 1982).

And how did women of earlier eras regard sex?

Is Sex a Right of Marriage?

Several accounts of women's sexual experiences in marriage in the nineteenth century were written by social scientists of the time. An early study, conducted between 1892 and 1920 by Dr. Clelia Duel Mosher, a physician, uncovered a pattern of wifely resignation to their husbands' right to totally control the course of marital sexuality. The women in Mosher's study repeatedly explained that they wanted to limit marital intercourse to times when it was mutually desired by wives and husbands, but they reported that they routinely submitted to unwanted sex. One woman talked about "having intercourse on average once a week," even though sexual relations were very painful for her because of injuries she had sustained during pregnancy and child birth (cited in Hasday, 2000).

In 1929, Katharine Bement Davis, a social scientist and penologist (that is, a scholar who studies the penal or prison system) sent 10,000 letters to selected wives, asking if they would be willing to answer (anonymously) and return a questionnaire about their sexual experiences. Her questionnaire was very thorough. She ultimately received complete responses from nearly 1,100 married women, most of whom were from the middle class, and thus, were not representative of all married women at the time. However, Davis's study provides a rare glimpse into the sexual dimension of marriage of the late nineteenth century (cited in Hasday, 2000).

The women who responded to Davis's survey made it clear that they had entered into marriage with the knowledge that their husbands had the right to control the terms of marital intercourse, but they were not enthusiastic about the situation. One woman wrote in response to Davis's questions: "My mother taught me what to expect. The necessity of yielding to her husband's demands had been a great cross in her own life." Davis's study also suggests that women's marital happiness in this historical period depended on how their husbands chose to wield their authority over marital intercourse—whether they fully exercised their "rights" or restrained themselves voluntarily. Women whose husbands had been "considerate" and/or "unselfish" when they engaged in sexual intercourse with their wives for the first times were most satisfied with this aspect of their marital relationships. Those whose husbands had ignored their sexual sensitivities, on the other hand, wrote that they were "repelled" by their introduction to sexual intercourse. They were "unprepared, shocked at the strength of (their) husbands' passion; their husbands were . . . inconsiderate, uncontrolled." A long period of sexual and marital adjustment followed, often unsuccessfully, which in turn produced marital unhappiness for both. Women in both of these early studies made it clear that unwanted sex in their marriages had caused them real harm and that they would have greatly preferred it if their husbands had respected their desires about sexual intercourse (summarized in Hasday, 2000).

Nineteenth century feminists were well aware of the negative consequences of husbands' legal right to totally control the sexual dimension of marriage and they campaigned ardently to change the laws so that men could be prosecuted for raping their wives. In the 1850s, feminist leader Elizabeth Cady Stanton wrote that the key to women's ability to reach full equality with men rested on their ability to control their own bodies. She was convinced that a wife's right to refuse her husband's sexual demands was the foundation needed to support equality. "Women's degradation is man's idea of his sexual rights" (quoted in Hasday, 2000, p. 17). Feminists of that era used the term *legalized prostitution* to refer to the situation in which married women had to acquiesce to marital intercourse because they had no practical alternative, no place to go, and no other means of negotiating their relationships with their husbands. They argued that there was no meaningful difference between married women who traded sexual access in return for their husbands' economic support and prostitutes who explicitly sold their sexuality to strangers because they had no better way to earn a living. In spite of ongoing feminist efforts in the nineteenth century, however, the legal exemption from rape for husbands who forced their wives to engage in sexual intercourse against their will continued into the last quarter of the twentieth century.

Rape and Marriage

In fact, there was no serious legal challenge to the marital exemption law until the late 1970s. But even now, a majority of states still retain some form of the rule exempting a husband from prosecution for raping his wife. Some states require a couple to be separated at the time of the assault, and sometimes they extend the exemption to cover unmarried cohabitants. Some states only recognize **marital rape** if it involves physical force and/or serious physical harm. Some provide for vastly reduced penalties if a rape occurs in marriage or create separate procedural requirements for marital rape prosecutions. Enforcement of existing statutes recognizing some forms of marital rape has been very infrequent (Hasday, 2000, p. 40).

The exemption from prosecution for husbands who force their wives to have sex against their will is defended on the principle of marital privacy. Proponents of this position argue that "there is something inherent in the nature of the relationship between husband and wife that makes legal intervention inappropriate, misguided, and ultimately self-defeating. It contends that the marital relation depends on intimacy protected from outside scrutiny, intimacy that could not survive if the law intervened to investigate and prosecute marital rape charges" (Hasday, 2000, p. 41). Furthermore, the proponents of this position argue, legal intervention into charges of marital rape would prevent the couple from working out their problems. "Once the state appears on the scene, the delicate shoots of love, trust, and closeness in a marriage will be trampled in a way unlikely ever to be undone" (Hasday, 2000, p. 42). A final defense of the exemption from prosecution of men who rape their wives is the claim that women will falsely accuse their husbands of this crime in order to gain leverage in a divorce suit. There is, of course, no empirical evidence to support the proposition that wives are prone to make false charges of marital rape. To the contrary, evidence available from states that allow marital rape prosecutions suggests that the incidents women report to law enforcement officials tend to be very brutal and relatively easy to prove (Hasday, 2000, p. 43).

Problems associated with initiating (and refusing) sex may be diminishing in many marriages today because of greater sexual freedom for women and more openness about sex. As men and women are less constrained by traditional gender-related notions about sex, their sex lives may improve.

Unwanted But Noncoercive Sex in Dating

It is commonly assumed that if an individual engages in sexual activity voluntarily, that is, without verbal or physical coercion, then she or he must have wanted to do so. There are many reasons people would have sexual intercourse when they really don't *want* to. One of the primary reasons is that they are involved in an ongoing relationship with the sexual partner and wish to do what they can to maintain it. Engaging in sex can satisfy a partner's needs, promote intimacy, and avoid conflicts. Partners learn to resolve differences in their levels of sexual desires through negotiation. They often make an implicit agreement that they will engage in sexual intercourse whenever one feels the desire to do so, even if the other partner isn't all that interested. In many newly dating couples, having sex has an important symbolic impact on further establishing the relationship as something more than friendship (O'Sullivan and Allgeier, 1998).

There are other reasons why individuals might engage in sexual intercourse even when they don't particularly want to. Women who endorse traditional female roles may feel that they are obligated to put their partner's sexual desires ahead of their own and, even further, that their primary value in a heterosexual relationship is sexual. They may also feel pressured to respond to men's sexual overtures out of a sense of guilt or a desire to conform to peer behavior, to avoid hurting their partner's feelings, and/or to avoid conflict or confrontation (Sprecher et al., 1994).

A final set of factors that might push a woman into having sexual intercourse even when she doesn't have a strong desire to do so is related to the changing sexual climate in our society. In the years before the second sexual revolution in the late 1960s, women could invoke traditional ideas about chastity to avoid engaging in sexual intercourse. Today, the social norms don't support this reason to refrain from having intercourse. Additionally, young women may not have developed effective strategies for telling their romantic partners that they don't want to have sex without offending them or threatening the relationship (Sprecher et al., 1994). Contemporary **sexual scripts** (that is, the set of guidelines about appropriate times and places, partners, and reasons for engaging in sexual activity that people are supposed to follow when they become sexually active) don't include specific words that can be used to indicate a lack of desire (Mitchell and Wellings, 1998). Rather than coming right out and saying "no" to partners' attempts to initiate sexual activities, individuals indicate their "consent" by not resisting. The person who doesn't say no or yes may be too confused or embarrassed to stop the process (Hickman and Muehlenhard, 1999).

In spite of the importance of this issue, not much social research has examined factors that lead women to engage in *unwanted, but noncoercive* sexual intercourse. Researcher Leslie Houts used data from a national survey to address this question. Houts analyzed responses from nearly 600 randomly selected young women, aged 15 to 24, who were asked to indicate how much they had wanted their first sexual intercourse to occur, on a scale of 1 (indicating that they didn't want it to happen at all) to 10 (indicating that they really wanted it). Eighty percent of the study participants were between the ages of 14 and 18 when they had sex for the first time and over 75 percent were involved in a committed relationship. Women who indicated that their first episode of sexual intercourse was a result of rape were excluded from this analysis.

The most common response given by the women in this study was a score of 5, indicating that they felt a great deal of ambivalence about their first experience of sexual intercourse. More than one out of every four (28 percent) fell below the midpoint in terms of the "wantedness" of their first sexual intercourse experience. Two factors—the age at which they had sex for the first time and the type of relationship they had with their first sexual partner—were the most important determinants of how much the women in the study wanted to have sexual intercourse the first time they did it. Those who postponed their first sexual encounter until a slightly older age and those who were involved in a committed relationship with their first partner were most likely to report a higher degree of "wantedness" of the experience. It is important to keep in mind that some of the young women may have been reluctant to say that they really wanted to have sex the first time it happened because of lingering beliefs that women should not really be that interested in sex. So the findings of this study may underestimate somewhat the extent to which the first sexual intercourse was desired (Houts, 2001).

Sexual Orientation

Sexual
Orientation

Sexual orientation is one of the four primary components of sexuality, along with *biological sex, gender identity,* and *gender.* It is defined on the American Psychological Association web site as "an enduring emotional, romantic, sexual, and/or affective attraction to individuals of a particular sex/gender." Three sexual orientations are commonly recognized: **homosexual** (that is, attracted to individuals of one's own gender); **heterosexual** (that is, attracted to individuals of another gender); and **bisexual** (that is, attracted to members of more than one gender). Individuals who have a specific sexual orientation do not always act on their feelings of attraction, for various reasons, including lack of opportunity and fear of the social stigma. Thus, constructing a precise and unambiguous definition of homosexuality is more difficult than might be supposed.

Sexual orientation emerges for most people in early adolescence, before they've even had any sexual experiences with other persons. The way in which a particular sexual orientation develops is not well understood by scientists. Various theories have been proposed, some emphasizing biological causes and others emphasizing social factors. Today, most scientists and therapists recognize that sexual orientation is shaped for most people through complex interactions of biological, psychological, and social factors.

Because of numerous stereotypes and much discrimination toward them, *coming out* can be a very challenging and emotionally painful process. Lesbians and gay men often feel different and alone when they first become aware of their attraction to persons of the same gender as themselves. They may also fear being rejected by family, friends, co-workers, and religious institutions if they do come out.

Some homosexual and bisexual individuals want to change their sexual orientation. The American Psychological Association has concluded that there is no scientific evidence to show that *conversion therapy* is effective. Changing an individual's sexual orientation is not simply a matter of changing his or her sexual behavior. It also requires altering the person's emotional, romantic, and sexual feelings and restructuring one's self-concept and social identity. Although some mental health providers do attempt to convert homosexual and bisexual individuals to heterosexuality, many others question the ethics of trying to alter a trait that is so fundamental to an individual's identity. Since the mid 1970s, neither the American Psychiatric Association nor the American Psychological Association has regarded sexual orientations other than heterosexuality to be pathological.

Over the past twenty years, social and legal constraints against same-gender sexual activity have declined. For instance, sodomy laws have been repealed by state legislatures in twenty-five states and the District of Columbia and struck down by state courts in six others (ACLU, 1999). A number of state and local governments have begun to prohibit discrimination based on sexual orientation in private employment (Human Rights Commission, 1999). By the close of the 1990s, hundreds of businesses provided domestic partnership benefits to same-sex couples. Additionally, the visibility of gay men and lesbians has increased in the media, and their portrayal has become more favorable (Kaiser, 1997). Attitudes toward same-gender sexual behavior have become more tolerant among the general public over this period. Thus, as our culture has become more accepting of a variety of forms of sexual expression, including homosexual relationships, it may have become easier for people to recognize and act on their sexual attraction to persons of their own gender. Unfortunately, however, hate crimes directed at homosexuals are still occurring in our society today.

Analyses of data from the General Social Survey, covering the years between 1988 and 1998, revealed that there was an increase in the likelihood that American men and women had a sexual partner of the same gender as themselves. Of the more than 11,000 randomly selected respondents in the surveys (roughly 5,000 men and 6,300 women), 271 reported that they had engaged in some type of same-gender sexual activity during the previous year and during the previous five years. A higher proportion of same-gender sexual activity was reported at the end of the 10-year period. However, it is important to note that even at the end of the 1990s, after a decade of more tolerant attitudes toward homosexuality, only 4.1 percent of the men and 2.8 percent of the women in this study reported that they had engaged in some type of sexual activity with a person of the same gender as themselves (Butler, 2000; see also Black et al., 2000).

A number of demographic factors were associated with the likelihood that men and women would report having engaged in same-gender sexual activity. Individuals who lived in larger towns or cities at age 16 were more likely to report this type of sexual activity, especially among men. Women whose mothers had higher levels of education were also more likely to report having engaged in some type of sexual activity with other women. Age is also associated with the likelihood that an individual will engage in same-gender sexual activity. Among men, the likelihood increases until the mid-thirties and then declines. Among women, the age difference occurs at a later age. Among women aged 18 to 49, the likelihood of experiencing some type of sexual activity with other women is fairly stable. Women in their 50s were significantly less likely than those in the younger group to report having had some type of sexual interactions with other women (Butler, 2000). The final demographic characteristic associated with same-gender sexual interaction among men was race. African American men were more likely than white men to report that they experienced some sexual activities with other men. Table 6.3 summarizes responses to questions about engaging in sexual activities with persons of the same sex.

The proportion of men and women in this study who reported that they had participated in sexual activities with persons of their own sex or gender should not be interpreted as an estimate of the male and female population that is gay, lesbian, or bisexual. Some people may identify themselves as heterosexual but occasionally have sexual interactions with persons of their own sex. Others may identify themselves as gay or lesbian but not engage in any sexual activity with persons of their own sex.

ConTentSELECT

Homosexual and
Attitude

TABLE 6.3

Trends in Percent of Men and Women Who Reported Having Engaged in Sexual Behavior with Persons of the Same Sex and Opposite Sex during Previous Year (1988–1998)

	INTERVIEW YEAR								
SEX PARTNERS	1988	1989	1990	1991	1993	1994	1996	1998	p
Male respondents									
Same gender	1.7%	1.6%	1.9%	2.7%	2.0%	2.5%	3.7%	4.1%	.0003
Opposite gender only	82.4	85.4	88.5	82.4	83.0	84.3	84.2	81.0	n.s.
No partners	11.7	9.9	6.8	11.2	9.5	10.1	7.2	10.8	n.s.
Did not answer	4.2	3.0	2.8	3.7	5.4	3.0	5.0	4.1	n.s.
	100.0%	100.0%	100.0%	100.0%	100.0%	100.0%	100.0%	100.0%	
N (unweighted)	458	479	400	419	505	963	963	876	
Female respondents									
Same gender	0.2%	1.5%	0.5%	0.4%	1.8%	2.2%	2.6%	2.8%	<.0001
Opposite gender only	82.9	82.7	84.7	84.1	83.8	81.4	81.1	82.2	n.s.
No partners	12.4	13.5	10.9	11.2	10.2	12.4	11.3	12.2	n.s.
Did not answer	4.5	2.2	3.9	4.3	4.2	3.9	5.1	2.8	n.s.
	100.0%	100.0%	100.0%	100.0%	100.0%	100.0%	100.0%	100.0%	
N (unweighted)	556	581	488	560	645	1,212	1,177	1,073	

Source: Adapted from Butler, 2000, Table 2, p. 338.

Summary

Sexual behavior has a biological basis, but biology alone does not explain sexual behavior. A person's sexuality and sexual behavior are more influenced by the culture in which he or she has been socialized. Individuals learn sexual scripts, which include cultural scenarios, interpersonal sexual relationships, and the personal desires and fantasies individuals have about their sexual activities.

Substantial evidence comes from historical records that premarital sex has occurred in all periods of U.S. history, even in the Puritan colonial period. Evidence from the first half of the twentieth century, especially coming from interviews and questionnaires, shows that a substantial minority of women (25 percent or more) had premarital sex.

Premarital sexual behavior in the United States has increased greatly in the last twenty-five years. Surveys show that the most rapid increases occurred in the 1970s,

but the percentages of teenagers who had sex continued to increase into the 1990s. By age 20, more than two-thirds of women and probably as many as 80 percent of men have had sexual intercourse. Factors associated with teenage sexual activity include race and ethnicity, socioeconomic status, educational experiences, religious beliefs, family contexts, and the use of alcohol, cigarettes, and drugs.

The first sexual intercourse experience is different for men and women. Women are more likely than men to have committed or love relationships with their first partners. First sexual experience for men is more often a measure of achievement; first sexual experience for women is more likely to be an expression of love. Studies show that for both genders the first sexual experience is likely to be more negative than enjoyable.

The traditional double standard of sexual behavior may not be as strong as in the past, but research evidence from many different studies shows that it still prevails. Women are still restricted and controlled by the double standard, which is enforced primarily by men.

Marital sex in the nineteenth century was primarily controlled by husbands, and many married women of that era probably thought of sex with fear and dread. Nineteenth-century marriage manuals generally depicted sex as being a duty for women and as being for procreation. Some of these views began to change in the twentieth century, when it became more acceptable for women to enjoy sex.

The frequency of sexual intercourse for married couples diminishes as couples are married longer. A part of this decline comes from the disintegration of some marriages, but even happily married couples report that sex gets lost in the stresses and pressures of daily life. Sex is related to power in a variety of ways—sometimes as sexual coercion, but both men and women report using sex as a way of gaining control over their partners.

Sex outside of marriage is nearly universally disapproved of by Americans, but some people do engage in extramarital sex. Men are more likely than women to have sex with someone other than their spouses. Recent evidence suggests the percentage estimates of the 1980s may have been high, but taking into account underreporting, about 15 to 17 percent of people who have ever been married have had sex with someone other than their mates.

Key Terms

Bisexual (p. 184)

Double standard (p. 172)

Habituation (p. 175)

Heterosexual (p. 184)

Homosexual (p. 184)

Hymen (p. 164)

Hymenotomies (p. 164)

Infidelity (p. 179)

Marital rape (p. 182)

Sexual orientation (p. 184)

Sexual revolution (p. 163)

Sexual scripts (p. 183)

Swinging (p. 178)

Vagina (p. 164)

Vulva (p. 164)

Review Questions

1. Briefly outline the history of the sexual revolution in the United States, noting key events in each decade of the twentieth century.

2. Identify the ways in which women's sexual attitudes and behaviors have changed over the past 100 years. Has women's sexual behavior become more or less like men's?

3. Describe the sexual behavior of American teens since World War II, including the age at which they become sexually active, the number of sexual partners they have, and their use of contraception.

4. Summarize findings of recent research regarding extramarital sexual relationships.

Critical Thinking Questions

1. Over the past few decades, there have been two broad *camps* in regard to sex education in the public schools: the pragmatist (or practical) camp and the abstinence camp. How might the sex education programs developed by people in these two camps differ?

2. What factors are pushing adolescents in our society to engage in sexual behavior at younger and younger ages?

3. How do today's teens and preteens learn about sex? What role do their parents play? Why might young

people be reluctant to turn to their parents for sexual information?

4. Is there a sense of *sexual entitlement* among adolescent boys today? Why or why not?

5. For some married couples, sex becomes goal directed (that is, they are trying to become pregnant).

What might be some of the positive and negative consequences of goal-directed sex for the marriage? Why might sex become depersonalized or mechanical under these circumstances? How might it lead to conflict between the spouses?

6. Outline the arguments for and against the statement that "sex is a necessity of life."

Online Resources Available for This Chapter

www.ablongman.com/marriageandfamily

- **Online Study Guide with Practice Tests**
- **PowerPoint Chapter Outlines**

- **Links to Marriage and Family Websites**
- **ContentSelect Research Database**
- **Self-Assessment Activities**

Further Reading

Books and Articles

Bullough, Vern L., and Bullough, Bonnie. *Sexual Attitudes: Myths and Realities.* Amherst, NY: Prometheus Books, 1995. An attempt to explore and come to terms with cultural and historical traditions on sexual attitudes in the United States.

Christopher, F. Scott, and Sprecher, Susan. "Sexuality in Marriage, Dating, and Other Relationships: A Decade Review." *Journal of Marriage and the Family* 62, 2000: 999–1017. A comprehensive review of social science research on sexuality conducted over the 1990s.

Kinsey, Alfred C., Pomeroy, Wardell, and Martin, Clyde E. *Sexual Behavior in the Human Male.* Bloomington, IN: Indiana University Press, 1998. A reprint of the original study that was first published in 1948. The pioneering scientific study of human sexuality that introduced a new way of thinking and talking about sexuality world-wide.

Kinsey, Alfred C., Pomeroy, Wardell, and Martin, Clyde E. *Sexual Behavior in the Human Female.* Bloomington, IN: Indiana University Press, 1998. Originally published in 1953, this was the companion volume to Sexual Behavior in the Human Male.

Laumann, Edward O., Gagnon, John H., Michael, Robert T., and Michaels, Stuart. *The Social Organization of Sexuality: Sexual Practices in the United States.* Chicago: University of Chicago Press, 1994. A comprehensive survey of sexual behavior based on a probability sample of 3,432 American women and men aged 18 to 59.

Reiss, Ira L. *An End to Shame: Shaping Our Next Sexual Revolution.* Buffalo, NY: Prometheus Books, 1990. A sociologist who devoted his life to the study of sexuality suggests ways of alleviating the major sexual crisis the United States is facing.

Rossi, Alice S. (ed.). *Sexuality Across the Life Course.* Chicago: University of Chicago Press, 1994. A multidisciplinary team presents fourteen articles dealing with the biopsychological perspective, sexual diversity in history and lifestyle, sexuality at different phases in the life course, and health issues.

Schwartz, Pepper, and Rutter, Virginia. *The Gender of Sexuality.* Thousand Oaks, CA: Pine Forge Press, 1998. Explores the ways in which sexual experiences are shaped by gender expectations.

Sprecher, Susan, and McKinney, Kathleen. *Sexuality.* Newbury Park, CA: Sage Publications, 1993. A focus on attitudes, behaviors, and satisfactions of same-sex and heterosexual relationships.

Whitaker, Daniel, Miller, Kim S., and Clark, Leslie. "Reconceptualizing Adolescent Sexual Behavior: Beyond Did They or Didn't They." In *Family Planning Perspectives* 32, 2000: 111–117. Offers a more sophisticated approach to studying adolescent sexuality from a social science perspective.

ContentSELECT Articles

Boekhout, B., Hendrick, S., and Hendrick, C. "Relationship Infidelity: A Loss Perspective." *Journal of Personal & Interpersonal Loss* 4(2), 1999: 97–124. **[Database: Psychology]** That loss is experienced following the discovery of infidelity is not unexpected. When emotional and physical boundaries of a primary relationship are crossed, the current study's results suggest men more often than women sought to end the relationship, sought revenge, or to have their own affair. Conversely, women more often than men sought to confront the unfaithful partner, discuss or talk it over, forgive the partner, and work to improve the relationship. Study participants indicate overall negative relationship consequences resulting from infidelity.

Ewoldt, C., Monson, C., and Langhinrichsen-Rohling, J. "Attributions about Rape in a Continuum of Dissolving Marital Relationships." *Journal of Interpersonal Violence* 15(11), 2000: 1175–1183. **[Database: Social Work]** One of the most common forms of rape is marital rape, with the prevalence estimated to be between 6 percent and 14 percent. Historically, marital rape was viewed differently than other incidents of rape, as it was thought legally impossible to rape one's own wife. In this study, Ewoldt and his cohorts examine attributions (perceptions) of whether "rape" occurs in varying levels of dissolving relationships. Rape-supportive attributions were made in the instances of intact marriages; less rape-supportive attributions were made in other varying levels of dissolving relationships (separated, living apart, seeking divorce, or divorced).

Milhausen, R., and Herold, E. "Does the Sexual Double Standard Still Exist? Perceptions of University Women." *Journal of Sex Research* 36(4), 1999: 361–369. **[Database: Sociology]** The aim of this study was to determine the attitudes of 165 university women concerning the sexual double standard. Analyzing data gathered from a self-report questionnaire, Milhausen and Herold's findings indicate that women's sexual behaviors are perceived more harshly judged by society than similar sexual behavior by men, suggesting that women believe a sexual double standard does exist. None of the study participants endorsed the sexual double standard.

Shackelford, T., and LeBlanc, G. "Courageous, Compassionate, and Scholarly: An Evolution Analysis of Rape and Male Sexual Coercion." *Journal of Sex Research* 38(1), 2001: 81–84. **[Database: Sociology]** Shackelford and LeBlanc present a thorough and articulate review of the book, *A Natural History of Rape: Biological Bases of Sexual Coercion* (Thornhill & Palmer, 2000). Discussed within an evolutionary framework, key questions about both the causes and consequences of sexual coercion and rape are reviewed.

Conflict, Communication, and Relationship Quality

When Iris Krasnow was doing the research for her book Surrendering to Marriage, *she asked a number of people to suggest couples who seemed to have particularly successful marriages so that she might interview them. One of the wives Krasnow interviewed shared the secrets of her 40-year marriage:*

What made our marriage work for so many years? I did comb my hair and put on lipstick when I knew Dick was coming home, but of course it's much more than that.

From the very beginning of our relationship, I was sure that Dick was smarter than I was, and therefore had to be right. Marriage for me was a process of discovering that I was at least as right, if not more right, some of the time. Our life together wasn't a competition, but a process of listening carefully, and respecting—respect is a very important factor. You need to respect, as well as love each other. Respect to me means having an enormous regard for the integrity of your mate's opinions and ideas, and absolutely never belittling or shooting the other down. . . .

The hardest part about being married to Dick was coaxing him to express his feelings; remember, this generation of men was disconnected from their emotions and their feelings. It was the most puzzling part of my marriage, to get this area to function. You know, when you get married you do not sit down with a syllabus: Making Marriage Work, semester one.

My marriage lasted nearly forty years; Dick died seven years ago, just three months shy of our anniversary. Happiness is a very elusive quality, but I would say our marriage was rich, very rich. . . . When we had a problem, I was fortunate that Dick would listen quietly to my dissecting, he would always hear me

Key Questions

1 To what extent, if any, do women and men have different styles of interpersonal communication?

2 Is conflict inevitable in intimate relationships?

3 Is effective listening the key to successful conflict resolution in intimate relationships?

4 How does the birth of children affect the quality of their parents' marriage?

5 How can researchers most effectively study the dynamics of intimate relationships?

out. And then we would redirect the compass a little. There were never great re-directions, just adjustments. He would fine-tune me and I would fine-tune him. You know, we grew each other up, and we grew up with each other. . . . Marriage is not a contest of who is going to win the round. It's a delicate balancing of needs and costs to both parties. . . .

We were each other's best friends. . . . We told each other we loved each other every day, every single day. When he died, I didn't have to feel guilty that he didn't know I loved him. I absolutely knew he loved me, and he absolutely knew I loved him. . . .

Maybe this sounds goofy to you, that it was all so picture perfect, and of course it wasn't; there were days that I would be irritated because he said he'd be home at 6:30 and wouldn't arrive until 8:30. He had no sense of time, and there is no use in trying to change such a fundamental characteristic. . . .

Dick was my other half, more than half, and it has been with great, great pain and effort that I have learned to live without him. I needed help in thinking, doing both parts of the dialogue myself. That was where I had to begin—to reach a point where I could decide something without talking it over. That was how we made life decisions—dialogue, the back and forth. . . .

With luck, I could live another thirty years, but I cannot imagine spending all that time without Dick. Even with my wonderful children and grandchildren and friends, it is just so alone now. Our marriage, it was just one of those little miracles.

Source: Krasnow, Iris. *Surrendering to Marriage: Husbands, Wives, and Other Imperfections.* New York: Hyperion, 2001, pp. 134–139.

*W*hat determines the quality of a marriage or any other type of intimate relationship? Are love and attraction enough? What does it mean when people say that it takes a lot of work to make intimate relationships successful? For that matter, what *is* a successful relationship anyway? Are successful relationships the ones that last, as Dee and Dick's did, until one partner passes away? Is the length of a marriage, in itself, the key? Can we simply say that a long-lasting relationship is successful, even if one or both partners is terribly unhappy?

As Dee and Dick's story attests, successful marriage involves a great deal of patient and respectful listening; it requires negotiation and compromise when important decisions must be made and tough problems tackled. And perhaps most of all, it involves forgiveness and understanding when anger and disappointment arise. In this chapter, we look at the underlying and ongoing factors that contribute to the quality of intimate relationships—the ways in which decisions are made and conflict is handled when it arises. In some heterosexual relationships, as we discuss, religious beliefs or grossly unequal economic contributions by the partners swing the decision-making power and the right to have the final say to the man. While gender privilege is typically removed from the conflict and communication processes that occur among same-sex couples, there are, nonetheless, differences of opinion that are resolved through interpersonal influence processes that can involve power differentials.

In this chapter we also look at the communication styles and strategies that can develop between intimate partners. Good communication between partners often includes special catchwords or private phrases, as well as inside jokes, idiosyncratic words, and customary rituals. As we discuss later in the chapter, these subtle parts of the communication and interaction between partners can help to reduce conflict, but conflict is never completely avoidable. Even though every couple has conflicts, these need not lead to angry arguments and traded insults. Conflict generally grows out of competing needs and interests, so it is unavoidable unless one person is completely subservient to another.

Relationships are shaped and influenced by patterns of control and power, with one partner having a greater ability to affect outcomes than the other. We consider the bases on which interpersonal power rests, emphasizing that many of these bases swing the balance of power in heterosexual relationships to male partners.

We also examine the many sources of conflict in intimate relationships, emphasizing that factors outside the relationship may cause problems between the partners. We offer a list of rules for fighting fair that can be used not only by intimate partners but also by others who come into frequent contact. Finally, we review some obstacles to effective communication, including difficulties related to women's and men's differences in communication styles.

Although much scientific research about power, conflict, and communication has focused on married couples, we believe the same dynamics occur in all types of intimate relationships, including dating couples, cohabiting heterosexual couples, and gay and lesbian couples.

We'll also take a special look at relationships in which partners approach each other as equals, still a unique situation among American couples today. We end the chapter with a discussion of the ways in which conflict and communication affect partners' degree of satisfaction with their relationships. How do couples create "little miracles" that give them a lifetime of joy? Social science researchers—as well as poets and artists—have given these questions a great deal of attention over the past 100 years. We discuss the advances that have been made by social scientists in recent decades to uncover the keys to developing and maintaining successful intimate relationships.

Methods Used to Study Intimate Conflict and Communication

*I*n Chapter 2, we reviewed the various methods used by social scientists to study marriages, families, and other intimate relationships. In that chapter we mentioned that sociologists tend to—but don't always—use verbal information provided by the persons involved in their studies (that is, **self-report data**). Typically, study participants provide written answers to questionnaires or spoken responses to an interviewer's questions. Ideally, a randomly selected national sample is used in survey research. Social scientists also collect information by observing people engaging in the behaviors in which they're interested (that is, **direct observation**). Both of these ways of gathering data have strengths and weaknesses. Survey research that collects self-report data runs the risk of response bias that results from poor memories and/or deliberate deception. But it is an efficient method of getting information from a large number of respondents. Observation research, on the other hand, bypasses the problem of respondents' faulty memory or attempts to provide what they believe is the acceptable response because it relies on information gathered by well-trained and supposedly objective researchers. Often, however, the observations take place in laboratories, which are artificial settings for most study participants, and involve minute and mundane tasks that do not approximate the complex behaviors and interactions that take place in everyday relationships (Ridley, Wilhelm, and Surra, 2001).

The detailed observations and analysis of interactions between spouses in laboratory settings began nearly thirty years. The focus of this type of research has been on the behaviors that take place during marital conflict and problem-solving discussions (Bradbury, Fincham, and Beach, 2000). This type of research was prompted by some psychologists' beliefs that spouses' reports of the extent, processes, and outcomes of marital conflict and communication were not good indicators of what actually happens. Rather than relying on the information provided by the couples themselves, laboratory observations rely on the data gathered by researchers as they watch couples engage in problem-solving discussions.

Over the past decade or so, researchers who put couples in laboratories to study their interactions have gone beyond simply focusing on what they say and do to each other. They've begun to gather information about the aspects of interactions that are not directly observable. This includes asking couples to watch videotapes of their discussions and asking them to describe their feelings at various points in the interactions, as well as providing their interpretations of their own and their spouse's behaviors and comments. Some researchers are even collecting data on the physiological responses that occur throughout the course of a discussion. Technological measuring devices are used to provide data about changes in heart rate, skin responses, and even hormonal fluctuations. While this type of research continues to provide interesting and important information about communication and conflict resolution in intimate relationships, it has not yet provided clear *answers* to clinicians' questions about the factors that doom some couples to dissatisfaction and divorce and others to prosperous marriage (Ridley, Wilhelm, and Surra, 2001). Research that moves out of the laboratory and into real-world settings, gathering data about a wide range of couples—including nondistressed as well as distressed relationships—is greatly needed. Studies that examine the broader sociocultural context in which intimate relationships are formed and maintained is also critical. Thus, most experts agree that sociological and psychological research perspectives that gather information about individual couple dynamics as well as social environmental factors are needed. Much of the information about conflict and communication processes that is summarized in this chapter comes from laboratory observation studies. Data pertaining to the correlates of relationship satisfaction come primarily from self-report data.

Another critical issue in research concerns the definition and measurement of key concepts and variables. We turn to this issue next.

Defining Marital Quality

We all probably know at least one married couple whom we would describe as having a good marriage. We often describe such couples as being *happily married*. Marital happiness seems to be a simple and obvious concept. And yet scholars and researchers continue to debate what it means to say that a marriage is happy. The problems associated with understanding marital happiness were foreseen by one of the earliest researchers of the subject, who wrote seven decades ago:

> Who is wise enough to say what constitutes a happy marriage? There are so many kinds of happiness and unhappiness incident to marriage that no weighing in the balance, one kind against another, can do justice to the complex of emotional facts in question. (Terman, 1935, p. 167)

Since these words were written, there has been a steady outpouring of research and writing on the subject of marital happiness. Yet there is still considerable diversity in how the subject is studied, and there are disagreements on how to define and measure a good marriage (Sabatelli, 1988; Glenn, 1990; Bradbury, Fincham, and Beach, 2000).

We use **marital quality** as a generic term to cover how happy, satisfactory, or stable a marriage is. This is the term now used by most family sociologists. However, several other terms also need to be identified and described because they are also widely used (Sabatelli, 1988; Bradbury, Fincham, and Beach, 2000). These terms are *marital happiness, satisfaction, adjustment, stability,* and *success.*

Marital happiness is a concept that most people intuitively understand, but social researchers continue to have debates about how it should be measured.

Marital happiness and marital satisfaction have one element in common—they both concern the way people *feel* about their marriages. Researchers sometimes use only a single question to get at a person's feelings about her or his marriage. For example, researchers might ask, "Taking things all together, how would you describe your marriage? Would you say your marriage is very happy, pretty happy, or not too happy?" Or "How satisfied are you with your marriage?" Both these questions (or others like them) indicate how a person feels about her or his marriage, but some researchers have found that happiness and satisfaction are not quite the same thing.

Some married people say they are satisfied with their marriages, but that does not necessarily mean they are happy; their marriages may not give them happiness, but do give them other satisfactions such as economic security, the comforts of a home life, companionship, and so on (Campbell, Converse, and Rodgers, 1976). Despite this distinction, many family scholars use the terms *marital happiness* and *marital satisfaction* more or less interchangeably (Glenn, 1990).

Some measures of marital quality focus on what couples actually do in their relationship rather than on their feelings about their marriage. Researchers who focus on the marital relationship ask questions about how much time the spouses spend interacting with each other, how often they disagree on issues, or how often they have considered ending their marriage (Glenn, 1990; Johnson, Amoloza, and Booth, 1992).

One widely used measure of marital quality combines questions that reflect feelings *and* questions about interaction, communication, and conflicts (Spanier, 1976). This measure, labeled **marital adjustment** by its originator, has been criticized *because* it combines, in a single scale, both feelings and behavioral characteristics (Glenn, 1990; Sabatelli, 1988).

One unambiguous term related to marital quality is **marital stability,** which refers to whether or not a couple stays together. Separation and divorce are the typical manifestations of marital instability, though marriages can also be intentionally terminated by other means, such as legal annulment, desertion, and even, in the extreme case, murder (Lewis and Spanier, 1979).

A newer term, **marital success** combines the ideas of marital stability and marital happiness/satisfaction (Glenn, 1991). It refers to marriages that have not ended in separation or divorce *and* are satisfactory to both spouses (Glenn, 1990, 1991). The overall level of marital success in a society is measured by the amount of divorce (and separation) and the average level of marital satisfaction/happiness reported by couples in social surveys.

By combining divorce statistics and measures of marital quality obtained in social surveys, Glenn (1991) has shown that there was a distinct decline in marital success in the United States from the 1970s to the early 1990s. Some of that decline was produced by the rapid increase in divorce during the 1970s, but some of it was also produced by the lower levels of marital quality among those who stayed in their marriages (Glenn, 1990).

In a study designed to examine whether marital quality in America was declining, Rogers and Amato (1997) compared two generations—the parents (who were between 20 and 35 in 1980) and their adult children (aged 20 to 35 in 1992). The younger generation scored lower than their parents on three of five dimensions of marital quality. They reported lower levels of interaction and more marital problems and conflict. They did not, however, report lower levels of marital happiness or display a greater likelihood of moving toward divorce. Rogers and Amato interpreted their findings by concluding that the younger generation was committed to the idea of having a life-long marriage but that it wasn't easy for them to do, given all of the challenges presented by a rapidly changing society.

Results of another study conducted in the 1990s support the idea that American's expectations for marriage are changing. Respondents in the study were

---

TABLE 7.1

Personal and Background Characteristics Associated with Marital Quality

Factors most consistently associated with higher marital quality

Later age at marriage
Greater educational attainment
Greater economic resources
Higher occupational status
Good physical and mental health
Parents' marital relationship good
Approval of spouse by family and friends

Factors moderately or sometimes associated with lower marital quality

Socioeconomic, religious, and racial dissimilarity

Factors most consistently associated with lower marital quality

Previous cohabitation
Previous marriage
Race (African Americans have lower levels of marital quality)

---

asked, in 1967 and 1994, to rank the relative importance of the following characteristics in making marriages successful: love and affection, healthy and happy children, companionship, emotional security, satisfactory sexual relations, common interests and activities, personal development, economic security, moral and religious unity, maintenance of a home, and a respected place in community. The rankings were fairly similar in the two time periods. Love and affection ranked as most important in both time periods. Companionship was also near the top in both periods. The least important characteristics in both periods were moral and religious unity, maintenance of a home, and a respected place in the community. There were some notable changes in the relative importance of the characteristics over the 25-year period. Emotional security became more important while a satisfactory sexual relationship became less important. Having healthy and happy children also declined in importance. The drop in the importance of the sexual component of marriage may be a reflection of the increase in premarital sexuality and non-marital cohabitation over the 25-year period, making marriage less important in legitimizing sexual activity (Barich and Bielby, 1996).

It is important to know as much as possible about the factors that enhance marital quality. The many studies that have examined the determinants of marital quality have found that a number of personal and family background characteristics as well as characteristics of the marital relationship and family situation are important. These are summarized in Table 7.1.

Correlates of Marital Quality

Research has found that differences between partners in such personal and background factors as religion, race, socioeconomic status, and age can affect marital quality.

Personal and Background Characteristics. The tendency for people who marry to have similar personal and background characteristics—*homogamy*—is associated with higher marital quality (Lewis and Spanier, 1979). Couples coming from the same religious background have been found, in many studies, to have higher marital quality than couples from different religions, but the effects of religious differences may be diminishing. Although some studies continue to find religious homogamy associated with higher marital quality (Ortega, Whitt, and Williams, 1988), others have found no differences, for example, between Catholics who marry other Catholics and those who do not (Heaton, 1984; Shehan, Bock, and Lee, 1990).

Even when lower marital quality is found among Catholics who marry outside their faith, the difference can sometimes be accounted for by a lower level of religious participation, that is, lower church attendance (Heaton, 1984; Shehan, Bock, and Lee, 1990). Numerous studies have shown that couples who are *more religious* are more likely to be happily and satisfactorily married (Filsinger and Wilson, 1984; Heaton, 1984; Wilson and Filsinger, 1986; Shehan, Bock, and Lee, 1990; Veroff et al., 1993).

Even though studies of Catholic–non-Catholic marriages show a lessening importance of religious *heterogamy* (different backgrounds) on marital quality, there may be more to the story. Couples who have greater religious differences, such as those in Christian–Moslem or Moslem–Jewish marriages, may experience lower marital quality. Although such marriages are occurring in greater numbers in the United States, there has not been any systematic research on the effects of this level of religious heterogamy on marital quality.

Marital quality is also related to several personal characteristics and individual abilities. Higher levels of education and occupational status, and greater economic resources, all of which reflect higher socioeconomic status, are related to higher marital quality (Kurdek, 1993; Larson and Holman, 1994). Couples who are older when they marry generally experience higher marital happiness and satisfaction. Good physical and mental health are also related to marital quality (Glenn and Weaver, 1979; Lewis and Spanier, 1979; Filsinger and Wilson, 1984; Clark-Nicolas and Gray-Little, 1991).

Good relationships with parents, especially if parents are happily married, increase adult children's chances of having high marital quality themselves (Larson and Holman, 1994). The approval and support of friends and community members are also related to higher marital quality.

Previous experience with intimate relationships has not been shown to improve marital quality. Cohabitation before marriage is related to lower marital quality and greater marital instability (Booth and Johnson, 1988; Hall and Zhao, 1995). Studies generally find that people in second marriages have lower marital quality than people in first marriages (Vemer et al., 1989), and that, in general, husbands in remarriages are more satisfied than are remarried wives.

Race is also related to marital quality, with African American couples generally exhibiting lower marital quality than other Americans. This racial difference may be the product of economic stress and lower educational status among many black couples. African American couples may also experience the stresses associated with racism, which could contribute to more marital difficulties (Broman, 1993; McLoyd et al., 2000). Additional research is needed on this question, however.

Greater religiousness has been found to decrease individuals' thoughts of divorce. It does not, however, decrease marital problems or conflict or increase marital happiness (Booth et al., 1995).

Agreement about Marital Roles.   Marital quality is greater when spouses agree about the roles of husbands and wives (Glenn, 1990; Lye and Biblarz, 1993). When husbands hold traditional attitudes about gender roles and wives have modern or egalitarian views, marital quality is negatively affected (Lye and Biblarz, 1993). Studies also show that when married couples are satisfied with the division of household labor (cooking, cleaning, child care) their marital quality is higher (Suitor, 1991). When the husband and wife share resources and are both caring, nurturing, affectionate, and devoted to each other, marital satisfaction is greater (Ickes, 1993).

Children and Marital Quality.   Studies covering a span of at least thirty years show that when couples have children they experience a decline in marital quality (Belsky, 1990a; Glenn, 1990). The decline is modest, but it is well documented (Rollins and Galligan, 1978; Anderson, Russell, and Schumm, 1983; Belsky, Spanier, and Rovine, 1983; Feldman and Nash, 1984; Belsky, Lang, and Rovine, 1985). It occurs among African American couples as well as white couples (Crohan, 1996).

Marital quality generally decreases with the birth of the first child. It often decreases even further as children reach school age and continues to be low through their teenage years. Some studies have shown that marital happiness increases again with the departure of the last child (Menaghan, 1983; White and Booth, 1985).

The birth of a first child reduces marital quality primarily because of changes in the interaction of husbands and wives (Kurdek, 1993). It is an indisputable fact that a newborn child takes a great amount of time and energy, which is almost certain to detract from the relationship between husbands and wives. Women generally report a decline in marital quality sooner and more sharply than men (Belsky, 1990).

Some additional evidence that children affect marital quality comes from a study that compared childless women with mothers. Two groups of fifty women were carefully matched on the basis of education, religion, and participation in the labor force. Women who were voluntarily childless scored higher on marital quality than mothers. Childless women had higher scores on *marital cohesion*, which reflected more active involvement with their husbands, as well as more frequent exchanges of ideas and discussions with their husbands (Houseknecht, 1979).

Marital Quality and Duration of Marriage.   Many studies have found that marital quality is high in the early years of marriage but declines and remains at a relatively low level until later in the marriage, when it may rise again, especially after children leave home. More recent research suggests that the steepest decline in marital satisfaction occurs shortly after marriage. The primary reason for the decline is a decrease in positive sentiments rather than an increase in negative behaviors (Berscheid and Reis, 1998).

When marital quality starts at a relatively high point, moves downward over time, and then upward again, the pattern is described as a U-shaped curve. This U-shaped curve has been much debated among family sociologists, because while some researchers have found the upturn in the later years of marriage, others have not (Belsky, 1990; Glenn, 1990, 1998).

An important criticism of the U-shaped curve is that cross-sectional research has typically been used to establish it. In cross-sectional studies, couples who have been married for different lengths of time are asked about the quality of their marriages. The long-time married couples, showing somewhat higher levels of marital quality, may be a select group because they are the ones who have remained together. Many of the less satisfying marriages may have ended in divorce, leaving only the couples who had better marriages remaining in the study.

To demonstrate that a typical marriage has a decline during the middle years and then rises again, it is necessary to follow some marriages over their entire lifetimes. Research that follows the same individuals or couples over time is called *longitudinal.* There are few long-term longitudinal studies because of the difficulty of maintaining contact with couples over thirty or forty years. Those that have been done generally do not show an increase in marital quality in the later years of marriage. Two early studies simply found continuing declines in marital quality in the

in the media

Real-Life "Frasier Cranes"

From her KPIX-FM studio in Oakland, California, psychologist Tara Fields sits watching the electronic monitor as dozens of callers line up waiting for her advice. But Fields is busy, listening to a woman tearfully tell the radio audience how she was repeatedly beaten by her partner. "You don't deserve that," Fields says in determined tones, glaring and shaking a finger like a lecturing schoolmarm. "Repeat after me. I don't deserve that."

The distraught caller. The concerned listener. The quick resolution. The closest most people have ever come to this scene is watching NBC's hit sitcom *Frasier*. But over the past few years, radio psychology has been blossoming nationally. . . . These programs are an outgrowth of shock-talk radio, which has dominated the talk radio field in the past decade. While the interest has pleased radio execs, it doesn't sit well with some psychologists who question the ethics of these programs. Others, however, say allowing people to talk about their problems, even in the radio venue, can be a help. "Although radio psychologists have been on the air for many years they appear to be more bold and prominent in the past few years," says Dr. Muriel L. Golub, who chairs the California Psychological Association's Ethics Committee. "They also appear to be more oriented in the direction of only-the-solution-matters.

They tell listeners that they can give them the solution to their problems, and that simply is not true." These shows have become so popular, she says, because people are searching for the "quick fix." The anonymity of a phone call also avoids having to deal with someone face to face. "Many people don't want to deal with their fear and shame at revealing their most secret thoughts," Golub says. "On the other hand, there are those who find it exciting to hear oneself on radio and to interact with a celebrity. [The calls] may also be used in a manipulative manner, by saying 'I was so upset with you, I even called Dr. So-and So about it.'" But Fields and others believe there can

---

later years of marriage (Burgess and Wallin, 1953; Pineo, 1961). The study by Pineo (1961) described the later years of long-term marriage as years of "disenchantment."

One longitudinal study of couples in which the husband attended Harvard (from 1938 to 1942) covered a nearly 50-year period (Vaillant and Vaillant, 1993). When these couples were asked about their marital satisfaction at different times over their marriage, a general decline was seen. The decline was somewhat more pronounced for wives than for husbands. This research did not confirm an increase in marital quality in the later years of long-term marriages. However, when the couples were asked later in their lives to think back over their entire marriage and describe their marital satisfaction at different stages, both husbands and wives, but especially wives, saw the middle years of marriage (between eleven and twenty-five years) as the *least* enjoyable (Vaillant and Vaillant, 1993).

Sexual Orientation.   "Despite prejudice and discrimination, lesbians and gay men have often succeeded in creating and sustaining family relationships. Research over the 1990s has shown that same-sex relationships are characterized by positive adjustment even in the face of stressful conditions. Many, if not most lesbians and gay men express the desire for an enduring love relationship with a partner of the same gender. . . . (R)esearch findings suggest that many are successful in creating such relationships. (Approximately) 40 to 60 percent of gay men and 45 to 80 percent of lesbians are currently involved in steady romantic relationships" (Patterson, 2000, p. 1052).

be positive outcomes from talking to a therapist on the air. "I'm not saying it should be used in the place of therapy, but it gives people a chance to tell their story, and that can be a positive first step," Fields says.

"With a show like *Frasier,* you know it's just entertainment," says Berkeley psychologist Steve Allen. "With these (radio) talk shows, the lines between entertainment and help are more blurred." [Radio psychologist] Fields has been a practicing psychologist for 15 years, has a private practice in Marin County, and teaches at the College of Marin. She says her show doesn't exploit anyone but does provide a springboard for people seeking help.

With her knowledge of Bay Area resources, she makes a point of referring callers with serious problems to those who can help them. Lists of crisis intervention centers and psychologist referral services are kept close by producer Geller's phone. . . . Fields has

strong opinions and isn't afraid to share them with her callers. But she draws the line at pronouncing judgments the way her fellow psych-talker Laura Schlessinger does. Fields considers the show to be entertainment, a step removed from the "real" patients she sees in her private practice.

Dr. Alan Siegel, a clinical psychologist working in the San Francisco area, says he has some strong ethical concerns about radio therapists who launch into on-line solutions without offering follow-ups. "In a proper mental health development, we come up with a plan, then tailor the intervention based on the person's ability to handle it and the resources available to them to follow through with treatment," Siegel says. "A premature suggestion could aggravate the situation." "To me, Dr. Laura is a little too forceful in the advice she gives. Ethically, not knowing that person and just interacting for a couple of minutes, she could misread the situa-

tion and cause real harm." Fields, on the other hand, does not dispense advice like so much Pez. And she's careful about following up with callers who she believes need additional help, referring them to local agencies. . . . Fields says she isn't doing therapy on her show and believes it's unethical to give listeners snappy answers or glib criticism. "I give some strong opinions, but the ball is in their court," Field says. "You can't take a person's self-confidence away just to get ratings. My intent with the show is to just to get people on the right path, to open up about their problems. There are no quick fixes and I remind my listeners they need to seek help for tougher problems." Fields says listeners need to know that these programs are entertaining, but can be helpful as well.

Source: Young, Susan. "Radio psychologists provide listeners with a therapeutic blend of sympathy and insight." *The Oakland Tribune,* www.drtara.com/couch/housecalls.html

Lesbians and gay men report as much satisfaction as do heterosexual couples. The great majority describe themselves as happy (Patterson, 2000; see also Peplau and Cochran, 1990). The factors that contribute to satisfying relationships among lesbian and gay couples include having equal power, seeing many attractions in the current relationship and few attractive alternatives to it, placing high value on the relationship, and engaging in shared decision making (Blumstein and Schwartz, 1983; Kurdek, 1994, 1995).

Much has been written in recent years about the benefits of legal marriage for health and well-being. Sociologist Catherine Ross, however, has found that it is the social attachment to a significant other, rather than legal marriage per se that is beneficial. She found no significant difference in well-being between cohabiting and married persons.

Marital Scripts

The expectation a person has about what is appropriate behavior for husbands and wives is referred to as a **marital script.** Both partners have marital scripts, but they are not usually clearly stated and they certainly may not be in agreement (Broderick, 1979, 1989). During the early stages of marriage, husbands and wives may be disappointed because they have different (or conflicting) marital scripts. Family sociologist Carlfred Broderick, who developed the concept of marital scripts, gave this illustration from his own life: Even though Broderick had known his wife since they were both in kindergarten and they had dated from the time they were in the tenth grade, not until they were married did he learn that he and his wife had mismatched scripts regarding what happens when someone gets sick:

> Every right-thinking person knows what you should do when you get sick—you go to bed. That is your part. Then your mother, or whoever loves you, pumps you full of fruit juice.

> Well, I married this woman I had known all my life, and in the natural course of events I caught the flu. I knew what to do, of course. I went to bed and waited. But nothing happened. Nothing. I couldn't believe it!

> I was so hurt, I would have left if I hadn't been so ill. Finally, I asked about juice and she brought me some—in a little four-ounce glass. Period. Because, as I learned later, the only time they drank juice at her house was on alternate Tuesdays, when they graced breakfast with a drop in a thimble-size glass. My family's "juice glasses" held 12 ounces and there was always someone standing by to refill them.

In regard to cultural expectations, five different types of marriages have been identified: marriage as conflict, patriarchal marriage, role-segregated marriage, companionate marriage, and peer marriages. In the United States today, the companionate marriage is generally the cultural ideal, but individual couples fall into different types.

Marriage as Conflict. In a few societies, the typical marriage is based primarily on a conflict relationship between husbands and wives (Mernissi, 1987, p. 108). Conflict marriages are based on built-in antagonisms between husbands and wives, which are very different from the American cultural ideal of marriage based on affection and mutual support. One extreme example of the conflictual marriage is found among the Pakhtun people of northwestern Pakistan. Anthropologists have described the Pakhtun marriage as lifelong *warfare* (Lindholm and Lindholm, 1979, p. 11).

The Pakhtun people are Islamic and follow a prevalent Islamic practice called **purdah,** which means that a woman must not leave her home, except with her husband's permission and then only with her face and body fully covered by loose garments (Mernissi, 1994). Not only are Pakhtun women virtual prisoners in the family home, but they are also in constant danger of being beaten by their husbands. Pakhtun men believe that wives who are seen in public places will bring dishonor and shame to the family. Since wives can bring shame on their husbands, they are viewed as threatening and treacherous enemies living inside the household (Lindholm and Lindholm, 1979).

Throughout their married lives Pakhtun spouses continue to see each other as enemies, although they do eventually develop a kind of respect and even fondness for each other. "Each admires the other's resolute pride and fighting ability. But the man cannot show his affection, for to do so would give the wife courage to dishonor him" (Lindholm and Lindholm, 1979, p. 19).

Only a few cultures base marriage relationships on conflict, but many build marriage around male dominance and, often, as a part of that dominance, male violence as well. The next cultural type of marriage is based on male dominance.

Patriarchal Marriage. A **patriarchal marriage** is one in which the husband is given absolute authority over his wife. Only a few decades ago, the marriage vows at most American weddings asked the bride if she would pledge to "love, honor, and *obey*" her husband. Even today there are American brides who take this traditional vow, while their husbands are asked if they will "love, honor, and cherish"

In many patriarchal cultures, men often exercise their right to control women, which may include physical beatings.

their wives. There is a big difference between obeying and cherishing, and the difference signals the essence of patriarchy.

Patriarchal marriage begins with the assumption that a husband is the senior partner, the master of the household; he is the boss. Christian theology provides an often-quoted statement that supports patriarchal marriage: "[T]he husband is the head of the wife, even as Christ is the head of the church" (Ephesians 5:23). Similar statements can be found in the Koran of Islam and are echoed in Islamic law, both of which require Muslim wives to obey their husbands (Mernissi, 1987).

A patriarchal marriage relationship does not mean that wives have no voice at all in their lives. Even within patriarchal marriages wives make some decisions about their children and their homes, but in any confrontation or dispute husbands have the final authority.

Role-Segregated Marriage.   Marriages in many societies are not so much characterized by absolute male dominance as they are by the separation of husbands and wives in most of their activities. Such marriages are referred to as **role segregated,** because husbands' and wives' activities, including leisure, are conducted separately (Bott, 1957; Rainwater, 1965). It is generally true that men are dominant in role-segregated marriage, but segregation gives women somewhat more freedom, simply because they have their own domain.

Role-segregated marriages were first identified in a classic study of working-class London families (Bott, 1957). The English wives remained in their homes, caring for their children, cleaning, and preparing food. Their leisure time was spent with their mothers, sisters, and other female kin who lived close by. Their husbands worked outside the home, usually in industrial or blue-collar occupations.

Their leisure time was spent with male friends and relatives, often in bars or at football games.

When married couples have role-segregated relationships, their demands on each other are limited. Both husbands and wives in these relationships get their social support from same-sex relatives and friends more than from each other.

Companionate Marriage.   **Companionate marriages** are those in which husbands and wives focus on each other more than on other family members and friends (Burgess and Locke, 1945). Ideally, the companionate marriage emphasizes a personal closeness between husband and wife that is based on trust, communication, mutual interests, and love (Goldscheider and Waite, 1991). This type of marriage is one in which husbands and wives spend as much of their time together as they can, especially when they are at home or engaged in leisure activities. Trends toward urbanization, suburbanization, and modernization have pushed many marriages toward companionate relationships (Kerckhoff, 1972). As couples form households away from their parents' homes, and separate from the friends they had as adolescents, they are more likely to turn to each other for companionship and social support.

Spouses in companionate marriages are sometimes characterized as equal partners. The assumption is that couples adopt new values and nontraditional ways of thinking about husband and wife roles as they move away from their families and kin groups. In particular, companionate marriage partners are expected to reject the traditional views of husband dominance and the strict gender division of labor.

Many feminists are skeptical of the presumed equality of companionate marriages. When wives are not employed, or are in lower paying, less prestigious occupations than their husbands, their relationships may not be equal (Goldscheider and Waite, 1991). Wives in companionate marriages continue to have most of the responsibility for taking care of the home and children, while their husbands focus on their jobs. This, too, reveals some persistent gender inequalities in the companionate marriage.

Peer Marriage.   Traditional couples (those who divide male and female roles into separate spheres of influence and responsibility, with final authority given to the male partner) sacrifice intimacy, deep friendship, and mutual respect, according to sociologist Pepper Schwartz, who completed an in-depth study of nontraditional couples. **Peer marriages**—Schwartz's label for relationships that are built on *equity* (each partner gives to the relationship in the same proportion that she or he receives) and *equality* (each partner has equal status and is equally responsible for emotional, economic, and household duties)—achieve true companionship and a deeply collaborative marriage. They are able to get past marital traditions based on gender and demonstrate a "profound psychological connection" (Schwartz, 1994a, p. 56).

There are four important characteristics of peer marriages (Risman, 1998; Schwartz, 1994a). The first is a nearly *equal division of household labor and child care*. Partners are very careful to do their fair share (never less than 40 percent) of the work of family life. If the division gets slightly out of balance, they don't get angry. Instead, they work to restore the balance. The second characteristic is that each partner believes the other has *equal influence over important decisions*. This is in direct contrast to traditional marriages, in which husbands often have final say, even though both partners discuss issues before reaching a decision. The third, and closely related, characteristic of peer marriage, is that both partners feel they have *equal control over the family money.* The male partner does not have automatic veto power over the female's decisions. As we saw earlier in this chapter, when money is allowed to determine status in a relationship, it destroys equality and friendship between the partners. Fourth, each partner's work is given *equal weight in the couple's life plans*. One person's work is not sacrificed for the other's. The person who earns the lower income is not always the one who is expected to do the most child care and housework. The marriage always takes precedence in decisions that pertain to career advancement or other types of job changes (Schwartz, 1994a).

Because of these characteristics, peer marriage has several benefits. The first is the *primacy* of the relationship. Because the marriage takes priority over work and all other relationships, each partner feels secure about the other's regard and support. Second is *greater intimacy*. Because they share housework, child care, and economic responsibility, peer partners experience the world in a similar way, understand each other better, and communicate more effectively. They negotiate more than other couples, share more conversations, and are not likely to dismiss each other. Finally, peer marriages offer *high levels of commitment*. Because partners find each other irreplaceable and describe the relationship as unique, they become highly interdependent on each other and the relationship. They are unlikely to separate, because the costs would be too great (Schwartz, 1994a).

Although peer marriages sound appealing, they are not without their difficulties. Schwartz has identified some of the major problems partners encounter in such marriages. The first is the *absence of external validation*. Outsiders (such as friends, parents, and co-workers) may criticize, even oppose, the relationship. They may refuse to provide the type of support that all marriages need to survive. The husband's parents, for example, may feel that he is being stripped of his "rightful" role as family provider and authority figure. A second problem is that others may resent the obvious companionship and intimacy of the peer marriage. "Most people like married couples to [quarrel with] their spouse occasionally" (Schwartz, 1994a).

There can also be *career costs* associated with peer marriage. Both partners need jobs that will let them coparent and give priority to their marriage and family life. In some cases, peer partners may have to modify their career aspirations in order to maintain the equity and equality in their marriage.

Schwartz has discovered that a new sexual dynamic emerges in peer marriages. Because they have so much intimacy in their everyday life, peer partners don't need sexual interaction to fulfill their emotional needs. They often relate as best friends rather than lovers. They may have to go out of their way to put eroticism back in their relationship. This may be a major cost of peer marriage for some partners (Schwartz, 1994a).

Finally, because there is no preexisting blueprint for success in this type of marriage, peer partners must work diligently to figure out the best way to do things so they can maintain the equity and equality in their relationship. They have to create their own rules, which can be very tiring (Schwartz, 1994a).

Peer marriages are rare. When sociologist Barbara Risman and her colleagues undertook a study of peer marriage using criteria similar to those identified by Pepper Schwartz, they had a great deal of difficulty finding them, even though they cast their net widely. They advertised in PTA newsletters and posted fliers in daycare centers, libraries, fitness centers, and grocery stores. As a result of these exhaustive efforts, 75 families volunteered for the study. But when Risman and her colleagues examined these families more closely, they found only 15 who actually fit the criteria and shared the household labor in a 40/60 split (or better), shared childrearing and bread-winning responsibilities equally, and felt their relationships were fair. The 15 families who did fit Risman's criteria were exceptionally well-educated. Over half of the parents had a Ph.D. or M.D. degree; another eight had Masters degrees. Only one partner had not completed a college degree. In all families, spouses held equally prestigious jobs and earned comparable incomes. Risman and her colleagues concluded that peer marriages depend on both partners having strong beliefs in gender equality (Risman, 1998, pp. 98–100).

ContentSELECT

Marriage and Intimacy

Power and Decision Making in Intimate Partnerships

*I*n the course of every intimate relationship, couples must make decisions that affect them jointly. Decisions range from the more mundane—such as whether to buy chocolate or strawberry frozen yogurt or which TV program to watch at 9 P.M. on Wednesday nights—to the more significant—whether to have a baby or buy a new home. Decision making involves communication and frequently some amount of conflict. The ways in which couples make decisions both affects and is affected by the quality of the relationship. It also reflects the balance of power between the partners. Before we turn to a discussion of communication and conflict in intimate relationships, we'll look first at the balance of power, because it is so important in shaping the ways in which couples interact.

The word **power** is used regularly when people speak of governmental or economic matters ("The prime minister exerts power over members of her political party"; "Corporate executives battle for power in the organization"). But when people speak of intimate relationships, they are less inclined to think in terms of power. Yes, people sometimes acknowledge that parents have power over children, but in the everyday relationships between two adults who love each other, the idea of power seems somehow inappropriate. The ideal American relationship between intimate partners is based on love and caring, cooperation and mutual support, not on self-interest and attempts to impose one's will on the other. If partners have a difference of opinion, most believe they should resolve the matter through compromise.

Sociologists have been studying power in intimate relationships, especially between wives and husbands, for over forty years. We now understand that despite cultural ideals, power is an important dimension of intimate relationships. Clearly, there are ongoing attempts by intimate partners to persuade—sometimes even coerce—each other to act in specific ways. Successful persuasive attempts are what we refer to as *intimate power*. Social scientists usually determine which partner in an intimate relationship has more power by asking who makes the final decision about a number of important issues.

One of the earliest and most influential studies was conducted by Blood and Wolfe (1960), who presented the married women in their study a list of the following decisions: what job the husband should take, what car to get, whether or not to buy life insurance, where to go on vacation, what house or apartment to take, whether or not the wife should go to work or quit work, what doctor to have when someone is sick, and how much money the family could afford to spend each week on food.

Blood and Wolfe realized that many couples talk over an issue before making a decision, but they believed the final decision must be made by either the husband or wife. They asked the participants in their study to indicate which of four statements best described decision making about each issue in their own household: The husband always makes the final decision, the husband makes the final decision more often than the wife, the husband and wife have exactly the same amount of say in the final decision, and the wife always makes the final decision.

Although the Blood and Wolfe study only applied to married couples, it would seem that their measure of intimate power could also be adapted for use with unmarried couples who live together (homosexual as well as heterosexual) because similar types of decisions would be faced. For couples who are dating, rather than cohabiting, more relevant decisions might include how fast the relationship should develop; how much time the couple should spend together; how quickly they should become sexually involved; how often they should have sexual intercourse; who should initi-

Marriage and
Decision Making

ate sexual activities; whether they should use contraceptives, and if so, who should have the responsibility for providing contraception; how they should demonstrate their commitment for each other; what types of relationships they will have with other people; and how they will divide dating expenses.

The "final say" measures of decision making, such as the ones used by Blood and Wolfe, have been criticized as being inadequate indicators of relative power in intimate relationships. For one thing, all the decisions are treated as though they are equal in their implications for family life and in the frequency with which they are made when, most likely, they are not. The particular decisions that are presented to study participants can also influence the conclusions that are drawn about the balance of power in a relationship. If more decisions that have traditionally been made by men are included, then it may appear that male partners are more dominant. The reverse may be true if "female" decisions are overweighted. For instance, in blue-collar couples decision making often breaks down along traditional gender lines. Men typically have the final say in decisions pertaining to the purchase of automobiles and insurance, and women are more likely to have a greater say in decisions relating to internal household matters and childrearing. Finally, when people identify who in their family or household makes specific decisions, they may be strongly influenced by prevailing norms about who is *supposed* to make those decisions rather than by who *actually* does (Shehan and Lee, 2001).

Self-report methods of collecting data—such as the one used by Blood and Wolfe to determine who had the final say in decision making—cannot capture the discussion and negotiation that go on between partners before the final decision is made. As we discuss later in this chapter, observational research conducted in laboratories is much better able to examine the evolving processes through which partners attempt to influence each other.

Lillian Rubin's study of blue-collar couples illustrates the limitations of the "final say" measures of decision making. When she asked wives and husbands how decisions were made in their families, most said that it was fifty–fifty. But Rubin discovered that this meant something other than equal say in decision making. When couples said they decided something *together,* what actually happened was that husbands *made* the decision and wives *carried it out* (Rubin, 1976, pp. 110–111).

RUBIN: How are decisions made in the family?

HUSBAND: They're mutual, you know, fifty–fifty. She asks me whether we can buy some furniture, let's say. If I say okay, she goes out and looks around. When she picks out something she likes, she asks me to go look at it. If I approve of it, she buys it. If not, she looks some more. (Rubin, 1976, p. 111)

Rubin found that women made the "smaller" decisions such as what to have for dinner, when to buy shoes for the kids, and when to see a doctor. Men made the other—bigger—decisions: what kind of car the family will own, when to buy a house, and sometimes even whether their wives will work for pay or not. There may be more discussion in today's marriages, but when a difference of opinion remains it is often the man who decides.

In working-class households, women often have the responsibility for paying bills but men make the decisions about how the couple's money will be spent. A 33-year-old housewife described the situation to Rubin:

I handle the money, but he makes the decisions. Like, he decided about whether we were going to buy this house or not, or whether we should buy a car, and how much we should spend for it. Some things I decide, like when the kids need shoes. But he watches out for what we're spending money on, and I pretty well know what it's okay for me to do and what's not okay. (1976, p. 113)

Working-class wives may go along with this type of male-dominated decision making because they believe it is important for men's self-esteem and sense of manliness. But underneath, they may feel a great deal of ambivalence because they have to give up many of their own needs and preferences in order to give their husbands' needs and preferences priority.

The preceding quotation also points to another important aspect of decision making in many working-class families: the fact that husbands may have veto power over decisions, as the following remarks indicate: "It's kind of a joint effort up to a point. We'll talk it over and, if we agree, we do it. But if I say a flat 'Forget it,' that's it" (Rubin, 1976, p. 110). Even in regard to issues that are typically thought of as falling in the *female* domain, such as the home, the husband's preferences usually take precedence:

> WIFE: I wanted to live someplace further from the Bay, someplace where it's sunnier. I'm always cold here, and I just feel a lot better in a warmer place. But he wanted to live someplace that wasn't too far to go to work, so we bought this place. (Rubin, 1976, p. 111)

> HUSBAND: She wanted to get a house right away, but I wanted to get some other things before we bought the house. I knew we'd get the house someday but I wasn't so sure about the other things. I thought we ought to have a nice car, and I wanted a boat before we got the house. Patty still doesn't like this house, she wanted a nicer one. She doesn't like the neighborhood either, but I don't see anything wrong with it. I'd like to get her a house she likes better someday, but this is plenty good enough for us for now. (Rubin, 1976, p. 112)

It is clear from the preceding quotations that power should be seen as a process of discussion and negotiation and of attempts at manipulation, which means that there are certain situations that allow one person to achieve the outcomes he or she desires (Komter, 1989). Three such situations have been identified: (1) *Direct exercise of power* occurs when there is an explicit conflict of interests and the more powerful person gets what she or he wants; (2) *indirect exercise of power* occurs when the less powerful person anticipates what the more powerful person will want and withdraws from a conflicted issue; and (3) *invisible power* occurs when the less powerful person so completely accepts the rightness of the more powerful person's position that he or she does not recognize any conflict of interest.

The Sources of Interpersonal Power

What determines each person's power in a particular relationship? Four major sources can be identified: *authority, resources, ability,* and *physical force.* All these sources of power may seem quite remote from the relationships between intimate partners, but as we will see, they influence intimate partners as well as business or political rivals.

Legitimate Authority. Built into the traditional husband role in western societies is **legitimate authority**—the right and responsibility to exercise control over wives (Shehan and Lee, 2001). "Historically, men have been given the right to control women through abusive means, if necessary, because women and children have often been seen as chattel along with farm animals and property" (Steinmetz, 1987, p. 727). Men have the right to command, and women have the obligation to obey those commands. The term **patriarchy,** which literally translated means "rule of the father," refers to the nearly universal belief that men have a "natural" right to be in control. This right is often attributed to God's will.

All the world's major religions emphasize patriarchal authority. Some Christian leaders, for instance, cite the teachings of St. Paul when delineating the proper roles of women and men. One Bible passage that is frequently quoted is from Ephesians 5, verses 22 to 24:

> Let the wives be subject to their husbands as to the Lord; because a husband is head of the wife, just as Christ is head of the Church, being himself savior of the body. But just as the Church is subject to Christ, so also let wives be to their husbands in all things.

In Islam, men are the undisputed heads of both the sacred and secular realms, including the household (Renzetti and Curran, 1995). The Koran pronounces that God made men superior to women and admonishes wives to obey their husbands.

Patriarchy is also built into civil laws. For instance, marriage laws in the United States have granted husbands the right to select the family's place of residence and to demand that wives live where their husbands desire. In some states, if a woman refused to move to another state with her husband, *she* was regarded by the law as having deserted *him*. If a wife moved to another city and her husband refused to move with her, she was also regarded as abandoning him.

Today, in most western societies, patriarchal authority in families and households does not have the same influence it once had, but it still exists and in certain segments of our society, it continues to be strongly supported (Thorne and Yalom, 1992). Evangelical Christians, for example, often adhere to a patriarchal ideology. When sociologist John Bartkowski visited the home of the female teacher of a woman's Bible study group to gather information for his research on evangelical families, he saw a large mobile hanging from her kitchen ceiling. The mobile was composed of several capital A's suspended from connecting wires. The mobile, his host told him, represented the theme of her Bible study class. The mobile reminds women how the Bible wants them to act toward their husbands. The largest capital A stands for attitude, which is the most important. The first of the smaller A's is for acceptance, which is defined as unconditional love. The next A is for admiration and the final A stands for authority, which refers to wifely submission to their husbands (Bartkowski, 2001, pp. 101 and 116).

Other religious subcultures also continue to subscribe to a patriarchal ideology. Prominent examples include the Hasidic Jews (Harris, 1986), the Old Order Amish (Kephart and Zellner, 1994), and to a lesser extent, the Mormons (Mauss, 1984).

Some ethnic and nationality groups in the United States also adhere fairly closely to a patriarchal ideology. These include people who have recently emigrated from the traditionally patriarchal cultures of the Middle East, Africa, Latin America, and Asia. African American and Latino populations have cultural elements that support patriarchy, although other aspects of their lives (such as the necessity for women to be employed) may counterbalance the traditional view of male dominance.

There has also been research suggesting that blue-collar families have more traditional views of gender. This was borne out by Rubin's study of working-class couples and is revealed in the words of one of the wives:

> He kept saying that I was too independent and that I had to learn to listen to him. He used to say he wanted me to be more feminine, to act more like a *real* woman. What that meant was that he wanted to order me around and have me listen all the time. I told him I wasn't his mother and he wasn't his father. (p. 92)

Little research has been conducted on this issue, however, so it is not clear whether today's blue-collar families are more likely than those from other social classes to adhere to patriarchal beliefs.

ContentSELECT

Patriarchy

Resources.   A second important source of interpersonal power is control over valuable **resources.** When one partner has the greater ability to give or withhold resources (that is, any objects, services, or personal qualities that are highly valued) to the other, he or she usually has a greater amount of power in the relationship. The person who receives more resources than the other becomes dependent to some degree. Among the most frequently mentioned resources in intimate relationships are income, educational attainment, and occupational or social status. In many heterosexual relationships, male partners possess more of these resources than female partners. For example, when there is a difference in the educational attainment between male and female partners, it is more likely that the man will be better educated (the exception is among the African American population, in which women reach higher average educational levels than their male partners). Even when both the male and female partners are in the labor force, women are likely to be in lower status occupations and earn less money. (We discuss this in detail in Chapter 12.) Of course, when women are not in the labor force, and their male partners are, their economic contributions are much lower than their male partners.

Resources need not be limited to money and other economic factors. Anything of value, even the pleasure of being in the company of an attractive person, can be rewarding. Noneconomic resources that are exchanged between intimate partners include sex, companionship and emotional support, childbearing and childrearing, kin keeping, and homemaking. These nonmaterial rewards, however, may not be valued as highly as the material and economic resources. It is generally agreed that Americans place great value on money and occupational status, and to the extent that men control more of these they are likely to have an advantage over their female partners.

Ability.   Knowledge, expertise, information, or even a talent for persuasion can be a source of interpersonal power. Two representatives in Congress may be equal in status, but if one has greater knowledge (about the rules of Congress or the tax code, for instance) or persuasive ability, that one will generally have more power. Gender stereotypes may come into play when decisions are being made about issues that fall into what are considered male or female domains of expertise. The purchase of an automobile may be regarded as a "male thing," and presumed expertise swings the balance of power in that decision to a male partner. And, as we discuss in a later section of this chapter, gender differences in communication styles may also affect processes of negotiation and decision making between intimate partners.

Physical Force.   When other sources of power are ineffective, some people turn to physical force to get their way. Nations with superior military forces use them to make weaker nations do what they want them to do, just as bullies on the playground do. This may be as true in intimate relations as in relationships between nations. We discuss the abuse of power and the use of force in the next chapter.

◼ Theoretical Perspectives on Intimate Power Relations

The major explanations of power in intimate relationships have emphasized the first two sources just discussed: legitimate authority and resources. In their study of power relations in marriage, researchers Robert Blood and Donald Wolfe (1960) adopted **resource theory** as a way of accounting for what they perceived as a long-term movement away from patriarchal marriages, in which husbands'

Around the World

In One Chinese Village, Women Rule

Yongning, a Chinese village of 18,000 residents, is home to the Mosuo minority, one of the world's few thriving matriarchies. Mosuo women head the households and most of the businesses. They control the family purse strings and inherit their clans' assets. They pass their names on to their children. In traditional families, grown children live with their mothers, even after having their own offspring.

No one knows exactly why the Mosuo—who number about 50,000 in several villages scattered around the Yunnan and Sichuan provinces—cling to a matriarchy in a male-dominated country. But 62-year-old Sunami Anna, the head of an extended family of eighteen, has a theory: "If a family's to be run well, a woman must be in charge." The status of these women is remarkable in a country that has always been run by men, and where girl babies are often aborted or abandoned because so many couples prefer sons. Although the rest of China now faces a serious deficit of women, Mosuo society has no shortage of confident, capable women.

One sphere men dominate is local politics. That is largely because in the past, Chinese officials outside the region refused to take seriously the women sent by the Mosuo. In Yongning village, however, that isn't a problem. "The men do what I say," says Ms. Sunami. Men in her clan hand over their earnings to her, and she decides how to spend the money. They obey her orders to run errands or do labor-intensive tasks, like chop firewood.

Ms. Sunami also has the power to appoint her successor once she gets too old to run the household. Although she has two sons, the choice is clear: "My daughter will do it. I love having daughters. It's enough to have two or three sons, but to have more daughters—I'm not afraid of that," she laughs.

Women's dominance extends outside the home: Virtually all the stores on the village's main street are owned by women. The advantages of a matriarchal society are obvious, say the Mosuo women. They contend that women fight less than men do and aren't prone to crime. And couples who opt to split up don't engage in messy fighting over marital assets, because women control their own finances.

Many men seem happy with the arrangement, too.

Source: Adapted from Chen, 1995.

power was *normatively* prescribed, to modern marriages, in which husbands' greater power was believed to be derived from their greater success in bargaining. They presented resource theory as an alternative to *ideological theory*, which held that cultural ideas about who *should* have control over household decisions influence who actually *does* have control. Blood and Wolfe believed their findings supported resource theory, and they concluded that patriarchy no longer affected the balance of power in marriages (Shehan and Lee, 2001). Our earlier discussion suggests that this conclusion was a bit premature.

Studies of marital decision making in other societies, such as Denmark, Greece, the former Yugoslavia, and Turkey, have found that husbands' economic resources do not increase their power relative to their wives. They either decrease it or have no effect on it. These findings led theorists to revise resource theory somewhat to predict that in modernizing societies (those changing from patriarchal to **egalitarian beliefs**—those that promote equality between the sexes), families in the middle and upper classes are the first to accept ideas about equality between women and men in intimate relationships. Higher status men in these societies are likely to believe that they should share control over household decision making with their female partners (Shehan and Lee, 2001). Once societies have fully adopted the idea of equality between women and men, resources become the determining factor in marital power relations.

The Balance of Power in Intimate Relationships

Power in heterosexual relationships typically favors male rather than female partners. Whenever aspects of patriarchy remain in the culture, male partners are the beneficiaries; it gives them some legitimate authority over their female partners. With respect to resources, male partners are usually more highly rewarded economically by their occupations and professions. (This discrepancy is due, at least in part, to the outright and institutional sexism women confront in the work world.) But men often gain another advantage from their occupations and from their generally higher educational attainment: They gain an advantage in expertise, knowledge, and the ability to persuade through communication skills, and these, too, enhance their power within intimate relationships.

We can modify this rather harsh and one-sided picture of male power in several ways. For example, among couples who emphasize egalitarianism, cooperation, and compromise, the power differential may be reduced. At a cultural level, the belief systems that automatically give men more power (patriarchy) have been under attack and, it seems, are diminishing in importance. As women make gains in education and employment relative to men, they are likely to gain power in their intimate relationships. In contemporary societies, however, women are still at a distinct power disadvantage (Chafetz, 1991; Huber, 1991).

The great majority of lesbian and gay couples believe that an equal balance of power is desirable (Peplau and Cochran, 1990). Some studies show that less than half of all gay male couples and heterosexual married couples—but a near majority of lesbian couples (59 percent)—report that they have equal power in their relationships. Other studies have found that the majority of both gay and lesbian couples report equal power (Peplau et al., 1996). Clearly, this is an important question that still hasn't been answered satisfactorily by existing research.

When power is unequal in gay and lesbian relationships, which partner tends to be the more powerful and what factors contribute to his or her greater power? Social exchange theory predicts that the partner with the greater personal resources (e.g., income and education) should have greater power and a number of studies have supported this hypothesis among gay and lesbian couples. For example, in gay couples, older, wealthier men tend to have more power than their intimate partners (Harry, 1984; Harry and DeVall, 1978). Similar results have been found among young lesbian couples (Caldwell and Peplau, 1984). Much more research is needed, however, to determine the extent to which financial resources affect the balance of power in gay and lesbian relationships (Peplau et al., 1996).

Other predictions from social exchange theory have been supported by existing research (Kurdek, 1995; Peplau, 1991; Peplau et al., 1996). The **principle of least interest,** which predicts that when one partner in a relationship is more dependent or involved in the relationship, he or she will have less power, has been supported in research among lesbian couples.

Conflict in Intimate Partnerships

*I*t is often assumed that the *ideal* family or intimate partnership is one with no conflict, but that is neither realistic nor necessarily desirable. Researchers and therapists, alike, have come to the conclusion that conflict is *inevitable* in intimate relationships. Whenever individuals live in close contact with each other, they are bound to occasionally disagree or have different opinions about something.

Families in which some members (usually wives and children) have virtually no ability to press for their interests are not healthy. Conflict in such families is suppressed, and hostility builds up. When suppressed hostility finally breaks out, it can be explosive. Of course, persistent and pervasive conflict is not a good family environment, either. But the total absence of conflict can be detrimental to family members.

When families were organized along patriarchal lines, there was less open expression of conflict than there is in families today. As patriarchy declined over the twentieth century, and as women (and children) gained relatively more power, the open expression of conflict has increased. Greater equality in families has led to greater amounts of overt conflict among family members. We should keep this in mind as we examine conflict between intimate partners.

Conflict Theory

An essential premise of the sociological theory called conflict theory, which we introduced in Chapter 2, is that there will always be conflicts of interest between intimate partners and family members. People in every social group, including families, have different amounts of power, due in part to the positions they occupy and to the resources they contribute (Ritzer, 1997). This unequal power is a major source of conflict, since those who have power try to keep it and those who do not, try to get it.

Unlike structural-functionalism, which proposes that social systems such as families are held together by voluntary cooperation or general consensus, conflict theory proposes that order is maintained through the use of power. People in authority are expected to control subordinates. Those who don't comply with the demands of the person in control can be punished. Those who are in positions of authority and those in subordinate positions have conflicting interests. Those in control try to maintain the status quo, while those "beneath them" strive for change. People who have considerable economic resources are also likely to exploit those who lack resources. As noted, power relations between partners often favor men. The ideology of patriarchy gives men power over their wives and children. This power can be a source of conflict between the genders and the generations.

Sources of Conflict

Conflict over Money. Couples at any income level can argue about how they spend their money. "Couples argue more about how [their] money is managed than about how much they have—and this holds true despite their actual income level" (Blumstein and Schwartz, 1983, p. 77). Conflicts about money are most likely to occur when one spouse is the "provider" and the other is the "spender" (Millman, 1991).

Attitudes about money and the use of money are often deeply ingrained, and may have their origins in early family life experiences. When two people marry or form a joint household, they must somehow learn to agree about how to spend their money. If not, money may be a persistent source of conflict between them. In U.S. society, money is often a symbol for other feelings and emotions (Millman, 1991). It can be a symbol for security; it is often a symbol of success; it can even be a symbol of love (Blumstein and Schwartz, 1983; Millman, 1991). Therefore, arguments over money can be, in fact, arguments over deeper feelings.

The yearly task of completing income tax forms often stimulates discussions about money, and may be a source of conflict for some couples.

Conflict about Sex.   Couples may disagree, even argue, about how often they have sexual relations. Partners may use sex to influence each other: to win favors, to show anger or disapproval, or to gain power in other areas (Blumstein and Schwartz, 1983). "When initiating sex, a partner is making something between a request and a demand: he or she may be invoking a right or seeking a special privilege. When refusing sex, a partner may be exercising an established prerogative or declining a sacred duty" (p. 206). Refusing to have sex is one way a person can gain more power in a relationship as well as a way to use the power she or he already possesses. In this respect, sexuality is clearly a valued resource, control over which gives a person power. "When a person refuses sex, he or she can be a force to be reckoned with. The initiator becomes more clearly the supplicant and may have to comply with his or her partner's wishes" (p. 219).

Initiating sexual activity still tends to be a male responsibility among heterosexual couples, especially among those who are married. Wives may not feel they have a legitimate right to ask for sex. Husbands have traditionally had the right of sexual access to their wives, established in both civil and religious laws. They may become angry when their wives refuse to have sex. Refusing to have sex, however, is one of the rights women have been given as a result of the persistent stereotype that women are "less sexual" than men. When a woman refuses to have sex, her male partner can simply attribute it to her "femaleness." In contrast, men may feel guilty if they do not initiate sex. Wives may be reluctant to initiate sex for fear that they will not only violate gender roles but will also hurt their husbands' ego. When couples reverse the traditional sexual roles (the woman initiates), they often experience problems in their relationship. Graduate students Greta (aged 27) and William (aged 30), for instance, have lived together for nearly two years. Greta describes an episode in which she tried to initiate sexual activity with William:

> We were lying in bed on Sunday morning and I was feeling really like having sex. We were talking and it was nice and relaxed, and so I reached over and started to touch his penis. He withdrew from me real sharply and angrily and moved to the other side of the bed. He said, "You never give up, do you?" I was embarrassed and angry. So even if I feel like it, I wait until he gives all the signals. (Blumstein and Schwartz, 1983, p. 224)

Same-sex couples can also encounter problems related to initiation of sexual activities. They usually don't want to pattern their relationships after traditional heterosexual marriages by having an initiator and a responder role. But they may find it difficult to take on the role usually assigned to a person of the opposite sex. Thus, while lesbian partners may be uncomfortable in the role of sexual initiator, gay partners compete for that role. What often develops in same-sex couples is that the more emotionally expressive partner is the one who initiates.

Other Sources of Conflict.   Money and sex may be the principal issues about which intimate partners have conflicts, but there are many other sources of conflict. Either partner's parents; differences in political, religious, moral, or philosophical views; and a wide array of personal characteristics can all precipitate conflict between intimate partners. Arguments may arise as a result of factors that originally had little or nothing to do with the relationship, itself. For instance, the frustrations of dealing with other people—at work, on the highways, in the supermarket—may carry over into the way a person communicates with a loved one after a long day apart. *Personal problems* (such as low self-esteem) may be associated with ongoing conflict in a relationship, although the partner may actually be fighting with his or her own shortcomings rather than with the loved one. *Physical conditions*—such as fatigue, illness, or excessive alcohol use—may turn a discussion into an argument. A popular television commercial for aspirin once showed a person coming home from work and yelling at his family. The theme line was "Sure,

Marital Conflict

you've got a headache, but don't take it out on them!" And although we may think that alcohol consumption makes us more articulate and courageous, it is best not to attempt an important discussion after drinking.

Finally, *unexpected life events or undesirable living conditions* may produce ongoing conflict as well as periodic outbursts between partners. A job loss, unintended pregnancy, or natural disaster such as a hurricane, flood, or fire may cause so much stress in partners' lives that it comes out as conflict between them. Similarly, living in crowded, noisy conditions can produce ongoing stress as well as occasional fights between partners.

Early research suggested that African American couples have more conflict in their relationships and are more tolerant of open, intense disclosure than are white couples. But this research had a number of methodological problems, such as a failure to take social class (particularly income) and family size into consideration, biased sampling, and faulty measurement. While more recent researchers have attempted to correct these problems in research that examines marital interaction and marital quality among African American couples, few generally accepted conclusions about the ways in which couples manage conflict, or in the amount of negativity or hostility that are expressed during marital interactions have yet been reached (McLoyd et al., 2000). Data are equally scarce on Hispanic couples; it appears that they do not differ significantly from white couples in terms of the frequency of major conflict (Lindahl and Malik, 1999; Mackey and O'Brien, 1998).

When lesbian and gay couples experience problems in their relationships, some of them stem from the same basic causes as those in heterosexual couples (e.g., differences in values that can result from growing up in different religious, racial, ethnic, or social class backgrounds; problems resulting from either partner's job; financial pressures; friction with members of extended families). The top five areas of conflict for lesbian and gay couples that have been found in recent research include finances, driving style, affection and/or sex, excessive criticism, and division of household tasks (Kurdek, 1994, 1995). There are some conflicts that are undoubtedly unique to gay and lesbian couples due to the negative attitudes toward homosexuality in our society. One of the most common problems is whether the homosexual nature of the relationship should be revealed to friends and family (James and Murphy, 1998; Peplau et al., 1996).

It is no wonder, then, that conflict is inevitable in close relationships. The key is to learn how to deal with differences of opinion or conflicts of interests so they don't erupt into violence or undermine the positive feelings of trust and intimacy that make the relationship special. Table 7.2 presents some rules for fighting fair that may help couples learn to manage intimate conflict more effectively.

TABLE 7.2

Rules for Fighting Fair

1. Choose your times for discussion wisely.
2. Deal with one issue at a time.
3. Deal with issues as they come up—don't save them until later.
4. When you bring up an issue for discussion, be prepared to discuss it.
5. Don't try to win at all costs. Consider compromise.
6. Don't hold grudges.
7. Don't fight just for the sake of fighting. Choose your battles carefully.
8. Don't attack your partner's vulnerable issues.

Source: Adapted from Edens, 1982.

In the final section of this chapter, we discuss communication patterns in intimate relationships, once again recognizing that gender shapes, and is shaped by, interactions between partners.

Communication in Intimate Partnerships

Communication is an important component of intimate relationships (Noller and Fitzpatrick, 1990; Weiss and Heyman, 1990). It is the key in managing conflict and resolving differences. When communication between partners is positive and effective, both are likely to be satisfied with the relationship. When communication is negative or ineffective in resolving problems, partners are much more likely to view the relationship as unsatisfactory.

Communication Styles of Happy and Unhappy Couples

In the last three decades, many psychologists and family therapists have studied communication patterns of married couples (Fincham and Bradbury, 1990). The aim of much of this research has been to help couples improve their communication so that they might resolve relationship problems (Gottman, 1979; Noller and Fitzpatrick, 1990). Researchers examine differences in communication between distressed and nondistressed couples (Noller and Fitzpatrick, 1990; Weiss and Heyman, 1990). If the communication patterns of happy couples differ from those of unhappy couples, then it is important to know what the happy couples are doing differently. Or, from another perspective, it is important to learn what it is about the communication of unhappy couples that contributes to their unhappiness.

Many research findings on the differences in communication between happy and unhappy couples have not been surprising. Happy couples *spend more time in conversation* than unhappy couples (Kirchler, 1988). Similarly, when distressed couples express their feelings they are more likely to be *hostile*. But researchers have also found that distressed couples have more *difficulty interpreting* their partners' expressions of affection. They accurately interpret expressions of hostility, but are less accurate in interpreting expressions of love and other positive feelings. Among unhappy couples, even when a partner is trying to express love, the other often misinterprets it as hostility. The inaccurate interpretation leads to an inappropriately hostile response (Gaelick, Bodenhausen, and Wyer, 1985).

This pattern of misunderstanding in unhappy couples is a common thread in the research on intimate communication. Distressed couples are much more likely than nondistressed couples to expect negative behaviors from their spouses, and thus to perceive them as hostile (Baucom and Epstein, 1990). Moreover, distressed partners often have highly developed expectations about how their spouses will behave in different situations (Vanzetti, Notarius, and

▲ *Conflict is inevitable in intimate relationships. The key is learning how to express oneself effectively and discuss differences of opinion.*

NeeSmith, 1992). Even when their partners behave in positive ways, distressed partners may misperceive these positive behaviors.

In one experimental study of forty couples, husbands and wives were asked to predict how their spouses would react in a discussion of their problems. The predicted reactions could range from "extremely calm" to "extremely upset." As expected, distressed partners were more likely to predict negative reactions from their spouses. When they responded positively, their spouses were more likely to explain it in terms of the situation ("It doesn't mean anything, he's on his best behavior here") (Vanzetti, Notarius, and Neesmith, 1992, p. 174).

Thus, experiments and clinical observations of couples in therapy all lead to the conclusion that marital partners in unhappy or distressed relations have negative expectations about how their spouses will behave. These beliefs are not easily changed, even in the face of contrary evidence. One partner's positive behaviors should cause the other partner to reevaluate his or her views, but that seems to be difficult once the negative expectations are firmly embedded (Vanzetti, Notarius, and NeeSmith, 1992; Weiss, 1980).

Researchers have identified some additional qualities that differentiate the communication patterns between distressed and nondistressed couples. Unhappy couples are more likely to command, disagree with, criticize, and put down their partners. Happy couples, in contrast, are more likely to give their approval and show empathy, caring, agreement, and support. Happy couples are also more willing to reveal their feelings through self-disclosure and to use humor and laughter in their interactions (Noller and Fitzpatrick, 1990; Weiss and Heyman, 1990).

Not all types of communication between intimate partners are beneficial to relationships. When communication helps move the relationship in a positive direction, leads to growth and development, helps partners resolve differences, and provides them with emotional support, it is said to be **constructive.** When communication puts a greater distance between partners, makes them feel alienated from each other, or causes hurt feelings, it is said to be **destructive.** There are many examples of destructive communication.

Communication Problems

Since communication has proven to be such an important element in successful relationships, it is useful to examine common communication problems. Let's begin with a discussion of barriers to effective communication.

Obstacles to Effective Communication.   Why do intimate partners have so much difficulty communicating with each other? There are a number of major obstacles to intimate communication. In some cases, the *physical environment* can interfere with attempts to communicate with a partner. If the location is too noisy or if the partners are not close enough to hear or see each other clearly, communication can be hindered. *Situational characteristics,* such as a prolonged separation due to military service, illness, or employment, or lack of privacy associated with crowded living quarters can also make it difficult for partners to communicate as intimately as they would like. For many couples, *cultural differences* due to discrepancies in educational attainment, age, racial and ethnic background, or gender can produce a communication gap. As discussed later, women and men have quite different communication styles and may actually speak what some experts have called different dialects of the language (Rice, 1990, pp. 423–425).

The final, and perhaps most important, obstacle to intimate communication is *psychological,* involving fear of rejection, ridicule, embarrassment, or lack of trust. Although it may not be possible to modify communication defects that stem from psychological disorders, it is possible to recognize destructive forms of communication and to do something about them (Rice, 1990, p. 425).

Ineffective Communication.   When one person's verbal and nonverbal behavior give conflicting messages, he or she can confuse the other person. A *double message* occurs when a person's words do not correspond with the tone of voice used or the body language being displayed. An illustration of a double message might be a man who says to his partner, "No, I *don't* mind if you go to the hockey game with your friends." But while he says these words, he pouts and shrugs, indicating that he really doesn't want her to go.

In some cases, incongruence between one's facial expression or body language and one's words may lead the listener to conclude the speaker is lying. Not all double messages, however, involve deliberate deception. They may simply reflect discomfort or lack of awareness of his or her own nonverbal behavior.

Frequently, in attempts to explain frustration with a partner's habits or patterns of behavior, people may also *exaggerate or overgeneralize.* They may use words such as "always" or "never," as in "You *never* hang your clothes up when you come home from work" or "You *always* flirt with the flight attendants when we go on vacation."

Some people engage in *mind reading*. They announce what their partners think about something or feel about an issue, rather than allowing partners to state their own feelings. This type of communication pattern prevents them from receiving new, more accurate information from partners.

When people find themselves losing an argument, they may resort to unfair tactics to win. They may engage in *put-downs* of partners to throw them off guard or to win by intimidation. Or they may engage in *fault finding*, blaming a partner for all the problems in the relationship so they need not take responsibility for their own shortcomings. Sometimes people *gunnysack*—dump all the grievances and annoyances collected over the course of a relationship, on an unsuspecting partner in the middle of what was supposed to be a discussion of a specific issue. People may attempt to demonstrate their own superiority in regard to a particular issue rather than show respect for a partner's opinion and independent judgment.

Finally, in some cases communication fails because one or the other partner has an *annoying mode of delivery*. Perhaps it involves rapid speech or excessive swearing or soft, barely audible speech. Sometimes it stems from a vocal monotone or an annoying accent. Whatever the cause, the effect is that the listener tunes out and fails to pay attention to the messages being conveyed.

Observations of Troubled Couples' Communication.   One of the primary ways in which social scientists study the inner workings of intimate relationships is through direct observation of couples in a laboratory setting. Psychologist John Gottman and his colleagues have studied hundreds of couples in their laboratory at the University of Washington (in Seattle), known as the Love Lab. Gottman also has a very busy counseling practice in which he helps troubled couples try to learn how to improve their communication styles and strategies.

Based on frequent, in-depth observations of more than 600 couples who were studied over a nine-month period, Gottman and his colleagues have identified six communication patterns that indicate a couple is in trouble. Dr. Gottman reports that within the first three minutes of a fifteen-minute discussion, he and his colleagues can predict how the discussion will end in terms of whether it will have a positive or negative tone and will result in a resolution of the conflicted issue just by noting the extent to which each of these six destructive communication patterns occur. Answers to the following questions are key in predicting not only the out-

ContentSELECT

Couples and
Communication

come of a specific discussion but most likely the long-term prognosis for the relationship (Gottman and Silver, 1999, pp. 26–46).

1 *Does the discussion have a **harsh set-up**?* Does one or the other spouse, or perhaps both, open the discussion with criticism, sarcasm, and/or contempt?

2 *Do the "four horsemen of the apocalypse" show up during the course of the discussion?* Do the partners' verbal and nonverbal behaviors include criticism, contempt, defensiveness, and/or stonewalling? Gottman refers to these as the **four horsemen of the apocalypse** because they signal that the end of the relationship may be near (just as four horsemen appear in the Bible to indicate that the apocalypse is near).

a. The first horseman, *criticism,* goes beyond the straightforward stating of a complaint or dissatisfaction to an attack on the partner's character or personality.

b. *Contempt,* which Gottman regards as the most destructive of the four horsemen, includes a number of ways in which one partner shows disgust or disrespect for the other: name calling, eye rolling, sneering, mocking, or hostile humor.

c. *Defensiveness,* the third horseman, refers to one partner's attempt to explain his or her actions in response to the other's attacks. Typically, however, defensiveness is not effective in stopping conflict. Partners who are on the attack don't apologize or back down in response to his or her partner's defensiveness. They aren't looking for an explanation. The specific issue isn't necessarily of importance to them. They are simply using it as an opportunity to start or increase conflict and to hurt their partner.

d. *Stonewalling,* the fourth of the four horsemen, is used to describe the situation in which one partner tunes out the other's comments. Stone-wallers blatantly signal their lack of interest in the conversation, and thus, their concern for the partner, by refusing to provide any kind of common feedback that listeners typically provide to indicate that they are, indeed, paying attention, following the conversation, and caring about the speaker's feelings (e.g., nodding or muttering *listening noises* such as "uh huh").

One of the couples Gottman observed in his lab, Peter and Cynthia, provides a clear example of a relationship in trouble, as the four horsemen ride into their discussion (Gottman and Silver, 1999, pp. 29–31):

> Peter, the manager of a shoe store, showed a great deal of contempt when he interacted with Cynthia. When he and Cynthia were asked to discuss their disparate views about spending money, Peter made the following comment: "Just look at the difference in our vehicles and our clothes. I think that says a lot for who we are and what we value. I mean, you tease me about washing my truck, and you go and pay to have somebody wash your car. We're paying through the nose for your car and you can't be bothered to wash it. I think that's outrageous. I think that's probably the most spoiled thing that you do."
>
> Cynthia responded by telling him that it's physically difficult for her to wash her car herself. Peter dismissed her explanation and continued to take the tone of the morally superior human being: "I take care of my truck because if you take care of it, it'll last longer. I don't come from the mentality of 'ah, just go out and buy a new one' that you seem to."
>
> Still hoping to get Peter to understand her perspective, Cynthia said, "If you could help me to wash my car, I'd really love that. I'd really appreciate it." But instead of stepping back and taking this opportunity to restore some good feelings to the discussion, Peter made another comment that further escalated the hostility:

"How many times have you helped me wash my truck?" Cynthia tried once again to make things right with Peter: "I will help you wash your truck if you will help me wash my car."

But Peter's goal was not to resolve this issue but to put her down. So he says, "That's not my question. How many times have you helped me?" "Never," says Cynthia. "See?" says Peter. "That's where I think you have a little responsibility, too. It's like, you know, if your dad bought you a house would you expect him to come over and paint it for you, too?"

"Well, will you always help me wash my car, then?" Cynthia asks. "I will help you when I can. I won't give you a blanket guarantee for life. What are you gonna do, sue me?" asks Peter. And he laughs again.

It's pretty easy to see that this couple has some basic problems which must be resolved if they are to save their relationship. We'll come back to them again in a few paragraphs. Let's consider the four remaining questions Gottman uses to determine whether a couple has severe communication problems.

3 Has either of the partners begun to experience the sensation of "flooding"? This emotional state develops when a spouse's negativity is so overwhelming that it leaves the other totally overwhelmed and thrown off balance. When this happens, the flooded partner begins to monitor every moment of interactions with his or her partner so that he/she can be prepared for the next emotional outburst. Eventually, flooded partners reach a point where they can't remain engaged in the discussion. They need a "time out" to compose themselves.

4 Is either partner showing signs of severe physiological stress? Emotional upset is often accompanied by physiological changes such as an increase in heart rate, secretion of adrenaline, and blood pressure. Many of the bodily sensations partners experience resemble the fight-or-flight response that occurs in situations of extreme risk. These bodily changes make it very difficult for an individual to engage in a productive, problem-solving conversation.

5 Are repair attempts failing to stop the hostility? Gottman uses the term **repair attempt** to refer to any statement or action that prevents negativity from escalating out of control. They can help decrease the amount of tension in the air and also reduce the physiological signs of stress. Repair attempts can range from simple, even silly, gestures (such as grinning or sticking out your tongue) to eloquent verbal responses. Obviously, in some situations, sticking your tongue out or grinning could have the opposite effect of de-escalating tension. The effectiveness of a repair attempt depends on the overall quality of the couple's relationship. Couples who have a **positive sentiment override** (meaning that the positive emotions shared by the couple far outnumber the negative) will recognize what the partner is attempting to do with the gesture or comment. Those who have **negative sentiment override** will not. In fact, in the latter situation, such attempts not only fail to stop the negative exchange, they may make it worse.

Gottman offers the following example of a couple who have an overload of positive sentiments in their very close relationship and are able to stop discussions from erupting into hostility even when they strongly disagree with each other (p. 22): Nathaniel and Olivia are moving from the city to the suburbs. They have agreed about which house to buy and how to decorate it. They are asked in the laboratory to discuss an issue about which they do not agree—what car to buy. Nathaniel wants an SUV while Olivia wants a mini-van. The more they talk about this issue the more heated their discussion becomes and the louder their voices get. To an amateur in the marital observation business, their marriage might look doomed. But suddenly, Olivia puts her hands on her hips and sticks her tongue out, imitating their four year old son. Nathaniel anticipates that she is going to do this so he does it first. Then they both start to laugh. They have used this repair attempt in the past successfully. Once again, it helps them put things into perspective and stops the increasing tension they were experiencing.

6 *Do the partners have difficulty recalling happy memories from their early life together?* When couples are in the middle of a heated discussion, they may find it difficult to identify any of the aspects of their relationship or any qualities of their partner that they find appealing. But those who have an override of positive sentiments will be able to step back and talk about what attracted them to each other initially. Cynthia and Peter—the couple whose conversation about washing their cars was used to illustrate the four horsemen above—had difficulty remembering anything positive about their history together. They could provide the facts about the first time they met but very little else. When asked about the kinds of things they liked to do together earlier in their relationship, they had a hard time remembering. "Didn't we go on picnics or something?" Cynthia asked him and he shrugged, indicating that he didn't remember. Their memories of their wedding were just as empty. Peter had pneumonia and a temperature of 103 degrees at the wedding. His main memory, other than feeling sick, was being in the limo afterwards with Cynthia and his best man. His friend turned on the stereo, and the Motley Crue song, "Same Old Ball and Chain" came blasting out. Cynthia remembered feeling hurt because many guests left right after dinner. Peter recalls that at the reception the guests kept banging on their glasses with spoons to make him and Cynthia kiss. "I was getting really annoyed," he recalled. To sum up their wedding day, he said, "It was your basic tragedy" (Gottman and Silver, 1999, p. 43).

Debriefing Conversations

One of the most commonplace forms of communication between intimate partners is the debriefing talk at the end of the day (Vangelisti and Banski, 1993). After being separated many hours each day, as most couples are, they return home to engage in **debriefing conversations**—talks in which they tell each other about the events of the day. Studies of both married and unmarried couples show that the more time partners spend in debriefing conversations, the happier they are with their relationship (Vangelisti and Banski, 1993).

Debriefing conversations show that each partner cares about the other. As one partner told an interviewer, "It's important to show that you care what the other is doing . . . show some interest in what they are doing in their lives" (Vangelisti and Banski, 1993, p. 155). Men and women approach debriefing conversations differently. Men often see the debriefing talk as a source of information (**report talk**); women may see it as a way of strengthening the rapport between partners (**rapport talk**) (Tannen, 1990). In their debriefing conversations women offer intricate details about their day (Vangelisti and Banski, 1993). We return to gender differences in communication later in the chapter.

End-of-the-day conversations are just one form of communication between intimate partners. Another version of the debriefing conversation is "pillow talk," which refers to the exchange of information couples have at night, in bed, before they fall asleep. There have been news reports and speculations over the years, charging that the wives of U.S. presidents (in recent years, Rosalyn Carter, Nancy Reagan, and Hillary Rodham Clinton) have used pillow talk to influence their husbands' views and decisions. President Franklin D. Roosevelt and his wife Eleanor had a distant and cold marriage, so instead of engaging in pillow talk, Eleanor produced a steady flow of written memoranda that the president read in bed at the end of the day (Goodwin, 1994).

Self-Disclosure

Self-disclosure (revealing one's thoughts and feelings to another person) has been shown by a number of different researchers to be an important part of communication between partners (Jourard, 1971; Hendrick, 1981). Some part of every person's life is secret—known only to him- or herself. We all have thoughts and feelings that we do not reveal to other people because doing so would make us feel too vulnerable. If we are to have close and intimate relationships, however, we must reveal ourselves to the other person. It is the very essence of a close, intimate relationship that we feel safe enough to reveal things that could be "used against us."

Self-Disclosure

Self-disclosure is in many ways nothing more or less than honest, open communication; but in self-disclosure the feelings and emotions are much stronger. Lillian Rubin (1983) has used the term *intimacy* as her way of describing self-disclosure and emphasizing the exchange of intimate feelings: "Intimacy is some kind of reciprocal expression of feeling and thought, not out of fear or dependent need, but out of a wish to know another's inner life and to be able to share one's own" (Rubin, 1983, p. 90).

Partners in happy, nondistressed relationships are likely to have higher levels of self-disclosure than unhappy, distressed couples (Hendrick, 1981). In a study of long-term married couples, husbands and wives were much more satisfied with their marriages when they confided in each other (Lee, 1988). The causal link between self-disclosure and marital satisfaction may, of course, go in either direction. Couples satisfied with their marriages are more likely to share confidences; in contrast, couples who share confidences may achieve greater satisfaction in their marriages.

Is Honesty Always the Best Policy?

Self-disclosure in an intimate relationship is generally related to greater satisfaction, but some research has revealed that when these are expressions of self-doubt or fear, however, they may *decrease* satisfaction with the relationship (Cozby, 1973). When partners are in conflict-ridden relationships, their self-disclosures may be largely negative. Partners who persistently disclose their feelings of anger, disappointment, disapproval, suspicion, jealousy, and other negative emotions are not thereby likely to improve their relationship. Clearly, self-disclosure, in itself, is not unconditionally positive for a relationship.

The positive, or negative, effect of self-disclosure depends on several factors. First is the type of information divulged. Information about a sexual indiscretion or sexual dissatisfaction with a partner is likely to harm the relationship.

A second, closely related, factor concerns the spouse's motivation for revealing the truth. If the purpose of disclosing an extramarital affair, for instance, is to ease one's own guilty conscience, it would be kinder to confess to a professional counselor rather than to one's spouse. If, in contrast, the reason for concealing dissatisfaction with the sexual aspects of the relationship is to protect the partner's feelings, it would be more beneficial to the relationship to gently reveal one's honest reactions. When stated in terms of one's own needs rather than the spouse's failures, loving, honest communication about one's dissatisfaction is acceptable—in fact, necessary—for a mutually enjoyable relationship. Pent-up frustrations, rather than protecting the partner's ego, may be more damaging to the relationship over the long run (Shehan, 1982, p. 66). Other negative motivating factors that should discourage a person from telling all are revenge and self-defense.

The third factor that should be considered when deciding about "telling all" concerns the timing of the potential disclosure. Honesty about a sexual indiscretion, for instance, may have different effects depending on the amount of time that

HEAD*line*   Keeping Secrets

About 40 percent of married Americans admit keeping a secret from their spouses, but most have nothing to do with an affair or fantasy, a new poll has found. The most common type of secret is how much money they spend. Of those with a secret, 48 percent said they had not told their spouses about the real price of something they bought, according to the poll published in the August 2001 issue of *Reader's Digest.* "I don't think there's a marriage where that didn't happen," said one respondent, a woman married for 26 years. "You always get those good bargains, you know?" Another wife said: "I don't like to tell him how much I spend when I go shopping. I'm afraid he'll cut back on the budget." It wasn't just women who concealed information about their spending habits from their spouses; the percentage was about the same for husbands. One man concealed the price of one small purchase: "The item wasn't very big but the price of it was."

The second most common type of secret, at about 15 percent, pertained to failure at work or children's misbehavior. "There are times your kids do things that you know would make the other party ballistic," one woman said.

Only two percent of all respondents, equally split between men and women, said they had an extramarital affair that remained a secret. Fourteen percent kept mum about being attracted to another person.

In response to another question, 16 percent of both men and women admitted that at least once during their marriage they wished they could wake up and not be married any more.

Some people kept secrets not out of guilt but to avoid hurt feelings. For example, one woman said her husband told her for years that her cocker spaniel had been stolen to spare her the knowledge that it had been killed by a car.

The poll, conducted by Ipsos-NPD, an Illinois-based research group, has a margin of error of plus or minus 3 percentage points.

Source: Reprinted with permission of the Associated Press, wire story, July 23, 2001.

---

has passed since the incident. Whether it is better to confess immediately or long after the potential threat has vanished depends, again, on one's motivation for confessing and on the state of the relationship at the time of the revelation. In an unstable relationship, information about a long-ago affair may strain a partner's trust or may be used as a weapon against the "guilty" party in conflicts (Shehan, 1982, p. 66). It seems, then, that honesty is never the best policy if a person's purpose is to ease his or her own conscience or to seek revenge. Honest, open communication between partners, in contrast, is always desirable (Shehan, 1982, p. 70). In spite of the desirability of honest communication, however, many partners keep secrets from each other, as the Headlines box shows.

Effective Listening

Effective communication involves not only the ability to relay information to another person, but also the ability to understand and respond to the information being presented. Communicating depends on being a good listener, which requires commitment, practice, patience, and skill. Learning to be an empathic listener means going beyond simply trying to absorb the information being presented, to trying to understand the feelings behind the speaker's words.

A number of sources of interference can prevent a person from listening effectively. Doing something else (such as watching television or reading the mail)

TABLE 7.3

How to Be a Good Listener

Communication Goal	Actions to Take	Actions to Avoid
Affirm the speaker's feelings	Make comments that show you recognize the speaker's actions	Don't deny or reject the speaker's feelings
Receive and provide accurate information	Ask the speaker for clarification if you don't understand what she or he is saying	Don't use humor inappropriately if you don't understand or feel uncomfortable with what is being said
Be appropriately engaged in the conversation	Share similar experiences or feelings you have had	Don't give advice unless the speaker asks for it; don't tell the speaker what you would do
Pay attention to the speaker	Maintain good eye contact with the speaker	Don't look at your watch or a clock; don't yawn or tap your fingers while the speaker is talking
Provide socioemotional support for the speaker	Make comments that show you think the speaker is a good person	Don't give feedback that criticizes the speaker

while another person is trying to speak to you not only interferes with your ability to listen effectively, it also sends a message to the speaker that you're not interested in what he or she has to say. A good listener gives the speaker his or her full attention. External noise (such as loud music or the sound of a dishwasher in the background) can also interfere with a person's ability to listen well. It's important to find a quiet setting for intimate conversations.

Anticipating what will happen next in a conversation and mentally rehearsing your response also can distract you from what is being said at the moment. And a high level of personal stress not only decreases the ability to focus on what is being said, but can also impair the ability to remember what has been said.

When you communicate with someone, you are not only exchanging *information* but also your *feelings* about the information and the person (the metamessage). Sometimes people call this "reading between the lines" or understanding what has been left unsaid. Listeners can realize that feelings are being disclosed and seek to acknowledge them, rather than simply responding to the information being presented. There are a number of techniques people can practice to become better listeners, to learn how to hear the underlying message being sent and to convey interest and concern for a speaker. Table 7.3 summarizes some of these techniques.

Gender Differences in Communication Styles: Barriers to Intimacy

Scientific research, case studies of couples in marriage counseling, and innumerable stories in popular magazines all reach a similar conclusion: Men do not easily express their feelings, at least not as easily as their female partners would like. The resulting lack of intimate communication between many men and women has led one researcher to describe marital partners as "intimate strangers" (Rubin, 1983). The problem is often identified by women when they plaintively say, "He won't talk to me." In the following quotation, one wife describes her frustration in getting her husband to talk to her. Ironically, she was first attracted to him because he appeared to be the "strong and silent" type. She was impressed by "his quiet power and his cool way of staying in control of his feelings. I remember thinking, 'This must be what a real man is like.' Then for twelve years I begged him to talk to me" (Pogrebin, 1983, p. 90). This woman longed for her husband either to ask her how she felt or just to sit around and talk about their lives. It was only when she reached a state where she would "get crazy" that he would say, "'Okay, you want to talk, *talk*!' But then she says she felt like a jerk saying, 'I just want you to say you care'" (Pogrebin, 1983, p. 90).

How do these silent, noncommunicative men feel about women's requests for communication? One perplexed and exasperated man vehemently expressed his feelings to an interviewer:

> The whole goddam business of what you're calling intimacy bugs the hell out of me. I never know what you women mean when you talk about it. Karen complains that I don't talk to her, but it's not talk she wants, it's some other damn thing, only I don't know what the hell it is. Feelings, she keeps asking for. So what am I supposed to do if I don't have any to give her or talk about, just because she decides it's time to talk about feelings? Tell me, will you; maybe we can get some peace around here. (Rubin, 1983, p. 66)

Female and Male Dialects.   A large and growing body of research on interpersonal communication shows that women and men have different styles of communicating, not only in presenting information but in receiving it, as well (Tannen, 1990, 1994). In fact, some linguists have concluded that there may even be distinct female and male dialects (Lakoff, 1975), which can be thought of as the speech characteristics of a geographic region or social group. The verbal and nonverbal components of women's and men's communications styles differ in a number of ways (Pearson, Turner, and Todd-Mancillas, 1991). For instance, women and men use slightly different vocabularies, reflecting their different socialization patterns and life experiences. They also use questions differently, as discussed later. Gender patterns are also reflected in what Sapiro (1990) has called the "right-of-way" in space (such as touching, eye contact, and staring) and in speech (such as amount of talking, turn taking, interruptions and overlaps, control of topics, and use of silence) and in listening styles. Let's discuss these patterns in more detail.

Conversational Right-of-Way.   A persistent myth in our society is that women talk more than men. Much research has shown, however, that in mixed-sex groups men talk more than women. Men also control the topics and direction of conversation, use interpersonal techniques that discourage women from speaking, and attempt to restrict the amount of influence women can exert on others in the group. This pattern of control is referred to as the **conversational right-of-way.** For instance, studies have found that men interrupt other people considerably more often than women do. They are especially likely to interrupt women (Zimmerman and West, 1975; Eakins and Eakins, 1978; Hall, 1984). And when challenged by other speakers, men are more likely to continue speaking simultaneously with the challenger. Men are also more likely to overlap their comments with women's, which means that they anticipate the end of women's comments and begin their turn just as women are ending, so that their remarks overlap by a few words (Zimmerman and West, 1975).

Listening.   Women "listen" with their eyes and mouths, as well as their ears. That is, they are much more likely to look intently at the person who is speaking, as a way of showing interest. They also make listening noises (the ever-present "Hmm," "Really?" and "Right" that dot women's conversations) and nod their heads while another person is speaking, once again as a way of showing their interest in the speaker. Men use these listening patterns less frequently than women and may mis-

Research has shown that women are more active listeners than men, insofar as they look directly at the person who is speaking to indicate their interest in what is being said.

interpret them when they appear in women's interactions with them. To a man, head-nodding indicates agreement. But he may discover, when it's the woman's turn to talk, that she actually disagrees with him. This can be frustrating, even infuriating to those who don't understand the purpose of the nod or the softly murmured "Uh-huh." It may be tempting to attribute the mismatch between the nonverbal behavior and the verbal behavior to indecisiveness on the woman's part. This, of course, may contribute to the stereotyping of women as fickle. In actuality, women's active listening style may be simply a way of showing they care about the speaker.

Women, in contrast, expect the people to whom they're talking to look at them. When a man continues to watch television or read the newspaper when a woman is talking, she may mislabel his failure to look at her as a lack of interest.

Use of Questions.   Women and men also use questions in different ways. You may think that the only reason for asking a question is to get information that is relevant to a specific issue. If you think this way, you are most likely a man. Men use questions primarily as a way of getting information. Women, on the contrary, also use questions as a way of inviting another person to talk or to indicate interest in what the person is saying, to avoid offending another person, or to indicate flexibility. Rather than stating their opinions or observations directly, or making direct demands, women phrase demands as requests, or hide them in long, complex sentences to soften them. For instance, the most direct way to ask someone to close a door is to simply say, "Please close the door." Women are more likely to phrase this request in an indirect way, such as "If you don't mind, would you close the door, please?" They may also be more likely to use "tag" questions (follow a declarative statement with a related question; for instance, "It's hot in here, isn't it?").

Women also personalize statements ("In my opinion . . . "), use disclaimers ("I may be wrong, but . . . "), or rising intonations when stating an opinion, as though asking a question or asking for permission. This type of hesitancy in speaking is typical of subordinates, and both reflects and reinforces the system of dominance and deference characteristic of communication between superiors and subordinates (Sapiro, 1990, p. 258).

Overall, research shows that women work harder to initiate and maintain communication, but that men actually control the course of a conversation. Women ask questions as a way of starting a conversation. Men veto topics (and thus stop conversation) by failing to respond to the questions or by giving only short, factual answers. Lack of awareness of gender (and status) differences in communication styles can result in considerable frustration and negative stereotyping. Although men's speech is described as rational, authoritative, decisive, dominant, and forceful, women's is described as emotional, tentative, soft, and *trivial* (Kramarae, 1981).

The Source of Gender Differences in Communication Styles.   Many differences in women's and men's communication styles are the result of differences in power and authority associated with being female or male in our society (Lakoff, 1975; Kramarae, 1981). In fact, gender-based communication patterns parallel those between superiors and subordinates in the workplace or military. In such organizations, and in informal groups, as well, status and hierarchy rankings are associated with communication rights and duties. Superiors have a number of rights in regard to communication: the right to veto or affirm the proposals of subordinates, to expect loyalty and obedience from subordinates, to monopolize communication within the organization (or group) and between the organization and the outside, to be insensitive to the personal needs of subordinates, and to speak out on all sorts of issues, even with little knowledge of those issues (Thompson, 1961). Subordinates, in contrast, operate under a number of communication obligations: to leave the final word to superiors, to defer to superiors, to be obedient to superiors, and to be responsive to superiors' personal needs. As emphasized throughout this text, men are assigned the role of superior and women, of subordinate, in nearly every society. Thus, men's communication styles follow the one prescribed for superiors, while women's follow the one prescribed for subordinates.

Intimate Communication as Socioemotional Support

Although too much self-disclosure may have a negative effect on some relationships, the more serious problem for many couples is unequal self-disclosure. When one partner is revealing more emotions and feelings than the other, this may have a negative effect on their relationship. Even when one partner perceives an imbalance in the amount of self-disclosure, the effect on the relationship can be negative (Davidson, Balswick, and Halverson, 1983). Men are generally less able, or willing, than women to reveal their emotions and feelings (Snell et al., 1988). The tendency of men to be less revealing about themselves in an interpersonal relationship has led to men being labeled *inexpressive* (Balswick, 1986; Snell, Miller, and Belk, 1988).

Supportive communication from a loved one is not only important to the success of the relationship but may also be critical in helping a partner deal with persistent personal problems. Yet in some cases these personal problems may, in themselves, pose a significant psychological barrier to communication. The extreme stress associated with involvement in a natural disaster or in a trauma (such as floods, earthquakes, plane crashes and automobile accidents, combat, and violent personal assaults such as rape) can seriously impede the development of intimacy.

Working through the delayed stress associated with the trauma can be facilitated by intimate communication in which the victim is shown that he or she is cared for and loved, esteemed and valued (Cobb, 1976, p. 30). However, this type of communication may be extremely difficult when one partner suffers from posttraumatic stress disorder (PTSD), which can discourage intimacy in several ways. It reduces the victim's willingness to self-disclose, increases the victim's use of defensive communication behavior, and causes intimate partners to develop communication apprehension, which leads to defensive responses (Shehan, 1987).

The feeling of mistrust associated with PTSD causes victims to closely guard the amount of information they give other people. Victims want to maintain the personal distance between themselves and others because they fear they will be condemned and rejected. Nonverbal behavior (avoiding prolonged eye contact, hesitating to touch, and using menacing or threatening facial expressions, stances, and postures) is particularly useful in creating and maintaining this distance (Shehan, 1987, p. 58).

Victims of PTSD have defensive styles of communication, which include threatening and trying to control other people, giving judgmental and dogmatic responses, and acting indifferent or superior. Victims' fear of communication reduces their amount of self-disclosure, their trust in other people, and their over-all amount of communication (Powers and Hutchinson, 1979). Partners of PTSD victims may reach the point at which they dread speaking to him or her, even to ask straightforward, impersonal questions about everyday life, such as in the debriefing talks described earlier in this chapter (Shehan, 1987, p. 58).

As a result of one partner's psychological distress, then, intimate communication can become defensive rather than supportive. This not only lessens the victim's chance of successfully working through the trauma, but also reduces the partner's satisfaction with the relationship (Derlega and Chaikin, 1977; Jorgensen and Gaudy, 1980).

Therapists who work with victims of this and other psychological disorders, then, must design treatment programs based on providing socioemotional support. Partners must be taught how to resist the impulse to withdraw and to return hostile and inattentive responses with tolerance and encouragement. This type of communication can begin to chip away a partner's resistance to open communication.

Summary

Marital quality has been conceptualized and measured in several different ways. Research has shown which personal and background characteristics are most likely to lead to high or low marital quality. Couples who have higher socioeconomic status, have similar background characteristics, and who agree about marital roles are likely to have higher levels of marital quality. Having children tends to reduce marital quality, as does the length of time in marriage.

Types of marital relationships are produced by cultures and by the interactions between individuals. At a cultural level, marriage may be conflictual, patriarchal, role segregated, companionate, and peer.

All intimate relationships are characterized by three dynamic processes: power, conflict, and communication. Power, which is the ability of an individual to produce intended effects on the behavior of others, is found in all intimate relationships, just as in other parts of society. In working-class couples, power is typically held by husbands, although they often claim that decisions are made on a fifty–fifty basis. Working-class women may make gender-related decisions having to do with household labor and childrearing.

Sources of power include legitimate authority, which is often embedded in patriarchy or religious beliefs. Resources, or things of value that can be given to other people, are a second source of power. In contemporary societies, the primary resources are economic. Expertise or ability can also be a source of power, as can physical force. Men often have the advantage over women in gaining power from some combination of these sources.

Resource theory, which emphasizes the importance of educational attainment and income as sources of power, explains some of the differences in power among U.S. couples. In more traditional societies, however, belief in male superiority (patriarchy) may be more important than resources in determining marital power. A study of U.S. couples found that lesbian partners tried not to base decision-making rights on the partner's individual income.

Conflict occurs in all intimate relationships, unless one partner is exercising absolute control over the other person. The breakdown of traditional families, in which fathers had patriarchal authority, may have actually increased the amount of conflict because other family members feel they have a right to challenge their husbands or fathers.

At a general level, conflict arises when less powerful people struggle for more power, while the more powerful resist their efforts. The issues found by researchers to produce the most conflict among married couples are money, children, housekeeping, and sex.

Communication is a crucial component in successful intimate relationships. Studies of happy and unhappy couples have found significant differences in the way partners communicate with one another. Happy couples are more considerate and view each other more accurately, while unhappy couples are skeptical and critical of their partners and often misperceive or misinterpret communications.

Debriefing conversations at the end of the day help couples maintain their relationships. Men and women tend to view and use debriefing conversations differently—men for information, women for maintaining closeness.

Self-disclosure (revealing one's intimate thoughts and feelings) is an important part of intimate relationships, but an excessive amount can have a negative effect. Total honesty is similarly important, but must be done with consideration, care, and sensitivity, and after some introspection.

Communication problems can result from the physical environment, situational characteristics, cultural and social differences, and psychological disorders. Communication can be destructive or constructive. Destructive communication involves introducing negative and unnecessary information into the conversation. An important part of communication is the ability to listen effectively.

There are important gender differences in communication, including styles of communication, in which women customarily soften their messages. Men use more assertive conversational styles, including interrupting others and controlling the topics of conversation. Women are much more willing to self-disclose, and they generally want more self-disclosure from their partners than men are willing to give. Serious communication pathologies, such as those experienced by individuals who have gone through traumatic events (military combat, rape, natural disasters) accentuate the importance of communication in intimate relationships.

Peer marriages represent a new form of intimate relationship in which traditional gender roles have been discarded and partners relate to each other in equitable and equal terms. Although rare at the present time, they may become more common in the future as couples realize their benefits over traditional marriage.

Key Terms

Companionate marriage (p. 204)

Conflict marriage (p. 202)

Constructive communication (p. 217)

Conversational right-of-way (p. 225)

Debriefing conversations (p. 221)

Destructive communication (p. 217)

Direct observation (p. 194)

Egalitarian beliefs (p. 211)

Flooding (p. 220)

Four horsemen of the apocalypse (p. 219)

Harsh set-up (p. 219)

Legitimate authority (p. 208)

Marital adjustment (p. 196)

Marital quality (p. 195)

Marital scripts (p. 201)

Marital stability (p. 196)

Marital success (p. 196)

Negative sentiments override (p. 220)

Patriarchal marriage (p. 202)

Patriarchy (p. 208)

Peer marriage (p. 204)

Positive sentiments override (p. 220)

Power (p. 206)

Principle of least interest (p. 212)

Purdah (p. 202)

Rapport talk (p. 221)

Repair attempts (p. 220)

Report talk (p. 221)

Resource theory (p. 210)

Resources (p. 210)

Role-segregated marriage (p. 203)

Self-disclosure (p. 222)

Self-report data (p. 194)

Review Questions

1. Identify the major sources of conflict in intimate relationships.

2. List and briefly discuss the major obstacles to effective communication in intimate relationships.

3. List and briefly discuss the sources of interpersonal power that operate in intimate relationships.

4. Identify the ways in which being male can give a partner more power in a heterosexual relationship.

5. In what ways can gender differences in communication styles impede our efforts to communicate with each other?

Critical Thinking Questions

1. Why is money so often a source of conflict in intimate relationships? What can be done to help couples resolve their differences about money and budgeting?

2. How does power emerge as an aspect of sexual relationships? Is it possible for sexual relationships to be devoid of power struggles? Why or why not?

3. Has patriarchy been declining in western societies?

4. Compare and contrast various ways in which social researchers attempt to determine who holds the most power in intimate relationships.

Online Resources Available for This Chapter

www.ablongman.com/marriageandfamily

■ **Online Study Guide with Practice Tests**

■ **PowerPoint Chapter Outlines**

■ Links to Marriage and Family Websites

■ ContentSelect Research Database

■ Self-Assessment Activities

Further Reading

Books

Bartkowksi, John P. *Remaking the Godly Marriage: Gender Negotiation in Evangelical Families.* New Brunswick, NJ: Rutgers University Press, 2001. This book presents results of a study that examined debates over gender and the family as they are manifested within contemporary evangelicalism.

Bem, Sandra Lipsitz. *An Unconventional Family.* New Haven: Yale University Press, 2001. Offers an autobiographical account of psychologists Sandra and Daryl Bem's nearly 30-year marriage in which they developed a nontraditional gender arrangement.

Blood, Robert O., and Wolfe, Donald M. *Husbands and Wives: The Dynamics of Married Living.* New York: Free Press, 1980. This book is in part a report of the findings gained through interviews with 732 city families and 178 farm families, identifying key aspects of marital dynamics.

Blumstein, Philip, and Schwartz, Pepper. *American Couples: Money, Work, Sex.* New York: William Morrow, 1983. A groundbreaking study of married heterosexual, cohabiting heterosexual, and same-sex couples focusing on economics and sexuality.

Gottman, John M., and Silver, Nan. *The Seven Principles for Making Marriage Work.* New York: Three Rivers Press, 2000. Psychologist Gottman reports on results of observation studies of marriages he has conducted in his laboratory at the University of Washington.

Rubin, Lillian. *Intimate Strangers: Men and Women Together.* New York: HarperCollins, 1990. Rubin explains not just how the differences between women and men arise but how they affect such critical issues as intimacy, sexuality, dependency, work, and parenting.

Schwartz, Pepper. *Peer Marriage: How Love Between Equals Really Works.* New York: Free Press, 1994. An examination of modern egalitarian marriage that identifies the distinguishing characteristics, assets, and liabilities of traditional versus peer marriages.

Tannen, Deborah. *You Just Don't Understand: Women and Men in Conversation.* New York: Morrow, 2001. Reviews research that shows that women and men tend to use different communication styles that can interfere with effective cross-gender communication.

*Content*SELECT *Articles*

Guilbert, D., Vacc, N., and Pasley, K. "The Relationship of Gender Role Beliefs, Negativity, Distancing, and Marital Instability." *Family Journal* 8(2), 2000: 124–133. **[Database Psychology]**   What is the process by which couples move from marital stability to marital instability? Based on an assumption that gender role beliefs are a primary initiator of negativity in marital relationships, Guilbert and his colleagues investigated the relationships among gender role beliefs, negativity, and distancing to determine if they are key factors in marital instability.

Halloran, E. "The Role of Marital Power in Depression and Marital Distress." *American Journal of Family Therapy* 26(1), 1998: 3–15. **[Database: Psychology]**   Are marital power, depression, and marital distress interrelated? The author of this study posited that marital power inequities play a significant role in depression and subsequent marital distress. A comprehensive review of the relevant literature supports the author's supposition that marital power is a moderator of sorts—when there are great inequalities in marital power, a stronger relationship between depression and marital distress exists. Conversely, when more equal power balances are exhibited, depression and marital distress may not be as strongly associated.

Haws, W., and Mallinckrodt, B. "Separation-Individuation from Family of Origin and Marital Adjustment of Recently Married Couples." *American Journal of Family Therapy* 26(4), 1998: 293–307. **[Database: Psychology]** Examining the connection between separation-individuation from parents and marital adjustment of newlyweds to marriage, Hans et al. found that increased levels of separation from family of origin resulted in better adjustment. Specifically, the husband's continued bonds with his parents predicted marital adjustment in both spouses. When a husband is more conflictually dependent on his mother and more functionally dependent on his father, lower marital adjustment occurs.

Lauritsen, J. "The Age–Crime Debate: Assessing the Limits of Longitudinal Self-Report Data." *Social Forces* 77(1), 1998: 127–155. **[Database: Social Work]**   Self-reports, typically gathered from surveys, questionnaires, and interviews, are perhaps the most common form of gathering information in social science fields; however, the generated responses may change based on interpretation of the assessment items. This current study addresses the reliability of self-reports in assessing the relationship between age and delinquency, serious offending, and victimization. Specifically, the author sought to determine if, as subjects matured, interpretations of the assessment items changed.

Rogers, S., and Amato, P. "Have Changes in Gender Relations Affected Marital Quality?" *Social Forces* 79(2), 2000: 731–754. **[Database: Social Work]**   In an attempt to examine the relationship between gender relations and marital quality, Rogers and Amato compared dimensions of marital quality from respondents married between 1981 and 1997 and subjects married between 1964 and 1980. While contemporary husbands and wives held to less traditional gender beliefs, they reported higher levels of marital discord than those from the less recent cohort. In spite of changes in gender relations and the apparent marital discord, overall marital quality remains high in contemporary marriages.

8

Violence and Abuse

*Mother ordered me to strip off
my clothes and stand by the
kitchen stove. I shook from a
combination of fear and
embarrassment. . . .*

She then reached over and turned on the gas burners to the kitchen stove. Mother told me that she had read an article about a mother who had her son lie on top of a hot stove. I instantly became terrified. My brain became numb, and my legs wobbled. I wanted to disappear. I closed my eyes, wishing her away. My brain locked up when I felt Mother's hand clamp my arms as if it were a vise grip.

"You've made my life a living hell!" she sneered. "Now it's time I showed you what hell is like!" Gripping my arm, Mother held it in the orange-blue flame. My skin seemed to explode from the heat. I could smell the scorched hairs from my burnt arm. As hard as I fought, I could not force Mother to let go of my arm. Finally I fell to the floor, on my hands and knees, and tried to blow cool air on my arm. "It's too bad your drunken father's not here to save you," she hissed. Mother then ordered me to climb up onto the stove and lie on the flames so she could watch me burn. I refused, crying and pleading. I felt so scared I stomped my feet in protest. But Mother continued to force me on top of the stove. I watched the flames, praying the gas might run out.

Suddenly I began to realize the longer I could keep myself off the top of the stove, the better my chances were for staying alive. . . . To keep Mother off balance, I began to ask whining questions. This infuriated her even more, and Mother began to rain blows around my head and chest. The more Mother

Key Questions

1 Are women as violent as men within the family context?

2 Does spanking contribute to children's likelihood of becoming violent?

3 Is family violence declining or are people becoming more reluctant to report suspected cases of abuse and neglect?

4 In what ways do social institutions and cultural norms contribute to family violence?

5 In what ways is family violence transmitted from one generation to another?

slugged me, the more I began to realize I won! Anything was better than burning on the stove.

Finally, I heard the front door fly open. It was Ron. My heart surged with relief. The blood from Mother's face drained. She knew she had lost.

Source: Pelzer, Dave. *A Child Called "It": One Child's Courage to Survive.* Deerfield Beach, FL: Health Communications, Inc., 1995, pp. 40–42.

*I*t can hardly be a surprise to anyone that violence exists in many American families. Television gives us vivid images of family violence through made-for-TV movies, dramas, talk shows, and real-life scenes on *Cops*. We see battered wives and girlfriends, abused children, and mistreated elders. Yet even though we know how frequently violence occurs, we often dismiss it as the unusual case. We dismiss conflict and violence as things that happen to "other" people; other people who are "sick" or mentally ill, deviant, or even criminal. But violence should not be dismissed as something "committed by horrible or bizarre people" (Gelles, 1993, p. 40).

In the pages ahead, we show that violence in families takes many different forms and any family members may be the victims of violence. Most often, though, the weaker members are the victims. Women are more likely to be hurt than men, children are more likely to be abused than adults, and the elderly are more likely to be victims than the middle aged. Physical violence, including punishment for misdeeds, is most likely to be used by the stronger against the weaker.

In this chapter we consider various forms of violence, abuse, and mistreatment in families and other intimate relationships. Family violence across cultures is examined first, before we turn to a consideration of family violence in the United States. The most prominent forms of family violence are intimate partner violence, the physical and sexual abuse of children, violence between siblings, and the mistreatment and abuse of elderly family members. We conclude this chapter with an assessment of trends in family violence.

Defining Intimate Violence

*T*here is little consensus among researchers regarding the most appropriate way to define the term **intimate partner violence.** One of the aspects on which researchers disagree centers on the desirability of limiting the definition to acts that are carried out with the intention, or perceived intention, of causing physical pain or injury to another person. Limiting the term to acts *intended* to cause harm ignores the wide range of behaviors that individuals use to control, intimidate, or dominate another person within the context of an intimate relationship. Such behaviors include verbal abuse, imprisonment, humiliation, stalking, and denial of access to financial resources, shelter, or services. Another contested aspect of the definition centers on the limitation of the term to actions that occur between persons who are married or living together as a couple. Not all researchers are willing to include persons who are dating or who consider themselves to be a couple but who are not living together.

In this chapter, we use the definition of intimate partner violence that was adopted by the National Violence Against Women Survey (which is discussed in this chapter). Our definition is broader than the ones that emphasize the intent or perceived intent behind acts. We include rape, physical assault, and stalking perpetrated by current and former dates, spouses, and cohabiting partners. Both same-sex and opposite sex cohabitants are included. **Physical assault** is defined as behaviors that threaten, attempt, or actually inflict physical harm. A wide range of behaviors can fall under this term, from slapping, pushing, and shoving to using a gun. **Stalking** is defined as "a course of conduct directed at a specific person involving repeated visual or physical proximity; nonconsensual communication; verbal, written, or implied threats; or a combination thereof that would cause fear in a reasonable person" (Tjaden and Thoennes, 2000, p. 5). This definition of stalking does not require stalkers to make a credible threat against the victim, but it does require the victim to feel a high level of fear. Finally, **rape** is defined as an event that occurs without the victim's consent and that involves the use of threat or force to penetrate the victim's vagina or anus by penis, tongue, fingers, or object or the victim's mouth by penis. This includes both attempted and completed rape (Tjaden and Thoennes, 2000, p. 5).

We begin our consideration of family or intimate violence by examining some of the research that has been done in different cultures and societies around the world.

Cross-Cultural Perspectives on Intimate Violence

"Violence against women is the most pervasive yet least recognized human rights abuse in the world. It also is a profound health problem, sapping women's energy, compromising their physical health, and eroding their self-esteem. Despite its high costs, almost every society in the world has social institutions that legitimize, obscure, and deny abuse. The same acts that would be punished if directed at an employer, a neighbor, or an acquaintance often go unchallenged when men direct them at women, especially within the family" (Heise, Ellsberg, and Gottenmoeller, 1999, p. 3).

Partner violence occurs in all countries, crossing social, economic, religious, and cultural boundaries. There is a growing agreement among researchers and practitioners that intimate violence against women is generally part of a pattern of abusive behavior and control, rather than an isolated act of physical aggression.

In nearly fifty population-based surveys from around the world, anywhere from 10 to 50 percent of women report being hit or otherwise physically harmed by an intimate male partner at some point in their lives. Many cultures believe that men have the right to control their wives' behavior and that women who challenge that right—even by asking for household money or by expressing the needs of the children—may be punished. In countries as different as Bangladesh, Cambodia, India, Mexico, Nigeria, Pakistan, Papua New Guinea, Tanzania, and Zimbabwe, studies find that violence is frequently viewed as physical chastisement—the husband's right to *correct* an erring wife. Justifications for violence frequently evolve from norms about the proper roles and responsibilities of men and women. Typically, men are given free reign as long as they provide financially. Women are expected to tend the house and mind the children and to show their husbands obedience and respect. If a man perceives that his wife has somehow failed in her role, stepped beyond her bounds, or challenged his rights, he may react violently. A number of women's behaviors are regarded as "just cause" for men to abuse their female partners, including her failure to obey, talking back, not having food ready on time, failing to care adequately for children, questioning her husband about money or girlfriends, going somewhere without his permission, refusing him sex, or expressing suspicions of infidelity (Heise, Ellsberg, and Gottenmoeller, 1999; Levinson, 1989; Morley, 1994).

TABLE 8.1

Cross-Cultural Approval of Wife-Beating: Percentage, by Rationale, Selected Studies, 1985–1999

Country and Year	Respondents F = Female M = Male	She Neglects Children and/or House	She Refuses Him Sex	He Suspects Her of Adultery	She Answers Back or Disobeys
Brazil (Salvador, Bahia) 1999	M	—	—	19[a]	—
	F	—	—	11[a]	—
Chile (Santiago) 1999	M	—	—	12[a]	—
	F	—	—	14[a]	—
Colombia (Cali) 1999	M	—	—	14[a]	—
	F	—	—	13[a]	—
Egypt 1996	Urban F	40	57	—	59
	Rural F	61	81	—	78
El Salvador (San Salvador) 1999	M	—	—	5[a]	—
	F	—	—	9[a]	—
Ghana 1999[b]	M	—	43	—	—
	F	—	33	—	—
India (Uttar Pradesh) 1996	M	—	—	—	10–50
Israel (Palestinians) 1996[c]	M	—	28	71	57
New Zealand 1995	M	1	1	5[d]	1[e]
Nicaragua 1999[f]	Urban F	15	5	22	—
	Rural F	25	10	32	—
Papua New Guinea 1985	High school F	—	—	—	59[g]
	High school M	—	—	—	63[g]
Singapore 1996	M	—	5	33[h]	4
Venezuela (Caracas) 1999	M	—	—	8[a]	—
	F	—	—	8[a]	—

Note: — indicates this question not asked.

[a] "An unfaithful woman deserves to be beaten."

[b] Also, 51 percent of men and 43 percent of women agreed: "husband is justified in beating" his wife if she uses family planning without his knowledge.

[c] Also, 23 percent agreed "wife-beating is justified" if she does not respect her husband's relatives.

[d] "He catches her in bed with another man."

[e] "She won't do what she is told."

[f] Also, 11 percent of urban women and 23 percent of rural women agreed "husband is justified in beating" his wife if she goes out without his permission.

[g] "She speaks disrespectfully to him."

[h] "She is sexually involved with another man."

Source: Heise, L., Ellsberg, M., and Gottenmoeller, M. "Ending Violence against Women." *Population Reports,* Series L, number 11. Baltimore: Johns Hopkins University School of Public Health, Population Information Program, December 1999, Table 2, p. 6.

In many developing countries, women share the belief that men have the right to discipline their wives by using force. In rural Egypt, for instance at least 80 percent of women say that beatings are justified under certain circumstances, such as refusing a man sex. Societies often distinguish between just and unjust reasons for violence, as well as between acceptable and unacceptable amounts of aggression. Certain individuals, usually husbands and elders, may have the right to chastise a woman physically for certain transgressions but only within limits. If a man oversteps these limits by becoming too violent or for beating a woman without just cause, other people may have cause to intervene (Heise, Ellsberg, and Gottenmoeller, 1999). Table 8.1 summarizes the findings from recent studies in thirteen different countries in which respondents were asked under what conditions it would be acceptable for men to beat their wives.

Family Violence in the United States

Social scientific studies of family violence in the United States started in the 1960s and expanded rapidly in the subsequent decades (Steinmetz and Straus, 1974; Gelles and Conte, 1990; Johnson and Ferraro, 2000; Tjaden and Thoennes, 2000). Research interest was stimulated greatly by the feminist movement because those who were harmed by family violence were often women and children, the victims of a patriarchal family system and society (Finkelhor, Hotaling, and Yllo, 1988).

We begin our consideration of what that research has found with a discussion of couple violence and wife abuse.

Couple Violence and Wife Abuse

Whenever people are in an intimate relationship, the possibility of violence between them exists. Intimate relationships are emotional, and emotions can be negative as well as positive. Highly negative emotions can lead to violent behavior (Gelles and Straus, 1979).

Husbands and wives are so likely to inflict violence on each other that one set of researchers has referred to the marriage license as a "hitting license" (Straus, Gelles, and Steinmetz, 1980, p. 31). In our society, just as in the societies discussed in the previous section, many people believe they have a right to hit members of their family. Gelles and Straus (1979) have pointed out that violence in the home, against children as well as spouses, can reach levels that would not be tolerated in more public settings. An adult would be sued or arrested for doing to a co-worker what he, or she, might do to a spouse or child in the home.

Researchers who study attitudes toward violent acts found in earlier decades that some Americans were willing to accept as legitimate a certain amount of violence in families. A 1970 study found that about one out of four men thought it was "all right for a husband to hit his wife" and "all right for a wife to hit her husband." Women were less likely to agree with these statements, although nearly 20 percent did so (Stark and McEvoy, 1970). A decade later, in 1980, American adults were asked to evaluate the phrase "couples slapping each other around." Approximately one out of three husbands and one out of four wives saw this type of behavior as at least "somewhat necessary," "somewhat normal," or "somewhat good" (Straus, Gelles, and Steinmetz, 1980, p. 47). Another study, conducted in Tuscaloosa, Alabama, in the mid 1980s found 20 percent of the adult respondents saying, in effect, that "hitting [a wife] occasionally with an open hand" was not *always* spouse abuse (Sigler, 1989). Even after two decades of negative media treatment of spouse

Around the World

Personal Accounts about Incidents That Led to Wife Beating

Victim, Northern Ireland: "Mostly . . . it was him coming back late at night and getting me up to get something to eat and I'd refuse."

Victim, Papua, New Guinea: "On one occasion . . . he came in at three o'clock in the morning, dragged me out of bed and beat me because he was hungry and no food awaited him."

Victim, Australia: "Say nine times out of ten it was because he was drinking. He'd come home from work about 11 P.M. drunk and complain about the dinner."

Victim, England: "He asked me to make him a cup of tea, and I was doing the party things. So I said, 'Well, wait a minute,' and he said, 'I told you to do it now.'"

Student researcher's account, Papua, New Guinea: "The husband had left [a] pig for his wife to look after. . . . However, the wife failed to look after the pig properly . . . the husband returned . . . and found that the pig was lost. He was so angry that he started arguing with his wife. The wife did not reply properly, which made the husband even angrier . . . he started hitting the wife with his hand. He then used an axe handle to beat her."

Batterer, United States: "You know [the children would] tell me to shut up. 'You're not going to tell me to shut up.' And then [my wife] would tell me, you know, 'Let me handle this.' I said, 'I'm the man of the house.' Then we'd start arguing. That's basically how they used to happen."

Batterer, Papua, New Guinea: "I stopped her from going to see her parents, she threw a stone at me, so I beat her up."

Batterer, United States: "She's going on and on about how much money we need . . . I'll listen to it for a while, but then, you know, you gotta get up and do something, you know, that's the way I felt, the way to do it was to go over and try to shut her up physically."

Victim, Papua, New Guinea: "I scolded him for taking girls around in his taxi, then he turned around and hit me."

Victim, Australia: "He accused me of running around . . . If I just looked at another man I was having an affair with him."

Victim, Australia: "If I had my periods and I didn't want sex he used to bash me up."

Source: Morley, 1994. Published in the *Journal of Comparative Family Studies*, 25(1), 1994. A special issue on family violence. University of Calgary, Dept. of Sociology, Calgary, Alberta T2N 1N4, Canada.

abuse and wife battering, it seems that some Americans, both men and women, still consider a certain amount of physical abuse acceptable within the family.

British social scientist Rebecca Morley (1994) has collected statements made by both the victims and perpetrators of wife beatings in a variety of societies and cultures, ranging from Australia, Ireland, England, and New Guinea, to the United States. These statements have striking similarities, and what "unites them is the wife's sometimes defiant failure to do her husband's bidding and/or her questioning of his actions or authority, and the husband's attempt to beat her into submission" (Morley, 1994, p. 46). Some of the statements collected by Morley come from her own research, while others come from the data of other researchers; selected statements appear in the Around the World box.

The Prevalence of Intimate Partner Violence

The question of how much violence occurs behind the closed doors of American households is difficult to answer, because the home is considered a very private place. Outsiders—relatives, friends, neighbors, and the police—are reluctant to get involved in the private lives of families, especially if they believe there is trouble. It is this privacy, however, that allows family members to use violence against each other with relative impunity.

In common couple violence—unlike patriarchal terrorism where men use physical force to control women—female partners may be perpetrators as well as victims of abuse.

The two basic sources of information about family violence are clinical samples and social surveys (Straus, 1990a, 1991). **Clinical samples** are cases of abuse that come to public attention, because victims seek help from women's shelters, police, treatment programs, or counseling services. Social surveys are, of course, inquiries in the general population using questionnaires or interviews. As might be expected, the picture of domestic violence coming from clinical samples differs from the results of social surveys.

From the differences between clinical and survey data, one of the major controversies about domestic violence has emerged (Gelles and Conte, 1990; Straus, 1990b; Tjaden and Thoennes, 2000). Clinical data find women the victims of abuse in the overwhelming majority of cases. Social surveys, however, find that women also engage in violent acts. Indeed, the rates of female-initiated and male-initiated violence are about the same. To understand this conflicting evidence and the furious debate that has resulted from it, we must first review some of the features of social surveys. Second, we must analyze the principal measure of family violence used by survey researchers.

Social surveys, when they are done properly, collect information from random samples of the general population. A random sample ensures that everyone in the population has had an equal chance of being selected for the sample. The people who are selected randomly are generally quite different from clinical populations. Surveys, by their nature, generally use quantitative measures, which can be described in detail, and therefore subjected to critical examination and analysis.

The most widely used measure of family violence comes from the work of Murray A. Straus, Richard J. Gelles, Suzanne K. Steinmetz, and others associated with the Family Research Laboratory at the University of New Hampshire. These researchers were pioneers in the study of family violence. On the basis of their early research, they developed a measure of family violence, which they called the Conflict Tactics Scale (Straus and Gelles, 1990b, Chapters 1–4). This measure, because it has been used in two major national surveys (1975 and 1985), has been the focus of some controversy and requires some special attention.

The Conflict Tactics Scale.   The **Conflict Tactics Scale** consists of a list of behaviors that family members might use in conflicts with other family members.

Three basic methods (tactics) used to resolve conflicts with other family members include (1) rational discussion or reasoning; (2) verbal aggression, symbolic acts that may hurt another person, such as curses, humiliation, or ridicule; and (3) physical aggression or violence. The Conflict Tactics Scale lists nineteen specific tactics that people might have used during the past year when they had conflicts with a family member, ranging from "Discussed an issue calmly" (reasoning) to "Used a knife or fired a gun" (the most extreme form of physical violence). The mildest form of physical violence, defined as assault, is a threat to hit a person or to throw something at that person. Other acts of physical violence include what is defined as battery: actually throwing something at the person; pushing, grabbing, or shoving; slapping; kicking, biting, or hitting with a fist; hitting or trying to hit with some instrument; beating a person up; choking a person; and threatening with a knife or gun (Straus and Gelles, 1990b).

A respondent is asked how many times he or she has used each tactic during the last twelve months, or how many times during the course of a marriage. The scale thus measures what people are willing to report about their violent acts. Straus and Gelles, the developers of the Conflict Tactics Scale, readily acknowledge that this method may underestimate the actual amount of violence; however, the violence people report is very likely to have happened, since they would have little reason to exaggerate such acts.

The Conflict Tactics Scale has been used in many studies since 1972, involving more than 70,000 participants from the United States, including many from diverse cultural backgrounds. It has also been used in at least twenty different countries, including Hong Kong, India, Japan, Israel, Spain, and Sweden. It is increasingly being used as a diagnostic aid in family therapy. In 1996, the Conflict Tactics Scale was revised. The new scale has more items than the original. The addition of items increases its validity and reliability. The new items were added to each of the three original subscales: reasoning, psychological aggression, and physical assault. A number of items have also been reworded to increase its clarity and specificity. The revised version of the Conflict Tactics Scale also has two new subscales, one that measures *sexual coercion* and a second that measures *physical injury*. A major change involves a better differentiation between minor and severe acts of physical assault, psychological aggression, sexual coercion, and extent of injury. A final change in the Conflict Tactics Scale is a new format that makes administration of the questionnaire easier and reduces respondents' likelihood of answering according to a random pattern (Straus et al., 1996).

The original Conflict Tactics Scale was the primary method of measuring violence in two national surveys of U.S. adults, the National Family Violence Surveys.

Family Violence

The National Family Violence Surveys.   The first national survey of family violence was conducted in 1975 (2,143 respondents) and the second in 1985 (6,002 respondents). These two surveys provided significant insight into the amount of violence in American families at that time. The 1985 survey found that about 16 percent of all married couples reported a violent incident in the previous twelve months. This may, of course, be an underestimation of the incidence of violent acts, since some incidents may not have been reported. The researchers divided the violent acts into two types: minor and severe. Severe violence included "kicked, bit or punched; hit or tried to hit with an object; beat up; choked; threatened with a knife or gun; and used a knife or gun" (Straus, 1990b, p. 6). Minor violence included throwing an object that could hurt; pushing, grabbing, or shoving; pulling hair; slapping, or hitting. The 1985 survey found 6.3 percent of the respondents reporting *severe* violence during the past twelve months. Almost everyone reporting severe violence also reported minor violence.

When respondents were asked if there had *ever* been a violent incident over the course of their marriage, the percentage rose to 30 percent. The researchers estimated, however, that because of a tendency to forget incidents that occurred years earlier, the true percentage might be much higher. Perhaps as many as 60 percent of couples experience at least one violent incident during the course of a marriage (Straus, 1991, p. 21).

The 1985 survey reconfirmed one of the surprising and controversial findings of the 1975 survey: Namely, wives in the study had rates of violence against their husbands that were as high as, or higher than, the rates of violence by husbands against wives. This was true for all types of violence including severe violence. Other studies, but not all, have found similar patterns (McNeely & Robinson-Simpson, 1987; Straus and Gelles, 1990a).

The equal rates of violence were surprising because data from clinical studies and police reports show that women are much more likely to be beaten and abused by men than vice versa. One study of domestic violence found that in 91 percent of all reported violent crimes between intimate partners, women were the victims of acts committed by husbands or ex-husbands (Frieze and Browne, 1989, p. 182).

Critics charged that the research showing equal amounts of violence by men and women was not valid and warned against the potentially negative repercussions. They feared that the public would use the results to minimize the problem of wife battering, or to claim that there was an equal amount of husband battering (Dobash and Dobash, 1992). Feminist writers were especially concerned about how this research result might be used to the disadvantage of women (Brush, 1990).

The impact or damage caused by women's acts against men is generally much less than that caused by men. Men's greater average size and strength makes them more powerful. Thus, a woman may hit a man, even with her fist, but it generally does much less harm than when a man uses his fist. This is especially true if the man strikes with greater aggressiveness (Straus, Gelles, and Steinmetz, 1980; Brush, 1990). Also, many assaults against men are acts of retaliation or self-defense.

A more recent national survey, the National Violence Against Women Survey (NVAW), has found that women are not only more likely than men to be victims of intimate partner violence, they are also more likely to be injured by the assaults.

The National Violence Against Women Survey.   A third national survey about family violence began in November 1995 and continued through May 1996. It was co-sponsored by the National Institute of Justice and the Centers for Disease Control and Prevention. The NVAW survey consisted of telephone interviews with a national representative sample of 8,000 U.S. women and 8,000 U.S. men about their experiences as victims of various forms of violence, including intimate partner violence. Three types of intimate partner violence were studied: rape, physical assault, and stalking. The survey compared intimate partner victimization rates among women and men, specific racial groups, Hispanics and non-Hispanics, and same-sex and opposite-sex cohabitants. It also examined risk factors associated with intimate partner violence, the rate of injury among rape and physical assault victims, injured victims' use of medical services, and victims' involvement with the justice system (Tjaden and Thoennes, 2000).

The NVAW survey revealed that intimate partner violence is quite prevalent in the United States today. Table 8.2 summarizes the percent of women and men who have been the victims of rape, physical assault, and stalking *over their lifetimes,* and within the *twelve months preceding the survey.* Nearly 25 percent of the women and 8 percent of the men in the survey said they were raped and/or physically assaulted by a current or former spouse, cohabiting partner, or date at some point in their lifetimes. A considerably lower percent reported having experienced this type of violence in the previous year (1.8 versus 1.1 percent for women and men, respectively). According to rates of victimization obtained in this survey, an estimated 1.5 million women and over 800,000 men are raped and/or physically assaulted by an intimate partner each year in this country. Stalking by intimate partners is also

---

TABLE 8.2

Persons Victimized by an Intimate Partner in Lifetime and in Previous Twelve Months, by Type of Victimization and Gender

	PERCENT		NUMBER[a]	
	Women (n = 8,000)	Men (n = 8,000)	Women (100,697,000)	Men (92,748,000)
In lifetime				
Rape[b***]	7.7	0.3	7,753,669	278,244
Physical assault[b***]	22.1	7.4	22,254,037	6,863,352
Rape and/or physical assault[b***]	24.8	7.6	24,972,856	7,048,848
Stalking[b***]	4.8	0.6	4,833,456	556,488
Total victimized[b***]	25.5	7.9	25,677,735	7,327,092
In previous twelve months				
Rape	0.2	—[c]	201,394	—[c]
Physical assault[b*]	1.3	0.9	1,309,061	834,732
Rape and/or physical assault[b*]	1.5	0.9[d]	1,510,455	834,732
Stalking[b**]	0.5	0.2	503,485	185,496
Total victimized[b***]	1.8	1.1	1,812,546	1,020,228

[a] Based on estimates of women and men 18 years of age and older: Wetrogen, S.I. "Projections of the Population of States by Age, Sex, and Race: 1988 to 2010." *Current Population Reports,* Washington, D.C.: U.S. Bureau of the Census, 1988: 25–1017.

[b] Differences between women and men are statistically significant: χ^2, *p ≤ .05, **p ≤ .01, ***p ≤ .001.

[c] Estimates not calculated on fewer than five victims.

[d] Because only three men reported being raped by an intimate partner in the previous twelve months, the percentage of men physically assaulted and physically assaulted and/or raped is the same.

Source: Tjaden, P., and Thoennes, N. *Extent, Nature, and Consequences of Intimate Partner Violence: Findings from the National Violence Against Women Survey.* Washington, D.C.: National Institute of Justice and Centers for Disease Control and Prevention, 1999, p. 9.

---

much more common than previously believed. Over 500,000 women and 186,000 men are stalked by an intimate partner each year in the United States.

Table 8.3 provides detailed information about physical assaults. The NVAW survey adapted the original Conflict Tactics Scale to measure physical violence. The data show that most physical assaults committed against women and men by intimate partners are relatively minor and consist of pushing, grabbing, shoving, slapping, and hitting. Fewer reported that an intimate partner threw something at them that could hurt them, pulled their hair, kicked or beat them, or threatened them with a knife or gun. A negligible number reported that a partner actually used a gun or knife on them (Tjaden and Thoennes, 2000, pp. 10–11).

Gender and Intimate Victimization

The NVAW survey concluded that women are significantly more likely than men to report being victims of intimate partner violence, whether it is rape, physical assault, or stalking. These findings are consistent with those of the Bureau of Justice Statistics' National Crime Victimization Survey, but contradict data from the National Family Violence Surveys, which reported that men and women were equally likely to be physically assaulted by an intimate partner. Additional

TABLE 8.3

Persons Physically Assaulted by an Intimate Partner in Lifetime, by Type of Assault and Victim Gender

Type of Assault[a]	Women (%) (*n* = 8,000)	Men (%) (*n* = 8,000)
Threw something that could hurt	8.1	4.4
Pushed, grabbed, shoved	18.1	5.4
Pulled hair	9.1	2.3
Slapped, hit	16.0	5.5
Kicked, bit	5.5	2.6
Choked, tried to drown	6.1	0.5
Hit with object	5.0	3.2
Beat up	8.5	0.6
Threatened with gun	3.5	0.4
Threatened with knife	2.8	1.6
Used gun	0.7	0.1[b]
Used knife	0.9	0.8
Total reporting physical assault by intimate partner	22.1	7.4

[a] With the exception of "used gun" and "used knife," differences between women and men are statistically significant: χ^2, $p \leq .001$.

[b] Relative standard error exceeds 30 percent; statistical tests not performed.

Source: Tjaden, P., and Thoennes, N. *Extent, Nature, and Consequences of Intimate Partner Violence: Findings from the National Violence Against Women Survey.* Washington, D.C.: National Institute of Justice and Centers for Disease Control and Prevention, 1999, p. 11.

research must be conducted to determine how the different methodologies used by these two surveys might account for the differences in their findings.

Women also experience more chronic and injurious physical assaults at the hands of intimate partners than do men. The NVAW survey found that women who were physically assaulted by an intimate partner averaged 6.9 physical assaults by the same partner, but men averaged 4.4 assaults. Over 41 percent of the women, but slightly under 20 percent of the men who were physically assaulted were injured during their most recent assault.

Patriarchal Terrorism versus Common Couple Violence. Sociologist Michael Johnson argues that women who come to the attention of public agencies, especially through police or women's shelters, are the victims of what he calls patriarchal terrorism. **Patriarchal terrorism** is violence almost exclusively initiated by men as a way of gaining and maintaining total and absolute control over their female partners. The violence these men use may be frequent and severe, or in some cases infrequent, but in either case violence "reinforces the power of other tactics" (Pence and Paymar, 1993). Other control tactics include emotional abuse, threats, intimidation, blame, isolation, and others. Figure 8.1 shows the types of control tactics battered women experience when men engage in patriarchal terrorism (Pence and Paymar, 1993; Johnson, 1995; Johnson and Feraro, 2000).

The victims of patriarchal terrorism are often the battered women who end up in women's shelters or in hospitals or, in the most tragic cases, murdered. But they

Figure 8.1 Control Tactics Used by Men Who Want to Maintain Complete Control over Their Women Partners

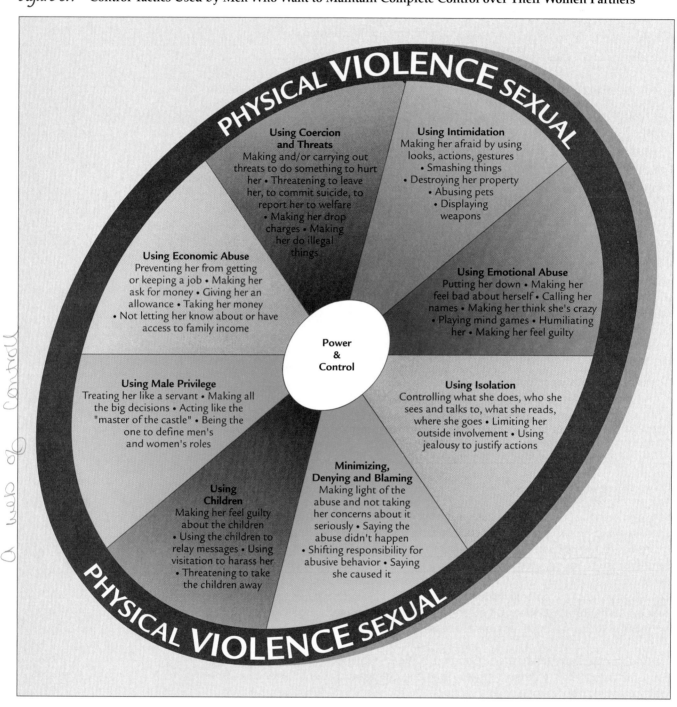

(*Source:* Pence and Paymar, 1993, p. 3.)

are not very likely to be respondents in random-sample surveys of the general population (Johnson, 1995). All surveys have nonrespondents who refuse to be interviewed, and men who terrorize their families are probably going to refuse to participate and are hardly likely to allow their wives to participate.

The family violence that social surveys uncover is probably the type Johnson calls "common couple violence" (Johnson, 1995, p. 287). **Common couple violence** is the product of conflicts that occur in many couple relationships; conflicts that sometimes "get out of hand" and in a significant number of families lead to violence (Johnson, 1995, p. 287). These are the violent acts that are more likely to be revealed by surveys, and, as it turns out, are as likely to be initiated by women as by men. Common couple violence may be mild or severe, but social surveys are most likely to reveal the mild cases (Johnson, 1995). Perpetrators and victims of severe violence are not likely to participate in surveys on violence or, if they do, they are less likely to tell the truth.

The distinction between patriarchal violence and common couple violence may account for much of the difference in views about violence against women. Workers in women's shelters, leaders of educational programs for battered women, and police and medical personnel are likely to see the results of patriarchal terrorism. Survey researchers are more likely to uncover a different kind of domestic violence, and thus their data provide a different picture of its nature and intensity. Nonetheless, any form of violence between intimate partners is likely to be more damaging to women and be, to some degree, the product of male assumptions about their rights to control their partners.

Violence among Gay and Lesbian Couples. Most research on violence in intimate relationships has focused on traditional family relations, especially husband–wife relations, or on heterosexual dating and courtship relations. Some recent studies, however, have broadened the scope of research on intimate-couple violence by studying lesbian and gay couples (Island and Letellier, 1991; Renzetti, 1992).

▲ *Dating violence among teens has become increasingly recognized as a serious social problem.*

Violence among lesbian couples bears some similarities to that found in heterosexual married couples, and some differences. Violence is associated with high levels of dependence on one's partner and concurrent feelings of jealousy, which often plays a part in heterosexual violence. Batterers in lesbian relationships tend to be the partners with the most power; their power is based on the combined influences of age, education, social class, and intelligence differences. Drug abuse is also highly associated with partner abuse (Renzetti, 1992).

Partner abuse among gay men has been studied by Island and Letellier (1991) who also found similarities with and differences from heterosexual abuse. The authors claim that partner abuse is "not a gender issue. It is a power issue, a legal issue, and a mental health issue" (p. 16). The perpetrators in the cases studied by these researchers most resemble wife-beating husbands. They explode with violence over minor issues and then go through a period of remorse, during which they beg for forgiveness and promise not to repeat their acts. Just as in the case of wife batterers, however, they often repeat their acts, and in a more violent form.

Table 8.4 summarizes the findings of the NVAW survey that pertain to sex of partners. Women who live with female partners experience less violence than those who live with male partners. Slightly more than 11 percent of women with female partners but 30 percent of those with male partners reported being raped, physically assaulted, and/or stalked. This suggests that lesbian couples experience less intimate violence than do heterosexual couples. The opposite pattern occurs among men. Those who live with male partners experience more intimate violence than those who live with female partners. Approximately 15 percent of the men who had lived with male partners reported being raped, physically assaulted, or stalked while less than 8 percent of those with female partners reported the same

---

TABLE 8.4

Persons Victimized by an Intimate Partner in Lifetime, by Victim Gender, Type of Victimization, and History of Same-Sex/Opposite-Sex Cohabitation

VICTIM GENDER/ TYPE OF VICTIMIZATION	PERSONS VICTIMIZED IN LIFETIME (%)	
	History of Same-Sex Cohabitation[a]	History of Opposite-Sex Cohabitation[b]
Women	(n = 79)	(n = 7,193)
Rape	11.4[c]	4.4
Physical assault[d*]	35.4	20.4
Stalking	—[e]	4.1
Total victimized[d**]	39.2	21.7
Men	(n = 65)	(n = 6,879)
Rape	—[e]	0.2
Physical assault[d*]	21.5	7.1
Stalking	—[e]	0.5
Total victimized[d**]	23.1	7.4

[a] Subsample consists of respondents who have ever lived with a same-sex intimate partner.

[b] Subsample consists of respondents who have ever married and/or lived with an opposite-sex intimate partner but never with a same-sex intimate partner.

[c] Relative standard error exceeds 30 percent; statistical tests not performed.

[d] Differences between same-sex and opposite-sex cohabitants are statistically significant: χ^2, *p ≤ .01, **p ≤ .001.

[e] Estimates not calculated on fewer than five individuals.

Source: Tjaden, P., and Thoennes, N. *Extent, Nature, and Consequences of Intimate Partner Violence: Findings from the National Violence Against Women Survey.* Washington, D.C.: National Institute of Justice and Centers for Disease Control and Prevention, 1999, p. 29.

---

type of victimization. These findings provide further evidence that intimate partner violence is perpetrated primarily by men, whether it is against female or male partners (Tjaden and Thoennes, 2000).

Violence perpetrated against women by their intimate partners is often accompanied by emotionally abusive and controlling behavior. Women whose partners were jealous, controlling, or verbally abusive were significantly more likely to report being raped, physically assaulted, and/or stalked by their partners even when other sociodemographic and relationship factors were controlled. In fact, having a verbally abusive partner was the factor most likely to predict that a woman would be physically victimized by a partner. These findings support the theory that violence perpetrated against women by intimate partners is often part of a pattern of systematic dominance and control. We discuss this in more detail in a following section.

Race and Ethnic Differences in Intimate Violence.   Table 8.5 summarizes findings pertaining to race and ethnicity differences in victimization rates. The NVAW survey found that intimate partner violence varies significantly among women of diverse racial backgrounds. Asian/Pacific Islander women and men reported lower rates of intimate partner violence than women and men from other minority backgrounds. African American and American Indian/Alaska Native women

TABLE 8.5

Persons Victimized by an Intimate Partner in Lifetime, by Victim Gender, Type of Victimization, and Victim Race

VICTIM GENDER/ TYPE OF VICTIMIZATION	White	African American	Asian/ Pacific Islander	American Indian/ Alaska Native	Mixed Race
			PERSONS VICTIMIZED IN LIFETIME (%)		
Women	(n = 6,452)	(n = 780)	(n = 133)	(n = 88)	(n = 397)
Rape[a]	7.7	7.4	3.8[b]	15.9	8.1
Physical assault[c,d]	21.3	26.3	12.8	30.7	27.0
Stalking	4.7	4.2	—[e]	10.2[b]	6.3
Total victimized[c]	24.8	29.1	15.0	37.5	30.2
Men	(n = 6,424)	(n = 659)	(n = 165)	(n = 105)	(n = 406)
Rape	0.2	0.9[b]	—[e]	—[e]	—[e]
Physical assault	7.2	10.8	—[e]	11.4	8.6
Stalking	0.6	1.1[b]	—[e]	—[e]	1.2[b]
Total victimized	7.5	12.0	3.0[b]	12.4	9.1

[a] Estimates for American Indian/Alaska Native women are significantly higher than those for white and African American women: Tukey's B, p ≤ .05.

[b] Relative standard error exceeds 30 percent; estimates not included in statistical testing.

[c] Estimates for Asian/Pacific Islander women are significantly lower than those for African American, American Indian/Alaska Native, and mixed-race women: Tukey's B, p ≤ .05.

[d] Estimates for African American women are significantly higher than those for white women: Tukey's B, p ≤ .05.

[e] Estimates not calculated on fewer than five victims.

Source: Tjaden, P., and Thoennes, N. *Extent, Nature, and Consequences of Intimate Partner Violence: Findings from the National Violence Against Women Survey.* Washington, D.C.: National Institute of Justice and Centers for Disease Control and Prevention, 1999, p. 26.

and men reported higher rates. However, the differences among these minority groups weakened when other sociodemographic characteristics and relationship variables were controlled. More research is needed to determine how much of the differences can be explained by respondents' willingness to disclose intimate partner violence and how much can be explained by social, demographic, and environmental factors (Tjaden and Thoennes, 2000).

Medical Treatment of Victims of Intimate Violence. The medical community treats millions of victims of rapes and physical assaults committed by intimate partners each year. Of the estimated 4.8 million rapes and physical assaults perpetrated *against women* by intimate partners each year, approximately 2 million result in an injury and over half a million result in some type of medical treatment. Of the 2.9 million assaults perpetrated *against men* by intimate partners each year, about 580,000 result in injuries and 125,000 result in some type of medical treatment. Many victims receive multiple forms of care (e.g., ambulance service, emergency room care, or physical treatment) and multiple treatments (e.g., several days in the hospital) for the same victimization. As a result, the number of medical personnel who are treating injuries that resulted from intimate partner violence is in the millions (Tjaden and Thoennes, 2000).

Police Involvement.   Most intimate partner victimizations are not reported to the police, according to findings of the NVAW survey. Approximately one-fifth of all rapes, one-quarter of all physical assaults, and one-half of all stalkings perpetrated against women by intimate partners were reported to the police. Even fewer of the victimizations against men were reported. The majority of victims who didn't file police reports said they thought the police would not or could not do anything on their behalf. These findings suggest that victims of intimate violence do not consider the justice system an appropriate vehicle for resolving conflicts with intimate partners.

The new research results on the deterrent effect of arrest on domestic violence show that, on average, it is no more effective than other responses in reducing subsequent violence. In fact, for certain offenders arrests were related to *increases* in violence, not decreases. When, for example, unemployed suspects are arrested they are more likely to repeat the offense; in contrast, employed suspects who are arrested are less likely to be repeat offenders (Berk et al., 1992; Pate and Hamilton, 1992; Sherman and Smith, 1992).

The researchers believe these results reflect the fact that arrested suspects who are employed are more "socially bonded" and therefore have more to lose by being arrested (Sherman and Smith, 1992, p. 681). Having been arrested once, they may wish to avoid a second arrest because it may lead to negative reactions from employers and possibly even job loss. Those men who are not employed, by contrast, are less socially bonded, and another arrest may have fewer negative social consequences for them. A first arrest does not deter them from further violence; indeed, an arrest may anger, upset, or further alienate them, which may lead to more violent acts against family members.

The results of these latest studies produce a policy dilemma for law enforcement agencies. Arrest deters those perpetrators who are socially bonded, but aggravates those, such as the unemployed, who are not (Berk et al., 1992; Sherman, Schmidt, and Rogan, 1992). The research that has been completed, up to the present time, leaves us with one conclusion: There is no single, simple way, such as arrest, to reduce domestic violence (Buzawa and Buzawa, 1993).

Child Abuse and Maltreatment

T**he European and American history of child abuse within families is long and deplorable (deMause, 1974). Yet through much of the twentieth century little was said about the harsh treatment of children. In the United States, the abuse of children came to the attention of the public only after the 1962 publication of an article in the *Journal of the American Medical Association,* titled "The Battered Child Syndrome" (Kempe et al., 1962). As the title suggests, in this early awareness period, the battering or abusing of children was viewed from a medical or psychiatric perspective and labeled a psychopathology (Gelles, 1993). This early view of child abuse has been expanded in two ways. First, a much wider range of child mistreatment has emerged, including physical abuse, sexual abuse, and physical neglect. Second, the abuse and mistreatment of children is no longer seen as simply a psychiatric or medical problem. Social factors and a broader range of psychological factors are now routinely part of the analysis of child abuse (Gelles, 1993; O'Leary, 1993). Again, as we noted earlier, abusiveness within families, even the abuse of children, is not explained simply by assuming all such acts are committed by sick, pathological, or mentally ill individuals.

Child abuse in contemporary American families is even more hidden from public view than intimate partner abuse. When adults are abused, they are usually fully aware of what is happening and they know it is wrong. Abused children, however, are much less likely to understand the wrongness of the acts against

Child Abuse

them. They are essentially trapped in a life that, to their knowledge, has no alternatives. In recent years, doctors, teachers, and other professionals have become sensitized to the signs of children being beaten and often uncover cases of child abuse. However, unless the child is severely hurt, or there are repeated injuries of a suspicious nature, the abuse may go undetected for years. Some cases of child abuse come to light only when the child dies. In other cases, the child becomes old enough to retaliate against the abusive parent, perhaps by using a weapon.

An added problem of detection comes from the fact that parents are given a great deal of latitude in how they may punish or discipline their children. There is no prohibition against physical punishment in the United States and no limits on how severe physical punishment may be. Sweden, in contrast, does have a law that prohibits a parent (or any other adult) from using corporal punishment on a child. A poll conducted by Daniel Yankelovich in the summer of 2000 found that of 3,000 adults (including 1,066 parents with children under age 6), 61 percent condoned spanking as a regular form of punishment (CNN.com, posted on October 5, 2000).

In the United States, 80 percent of adults agree with the statement "[I]t is sometimes necessary to discipline a child with a good, hard spanking" (Flynn, 1994, p. 316). For differences in the acceptance of spanking in different regions of the United States, see Figure 8.2.

The physical punishment of children ranges from mild spankings or slaps to severe whippings or beatings with belts, sticks, or paddles. Exactly where abuse begins on this continuum of physical punishment is unclear. Parents are given great latitude, because outsiders are generally reluctant to interfere with a parent's right to discipline his or her children.

When the 1940s Hollywood actress Joan Crawford reared her two children, she punished and restricted them in a variety of ways. When her daughter published the autobiographical *Mommie Dearest,* the book revealed how often and severely she and her brother had been punished as children (Crawford, 1978). At the time, it seems that Joan Crawford's colleagues, friends, and visitors saw her only as a strict and demanding mother whose children always behaved perfectly. Most observers today would say these children were abused, yet some people might still argue that parents have the right to rear their children as they see fit, even if that involves some severe punishments. The issue of when punishment becomes abuse is difficult to resolve.

So there really was a monster in her bedroom.

For many kids, there's a real reason to be afraid of the dark. Each year in Indiana, there are thousands of substantiated cases of sexual abuse. (Not to mention the number that goes unreported.)

The trauma can be devastating for the child and for the family. So listen closely to the children around you. If you hear something that you don't want to believe, perhaps you should. For information on child abuse prevention, contact: Dunebrook Prevent Child Abuse LaPorte County, 7451 Johnson Road, Michigan City, IN 46360.
1-800-897-0007
Or visit **www.dunebrook.org**

DUNEBROOK
Prevent Child Abuse
LaPorte County

▲ *As this poster suggests, awareness of child abuse has increased greatly, which may help to reduce the number of severe cases.*

The Extent of Violence against Children

The federal government has been publishing national data on the maltreatment of children by their caregivers since the late 1980s. The National Child Abuse and Neglect Data System (NCANDS), which is sponsored by the Children's Bureau of the Administration on Children, Youth, and Families, collects accurate, timely information on child maltreatment and provides information to policy makers, child welfare practitioners, researchers, and concerned citizens. NCANDS asks each state to report the number of children and families receiving preventive services; the

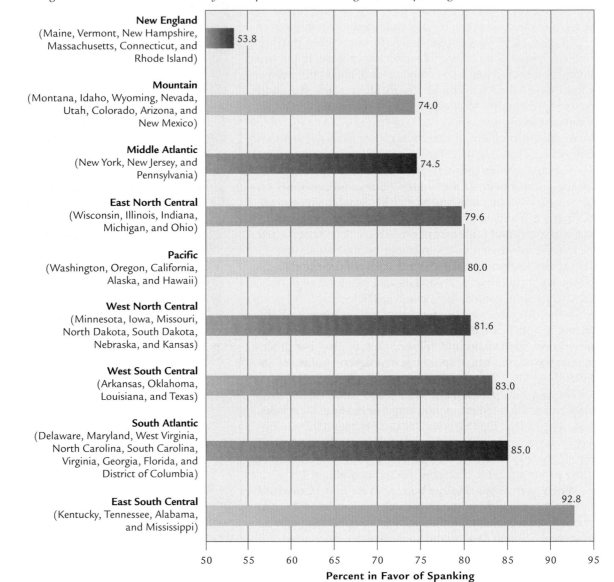

Figure 8.2 **Regional Differences in Attitudes about Spanking Children.** *Percentage who Agree Strongly or Agree that it is sometimes necessary to discipline a child with a good, hard spanking*

(*Source:* Flynn, 1994, p. 317)

number of reports and investigations of child abuse and neglect; the number of children who were subjects of reports of abuse or neglect; the number of child victims of maltreatment; and the number of child fatalities due to abuse or neglect.

Every day, child protective service agencies receive referrals alleging that children have been abused or neglected. The sources of these referrals include educators, law enforcement personnel, social workers, parents, and concerned neighbors. Many referrals are investigated, indicating that the referral was considered serious enough to warrant further consideration. Once a referral has been *screened in* (put into the investigation process) the agency determines whether the child has been maltreated or is in danger of being maltreated. The child protective service agency must then decide whether to take further action to protect the child. Data presented here were provided to the NCANDS by individual states in 1999 (U.S. Department of Health and Human Services, Administration on Children, Youth,

HEAD*ine* Spanked Children Removed from Their Homes

On July 4, 2001, seven children, aged 6 to 14, were forcibly removed from their home in Aylmer, Ontario, by police and child welfare workers. They were removed because their parents, who are members of the fundamentalist Church of God, refused to promise that they would stop spanking their children with paddles, sticks, belts, or other objects. Child welfare workers feared the children were endangered by this type of physical discipline. The Church of God members interpret the Bible literally and lead their lives according to its principles. They believe that Proverbs 13:24, which says "Those who spare the rod hate their children but those who love them are diligent to discipline them," requires them to use physical punishment. Canadian law allows parents to spank their children but only with their bare hands. It prohibits the use of unnecessary force by parents against their children. Church of God members argue

that a parent's hand is intended to show affection and that objects should be used for spanking.

After a preliminary investigation, Canadian authorities allowed the children to go back to their homes temporarily. Several conditions were imposed on the parents and on the child welfare workers, however. The parents of the children who were removed had to agree not to spank their children. They also had to allow child welfare workers to make unannounced and unsupervised visits with their children in their home and school. The parents also had to submit to counseling sessions to learn about alternative methods of discipline, while the child welfare workers were required to learn more about the family's religious and cultural backgrounds.

After the initial investigation of the case, which involved interviews with a number of other families who belonged to the local Church of God congregation, twenty-six mothers fled Canada

with seventy-four children because they were afraid the authorities would take their children, too.

This case has generated a great deal of controversy in Canada and the United States and Mexico, where several of the families fled for refuge. Members of the Church of God and similar fundamentalist denominations who believe the Bible requires parents to spank their children with sticks and other objects argue that they are experiencing a type of religious persecution. Some conservative family organizations are outraged that the Canadian government stepped in and disrupted a family in this way. Still other Canadians are hoping that this case will result in a major change in the country's tolerance toward physical punishment of children, which they regard as a form of child abuse.

Source: Canadian Press, canews.yahoo.com, downloaded on October 25, 2001.

and Families, Child Maltreatment 1999. Washington, D.C.: U.S. Government Printing Office, 2001).

Figure 8.3 summarizes the rates of child maltreatment in the United States from 1995 through 1999. Rates are presented separately for six different categories of maltreatment as the number of child victims for every 1,000 children in the population. The highest rate of maltreatment occurred in the category of neglect (6.5 victims per 1,000). The next highest rate was reported for other types of abuse (e.g., abandonment) at 4.4 victims per 1,000. The physical abuse rate in 1999 was 2.5 victims per 1,000 children.

There were an estimated 826,000 victims of maltreatment nationwide in 1999, resulting in an overall rate of 11.8 per 1,000 children. The 1999 rate was actually lower than the previous years' rates. Almost three-fifths of all the child victims suffered *neglect*, while one-fifth suffered from *physical abuse.* Slightly more than one-tenth were *sexually abused.* More than one-third of all the victims *experienced more than one type of maltreatment.*

The highest victimization rates were for the 0 to 3 age group (which has a rate of maltreatment of 13.9 incidents per 1,000 children). Figure 8.4 shows the rates of

Figure 8.3   **Child Victimization Rates by Maltreatment Type, 1995–1999**

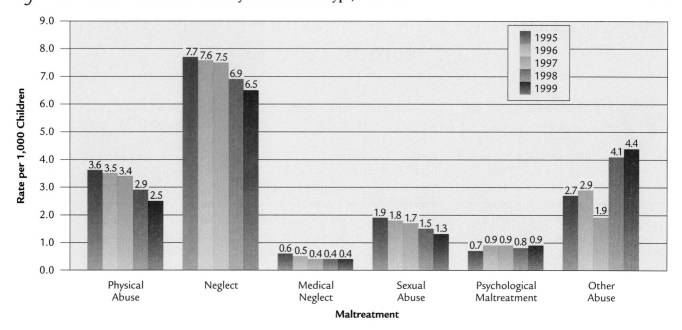

(*Source:* U.S. Department of Health and Human Services, Administration on Children, Youth, and Families 2001. *Child Maltreatment 1999.* Washington, D.C.: U.S. Government Printing Office, 2001, p. 12.)

maltreatment for the five different age groups. As the figure shows, rates of maltreatment decline with age. On many types of maltreatment, rates for girls and boys were similar. But the sexual abuse rate is higher among girls. Victimization rates by race and ethnicity (which are shown in Figure 8.5) ranged from a low of

Figure 8.4   **Child Victimization Rates by Age, 1999**

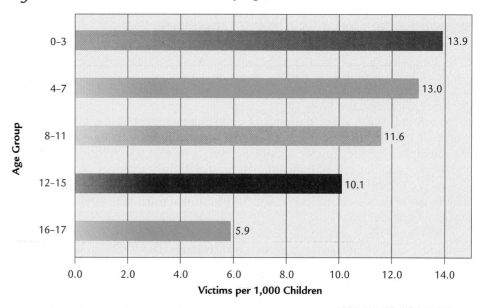

(*Source:* U.S. Department of Health and Human Services, Administration on Children, Youth, and Families 1001. *Child Maltreatment 1999.* Washington, D.C.: U.S. Government Printing Office, 2001, p. 12.)

Figure 8.5   **Child Victimization Rates by Race and Ethnicity, 1999**

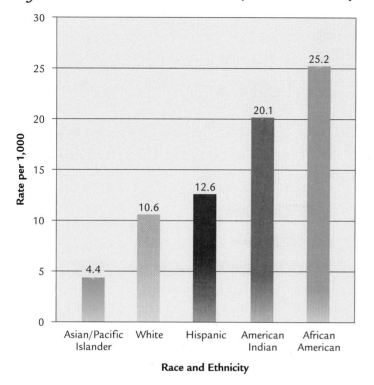

(*Source:* U.S. Department of Health and Human Services, Administration on Children, Youth, and Families 2001. *Child Maltreatment 1999.* Washington, D.C.: U.S. Government Printing Office, 2001, p. 14.)

4.4 among Asian/Pacific Islander children to a high of 25.2 among African American children.

A **perpetrator** of child abuse and/or neglect is a person who has maltreated a child while in a care-taking relationship to that child. As Figure 8.6 indicates, about 90 percent of child victims were maltreated by a parent, either acting alone or with someone else. The most common pattern of maltreatment was a child victimized by a female parent acting alone (44.7 percent). When the type of maltreatment is examined separately, as shown in Figure 8.7, female parents were identified as the most common perpetrators of neglect and physical abuse. In contrast, male parents were identified as the most likely perpetrators of sexual abuse.

A number of children die every year as a result of maltreatment. Child fatality estimates are based on data recorded by Child Protective Service agencies and/or other agencies. An estimated 1,100 children died of abuse and neglect in 1999, a rate of approximately 1.62 deaths per 100,000 children in the general population. Slightly more than 2 percent of all fatalities occurred while the victim was in foster care. Children younger than 1 year old accounted for 42.6 percent of the fatalities, and 86.1 percent were younger than 6 years of age. Maltreatment deaths were more often associated with neglect (about one-third) than with any other type of abuse.

Factors Related to Child Abuse

No single factor accounts for child abuse; instead, many closely related factors are associated with using severe violence against children (Straus and Smith, 1990). Two prominent factors associated with child abuse are gender and socioeconomic status.

Figure 8.6   **Perpetrator Relationship to Child Victim, 1999**

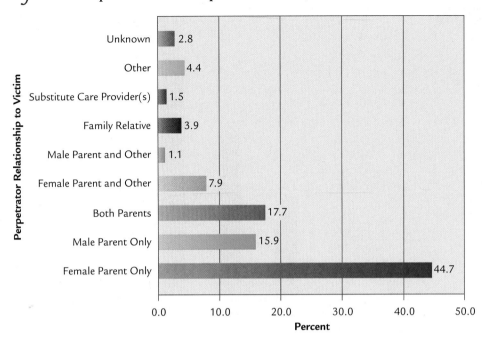

(*Source:* U.S. Department of Health and Human Services, Administration on Children, Youth, and Families 2001. *Child Maltreatment 1999.* Washington, D.C.: U.S. Government Printing Office, 2001, p. 34.)

Figure 8.7   **Perpetrator Relationship to Child Victim by Maltreatment Type, 1999**

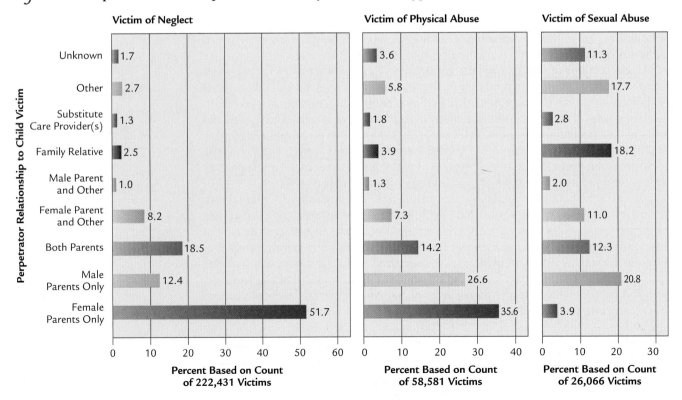

(*Source:* U.S. Department of Health and Human Services, Administration on Children, Youth, and Families 2001. *Child Maltreatment 1999.* Washington, D.C.: U.S. Government Printing Office, 2001, p. 34.)

In both the 1975 and 1985 National Family Violence Surveys and the 1999 NCANDS data, women were more likely to commit acts of child abuse than men. The reason for the higher levels of child abuse by women is obvious: Women spend more time caring for children and being in contact with children—they have much more time "at risk." Researchers also speculate that women, following the expectations of the traditional female gender role, may feel more responsible for disciplining and controlling their children—hence, more child abuse. Women may also resent the fact that they are charged with the major responsibilities of child care, and this resentment may contribute to the physical abuse of children (Straus and Smith, 1990, p. 247). In line with this speculation is a finding from the 1975 survey that women who were keeping house full-time were slightly more likely to abuse their children than women who were employed.

Child abuse is found at all socioeconomic levels, but the rates of child abuse are higher among lower status parents. The family's annual income, husband's occupation, and wife's occupation are all associated with child abuse. Among both fathers and mothers, higher rates of child abuse are found in lower income and lower occupational-status families (Straus and Smith, 1990, p. 250).

That African American children in the United States are abused at a higher rate than white children may stem from declining economic conditions among African Americans, as compared with whites, as well as changing family conditions of African Americans in this period (Straus and Smith, 1990, p. 252).

The Connection between Domestic Violence and Child Abuse

The two National Surveys of Family Violence clearly demonstrated that violence in one family relationship is related to violence in other family relationships (Straus and Smith, 1990, p. 254). For example, child abuse by parents is strongly related to violence between husbands and wives. Families in which husbands use violence against wives—even mild forms such as slapping, pushing, and throwing things—have an incidence of child abuse that is 150 percent greater than in other families. In families in which wives hit their husbands, the level of child abuse is 120 percent higher. Even verbal aggression between parents is associated with higher levels of child abuse in the family (Straus and Smith, 1990, pp. 253, 254).

Researchers who have studied family violence frequently conclude that the family itself provides the training ground for future violent behavior (Steinmetz and Straus, 1973; Straus et al., 1980; Egeland, 1993). That is, children learn about violence when they themselves are struck or beaten, or when they see their parents hitting each other—"violence begets violence" (Egeland, 1993, p. 197). Children who experience violence within the home, whether it is directed toward them or toward other family members, are also more likely to engage in antisocial acts outside the home, such as delinquency (Widom, 1989a, 1989b).

Intergenerational Violence

Violence is also transmitted from one generation to another. Parents who received physical punishment as children are more likely to abuse their own children. Both mothers and fathers who report that their fathers used physical punishment against them at age 13 are nearly twice as likely as parents who were not physically punished at that age to abuse their own children. Similarly, both women and men who report that their mothers used physical punishment against them at age 13 are more likely to abuse their own children (Straus and Smith, 1990, pp. 253, 255).

When parents report that their fathers hit their mothers, or their mothers hit their fathers, they are also generally more likely to abuse their children. The only exception is the case of men whose fathers hit their mothers; they are slightly more likely to abuse their own children, but the relationship is not statistically significant (Straus and Smith, 1990, pp. 253, 256).

▲ *Domestic violence may be decreasing because more and more women know they can find a safe haven when they need to escape from abusive partners.*

Adding to the picture of intergenerational family violence is the *double jeopardy* women face as the victims of violence. Studies consistently show that women who were physically punished as children are more likely to have abusive husbands or boyfriends as adults (Downs et al., 1992; Simons et al., 1993). The fact that women who have been abused as children marry men who are more likely to abuse them does not necessarily mean that these women seek out violent men. An alternative explanation offered by one set of researchers is that women who were abused when they were young "develop a hostile, defiant orientation . . . [and] are attracted to activities and events that bring them into contact with aggressive, antisocial boys" (Simons et al., 1993, p. 721). Such boys may be more likely to use physical violence against their girlfriends and, later, their wives.

Even though the intergenerational transmission of violence is supported by research, the transmission is not inevitable (Kaufman and Zigler, 1987, 1993). Not every abused child becomes an abusive parent, and not every abusive parent was subjected to abuse as a child. Research shows that the continuation of violence is not inevitable.

One study found that only 18 percent of parents who were abused themselves became abusive parents (Hunter and Kilstrom, 1979). However, Egeland and Jacobovitz (1984) found that most mothers who were severely abused showed some degree of abusiveness with their own children. The best estimates are that 30 to 40 percent of adults who were abused as children also abuse their own children (Egeland, 1993; Kaufman and Zigler, 1993). This is a much higher percentage than the estimated 2 to 4 percent of parents in the population who abuse their children (Gelles and Conte, 1990). In round numbers, people who were abused as children are about ten times more likely than the national average to become abusive parents.

Both the critics and the supporters of the generational transmission hypothesis agree that it is possible to break the cycle of violence and abuse (Egeland, 1993; Kaufman and Zigler, 1993). One study focused on women who had been abused as children and found that those who were not abusive mothers, and thus were breaking the cycle of abuse, were more likely to have had emotionally supportive individuals in their lives when they were young (other relatives and foster parents, for example) (Egeland, Jacobovitz, and Sroufe, 1988). Nonabusing women were also more likely to have had some sort of therapy or professional counseling in the course of becoming adults; they were also more likely to be currently involved in relationships with supportive husbands or boyfriends, to have more social supports generally, and to have fewer stresses in their lives (Kaufman and Zigler, 1993).

The Sexual Abuse of Children

Sexual abuse is a separate form of child abuse (Garbarino, 1989; Gilgun, 1995). The definition of **sexual abuse of children** is based on three criteria: (1) an age difference of five years between the child and the offender, (2) specific sexual behaviors, and (3) the sexual intent of the older person (Conte, 1993, p. 60). The five-year age differential between a child and an offender is established to exclude what might be called "normal" sexual experimentation and exploration by children. The required age difference between the offender and the child also reflects the idea that in sexual abuse cases the offender has more power than the child who is being sexually abused (Finkelhor, 1986).

The specific behaviors associated with child sexual abuse include exhibitionism, voyeurism, kissing, fondling, fellatio or cunnilingus, penetration of the vagina or anus with sexual organs or objects, photographing a child in sexually explicit ways, and exposing a child to pornography (adapted from Conte, 1993, p. 60). In general, these behaviors with a child are clearly inappropriate, but there can sometimes be ambiguity. Nudity, for example, is not seen as improper in some families, and appearing nude before children carries no sexual connotations. Photographing children nude is also acceptable in some families, again with no sexual implications.

The sexual intent of adults is sometimes difficult to establish with certainty (Conte, 1993, p. 60). An adult may claim that his behavior has no sexual intent, as the following example illustrates:

> a 3-year-old child describes what sounds like her grandfather's limited (a few times) touching her labia (no penetration). The grandfather, who has cared for the child on a number of occasions, indicates that he was checking for a diaper rash (which the child has in fact had during the time the grandfather took care of the child). (Conte, 1993, p. 60)

In this example, the grandfather claims that his intent was not sexual, but was part of the normal care that an adult would give a small child. His intention, he might say, was to ensure the well-being or comfort of the child entrusted to his care. Such a case, in which intent is the issue, is filled with uncertainty about whether his behavior was sexual abuse or not.

Professionals who deal with cases of child sexual abuse are becoming increasingly sensitive to the problem of balancing the welfare of children against the dangers of false accusations against adults (Fincham et al., 1994). Children must be protected against the predatory behaviors of sexual abusers, but at the same time professionals who interview children must be aware that children can be highly suggestible and may sometimes be conforming to the interviewer's preexisting ideas about what happened (Ceci and Bruck, 1994).

Incidence of Child Sexual Abuse

"Of all crimes against children, sexual abuse has arguably captured the greatest share of attention from child advocates, professionals, policy makers, and the general public" (Jones and Finkelhor, 2001, p. 1). During the 1980s, increasing numbers of victims were identified each year (American Association for the Protection of Children, 1988) and concerns about this crime intensified. However, a dramatic shift in child sexual abuse trends has occurred. Over the fifteen-year period between 1977 and 1992, the number of cases increased 10 percent each year. Data from child protective services agencies across the United States indicate that the increases of the late 1970s and 1980s, however, were followed by an extensive period of marked decline in the 1990s (Jones and Finkelhor, 2001). Data provided by the NCANDS and the Annual Fifty State Survey conducted by Prevent Child Abuse America indicate that the number of substantiated cases of child sexual abuse decreased from a peak of estimated 149,800 cases in 1992 to 103,600 cases in 1998, which represents a decline of 31 percent. Along with the decline in the number of substantiated cases of child sexual abuse, the number of reported cases also decreased, from 429,000 in 1991 to 315,00 in 1998.

Why has there been a decline in the number of reported and substantiated cases of child sexual abuse over the past ten years? The decline could be real or it could be a reflection of increasing reluctance to report and investigate cases. There is considerable reason to believe that there has been a real decrease in child sexual abuse in the past decade. During the 1980s, there was a significant increase in public awareness about child sexual abuse. Perpetrators were increasingly incarcerated for their crimes. Treatment programs for offenders were developed and laws were changed, particularly those that involved the monitoring of convicted sex offenders in residential neighborhoods. Additionally, as our previous discussion has shown, there have been declines in other types of victimization. Over the 1990s, cases of female victimization by intimate partners declined 21 percent, cases of forcible rape declined by 60 percent, and the overall rate of violent crime has declined by 31 percent since 1994.

However, the decline in substantiated cases of child sexual abuse may also reflect an increasing reluctance to report suspected child sexual abuse incidents. Media coverage has been more skeptical over the past ten years, highlighting false allegations and unfounded stigmatization of alleged abusers. Child protective service investigators may have become more conservative in their pursuit of allegations. Perhaps professionals have become less vigilant about reporting suspected cases of abuse, as well (Jones and Finkelhor, 2001). At this point, it is difficult to untangle the effects of these societal changes on the number of child sexual abuse cases. But there is some reason to hope that the decline is real and will continue over the next decade.

Child Sexual Abuse

The Victims of Child Sexual Abuse

Sexual abuse of children can occur either in or outside the family. The most likely victims in both cases are young girls. Data collected from state governments and reported by the American Humane Association found that 78 percent of sexually maltreated children in 1984 were girls; the remaining 22 percent were boys (Garbarino, 1989). The average age of children who were sexually abused is 9.3 years (Garbarino, 1989, p. 228).

Beyond gender itself, we do know that girls are more likely to be victims of sexual abuse if they have been separated from their mothers at some time, especially if the mother has been out of the home or if she is ill or disabled. Girls who report poor relationships with their mothers are also more likely to be sexually abused (Gelles and Conte, 1990, p. 1052). Girls are also at greater risk if the natural father is gone from the home, or if the marriage of their parents is full of conflict (Finkelhor, Hotaling, and Yllo, 1988). Unlike physical abuse, poverty and economic stress are *not* associated with higher rates of child sexual abuse (Finkelhor and Baron, 1986).

Who Are the Sexual Abusers?

As Figure 8.6 reveals, the most likely sexual abusers of children are men (in the family—fathers, stepfathers, mothers' boyfriends, brothers, or other male relatives). Women, including female family members, may also be the sexual abusers, but their numbers are very small compared with men (Conte, 1993, p. 65).

Sex offenders, especially men, who abuse young children have generally been divided into two types: fathers (or stepfathers) who sexually abuse their *own* children (thus committing incest), and pedophiles who prey on any young children (Gelles and Conte, 1990; Conte, 1993). Recent evidence suggests that these two categories may overlap considerably, with a high percentage of incestuous fathers and stepfathers having also committed other sex offenses. Nearly half of a group of men (49 percent) who were being seen in an outpatient clinic for sexual abuse within their families had also abused children outside their families. Furthermore, 18 percent of these men had also raped adult women (Abel et al., 1988). This finding suggests that men who sexually abuse their own children are part of a population with a fundamental sexual pathology.

The fact that men who sexually abuse females in their own families are also likely to commit other sexual crimes is an important point, because research on incest has so often focused on internal family processes and family structures. Father–daughter incest was believed to occur in problem families, especially where the mother has abrogated her role. According to this line of thinking, a daughter, often the oldest daughter, took on the responsibilities of her mother. The father then exploited this situation and used his daughter for sexual gratification. This scenario is based largely on clinical studies and may be overlooking the predatory sexual pathologies of some fathers; the same sexual pathology found in other pedophiles and rapists (Conte, 1993).

Men who sexually abuse children, including those in their own families, may have psychological problems, but home and family characteristics also seem to be implicated in sexual abuse. As we noted, the most likely victims are girls who are separated from mothers, have conflict with parents, and so on. Much more research is needed on people who sexually abuse children, as well as on the families of the victims of sexual abuse, if we are to gain an understanding of this deplorable behavior against children.

Family Violence between Siblings

Anyone who has grown up with brothers and sisters is likely to know that conflict is a defining feature of sibling interaction (Raffaelli, 1992). Sibling violence is, in fact, the most common form of family violence in the United States (Noland and Liller, 2000). Yet most people, including parents, do not take sibling violence very seriously. In one survey of American parents only 7.4 percent considered fights between the children of the family a problem (Straus, 1990a, p. 451).

A common psychological explanation for why siblings fight is **sibling rivalry,** the notion that siblings contend for the attention of their parents and are jealous of any attention given to their brothers and sisters (Raffaelli, 1992). Sibling jealousy may lead to **sibling aggression,** which is characterized as angry, expressive conflict that does not have a realistic basis (Felson, 1983). **Realistic conflict** is conflict over different interests, values, or goals. If, for example, a brother uses his sister's blouse to clean his bicycle, this constitutes a realistic basis for conflict. When siblings have fights, they are almost always over real issues (Felson, 1983). A study of preadolescent boys and girls found that conflict between siblings was realistic rather than based on sibling rivalry. Conflict among preteens was primarily over power issues, personal property, verbal and physical provocations, and relationship betrayals— for example, revealing secrets, especially to parents (Raffaelli, 1992, p. 656). The conflicts between siblings reflected "age-appropriate issues of self-definition and personal boundaries" according to the researcher (Raffaelli, 1992, p. 660).

The things siblings fight over are not surprising. They fight most often over the use of property such as toys, television, the telephone, or clothes. The second most frequent cause of fighting is the division of work. The third most frequent cause is objectionable behavior—teasing, insulting, spying, and so on (Felson, 1983).

A recent study of college students that was designed to explore university students' experiences with sibling violence during adolescence found that most had been involved in conflict that involved "loud talking," yelling, or screaming.

ContentSELECT

Sibling Rivalry

in the media

Pediatricians Warn of the Impact of Television Violence on Children

The amount and influence of violence on television has long been the subject of study and debate. In 1993, however, public concern over TV violence became so politicized that it reached the U.S. Congress, where Senator Paul Simon demanded that the television industry control and regulate the amount of violence in its programming. In response, the National Cable Television Association funded a $3.5 million, three-year research study. An advisory panel composed of physicians, health professionals, and educators monitored the study. From 1994 to 1997, the National Television Violence Study gathered data from nearly 10,000 hours of television programming, the largest sample and most detailed analysis of television content ever examined. Researchers randomly sampled cable and network TV programming seventeen hours per day, seven days each week, for nine months over the three-year period. Beginning in June 1994, drama, comedy, movies, music videos, children's shows, cartoons, and reality programs (e.g., news magazines, documentaries, police shows, and talk shows) were analyzed. Only news, sports, and entertainment sports programs were excluded from the sample (Shifrin, 1998).

Over the three-year period of the study, 60 percent of the sampled programs contained violent scenes. Violence was defined as "the involvement of animate beings, a clear intent to harm, and harm that is physical in nature as opposed to psychological or emotional." But more important than the actual frequency of violence was the way in which it was often portrayed, in a manner that could increase the likelihood of negative effects on viewers. More than one-third of violent scenes featured *bad* characters who were never punished for their actions. Seventy percent showed no remorse or punishment at the time the violence occurred. Forty percent of all violence included humor; more than 50 percent showed no pain cues; and 50 percent of the violent behaviors would be lethal or incapacitating if they occurred in real life. Forty percent of the violence was perpetrated by heroes or role models. This is especially harmful for young viewers. The study concluded that TV violence is glamorized, trivialized, and sanitized. It teaches that violence is a solution to interpersonal problems. Viewers can learn aggressive attitudes and behaviors from watching violence, become desensitized to the seriousness of violence, and become especially frightened of becoming a victim of real-life violence.

Many of the most harmful depictions of violence were seen most often in cartoons. The typical preschooler who watches about two hours of cartoons per day is exposed to 10,000 acts of televised violence each year. Depending on a child's developmental level, cartoon and fantasy-type violence cannot be dismissed simply because it is unrealistic because children may not be able to distinguish fantasy from reality (Shifrin, 1998).

In 1997, largely in response to the findings of the National Television Violence Study, the American Academy of Pediatrics launched a Media Matters campaign to help pediatricians, parents, and children become more aware of the influence the media have on children and adolescents. The campaign developed a media history form that pediatricians can use during well-child visits to determine parental involvement and the amount and effects of children's exposure to the media. In 2001, the Academy issued a revised Policy Statement entitled "Children, Adolescents, and Television," which includes recommendations for pediatricians such as persuading parents to discourage TV viewing for children under age 2; remove television sets from children's bedrooms; and work with television writers, directors, and producers to develop appropriate programming for children. The Policy Statement concludes that nearly every aspect of children's development (e.g., sexuality, academic performance, body concept and self-image, nutrition, dieting and obesity, and substance abuse) is touched by the media and that many effects of the media have public health implications (O'Keefe, 2001).

Sources: Shifrin, D. "Three-Year Study Documents the Nature of Television Violence." *AAP News,* August 1998 (reprinted on AAP website: http://www.aap.org/advocacy/shifrin898.htm); O'Keefe, L. "Academy Supports Efforts to Loosen Grip of Media Violence on Children." *AAP News,* February 2000 (reprinted on AAP website: http://www.aap.org/advocacy/shifrin898.htm).

Nearly two-thirds had been involved in arguments with brothers or sisters that resulted in hitting or throwing objects at each other. Almost one-fifth of the students said their fights with siblings had involved threats of violence with objects. And nearly one in every ten said they had actually had an argument with a brother or sister that had involved the use of a weapon (Noland and Liller, 2000).

One unusual finding from studies of sibling aggression is the role that parents play in a particular situation. Younger siblings are more likely to call for help from their parents than older siblings. If parents respond to the younger sibling—especially if they *punish* the older sibling—there is apt to be more subsequent fighting. It seems that when parents intervene, the younger sibling is more willing to fight with an older, stronger sibling. Parental intervention, in this case, leads to more aggression (Felson, 1983).

Abuse of Elderly Family Members

Sociologists, psychologists, social workers, and doctors became aware of the widespread mistreatment of the elderly somewhat later than they became concerned about child and spouse abuse. One of the earliest attempts at data collection came in the late 1970s (Rathbone-McCuan, 1980). But during the 1980s, research and writing on the mistreatment, abuse, and neglect of the elderly increased rapidly (Glendenning, 1993).

Abuse of elderly family members—generally those who are 65 years and older—is similar to the abuse of other family members we have been considering, but with some differences. Of all the types of family violence, the strongest negative feelings by the public are held about elder abuse (Webster, 1991). Since the next strongest negative feelings are about child abuse, it appears that people are reacting to the relative powerlessness of the victims.

ContentSELECT

Elder Abuse

There is a lack of consensus regarding a definition of elder abuse. Two experts on the subject have described the inability to agree on exactly what constitutes elder abuse as "definitional disarray" (Pillemer and Finkelhor, 1988). The disarray comes from a tendency to include an especially wide range of behaviors under the label of elder abuse (see Glendenning, 1993, p. 6). An added complication comes from the fact that elderly persons who are in institutions (nursing homes and long-term care facilities) may be abused by nonfamily members, such as staff members or other residents (Pillemer and Moore, 1989).

Physical abuse is the clearest dimension of elder abuse, and the dimension that is most consistent with the other forms of family abuse. Physical abuse of the elderly involves, once again, hitting, beating, kicking, and other forms of behavior that cause pain or threaten to do so. Most specialists on elder abuse also include neglect, a failure to provide food, medication, clothing, or help with personal hygiene when an elderly person cannot provide these for herself or himself. The most extreme version of neglect is abandonment (Pagelow, 1989; Glendenning, 1993). In the case of the elderly, neglect can be life threatening.

Elder abuse also sometimes includes fiscal abuse. Family members may steal an elderly relative's financial resources, such as savings, pensions, or Social Security income. Finally, mental abuse is often included as a part of elder abuse. Mental abuse is variously described, but one description used by the California Department of Social Services includes, "deliberately causing fear, agitation, confusion, severe depression, or severe emotional distress through threats, harassment, or intimidation" (Pagelow, 1989, p. 266). Mental abuse can be very difficult to identify because it is easily hidden from outsiders.

The Prevalence and Characteristics of Elder Abuse

The National Elder Abuse Incidence Study (NEAIS), which was conducted in 1996 by the National Center on Elder Abuse and funded by the Administration for Children and Families and the Administration on Aging has shed new light on the significant problem of elder abuse.

The groundwork for the NEAIS was laid in 1992 when Congress, through the Family Violence Prevention and Services Act of 1992 (P.L. 102-295), directed that a study of the national incidence of abuse, neglect, and exploitation of elderly persons be conducted under the auspices of the Administration for Children and Families. The Administration for Children and Families consulted with the federal Administration on Aging, resulting in the two agencies combining resources and expertise to support the national study. The NEAIS focused only on the maltreatment of noninstitutionalized elderly. Elders living in hospitals, nursing homes, assisted-living facilities, or other institutional or group facilities were not included in the study.

In the NEAIS, *elder maltreatment* refers to seven types of abuse and neglect: physical abuse, sexual abuse, emotional or psychological abuse, financial or material exploitation, abandonment, neglect, and self-neglect. The NEAIS gathered data from a nationally representative sample of twenty counties in fifteen states. For each county sampled, the study collected data from two sources: (1) reports from the local Adult Protective Services (APS) agency responsible for receiving and investigating reports in each county and (2) reports from specially trained individuals in a variety of community agencies having frequent contact with the elderly. The NEAIS research is groundbreaking because it provides, for the first time, national incidence estimates of elder abuse, which can serve as a baseline for future research and service interventions. Its findings confirm some commonly held theories about elder abuse and neglect, notably that officially reported cases of abuse are only the "tip of the iceberg," or a partial measure of a much larger, unidentified problem. The NEAIS final report offers insight into critical questions, including who are the victims of elder abuse and neglect, and who are the perpetrators? Who are the reporters of abuse and neglect? What are the characteristics of self-neglecting elders? What is the extent of abuse, neglect, and self-neglect in our communities and what forms do they take?

The best national estimate of elder abuse obtained from the NEAIS is that a total of 449,924 elderly persons, aged 60 and over, experienced abuse and/or neglect in domestic settings in 1996. Of this total, 70,942 (16 percent) were reported to and substantiated by Adult Protective Services agencies, but the remaining 378,982 (84 percent) were not reported to Adult Protective Services. From these figures, one can conclude that over five times as many new incidents of abuse and neglect were unreported than those that were reported to and substantiated by Adult Protective Services agencies in 1996. The margin of error for this study, however, indicates that as many as 688,948 elders or as few as 210,900 elders could have been victims of abuse and/or neglect in domestic settings in 1996. Additional findings of this study indicate that:

- Female elders are abused at a higher rate than male elders, after accounting for their larger proportion in the aging population. Emotional abuse is the category of abuse in which elderly women are most heavily overrepresented.
- Our oldest elders (80 years and over) are abused and neglected at two to three times their proportion of the elderly population.
- The most common type of maltreatment among the elderly is neglect (48.7 percent of victims experience this). The second most common type of abuse is emo-

tional or psychological abuse (35.4 percent), followed by financial/material exploitation (30.2 percent) and physical abuse (25.6 percent).

■ In almost 90 percent of the elder abuse and neglect incidents with a known perpetrator, the perpetrator is a family member, and two-thirds of the perpetrators are adult children or spouses.

■ Victims of self-neglect are usually depressed, confused, or extremely frail.

Summary

Violence and abuse occur in American homes and families. Abuse may be directed at all family members, but weaker members are the most likely victims.

Family violence is found in many other societies besides the United States, including nonliterate and peasant societies, where wives and children are the most likely victims. Women in these societies are most likely to be victims when they are economically disadvantaged in comparison with men. Physical punishment of children is found in some, but not all, nonliterate and peasant societies. In modern developed societies, the data on family violence are limited, with the United States and Great Britain providing the most complete data.

Studies of family violence in the United States started in the 1960s and has expanded rapidly since then. Research shows that violence against family members is widely accepted as appropriate behavior in some circumstances. Because many people believe the privacy of the home must be respected, it is difficult to learn just how much violence occurs in American families. Research based on clinical populations often differs from data coming from social surveys. The Conflict Tactics Scale is the most widely used measure of family violence. A number of national surveys using this measure have been conducted.

Survey research finds that women are less likely to use violence against male partners. Most observers agree that regardless of who initiates intimate partner violence, women are more likely to be seriously hurt. Violence occurs in gay and lesbian couples, just as in heterosexual couples, and often for many of the same reasons.

Police response to domestic violence can influence the recurrence of violence. Early research found that arresting the perpetrators of violence reduced repeat incidents. Further studies show that arrest is a more effective deterrent when the perpetrator is employed and socially bonded.

Child abuse and maltreatment are often hidden from public view because many people believe parents have the right to punish their children physically. Surveys show that almost all American parents use some violence in rearing their children; this is especially true for children under age 3. Mothers are more likely to use violence with their children than fathers, probably because they spend more time with them. Parents in lower socioeconomic classes use more violence with their children than other classes.

Violence in one family relationship is often related to violence in other family relationships. For example, parents who received physical punishment as children are more likely to abuse their own children, and women who received physical punishment as children are more likely to have abusive boyfriends and husbands. Some researchers view the family as a training ground for violence, but not everyone who is abused as a child goes on to be an abuser.

The sexual abuse of children is a problem that affects large numbers of children, but the number of reported and substantiated cases has dropped since the early 1990s. Girls are more likely to be sexually abused than boys, especially when they have been separated from their mothers at some time. Men are the most likely sexual abusers of children. Incest and pedophilia are the two major forms of sexual child abuse.

Violence among siblings is the most common form of family violence, but many people regard this form of violence as normal and acceptable. Conflict among siblings is most likely to be over power, personal property, verbal or physical provocations, and relationship betrayals.

Abuse of elderly family members can take many different forms. Physical abuse and neglect are the clearest violations of societal norms. The most common abuse of elders is by their spouses, with the next most common by their children.

The declines in various acts of family violence over the 1990s may indicate a real decline or simply a greater sensitivity to the inappropriateness of violence. In any case, much family violence persists in American society.

Key Terms

Clinical samples (p. 239)

Common couple violence (p. 244)

Conflict Tactics Scale (p. 239)

Intimate partner violence (p. 234)

Patriarchal terrorism (p. 243)

Perpetrator (of child abuse) (p. 253)

Physical assault (p. 235)

Rape (p. 235)

Realistic conflict (p. 259)

Sexual abuse of children (p. 256)

Sibling aggression (p. 259)

Sibling rivalry (p. 259)

Stalking (p. 235)

Review Questions

1. Discuss the various ways in which family violence is defined. What behaviors or actions are typically included in measures of the various forms of family violence?

2. What are the various sources of statistical information about the incidence of domestic violence? Why might these different sources give slightly different pictures of perpetrators and victims?

3. How many women are killed each year by their intimate partners? How many children are killed each year by a parent or other adult caregiver?

4. Are same-sex partnerships as violent as heterosexual partnerships? Why/why not?

Critical Thinking Questions

1. How do social institutions such as religion, economy, and medicine work to encourage a victim of intimate partner violence to stay in a relationship with the abuser? What could these institutions do to enable victims to live independently of their abusers?

2. Why are victims of intimate partner violence reluctant to report their crimes to the police?

3. In what ways is family violence transmitted from one generation to the next?

4. Why aren't children who are at risk of maltreatment taken from their parents automatically?

Online Resources Available for This Chapter

www.ablongman.com/marriageandfamily

- Online Study Guide with Practice Tests
- PowerPoint Chapter Outlines

- Links to Marriage and Family Websites
- ContentSelect Research Database
- Self-Assessment Activities

Further Reading

Books and Articles

Gelles, Richard J. *Intimate Violence in Families*. Thousand Oaks, CA: Sage, 1997. A discussion of various theories of intimate violence and the contributing social factors.

Jasinski, Jana L., and Williams, Linda M. *Partner Violence: A Comprehensive Review of 20 Years of Research*. Thousand Oaks, CA: Sage, 1998. Summarizes the major findings of research on family violence over a 20-year period.

Johnson, Michael P., and Ferraro, Kathleen. "Research in Domestic Violence in the 1990s: Making Distinctions." *Journal of Marriage and the Family* 62, 2000: 948–963. A comprehensive review of research conducted on domestic violence over the decade of the 1990s.

Kanter, Glenda K., and Jasinski, Jana. *Out of the Darkness: Contemporary Perspectives on Family Violence*. Thousand Oaks, CA: Sage, 1997. Using information from the international arena, the editors provide an interdisciplinary look at family violence.

Lloyd, Sally A., and Emery, Beth C. *The Dark Side of Courtship: Physical and Sexual Aggression*. Thousand Oaks, CA: Sage, 2000. Reviews factors that contribute to violence in developing relationships.

Renzetti, Claire M., and Miley, C. H. *Violence in Gay and Lesbian Partnerships*. New York: Haworth Press, 1996. One of the first comprehensive studies of violence in same-sex partnerships.

Straus, Murray A., and Gelles, Richard J. *Behind Closed Doors: Violence in the American Family*. Newbury Park, CA: Sage, 1988. A ground-breaking report of the extent of violence in American homes.

Straus, Murray, and Gelles, Richard. *Physical Violence in American Families*. New Brunswick, NJ: Transaction, 1990. Extensive report of violence in American families based on two national surveys conducted a decade apart (in the mid 1970s and mid 1980s).

Tjaden, P., and Thoennes, N. *Extent, Nature, and Consequences of Intimate Partner Violence: Findings from the National Violence Against Women Survey*. Washington, D.C.: National Institute of Justice and Centers for Disease Control and Prevention, 1999. Reports on the findings from the national study of family violence sponsored by the federal government.

U.S. Department of Health and Human Services, Administration on Children, Youth, and Families. *Child Maltreatment 1999*. Washington, D.C.: U.S. Government Printing Office, 2001. Reports the findings of the annual survey of child abuse and maltreatment conducted by the federal government.

ContentSELECT Articles

Humphrey, S. "Fraternities, Athletic Teams, and Rape." *Journal of Interpersonal Violence* 15(12), 2000: 1313–1323. **[Database: Social Work]** In this study, 182 men from fraternities and athletic teams were surveyed to assess sexual aggression, hostility toward women, and male peer support that approved of sexual aggression. While membership in these groups alone did not distinguish men in these aggression areas from non-group members, differences did exist in that environments were created (parties with more women than men; gender segregation; less opportunity for conversation; degradation of women) that posed a high risk for sexual assault to occur.

Langley, J., and Martin, J. "Physical Assault among 21-Year-Olds by Partners." *Journal of Interpersonal Violence* 12(5), 1997: 675–685. **[Database: Social Work]** Seeking to answer such questions as: Do women experience more physical assaults from their partners than men? Is the resulting physical harm more severe for women assaulted by partners than the physical harm experienced by men from partners? Do women physically assault their male partners? Utilizing data obtained from a cohort of 21-year-olds, research results indicate that women do, indeed, suffer more serious injury. In addition, four times more women reported physical assault by partners than did men.

McCloskey, L., and Bailey, J. "The Intergenerational Transmission of Risk for Child Sexual Abuse." *Journal of Interpersonal Violence* 15(10), 2000: 1019–1036. **[Database: Social Work]** Existing research has demonstrated that a link exists between women who were sexually abused in their own childhood (maternal sexual abuse) and later child abuse of their own children. This present study sought to examine whether parental history of sexual abuse heightens the risk of sexual abuse in offspring. Numerous variables were also investigated. Study results indicate that when maternal sexual abuse history exists concurrently with maternal drug use, 83 percent (10 out of 12) of the girls reported sexual abuse.

Mustaine, E. "A Routine Activity Theory Explanation for Women's Stalking Victimizations." *Violence Against Women* 5(1), 1999: 43–63. **[Database: Sociology]** It is estimated that one in twenty women will be a victim of stalking at some point during her lifetime. Stalking—almost always directed at women—includes victimizations of the target's personal life, her family and friends, and is oftentimes associated with threatening behaviors that can include homicide. But what places one woman at greater risk to be a stalking victim than another? Mustaine, with a comprehensive review of the literature and an analysis of university women's lifestyle behaviors, identifies in this study those behaviors and activities that place women in greater danger of being the victim of stalking; routine activity appears to place women at greater risk.

Parenting Desires and Decisions

*P*arenting can take many forms and may not reflect biological connections. The Hughes family described in the vignette illustrates the complexities that family formation can involve. Shirley and Van Hughes gained such satisfaction from rearing their two biological sons that they wanted to extend their parenting experiences by sharing their home with foster children. In their situation, the interconnection between the family system and the governmental institution in the form of the state's foster care system reveals one method of providing for the health and welfare of children in need of parenting. In this chapter and the next, we examine individuals' desires to become parents, the decisions they make regarding the options available to them, and the ways in which they relate to their children once they've joined the family.

Childbearing Trends in the United States

*W*e begin our discussion of childbearing by looking at the trends in the United States, giving consideration to variation in childbearing across racial, ethnic, social class, and religious groups. We then turn to the decision to have children, framing it in terms of the rewards and costs of parenthood. Then women's descriptions of their pregnancy and childbirth experiences are presented, to provide a realistic perspective on this initial stage of family formation. The decision-making processes of voluntarily childfree couples contribute to our understanding of the social pressures for parenthood. At the end of the chapter we examine the reproductive technologies now available for couples who find it difficult to have children and conclude with a discussion of adoption.

In 2000, more than 4,059,000 babies were born in the United States (Martin et al., 2002). This is comparable to the high number of births in the later years of the baby boom (1960 to 1963). It does not mean, however, that the average American woman is having more children than ever before. There are simply more women of childbearing age in the population. To get a clearer picture of the childbearing patterns, we must calculate fertility rates, since they take into account the number of childbearing women in the population.

Measures of Childbearing

Demographers use the term **fertility** to refer to the childbearing patterns of a population. One useful measure of fertility is obtained by comparing the yearly number of births to the number of women of childbearing age in the population. For statistical purposes, the childbearing ages are identified as 15 to 44, although women who are older and younger do, of course, have babies. The resulting statistic is called the **general fertility rate.** In 2000, the general fertility rate was 67.5 births per 1000 women between ages 15 and 44 (Martin et al., 2000). Figure 9.1 presents data about childbearing in the United States since 1930.

In the last half century, childbearing rates in the United States reached a peak in 1957. After that year, fertility declined quite rapidly for nearly twenty years. Since the middle 1970s, the fertility rate has been fairly constant, although there was a minor upturn in the late 1980s.

Another way to look at the childbearing level of a society is to use the **total fertility rate.** This rate predicts the total number of births that each woman in the population would have if the current year's fertility patterns continued. The number that is given in this type of rate is hypothetical but still useful for comparison purposes. In 2000 the total fertility rate in the United States was 2.13 babies per

Figure 9.1 Live Births and Fertility Rates: United States, 1930 to 2000

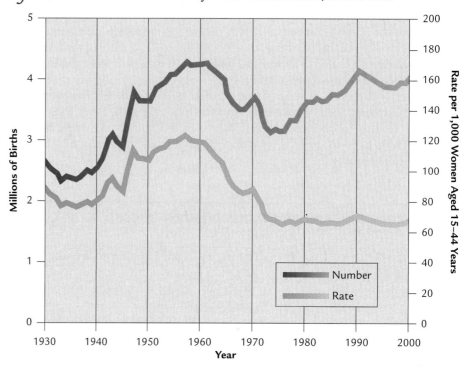

Note: Beginning with 1959, trend lines are based on registered live births; trend lines for 1930 to 1959 are based on live births adjusted for underregistration.

(*Source: National Vital Statistics Reports,* Volume 50, number 5, February 12, 2002, p. 1.)

woman. This number suggests that each woman in the population would have just over 2 babies if 2000 fertility rates continued. It is estimated that a *replacement level* of fertility in the United States would be about 2.11 births per woman (because of infant and child deaths).

The total fertility rate in 2000 was above replacement level for the first time in thirty years (Martin et al., 2002). Differences by ethnic and racial groups can be observed, however. The total fertility rate was above replacement level for American women of Mexican, Puerto Rican, and other Hispanic descent, as well as for non-Hispanic blacks and American Indians. But it was below replacement levels for those of Asian or Pacific Islander descent, non-Hispanic whites, and Cuban Americans.

The total fertility rate in the United States is high relative to those of other *developed* countries. Table 9.1 shows how the U.S. rate compares with those of other nations.

Current fertility rates suggest that childbearing in the United States today is at a relatively low level compared with the past. Certainly that is true when current rates are compared with childbearing in the eighteenth and nineteenth centuries.

Historical Declines in Fertility

Over the past 200 years, the average number of babies born to American women has decreased from seven births to two. During this period, childbearing has made some dramatic swings, but the general trend has been downward. During certain times, such as the Great Depression of the 1930s, the rate of decline was much more pronounced, while at other times, most notably during the post–World War II baby boom, the number of births per woman actually increased. In 1936, the middle of the Depression, American women were giving birth to two children, on the average, while in 1957 the number reached 3.6 births per woman.

Why has the average number of births per woman decreased over the past 200 years? One reason is that in the past women had little control over their fertility. Through the eighteenth and nineteenth centuries, many women had about as many children as they were biologically capable of having. Married women generally had children as a natural outcome of sexual intercourse. This pattern persisted into the twentieth century for many women, although by the end of the nineteenth century many middle-class women were beginning to use birth control. Childbearing in the United States is now largely controlled. Most people have the number of children they want to have, and generally they want no more than two. Only a small percentage of couples want, and have, more than two children.

A second reason for the historical decline in childbearing is that children have changed from being economic assets to being liabilities. Through much of the nineteenth century, the labor of children helped families survive. Most Americans lived on farms where children could help out in many ways. Even the children who lived in small towns and cities often worked at young ages to help support their families.

When child labor laws and compulsory education laws were passed in the nineteenth century, children became less valuable economically to their parents. Today children require large economic expenditures from their parents. (We discuss the costs of childbearing later in this chapter.) Most people have the number

TABLE 9.1	
Total Fertility Rates for Selected Developed Countries*	
Country	**Total Fertility Rate**
Spain	1.2
Germany	1.3
Japan	1.5
United Kingdom	1.7
Australia	1.8
Ireland	1.9
Norway	1.9
Iceland	2.1
United States	2.1

*Data pertain to 1994, 1995, or 2000.

Source: Martin et al., 2002.

In the late 1950s, during the peak of the Baby Boom, average family size was larger than it is today.

of children they think they can afford, and thus the number they have is much lower than in the past.

One other reason for the current low fertility rate is that women are marrying at later ages than they did during the 1950s, the baby boom years. As a result, the number of childbearing years spent in marriage is lower, and the number of children that can be born to married couples is also lower. The relatively high divorce rate has had a similar effect on fertility. Another major reason for the low fertility rate is the large number of women in the labor force. Childrearing duties decrease the amount of time and energy mothers can devote to their jobs; therefore, women who are career oriented often choose to give up childbearing altogether or to limit the number of children they have. A final factor that has reduced the average number of births per woman is the legalization of abortion. Currently, 30 percent of all pregnancies that don't end in stillbirth or miscarriage are aborted.

■ *Different Patterns of Childbearing*

Not all women in the United States are having babies at the same rate. Race, ethnicity, socioeconomic status, and religion affect childbearing, although not always in the expected ways.

Race and Ethnicity.   Racial and ethnic groups in the United States continue to have different fertility levels, but they are not especially great. Fertility rates among American women of Hispanic origin are higher than those of non-Hispanic women (105.9 versus 61.8 babies per 1000 women of childbearing age, respectively). Within these two ethnic origin categories, however, rates vary considerably. The 2000 fertility rates for women of Hispanic origin are highest among Mexican women (115.1), next highest among Puerto Rican women (84.3), and lowest among women of Cuban origin (57.3). Among non-Hispanic women, the fertility rate is higher among African Americans (73.7) than whites (58.5).

Socioeconomic Status.   A person's position in the socioeconomic structure of a society is one of the most enduring factors related to childbearing. Women in lower social classes generally have more children than women in the middle and upper classes. That was true throughout the twentieth century in the United States, and continues to be true today, regardless of whether socioeconomic status is measured by educational level, occupational prestige, or income.

Religion.   Because the Roman Catholic church disapproves of mechanical (barrier) and chemical methods of birth control and sterilization, it is often assumed that the Catholic birth rate is much higher than the birth rates found among other religious groups. That is not the case, however. For several decades, Catholic fertility in the United States has been about the same as non-Catholics.

A national survey of American women aged 15 to 39 found Catholic women were having *fewer* children than Protestant women (Mosher, Williams, and Johnson, 1992). The apparent reason for the lower fertility among Catholic women is their later entry into marriage. This same survey found that Catholic women expected to have more children in the future than do Protestant women, but previous studies have shown that unmarried Catholic women overestimate the number of children they will have.

The fact that Catholic fertility is no higher than Protestant fertility (and is actually lower in the national survey just described) is not too surprising when one understands that there are no longer great differences in contraceptive use between Catholics and non-Catholics. American Catholics generally use the same contraceptive measures as non-Catholics, and the overall pattern of contraceptive use by

Catholics and Protestants is very similar. The major difference is that Catholic women are somewhat less likely to use sterilization as a method of contraception.

Across the entire spectrum of religious and ethnic groups, some groups fall at the extremes. The lowest fertility in the United States is found among whites who have *no* religious affiliation; Jews have the next lowest fertility. The highest levels of fertility are found among Hispanic Catholics, fundamentalist Protestants, and Mormons (Mosher, Williams, and Johnson, 1992).

Changes in Women's Average Age at the Birth of a First Child

In addition to the lower average number of children born per woman, the age at which women begin to have children has also changed. The childbearing period seems to be expanding, as some women continue to become mothers in their teens while others wait until they are in their early forties or beyond. The average age at which women give birth for the first time reached 24.6 in 2000 (Martin et al., 2002). In the past twenty years, more and more people have been postponing parenting. This can be explained by educational advancement and the growth of economic opportunities in the labor market, which are postponing marriage, as well.

Birth rates for teens aged 15 to 19 have generally declined since the late 1950s, except for a brief but steep upward climb from the late 1980s through the early 1990s. The 2000 rate (49 births per 1000 women aged 15 to 19) is just over half of the peak number that was recorded in 1957 (96 births per 1000 women in this age group). In spite of this decline, the teen fertility rate in the U.S. is considerably higher than the rates for other developed countries. During the 1990s, the decline in rates was especially large for black teens. The factors accounting for these declines include decreased sexual activity reflecting changing attitudes toward premarital sex, increases in condom use, and adoptions of recently available forms of hormonal contraception that are implanted or injected (Ventura, Matthews, and Hamilton, 2001, p. 1).

The birth rates for women aged 20 and over have increased over the past several decades. For those aged 20 to 24, the birth rate increased to 112.3 babies per 1000 women. Among those aged 25 to 29, the birth rate reached 121.4, its highest

The arrival of a baby—while often eagerly awaited—brings many changes to its parents' daily lives.

point since 1971. Rates for women in their thirties and forties have also increased over the past several decades. In fact, for women aged 30 to 34, the birth rate in 2000 was higher than for any year since 1965. For women aged 35 to 39, the rate has doubled since the late 1970s, reaching a record high in 2000. Similar increases have occurred among women in their forties, reaching their highest levels since 1970.

Changes in Births to Unmarried Women

Most teenage births today occur outside of marriage—79 percent in 2000—compared with only 14 percent in 1957 (Ventura et al., 2001).

The rapid increase in births to unmarried women is a major change in U.S. childbearing patterns. In 1960 only slightly over 5 percent of all births were to unmarried women. By 1980, the percentage increased to 18.4 percent. Today one-third of all births in the United States are to unmarried mothers. Figure 9.2 shows changes in birth rates for unmarried and married women since 1960. Nonmarital birth rates differ considerably by race and Hispanic origin. The level is higher among African Americans than among whites. In 2000, 69 percent of all African American births were to unmarried women. This is three times higher than the percentage among white women (22 percent). The proportion of children born out of

Figure 9.2 **Birth Rates for Married and Unmarried Women: United States, 1960 to 1999**

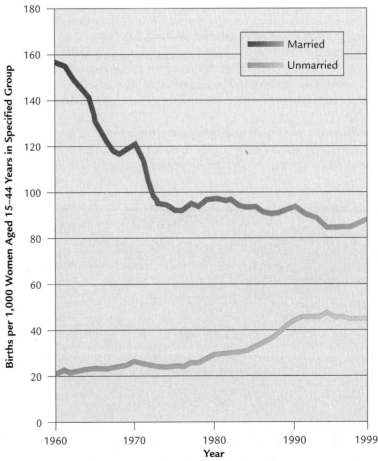

(*Source: National Vital Statistics Reports,* Volume 48, number 16, October 18, 2000, p. 5.)

Figure 9.3 **Percent of All Births to Unmarried Women by Racial and Ethnic Groups, 1980, 1990, and 1999**

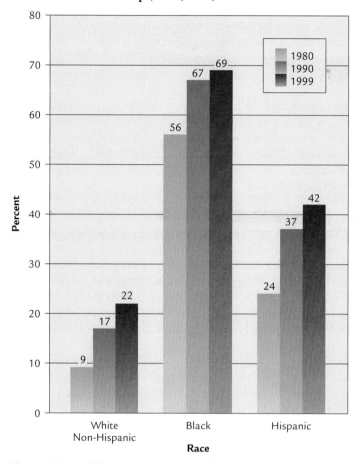

(*Source: National Vital Statistics Reports,* Volume 48, number 16, October 18, 2000, p. 6.)

wedlock among Hispanic women was 42 percent (Ventura and Bachrach, 2000). Figure 9.3 presents racial and ethnic differences in the percent of births to unmarried women.

Motherhood among never-married women has increased across all races and at all educational levels from the 1940s to 1990, but it has leveled off since then. Unmarried motherhood, especially among women beyond the teenage years, may indicate a declining importance of marriage in women's lives. Many women, especially those who are well educated and in professions, may not consider the absence of a husband a reason to be without children.

The Decision to Have Children

Since individuals today can largely control their childbearing, with the advances in contraceptive technology and access to legal abortion, it is clear that having children is largely a matter of personal choice. Therefore, it is important to examine the reasons why the majority of Americans choose to become parents.

Social Pressures to Have Children

The United States is often referred to as **pronatalist,** which means that dominant values and attitudes of our culture encourage childbearing. Not all cultures have such strong positive feelings about children (Peterson, 1995). In our society, the strongest social pressures to have children come from family members and from religious affiliations.

Pressures from Family Members.   When a young couple marries today, parents are likely to encourage them to wait to have a family until they have had a chance to get to know each other. However, if a couple has not had a child after four or five years, they are likely to be questioned by their parents and grandparents, who inquire if "something is wrong" or jokingly ask about when they are going to be presented with a grandchild.

Religious Pressures.   Almost all religions treat childbearing positively. Some religions take the view that a major purpose of marriage is procreation, whereas others simply encourage married couples to have children.

As a general rule, the newer and smaller religious groups place more emphasis on having children. The Nation of Islam, an African American Muslim faith that came into prominence in the 1960s, strongly urged members to have large families (Edwards, 1968). It is understandable that these newer or smaller religious groups would want to encourage having children, since it would contribute to their future growth.

Other Social Pressures.   In addition to family and religious groups, ethnic groups frequently encourage their members to have large numbers of children. Government policies, from income tax deductions for children to child welfare payments, also encourage childbearing. In the economic realm, it would be difficult to ignore the vast amount of advertising devoted to portraying babies and children in a positive way. Although these images presented in the mass media may not cause people to have children, they are certainly consistent with the other types of encouragement for childbearing.

The entire set of family, religious, ethnic, and economic pressures to have children can be characterized as a **cultural press for childbearing** (Daugherty and Kammeyer, 1995). Because of the cultural press, 90 percent of Americans over age 40 have had children.

Personal Rewards of Having Children

People generally believe they will get personal rewards and satisfactions from having children. In U.S. society, parents do not usually expect their children to be economically rewarding, but they do expect children to be psychologically, emotionally, and socially rewarding.

Becoming a parent can lead to much desired changes in social identity. Having a child grants adult status, which suggests to others that a person is now mature and stable. In fact, for many people parenthood is *the* event that gives a sense of feeling like an adult and provides a sense of being a family. Having children may also produce a sense of personal fulfillment. Having children of one's own often provides individuals with desired primary group ties and affection. Children are expected to provide love and companionship to their parents.

The stimulation and fun that childrearing promises are also considered rewards of parenthood. A new baby in the home is an immediate source of novel-

(*Source:* Reprinted with special permission from King Features Syndicate.)

ty. As babies grow and mature, they are expected to provide new experiences and satisfactions for their parents.

Finally, some people regard childbearing as a sacred duty. The duty may be to their family, their religion, or simply to some higher moral or spiritual authority. The physical and symbolic sacrifices that are required of parents make some people feel virtuous and altruistic.

Although having children is undoubtedly both personally and socially rewarding for most people, the rewards must be balanced against the costs of having children. In today's society, these costs may limit the number of children people have, or in some cases, keep them from having any children at all.

The Costs of Parenthood

There are both financial and socioemotional costs associated with parenting. The costs may be direct (such as food, clothing, shelter, medical and dental care, toys, recreation, leisure, and education) or indirect (such as forgone savings and investments, lower standards of living, and loss of potential income for parents who leave the labor market to care for the child). The costs of childrearing have been rising steadily.

Economic Costs. The U.S. Department of Agriculture annually makes estimates of the total expenditures for rearing an American child through age 17. According to their estimates, a child born in 1997 will cost between $220,000 and $440,000 by age 18. Average expenditures on children vary greatly by the parents' income. Higher-income parents spend nearly twice as much as lower-income parents. Two-parent families with annual incomes of more than $59,000 spend at least $430,000 per child through age 17. Low-income families (below $35,000 in annual income) spend more than $220,000 (Longman, 1998).

These cost estimates do not include the substantial expenditures many parents make after their children reach age 18. The greatest expenditure, of course, is for post-secondary education. College costs can easily run into the tens of thousands of dollars. To send their children to elite private colleges and universities, parents may have to spend $100,000 or more.

Although couples may be aware of the magnitude of financial costs associated with childbearing, most are not deterred by it. Economic considerations play only a small role in the decision to become a parent, at least for the first and second children. But when it comes to having a third or fourth child, parents may be more likely to consider whether they can afford more children.

Beyond the actual dollars required to raise a child, still other costs are associated with parenting. Children restrict the activities of parents, resulting in a loss of

▲ *Parents can spend a large amount of money to provide their babies with the necessities and the niceties of life.*

freedom. For women, having children can be costly because of lost career opportunities. The **opportunity costs** of having children (the lost wages, lost promotions, and lost seniority that may come from dropping out of the labor force to have a baby) are often considered carefully by women who have advanced or professional degrees and career ambitions. If they want children, women who have career aspirations must decide *when* to have them, so they can minimize the potential damage to their careers. Should they have children early, before they get immersed in their careers, or should they get established in their careers first, and then take time to have a child or children? This is the kind of calculation that many women must make when they estimate the opportunity costs of having a baby.

The lost opportunities that result from having children are often far less for men than for women. Men obviously do not have to go through the potentially limiting aspects of pregnancy and childbirth. After a child is born, traditional gender roles and social customs place the major responsibility for child care on women. Men are expected to be supportive, but they are often excused, because of their paid work outside the home, from the primary responsibility of caring for babies.

Very few men take time from their work or put their careers *on hold* after the birth of a baby. In fact, men may work more intensely and give increased attention to their careers after they become fathers. Employers often view men who become fathers as more dependable and reliable because of their new responsibilities. The opportunity costs are much less for men than for women.

Social and Emotional Costs of Childbearing.   Parents are responsible for the mental, emotional, physical, spiritual, and social development of their children. Obviously, such responsibility consumes considerable time and attention and may require that parents adjust their lifestyles to accommodate their children's needs. Children may also negatively affect the relationship between their parents. The birth of children often results in **role segregation,** which means that spouses engage in fewer joint activities as they attempt to fulfill their parental responsibilities.

Despite the financial, emotional, and other costs of having children, our society emphasizes the positive outcomes of parenting while playing down the negative. It may be that societies must do this to ensure that adults take on this difficult, but essential, societal function (LeMasters and DeFrain, 1983). The folk beliefs that depict children as fun, cute, clean, healthy, and intelligent, and childrearing as easy and enjoyable are not always supported by facts. Indeed, most studies reveal that adults believe these overly positive depictions of children and childrearing only until they become parents themselves and reality sets in.

Up to this point in the chapter, we have considered trends in childbearing and the rewards and costs of having children. We have given little attention to the very personal experiences of pregnancy and childbirth.

Pregnancy and Childbirth

*I*n television situation comedies and, it seems, in most movies, pregnancy is handled through a series of stereotypes. First there is the "pregnancy announcement," when the woman informs her male partner, who reacts with a combination of excitement, joy, and bewilderment. The second stereotyped scene is at the beginning of labor, when the nervous and rattled father-to-be falls apart, leaving his calm and slightly bemused female partner to handle the situation. Then, after the birth of

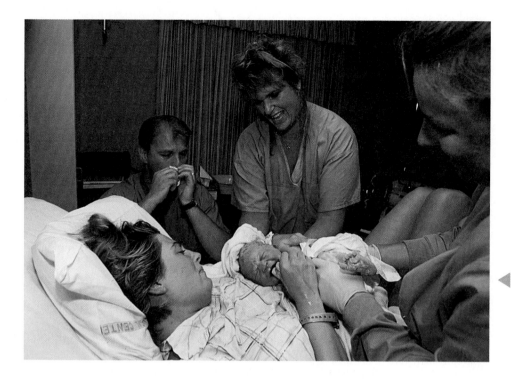

Some new parents today are having their babies at home or in birthing centers attended by midwives rather than physicians; fathers are usually present to support their partners.

the baby, the beaming father stands with the glowing new mother, who is usually holding the baby. In real life there may be occasions similar to these fictional scenes, but reality usually has a way of being a bit less sugar-coated.

When mothers in one study were asked to describe their pregnancy experiences, including both negative and positive aspects, slightly more than one-third said pregnancy was everything they thought it would be—a physical and emotional high, the ultimate female experience:

> Wonderful! Sexy. Super-fulfilling emotionally. Improved closeness with husband. Lots of attention from friends and strangers. I think being pregnant was the best thing that ever happened to me. I felt beautiful. For the entire nine months I was on an emotional high. (Genevie and Margolies, 1987, p. 101)

The majority, however, found pregnancy was far from rapturous. A small minority even hated being pregnant because of intense physical and emotional discomfort, combined with a fear of the unknown and a feeling of being out of control of one's own body.

> I felt awful—all day sickness, too much weight gain, swollen ankles, constant sleepiness. I felt large, tired, unattractive, sickly, hurt somewhere most of the time, and couldn't do all the things I wanted. I couldn't wait for the baby to be born to be over this miserable part. (p. 103)

About 40 percent of the women described their pregnancies with great ambivalence:

> Physically, I felt sick. Morning sickness for three or four months, tired, flu, heartburn, the last few months with vomiting! At the same time, I felt complete, whole as a woman. It's hard to explain. (p. 105)

Thus it appears that emotional and physical experiences of pregnancy are closely intertwined. The physical changes such as weight gain, swelling, and fatigue affect psychological well-being. Moreover, women who are concerned about the circumstances of the birth or the relationship they have with the baby's father may find it more difficult to put the physical discomfort into a positive perspective.

Around the World

Japan's Ancient Traditions Are Wrapped Up in the Birth of a Prince or Princess

A celebration swept Japan when the palace announced that the Crown Princess Masako was pregnant. Concern about the Japanese royal line developed after Masako suffered a miscarriage two years earlier. The Chrysanthemum Throne is the world's oldest monarchy, dating back 2600 years. Under Japanese law, only men can ascend to the throne. No male heir has been born in more than thirty years.

A number of ancient rituals surrounded Masako's pregnancy and delivery. At the beginning of her fifth month of pregnancy, Masako participated in a fifteen-minute ceremony that involved the donning of a belly belt and a trip to a Shinto shrine where she and other pregnant women asked the deity to watch over their unborn babies and ease the pain of childbirth.

In anticipation of the baby's arrival, a master sword-smith made a sword that the Emperor presented to the baby to protect it from harm. A bathtub made of fresh cypress was built for the new prince or princess's first bath. Buddhist priests delivered a paper amulet, and literature professors were asked to search ancient texts for an appropriate name.

On December 1, 2001, Princess Masako gave birth to a daughter, Aiko ("child of love"). Had the baby been a boy he would have automatically been second in line to the throne. When baby Aiko was born, however, Japan's ruling party started the process of changing the rules of succession, paving the way for Japan to have its first female monarch since ancient times.

Sources: Associated Press. "Pregnant Princess Joins Tradition of 'Belly Belt.'" *Gainesville Sun,* July 11, 2000, p. 2A; Larimer, Tim. "A Fairy-tale Ending: Japan's Princess Masako Gives Birth to a Girl." *Time Asia,* January 27, 2002.

Women who go through labor and deliver a baby are in nearly universal agreement that it is an unforgettable event. But when a sample of wives was asked how they felt about the birth process and their newborns, 30 percent were negative about the emotional aspects and almost half were negative about the physical (Entwistle and Doering, 1981). Similar results were found in a study of English women having their first child, with approximately half saying that the birth experience and the pain connected with it was worse than they expected (Oakley, 1980).

> Childbirth was long and painful. At first I wasn't frightened, just anxious. Since it took over sixteen hours, toward the end I screamed, 'Enough, get me out of here!' The pain was excruciating. . . . All I could think of was getting it over. (Genevie and Margolies, 1987, p. 118)

Nevertheless, six out of ten mothers in this study remembered childbirth as a very positive experience, despite the fact that nearly all suffered from varying degrees of pain. Some described their pain as "nightmarish" but "worth it."

> It hurt more than anything I could have ever imagined. The pain is severe and agonizing, but when you think about what that pain is producing—bringing a new life into this world—it makes it all worthwhile. It was like having a nightmare turn into a wonderful dream. The pain was quickly forgotten. (p. 116)

When author Naomi Wolfe became pregnant with her first child in the 1990s, she was surprised by her negative experiences. Wolf and her husband spent quite a bit of time and energy—and money—to find an obstetric/gynecological practice that worked with nurse midwives and promised to use the *modern* methods of childbirth. They were shown the hospital's beautiful birthing room where they thought she would give birth. She expected to have a *natural* (that is, nontechnological) delivery. Her experiences, which she describes in a book, *Misconceptions* (2001), were quite different from what she expected. In the book, she criticizes the failure of the medical establishment to provide her and other pregnant women with a safe, effective, and supportive environment in which to give birth. In the following paragraph Wolfe describes her own experience of giving birth in a hospital setting:

> When I gave birth, nothing happened the way I had imagined. . . . In my delivery, I was an adjunct; I had almost no role. There was nothing I could do to contribute to the birthing process if I wanted to, which I badly did before the epidural essentially neutered my faculties and my will. . . . I did not dare risk doing anything other than what the doctors and nurses told me I must do. I lay passively on the birthing bed, letting them tie me and tether me down, and anesthetize me. I was told that I would have 24 hours to deliver before they would have to perform surgery. . . . I did not feel safe in the hospital. I did not feel safe. In spite of my best intentions, I could not labor. . . . After 24 hours, I am wheeled into the surgery room (pp. 137–138).

Wolfe interviewed other women about their birth experiences, which she describes in her book, as well. She concludes that the administrators and doctors who run the hospitals view childbirth as a medical crisis that they have to solve through the use of complicated technological devices rather than a natural process that occurs at its own pace. "A number of women who had given birth described a moment at which they felt the medical institution simply took over, oblivious to the mother's wishes, experience, or concerns; many new mothers dissociated from their birth experience because it was so distressing" (p. 145).

Seeing the baby for the first time in the delivery room is not a positive experience for all women. One-third of the women in a study of motherhood said they had either negative or *very* negative reactions to the appearance of their babies. And when asked about their initial feelings toward their newborn, 8 percent said they had negative feelings, and 22 percent, neutral (Entwistle and Doering, 1981).

The research findings on pregnancy and birthing experiences are more negative than we might have supposed, but it may be that many women, especially those who found the childbearing experience more difficult than they had been led to believe, feel that a realistic portrait is better than a totally rosy one. Ann Oakley, a British researcher who has studied mothering, supports the realistic approach:

> Some readers may feel that the portrait of motherhood given here is too bleak, too depressing, an inaccurate rendering of the satisfaction many women derive from having . . . a baby . . . But many of the women who were interviewed said . . . that they were misled into thinking childbirth is a piece of cake. (Oakley, 1980, p. 6)

For some people today, the difficulties of childbearing followed by the task of childrearing do not seem sufficiently rewarding. Therefore, they choose, voluntarily, to be childfree. We next consider the experiences of voluntarily childfree individuals and couples.

Voluntarily Childfree Couples and Individuals

*T*hroughout the twentieth century, the proportion of childless or childfree marriages in the United States has ranged from 5 to 10 percent. The percentage has increased since 1980. Estimates of childlessness are often made for women who are aged 40 to 44 years old, the assumption being that few women will have children after age 44. The proportion of childless women in this age group has nearly doubled since 1980, from 10 to 19 percent. Women who have the highest levels of education, those who are employed in managerial and professional occupations, and those with the highest family incomes have the highest levels of childlessness. White women are more likely than black women to be childless—20 versus 17 percent, respectively (Bachu, 1999).

Childless

The decision to remain childfree runs counter to the cultural pressure toward childbearing. In fact, our use of the term *childfree* to refer to those who have voluntarily chosen not to become parents may be more appropriate than the customary term *childless*. The former term is used to reflect their perception that parenting places many restrictions on adults that they would prefer to be without.

For the very small minority of people who are voluntarily childfree, the anticipated costs of having children outweigh the anticipated rewards. Those who choose to remain childfree may believe that having children would interfere with their ability to achieve in their careers or in other types of activities. They may feel that caring for children would drain time and energy that could be devoted to other highly valued pursuits.

Some couples choose to be childfree because parenthood would reduce the time available to devote to each other. For them, marriage is the primary source of affection and sense of belonging, and children are not needed to provide such rewards. Finally, some couples decide against having children because they believe that the demands of parenthood would be monotonous.

Childfree by Deliberation

Studies of voluntarily **childfree couples** show that the decision to forgo parenthood is basically made in one of two ways. Some people decide at an early point in their lives, perhaps long before, not to have children. Others don't reach this point until much later, after they've lived without children for a long time. One of the early studies of childfree women conducted in Canada found that about a third had decided early in their lives not to have children (Veevers, 1980). A national study of U.S. women conducted at about the same time similarly found that 43 percent of the childfree couples entered marriage agreeing that they would not have any children (Mosher and Bachrach, 1982).

Women who choose early in their lives not to have children offer different reasons. One woman gives the following account of her experience:

> My first decision never to have children was formed when I was fifteen and all us girls sat around talking about sex and marriage and husbands. Everyone else would always talk about the kids they were going to have, like it was just taken for granted. I couldn't sit and talk about it with the same enthusiasm as the others did. It finally came to me that I just didn't want to have children. It was a shock because all my life, you know, you're sort of groomed for it. (Veevers, 1980, p. 18)

Childfree by Default

Since the early decision makers are only a minority of the voluntarily childfree couples, what about the others? How do they come to be childless? In many ways they are the more interesting and revealing decision makers, because they share some of the characteristics of the couples who do go on to have children. They certainly begin at the same place, because they enter marriage with the conventional expectation that they will eventually have one or two children. Typically, they have not given the matter very much serious thought, and in this regard they are also like most couples.

For the couples who eventually end up being childless, the process of decision making involves a series of stages. In a sense, these stages do not represent decisions so much as a series of postponements, each of which involves another assessment of the costs and benefits of parenthood. We can see this more clearly if we examine the four stages that typify the experience (Veevers, 1980).

Stage 1: Postponement for a Definite Time. In the first stage on the path to childlessness, these voluntarily childfree couples are, again, like most other contemporary couples. They avoid pregnancy through careful contraception in order to achieve certain goals before starting a family. The typical goals may be graduating from school, buying a house, saving a nest egg, or simply getting adjusted to one another. They do not become careless about contraception, as is so often the case among couples who become parents not long after marriage.

Stage 2: Postponement for an Indefinite Time. The second stage is marked by increasing vagueness about the length of the postponement and the reasons for it. Although the couple may still believe they will have children someday, they no longer have a notion of when that will be. Their reasons for postponement become vague, such as "when we can afford it" or "when we're ready."

Stage 3: Deliberating the Pros and Cons of Parenthood. Stage 3 is the first time that the couple openly considers the possibility that they might remain childless. It is a time of considerable ambivalence. As one woman said, "We haven't decided to have children right away, and we haven't decided never to have them either. We just keep postponing the whole thing. We might or might not. We can worry about that later" (Veevers, 1980, p. 23). For the couples who remain childless, the "later" comes with the fourth and final stage of the process.

Stage 4: Accepting Permanent Childlessness. The fourth stage of the process is the recognition that a decision has already *been* made. It might more aptly be described as a retrospective acknowledgment that all the postponements of the past have added up to a decision to be permanently childless.

Numerous studies have shown that whatever their reason for deciding not to have children, voluntarily childless women are stigmatized. They are perceived as less well-adjusted, less nurturing, independent, and socially distant than women who are mothers. Childless women are also seen as selfish, moody, bitter, and insensitive. A study conducted in the late 1990s asked four groups of married women—those with no children, those with only one child, those with two or three children, and those with four or more—to discuss the social responses they have received about their family size. All of the women in the study had been married for at least ten years and were under age 50. Interestingly, many of the women in the *nonnormative* family situations (those who didn't have two or three children, which is viewed as the ideal number in our society) felt some type of social pressure. They believed that other people had preconceived notions about what motivates women to make their decisions about childbearing. The women who had no children reported that they began to feel social pressure to have children during the third and fourth years of their marriages. Those who had only one child began to feel pressured to have another child when their child was 5 years old. Women with four or more children began to feel pressure to *stop* having children.

Childfree women reported that they encountered intrusive, inappropriate questioning regarding their decision to forego childbearing. The questions they received ranged from direct ones, such as "Why wouldn't you want to have kids?" to somewhat more indirect questions (that is, "Was this your husband's decision? Or "Are you able to have children?"). Some of the childfree women even reported that they received unsolicited advice from medical professionals regarding their parenting status. One young woman, in her late twenties, brought up the topic of having a tubal ligation (the female form of sterilization) to her gynecologist, who responded by saying that she would change her mind when she was older. The situation of women who do not have children remains difficult. Many report that they feel denigrated by others for their decisions, but they still feel satisfied with their childfree status (Mueller and Yoder, 1999).

Social Pressures on Childfree Couples

Regardless of how the decision to remain childfree is made, couples with no children report social pressure and negative, or even hostile, responses to any indication that they may remain childless forever. Negative reactions often reach a peak in the fourth and fifth years of marriage. Apparently, parenthood is so positively valued that relatives, friends, and even strangers feel justified in asking a childless couple why they are not having children. When couples admit that it is their preference, they are usually told to think carefully about their decision and not wait until it is too late.

Most childless couples use different strategies to conceal their intentions from well-meaning friends, co-workers, and strangers, but it is parents who present the most persistent problem. With them, the most common strategy is not to talk about any *final* decisions, holding out the possibility of parenthood at some later date. In practice, this often means that parents are "literally the last to know" (Veevers, 1980, p. 145).

Contraception and Abortion

*P*eople who live in modern, industrialized countries now have access to various means to control their childbearing and limit the number of children they have. The fundamental ways of controlling childbearing are avoiding conception by using birth control methods and terminating pregnancy after conception has occurred. (See Appendixes C and D.)

Contraception

Contraception

Contraceptive methods of various types have been used for thousands of years, but the major technological improvements and medical advances have come in the last century. Condoms, for instance, date back to the ancient Egyptians, but in earlier years were usually made of animal intestines. In the late 1800s, improvements in the production of latex rubber led to the development of more comfortable and reliable condoms and, somewhat later, the diaphragm. Spermicides and douches became more effective as their chemical composition changed in the twentieth century. The effectiveness of the *rhythm method,* or periodic abstinence, which is an effort to limit sexual intercourse to those times of the menstrual cycle when conception is least likely, has improved as people have been taught to chart basal body temperature in order to determine the time of ovulation. The birth control pill, first approved for use by the Food and Drug Administration in 1960, quickly became one of the most widely used forms of contraception.

As new birth control methods became more widely used in the United States, they were met with growing opposition, and laws were passed to prohibit the distribution of contraceptives. Information about birth control methods was considered pornographic, and those who violated the law were subject to imprisonment of up to five years and fines of up to $2,000. In the early twentieth century, activists such as Margaret Sanger and Emma Goldman were arrested for helping poor, working-class, and immigrant women control their fertility.

Although many young people today take birth control for granted and are urged by government agencies to use certain methods, the complete legalization of contraception did not occur until forty years ago. Supreme Court rulings in the 1960s established the right of all Americans to purchase and use the available birth control methods.

Today the majority of all women in the United States between the ages of 15 and 44 use some kind of contraception. The two most popular methods are female sterilization and the birth control pill. But these two methods are used very differently by women as they go through their reproductive years. The pill is most widely used when women are in their teens and twenties; the use of female sterilization increases rapidly after women reach age 30. By the time women reach age 40 to 44, just over half have chosen sterilization. At the same age, about one in five couples (22 percent) is relying on male sterilization. Table 9.2 shows the use of the methods of contraception in the United States today. The pill and, to a lesser extent, the condom are replaced by sterilization as women and their partners reach age 30.

Among the more recent additions to contraceptive technology is Norplant. Norplant consists of six flexible capsules (each about the size of a paper match) implanted under the skin on the inside of the woman's upper arm. The hormone in the capsules gradually enters the woman's body and prevents conception for a period of up to five years (McCauley and Geller, 1992).

Information about effective methods of contraception may lead to increased use, as the Media box on the next page shows. When women in Cameroon were exposed to an ad campaign promoting reproductive health services, they were more likely to use modern contraceptives.

TABLE 9.2

Current Contraceptive Status and Method Used, U.S. Women Aged 15 to 44

	Percent
Using contraceptives	64.2
Type of contraceptive used	
Female sterilization	17.8
Male sterilization	7.0
Pill	17.3
Implant	0.9
Injectable	1.9
Intrauterine device	0.5
Diaphragm	1.2
Condom	13.1
Female condom	0.0
Periodic abstinence	1.5
Withdrawal	2.0
Other methods*	1.0

*Other methods include the "morning after" pill, spermicidal foam, cervical cap, sponge, suppository, spermicidal jelly and/or cream without diaphragm.

Source: Abma, J.C., Chandra, A., Mosher, W.D., Peterson, L., Piccinino, L. "Fertility, Family Planning, and Women's Health: New Data from the 1995 National Survey of Family Growth. National Center for Health Statistics." *Vital Health Statistics* 23, 1997: 19.

Abortion

If contraception is not used, or if it is used and fails, it is still possible to avoid childbirth through abortion. **Abortion** is the expulsion of a fetus or embryo from the uterus. Such an expulsion can happen spontaneously (referred to as *natural abortion*) or medically (which is referred to as *induced abortion*). Different methods of medically induced abortion are currently in use. For early (first-trimester) abortions, the most common method is vacuum aspiration (or suction). Dilation and curettage (D and C), or scraping the inside of the uterus, is also used. In second-trimester abortions, a saline or prostaglandin (a hormone) injection is used to cause the uterus to contract and expel the fetus. Hysterotomy, a procedure in which the fetus is surgically removed through the abdomen, may be performed.

A pharmaceutical innovation is the drug mifepristone or, as it is identified by its developer, RU486. The public often calls this drug simply "the French abortion pill," because it was developed by the French pharmaceutical company Roussel UCLAF and has been most widely used in France. Mifepristone is an antiprogestin that is administered to a woman who knows or believes she is pregnant. After the woman receives the drug, the fertilized ovum is expelled from the uterus.

Media Campaign in Cameroon Linked with Increased Contraceptive Use

In the late 1990s, the U.S. Agency for International Development, in conjunction with the Sante Familiale et Prevention du SIDA project, launched the Gold Circle Initiative in four countries in sub-Saharan Africa. The goals of the initiative were to increase the availability of family planning methods and to improve clinic management, client–provider interactions, and infection prevention practices. Its media campaign promotes sites where women can obtain quality reproductive health services. The cost of implementing the Gold Circle Campaign in Cameroon, including materials, distribution, community events, and consultants' time, was only $36,000 over a one-year period, or about 3 cents per woman reached.

Data obtained in the 1998 Cameroon Demographic Health Survey revealed that more than one-third of the estimated 3.5 million women of reproductive age said they had been exposed to the campaign. Women who had seen the campaign reported an increased use of modern contraceptives. The year before the survey, less than one-fifth had used modern contraceptives. After the campaign over one-fourth were using them. Among women who had not seen the media campaign, there was only a 4 percent increase over the same period in the proportion who reported using modern contraceptives.

Source: Babalola, Stella. "The Impact of a Regional Family Planning Service Promotion Initiative in Sub-Saharan Africa: Evidence from Cameroon." *International Family Planning Perspectives,* December 2001.

Mifepristone entered clinical trials in 1981 and was approved in France in 1988. The French manufacturer decided not to try to distribute it in the United States because of threats of boycotts. President George H. W. Bush banned imports of the abortion pill in 1989. In 1993, President Bill Clinton signed an executive order that lifted the ban on imports of RU486. Testing by the Food and Drug Administration began in the United States. Over 10,000 women participated in clinical trials of the drug. In the fall of 2000, the Food and Drug Administration approved the use of RU486 to terminate pregnancies in the United States. One primary restriction placed on the use of RU486 is that no more than forty-nine days can have passed since the start of a woman's last menstrual period and that she does not have any of the health conditions that indicate against its use (e.g., chronic adrenal failure or bleeding disorders).

In order to terminate a pregnancy through mifepristone, a woman must make three visits to her physician. On the first visit, she is given three pills to take while in the doctor's office. Forty-eight hours later she is given two different pills that lead to a miscarriage, typically within four hours. On the third visit, a physician confirms that the pregnancy has been terminated. Studies have shown that the drug is effective in terminating pregnancies 92 to 97 percent of the time. Women whose pregnancies are not terminated after taking the drug regimen must follow through with traditional surgical abortion techniques (France and Rosenberg, 2000, pp. 26–30).

A Brief History of Abortion in the United States.   The history of abortion in the United States is more complex than most people suppose. It might be surprising to learn that abortion was legal earlier in our history. In the first part of the nineteenth century, American women were able to use various substances and techniques to "restore their menstrual flow" after they had missed a period or two. As long as the fetus had not yet been felt to move in the uterus (referred to as *quickening*), these methods were accepted and apparently widely used. In effect, these early methods allowed abortion until sometime in the fourth month of pregnancy.

But as the nineteenth century progressed, abortions were gradually outlawed. The newly developing medical profession argued that abortions could pose a threat to the health of women, especially if performed by midwives—the chief competitors of doctors. Lawmakers were also concerned about decreased childbearing among native-born Protestant white women, perhaps due to their use of abortion.

By the beginning of the twentieth century, abortion had become illegal in the United States. As a result, for the first two-thirds of the twentieth century, few *legal* abortions were performed in the United States, but countless illegal and self-performed abortions occurred.

American abortion policies started changing again in the 1960s as a number of state legislatures passed laws that liberalized conditions under which abortions could be performed. The situation changed dramatically in 1973, when the U.S. Supreme Court ruled in *Roe* v. *Wade* that women could, in consultation with their physicians, have a constitutionally protected right to have an abortion in the early stages of pregnancy—that is, before the fetus can live on its own outside the mother's body—free from government interference. In 1992, the Supreme Court upheld women's right to have an abortion in the case *Planned Parenthood* v. *Casey*. However, the ruling significantly weakened the legal protections that had been given to women and their physicians by allowing states to pass laws that restrict women's rights, as long as they do not create an "undue burden" for those who seek an abortion. The most common restrictions now in effect are those that require minors (that is, women under 18) to involve their parents in the decision, to undergo mandatory counseling, and to wait a minimum amount of time between contacting an abortion provider and actually undergoing the procedure. Thirty-one states now enforce laws that require minors to notify and/or obtain consent from their parents before undergoing an abortion. Recognizing, however, that this restriction might cause an undue burden for some minors (e.g., those who are victims of abuse or parental violence), the Supreme Court ruled that in states that require parental notification and/or consent, they must also allow young women the option of obtaining a local court's permission to obtain the abortion rather than getting such permission from a parent. The majority of young women who undergo a medical abortion procedure do so with at least one parent's knowledge. Over 60 percent of parents whose daughters decide to have an abortion support the decision (Alan Guttmacher Institute, 2001).

Abortion rights continue to be a heated topic in the United States. The *Roe* v. *Wade* decision figured prominently in the 2000 presidential election. Should new justices be appointed to the U.S. Supreme Court, it is possible that new judicial rulings on abortion rights will be made. The majority of Americans, however, continue to support *Roe* v. *Wade,* according to a Gallup poll conducted in October 2000. And in January 2001, the same polling organization asked a random sample of Americans whether they believed the laws governing abortion should be changed. About a third said they thought that laws should be stricter, nearly half wanted to keep the laws as they are, and the remaining 17 percent wanted the laws to be made less strict (Carroll, 2001).

Although the right to have an abortion has been vigorously attacked by some individuals and groups, it is nonetheless a very important factor in U.S. childbearing patterns today. Over the 1990s, the number of medically induced abortions that were performed in the United States dropped. In 1997 (the most recent figures that were available in late 2001), slightly more than 1.3 million abortions took place,

HEADline **The Dutch Abortion Ship Sails to Ireland**

D r. Rebecca Gomperts, a Dutch physician and her abortion rights organization, Women on Waves, rent the ship *Aurora* for $1000 a day. The *Aurora* is a 1130-foot long fishing trawler that is outfitted with a medical clinic. The mission of Dr. Gomperts and Women on Waves is to sail the *Aurora* to countries where abortion is restricted or strictly controlled to provide women with birth control counseling, contraceptives, and to terminate pregnancies, through RU486, if necessary.

During the summer of 2001, the *Aurora* and her medical crew sailed to Ireland where it was going to drop anchor just 12 miles off the coast in international waters. There the doctors and their medical assistants planned to provide the abortion pill RU486 to Irish women who wished to terminate their pregnancies. Women on Waves chose Ireland because it has one of the toughest antiabortion laws in Western Europe. As it turned out, however, the doctors on board the *Aurora* did not have the required licenses, so they

were not able to provide the medical services as planned. But abortion rights activists in Ireland hoped that the presence of the ship would influence Irish public opinion toward a more permissive policy.

Sources: Grose, Thomas K. "An Abortion Ship on the High Seas." *US News & World Report,* June 25, 2001, p. 30; Lavery, Brian. "Ship's Irish Stop Largely Symbolic." *Gainesville Sun,* June 17, 2001, p. 8A.

compared with 1.61 million in 1990. Each year, two out of every 100 women who are between the ages of 15 and 44 have a medically induced abortion. Nearly half of these women have already had at least one previous abortion and well-over half have had at last one previous birth. It has been estimated that over 40 percent of women in the United States will have at least one abortion by the time they reach age 45 (Alan Guttmacher Institute, 2001).

Nearly all of the women who are at risk of an unintended pregnancy (that is, they are sexually active but do not intend to have a child at the present time) use a contraceptive method. In fact, the majority of women who have abortions reported that they were using a contraceptive method during the month they became pregnant. Just under half of the 6.3 million pregnancies that occur each year in the United States are unplanned (Alan Guttmacher Institute, 2001).

Characteristics of Women Who Have Abortions. Slightly over half of all women who have abortions in the United States each year are under age 25. Women aged 20 to 24 obtain about one-third of all abortions, and teenagers obtain one-fifth of them. Two-thirds of all abortions are performed on unmarried women. There are racial differences in women's likelihood of terminating a pregnancy through medical abortion. Black women are over three times more likely than white women to have abortions. Hispanic women are about twice as likely. There is a significant difference by religious affiliation as well. Catholic women are 29 percent more likely than Protestant women to have a medically induced abortion (Alan Guttmacher Institute, 2001).

Reasons for Obtaining Abortions. The most frequent reason women give for having an abortion is that a birth would interfere with work, school, or other responsibilities. The second most common reason is that the woman cannot afford to have a baby. In about half of all abortion cases, the woman either has no relationship with the baby's father or has a problematic relationship with him and feels she cannot raise a child on her own. Less common reasons include fear that the fetus has been harmed by exposure to toxic substances, knowledge that the fetus actually has a physical defect, or the fact that the pregnancy resulted from rape or incest (Alan Guttmacher Institute, 2001).

When Do Women Have Abortions?   Nearly all of the abortions performed in the United States occur in the first trimester (the first three-month stage) of pregnancy. Over half occur before the end of the second month of pregnancy. Only 5 percent are performed after the fifteenth week of pregnancy. In the small number of cases in which abortion is performed after the first trimester, the delay is associated with problems in arranging for the abortion. Many women who live in rural areas must travel long distances to find a doctor who is willing to perform abortions, even though abortion is legal in this country. The number of medical facilities that provide abortion services declined over the 1990s. Most counties in the United States do not have an abortion provider (Alan Guttmacher Institute, 2001).

Safety of Induced Abortions.   The risk to women of medically induced abortion is minimal. Less than 1 percent of all abortion patients experience a major complication, such as pelvic infection or hemorrhage requiring a blood transfusion. The risk of death associated with abortion is many times smaller than the risk associated with childbearing and has even decreased over the past twenty years. There is no evidence that women who have early abortions through vacuum aspiration have later problems with childbearing (Alan Guttmacher Institute, 2001).

Attitudes toward Abortion in the United States.   For a number of years, public opinion polls have shown that the majority of Americans favor the availability of abortion, especially under some circumstances (e.g., if the mother's health is endangered by the pregnancy).

A Gallup poll conducted in August 2001 reported that 26 percent of respondents believe abortion should be legal under any circumstances, 56 percent believe it should be legal under certain circumstances, and 17 percent believe it should not be legal under any circumstances.

Social groups and categories in the population have different attitudes about abortion. The highest proportions supporting the legality of abortion are found among those with family incomes of $75,000 or more, the college educated, those who are 30 to 49 years of age, and residents of the east. Opposition to abortion (those most likely to say it is morally wrong) is greatest among political conservatives, Republicans, Southerners, rural residents, those with incomplete college educations, and incomes of less than $20,000 annually ("Legality, Morality, and Abortion," 1995).

weird wouldn't they favor abortion?

Infertility

Although most women are able to become pregnant quite easily, some women may have sexual intercourse for an extended period of time and not become pregnant. The more precise term for men and women who are unable to conceive is **infecundity** or **sterility** but the word *infertility* is also commonly used.

Incidence and Causes

When a woman fails to become pregnant after twelve months of unprotected intercourse, the couple is said to be **infertile.** Estimating the exact incidence of infertility is very difficult, because some couples use contraception consistently and have not yet "tested" their fertility. The National Center for Health Statistics estimates that over 15 percent of women aged 15 to 44 may have an impaired ability to have a child (Stephen and Chandra, 2000)

The percentage of women who have infertility problems didn't change significantly over the 1990s. But the actual number of women who reported difficulties with fertility increased simply because there were so many more women in the older years of the reproductive period due to the aging of the baby boomers. Over the same period, the range of available infertility treatments increased, as did the number of providers of assisted reproductive technologies (e.g., in vitro fertilization and related techniques) (Stephen and Chandra, 2000).

Primary infertility (the inability to conceive among those who have never had children) has increased, especially among the white middle class, but it is still less common than **secondary infertility,** a term that refers to the difficulties couples face when they try to have additional children. Currently, about 30 percent of infertile couples in the United States have no children, whereas about 70 percent already have at least one child (Greil, 1991, p. 28).

Infertility can be caused by any number of problems in the female or male reproductive systems. In approximately 35 to 40 percent of the cases in which a specific problem is identified, the difficulty is associated with the male partner, generally because he fails to produce the necessary number of healthy, active sperm or has blocked passages through which sperm must travel. Exposure to toxic chemicals in the workplace, cigarette smoking, excessive marijuana use, and some prescription drugs may produce infertility among men. Too much heat may cause a temporary reduction in sperm count as well. Varicocele (a varicose condition of veins above the testicles) can also lead to fertility problems.

In another 35 to 40 percent of the cases in which a cause is identified, the problems involve the female partner's reproductive system. Often the problem concerns ovulation. Some infertile women fail to release healthy eggs because of hormonal problems associated with the menstrual cycle. The most common source of difficulties in women involves blockage of the fallopian tubes, where fertilization of the egg occurs. Previous surgery and pelvic inflammatory disease are frequent causes of blockage. In other cases of infertility, the woman's cervical mucus prevents sperm from entering the uterus. Problems with the uterus itself, such as abnormal growths or developmental defects in the shape of the uterine cavity, may interfere with the implantation of the fertilized egg. Sometimes a woman develops an immunity to her partner's sperm and produces antibodies to it. The woman's age may also be a factor. By age 35, roughly one in four women is infertile. In approximately 10 to 20 percent of infertility cases, the cause of the failure to become pregnant is never identified (American Infertility Institute, 2001).

Psychological and Emotional Impact of Infertility

Most couples assume that pregnancy will occur whenever they desire it. But when they learn that they have a fertility problem, they frequently experience a feeling of loss of control over their lives. Sex now has to be programmed to coincide with the time of peak fertility and is thus robbed of its spontaneity.

Many who are infertile feel guilt that they are no longer as good as those who have children. Men with a low sperm count may doubt their masculinity. Women

Infertility

may feel cut off from the world of mothers: "Sometimes when I go shopping, I look through the infant clothes and other baby items. I feel guilty being in that department, sure that I will be spotted as an impostor and asked to leave the area" (Stout, 1990, p. 13). And many people with infertility problems, men as well as women, experience a drop in self-esteem.

Anger is also a common reaction to infertility. Sometimes it is directed at specific people or procedures; at other times it is a general frustration associated with the inability to achieve a pregnancy in spite of intense effort. One woman told a story about her reaction to her mother-in-law's repeated questioning about her plans to become pregnant:

> I remember my mother-in-law patting my stomach and asking, "Is there anything in there for me yet?" Once, after tolerating that a number of times, I went to the bathroom, slammed the door, and stayed in there a long time. She never said anything like that again. (Stout, 1990, p. 23)

Support groups have been springing up across the nation to help infertile couples. One of the largest is Resolve, a national nonprofit organization that provides a number of services for infertile couples, including telephone counseling, referrals to medical care and professional counseling, a network of support groups, and literature, including its own newsletter.

Couples typically go through several psychological stages after discovering their infertility. In the first stage, they try to determine why they are having trouble conceiving. This is when the damage to their self-esteem is most pronounced. In the second stage, after unsuccessful attempts to become pregnant, couples mourn for the children they will never have. In the final stage, they must decide what future action, if any, to take.

Donna, who waited until she was over 40 to start trying to have children, had the following reaction:

> I married later than some people do, when I was in my early 30s. Gene and I never felt the pressure to have kids right away, though it was something we knew we'd want to do someday. Now that someday is here. We didn't anticipate that it would be this hard to get pregnant, but we intend to take full advantage of all the recent advances that can help us fulfill our dream of having a child of our own. We're looking for a doctor who can help us try. (Resolve, 1999, p. 14)

Greg underwent surgery to repair a varicocele that had caused the infertility that he and his wife experienced:

> Guys aren't supposed to show their emotions. I have to be supportive of my wife and I have to stay calm and not feel my stuff until later," Greg asserts. "Society says it shouldn't be as hard for me as it is for her. But it is hard to fail. Every month was failing, every cycle a failure. Then it became like a challenge, like 'I'm going to beat this.' And then it became more of an issue of not failing than it was about a baby. These days, one day I feel great and the next. . . . Now with the surgery—it's something I can do. The waiting, though, to see if this will work for Jena and me is hard. (Resolve, 1999, p. 166)

Treatment for Infertility

Infertility treatment has become a big business. Millions of dollars are spent on fertility services each year in the United States. The National Survey of Family Growth (which is conducted by the National Center for Health Statistics) has shown that among individuals with self-reported fertility problems, those who seek medical help are a highly select group. Slightly over 40 percent of women with current fertility problems have used fertility services. Those who are married, older, more highly educated, and more affluent are more likely than other women with impaired fertility to seek help. Given the high costs of infertility treatment (most of which are not covered by private health insurance or public assistance), women of higher socioeconomic status are more likely to seek assistance for infertility. Examples of the type of fertility services that are sought by infertile women include advice and diagnostic tests on the woman or her male partner; drugs to stimulate ovulation; artificial insemination; assisted reproductive technology (e.g., in vitro fertilization, gamete intrafallopian transfer, and embryo donation, among others); and medical help to prevent miscarriage (Stephen and Chandra, 2000).

Artificial Insemination.   For couples whose infertility is caused by sperm production problems, **artificial insemination** can be the answer. In this procedure, a high concentration of sperm from the partner or from an anonymous donor is injected into the vagina with a syringe. The yearly number of artificial inseminations occurring in the United States is not precisely known, but it is estimated that about 60,000 babies a year are born as a result of this method (ISLAT, 1998).

The sperm used for artificial insemination can now be stored for long periods of time by freezing it. Sperm storage facilities, usually called *sperm banks,* are found in most metropolitan areas of the country.

Artificial Insemination

There are no federal regulations governing the operation of sperm banks, so each state sets its own guidelines. Most sperm banks obtain information about the donors' medical and family histories and do some type of genetic screening or chromosome analysis to detect hereditary diseases. More recently, steps have been taken to guard against donated sperm carrying the human immunodeficiency virus (HIV). Many sperm banks use medical or dental students as donors, paying them a nominal fee, and limiting the number of times each can donate sperm.

The absence of federal regulations to protect consumers who deal with sperm banks and other types of reproductive assistance has resulted in some serious abuses. Often the abuses revolve around fraudulent reports of success rates. One well-publicized case involved Dr. Cecil Jacobson, owner of a fertility clinic in Virginia, who used his own sperm to impregnate his patients. He also misled women into believing they were pregnant, by injecting them with hormones that produced the symptoms of pregnancy. Dr. Jacobson was found guilty of fifty-two counts of fraud and perjury (Howe, 1991).

In Vitro Fertilization.   For those whose infertility problems are associated with a blockage or scarring of the fallopian tubes, **in vitro fertilization** may be the appropriate treatment. In this process, fertility drugs are used to stimulate the production of eggs (in the mother or a donor), which are removed from the ovaries and placed in a petri dish. Sperm are added to the same petri dish and fertilization occurs outside the woman's body. The fertilized eggs, or embryos, are transferred to the woman's uterus. About 45,000 babies have been born from in vitro fertilization since 1981, when the technique was first used in the United States (American Society for Reproductive Medicine, 2001).

The success rate associated with the conventional form of in vitro fertilization is low—only about one in every five fertilized eggs that is inserted in the uterus actually becomes implanted in the uterine wall. To increase the odds that a fertilized egg will be implanted, a number of adaptations have been developed. Gamete intrafallopian transfer (GIFT) involves a procedure whereby both egg and sperm are placed directly in the fallopian tubes so they will meet, fertilize, and migrate to the uterus where they will be implanted for the duration of the pregnancy. The implantation success rate of GIFT is two to three times higher than that of the conventional method of in vitro fertilization. In zygote intrafallopian transfer (ZIFT), a woman's eggs are extracted and then fertilized in a petri dish just as in traditional in vitro fertilization. The fertilized egg (zygote) is then transferred to the fallopian tubes. In this procedure, fertilization is ensured and the natural migration of the fertilized egg from the fallopian tubes to the uterus is believed to increase the likelihood that it will be implanted. The implantation rate for ZIFT is comparable with that of GIFT, and both are higher than the rate for conventional in vitro fertilization.

In vitro fertilization is, however, only available for those who can afford the very high costs. Estimates are that it may cost anywhere from $67,000 to $114,000 for an average couple to be successful in having a child through in vitro fertilization (Neumann, Gharib, and Weinstein, 1994). The average costs are so high because each individual attempt has such a low chance of success (about 12 percent); thus, couples must try again and again. Also, there are costs associated with losing time from work to undergo treatment as well as the potential problems stemming from multiple births, which are common with this method.

One of the newest high-tech treatments for infertility is **direct sperm injection** into the egg. This technique is used when the man is not producing enough healthy sperm to impregnate his partner through regular sexual intercourse. In this procedure, fertility drugs are administered to the woman to stimulate egg production and the eggs are retrieved surgically. The male partner provides a semen sample from which sperm are obtained. The sperm are injected into the egg directly, under a microscope. Roughly half of the eggs are successfully fertilized. Once fertilization takes place in the laboratory, the embryo is reimplanted in the woman's uterus. After a ten-day waiting period, a blood test is performed on the woman to determine if she has, indeed, become pregnant.

This method was used to help a young widow become pregnant with the sperm of her husband, who was fatally injured in a car accident. Once her husband was declared brain dead, his sperm were surgically removed and frozen for later insemination of his widow ("Widow Hopes," 1994).

Surrogate Mothering.   Another technique that employs artificial insemination is called **surrogate mothering.** When couples cannot have a baby because the woman is infertile, the husband's sperm may be used to impregnate another woman. Frequently, female relatives volunteer to carry a baby for another family member.

In a relatively new form of surrogacy that is referred to as **gestational surrogacy** or host uterus, a woman can have her own eggs fertilized by her partner's sperm and have the fertilized egg implanted in another woman. Gestational surrogacy is an option for women who ovulate but cannot carry a baby to term. Perhaps the most well-publicized case of gestational surrogacy involved Arlette Schweitzer, a 45-year-old woman whose 24-year-old daughter had been born with no uterus but did have ovaries and could ovulate. After her daughter's marriage, Mrs. Schweitzer served as a surrogate mother for her daughter, giving birth to two babies, who were her own granddaughter and grandson (Dowling, 1993).

In both types of surrogacy, the surrogate mother agrees, through a legal contract signed in advance, that she will turn over the baby to the couple at the time of birth. Although there have been thousands of these arrangements, and organizations are springing up around the country to provide surrogate mothers, there are many unsolved problems and unanswered questions. Some of these problems and questions are legal, but others are personal and emotional. In several well-publicized cases, surrogate mothers have resisted giving up the babies they had carried and delivered. Under existing legal customs, it is extremely difficult for a father to obtain custody of a child if a mother wishes to keep it. This is true even when a mother has signed a contract agreeing to give up her rights to the child. Many states have passed legislation to regulate surrogacy, and in some cases to prohibit it altogether.

ContentSELECT

In Vitro Fertilization

Another problem with surrogacy may arise when a child is born with birth defects and neither the father nor the surrogate mother wishes to keep the child. Such a problem has already arisen in the case of a baby born in Michigan. The contractual father argued that the child was not his, and in this case the evidence from blood typing supported him, but that did not resolve the problem of who would care for the child (Krucoff, 1983).

Passing laws to govern surrogate mothering has been difficult. Opposition to such legislation has come from those who *favor* surrogate mothering as well as from those who disapprove of the practice.

Emotional Reactions to Infertility Treatment Procedures

The procedures associated with infertility treatments are often stressful. Men report how embarrassed they are when they must masturbate in a clinical setting in order to provide semen. Women say they find it degrading to go through gynecological examinations and treatment procedures within view of so many medical professionals and technicians. A woman named Lois described how she lost her sense of dignity as she pursued treatment for infertility: "[A]fter I had probably five or six tests—I swear I'd probably pull down my pants for anyone that walked by because I'd lost all of my dignity. I'm a very modest person, but I began to feel like I was a car being worked on" (Greil, 1991, p. 95).

In spite of the emotional trauma that may be associated with infertility treatment, many couples subject themselves to it, because the disappointment of childlessness is even greater. When the new reproductive technologies fail, many childless couples turn to adoption.

Adoption

Adoption is defined as the act of lawfully assuming the parental rights and responsibilities of another person, usually a child under the age of 18. It imposes the same rights and responsibilities on adoptive parents as are imposed on biological parents and grants social, emotional, and legal family membership to the adopted child (Adamec, 1991, p. 17).

Since the mid 1980s, it has been very difficult to obtain comprehensive data about adoption in the United States. The federal government agency that was responsible for collecting the data was abolished, and states were under no obligation to report the number of adoptions that took place in their jurisdictions. With the passage of the Adoption and Safe Families Act in 1997, there was a renewed effort to improve the data available about adoption. Under this act, states are required to collect data on all children in foster care for whom the state child welfare agency has responsibility for placement, care, or supervision and for all adopted children who were placed by the state child welfare agency or by private agencies under contract with the public child welfare agency. Most new statistical information about adoption and related areas is being gathered and analyzed by private organizations (such as the Alan Guttmacher Institute and Child Trends), through private surveys, and research. Based on the limited data available, the estimated total number of adoptions has ranged from a low of 50,000 in 1944 to a high of 175,000 in 1970. In the 1990s, there were approximately 120,000 adoptions each year. Some children are adopted by relatives, while others are adopted by nonrelatives. A growing number of children are being adopted from other countries (National Adoption Information Clearinghouse, 2002).

Transracial Adoption

Transracial or transcultural **adoption** means placing a child who is of one race or ethnic group with adoptive parents of another race or ethnic group. In the United States these terms usually refer to the placement of children of color or children from another country with white adoptive parents. Today, approximately 15 percent of all adoptions are classified as transracial or transcultural. People choose to adopt transracially or transculturally for a variety of reasons. Fewer young white children are available for adoption in the United States than in years past, and some adoption agencies that place white children do not accept singles or applicants older than 40. Some prospective adoptive parents feel connected to a particular race or culture because of their ancestry or through personal experiences such as travel or military service. Others simply like the idea of reaching out to children in need, no matter where they come from (National Adoption Information Clearinghouse, 2002).

Adoption experts have different opinions about this kind of adoption. Some say that children available for adoption should always be placed with a family with at least one parent of the same race or culture as the child. This is so the child can develop a strong racial or cultural identity. These people say that adoption agencies with a strong commitment to working with families of color and that are flexible in their procedures are very successful in recruiting same-race families. Other experts say that race should not be considered at all when selecting a family for a child. To them, a loving family that can meet the needs of a particular child is all that matters. Still others suggest that after an agency works hard to recruit a same-race family for a certain period of time but does not find one, the child should be placed with a loving family of any race or culture who can meet the child's needs. Public opinion in the United States is evenly split between those who do and those who do not support transracial adoption (Hollingsworth, 1998). For nearly twenty-five years, the dominant policies about adoption discouraged or, in some cases, forbid transracial adoption. But in 1994, the federal Multi-Ethnic Placement Act ruled that race cannot be the sole factor in determining the placement of a child in adoption.

In the United States today, there are two basic forms of adoption proceedings, closed and open.

Adoption and Child

Closed Adoption

Couples who wish to adopt a child born in the United States are carefully evaluated and counseled, usually by a licensed social worker, before the courts approve the request for adoption. In a **closed adoption,** the original birth certificate is sealed and a new birth certificate is prepared with the adoptive parents' names. This procedure essentially keeps the biological parents from knowing the names of the adoptive parents, and the adopted child from knowing the names of his or her biological parents.

The assumption underlying the closed adoption is that there should no longer be any contact between adopted children and their biological parents. This assumption has been questioned in recent years, particularly by adopted children who wish to know more about their biological parents (or, in other cases, by biological parents—usually mothers—who seek to reestablish contact with the children they put up for adoption). Although it may require an extended and arduous search, adoptive children are often able to identify, locate, and contact their biological parents. Sometimes the contact is satisfying and enjoyable to both sides, but other times it is not.

Open Adoption

An alternative to closed adoption is **open adoption,** in which the biological parents and adoptive parents are known to each other (Caplan, 1990). In open adoptions, the two sets of parents may remain in contact as the child is growing up, and biological parents may actually continue to play some part in the child's life. Even though open adoptions are being tried by some couples today, there are some obvious potential problems. Biological parents may become too intrusive into the lives of their children, and children may feel divided between their natural and adoptive parents. Despite the complexities of open adoption, advocates say it is no more problem laden than closed adoption (Caplan, 1990).

Summary

Calculating birth rates, such as the general fertility rate and the total fertility rate, is the most meaningful way to assess fertility trends in a society. The long-term trend in childbearing in the United States over the last 200 years has been dramatically downward. Over the last fifty years, the peak in childbearing occurred in 1957; but even in recent years, over 4 million babies are born each year in the United States. Fertility in the United States declined because it became possible to control childbearing, through contraceptive methods, and because children became less economically beneficial.

Differences exist in childbearing among racial and ethnic groups, religions, and socioeconomic classes. White women have lower fertility than African American women, and African American women have lower fertility than Latinas, but the difference between the average number of births to whites and Latinas is only about six-tenths of a child. Women in lower socioeconomic classes, especially as measured by educational attainment, have higher fertility than women in higher classes.

Fertility among U.S. Catholics is no longer higher than among Protestants (except that found among Latinas) and contraceptive use among Catholics is very similar to that found among non-Catholics. The highest fertility is found among Catholic Latinas, fundamentalist Protestants, and Mormons.

Teenage births have continued to be high in the United States, but today most teen births are to unwed mothers. Births outside marriage now constitute 30 percent of all births, and the level of unwed births is especially high among African American women (69 percent

of all births). Women in their thirties and forties have increased their first-time births in the last thirty years.

Family members and religions exert pressure on couples to have children. Government policies, such as income tax deductions and child support payments, also encourage childbearing. Only a small percentage of Americans do not want to have children.

At a personal level, children are rewarding because they give the parents adult status, produce a sense of fulfillment, provide primary group ties and affection, offer stimulation and fun, and fulfill social duties and responsibilities. The costs of having children are primarily financial, but children also restrict their parents' activities, including career and occupational opportunities. This is especially true for mothers.

The reality of the pregnancy experience is often quite different from the stereotypical image. Childbirth is an unforgettable memory for most women, often because it is a painful and difficult experience.

Voluntarily childfree individuals and couples may deliberately decide to be childfree, but many are childless by default. Those who reach the decision by default always assumed they would have children at *some* time, but eventually they recognize this will not happen. Over the years, they must withstand many pressures from families and others who urge them to have children.

Contraception allows many people to control their childbearing. The major birth control methods are condoms, diaphragms, oral contraceptives, and sterilization. Abortion—the expulsion of a fetus or embryo from the uterus—can occur naturally or medically. Medical abortions were not illegal in the first part of the nineteenth century, but they were gradually outlawed. After the 1973 court decision *Roe* v. *Wade,* abortion once again became legal under certain circumstances. Today nearly 30 percent of all pregnancies end in abortion.

The majority of women who have abortions are under age 25 and unmarried. Many are teenagers. The major reasons given for having an abortion are that parenting responsibilities would interfere with work or education, or that raising a child would be prohibitively expensive.

Infertility is experienced by over 8 percent of women. In about 40 percent of infertility cases, it is the male part-

ner who has the biological problem that prevents conception. For many men and women, the inability to conceive has a significant emotional impact. A number of treatments for infertility are available, but if treatment fails, couples may use the new reproductive technologies, which include artificial insemination, in vitro fertilization, and surrogate mothering.

Couples or individuals who are not able to have children often use adoption. Adoption proceedings can be open or closed.

Key Terms

Abortion (p. 285)
Adoption (p. 294)
Artificial insemination (p. 292)
Childfree couples (p. 282)
Closed adoption (p. 295)
Cultural press for childbearing (p. 276)
Direct sperm injection (p. 293)

Fertility (p. 269)
General fertility rate (p. 269)
Gestational surrogacy (p. 293)
In vitro fertilization (p. 292)
Infecundity (p. 289)
Infertile (p. 290)
Open adoption (p. 296)
Opportunity costs (p. 278)

Primary infertility (p. 290)
Pronatalist (p. 276)
Role segregation (p. 278)
Secondary infertility (p. 290)
Sterility (p. 289)
Surrogate mothering (p. 293)
Total fertility rate (p. 269)
Transracial adoption (p. 295)

Review Questions

1. Explain the differences between the crude birth rate, the general fertility rate, and the total fertility rate.

2. How and why have U.S. fertility patterns changed over the past 200 years? Be sure to identify periods in which fertility rates deviated from the general trend since 1800.

3. How has the age at which women have their first children changed over the past thirty years? How does the incidence of teen pregnancy today (in the United States) compare with the teen pregnancy rate of thirty years ago? How and why have the fertility rates for women over 35 changed over the past thirty years?

4. What is the medical definition of infertility? How common is infertility in the United States today? What are the possible causes of infertility in men and women? What procedures are used to diagnose and treat infertility? What are the common emotional reactions to infertility among women and men?

5. How have rates of voluntary childlessness changed in the United States in the past twenty years?

6. Summarize the characteristics of women who have abortions in the United States. What are the most common reasons for terminating a pregnancy?

7. Discuss the two positions regarding transracial adoption in the United States today.

Critical Thinking Questions

1. When a woman becomes pregnant unintentionally and decides to terminate the pregnancy, what rights, if any, should her male partner have in regard to this decision?

2. In what sense are teen pregnancy and teen parenting a *trap*? Are teens ready to be parents? What determines a person's readiness for parenting?

3. Some critics of assisted reproduction claim that the methods put too much pressure on couples to keep trying to get pregnant and make it impossible for them to stop. Do you agree with this statement? Why or why not? Are there circumstances under which a woman or a couple should not be encouraged to undergo infertility treatments?

4. What are the ethical issues associated with assisted reproduction?

5. Some people argue that adults who choose not to have children are selfish. Do you agree with this statement? Why or why not?

Online Resources Available for This Chapter

www.ablongman.com/marriageandfamily

- Online Study Guide with Practice Tests
- PowerPoint Chapter Outlines

- Links to Marriage and Family Websites
- ContentSelect Research Database
- Self-Assessment Activities

Further Reading

Books

Aronson, Diane, and the staff of Resolve. *Resolving Infertility.* New York: Harper-Collins, 1999. A comprehensive guide to the diagnosis, treatment, and alternative options in regard to infertility.

Carroll, Laura. *Families of Two.* Philadelphia: Xlibris Corporation, 2000. Using in-depth interviews with 15 child-free couples, the author addresses the major questions couples ask when deciding whether to have children.

Dowd, Nancy. *In Defense of Single-Parent Families.* New York: New York University Press, 1997. A look at single parents, what we know about them, how they can be positive role models, and how the law treats them.

Kaplan, E. B. *Not Our Kind of Girl: Unraveling the Myths of Black Teenage Motherhood.* Berkeley: University of California Press, 1997. Based on interviews with black teen mothers, this book offers proposals for rethinking and reassessing the class factors, gender relations, and racism that influence black teens to become mothers.

Luker, Kristin. *Dubious Conceptions: The Politics of Teenage Pregnancy.* Cambridge, MA: Harvard University Press, 1996. An examination of popular myths and misconceptions about teenage pregnancy and the social and economic changes that affect teenage pregnancy.

Marsiglio, William. *Procreative Man.* New York: New York University Press, 1998. Addresses gender issues associated with reproduction (such as men's role in birth control and abortion).

Mitford, Jessica. *The American Way of Birth.* New York: Penguin, 1993. A comprehensive examination and critique of the way in which physicians and hospitals have transformed childbirth into a crisis that must be managed through the use of high-tech equipment.

Morell, Carolyn. *Unwomanly Conduct: The Challenges of Intentional Childlessness.* New York: Routledge, 1994. A highly readable account of research based on intensive interviews with 34 married, intentionally childless women ranging in age from 40 to 78.

Pertman, Adam. *Adoption Nation: How the Adoption Revolution Is Transforming America*. New York: Basic Books, 2001. This book examines the history of adoption and discusses the way in which adoption proceedings are become less secretive.

Walzer, Susan. *Thinking about the Baby: Gender and Transitions into Parenthood*. Philadelphia: Temple University Press, 1998. Examines the ways in which women's and men's identities change with parenthood.

*Content*SELECT *Articles*

Eriksen, K. "Infertility and the Search for Family." *Family Journal* 9(1), 2001, 55–62. **[Database: Psychology]** This article depicts one woman's journey through infertility. The trials of high-tech interventions such as laparoscopic surgery in an attempt to unblock the fallopian tubes, artificial insemination, and in vitro-fertilization (embryo transfer after fertilization outside of the body) are discussed. Eriksen also depicts the complexities of her changing interpersonal relationships.

Moore, L., and Schmidt, M. "On the Construction of Male Differences: Marketing Variations in Technosemen." *Men and Masculinities* 1(4), 1999, 331–352. **[Database: Sociology]** Through analyzing data obtained from semen banks' donor catalogues, Moore and Schmidt delineate the distinguishing characteristics among semen donors and how these differences are advertised to potential consumers. The effects of semen marketing techniques and the selection of masculinity are also addressed.

Pyton, E. "Is Surrogate Motherhood Moral?" *Humanist* 61(5), 2001: 20–22. **[Database: Sociology]** Is surrogate motherhood morally wrong? Author Elizabeth Pyton explores the ethical and moral questions surrounding surrogacy—the process by which a woman carries a fetus to term for a couple that is typically infertile. Because cash payments are made to the surrogate, opponents of surrogacy parenting deem the practice "baby selling." Proponents assert that surrogacy satisfies innate biological and emotional needs to reproduce.

Varnis, S. "Regulating the Global Adoption of Children." *Society* 38(2), 2001: 39–47. **[Database: Social Work]** With higher rates of infertility in the United States, more and more couples are turning to global adoptions. Nearly fifty percent of all children adopted from the world over will have homes in the United States, making the United States the receiver of over 15,000 international orphans in 1998 alone. This article addresses the regulation of global adoption; specifically, the numerous aspects of the Hague Convention on Protection of Children and Cooperation in Respect of Intercountry Adoption are examined.

10

childrearing

In the following vignette, Maureen Reddy (who is white) talks about the difficulties she and her husband Doug (who is black) encountered in their attempts to raise their son, Sean, in a gender-neutral and multiracial way:

1 To what extent do parents determine their children's personalities, values, and behaviors?

2 Is childhood a fixed biological stage of life or a social construction?

3 How does the birth of a baby affect the relationship between its parents?

4 To what extent are the traditional mother and father roles shaped by biological factors?

5 How are young children affected by nonparental care?

One of the simpler pleasures of parenting, we thought, would be giving Sean toys and playing with him—wrong, wrong, wrong, as we learned on our first excursion to a toy store when Sean was just a few weeks old. Because Doug and I were among the first of our friends to have children, we had not been toy shopping since we were little more than children ourselves, and we therefore had no clear idea about what toys were available. Before our baby's birth, we had decided to buy toys on a gender-neutral basis—blocks, trucks, stuffed animals, and dolls, regardless of our child's sex—and to ban war toys and Barbie, for obvious reasons. We had guessed that black dolls would be hard to find, but otherwise we had given little thought to race as a factor in toy shopping. After all, what could race have to do with blocks? Plenty, we discovered.

That first trip to a big toy store was enlightening: we found aisle upon aisle of toys of all varieties in packages that depicted only white children playing with them. At most, one-fifth of the toys we saw incorporated no exclusionary race or gender codes on their packages. Even fancy yuppie toys, carefully aimed at both sexes—European crib mobiles and the like—came in packages adorned with pictures of white babies. In the doll aisle, blond, blue-eyed dolls outnumbered black dolls fifty to one, and the only black male dolls were Cabbage Patch Kids, which were new to the market the year Sean was born and almost impossible to get. In an effort to support progressive manufacturers, we tried to buy toys that showed some sensitivity to racial diversity in their packaging, but we also ended up buying a lot of things that had to be removed from their boxes before we gave them to Sean. Obviously, though, we could not control everything in Sean's life as easily as we discarded troubling toy wrappings, and we knew that he would be bombarded by images and messages quite contrary to the vision of self we hoped to foster. What effect would these images have on him? And how powerful would our parental influence be? We waited, and hoped.

Source: Maureen T. Reddy. *Crossing the Color Line: Race, Parenting, and Culture.* New Brunswick, NJ: Rutgers University Press, 1994, pp. 43–58.

*M*aureen and Doug, the parents in the opening vignette, approached parenthood with concern and good intentions, hoping to provide a world free of racist and sexist influences for their young son. They discovered early on, however, that their attempts at gender-neutral and race-inclusive socialization could be overshadowed by the other influences in the world outside their home, including commercial toy manufacturers. In this chapter, we discuss parents' role in the socialization of their children, including attempts by African American parents to prepare their children to survive in a racist world.

In this chapter on childrearing, we make no claim to have the answer to the question of how children *should* be raised. Ours is a more modest approach. We use the best knowledge available from social science research to identify and discuss the most important questions related to parenthood and childrearing.

We begin with a brief examination of what we know about the lives of children in the past. Scholars studying the history of childhood have found some surprising, and even shocking, facts. Contemporary childrearing, which we take up next, begins with the transition to parenthood, an experience that often has a negative impact on the marital quality of the parents. As parents and children interact, the children learn the ways of their society and develop human qualities and personalities. Mothers and fathers often relate to their children differently, primarily because fathers are often less involved in the parenting process. Many parents, because they are employed, must use child care services, the impact of which is still being debated among social scientists.

The History of Childhood

*M*ost people today assume that children are fundamentally different from adults. Children play rather than work; they are not completely accountable for their acts; they often behave irrationally and emotionally; and they are more likely to think in concrete rather than abstract terms. In a word, they are immature. Given this fundamental view of the nature of children, parents are expected to provide protection, love, nurturance, and training. If parents do these things, children move toward maturity and eventually into adulthood.

Some historians believe that the contemporary western view of childhood as a separate and immature stage of life is a relatively modern invention.

Using his interpretations of art as evidence, historian Philippe Ariès (1962) described changes in family organization, conceptions of childhood, and relationships between generations from the Middle Ages through the end of the eighteenth century. Today, many of Ariès's ideas have been refuted. However, his belief that childhood was a social construction rather than a fixed biological stage of life persuaded historians and other social scientists to begin to pay more attention to children (Corsaro, 1998). Ariès argued that in earlier centuries there was no recognition of the particular nature of children that distinguished them from adults. Children were almost totally absent from medieval paintings and when they were included they were depicted as miniature adults.

> In medieval society the idea of childhood did not exist; this is not to suggest that children were neglected, forsaken, or despised. The idea of childhood is not to be confused with affection for children: it corresponds to an awareness of the particular nature of childhood, that particular nature which distinguishes the child from the adult, even the young adult. In medieval society this awareness was lacking. (Ariès, 1962, p. 128)

Over time, the depiction of children in art changed, which led Ariès to conclude that the dominant cultural views of childhood changed as well. From the thirteenth through the sixteenth centuries, paintings began to include representations of children as angels. Ariès argued that the dominant view of childhood that emerged during this time was a period of innocence and sweetness. He referred to this as the **coddling period of childrearing.** Children were idolized and valued as a source of amusement for adults. A different view of childhood developed in the sixteenth through eighteenth centuries in reaction against the coddling period, primarily among scholars and moralists of the time. The emergent view—referred to as the **moralistic period of childrearing**—saw childhood as a period during which children must be disciplined and prepared for adulthood. Parents were taught that they were the spiritual guardians of their children, responsible before God for their souls (pp. 411–412). The moralistic period, according to Ariès, laid the groundwork for the development of child psychology, which has, in turn, had a major influence on contemporary conceptions of childhood and modern theories about childrearing. Contrary to what you might expect, Ariès did not view these changes in ideas about childhood as a positive development. He believed that as children were removed from adult society and *protected* from the evils of the larger society, they lost their freedom. Women's rights advocates in nineteenth century America made a similar argument about the status of women, that is, that laws that were designed to protect women from evils in the workplace actually restricted them in significant ways.

Since parents did not recognize childhood as a distinct stage of life, as parents do today, they treated their children very differently. Children were often expected to carry a heavier load than today. They worked from a very early age, on farms, in mines, and at crafts (shoemaking, baking, tailoring, and others). The coming of the Industrial Revolution meant that children were put to work in factories, a pattern that prevailed in England and the United States until the passage of child labor laws in the nineteenth century (Johansson, 1991).

It was not just working that made childhood different in the premodern age. Infant and childhood death rates were so high that in many places half the children born did not reach adulthood. Infectious diseases and various unidentifiable fevers were frequent killers of children. There were almost no effective defenses against these many causes of death. As one historian has said, "the history of childhood is a nightmare. . . . The further back in history one goes, the lower the level of child-care, and the more likely children were to be killed, abandoned, beaten, terrorized and sexually abused" (deMause, 1974, p. 1).

Infanticide

Infanticide and Abandonment

Infanticide (the murder of babies) and child abandonment are part of the history of many societies, existing in every country in Europe in earlier times and in Asia today. At the end of the nineteenth century, mothers in an eastern European village could send their babies to "killing nurses." The methods of doing away with the infants included "exposing them to cold air after a hot bath; feeding them something that caused convulsions in their stomachs and intestines; mixing gypsum in their milk, which literally plastered up their insides; suddenly stuffing them with food after not giving them anything to eat for two days" (deMause, 1974, p. 29).

Estimating the amount of infanticide is difficult because the intentional killing of an infant can easily be disguised, just as child abuse today is often covered up by claiming a child has suffered an accident. Furthermore, it appears that many infant deaths were, in fact, semiaccidental. Under crowded living conditions, many infants slept with their parents, other relatives, or a nurse. It was often reported that infants were suffocated during the night. Although suffocating an infant may have been accidental, it may also have been the result of wanton carelessness.

One indirect form of infanticide is abandonment. Abandoning babies was so widely practiced in Europe that it led to the establishment of foundling homes (babies that were found were called **foundlings**). Thomas Coram of London opened a Foundling Hospital in 1741 "because he couldn't bear to see the dying babies lying in the gutters and rotting on the dung-heaps" (deMause, 1974, p. 29).

Wet-Nursing and Swaddling

Although killing and abandoning infants are clearly deviant and even criminal behavior, a number of *normal* childrearing practices may also have been harmful to infant children. One of these was the practice of wet-nursing, which was widely practiced in Europe in medieval times and continued well into the eighteenth century. **Wet-nursing** is the practice of hiring another woman to breastfeed one's baby. Families with enough money would hire a woman from the lower classes (who had also recently had a baby) to nurse their baby. Since women who served as wet nurses were often poor, babies ended up living in homes with less healthy conditions than their own parents' homes.

Another common practice with infants was **swaddling** (wrapping a baby very tightly with strips of cloth, making it impossible for the baby to move its arms and legs). In many cases, the baby was wrapped against a board. A baby was typically swaddled for one to four months of its early life.

Ostensibly, the purpose of swaddling was to protect the newborn infant from thrashing around and hurting itself. Another concern was that if the legs weren't held in a straightened position, the child might walk on "all fours" like an animal. Swaddling or wrapping a baby was a time-consuming task, but it was thought necessary by many parents for the baby's own good. Yet perhaps parents and nurses found some personal advantages in swaddling, for babies that are swaddled are very passive and docile; swaddled babies cry less and sleep more. In fact, some experts recommend this today for frantic babies. Sometimes swaddled babies were simply placed in some convenient out-of-the-way place, or even hung on a hook.

There are also some incredible reports that swaddled babies were tossed about between adults as a kind of game or sport. The brother of King Henri IV of France (sixteenth century) was being passed from one window to another for amusement when he was dropped and killed (deMause, 1974). Doctors often complained that parents broke children's bones in the "customary" tossing of their babies.

Discipline and Punishment

Parents through the ages have used various means to control or discipline their children. Often physical punishment was administered routinely and severely. According to one historian, a very large percentage of children born prior to the eighteenth century were what would today be termed 'battered children'" (deMause, 1974, p. 40). One thirteenth-century law even said, "If one beats a child until it bleeds, then it will remember, but if one beats it to death, the law applies."

Well into the nineteenth century in the United States and Europe, children were routinely whipped by parents and teachers with brushes, straps, belts, or switches. One German schoolmaster estimated that he had, through his career, administered "911,257 strokes with the stick, 124,000 lashes with the whip, 136,715 slaps with the hand, and 1,115,800 boxes on the ear" (deMause, 1974, p. 41).

Child and
Discipline

Parents of the past justified hitting their children by saying it was necessary "to break their will or spirit." Children were viewed as wild and willful little animals, who might never be brought under control if they were not broken early. *Early* often meant in infancy, as soon as the child showed signs of independence or will-fulness. Esther Burr, the wife of a Princeton College president, described in her 1755 journal how she had already "whipped" her ten-month-old daughter. She believed her daughter understood when she had done something wrong, and con-cluded, "'Tis time she should be taught" (Walzer, 1974, p. 366). Another mother of that period said about her children, "When turned a year old (and some before), they were taught to fear the rod, and to cry softly" (deMause, 1974, p. 41).

By the 1840s in the United States, whipping children, as an automatic and rou-tine part of childrearing, had fallen out of favor. Of course, corporal punishment of all types continued to be used, just as it continues today.

In summing up the history of childhood, we can conclude that until fairly recently, children led harsh lives and a good many did not survive to adulthood. Life for everyone was more difficult and dangerous before the modern era. Today, at least in developed societies, life for nearly everyone is easier, and childhood has come to be a very different experience for most children.

The work of Ariès and deMause has been criticized by other historians. Some argue that better evidence about childhood in earlier times can be found in diaries, autobiographies, and newspaper reports of court cases regarding child abuse. When this type of evidence is examined, a much less negative picture of childhood emerges. In an analysis of 500 diaries and autobiographies from the United States and Britain, Linda Pollock (cited in Corsaro, 1997) found little support for the claim that there was indifference to children or widespread maltreatment or abuse prior to the eighteenth and nineteenth centuries. Most children were wanted by their parents. When they died, their parents showed a great deal of anxiety and distress, rather than indifference. Relations between parents and children were not as for-mal and one-sided as formerly believed. Children were close to their parents and were influenced by them, but parents were influenced by their children as well. Pollock's work has been criticized because it relied on information that came pri-marily from upper-class elite members of these societies. But it does throw into question some of the conclusions drawn about children's lives presented by histo-rians such as deMause.

Childhood in Modern Times

*T*he twentieth century was supposed to have been the *century of the child.* In 1900, Swedish feminist Ellen Key predicted that the primary problems that plagued the world's children in earlier centuries would be solved and children would live a protected life of leisure (Shehan, 1999). At the beginning of the twentieth century, the boundaries between childhood and adulthood were clearly drawn. Children were seen as innocent and in need of protection. It was believed that the preservation of childhood depended on (1) the restriction of children's awareness about and involvement in the adult world of sexuality, sweatshops, and criminality, and (2) the provision of loving parents, time to play, protection, and free education. In the ensuing decades, laws restricting child labor were passed; mandatory education was established; and the juvenile justice system was developed. These changes "codified as never before the ways in which children were different from adults" (Applebome, 1998, p. 3).

There were many positive developments in children's lives during this period: Educational attainment increased, health improved, infant mortality declined, and life expectancy increased. But there were many negative developments, as well: exposure to and involvement in crime and violence increased; sexual involvement started earlier and became riskier; and the likelihood of living in poverty increased. Some observers have argued that the changes that have transpired over the past fifty years have resulted in a type of childhood that is encumbered by anxiety and overprotection (Marriott, 1995; Wright, 1999). As the century closed, the promise of a perfect childhood had not yet been realized. In fact, the boundaries between childhood and adulthood are once again blurred, and children are treated simultaneously as both children and adults, or what one psychologist calls **kinderdults** (Diane Ehrensaft, 1998). The institutions that appeared early in the twentieth century are being abandoned. We are witnessing a noticeable change in the juvenile justice system, insofar as increasing numbers of teens are being tried as adult offenders. Sexual activity among the young has become more commonplace. High employment rates among teens are once again raising concern about premature entrance into economic adulthood. Public schools are becoming more like a workplace. In some school districts recess has even been eliminated and the school year has been extended from nine to twelve months. Children's lives are anything but worry free. Parents struggle, but often fail miserably, to prevent their children from knowing about and participating in the adult world outside the home (Coontz, 1997).

Contemporary Childrearing

*C*hildren today are viewed very differently from the way they were viewed in the past. Beginning in the latter part of the nineteenth century, in England and the United States, parents were urged to practice altruistic parenthood (Johansson, 1991). The term **altruistic parenthood** suggests that parents are expected to take good care of and provide for all the children they bring into the world.

As practiced in the United States and other developed countries today, altruistic parenting means parents make great emotional and financial investments in the children they have. They feel responsible for the care, development, and long-term well-being of their children. One result of this contemporary view of childrearing is that couples have far fewer children than they did in the past.

Contemporary parenthood is thus a great responsibility, but, at the same time, parents also expect their role to be a source of pleasure, satisfaction, and accomplishment. Most contemporary parents enjoy the rewards of parenthood, but they may also experience doubts, uncertainties, and problems. Some of the problems of parenthood come in the very earliest weeks and months of childrearing.

The Transition to Parenthood

Probably no event has more impact on a marriage and on the marriage partners than the addition of a child. This momentous event affects the career patterns of the parents, the pattern of housework, the distribution of power, marital satisfaction, and the economic well-being of the unit. Significantly, when spouses become parents, they shift to responding to each other in terms of role obligations rather than as intimates (Baca Zinn and Eitzen, 2002, p. 314).

Generation after generation, a continuing drama plays out: People who have already had children tell (or warn) prospective parents how much having a child will change their lives. The parents-to-be say, "Yes, we know," and they do believe they know. Or they may think that they will be different, handling the adjustments to parenthood better than others. Then, after having the baby, they say, "We knew it would be difficult, but not *this* difficult."

It is nearly impossible to communicate to others what it is really like to make the **transition to parenthood.** The strongest way to describe the transition is to call it a *crisis*. Whether or not it is a crisis, becoming a parent abruptly changes a person's daily routine and overall lifestyle. Taking care of a baby is a twenty-four-hour-a-day job for which few new parents have realistically prepared.

The high level of physical demands in caring for a baby is one thing that most new parents comment on first. "Couples say there are simply not enough hours in the day to look after the baby, keep the household running, go to work, talk with a co-worker or friend, and have any time left over to nurture their relationship" (Cowan and Cowan, 1992, p. 105).

There is considerable evidence that children have a negative impact on marital happiness (Heaton et al., 1996). Both men and women report a decline in happiness in the first year after the birth (Demo and Cox, 2000). Having a baby pushes the parents into traditional gender roles (Walzer, 1998). Women's identity shifts to caregiving responsibilities while men find themselves preoccupied with wage earning. The division of labor also changes. Men tend to do more paid work after the birth of a baby while women do less. Women tend to do more household labor while men continue to do less (Sanchez and Thomson, 1997). These gender-typed changes occur regardless of the mother's employment status before the birth, her educational level, the couple's division of labor before the birth, or their attitudes toward gender roles. The changes that occur with the birth of a child generate marital conflicts that do not occur among childless couples. African American couples as well as whites experience declines in marital happiness and increases in marital conflict (Crohan, 1996). Men sometimes have more difficulty with the transition to parenthood than do women (Arendell, 2000).

Not all marriages are affected to the same degree by the birth of a baby. Belsky and Kelly (1994) identified four different patterns in the quality of marriage after a baby is born. About 13 percent of marriages go into *severe decline.* They become so estranged as a result of their different experiences with parenthood that they lose faith in each other and in their marriages and their communication decreases. They may feel a loss of love. Thirty-eight percent go into *moderate decline.* They are able to avoid catastrophic conflict but they do experience a decline in marital communication and feelings of love. Another 30 percent experience *no change* in marital quality or interaction after the birth of a child. The remaining 19 percent actually experience an *improvement* in their marital cohesion, communication, and feelings

UNICEF Asks Children to Rate Their Country's Concern for Children's Rights

Children are not only our future, they are our present and we need to start taking their voices very seriously. We must listen carefully to what young people have to say and give them every opportunity to speak. We must reach out to them and encourage them to participate in the decision-making processes that affect their lives.

Carol Bellamy, Executive Director of UNICEF

Do adults really know what children think? Do the decision makers have any idea of children's hopes, ambitions, or concerns? And if they did, would they use this knowledge to tailor services at home, school, and in the community to better reflect children's real needs and desires?

The Convention on the Rights of the Child, adopted by the United Nations General Assembly in 1989 and now the most widely ratified international treaty, says that children have the right to express themselves freely. This is itself a major breakthrough. The Convention then goes on to say that adults must take the views of children and adolescents into account when making decisions that affect them. The first step is to find out children's views and insight into a wide range of important topics, which is what UNICEF has attempted to do through opinion polls. Through representative samples of boys and girls in seventy-two countries in East Asia and the Pacific, Europe and Central Asia, Latin America and the Caribbean, the polls reflect the views of the 500 million children and young people between the ages of 9 to 18 living in the three regions. Between late 1999 and early 2001, UNICEF regional offices conducted interviews with nearly 40,000 children asking them open-ended as well as targeted questions about their lives, families, schools, communities, and governments. UNICEF plans to use the rich and complex results of the polls to guide our advocacy and programming support efforts over the coming years.

What do the young people tell us about how the world is performing when measured against the ten imperatives for children—a set of overarching principles supported by millions of people who have pledged their support in the Say Yes for Children campaign?

1. Leave No Child Out

Children themselves are very aware of discrimination against themselves as well as against their peers. Roughly half of the children in each of the regions said that some children in their country (e.g., disabled children) were not well accepted and were treated unfairly.

2. Put Children First

All people must take responsibility for ensuring that the rights of children are respected, and all governments must meet their obligations to children and young people. While children may not always know their rights in detail, those polled by UNICEF spontaneously mentioned the right to express ideas, the right to play or amusement, and the right not to be hurt. Children in all three regions polled referred to the "right to be loved." Children also want their government to fulfill its promises, protect the poor, and show greater concern for youth. And yet, only 30 percent of the children in Europe and Central Asia feel they can trust their governments and nearly 20 percent of the children polled in this region feel that voting in elections is ineffective.

3. Care for Every Child

Children have the right to grow to adulthood in good health and with proper nutrition. It's an essential foundation of human development. No child should go hungry, and every effort should be made to ensure that children get the best possible start in life. The family is central in ensuring that all children have the best possible start in life.

of love. All new parents, however, undergo major life changes and may "find themselves riding the same roller coaster of elation, despair, and bafflement. [They approach] parenthood full of high hopes and soaring dreams [yet] six months or a year after the child's birth they . . . find themselves wondering, 'What's happening to us?'" (Belsky and Kelly, 1994, p. 4).

In East Asia and the Pacific, a quarter or more respondents explained an average/bad relationship with their father or mother in terms of the absence of good communication. When children in Latin America and the Caribbean were asked to spontaneously mention situations that concerned them the most, the family came top of the list: when something bad happens in the family (27 percent) and when there are fights or family quarrels (17 percent).

4. Fight HIV/AIDS

The lack of information about HIV/AIDS contributes to the vulnerability of children. A significant proportion in each of the global regions felt they had insufficient knowledge about AIDS.

5. Stop Harming and Exploiting Children

An appallingly high percentage of the children polled by UNICEF say they witnessed or personally experienced violence or aggressive behavior in their home. In addition, nearly 30 percent of the children polled in East Asia and the Pacific report that their home communities at night are always or sometimes unsafe. Twenty percent of those interviewed in Europe and Central Asia feel that their neighborhood is unsafe to walk around in. In Latin America and the Caribbean, the feeling of insecurity is even higher (43 percent).

6. Listen to Children

In the East Asia and the Pacific region, less than half the respondents feel that their opinion, and their friends' opinions, matter in decisions in their local community. More than 60 percent of children polled in Europe and Central Asia feel their opinion is not sufficiently taken into account by their government, and more than half the children in the Latin America and Caribbean region feel unheard at home and in school.

7. Educate Every Child

Children are very aware of the value of education. In every region polled, at least half spontaneously mentioned education as a child's right, and also that school was the main topic of children's conversations with friends. In all regions polled, children are clearly aware of the need for a mutually respectful and attentive relationship between teacher and pupil. Many children decry teachers' authoritarian attitudes and the lack of space for children to express themselves.

8. Protect Children from War

In Europe and Central Asia, almost 40 percent of the children polled by UNICEF say they would like their country to be at peace. In the Latin America and Caribbean region, 20 percent of children wish for a country of peace.

9. Protect the Earth for Children

When asked to name the rights they knew, about 7 percent of the children in East Asia and the Pacific spontaneously came up with the right to a clean environment. One-tenth of the children polled in Latin America and the Caribbean dreamed of a society without pollution. The figures rose to 26 percent in Europe and Central Asia and to almost a third in Western Europe.

10. Fight Poverty: Invest in Children

Awareness of the plight of the poor is very high among children themselves. When asked how they saw the future, almost half say they would like their country to be a place where there is a better economic situation and where everybody has a job.

Listening to Change the World

In listening to what these children and young people have to say, it becomes clear what changes are needed in the world to realize their basic rights and thereby ensuring that each child everywhere, without discrimination, has the right to survive; to develop to the fullest; to be protected from harmful influences, abuse, and exploitation; and to participate fully in family, cultural, and social life.

Source: Adapted from the UNICEF website: www.unicef.org/polls.

One key to reducing the stresses and problems of new parenthood is preparedness. Parents who underestimate how much energy and effort a baby will require are more likely to report problems after the baby is born (Oakley, 1980; Kach and McGhee, 1982). Unfortunately, it seems that most women do enter parenthood with romanticized notions of what it will be like.

One study of nearly 500 middle-class, first-time mothers found that expectations during pregnancy were usually more positive than their actual experiences one year after the birth of the child. For example, the relationship with their spouses was not as good as they had expected it would be, their husbands were not giving as much assistance as they had expected, and their relationships with friends were not as good as expected. Furthermore, those women whose experiences were most discrepant from their expectations had the most difficult adjustment to parenthood (Kalmuss, Davidson, and Cushman, 1992).

Research shows that several factors are related to the decline of marital satisfaction during early parenthood (Cowan and Cowan, 2000). First, couples who had some marital difficulties or expressed ambivalent feelings about their relationship *prior to the pregnancy* were more likely to experience conflict or dissatisfaction after the birth of their child. Second, wives who were disappointed with their husbands' level of involvement in caring for the baby were more likely to experience declines in marital satisfaction. A third factor associated with declines in marital satisfaction is that a husband and wife may experience parenthood very differently. Their different perceptions lead to emotional distance and conflict. One couple's conversation illustrates this last point:

BILL: I thought we were doing OK. I was pitching in at home. We'd started making love again . . .

PEGGY: Well, I know we're making love again, but it still hurts. . . . And we've got very different ideas of "pitching in." I don't consider changing a diaper once a month and feeding Mindy when you've nothing else to do, much of a "pitch." (Cowan and Cowan, 1992, p. 112)

The research on the transition to parenthood may at first seem discouraging, but two points should be kept in mind. First, for many new parents having a baby is an interesting and positive experience; parenthood does not always have a negative impact on the marriage relationship. Second, research consistently shows that couples who have the most realistic expectations about having a baby—those who are able to get beyond the romantic images of parenthood—make the easiest adjustment and experience the least stress.

The Importance of Family and Other Support

One thing that can make the experience of new parenthood more positive is the support and help of parents and other kin members. Many new grandparents (especially grandmothers) stay with the new parents and help care for the baby during the first few weeks. Even when young couples live great distances from their parents, the new grandparents are likely to give emotional and financial support. Parents and other kin, as well as friends, constitute the social networks of couples and are a source of valuable social support during the early difficult period of parenthood (Tinsley and Parke, 1984).

When family social support for new parents is not available, as it sometimes is not in contemporary urban life, organizations may spring up to fill the gap. One such group, Parents After Childbirth Education, was formed by two mothers who had what they called "bad bouts with the new baby blues" (Breathnach, 1983, p. C5). Reasoning that many other new mothers must experience similar stresses, they created a series of workshops for new mothers. Mothers, with their babies in tow, discuss their problems and fears. Through these group sessions, they learn they are not alone in their anxieties over mothering, which helps them make the difficult transition to parenthood.

Parent–Child Interaction and Socialization

*I*t is primarily the interaction with their parents that equips children to enter society. This process is labeled socialization. **Socialization** is, first, the process by which a person learns and generally accepts the ways of a particular group or society. A second dimension of socialization is that parents' peers, and other caregivers, through their interaction with children, contribute to the development of social beings with unique characters and personalities. We take up these two dimensions of socialization separately, beginning first with that part of socialization in which children learn about the ways of the society in which they live.

▮ Socialization: Learning the Ways of the Society

Generally parents (or other caregivers) are eager to teach their children about the ways of the society. They begin teaching the language of the society almost immediately, by talking to their children. Once children have language, parents start to teach, both directly and indirectly, what they interpret and understand to be the ways of the society.

Considerable agreement exists among the members of social groups about the kinds of things children need to know, so parents tend to socialize their children in similar ways. At the same time, differences do exist. Parents coming from different ethnic, racial, and religious groups or different social classes may have differing notions of what they should pass on to their children. As a rule, parents try to teach their children lessons that they themselves have found useful in life. This has been thoroughly documented by research on social class differences in the socialization of children (Gecas, 1990).

Parents are most likely to pass on to their children the strategies they have learned in the occupational world (Kohn, 1977). Higher-status jobs permit, even require, self-direction. People in these jobs are encouraged to be creative and to make independent decisions. Parents who hold such jobs come to value these traits and attempt to instill them in their children with the hope that they will bring them success in life. Lower-status jobs, in contrast, rarely provide opportunities for self-direction and require conformity to authority. Thus, lower-class and working-class parents believe the most important trait they can teach their children is obedience and conformity.

The differences in the values of middle-class and working-class parents can be seen in the ways they discipline their children. Middle-class parents expect their children to be self-directed and therefore to have inner sources of control, whereas lower- and working-class parents expect their children to be obedient to external sources of control. As a result, they are more likely to punish any disobedient acts, while middle-class parents are more likely to punish only those disobedient acts that they view as having wrongful intent.

Working-class mothers punish their children immediately after the child misbehaves, without asking questions. Middle-class mothers are more likely to punish or not punish their children according to how they interpret the child's intentions when the act is committed. Middle-class parents judge the child's misbehavior according to whether or not it seems to violate their long-range goal of making the child independent and responsible. Working-class parents punish misbehavior if it violates some rule they have set down. They want obedience to the rules, not a discussion of them. They are also more likely to use physical punishments such as hitting, slapping, or spanking.

Socialization: Human Qualities

The first feature of socialization is teaching a child the ways of the society; the second is the way socialization contributes to the human qualities and the personality development of children. Human babies cannot care for themselves when firstborn; they must have some other human present to provide care. Their physical dependence on other humans is accompanied by a strong attraction to their primary caregivers.

Evidence shows that interaction with other humans is absolutely essential for an infant to develop a social nature and a personality. We know this from the few documented cases of children who have had only a small amount of human contact. One highly publicized case of an isolated child occurred in Temple Hills, California. A father locked his daughter in a room from age 2 until she was discovered (in 1970) at age 13 (Rymer, 1992a). The girl, called Genie, was put in a restraining harness and seated on a potty chair during the day; at night she was put in a straitjacket. Genie's mother, terrorized by her brutal husband and further limited by blindness, had almost no contact with Genie after infancy. When Genie was discovered, she was unable to speak, because during her formative years her father had not allowed her to make any sounds. Genie was not mentally retarded, for she showed a quick mind in nonverbal ways and had good spatial skills. Nonetheless, even though psychologists and others worked with her intensively for many years, she was never able to achieve any kind of normal social life (Rymer, 1992b).

Socialization: Personality and Self-Image

It is a fundamental principle of contemporary sociology and psychology that parents or other primary caregivers influence the personalities of their children. Symbolic interaction theory (see Chapter 2) offers one explanation for how a child's personality is influenced by interaction with parents.

Symbolic interaction theory is based on the idea that human behavior is deeply influenced by the human ability to use language. It is through words and language that we comprehend and respond to the world around us and to our own selves. The words used by significant others (parents, other family members, friends) give us a sense of ourselves. Thus, a little girl who is told often enough that she is bright and intelligent will eventually come to take that attitude toward herself. That is, she will evaluate herself with the same words or symbols as do significant others in her life. Symbolic interactionists call this evaluation her **self-image.**

Most contemporary parents, especially those who have some knowledge of sociology and psychology, accept the idea that they influence the personalities of their children. But many parents extend this principle and believe they can actually *create* the personalities of their children. That is, they believe they can decide in advance the qualities and characteristics they want in their children and then, through their childrearing practices, produce them. That belief must be questioned, as we discuss later in the chapter.

Child and Socialization

Racial Socialization

One of the most important tasks of African American parents is **racial socialization** (McAdoo, 2002). This is the process by which parents help their children see where they fit into the racial context in their society. Children overhear parents' conversations about race; they notice how parents react to people of other races; and they receive direct instruction from their parents (Murray and Mandara, 2002).

They also receive related messages at school, from their peers and their teachers. neighbors & relatives. They begin to internalize the stereotypes, prejudices, and other racist beliefs of the society. About two-thirds of African American parents consciously engage in racial socialization with their children (Murray, Stokes, and Peacock, 1999). They can use one of four different racial socialization strategies. **Racial empowerment** reflects a proactive approach that stresses racial identity and the ability to overcome obstacles in life despite racial barriers. **Racial awareness** reflects an active strategy in teaching children to be proud of their racial group. **Race defensiveness** cultivates a dislike for other racial groups among children, but teaches them that it can be useful to imitate white American behavior. Finally, **race naivete** minimizes race issues (Murry and Mandara, 2002).

Whatever their particular stance, most black parents realize that they face an enormous challenge in raising their children to survive in a racist society. Families perform at least two important functions in the African American child's early development. They foster the development of a personal frame of reference for self-identity, self-worth, achievement, group identity, and other social behaviors. They also provide comfort and affection, which lessen the negative and often harmful consequences of prejudice and discrimination (Murry, 2002). But they do not completely control their children's exposure to, awareness of, or involvement in racially driven dialogue or behavior, as the vignette drawn from an intensive observation of preschoolers' interactions at a racially and ethnically diverse program illustrates:

> Debi (the researcher who had observed at the preschool for many months) is watching the children play outside . . . . There are two children at play with shovels and buckets in the sandbox a few feet away from her. As they both play in the sandbox, Brittany (3, white) informs Taleshia (3.5, black), "You're the same color as the rabbit poop." Taleshia stares at Brittany and frowns deeply. Brittany picks up a rabbit pellet from the sandbox, holds it up close to Taleshia's arm, and says, "See?" She smiles at Taleshia. "Your skin is shitty!" Brittany smiles triumphantly. "You have to leave. We don't allow shit in the sandbox." Taleshia stares at Brittany for a quiet moment, then slaps Brittany's hand away, retorting "Shut up!" and leaves the sandbox. She retreats to a bench about ten feet away and sits, glaring at Brittany, who continues to dig in the sand, supremely unconcerned with Taleshia. (Van Ausdale and Feagin, 2001, p. 109)

In her observations, Debi Van Ausdale saw many similar incidents where very young children invoked racial ideas to assert the status and privileges that come with being white and the lower status and fewer privileges that come with being a person of color. Van Audale and her co-author, Joe Feagin, note that even at the young age of 3 children are aware of the power of racist language. When incidents such as these came to the attention of the school administration, which was committed to the idea of racial and ethnic identity, they typically called in the parents of the children who were involved. In most cases, both the parents and the teachers and teachers' aides vehemently denied having taught the children racist attitudes. This suggests that children learn through observation and actively try to make sense of the world around them rather than simply soaking up direct lessons taught by their parents.

Do Parents Determine Children's Personalities?

Psychologist Judith Harris made headlines in the late 1990s with her book, *The Nurture Assumption: Why Children Turn Out the Way They Do*. She defines the **nurture assumption** as the belief that parents are the most important part of the child's environment, determining how the child turns out. Harris strongly contests the nurture assumption. She acknowledges that parents (or other adult caregivers) play an important role in a baby's life. Caregivers help babies learn their first language and provide their first opportunities to form and maintain relationships. Caregivers also present the initial need for children to learn to follow rules. Harris disagrees, however, with the idea that these early learning experiences determine the entire course of their lives. She argues that the content of what children learn in their homes may, in fact, be irrelevant to the world outside.

If parents are not the key in children's socialization, who is? According to Harris, it is in middle childhood (the elementary school years) when the core of their personalities is developed. It is interaction with their same-age peers that shapes children. From age 7 on, children become more like their peers. They learn how to behave in public. They also develop a self-identity by comparing themselves with other children who are in the same social category. Elementary school children initially take the things they've learned from their parents into their peer groups. But if the peer group's culture differs from their parents' the peer group always wins. This process can actually begin earlier than elementary school if children have the opportunity to interact regularly with same-age peers outside their home. Harris offers the following example:

> A baby we know had to face a dilemma very early on. From the age of about 12 months on, she was quite successful in requesting a bottle by saying, "Nai nai!" (the Chinese term for *milk*) to her parents. Meanwhile, she noticed that other babies at her day-care center got their bottles by saying "Ba ba!" and followed suit at age 15 months. The demands of leading a double life apparently were too great for her to bear. A day or two later, when her mother asked, "Nai nai?" she shook her head vigorously and said emphatically, "Ba ba!" (Savage and Kit-fong, cited in Harris, 1998, pp. 358–359).

Harris continues her argument by saying that even when their parents belong to the same culture as their friends, children can't count on being able to export the behaviors they learned at home. Behavior parents expect—or accept—may not be accepted by peers. Experiences in peer groups modify children's personalities in ways they will carry with them to adulthood. In summary, what is being argued is that it's the influence of peers, not parents, that matters most in the long run.

This obviously controversial position challenging the long-term influence of childrearing practices of the home environment on personality and intellectual development has been voiced by others. Rowe (1994), for example, questions the influence attributable to social and environmental factors such as social class, parental warmth, and family structure on child outcomes. Instead, he makes a persuasive case for the major role that genetic variations play in personality development as opposed to, in his view, the minimal effects of family environments.

In order for parents to produce, in some systematic way, a child with certain specific personality characteristics, several things would have to occur. First, the parents would have to decide on exactly the personality characteristic(s) they wanted to produce in their child. In a two-parent family, both parents would have to be in agreement. Next, the parents would have to develop a socialization strategy that would produce the personality characteristic(s) they wanted in their child. Finally, they would still face the daunting task of being uniformly consistent in carrying out their strategy. What if one parent did so, but the other did not? In fact, one might wonder, should both parents use the same strategy, or should mothers use one and fathers another? Should the same strategy be used for boys as for girls?

It is doubtful whether any parents, no matter how dedicated, could be intelligent enough, consistent enough, and in agreement enough to follow a regimen that will produce a child with some particular sought-after characteristics and qualities. And even if they were, there are other influences on children than the calculated socialization behaviors of their parents. Socialization is much more complex and subtle than many people suppose. Socialization goes on all the time, not just when parents are consciously teaching a lesson. Children learn as much by observation and deduction as they do from their parents' verbal directives ("Do this . . ." "Don't do that . . ."). There are also likely to be other socializing agents in children's lives besides their parents, as we discussed in Chapter 3. Siblings, other relatives, playmates, baby-sitters, preschool teachers, and others may play some part in the socialization process. At a fairly early age, children are also socialized by the mass media, especially television.

Finally, there is the possible influence of biological inheritance that might override all socialization efforts. (Nature may be as important as nurture.) Although the sociological and psychological models emphasize parental and social influences on personality, there is certainly the possibility that particular biological or inherited traits might neutralize or moderate socialization efforts by parents. A child's personality may actually be the product of the *interaction* between inherited traits and socialization (Dunn and Plomin, 1990).

For all these reasons, parents have little more than an average chance of success in producing a child with particular personality characteristics, even when they set out in the most calculated way. This does not mean, however, that parents have no influence on their children's personalities. It simply means that there are too many obstacles for parents to produce exactly what they want through their childrearing techniques.

Gender and Parenting

*E*veryone agrees that a child needs to be cared for and nurtured, and that parents should be the ones to provide that care and nurturance. But a parent's actual involvement in childrearing depends greatly on gender.

The relationship between gender and parenting can be viewed in one of two ways, in terms of the cultural image of what mothers and fathers are expected to do with respect to rearing children, or in terms of their actual behavior. We begin by looking at the images and behaviors of mothers, both historically and in contemporary society, and then we turn to the images and behaviors of fathers.

Mothers and Motherhood

To many people, parenting is synonymous with mothering, and many believe mothering to be instinctive in women. Although scientists have yet to find an instinctual motive for motherhood among humans, it is clear that many women show a strong interest in having children, which can be explained by the fact that motherhood is culturally expected of women. In U.S. society, most women choose to become mothers, and most women who already have children say they would do so again.

The image of motherhood has changed throughout history and varies from one culture to another. In American history the expectations placed on mothers and the presumed importance of mothers in their children's development have waxed and waned in different periods. Often it seems that what is expected of mothers is closely tied to prevailing economic conditions. When women's labor is not needed outside the home, the mother role is glorified; when their labor is essential to the economy, the importance of the mother–child bond is deemphasized (Margolis, 2000).

Earlier in American history, when the economy was agrarian, parenting was more of a joint venture. Childrearing was shared among a larger number of adults,

ContentSELECT

Motherhood

and the mother–child bond was not regarded as the primary one (Lopata, 1994). Only after industrialization and urbanization changed the nature of work and family life did the importance of the mother in child development become preeminent. As we discuss later, similar shifts have occurred with the father role.

In the preindustrial period, the home *was* the workplace and women were the primary manufacturers in colonial America. They "kept house, tended gardens, raised poultry and cattle, churned milk into butter and cream, butchered livestock, tanned skins, pickled and preserved food, made candles, buttons, soap, beer, and cider, gathered and processed medicinal herbs, and spun and wove wool and cotton for family clothes" (Margolis, 2000, p. 13).

Childrearing took place within these daily and seasonal rounds of activities. Fathers could also take an active role in childrearing, because they worked near the household. Artisans and tradespeople typically operated their businesses from their homes. Households often contained a number of adults: unmarried aunts, aged grandparents, apprentices or journeymen, older sons and daughters, and occasionally domestic servants. Thus, childrearing duties were not differentiated by gender, and parenting was not considered a distinct role in families. It was merely one part of ongoing daily life activities performed by either parent or others in the household.

During the early stage of industrialization (around 1790), when the factory system began in the United States, women's labor was essential in manufacturing, because men's labor was crucial to agricultural production. The first waves of European immigrants (during the period 1830 to 1840) greatly reduced the demand for native-born white female labor in the factories. At this point an ideological base for full-time domesticity for women was constructed to justify the displacement of native-born women from the factories. Full-time domesticity for women, including motherhood and the general management of the home, was elevated to a status symbol.

During the 1840s, motherhood emerged as a full-time role and as a distinct and special form of parenting. The bond between mothers and their children was proclaimed the most sacred and consequential of all human relationships. This ideology of motherhood flourished until the 1960s, and it generally kept women out of the labor force, especially if they had young children. (We discuss the relationship between women's work and family roles in more detail in Chapter 12.)

Since the 1960s, the percentage of women in the labor force, and especially mothers, has increased steadily. As female labor force participation went up and two-earner families became more common, women's economic contributions to their families were increasingly acknowledged and appreciated. The belief in full-time domesticity for women was being undermined. An increasing emphasis was placed on *parenting* rather than *mothering*. Fathers were rediscovered, and housework tips were designed to save time rather than to fill the day with "make-work" tasks for women (Margolis, 2000).

Some writers, such as historian Mary F. Berry (1993), have argued that there was a partial resurgence of the belief in traditional mothering during the 1980s. She sees a reemphasis on the importance of mothering reflected in the politics of that decade, especially during Ronald Reagan's presidency. During the 1980s, there was a strong "protraditional family" movement led by the right wing. One major political battle of the decade was between the profamily group and those who sought ratification of the Equal Rights Amendment to the Constitution. When state legislators in many states (mostly male) failed to ratify the Equal Rights Amendment, they seemed to be expressing a preference for the traditional woman's role.

In the 1990s, it was widely understood and accepted that women, even when they have small children, cannot leave the workforce for long periods of time. Though many people believe that mother care is vitally important for the development of children, most now recognize that the majority of women must be employed. In many cases, in both single-parent and two-parent homes, mothers must return to their employment soon after the birth of a baby because their families cannot get along without their incomes. There is, in fact, still a basic conflict in U.S. society over the role of women as mothers and their place in the labor force.

Employed mothers often feel they are being asked to "do it all." They try to achieve the mythical *supermom* role. The supermom is a woman who has sufficient energy to succeed in a career, carry out all the childrearing responsibilities expected of her, and be a perfect wife as well. Most women soon realize that it is impossible to consistently perform all these demanding roles perfectly.

In our culture today, the dominant view about women's role in parenting is referred to as **intensive mothering,** in which the woman is *supposed to be* devoted to the care of others. In this view, they are self-sacrificing and should not have any needs of their own. This ideal image of mothers and mothering, however, cannot easily fit into today's society. Most women cannot afford to devote their entire lives to their children. Other responsibilities compete for their time and attention. Those who don't conform to the ideal of full-time motherhood (that is, those who are single mothers, welfare mothers, immigrant mothers, lesbian mothers) are often targeted for ridicule and censure. Interestingly enough, the ideal is turned on its head for low-income mothers of color. They are expected to put employment above full-time mothering so they can get off welfare (Arendell, 2000). Current federal policy initiatives are pushing marriage as the solution to poverty.

▲ *Weekday mornings, as employed mothers attempt to get their children ready for day care, can be particularly stressful times.*

The experience of mothering can be a source of personal fulfillment, growth, and joy on the one hand and distress, depression, and anxiety on the other. Raising children can bring personal development, but it can also produce economic stress and a heavier work load. Women caring for dependent children can feel oppression and subordination as well as transformation and liberation. Mothers may experience all of these contradictory forces within one day (Arendell, 2000). Overall, mothers are more satisfied than fathers with parenting. But they also experience more strain due to their more intensive involvement in parenting work.

An alternative is for men to take on more of the family tasks, including parenting. Although there has been some movement in this direction, as we show later, mothers are still expected to take the major responsibility for child care. Recent decades have seen changes in men's and women's roles, but the change has been unbalanced. Women have assumed more and more economic responsibilities, but men have not fully reciprocated. "It has been far easier to convince husbands to share economic responsibilities with their wives than to assume domestic and child care responsibilities" (Furstenberg, 1988, p. 200).

Fathers and Fatherhood

The verb *to mother* calls up the image of nurturing and caring for children; the verb *to father* has a much more limited meaning. To most people, fathering a child

HEADline To Father a Child Means to Provide for It

Perhaps the most basic expectation of fathers today is that they provide financially for their children. Not all men, however, contribute to their children's economic well-being. Two well-publicized court cases in recent years have led some observers to debate whether men should have to prove that they can and will support any children they might have before they actually become fathers. One case involved David Oakley (of Wisconsin) who has a criminal record that spans more than fifteen years. Oakley had fathered nine children with four different women and owed $25,000 in back child support, even though a number of legal actions had been taken against him. In 2001, the Supreme Court of Wisconsin

upheld a lower court decision that said that Oakley would be sent to jail for eight years if he fathered any more children—unless or until he could prove that he would support all of the children he has already had. The court ruling has implications for any women who have sexual relations with Oakley. If any of them become pregnant, their babies will be tested to see if Oakley is their father.

A second case involved 20-year-old Robert Torres, who was convicted of having sex with a 13-year-old girl. During a parole violation hearing Torres admitted that he had impregnated two other teens. In 2001, a district court judge in Texas ordered Torres not to have sex with anyone, regardless of her age, until he married.

If he violates this ruling he will go to prison for life.

Not all judges agree with these rulings. Some argue that they strip men of their basic right to have children. The right to procreate (that is, reproduce) was declared a basic human right by the U.S. Supreme Court in 1942. Thirty-five years later the Court reaffirmed this right in a decision to overturn a Wisconsin law that forbid citizens who were delinquent in child support payments from marrying (or remarrying) if they couldn't show that their children would not end up on welfare.

Source: Van Beima, David. "When Father Equals Convict: Can Judges Jail Problem Dads Just for Procreating?" *Time* July 23, 2001, p. 64.

means impregnating a woman; fathering carries no strong suggestion of rearing or caring for that child. But fatherhood does have responsibilities associated with it, and just as the image of motherhood has changed over time, so has the image of fatherhood (Griswold, 1993). Today the responsibility most often associated with fatherhood is economic: To be a good father, a man must be a good provider (Marsiglio, 1993; Wilke, 1993). But in the colonial period, a father's primary responsibility was to serve as his children's *moral teacher.*

With increasing industrialization, wage earning became the primary responsibility of fathers. This new emphasis complemented the change in the image of the mother as one who stayed home to care for the children. Women increasingly took over primary responsibility for the moral development of the children, since fathers were working away from the home and were simply not around to interact with their children. By the end of the nineteenth century, mothers had become the upholders of moral authority in the home, and fathers, although still partially responsible for disciplining children, were moved almost exclusively into the breadwinner role (Demos, 1986).

The importance of the economic provider role for fathers has persisted until the present time, but two historical events in the first half of the twentieth century started to erode it somewhat (Griswold, 1993). First, the Great Depression of the 1930s left many men without work and prevented them from fulfilling their economic role. Sometimes husbands had to turn over the breadwinning role to their wives; in other cases, their families lived off public welfare funds. Some men, in the depths of the economic depression, simply stopped trying to support their families and abandoned them (Komarovsky, 1940). World War II, from 1941 to 1945, also limited the economic provider role of fathers. With many young fathers in the military, mothers often entered the labor force, both to help with the war effort and to support their families.

After the war, the male breadwinner role regained much of its prominence, especially during the 1950s. Certainly during that decade fathers had almost exclusive breadwinner responsibilities, since it was the ideal for women to be in the home caring for children.

By the 1960s, the economic supporter role of fathers again began to diminish, perhaps as a result of the new wave of feminism. As we have seen, women started entering the labor force, even when they had children. Today the economic provider role is no longer the exclusive province of fathers, and most couples recognize that two incomes are necessary.

The New Nurturant Father. The contemporary ideal of fatherhood has been called the "new nurturant father" (Lamb, 1987). This new father is earnestly involved in caring for his children to ensure their healthy development (Biller, 1993). The nurturant father's involvement begins during pregnancy with prenatal doctor's visits and childbirth classes. The new nurturant father is often in the delivery room when the baby is born. He is expected to follow through by being involved in the everyday care, feeding (if possible), and nurturing of the infant.

Comparing the first edition of Dr. Benjamin Spock's classic book on childrearing, published in 1945, with the 1980s edition shows the extent to which Americans' ideas about the father role had changed. In 1945, Spock suggested that fathers might help out with baby care by "preparing a formula on Sundays." By the 1980s, Dr. Spock admonished fathers to take on half of all child care and housework tasks (Spock and Rothenberg, 1985).

The twentieth-century trend has generally been to emphasize the nurturing father as much as the economic provider father, but an empirical analysis of popular magazine articles on fatherhood shows some interesting fluctuations from one decade to another. Magazine articles emphasizing the nurturant father over the provider father were found most often in the 1970s and, to a lesser extent, the 1980s, although some did appear as early as the 1940s (Atkinson and Blackwelder, 1993, p. 981).

The nonprofit organization called Child Trends has published a series of papers on fathers and their parenting activities using national data from several large surveys that were conducted in the late 1990s. They report that parental involvement tends to be assigned along traditional gender roles. For instance, fathers were more likely than mothers to help their children build or repair something and to play sports or engage in outdoor activities with them (Brown et al., 2001). Involvement of fathers with children is reported for four areas: general activities, school activities, limit-setting, and religious activities. All the fathers in the studies were living with their children.

▲ *Changing gender roles have moved some fathers into the nontraditional role of caring for children, but most child care is still done by mothers.*

General Activities. Contemporary fathers remain actively engaged in activities with their children. Figure 10.1 presents data pertaining to this issue. At least half of the men in the study reported that they played sports or engaged in outside activities, worked on homework, went to the store, or talked about their families with their children at least once each week. Two-fifths said they looked at books

in the media

Dagwood Bumstead and Other Comic Strip Dads

The comics have been part of our culture for more than 100 years. They often focus on domestic situations. More than 100 million people read the comics every day. Like television, comic strips occupy a central place in American society. Sociologists have begun to use comic strips as valuable sets of data that can be analyzed to get a better idea of prevailing ideologies surrounding family life.

Some researchers have used the comic strips to examine long-term changes in the image of American fathers. Analyzing nearly 500 comic strips published in the *Atlanta Journal and Constitution* every Mother's Day and Father's Day from 1940 to 1999, sociologists at Georgia State University looked at the way fathers have been depicted (LaRossa et al., 2000). They were specifically interested in whether fathers were depicted as incompetent (that is, ignorant, inadequate, incapable, ineffectual, inefficient, inept, stupid, unable, unfit, or weak) in their performance of more than twenty-seven different activities related to family and work life. They also looked at whether the comic strips attempted to mock fathers. And their final focus was on the extent to which fathers were depicted in nurturant and supportive roles.

The Georgia State researchers used a method known as content analysis, which involves a systematic coding of themes by independent coders. Their results indicated that the depictions of fathers and fatherhood in our culture has changed over time but not in a simple way. First, the amount of attention given to Father's Day in the comics has increased over time, especially in the 1970s. One interpretation of this finding is that Father's Day wasn't officially signed into law until 1972 (by then President Nixon). Mother's Day, on the other hand, was made an official federal holiday in 1914.

The 1970s seemed to be a period in which the comics honored fathers. According to the Georgia State study, fathers were less likely to be mocked during this decade. During the 1980s and 1990s, comic strips were more likely to portray fathers as nurturant and supportive, coinciding with the emphasis that was being give to the *new father* in other media.

Comic strips, in general, are devoting more space to family life, regardless of whether the strip appears on Mother's Day or Father's Day. In recent years more characters in the comics are parents. This change may reflect the entrance of new types of cartoonists onto the funny pages. As more women and more artists from younger cohorts entered the comic industry, the portrayals of fathers and mothers changed. Until recently, the majority of comics were white men. Some of the newer comics (e.g., *Cathy* and *For Better or Worse*) are written by women.

Also until recently, all the comic strip characters appeared to be white. It wasn't until the 1990s that new strips such as *Curtis*, *Jumpstart*, and *The Boondocks* had more people of color as major characters. The longevity of strips such as *Dennis the Menace* and the *Family Circle* (dating back to the 1950s) may mask some of the trends that are occurring, however, because they tend to take the same perspectives over time.

The most important question to ask about comic strips pertains to their connection with public attitudes and behaviors. The connection is certainly not simple. "Internalizing culture, of which comic strips are a part, is not akin to down-loading software on a computer. Rather, the socialization process is more selective and more interactive. . . . One could say that comic strips are part of a society's cultural supermarket. A strip's presence "on the shelves" makes its stories and vocabularies (e.g., "Good grief!" from *Peanuts*) available for selection and incorporation into the amalgam of norms, values, beliefs, and expressive symbols that influence people's perceptions and behaviors" (LaRossa et al., 2000).

Source: Adapted from LaRossa, Ralph, Jaret, Charles, Gadgil, Malati, and Wynn, G. Robert. "The Changing Culture of Fatherhood in Comic-Strip Families: A Six-Decade Analysis." *Journal of Marriage and the Family* 62(May), 2000: 375–387. Reprinted with permission.

Figure 10.1 **Fathers' Activities with Children.**

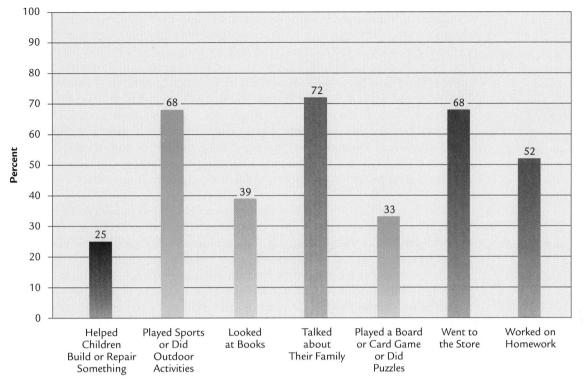

(*Source:* Brown, B., Michelsen, E., Halle, T., and Moore, K. *Fathers' Activities with Their Kids.* Child Trends Research Brief. Washington, DC: Child Trends, 2001. Figure 1, page 2.)

with their children and one-third played a board game or card game with their children at least once a week.

School Activities. Fathers are about half as likely as mothers to be highly engaged in their children's school activities (that is, highly engaged means that they participate in at least three of the following activities: attend a general school meeting, participate in a parent–teacher conference, participate in a class event, and/or volunteer at school). Of the fathers in the study who lived with their children, about one-fourth of those whose children were between ages 3 and 5 reported that they were highly engaged in school activities. A similar percentage of fathers whose children were between 12 and 17 reported being highly engaged. Men whose children were between 6 and 11 were the most likely to report that they were very engaged in school activities: One-third reported participating in at least three of the four primary activities mentioned previously. Fathers who have higher levels of education themselves are more likely to report high levels of involvement in their children's schooling. Fathers were more likely to provide support for their children's education by helping them with their homework. Over half said they did this at least once each week.

Setting Limits on Children's Behavior. Authoritative parenting (that is, parenting that is firm but responsive to a child's needs) helps children develop in positive ways. Parents who set limits on their children's behavior help them develop their judgment, their understanding of the surrounding environment, and their conscience. Setting limits also decreases children's risk of injury and increases their likelihood of complying with their parents' expectations. Fathers as well as mothers are highly involved in setting limits and providing structure for their children's lives. The majority of parents report that they limit the television programs their children watch. Less than half, however, say they limit the *amount of time* their children can watch television. Another way in which parents set limits on their children's behavior is by keeping close watch on who their children spend time with and what they do with their time. Again, both fathers and mothers set limits in this way. Forty percent of mothers and 46 percent of fathers who live with their children say they frequently perform this monitoring function. Other ways in which parents attempt to set limits for their children is to establish a specific time for them to do their homework. The majority of fathers who live with their children report that this is a parenting role they perform frequently.

Religious Activities. The Child Trend report shows that fathers and mothers of children in grades seven through twelve are involved in religious activities with their children. More than one-fourth of the children in this age group said they had gone to a church-related activities with their father in the month prior to the survey. A slightly larger proportion of the children (more than one-third) said they had gone to a church activity with their mothers during this time period. Previous research has shown that children whose parents are more involved in religious activities experience a number of benefits.

Father and Involvement

Factors Affecting Fathers' Involvement with Their Children. Many fathers today support the cultural ideal of the nurturant father, at least in principle, and many attend birthing classes and are present in the delivery room, but their participation in *everyday* child care is often very limited. Many new fathers think they are "pitching in," as we noted, but in reality they are falling far short of the nurturant father ideal.

Because fathers may not be as involved with their children as they would like to be, or as much as mothers would like them to be, we might ask what factors encourage or discourage fathers' involvement with their children. Four factors have been identified (Lamb, 1987):

1 *Motivation.* Do men want to spend more time with their children and participate more actively in childrearing tasks? In one survey, over half of the fathers said they did not wish to spend more time with their children (Lamb, 1987). Those who do want to spend more time with their children may not necessarily wish to change more diapers, prepare more meals, make more visits to the doctor, and so on.

2 *Skills and Self-Confidence.* Some men claim they do not have the abilities to do the necessary child care tasks. Especially when their children are infants, men may feel inept—but new mothers have no special instinct that tells them what to do, either. Nevertheless, new fathers often respond to the slightest discomfort or implicit criticism by handing the baby back to "the expert," as they often call their wives (Cowan and Cowan, 1992, p. 103). New fathers need to understand that many new mothers often feel incompetent and as terrified as they do.

3 *Social Support from Spouse, Family, and Friends.* Wives are most influential in determining how much their husbands participate in child care. Some evidence suggests that some men's low level of participation in the care of their children, especially very young children, may occur because their female partners do not want them to do more (Marsiglio et al., 2000). If wives want their husbands to take an active role in caring for their children, they must make their views clear and be supportive.

Other family members and friends can also influence how much men participate in the care of their children. If family members and friends expect and support a father in his childrearing efforts, the task may seem more natural to him.

4   Institutional Policies and Practices. If fathers are to take a more active part in the care of their children, from infancy onward, the external institutions of the society must make that possible. Employers are most important in this regard, since very few make provisions that allow men to be active fathers. More often employers *discourage* fathering activities. Even men who have access to paternity leave from work are unlikely to take it because they fear it signals to their boss that they place a higher priority on family life than on their job.

Types of Involvement with Children

Parents can be involved with their children in three different ways: engagement, accessibility, and responsibility (Lamb, 1987, p. 8). These three categories are useful for analyzing fathers' involvement with their children.

Engagement is the time spent in one-on-one interaction with a child. Engagement activities include feeding, dressing, talking to, playing with, helping with homework, and so on.

Accessibility is a lesser form of involvement, such as when a parent is in the presence of the child or in close proximity, but is not interacting directly with the child. If a parent is watching television or cooking and the child is in the same or an adjoining room, the parent is accessible.

Responsibility is the most intense kind of involvement with a child, since it requires planning, making decisions, and organizing. "Responsibility involves making childcare and babysitting arrangements, ensuring that the child has clothes to wear, and making arrangements for the child's supervision when she is sick" (Lamb, 1987, p. 8). The parent who has primary responsibility usually feels more pressure, anxiety, and worry.

To sum up, contemporary fathers have moderately increased their involvement with infants and small children, but the overwhelming amount of parenting is still done by mothers. Even though fathers are more engaged with their children, they are still not likely to consider child care their basic responsibility; mothers almost always retain the primary responsibility for child care (Darling-Fisher and Tiedje, 1990). One observer describes the situation by using a sports metaphor: "It appears that fathers are still pinch hitters and part-time players rather than regulars" (Furstenberg, 1988, p. 209).

The involvement of many fathers in the lives of their children is complicated by two important trends in U.S. society: divorce and births to unmarried women. In both instances, fathers are often not living in the same households as their children. Never-married and divorced fathers have been identified by some sociologists with the shorthand labels *good dads* and *bad dads.*

Good Dads versus Bad Dads.   **Good dads** are men who try, at least minimally, to be caring, supportive, and active fathers, even though they may not be living with their children. Although many fathers fall short of the ideal, they are still in the good dad category if they are *trying* to be "full partners in parenthood" (Furstenberg, 1988, p. 193). **Bad dads** are men who have little or no contact with their children and provide little or no economic support. These bad dads are often characterized in the popular press as *deadbeat dads.*

Nonmarried fathers often intend to provide for their children at the time of the pregnancy, and many do for a while. But as time goes on, and they have less and less contact with the mother, they see their children less and less often. When fathers do not see their children, they generally also stop providing financial support for them.

The pattern is somewhat similar for noncustodial fathers after divorce, where children, over the years, see less and less of their fathers. The pattern is so widespread that the term *disappearing dads* has been applied to many divorced fathers (Furstenberg and Harris, 1992). Divorced fathers often pay child support in the early years after divorce, but as time goes by many begin to default on their payments. (This issue is discussed more fully in Chapter 14.) Divorced fathers who remarry are especially likely to stop or reduce their child support payments, especially if they have children in their new marriage, either their own or stepchildren.

Some observers believe that *deadbeat dads* are part of a larger phenomenon that finds men retreating from fatherhood and their paternal obligations. From a demographic perspective, men are spending fewer years of their lives in family environments in which children are present (Eggebeen and Uhlenberg, 1985). This demographic fact can be accounted for by later marriage, later childbearing, fewer children, and high divorce rates, but they all lead to the same conclusion: Men today have less opportunity than in the past to become fathers and to live with their children.

A survey in Baltimore, Maryland, dramatized the male trend of retreating from fatherhood. When parents were asked to list their children, more men than women "forgot" some of them. Since these fathers often did not see their children or provide any financial support for them, they had apparently put them out of their minds also.

Many parents today, whether in one-parent or two-parent homes, need help in caring for their children. When parents are employed, they must turn to child care services.

Child Care Services

The majority of American mothers are employed. An estimated 15 million children under 6 and 23.5 million children between 6 and 13 have mothers who are in the labor force (Hofferth, 1992). For many of these parents, child care is a stressful issue.

Mothers, in particular, find arranging and handling child care for their children a special burden and a source of anxiety. Compared with unemployed mothers, "working mothers worry more about the time they spend with their children and feel guilty about leaving them when they have to go to work. They feel deprived of their children's company. They feel confused and worry about harm they might be doing to their children" (Clarke-Stewart, 1993, p. 3).

Alternatives

There are five types of child care arrangements: parental care; relative care (in the child's home or the relative's home); baby-sitters or nannies (in the child's home); family daycare homes (care in a nonrelative's home); and center-based care (for-profit and nonprofit daycare centers, Head Start, and before and after school programs). In two-parent households, it is sometimes possible for parents to work at different times, allowing one parent to care for the children while the other is working.

Child care arrangements for children under 5 years of age differ in expected ways when mothers are and are not employed: When mothers are not employed,

Finding good child care for infants and toddlers is a major challenge for most employed parents.

they are more likely to be the primary caregivers for their children, but even among these mothers, some of the primary child care is done by others (see Table 10.1).

In 24 percent of the cases in which the mother is employed, parents are the primary caregivers, which means that either the mother takes care of her children at her place of work (which is most likely her own home) or the father (or partner) cares for the children. Other relatives also care for the children of employed mothers (23 percent of the cases), either in their own or the child's home.

Middle-class parents, whether the mother is employed or not, often use preschools and nursery schools as a way of improving their children's skills before they enter school. Disadvantaged children are enrolled in Head Start programs for the same reasons. Seventy-six percent of preschool children whose mothers are employed are regularly cared for by someone other than their parents (Capizzano, Adams, and Sonenstein, 2000). Table 10.1 summarizes the use of the five different

TABLE 10.1			
Primary Child Care Arrangements for Children under 5 Years			
Type of Care	**All Children**	**Younger Than Three Years**	**Three to Four Years**
Center-based	32	22	45
Family daycare homes	16	17	14
Relative care	23	27	17
Parent care	24	27	18
Nanny/babysitter	6	7	6

Source: Capizzano, J., Adams, G., and Sonenstein, F. "Child Care Arrangements for Children under Five: Variation Across States," Number B-7 in Series, *New Federalism: National Survey of America's Families.* Urban Institute, excerpted from Table 1, "Primary Child Care Arrangements for Children under Five with Employed Mothers, by Selected Characteristics and State," 2000. Reprinted with permission.

types of child care by parents of preschool children. The types of care experienced by children under age 3 are compared with that experienced by children aged 3 and 4. Figures for preschool children in general (those under 5) are also included. Care provided in private homes (either in their own or another person's) is the most common type of child care arrangement for children who are under 3. Over one-fourth of the children in this age group are primarily cared for by a parent. The same proportion are cared for by a relative. About one-fifth of children under 3 are in child care centers. As preschool children age, they are more likely to be cared for in some type of child care center. This is the most common type of arrangement for 3 and 4 year olds (45 percent attend some type of child care center).

Over the last quarter century, the child care arrangements for employed mothers have changed. In-home care has decreased the most, probably because its cost has increased significantly. Care by relatives has also decreased, as has family day care because women who provide this type of care for others have also entered the labor force. The use of child care centers has increased greatly over the last twenty-five years.

Costs

Sixty percent of the American parents whose children are under age 5 pay for some type of child care. On average, they pay $325 per month for that care, or 10 percent of their monthly earnings. Parents of school-aged children are less likely to pay for child care and those who do, pay a lower amount each month (Giannarelli and Barsimantov, 2000). The Children's Defense Fund issued a report about the high cost of child care around the United States (Schulman, 2000). The major findings of the report are summarized below:

1 Child care for a 4 year old in a child care center costs between $4,000 and $8,000 per year (on average). Families with younger children or with more than one child in care pay even greater costs.

2 The average annual cost of child care for a 4 year old in urban areas is greater than the average annual cost of tuition at a public university in all states except one. In some cities, child care costs twice as much as college tuition. Table 10.2 lists fourteen urban areas in states where average child care costs exceed the cost of tuition at a public university in the state.

3 Low-income families have the fewest options. They cannot afford not to work, but even average-priced child care is unaffordable for many of them. Even if a two-parent family with both parents working full time at minimum wage ($21,400 a year before taxes) could put aside 10 percent of their wages for child care, they still would fall short of the amount needed for average quality care.

4 Many low-income families have no choice but to put their children in lower cost, often lower quality care. Because of this, many low-income children are cared for in unstimulating or even unsafe setting, deprived of opportunities to learn, grow, and thrive. These are the children most at risk for failing in school and most in need of the strong start that high-quality care can provide.

5 The dilemma posed by high child care costs cannot be resolved by asking child care providers to lower their fees. Most operate on extremely tight budgets. A large proportion of the budget of child care centers is spent on staff salaries, which are already too low. The average salary for a child care worker is under $15,000 per year. Lowering child care center fees would undermine their ability to

TABLE 10.2

States Where the Average Annual Cost of Child Care for a 4-Year-Old in an Urban Area Center Is at Least Twice the Average Annual Cost of Public College Tuition

State	Urban Area	Average Annual Cost of Child Care for a 4-Year-Old in a Center (in dollars)	Average Annual Cost of Public College Tuition (in dollars)
Alaska	Anchorage	6,019	2,769
Arizona	Tucson	4,352	2,158
Florida	Orange County	4,255	2,022
Georgia	Atlanta	4,992	2,442
Idaho	Boise	4,814	2,380
Iowa	Urban areas statewide	6,198	2,869
Kansas	Wichita	4,889	2,392
Massachusetts	Boston	8,121	4,012
Nevada	Reno	4,862	1,956
New Mexico	Albuquerque	4,801	2,180
New York	Rockland County	8,060	3,905
North Carolina	Durham	5,876	1,958
Utah	Salt Lake City	4,550	2,174
Washington	King County (Seattle)	6,604	3,151

Source: Schulman, Karen. "The High Costs of Child Care Puts Quality Care Out of Reach for Many Families," Children's Defense Fund, 2000, Table 1, p. 4.

hire a sufficient number of well-trained teachers, purchase adequate material and equipment, and afford a safe facility (Schulman, 2000).

Quality of Child Care Facilities

When parents place their children in the hands of others, their primary concern is that the setting is safe and beneficial. Most parents want child care that contributes to the social, emotional, and intellectual development of their children. Researchers studying child care services, especially daycare programs and child care centers, have concluded that the important features to consider when selecting care are the physical setting, caregivers' behavior, curriculum, and number of children. "Children do better in centers that are neat, clean, safe, and orderly, that are organized into interest areas and oriented toward children's activities" (Clarke-Stewart, 1992, p. 68). Parents should be especially careful to examine the sanitary conditions that exist in the center; they should look to see if there is a sink near the diaper-changing station and a sign reminding workers to wash their hands after changing a baby. One of the greatest risks children face in daycare centers is being exposed to contagious diseases, some of which are spread by workers who do not wash their hands between diaper changes.

Caregivers' behavior is significantly related to the development of children's social and intellectual skills. The best caregivers are stimulating, educational, and respectful, not custodial or demeaning. The caretakers who contribute least to development are those who direct, control, restrict, and punish the children. Another important consideration is the turnover rate among adult caregivers, that is, how frequently workers leave to take other jobs. Children need to form stable relationships with their caregivers.

The best curricula of daycare centers are those that are not too structured, organized, or supervised. Some kind of curriculum (planned activities and structure) is better than none, but too much is not beneficial.

When there are too many children in a center (say twenty or more), many children simply hang around watching the other children, instead of getting actively involved in their own activities. Yet it is important that there be *some* other children in a center, because they provide opportunities for interaction and for social and intellectual development. The key factor to consider is the ratio of adult caregivers to children. Ideally, there should be one adult for every three infants or seven older children.

The general lesson that researchers have learned about the quality of daycare centers is that "more is not necessarily better (whether it be more training, . . . more toys or more space, more structure or more academic activities, more direction or more physical contact from the caregiver, more children to play with or more time to play with them)" (Clarke-Stewart, 1992, pp. 72–73). Too much of any of these things can detract from the development of the children, rather than add to it.

Effects of Child Care on Children's Development

Child Care and
Development

The question that parents and researchers have been trying to answer for some time is whether it is a positive or negative experience for children to spend time in child care centers, in daycare, or with other nonparental caregivers.

It has now been fairly well established that children who spend time in *high-quality* child care facilities (using the criteria just discussed) often benefit, especially intellectually. They do as well as children reared by parents (Belsky, 1990b; Clarke-Stewart, 1992, 1993). But in order for children to benefit, the child care must be of high quality.

Preschool children in child care settings have the same, or even better, intellectual development as children who are reared exclusively by parents. Over thirty studies conducted in countries as widely dispersed as Canada, England, Sweden, Czechoslovakia, Bermuda, and the United States have found, with only a few exceptions, that preschoolers who have been in daycare have equal or better intellectual development. Children from disadvantaged backgrounds are especially likely to gain intellectually from being in daycare. This finding should not be exaggerated, however, since disadvantaged children who don't attend daycare catch up by the time they reach the first grade.

Most, but not all, studies of preschool children who attend daycare find them developing social skills earlier. They are more self-confident, outgoing, assertive and self-sufficient, more comfortable in new situations, less timid and fearful, more helpful and cooperative, and more verbally expressive. At the same time, some researchers have found children who have been in daycare are less polite, less agreeable, less compliant, louder, more boisterous, and more aggressive than children who have not been in daycare (Clarke-Stewart, 1992, p. 65).

One disturbing, but still controversial, research finding is that children who are placed in child care during the first year of their lives may be adversely affected socially and emotionally. Jay Belsky has assembled evidence suggesting that children who are placed in the care of others (child care centers, family daycare, or nanny care) more than twenty hours a week during their first year are more likely to be "classified as insecure in their attachments to their mothers at 12 or 18 months of age and of being more disobedient and aggressive when they are from 3 to 8 years old" (Belsky, 1990, p. 895). However, not all studies show this negative effect of first-year child care. A Swedish study, for example, did not find any negative effects of first-year child care among children when they reached 8 and 9 years of age (Broberg et al., 1989).

The basic conclusions drawn from years of research on childrearing are that when child care (whether provided by parents or others) is sensitive and responsive, children generally develop into cooperative, compliant, and achieving children. When child care is inconsistent, unsupportive, unresponsive, and negative, the result is likely to be uncooperative and problem-prone children.

Child development expert Dr. Stanley Greenspan believes that America's dependence on out-of-home child care poses a serious threat to the long-term outcomes for children. Greenspan fervently believes that preschool children need concentrated, one-on-one attention. He thinks parents should reconsider their priorities to find a way of making more quality time for their children even while they pursue careers. In a book he co-authored with journalist Jacqueline Salmon, Greenspan offers a solution to parents. Both should cut their work schedules back to two-thirds time and devote the extra time to their children. His solution, as a result, is called the **four-thirds solution.** In most contemporary workplaces, employees cannot easily work a two-thirds schedule without sacrificing benefits and the rewards of seniority. We talk about employment in Chapter 12.

Much of this chapter has focused on the nature of parenting when children are relatively young. We turn next to parenting and parent–child relations in the adolescent years.

Parents and Adolescent Children

Family scholars have examined the ways in which adolescents spend their time, particularly looking at the changing settings in which their activities occur (Furstenberg, 2000). As they increase their out-of-home activities, their in-home family time decreases. Along with this comes a decline in direct parental supervision. American adolescents spend a growing portion of time outside the control of adults. While this may seem to be natural step in development to many, opinion surveys reveal that Americans believe that parents provide too little supervision (Furstenburg, 1999).

Most surveys indicate that parents generally monitor their teenage children fairly closely, but the type of monitoring changes as the teens age. Direct watching declines as parents assume their older teens will follow their guidelines even when they are out of sight. While teens usually behave according to parental guidelines, they underreport their use of alcohol and drugs, school problems, and sexual behavior. Furstenberg suggests that "a developmental task of adolescents is learning what not to tell parents and how not to tell them" (2000, p. 901).

In the adolescent years, children become increasingly self-sufficient and independent, which makes the job of parenting easier in some ways but harder in others. Parents usually feel that they must continue to guide and control their teenage children, whereas children of this age are often striving for autonomy. These competing goals often lead to clashes between parents and children.

Parent–Adolescent Conflict

The popular view is that adolescence is a time of rebellion and disrespect. Clashes with parents are considered the dominant form of interaction, and much anecdotal evidence exists to support the popular image.

Many parents find their children's teenage years the most frustrating and least gratifying years of parenthood. Many mothers say they feel less love and appreciation at this stage of their children's lives than at any other. They report feelings of worry and self-doubt, of losing control over their children's lives.

At this stage parents experience the ultimate dilemma of parenthood: They have raised their children to be independent, and now their children may reject their standards and values. Parents often feel a combination of anger, frustration, and failure when their children, who once respected their every word, now seem to reject them totally.

Such experiences with teenage children, although not universal, are certainly commonplace. But it is sometimes necessary to go beyond the personal illustrations and examine the larger, more general, picture, especially as it is produced by systematic research (Gecas and Seff, 1990).

Research in the last decade has challenged the characterization of adolescence as a time of "storm and stress." Although conflict between parents and adolescents may increase about some things, such as money, it may decrease in regard to other issues, such as chores, appearance, and politeness (Galambos and Almeida, 1992). A number of studies have found that "for most young people, adolescence is not a particularly turbulent time; that relations with parents reflect more harmony than conflict" (Gecas and Seff, 1990, p. 942).

Whether or not adolescence is seen as a time of turmoil may depend on whose view is being reported. Adolescents may say this is not an especially troubling time for them, but their parents often see the situation differently. When parents are asked about the most difficult period of parenting, the majority name adolescence. Parents find this a stressful time because they feel they have lost control of their child. Children may see the same situation in a different light. For them it is a time of greater freedom and independence (Gecas and Seff, 1990).

How Well Are Parents Doing in Childrearing?

*P*arents in the United States, as a group, are under rather persistent attack for their alleged failures in childrearing. The news stories about parents abandoning their children, as well as some of the evidence presented on *deadbeat dads,* for example, seem to support the critics.

Parents are often blamed for the negative behaviors of their children. Violence and substance use among youngsters, for example, along with poorer school performance, births to teenagers, alcohol use while driving cars, and a host of other behaviors are often described as the products of poor parenting. Is this blanket criticism of parents valid? Are most parents doing a poor job of rearing their children? These questions are not easy to answer in a scientific way, since specifying what constitutes good parenting is nearly impossible. Moreover, even if young people today do display more negative behaviors than they did in earlier generations, does that necessarily mean that their parents are at fault? Or, is it primarily a reflection of the complexities of modern society?

Casual observation suggests that almost all parents do care about their children and take the job of parenting seriously. Parents almost always want their children to be happy, secure, and successful. Their children may not always achieve these objectives, and parental shortcomings may contribute to that outcome, but there may also be many other contributing factors.

There is some relevant scientific evidence that parental behavior has changed over the last several decades: American parents are placing less emphasis on the importance of obedience and more emphasis on autonomy and responsibility (Alwin, 1990). Parents today want their children to be responsible for their actions.

In many states, laws allow homosexual couples to adopt children.

One apparent outcome of this change in parental values is that children, especially adolescents, are less likely to be influenced by their parents and more likely to be influenced by their peers (Harris, 1998). This change in parental values, and the resulting changes in adolescent behavior, may be viewed by some as a surrender of parental responsibility, but others may see it as a positive trend in parenting.

Substantial empirical evidence also shows that "parents continue to value children positively, that children provide meaningful sources of happiness and social support, and that parents remain influential in the transmission of values, especially on important issues" (Demo, 1992, p. 111). Most parents are supportive and show their support in a variety of ways, both materially and emotionally. Yet parents are often detached from their children in the sense that parents and children do not spend much time interacting with each other. Young children are with babysitters or in daycare settings, later they are in school and participating in activities for much of the day. Children are often with their friends, watching television, participating in athletics or other activities, attending camps, and so on.

There has been growing concern that work is keeping parents away from their children and that they are spending less and less time with them than ever before. In fact, recent research shows that quite the opposite is true. A report released by the Institute for Social Research at the University of Michigan concluded that parents were spending four to six hours *more* per week with their children in the late 1990s than comparable parents did in the early 1980s (Sandberg and Hofferth, 2001).

One of the most important findings is that employed mothers today are spending as much time with their children as stay-at-home mothers did 20 years ago (26 hours per week). In spite of a large increase in employed mothers and a persistently high rate of divorce, parents seem to be making a concerted effort to spend more time with their children. In two-parent families, mothers are spending about 31 hours with their children per week and fathers are spending about 23 hours. The extra hours that parents are devoting to their children seem to be coming from time that was previously used to do housework. Today parents are either hiring someone to help with household chores or are simply letting some of them go undone. Figure 10.2 summarizes these findings.

Figure 10.2 Children's Mean Time with Parents in Two-Parent Families, by Year.

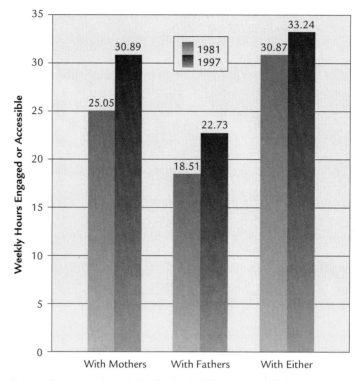

(*Source:* Sandberg, J., and Hofferth, S., "Changes in Children's Time with Parents: United States, 1981–1997." *Demography,* Volume 4, August, 2001. Figure 2, p. 428. Reprinted with permission.)

Simply increasing the amount of time parents and children spend together may be of more concern to parents than it is to their children, however. When 1000 American children were asked about their relationships with their employed parents, an interesting pattern emerged (Galinsky, 1999). Most of the children thought they had enough time with their parents. Only 10 percent wanted more time with their mothers and 15 percent wanted more time with their fathers. Well over half of the parents of these children, on the other hand, thought their children would say they wanted more time together. This is not to suggest that children don't regard spending time with their parents as important. Those who spend time with their mothers and fathers on week days and weekends regard them more positively, feel they are more successful at balancing work and family responsibilities, and believe that their parents put family life before work. The more time parents spend with their children—whether it involves eating meals together, participating in active leisure activities, doing homework together, or even watching television—the more favorably their children rate them. Many of the children (roughly 40 percent) in the study did say that the time they spend with their parents feels rushed and hurried. As a result, many wished their parents would give them more **focused time**; that is, they want time when parents are devoting their full attention to them, rather than simply being present physically but distracted mentally.

If the amount of time parents spend with their children is not the primary indicator of good parenting, what does make a good parent? In Galinsky's study, *Ask the Children,* eight critical parenting skills were identified:

1 making the child feel important and loved

2 responding to the child's cues and clues

3 accepting the child for who she or he is, but expecting success

4 promoting strong values

5 using constructive discipline

6 providing routines and rituals to make life predictable

7 being involved in the child's education

8 being there for the child.

The children were asked to grade their mothers and fathers on each of these critical skills. Table 10.3 summarizes the children's responses. Overall, the children gave their mothers higher grades than their fathers. Mothers were graded highest on their likelihood of being there for their children when they were sick and for raising their children with good values. They got the lowest grades from their children for failing to control their temper and for not knowing what was really going on in their children's lives. Fathers also scored lowest on controlling their temper and not really knowing what was going on in their children's lives. They did best on raising their children with good values and appreciating them for who they are really are (although their scores on these skills were lower than mothers' scores).

TABLE 10.3

Children's Evaluations of Their Parents (All Children Grades 7 through 12)

What grade would you give your mother or father on . . .	VIEWS ON MOTHERS (BY PERCENT)					VIEWS ON FATHERS (BY PERCENT)				
	A	B	C	D	F	A	B	C	D	F
Being there for me when I am sick?	81	11	5	2	1	51.5	20	16	8	4
Raising me with good values?	75	15	6	3	2	69	18	8	4	2
Making me feel important and loved?	64	20	10	5	1	57	22	13	6	2
Being able to attend important events in my life?	64	20	10	3	3.5	55	22	13	5	5.5
Appreciating me for who I am?	64	18	8	6	5	58	21	11	8	2
Encouraging me to want to learn and to enjoy learning?	59	23	11.5	3	3	57.5	24	12	4	2
Being involved with what is happening to me at school?	46	25	14	10	6	38	24	19	12	7
Being someone I can go to when I am upset?	46	22	14	8	9	38	22	15	12	13
Spending time talking with me?	43	33	14	6	4	43	24	19	10	4
Establishing family routines and traditions with me?	38	29	17	10	6	41	26	15	11	7
Knowing what is really going on in my life?	35	31	15	10	9	31	30	17	12.5	10
Controlling their temper when I do something that makes them angry?	29	27.5	20.5	12	11	31	27	20	10	12

Source: Galinsky, Ellen. *Ask the Children*, Tables 2.25 and 2.26, pp. 46–47. New York: William Morrow and Company, 1999.

Many parents *could* probably do a better job of parenting, and no doubt many wish they could do more for and with their children. But because of the pressure of other responsibilities or other circumstances, such as divorce, many parents cannot do as much for their children as they would like. This does not mean they do not care for their children, or that they are doing a poor job of parenting. Most do the best job they can, given their resources, circumstances, and abilities. When asked to evaluate their performance as parents most adults gave themselves a *B* (Gallup and Newport, 1990).

Summary

In premodern societies, children were seen differently from the way they are seen today; they were often viewed as miniature adults. Children were expected to work as soon as they were able, and they were often harshly treated. Infanticide and abandonment were widespread in medieval and early-modern Europe. Wet-nursing and swaddling were common. Children were routinely punished and disciplined to break their spirit.

In contrast, contemporary parents practice altruistic parenthood, which means that they feel responsible for the care, development, and long-term well-being of their children.

The first months of parenthood are often extremely stressful. The physical demands of caring for a new infant are often greater than expected. Marital quality often suffers during this early period. New parents can move more easily through this early period if they have the support of family members or a support group made up of other parents.

A key feature of parent–child interaction is socialization. Socialization is the process by which a person learns and generally accepts the ways of a particular group or society, and the process by which children become social beings with unique characters and personalities. Parents generally socialize their children according to their interpretation of the ways of the society. Sociologists have found that parents' occupations greatly influence the values they try to teach their children.

Socialization strongly influences the human qualities and personality development of children. Evidence coming from isolated children who have had little or no human contact shows how important social interaction is in development. Although parents influence the personalities of their children, it is doubtful that parents can produce exactly the type of child they set out to produce.

Gender is closely associated with parenting in two ways: cultural ideals of motherhood and fatherhood, and actual behaviors of mothers and fathers. In American history, the image of motherhood has changed from one period to another. In the middle of the nineteenth century, motherhood emerged as a full-time role for women. But as women began to enter the labor force in greater numbers over the last fifty years, the emphasis on full-time motherhood has diminished. Today it is widely understood that many women, even with small children, must work, out of economic necessity. With more mothers in the workforce, the image of fatherhood has also changed.

In the colonial period of American history, fathers were viewed as the moral teachers of children. But with growing industrialization, which called for fathers to work outside the home, moral teaching was left to mothers, and fathers were expected to be economic providers. The contemporary ideal for fatherhood is that fathers should play a greater part in the nurturance and care of their children.

Fathers are most likely to care for their children when they are motivated; have parenting skills and self-confidence; get social support from spouses, family, and friends; and when other institutions have policies and practices that make it easier. Compared with mothers, fathers still spend very little time engaged with their children, although some increases have occurred in the last two decades. Unmarried and divorced fathers have been labeled as *good dads* and *bad dads*. Good dads try to support and be involved with their children, while bad dads abandon or lose touch with their children.

Many parents today, because they are employed, must place their children in substitute care. Although some working parents can care for their children themselves, the majority must place their children in child care centers or family daycare homes. Research shows that if the quality of substitute care is high, there are no significant negative effects on children.

Parenting during adolescent years presents different problems and raises different issues from those in parenting younger children. The popular view is that adolescence is a time of conflict with parents, and the anecdotal evidence seems to bear out that image. Yet recent studies have found that adolescents do not see this as a particularly troubled time in their relations with parents. It may be that parents and adolescents see their relationship differently.

Some critics claim that contemporary parents are doing a poor job of meeting their parental responsibilities, and certainly some, such as deadbeat parents, are. Many parents, however, show supportive detachment toward their adolescent children, which means they support them both materially and emotionally but give them the freedom to be individuals.

Key Terms

Accessibility (parental) (p. 323)
Altruistic parenthood (p. 306)
Bad dads (p. 323)
Coddling period of childrearing (p. 303)
Engagement (parental) (p. 323)
Focused time (p. 332)
Foundlings (p. 304)
Four-thirds solution (p. 329)

Good dads (p. 323)
Infanticide (p. 304)
Intensive mothering (p. 317)
Kinderdults (p. 306)
Moralistic period of childrearing (p. 303)
Nurture assumption (p. 313)
Race defensiveness (p. 313)
Race naivete (p. 313)

Racial awareness (p. 313)
Racial empowerment (p. 313)
Racial socialization (p. 312)
Responsibility (parental) (p. 323)
Self-image (p. 312)
Socialization (p. 311)
Swaddling (p. 304)
Transition to parenthood (p. 307)
Wet-nursing (p. 304)

Review Questions

1. How and why have ideas about the nature of childhood changed over the past 500 years? How did the treatment of children change as ideas about childhood changed? How did social scientists gather information about children and childhood in the past? What are the limitations of these methods of data collection?

2. What impact does the birth of a baby have on the relationship between its parents? Why do many married couples experience a decline in marital satisfaction during the first year after a baby's birth?

3. How is *socialization* defined? What are the primary outcomes of socialization? What strategies do African American parents follow to racially socialize their children?

4. According to psychologist Judith Harris, what role do parents and peers play in the long-term development of children's personalities, values, and behaviors?

5. How have American ideals about the mother role changed over the past twenty years? What is meant by intensive mothering? What challenges does it pose for employed women?

6. In what ways have Americans' childrearing expectations for fathers changed over the past 200 years? To what extent are contemporary fathers engaged in various types of behaviors with their children? What factors influence men's involvement with their children?

7. What are the five major types of child care arrangements? What percentage of preschool children are cared for in each type? What is the average monthly cost of child care? How does this cost compare with other financial obligations of families?

8. What characteristics define good quality child care?

9. How does nonparental/nonrelative care affect the development of infants and young children?

10. How much time do American parents spend with their children? How has this changed over the past twenty years?

11. How do children grade their parents?

Critical Thinking Questions

1. To what extent do American adults regard and treat children simultaneously as both childlike and mature? Provide examples of this. Discuss why the line between childhood and adulthood might be blurring.

2. Can men *mother* children? To what extent do women and men have unique styles of parenting? Discuss possible reasons for gender-based differences in parenting styles.

3. How can social researchers more effectively inte-grate the perspectives of children in studies of parenting and family life?

4. Do you agree with the argument that parents' influences on their children early in life largely determine what type of adult they will become? Why or why not?

5. Discuss the policy implications of the ongoing debate about the impact of nonparental/nonrelative care on young children.

Online Resources Available for This Chapter

www.ablongman.com/marriageandfamily

- **Online Study Guide with Practice Tests**
- **PowerPoint Chapter Outlines**
- **Links to Marriage and Family Websites**
- **ContentSelect Research Database**
- **Self-Assessment Activities**

Further Reading

Books

Arrendell, Terry (Editor). *Contemporary Parenting Challenges and Issues*. Newbury Park, CA: Sage, 1997. A collection of papers written by scholars from a variety of disciplines that examine and attempt to redefine today's parenting roles.

Booth, Alan, and Crouter, Ann. *Men in Families: When Do They Get Involved? What Difference Does It Make?* Mahwah, NJ: Erlbaum, 1998. Examines the conditions under which men participate more fully in their family roles.

Chase, Susan, and Rogers, Mary. *Mothers and Children: Feminist Analysis and Personal Narratives*. New Brunswick, NJ: Rutgers University Press, 2001. A feminist exploration of mothers, mothering, and motherhood combining evaluations of empirical and theoretical work with personal narratives by mothers or caregivers.

Corsaro, William. *The Sociology of Childhood*. Thousand Oaks, CA: Pine Forge Press, 1997. One of the first major works in the "new" sociology of childhood which outlines an interpretive approach to understanding children's lives.

Dowd, Nancy. *Redefining Fatherhood*. New York: New York University Press, 2000. An analysis of contemporary fatherhood centered on legal issues.

Galinsky, Ellen. *Ask the Children: What America's Children Really Think about Working Parents*. New York: William Morrow and Company, 1999. The first comprehensive study that asked children and parents for their views on work and family life today.

Harris, Judith. *The Nurture Assumption: Why Children Turn Out the Way They Do*. New York: The Free Press, 1998. A critique of research in developmental psychology which assumes that parental treatment is the determining factor in the types of adults children become.

La Rossa, Ralph. *The Modernization of Fatherhood: A Social and Political History*. Chicago: University of Chicago Press, 1997. An in-depth examination of the changes in ideas about men's roles as fathers.

Margolis, Maxine. *True to Her Nature: Changing Advice to American Women*. Prospect Heights, IL: Waveland Press, 2000. Explores the changing ideologies about middle-class women's roles and asserts they can only be explained within a larger material context.

McAdoo, Harriette Pipes (Editor). *Black Children: Social, Educational, and Parental Environments*, 2nd ed. Thousand Oaks, CA: Sage Publications, 2002. A collection of papers, many of which report on original research, highlighting the process of racial socialization.

Walzer, Susan. *Thinking about the Baby: Gender and Transitions into Parenthood.* Philadelphia: Temple University Press, 1998. A qualitative study of the ways in which women and men view parenthood and shape their roles around gendered expectations of parents.

*Content*SELECT *Articles*

James, W. "Placing the Unborn: On the Social Recognition of New Life." *Anthropology and Medicine* 7(2), 2000: 169–189. **[Database: Sociology]** James provides a comprehensive review of the infanticide literature within anthropology. Central to her discussion is the issue of the status given to new life: At what point in time is "life" recognized? When is "personhood" to be recognized? Rivaling moral, ethical, and legal viewpoints confound the issue.

McCollister, B. "The Social Necessity of Nurturance." *Humanist* 61(1), 2001: 13–17. **[Database: Sociology]** Suggesting a link between negligent infant care and adolescent violence, the author discusses the significant role breastfeeding plays in child development. The author hypothesizes that the one, central difference between children of the past and children today is the breastfeeding variable: ". . . the dismal truth is that, on the whole, babies received more and better care 25,000 years ago, 250,000 years ago, even 2.5 million years ago, than many do today."

Neal, J., and Frick-Horbury, D. "The Effects of Parenting Styles and Childhood Attachment Patterns on Intimate Relationships." *Journal of Instructional Psychology* 28(3), 2001: 178–184. **[Database: Psychology]** The child's ability to form attachments with caregivers is known to significantly guide intimate interpersonal relationships as adults. This paper sought to discover whether parenting styles affect interpersonal relationship qualities in adulthood. Neal and Frick-Horbury discovered that parenting styles do not necessarily affect one's intimacy ability or the perception of others' intimacy/relationship capacities.

Romeo, F. "The Educator's Role in Reporting the Emotional Abuse of Children." *Journal of Instructional Psychology* 27(3), 2000: 183–187. **[Database: Psychology]** As mandatory reporters of suspected child abuse, educators are trained to know and understand the behavioral symptoms of physical abuse; however, the indicators of emotional abuse may go unnoticed. Romeo aptly delineates the numerous passive and aggressive behavioral signs of emotional abuse and the abuse's negative impact on a child's self-image. He further describes the impact of emotional abuse on the adolescent's and adult's self-concept.

Parents and Children in the Middle and Later Years

I retired from teaching six months before my mother started to lose her vision and had to come to live with us.

She was 85 years old then, and I was 62, retiring early for health reasons. My brothers, who live in other states, provided no support financially or emotionally for either my mother or for me, not that we ever thought to ask for their help. My mother lived with us for eight years before she died. At one point, both she and my husband were in the hospital at the same time. I had accidents, once falling down a whole flight of stairs, and on several occasions was unable to even manage my own care. At least twice, we three stayed for extended periods at my daughter's house, because I was ill or injured. My mother also stayed with my daughter and her family, when my husband and I went away for a rare weekend trip. At first, when my mother came to live with us, she was able to join us when my husband and I went out socially; she was never the sort to give up going or doing anything, and she didn't feel that she was intruding either. She loved music, so we would take her to every concert. Afterwards, my husband would go to get our car, and my mother and I would wait for him together, with her leaning heavily on me. I tried not to let her know how hard it was for me and I still don't think she ever realized. In the last few years, as she became more disabled, we gave up trying to take her to the concerts and had to hire help if we were going out for an evening, because she was not safe staying alone. She began to lose her hearing as well as her eyesight and needed more and more attention. Near the end of her life, it became too difficult for her to come downstairs to the kitchen for her meals, so I tried to bring them upstairs to her bedroom. I have a severe tremor. In

Key Questions

1 Are the stages of human development (e.g., adulthood, middle age, old age) socially constructed or biologically determined?

2 In what ways, if any, have social change (particularly those that have affected women's work and family roles) affected intergenerational relationships?

3 As the world's population continues to age, what challenges will national governments face?

4 Will the gender gap in life expectancy in developed countries continue into future generations?

5 To what extent are elderly family members isolated from younger generations of their families?

order to carry a tray of food to her when my husband was at work, I placed the tray two or three steps ahead of me on the stairs, advanced a few steps and repeated the process. It was very difficult, but I felt that there was no choice.

Source: Brandler, Sondra M. "Aged Mothers, Aging Daughters." *NWSA Journal* 10(1), 1998: 43–57.

*T*he relationship between adult children and their parents is just one of several important relationships that change as families reach middle and later life. The marital and the sexual relationships of husbands and wives in their middle years and later are equally important. Since the family in middle life is typically composed of three or more generations, there are many relationships to consider.

Today, at age 50, parents can expect to live, on average, nearly thirty more years. The parents of these 50 year olds, who are, by now, in their seventies, might expect to live another ten to fifteen years. Given current life expectancies, young adults today, say those at age 20, might expect their parents to still be alive when they themselves approach 50. They may also expect some or all of their grandparents to be alive for some years after they reach adulthood. Perhaps for the first time in history, most young people today are likely to have known at least some of their great-grandparents.

This chapter is about family and marital relationships when parents reach the middle and later years of life. We begin by discussing the important process of adult children leaving their parents' home—a process that may have many false starts as children sometimes return home again. This is followed by a discussion of how young adults relate to their middle-aged parents, and how middle-aged couples often serve as a bridge between the older and younger generations. We then consider the marital and sexual relationships of couples in middle and later life. The interactions between middle-aged people and their elderly parents, and between grandparents and grandchildren receive our attention at the end of the chapter.

Parents and Children in the Launching Stage

A key period in the relationship between parents and their children occurs in late adolescence, when the younger generation prepares to make the transition to adulthood. This period of family life is often referred to as the **launching stage.** One question that is of interest to many parents and their children pertains to the age at which launching typically occurs. When, in effect, does adulthood begin? How old are parents when their children are launched? It is important to keep in mind that both parents and their children are engaged in ongoing developmental pathways at any particular point in time. This means that when we consider the launching stage we must consider the developmental tasks of the parents as well as of their children. When do parental responsibilities to children end? What are the needs or concerns of parents who are in the launching stage of family life? Some may be in the peak years of their careers, with maximum occupational demands as well as maximum economic rewards. Others may be approaching retirement. Some parents of young adult children may be caring for elderly grandparents. These questions are important because the successful navigation through the transition to adulthood involves the development of functional and attitudinal autonomy from parents while maintaining positive relationships with them. We discuss autonomy and attachment in more detail later in this section.

Transition to Adulthood

Someone once said that "pinning down the threshold to adulthood is about as difficult as pinning Jello to a wall." In some societies there are clear markers for adulthood. Often these are tied to puberty (sexual maturity and the ability to reproduce). Religious ceremonies such as the bar or bat mitzvah emerged from biological definitions of adulthood. American ideas about adulthood have undergone substantial changes over the past 100 years. Early in the twentieth century, compulsory education led to the development of a standardized life course (that is, people were expected to undergo life transitions at specific ages). But this strictly aged-based definition of human development has given way to more individualized definitions, in large part because the conventional age-based legal markers of adulthood often conflict with each other. For instance, teens who marry before age 18 (which they can only do with their parents' consent in most states) can engage in sexual activity, but they cannot legally watch X-rated films. Other examples include the right to buy a car before you are old enough to legally drive one; and the right to *buy* and drive cars before you can *rent* one (age 25 for many rental companies).

The legal and/or chronological definitions of adulthood began to change in this country in the late 1960s, when the first wave of the baby boomers were in their late teens or early twenties. This was the Vietnam era. The age of *majority* dropped from 21 to 18. In 1971, the twenty-sixth amendment gave 18 year olds the right to vote. This constitutional change was prompted in large part by two forces—the involvement of the United States in the Vietnam war and the low average age at marriage. Eighteen-year-old men were being drafted and sent to southeast Asia to serve in the armed forces; many also married and became fathers at about the same age. Yet until the twenty-sixth amendment, they were not able to vote. Clearly, social and cultural factors affect the prevailing definitions of adulthood.

Young People's Ideas about the Transition to Adulthood. When nearly 500 young people (some of *typical* college age and others well into their twenties) were asked to indicate the characteristics necessary for a person to be considered an adult, a number of interesting findings emerged (Arnett, 1997). In both groups of young people, the most frequently mentioned qualities reflected an individualistic conception of adulthood: accepting responsibility for the consequences of one's actions; deciding one's own beliefs and values independently of parents or other influences; and establishing a relationship with one's parents as an equal adult. In contrast, **role transition events** (e.g., finishing school, entering the labor force, getting married, having children) were rejected as signs of adulthood by a large majority of young people in the study. Rather than relying on these external markers of adulthood, young people today seem to recognize that the transition from adolescent to adult is more gradual and is best defined in individual terms. Often, the individuals themselves are best able to gauge the intangible differences they feel as they leave adolescence behind. When the college students in the study were asked whether they considered themselves to be adults, only one-fourth said they did.

Among the slightly older persons in the study, one-third said they were adults in some ways but not others. They were still "in transition."

In fact, the transition to adulthood now extends well into the third decade of life and is not completed by a substantial fraction of young people until their thirties (Furstenberg, 2000). In the past (and still in many countries today), marriage was the primary event that set in motion the various role changes that made up the transition from adolescent to adult: school departure; entrance into the labor force; onset of sexual relationships; and departure from the parental home. All of these role changes—with the exception of the onset of sexual involvement—have begun to occur at significantly older ages in recent decades. The average age at which young people are leaving school, for instance, is now close to twenty-one (reflecting the fact that more young people are attending some type of postsecondary education). Similarly, the age by which young adults have found permanent employment has also increased. Even by age thirty fewer than 60 percent of a recent cohort of Americans had worked for two years or more in a full-time job. As a result of this, young people frequently live in their parents' home at least episodically while they attempt to develop some occupational and economic stability. The median age at marriage has also increased by about five years over the past several decades. Finally, young people's permanent departure from their parents' home has been occurring at increasingly older ages in recent years.

ContentSELECT

Transition and Adulthood

Parents' Responsibilities during the Transition to Adulthood. During the launching stage the parent–child relationship ideally evolves into one that involves increased independence (or autonomy) and continuing emotional attachment (Baumrind, 1991). Finding this careful balance is what Collins and Russell call a **modulation of dependency.** The young person needs to establish a sense of self-competence and independence with the support and encouragement of his or her parents. Therefore, parents, as well as the son or daughter, have to adjust to a new definition of the young person who is approaching adulthood.

One mother of a son who was a senior in high school told researchers Jean Whitney-Thomas and Cheryl Hanley-Maxwell (1996) that she felt her job wasn't done. "Tell that to a 17-year-old boy who thinks he's an adult. I want him to fly—with a parachute. Some of this 'chute comes from school, some from home." The authors of the study were interested in identifying the critical dimensions of the transition process as reported by parents whose children were within two years of leaving high school. Three aspects of parents' experiences in launching their children were highlighted in the study: parents' degree of *comfort* with the transition; their *visions of the child's future* (e.g., whether he or she will be able to live away from home, get a job, have reliable transportation, make independent decisions, and build adult relationships); and their *satisfaction* with the education and preparation provided by the schools.

When parent–child pairs were asked to describe their relationships as they navigated through the transition to adulthood, interesting differences between the two generations emerged. Parents gave significantly higher ratings to the overall quality of their relationships than did their young adult children. Parents also rated their relationships more positively on specific dimensions as well, most notably on humor and closeness and on shared activities. They also reported less tension in the relationship. Children reported more arguments and fights and were more likely to believe their parents wanted more influence over their lives. On two dimensions of conflict and control, however, children reported lower levels than did their parents. Parents rated their levels of disapproval of children's decisions higher than did children, who may not be fully aware of their parents' feelings. Parents may try to keep their feelings of disappointment about their children's decisions to themselves. The older generation also described higher levels of overt disagree-

HEADline Bringing up *Adultolescents*

Millions of Americans in their twenties and thirties are still supported by their parents. . . . Whether it's reconverting the guest room back into a bedroom, paying for graduate school, writing a blizzard of small checks to cover rent and health insurance premiums, or acting as career counselors, parents across the country are trying to provide their twenty-somethings with the tools they'll need to be self-sufficient—someday. In the process, they have created a whole new breed of child—the adultolescent.

For their part, these overgrown kids seem content to enjoy the protection of their parents as they drift from adolescence to early adulthood. Relying on your folks to light the shadowy path to the future has become so accepted that even the ultimate loser move—returning home to live with your parents—

has lost its stigma. According to the 2000 Census, nearly 4 million people between the ages of twenty-five and thirty-four live with their parents. And there are signs that even more moms and dads will be welcoming their not-so-little-ones back home. (In a survey conducted in mid-March 2002) by Monster-TRAK.com, a job-search firm, 60 percent of college students reported that they planned to live at home after graduation—and 21 percent said they planned to remain there for more than a year.

Most adultolescents no longer hope, or even desire, to hit the traditional benchmarks of independence—marriage, kids, owning a home, financial autonomy—in the years following college. The average age for first marriage is now twenty-six, four years later than it was in 1970, and childbearing is often postponed for a decade or more

after that. Jobs are scarce, and increasingly, high-paying careers require a graduate degree. The decades-long run-up in the housing market has made a starter home a pipe dream for most people under thirty. "The conveyor belt that transported adolescents into adulthood has broken down," says sociologist Frank Furstenberg.

Beyond the economic realities, there are some complicated psychological bonds that keep able-bodied college graduates on their parents' payroll. . . . "We are seeing a closer relationship between generations than we have seen since World War II," says psychologist Jeffrey Jensen Arnett. "These young people genuinely like and respect their parents."

Source: Excerpted from Peg Tyre. "Bringing Up Adultolescents." *Newsweek,* March 25, 2002, pp. 38–40.

ments than did their children. Young adults may assume that if their parents don't voice disapproval about the ways they dress or spend money, they must approve. Overall, these findings support what is known as the **generational stake theory,** which proposes that family members who are at different points in the life cycle may regard their relationships differently. Younger family members, particularly those who are going through the transition to adulthood, may feel a strong need to exaggerate differences between themselves and their parents in order to achieve a clear sense of emancipation and to make it easier to leave their parents. Parents, on the other hand, wish to maintain the continuity between generations and may be motivated to present a more positive picture of intergenerational relationships (Aquilino, 1999).

Are children *launched* then, or do they *leave the nest?* The choice of metaphors has some significance, because each reflects a particular view of the process. To *launch* children is to send them out onto the seas of life, just as a ship is launched. Children *leaving the nest* suggests fledgling birds flying away.

Actually, both metaphors are apt in some ways. First, the launching metaphor has parents taking the action, whereas the nest metaphor suggests that it is children who initiate the move away from home. It turns out, in fact, that parents can impede or facilitate the departure of their children, and they do both, depending on their own preferences (Goldscheider and Goldscheider, 1993b). This is not to say

Many young adults today make their first move from home when they go to college.

that children are without a voice in the decision to leave their parental homes, for their preferences and expectations are also influential.

The nest metaphor evokes a further image of an *empty nest,* implying that the parents left behind are alone and lonely. But research shows that it is far from true that most parents feel lost and alone when their children leave home. The empty nest image also suggests that once the children have left they have gone forever, but many do return home, and not just to visit, but to live. Indeed, it is increasingly acceptable, especially among men, to live with parents *after* college as a way of saving money.

As we note in the following discussion, when children leave home they are sometimes launched by parents, but also they are often eager to leave the nest (Goldscheider and Goldscheider, 1994).

Long-Term Trends in Leaving Home.   Throughout the twentieth century, the three major reasons for leaving home were marriage, school, and the military. Getting a job and living on one's own were other common reasons men and women followed different patterns (Goldscheider and Goldscheider, 1994).

During most of the twentieth century, women's most common reason for leaving home was to marry. However, the percentage leaving for this reason has declined steadily since the late 1950s.

For men, the transition to adulthood has been somewhat different. In the past, many young men left home when they entered the military, especially during World War II and the two decades thereafter. Today fewer young men leave home to enter the military. Before 1930, marriage was also a major reason for men leaving home, but today only a small percentage leave home to marry. More leave home to go to school, but the major reason is to start jobs or simply to be independent.

The age at which young people leave home declined over the twentieth century. Figure 11.1 provides the median age at which cohorts of young men and women have left home during much of this century. The major decline in age came in the 1930s and 1940s, with the average age for both men and women then remaining at about age 19 for about four decades (Goldscheider and LeBourdais, 1986). This

Figure 11.1   **Median Age at Leaving Home for Men and Women, 1920s to 1980s**

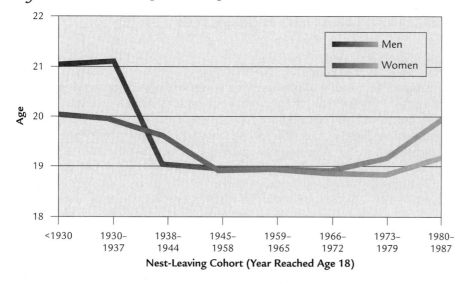

(*Source:* Goldscheider and Goldscheider, 1994, p. 18.)

same long-range downward trend was observed in other countries as well, for example, Germany, Denmark, Australia, and Great Britain (Buck and Scott, 1993).

However, beginning in the 1980s, there was a reversal of the long-term trend. Young men, especially, are remaining in their parents' homes longer than they did in the previous four decades (Goldscheider and Goldscheider, 1994).

Current Research on Children Leaving Home.   Recent studies provide a clearer picture of when and why young people leave home today. One major study was based on 60,000 high school seniors who were first interviewed when they graduated, and many were reinterviewed two, four, and six years after graduation (Goldscheider and Goldscheider, 1993a).

Expectations and Reality.   At the time of graduation, both students and parents were asked *when* they thought the children would leave home. Young people expected to leave home sooner than their parents thought they would, and as it turned out, the parents were closer to being right. Forty-one percent of young people thought they would be living away from home in two years, but, in fact, only 25 percent of them had actually achieved residential independence by then. Twenty-six percent of parents thought their children would be away from home in two years, so their overall estimate was much closer to reality (Goldscheider and Goldscheider, 1994). Some of these young people may have returned to live with their parents later, as other studies have shown (Aquilino, 1990; DaVanzo and Goldscheider, 1990).

Women Leave Sooner.   Women leave home at earlier ages than men, which is partially accounted for by the fact that women tend to marry at younger ages. But even when women are not marrying, and are simply establishing an independent residence, they tend to do so sooner than men (Buck and Scott, 1993).

Living Arrangements.   Most 18 year olds who leave home live first in group quarters (dormitories or military barracks) and then when they reach 19 and 20 they live with housemates. Thirty-eight percent of men and 33 percent of women experience this living arrangement at some time during their young adult years (Thornton, Young-DeMarco, and Goldscheider, 1993).

Group Differences. Religious, racial, and socioeconomic groups differ in the way they establish independent residence before marriage (Goldscheider and Goldscheider, 1993b). Young adults from higher social class backgrounds are more likely to live away from their parents than young adults from lower social statuses. Whites, Protestant, and Jewish young people are more likely to live away from their parents than Catholic, Hispanic, Asian, and African American young people. African Americans leave home at older age than members of other race and ethnic groups—nearly a year older than Hispanics, and a year and a half older than whites (Goldscheider and Goldscheider, 1994).

There are even regional differences in when young people leave home. Those who live in the southern region of the country are less likely to establish independent residence than young people in other regions of the country (Goldscheider and Goldscheider, 1993b).

Parental Influence. Parents use their economic resources to influence when their children leave home. They may, for example, try to delay what they consider to be premature marriages by their children. On the other hand, they may contribute their money to facilitate the departure of their adult children who have stayed at home too long (Avery, Goldscheider, and Speare, 1992).

Parents also influence, in another more indirect way, when their children leave home. When parents divorce and the custodial parent remarries, the children leave home sooner (Goldscheider and Goldscheider, 1993a). As a general rule, whenever there is a family structure that differs from the normative ideal (e.g., single-parent households, adoptive children, or those who live in foster homes, with other relatives, or in institutions) children are more likely to leave home before age 19 (Aquilino, 1991).

Coming Home Again. In the past, when most young people left their parents' homes to get married they were not very likely to move back in, except in cases of the death of a spouse or a divorce. Today most young adults do not leave home to marry, so there is more ambiguity associated with leaving home and living independently (Buck and Scott, 1993). In many families there is no discussion or decision that marks the first move away from home as a *permanent* move, so it is easier for children to return. The popular press has frequently published articles on "the return to the nest," and the "boomerang" generation (Riche, 1990).

Over the twentieth century there was a steady increase in the likelihood of young people returning to their parental home to live (Goldscheider and Goldscheider, 1993a, 1994). About 40 percent of young people who have lived away from home for four months or more returned home to live. Just as in the past, men did so more often than women.

The reasons for young people leaving home in the first place are related to the likelihood that they will return later. Those who leave home to marry are still the least likely to return home to live with their parents, but the percentage that does so has been creeping up. Military service, which is much more common for men, has often been followed by a period of living with parents again (more than half do so). Children who leave home to go to college or take a job return home to live between 40 and 50 percent of the time. When children do return, it is usually because of their economic needs or other circumstances—no job, not enough money, the breakup of a relationship, and so on (Ward, Logan, and Spitze, 1992).

Young people who leave home simply to be independent are more and more likely to return to live in their parents' home. In the early part of the twentieth century, only 10 to 20 percent of young people who left to be independent ever returned home to live again; today the percentage is between 40 and 50 percent. Even those who leave home to live with an intimate partner return home to live with their parents about 40 to 50 percent of the time (Goldscheider and Goldscheider, 1994).

Of course, when children return home to live with their parents, there are both advantages and disadvantages.

Disadvantages of Returning Home.   Many of the problems associated with returning home to live are caused by the ambiguity of the situation. Parents may wonder if they should establish and enforce rules governing their adult child's behavior (the most critical issues are curfews, guests, alcohol use, financial obligations, and so on). The absence of time-proven guidelines may lead to confusion, conflict, frustration, and stress for both parents and their children.

Both parents and their adult sons and daughters often return to the roles they played when the children were adolescents. For instance, children may revert to being emotionally, physically, and financially dependent on their parents. If they do, they are likely to find it stressful being "adult teenagers" (Shehan and Dwyer, 1989).

Parents are also likely to feel stress when their children return home to live. Children often return with special needs (no money, no job, no other place to live), and parents feel they have no choice but to help them out.

Parents are often forced to make changes in their daily routines when children return home. Their eating and sleeping schedules may be disrupted, and their leisure time diminished. They may be forced to take on such unwanted burdens as extra cooking, cleaning, and laundry. When adult children return with children of their own, the problems are further exacerbated.

In addition to the extra tasks, there may be financial strains caused by larger food bills, and greater telephone, electricity, and water costs. And conflicts between parents and children may also arise because of the sheer increase in household density. When children bring their household furnishings, recreational equipment, and clothing back home, the previously *empty nest* is more likely to be a *cluttered nest.*

Advantages of Returning Home.   Despite the potential problems that may arise when adult children live with their parents, both groups report that it also has benefits. For example, in one study that focused on children between 19 and 34 who were living with their parents about 70 percent of the parents thought coresidence worked out "very well" (Aquilino and Supple, 1991).

Parents may also benefit from having children living with them during their own times of crisis or illness. Adult children can provide general feelings of security and comfort. Young adults may also experience a feeling of security in the home of their parents, a security not easily obtained elsewhere. And when returning adult children have children of their own, grandparents and grandchildren experience a level of contact they could not otherwise enjoy. Grandparents in these circumstances often help in the rearing and socializing of their grandchildren.

The chance for a good relationship is increased when communication is open and there is goodwill on both sides. Observing the following guidelines can also help:

1 Establish—and follow—clearly stated house rules concerning division of household labor and access to family property and areas of the living quarters.

2 Develop a clear and mutual understanding of authority relationships, particularly if young children are in the home.

3 Reach a mutual agreement on the financial obligations of the adult children.

4 Guarantee all family members times and places where they can have privacy.

5 Adapt or discard inappropriate roles from earlier stages of family life. Create new roles through direct, open communication between adult children and their parents.

6 Develop tolerance for individual differences in tastes and viewpoints, since parents and their adult children are likely to have different tastes in music, television viewing, clothing, and hairstyles, and to hold different views about religion, politics, and cultural values.

Observing these guidelines can help reduce stress and interpersonal conflict as well as preserve the autonomy and privacy of family members living in the same household.

Almost all American adults do eventually live separately from their parents. They establish their own homes, and they maintain contact with their parents, but on a more limited basis than before. As they do, the relationship between middle-aged parents and their adult children may change again.

Relations between Middle-Aged Parents and Their Adult Children

Adult Children and Parents

Writer and humorist Mark Twain left his parents' home in his late adolescence, and when he returned home in his twenties he marveled at how intelligent his parents had become while he had been away. Twain's observation makes the point that whatever their earlier disagreements, children, as they get more worldly experience, are likely to see their parents in a better light. Parents, too, may see their children more positively after they have attained full adulthood.

In a study that explored the relationship between the generations, adult respondents were asked to evaluate their relationships with both their mothers and fathers when they were about 10, 16, and 25 years old. The evaluation was on a scale ranging from "very close and intimate" at one extreme to "very tense and strained" at the other. This research found parent–child closeness was at its lowest level when children were 16, but improvement occurred as children moved into their twenties (Rossi and Rossi, 1990). The improvement was especially great between mothers and daughters, an observation supported by other research (Fischer, 1986).

Daughters and Mothers

Studies of the relationships between adult daughters and their mothers have revealed four basic types of relationships (Fischer, 1986). **Mutual mothering,** the most common type, is characterized by mothers and daughters who have a mutual propensity to supervise each other's lives. Mothers who still view themselves as responsible for their daughters (and whose daughters accept this view) are referred to as **responsible mothers with dependent daughters.** Usually the daughters in this type are under age 25 and unmarried. In the third type, **responsible daughters with dependent mothers,** a relatively uncommon type, mothers are often emotionally unstable or have physical or medical problems. Their daughters take on the role of caring for their mothers out of necessity. In the final type, which is referred to as **peerlike relations,** mothers and daughters have developed a friendship. They take a deep interest in each other's lives but don't intrude beyond a certain point. Only a few mothers and daughters have this type of relationship.

Of course, some mother–daughter relationships do not fit any of these four types. But in general, mothers and daughters become close when daughters reach adulthood. Even though many report difficulties in their relationships during the adolescent years, they often grow closer when the daughter reaches her twenties, gets married, and has children of her own.

One example that illustrates this increasing closeness between mothers and daughters is provided here. In this case, the daughter did everything she could as an adolescent to shut her mother out of her life. Her mother described that period as "pretty bad." But then the daughter married, and the relationship changed. Even on her wedding day, the signs of change appeared. Her mother recalled the day of the wedding, and how her daughter cried nearly the entire time. And when it came time for her to leave on her honeymoon, it was nearly impossible to separate her from her family:

> It was time for them to go and friends were taking them to the airport. She could not leave. I am not kidding when I say they physically forced her in the car. "We've got to go. We're going to miss the plane." "I know . . . I know. Where's Jimmy?" (her brother). And then she had to come to see me first. And then she went to see her father. She went to Jimmy, who she adores. She's out of the car and I hear her scream: "I didn't say goodbye to Mummy!" . . . The fact that we have this beautiful relationship [now] is the high point of my life. (Fischer, 1986, p. 69)

When daughters become parents themselves, they often idealize their own mothers' parenting abilities. Young mothers can generally see their own mothers' qualities in the light of their own experiences. One daughter with small children expressed her feelings in the following way:

> Now that I had children I realized what she had been through. Before that . . . it just didn't dawn on me what kind of responsibility she had. (In what specific ways?) Well, her patience—she really understood. I never realized how much she did understand—what we were going through when we were teenagers and when we were younger. She was really almost, I consider, almost a saint. (Fischer, 1986, p. 74)

These positive sentiments expressed by adult daughters may explain why the mother–daughter relationship is likely to be the closest of all the relationships between middle-aged parents and their young adult children (Rossi and Rossi, 1990).

The Middle-Aged Couple as a "Generational Bridge"

When a couple reaches middle age, they may be called on to serve as a kind of bridge linking their adult children and their elderly parents. Because of its position between the two generations, the middle generation is sometimes called the **sandwich generation.** Often the middle generation is giving economic aid to both the younger and the older generations. The middle generation also provides emotional support and advice on a variety of matters. For example, middle-aged parents whose children are purchasing a first home may be asked for advice or financial assistance. The middle generation may, at the same time, be giving economic support to elderly parents. Even when elderly people have the economic resources to take care of their business affairs, they may still need help with confusing or incomprehensible bureaucratic regulations and requirements. Their middle-aged children may help them with Medicare regulations, supplementary health insurance programs, the Social Security system, insurance, investments, taxes, and other such matters.

Middle-aged parents also help their children get through difficult times in their lives. For example, children going through a divorce often turn to their parents for emotional support and economic assistance. Parents are often called on to inform grandparents and other family members about the separation and possible divorce of a grandchild.

Women as Kinkeepers

The middle generation also acts as a generational bridge by maintaining connections and communication between generations (Bengston, 1993). This task, which has been called *kinkeeping*, is very often a task that is carried out by women family members.

At *all* generational levels, it is women, in their roles as mothers, daughters, grandmothers, aunts, and nieces, who are more likely to maintain contact with family members and display higher levels of affection and intimacy (Rossi, 1993). Gunhild Hagestad (1987) calls women "the ministers of the interior." They carry much of the responsibility for maintaining family life and for intergenerational continuity. One demonstration of the work women do to keep families in contact is their use of greeting cards on holidays, birthdays, and anniversaries.

Women gain an interesting advantage from the fact that they generally act as the kinkeepers: People feel more obligations and greater emotional closeness to the women members of their families. Rossi and Rossi (1990) documented this pattern by measuring the obligations Americans feel toward various family members. They presented a series of vignettes to subjects and asked them to rate their degree of obligation to particular relatives. Two examples illustrate their method: "Your aunt has undergone major surgery. . . . How much of an obligation would you have to offer some financial help?" "Your cousin is going to have a birthday. . . . How much of an obligation would you have to give a gift?"

When women are the connecting links between two kin members, people feel greater obligations toward them. For example, children feel greater obligations to their mother's mother (maternal grandmother) than to their father's mother (paternal grandmother). The same pattern is found for their mother's sister versus their

Women are the kinkeepers in their families, providing companionship and assistance to those in need.

father's sister, mother's brother versus father's brother, and so on. Virtually without exception, respondents feel more obligations toward their mother's relatives than their father's.

Another reflection of the greater closeness toward maternal relatives is revealed in the way respondents rank a variety of relatives on whether or not they had been "particularly important to them while growing up." The rankings of importance always favor mother's relatives over father's. The lowest people in terms of importance are male relatives who are linked through another man. That is, their father's father and brothers are the least likely to be cited as "very important" in the earlier lives of respondents (Rossi and Rossi, 1990, p. 198).

Although women benefit from their kinkeeping activities, they may also pay a price, especially because they often end up caring for elderly parents. Later in this chapter we consider this issue, but first we turn to the marital and sexual lives of middle-aged couples.

Marital Life in Middle and Later Ages

Some cross-sectional studies have shown that marital quality is higher for long-term married couples than for couples in the middle years of marriage. However, longitudinal studies (following the same couples from their early years of marriage to their later years) show no increase (Vaillant and Vaillant, 1993).

One study, for example, studied couples who had been married for varying lengths of time, concentrating on their level of love as well as their problems. Love was measured by asking married couples about their actual behaviors toward each other, rather than just asking about their emotions. Researchers asked questions about "the things that people in love say to each other, do to or for each other, or feel for each other" (Swensen, Eskew, and Kohlhepp, 1981, p. 846). Couples who had been married longest had the lowest scores on this measurement of love. Other studies have confirmed this general decline in love over the years of marriage, especially for men (Peterson and Payne, 1975).

On the positive side, long-term marriages often show declines in marital problems. At the later stages of marriage, problems may be even less frequent than they are in the early years of marriage, a time when marital quality is usually highest. This is consistent with research showing that "negative sentiments" such as sarcasm, anger, and criticism diminish over the course of marriage (Gilford, 1984). Although couples who have been married many years express their feelings of love less often, they also express fewer negative sentiments.

Long-term married couples also experience increased levels of "positive interaction," which include working together, discussing things, laughing together, exchanging ideas, and having a good time together. As might be expected, couples in the earliest stage of marriage have the highest level of positive interaction. But in later stages, after the low levels of positive interaction in the childrearing years, it increases again, to an intermediate level (Gilford and Bengston, 1979).

In a study of marriages lasting fifteen years or longer, husbands and wives were asked (independently) to identify factors that best accounted for the duration of their marriages (Lauer and Lauer, 1985). One remarkable thing is that husbands and wives, in their first seven choices, selected exactly the same reasons, in the same order of importance. The two most frequently given reasons for the success of marriage reflected generally positive feelings about one's spouse—"my best friend" and "like [him or her] as a person." As one woman observed, "I feel that liking a person in marriage is as important as loving that person." It is worth noting that *love* is not mentioned by either husbands or wives as being among the rea-

Long-term married couples are likely to say that their spouses are their best friends.

sons for the success of their marriages. Some reasons, however, have nothing to do with the marriage relationship itself. They reflect personal values that tend to keep marriages intact, perhaps even when they are not satisfying: "Marriage is sacred" and "Marriage is a long-term commitment." The remaining reasons generally indicate that it is important for married couples to be in substantial agreement on goals, philosophy, and behavior.

Among couples who had been married more than forty years, on the average, the most important contributors to marital longevity included intimacy, commitment to making the marriage last, communication, and agreement on many issues (Robinson and Blanton, 1993). Husbands and wives in these long-term marriages gave sex a relatively low ranking among the reasons for their marital success. Yet most were still generally satisfied with their sex lives. In the next section we consider in more detail the sex lives of couples in the middle and later years.

■ Sexual Life

There are still many erroneous beliefs and misconceptions about the sexual interests and behavior of older people. Among the myths, which may have varying amounts of acceptance, are that older people are no longer sexual (have no interest in sex and do not engage in sexual behavior), that sexually active elderly people (particularly those who are unmarried) are abnormal or perverse, and that sexual activity in old age may be harmful (Palmore, 1981). There may also still be some taboos about discussing the sexuality and sexual behavior of older people, especially the very old. For many people, discussing sex among the elderly is an embarrassing, or even repulsive, topic.

It is clearly a myth that elderly people are no longer sexual or are uninterested in sex. Studies have shown that many, if not most, people from their fifties to their eighties, both married and unmarried, have an interest in sex and engage in sexual activity (Ade-Ridder, 1990; Marsiglio and Donnelly, 1991). At the same time, the amount of sexual activity declines as men and women get older. Both women and men, but especially women, are less and less sexually active *with a partner* after they reach age 50.

The lack of sexual activity with a partner should not necessarily be taken as proof that there is a reduction of sexual interest in later life. Many older men and women have less sexual activity simply because they lack partners. Many old people, especially women, do not have partners available to them for sexual intercourse. Those without partners can masturbate, and apparently many do, but they would be categorized as sexually inactive if frequency of genital intercourse were used as a measure of activity. Medical reasons, including the poor health of one's partner, also reduce sexual activity (Marsiglio and Donnelly, 1991).

A national study of *married* adults, 60 years of age and older, provides further information on the sexual activity of older people who have partners (Marsiglio and Donnelly, 1991). Married people were asked, "About how often did you and your husband/wife have sex during the last month?" Over half of those who answered the question said they had sexual intercourse at least once during the previous month. Among those 66 and older, the percentage that was sexually active was 44 percent. Among the oldest group, aged 76 and over, only 24 percent reported having engaged in sexual relations during the previous month. These figures do show that, as measured by frequency of sexual intercourse during the previous month, a substantial percentage of older married couples do not have active sexual lives. The percentage not having sexual intercourse increases as couples get older. However, a majority of all married people 60 and over are sexually active, and many have sexual intercourse more than once a month. One-half of all sexually active couples age 60 and over have sexual intercourse four times a month or more. The sexual lives of many elderly people are quite active, and clearly refute the myth of no sexual interest among the elderly.

A Broader Measure of Sexual Activity

Another perspective on the sexual activity of elderly people is that it is too narrowly defined. Measuring the sexual activity of older people by a sexual intercourse standard may be inappropriate because it is a "youth-oriented, genitally focused model" (Garza and Dressel, 1983, p. 105). Sexual relations among the elderly may not be described as well by frequency of sexual intercourse as by a more general standard of affectionate behavior that includes hand holding, hugging, caressing, touching, and other similarly stimulating activities. These activities are what one author has described as *sensuality,* as opposed to sexuality (Weg, 1989).

When a broader measure of sexual behavior is used, one finds that older people continue to be sexually active, although perhaps not always by genital sexual intercourse (Janus and Janus, 1993). Respondents in all age groups, from 18 to 65 and over, were simply asked to estimate the frequency of "*all* sexual activity" in which they engaged. Respondents who were 65 or over reported sexual activity at about the same level as the younger age groups. Among the older men, 53 percent reported that they engaged in sexual activity "daily" or "a few times a week." Women in the 65-and-over age group reported somewhat less sexual activity than men in this age group; 1 percent reported daily sexual activity, and 40 percent reported sexual activity a few times weekly. Some of the elderly reported little sexual activity, with 11 percent of the older men and 22 percent of the older women reporting that they "rarely" engaged in any sexual activity.

The general conclusion about the sex lives of elderly people is that sexual interest and activity continue to be a part of the lives of most, at least until advanced ages (75+). For those who do not have sexually active lives, the reasons may be as much due to external circumstances and a lack of opportunities as to a lack of desire.

Retirement and Marital Quality

Many people look forward to retirement with great positive anticipation because the stresses associated with work will be left behind. But a number of possible negative outcomes are also associated with retirement. Retired individuals may miss the meaningful activities they engaged in at work. They may also experience a sharp reduction in income and social status.

Identifying the impact of retirement on married couples is somewhat more problematic. On the one hand, retirement has been described as a period when married couples may once again experience a honeymoon stage. With their children launched, retired couples may have more leisure time to spend together, doing the things they did not have time for in earlier years. The alternative view of retirement and marital quality stresses that husbands and wives may be together *too much.* They may get on each other's nerves, which may lead to a lowering of marital quality. Wives, especially, may see the presence every day of their husbands as a mixed blessing, and may ask, "What do I do with him twenty-four hours a day?"

The research evidence suggests that the effect of retirement on marital quality may not be as clear-cut as either of these views. One study, using data from more than 1,000 men and 1,000 women aged 55 and over, did not find that retirement enhanced marital quality (Lee and Shehan, 1989b). Neither husbands nor wives reported higher levels of marital satisfaction in the early years of retirement. Rather,

Global Aging

The twentieth century witnessed a historical lengthening of the human life span. Over the last fifty years, life expectancy at birth has climbed globally by about twenty years to reach sixty-six years, thanks to advancements in medical knowledge and technology. Already about 1 million people cross the threshold of age 60 every month—80 percent of them in developing countries. The fastest-growing segment of the older population is the oldest one—comprising those 80 and older. That group numbers 70 million, and over the next fifty years it is projected to grow to five times its present number.

This demographic transformation, while celebrated by individuals and society at large, has profound implications for the quality of life, healthy aging, social integration, the situation of older women, and the provision of social services over the long course of life. These issues should not overshadow a troubling reality in parts of the developing world, where old age comes earlier for many people, who are worn down by poverty and disease. Prolonged economic and psychosocial hardships, compounded by the HIV/AIDS pandemic, have reversed life expectancy gains in some countries, particularly in sub-Saharan Africa.

Twenty years ago, the First World Assembly on Aging was held in Vienna. Already, the increasing number of older people and their issues were becoming apparent. The purpose of the Assembly was to bring much needed attention to the economic, psychosocial, and health-care concerns of the older person. As a result, the International Plan of Action, calling for humanitarian and developmental approaches to aging, was developed. Since then, additional factors have arisen, for example, the impact of HIV/AIDS on the aging.

In April 2002, a Second World Assembly on Aging was held in Madrid. Representatives from over 160 countries and international organizations met to discuss common problems and solutions. The Plan of Action calls for changes in attitudes; in national and international policies; and in community, corporate, and organizational practices, so that the positive aspects of aging in the twenty-first century are fulfilled. It seeks to ensure that people everywhere can age with security and dignity and continue to participate in their societies as citizens with full rights. The Plan's recommendations for action are organized according to three priorities: older persons and development; advancing health and well-being into old age; and ensuring

wives who continued to work after their husbands retired had significantly lower levels of marital satisfaction than other wives. Marital quality seems to suffer when a husband retires first while his wife continues to work (Lee and Shehan, 1989b).

The lower marital satisfaction of wives who are still working after their husbands have retired may come from their dissatisfaction with the division of household labor. Previous research has shown that husbands increase their household work only slightly when they retire, and this holds true even when their wives are still employed. Employed wives may view the limited household contributions of their retired husbands as inequitable and therefore be less satisfied with their marriages (Ward, 1993). One study found that husbands who retired while their wives continued to work felt more dependent on the marriage than did their wives (Szinovacz and Harpster, 1993). This situation could mean that retired husbands whose wives continue working feel a loss of power in the marital relationship. This, too, could contribute to a decrease in marital satisfaction, in this case on the part of the husbands.

In general, the studies just described, as well as others, have not shown that retirement is associated with a general decline in marital quality or satisfaction (except when a husband retires while his wife continues to work). Nor has research shown that retirement improves marital quality. In all likelihood, those couples who have had uneasy or difficult relationships during their working years will continue to experience marital problems after retirement. Couples who have had enabling and supportive environments. The recommendations reflect the central themes of the Plan of Action:

- The achievement of secure aging—to reaffirm the goal of eradicating poverty in old age and to build on the United Nations Principles for Older Persons;
- Empowerment of older persons to participate fully and effectively in the social, economic, and political lives of their societies;
- Provision of opportunities for individual development, self-fulfillment, and well-being throughout life as well as in late life;
- Guaranteeing the economic, social, and cultural rights of older persons as well as their civil and political rights;
- Commitment to gender equality in older persons through elimination of gender-based discrimination;
- Recognition of the crucial importance of intergenerational interdependence, solidarity, and reciprocity for social development;
- Provision of health care and support for older people, as needed;
- Facilitating partnership between all levels of government, civil society, the private sector, and older persons themselves in putting the Plan of Action into effect; and

- Harnessing scientific research and expertise to focus on the individual, social, and health implications of aging, particularly within developing countries.

The demographic revolution has spawned intense debate about how population aging should be viewed. The longevity breakthrough must be viewed as an achievement, and the resulting accumulation of knowledge, wisdom, practical experience, and human growth should be put to productive use. The rapid aging of the population is occurring along with two other powerful forces, globalization and urbanization, and will have a profound impact on our societies—one that cannot be measured or predicted, but one that we should prepare for. Social planners must include policies for the aging population, which must be innovative, creative, and flexible and likely to result in new plans and strategies. The best possible society will be "a society for all ages" where opportunities exist for older persons to act as mentors and advisers, where the value of their experience and wisdom is irreplaceable.

Source: The United Nations Department of Public Information DPI/2264, March 2002.

relatively good relationships during the working years may enjoy their greater time together after retirement.

The Elderly and Family Relationships

The last stage of family life occurs when the oldest members reach advanced ages. Today that means 75 and older, an age group sometimes called the *old-old*. At this age, many people begin to decline physically and mentally and may require more support and assistance from their middle-aged children.

There are two major dimensions of the relationship between adult children and their elderly parents: (1) their personal and emotional relations; and (2) caregiving (physical and economic support).

Personal and Emotional Relations

The personal and emotional relations between elderly parents and their adult children are overwhelmingly positive. Approximately 90 percent of adult children say they feel "close" or "very close" to their parents (Barnett et al., 1991).

in the media

Older Adults and the Electronic Media— Providing Ties That Bind

Although most of today's older adults spent their youth listening to the radio, only 58 percent of individuals over 65 report weekly radio listening, the lowest percentage for any adult group (Nussbaum et al., 2000). When older adults do listen to the radio, they prefer AM programming, with its emphasis on talk radio, news, and public affairs (Nussbaum et al., 2000). Thus, while younger adults frequently prefer music programs, older adults enjoy radio programs that provide information about other people and content that may be used in subsequent conversations. With their interest in talk radio, older adults also enjoy the only radio format that has the possibility for direct interaction, which enhances the likelihood of interpersonal connections.

More important to those of all ages is television. The average adult watches three to four hours daily, and that frequency increases with age, making television viewing the most frequently reported daily activity of older adults

(Nussbaum et al., 2000). Widowed older people watch more television than their married counterparts, suggesting that part of the age-related increase in television viewing is due to social isolation; however, most of this change is attributed to the increase in available time that usually accompanies retirement (Nussbaum et al., 2000).

As with radio, older adults prefer information-oriented television programs—news, documentaries, and public affairs (Nussbaum et al., 2000). Older adults are the largest single group of regular news viewers and are more likely to watch local news than are other adults. News and nonfiction programs enhance the viewer's engagement in the world and connections with other people. In addition, news programs, with their consistency in anchors, provide a personal connection. . . . Unlike actors, news anchors always appear as themselves, allowing viewers to feel that they know and are

connected with the people who often appear for decades on their television sets. Consequently, when older adults watch the news, they visit familiar people with whom they have shared some of the great events of their lifetimes. Thus, watching the news can provide various levels of connection, including feelings of having personal relationships with individual news anchors and bonds with the community and the world. Interpersonal relationships also may be enhanced outside the viewing experience, because of the information one gains from such programs. Radio listening may provide similar feelings of connection for the minority who are regular listeners. In conclusion, radio and television are readily accessible and provide older adults with valuable connections to their world.

Source: Excerpted from Roberts, Pamela. "Electronic Media and the Ties That Bind." *Generations* 2001 (Summer), pp. 96–98.

Almost all elderly parents say they have positive feelings toward their children. Older parents may have a particular stake in viewing their children positively, because their children are the products of their upbringing and socialization. But there is another reason relationships between elderly parents and their adult children are usually positive. Generally, both parents and children *want* to have good relations. They therefore make an effort to avoid topics that create problems for the relationship. Elderly parents and their middle-aged children have learned through the years which topics are potentially explosive, and they carefully avoid raising them. Their conversations have "demilitarized zones" (Hagestad, 1981, p. 30). Perhaps to take the place of these explosive topics, family members learn to pick their fights. They can argue and debate issues, and perhaps let off some steam, but everyone recognizes that these are issues of no great consequence.

The different generations in families may also manipulate the settings in which they interact with each other, thus enabling them to minimize conflict. Hagestad (1981) reports that many people she interviewed could tell her exactly the conditions under which they could get along smoothly with other members of the family. Sometimes it might be alone with the other person, other times it might be in a group. Sometimes certain other relatives are used as buffers. There are some indications that middle-aged children and their elderly parents use grandchildren in this way.

Although the vast majority of middle-aged children and their elderly parents get along well together, for a small number there is continuing conflict between these older generations. Five percent of Cicirelli's (1983) sample of adults reported frequent conflict with their elderly mothers, and 6 percent reported conflict with their elderly fathers. The most common reason for conflict was that one party was critical of or intruded into the activities or habits of the other party.

Many elderly parents and their adult children acknowledge that, while they get along well, they might have more conflicts if they were to live together. This is perhaps why most older people want to live *near* their children, but not *with* them (Brody, 1990). In fact, only a small percentage of elderly people do live with their adult children. Various estimates suggest that between 10 and 15 percent of elderly people share a household with an adult child. However, this is a cross-sectional picture of shared households and does not reveal how many elderly people will live with an adult child at some time during their lives. When an elderly parent becomes extremely disabled, there is a much higher likelihood that she (or he) will live with a child (Brody, 1990, p. 31).

The fact that elderly parents typically do not live with their adult children is not an indication that they are isolated or alone. The myth of the *isolated elderly* has been demolished for some time. Most older people have frequent contact with at least one child who lives nearby. The majority of elderly Americans have at least one adult child living within ten miles of their own residence; for those with two or more adult children, the second closest child is usually within thirty miles (Lin and Rogerson, 1995). When elderly family members need assistance, the majority of the help they receive comes from family members (Brody, 1990). Contrary to a prevailing myth, there has not been a decline in family values or norms in the responsibility children feel for their aging parents (Brody, 1990; Rossi and Rossi, 1990). In fact, younger people report higher normative obligations for their kin than do older people (Rossi, 1993).

When adult children provide aid and assistance to their elderly parents, parents often feel a loss of independence and autonomy. Caregiving children often adopt a paternalistic stance toward their parents, which means that they intervene in their parents' decision making. From the point of view of the children, they make decisions for their parents when they believe it is in their parents' best interests (Cicirelli, 1992). Elderly parents, however, often resent their loss of autonomy and find it demoralizing. The ideal is a kind of shared autonomy, in which elderly parents and their children make decisions jointly.

Women as Caregivers

When parents reach the *old-old* stage of life, they may experience physical and mental declines that require someone to care for them. When parents need assistance, it is most often daughters and daughters-in-law who provide the bulk of the work. "Daughters outnumber sons in a ratio of approximately four to one as primary caregivers to severely disabled parents and are about four times more likely

*Content*SELECT

Intergenerational
Relation

to share their homes with a parent when the latter can no longer manage alone" (Brody, 1990, p. 35).

Why do women provide most of the care for elderly parents, in-laws, and other relatives? The most commonly offered reason is that caregiving is part of the traditional role that women have in the family (Aronson, 1992). Sons also help their parents, but in general they do those things that are most closely associated with the male gender role, such as money management and home repairs. Sons may also get involved when there is a major decision to be made. When there are no daughters in the family, sons take on somewhat more caregiving responsibility, but if they are married, their wives often take over some of the caretaking tasks (Brody, 1990).

Sons are often excused from caregiving because their jobs and careers are deemed more important than their sisters' or their wives'. One woman explained (or rationalized) why she rather than her brother had taken responsibility for caring for their frail mother: "But, you see, he's in a different situation. He's head of a company. He's under a lot of pressure. . . . So I'm not going to put a load of anything on him" (Aronson, 1992, p. 19). This same woman had a full-time teaching job, and was herself in poor health, but she nonetheless excused her brother from the responsibility of caring for their mother.

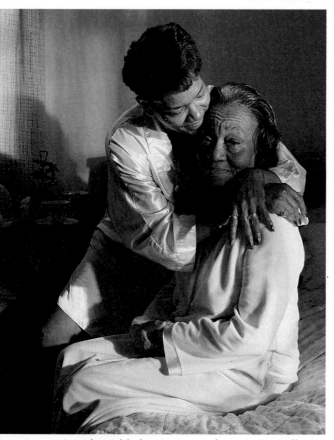

▲ *When elderly parents need care it is usually daughters or daughters-in-law who provide most of the help.*

When women are asked why they have taken on the major responsibility of caring for their parents (or even parents-in-law), a common response is "love and affection." Women may recognize their normative obligations, but as they see it, caring for an elderly parent is not based on obligations as much as their emotions and feelings. These feelings may come from gender differences produced by early socialization, which leads men to want more privacy and independence, while women are more inclined toward emotional connectedness with other people (Brody, 1990; Cicirelli, 1992).

The task of giving care to elderly parents often puts additional emotional and personal strains on women, especially those who are employed and have major responsibilities for taking care of their home and children (Stull, Bowman, and Smerglia, 1994; for a contrasting view, see Loomis and Booth, 1995). One employed woman described the schedule she had devised so that she could fit her caregiving around her job: "I would go over after work every day and feed them. . . . I would have to . . . make sure that they were having a meal . . . then on weekends go over and help them clean, take care of Medicare forms and things like that" (Stull, Bowman, and Smerglia, 1994, p. 323).

Some employed women find it necessary to give up their jobs when an elderly parent requires more help and time. They are forced to make a choice between their jobs and their parents. One woman said: "I began to worry about my mother at work when she began to do dangerous things. When she became irrational, I decided to quit. But I had enjoyed my career" (Brody, 1990, p. 221).

Other women find it necessary to forgo career opportunities altogether: "My boss said I had to work full time if he promoted me, but I couldn't. I had to have the time to take care of Mom" (Brody, 1990, p. 222). It would be unusual for a man to make this same statement.

A substantial proportion of caregivers, however, also receive help from the aging parents for whom they provide care (Ingersoll-Dayton, Neal, and Hammer, 2001). The four most common types of help elderly parents or in-laws provide their adult children are financial, emotional support, child care, and household help. For example, one self-employed daughter with two children described the give-and-take relationship she had with her elderly mother:

> Sometimes you feel like, well, you're exhausted emotionally after one conversation. But then the next one, they'll have some insight for you about dealing with your kids or something. So it's still, you know, it's still a really dynamic giving-both-ways relationship. (Ingersoll-Dayton, Neal, and Hammer, 2001, p. 265)

Another woman who cares for her mother and her own two sons, while holding two part-time jobs, also illustrates the kind of reciprocity she feels in her caregiving relationship with her mother:

> We rely on Mom, but it's kind of a two-way street, because she hates being alone. She can stay the night by herself, but she doesn't want to. Especially in the summer, she'll go every other night because she wants to have them (the children). They'll spend the night or work for her during the day or whatever. But that does help us out, too, because you don't have the sibling problems as much. You just know that they're kind of taken care of. (Ingersoll-Dayton, Neal, and Hammer, 2001, p. 265)

One woman who worked as a budget analyst had a frail elderly mother who required extensive personal care. The daughter described how she and other family members received financial reimbursement from her mother when they provided personal care for her:

> If you just go visit her, you're visiting her—but if you're there and you're doing the suctioning of her throat and changing her diapers and feeding (she's got the tube), if you're doing all that stuff, you're getting something for it. That's out of her estate—that's something she set up ahead of time. (Ingersoll-Dayton, Neal, and Hammer, 2001, p. 266)

Receiving help from the elderly family members for whom one provides care is often associated with costs as well as benefits. It is beneficial in terms of the quality of the relationships between elderly parents and their children. It is also beneficial in terms of improved ratings of oneself as a caregiver. But it can also be costly insofar as it can interfere with the caregivers' work because it increases the amount of worry for the elderly parents. Receiving monetary gifts or payments from elderly parents produces feelings of dependence and guilt for some adults. This appears to be particularly problematic for sons or sons-in-law. Child care assistance provided by elderly family members in return for the help provided by their caregivers appears to be most problematic for daughters or daughters-in-law, in terms of interfering with their ability to concentrate at work. These patterns parallel the traditional allocation of family tasks—financial responsibility to men and child care to women.

The Grandparent–Grandchild Relationship

One of the most interesting family relationships is between grandparents and grandchildren. In recent years, family scholars and researchers have devoted increasing attention to this topic.

The research consistently shows that there is no single or dominant way of grandparenting, but a variety of ways. It is usually the grandparent and not the grandchild who sets the pattern of the relationship, although at some stages in the child's life (adolescence, for example) the child may shape it.

Grandparenting behavior may change over the course of a child's lifetime. There is some tendency for grandparents to be closer to their grandchildren when the children are younger and become less involved when the children reach adolescence. Of course, the reduced involvement with adolescent grandchildren may reflect the priorities of the teenagers more than those of the grandparents. As many grandparents say about their adolescent grandchildren, "They are too busy," which seems to carry the meaning, "That's as much of a relationship as we are able to have at this time" (Cherlin and Furstenberg, 1986, p. 88).

Researchers have also found that grandparents seem to make selective investments in their various grandchildren, devoting more time and attention to those who promise the greatest emotional return. Nearly one-third of the grandparents in one study admitted that they had a favorite grandchild, even though making such a statement runs counter to the general norm of regarding all grandchildren as equal (Cherlin and Furstenberg, 1986).

Research has identified two distinct dimensions to grandparenting: (1) the closeness or frequency of interaction, and (2) the essential nature of the relationship.

Grandparent

Closeness or Frequency of Interaction.   Some grandparents are very involved in the lives of their grandchildren, interacting with them frequently. Other grandparents rarely see their grandchildren (at least some of them) and are emotionally and socially distant from them. Very often this distance exists because grandchildren live far from their grandparents. It can also happen because of the separation and divorce of the grandchildren's parents (Roberto, 1990). When parents and grandparents have not had a good relationship through their lives, the grandparents and grandchildren are also less likely to have a good relationship (Whitbeck, Hoyt, and Huck, 1993).

Essential Nature of the Relationship.   Many grandparents view their relationship with grandchildren as essentially one of fun and pleasure. They enjoy spending time with their grandchildren but they are ready to leave the tough work of parenting to the parents.

Other grandparents, at an opposite extreme, are intensely involved in shaping and directing the lives of their grandchildren, acting in many cases as substitute parents. African American grandmothers are more likely to take on surrogate parenting roles than white grandmothers. The greater involvement of African American grandmothers in the lives of their grandchildren reflects stronger cultural expectations for their doing so, as well as economic and family problems that require it (Kivett, 1993).

Grandparents may, in some cases, obtain legal custody of their grandchildren when the problems of their own children—often produced by alcoholism or drug addiction—leave grandchildren in danger (Jendrick, 1993). This is one reason why grandparents have sometimes been described as "family watchdogs" (Troll, 1983) or "safety nets" for their grandchildren. They are likely to get involved in their grandchildren's lives if circumstances call for it, such as in the case of parental neglect, illness, or death.

There have been a number of attempts to identify *styles* of grandparenting, based on these two dimensions. The following are the most common styles:

- **Remote-uninvolved.** The remote-uninvolved grandparents have relatively little contact or interaction with their grandchildren (often because of physical distance). Being a grandparent is not a central source of personal identity in their lives. The remote-uninvolved grandparent may do the things that grandparents are expected to do, but in a formal, stylized way; for example, giving gifts on birthdays, graduations, and holidays.
- **Companionate.** The companionate relationship reflects the fun and pleasure dimension, but in a very broad sense. It may mean engaging in conventional recreational activities with grandchildren—visiting theme parks, shopping,

TABLE 11.1	
What Grandparents Do with Their Grandchildren	
Activity	**Percent**
Eating together at home	72
Eating out together	65
Watching TV comedy	55
Shopping for clothes	43
Sports/exercise	41
Attending religious services	39
Gardening	29
Computer	24
Attending sports	20
Taking trips	17
Movies	10

Source: Waggoner, Glen. "The New Grandparents." *Modern Maturity,* 2000, March/April.

movies, sports—but it can also mean baby-sitting and occasional overnight visits. Grandparents in this style often say, "I can love them and then send them home" (Cherlin and Furstenberg, 1986, p. 56).

■ **Involved.** The involved grandparent engages directly and intimately in the life of the grandchild. Table 11.1 summarizes the various ways in which grandparents are engaged in their grandchildren's daily lives. In many cases, the involved grandparent shares a home with the grandchild and parent(s), but coresidence is not necessary for an involved relationship. The involved style of grandparenting can in some extreme cases be an interfering style, in which grandparents bypass the parents and their wishes. Involved grandparents might, for example, advise and discipline their grandchildren, even without the knowledge or approval of the parents.

Even though some styles of grandparenting may have negative qualities, the grandparent–grandchild relationship is generally mutually beneficial. In their study of grandparents, Cherlin and Furstenberg (1986) found over half (55 percent) fell into the companionate style, which seems to have the smallest potential for negative outcomes. Children, in particular, are likely to receive special benefits from having healthy relationships with their grandparents. This can be detected in the words of grandchildren when they responded to the question "What is a grandparent?":

> Granddad grows lovely raspberries and always pretends not to notice us eating them. (Tracey, age 8)

> She's the person who tells me all the things about my parents they would rather not have me know. (Sarah, age 15)

> Most of all she is a person who will always have time to see you when the rest of the world is busy. (Gill, age 14)

> (From *To Grandpa and Grandma* by Richard and Helen Exley, eds., cited in Tinsley and Parke, 1984, pp. 161–162)

In a small but growing number of families, grandparents are becoming the primary caregivers for their grandchildren. ▶

TABLE 11.2

U.S. Children Living with Their Grandparents

Year	Percent of Under-18 Population
1970	3.2
1980	3.6
1992	4.9
1997	5.5
1999	5.4

Source: "Speaking Graphically," *Population Today,* December 1999, p. 6.

These statements tell us that the relationship between children and their grandparents can be pleasant and supportive in a rich variety of ways.

Grandparents as Primary Caregivers.   Table 11.2 shows that the number and percentage of children who are being raised by their grandparents has increased substantially over the past three decades, from 2.2 million (or 3.2 percent of children under 18) to 3.9 million (5.5 percent) in 1997. By 1999, the percentage had dropped slightly, perhaps reflecting the declining birth rates among teens. Children who live in homes maintained by their grandparents are more likely to live in poverty than are children in traditional family households (Bryson and Casper, 1999).

The American Association for Retired Persons commissioned a study to find out how grandparents interact with their grandchildren—what values they want to pass on to them, what roles they play in their lives, and how they communicate (Waggoner, 2001). Over 800 grandparents were interviewed. When asked, "What do you think is the most important value or legacy you'd like to pass on to a grandchild?" the following answers were given: morality and integrity (42 percent); success and ambition (21 percent); religion (20 percent); being considerate of others (14 percent); and being a trustworthy person (10 percent). (Percentages do not sum to 100 because respondents could list more than one item.) Grandparents appear to be very satisfied with their relationships with their grandchildren. Eighty-one percent of the participants rated their relationships an 8 or higher on a scale of 1 through 10.

Widowhood

*T*here are nearly 14 million widowed persons in the United States. Seventy-five percent are over age 65. The large majority (80 percent) are women; given present trends, this will become increasingly true. Several factors account for this gender gap. First, women generally live longer than men. Second, wives are usually younger than their husbands, which contributes to their likelihood of outliving them. Third, remarriage rates after the death of a spouse are lower for women than men. Many men exit the status of widow by remarrying, but comparatively fewer women do this. The average age at which people experience the loss of a spouse is 56, but about half a million people lose a spouse before age 45 (Himes, 2001). Women typically spend twenty years of their lives as widows (Berardo, 2002).

The death of a spouse or intimate partner is one of the most stressful life events a person experiences. Most older adults are able to return to earlier levels of physical and psychological health within 18 months of their loss, however. The closer the marital relationship, the more depressed men and women are after their spouses die. Widows and widowers who are better off economically—as indicated by home ownership rather than rental—are more likely to be depressed than those who live in apartments or retirement communities. It could be due to the strains of maintaining a home on their own. It could also reflect greater isolation, loneliness, and fear of living alone. Women who were dependent on their husbands to perform *male* tasks (financial management and home repairs) are at higher risk of anxiety after the death of a spouse (Carr et al., 2001). Widowhood seems to be a more difficult experience for women because of their greater financial strains; but widowed men are in worse health, endure greater social losses, and have more difficulty developing social networks to replace the support and companionship that had been provided by their wives (Lee, Willetts, and Seccombe, 1998).

Bereavement and Anticipatory Grief

The initial stage of bereavement, for some people, is referred to as **anticipatory grief.** For some people, anticipatory grief may be as intense as the grieving that occurs after the actual death. It includes a range of emotions—depression, helplessness, anger, guilt, denial, confusion, rage, anxiety, and fear. For some family members, anticipatory grief may allow them to feel more in control of the situation, able to prepare for the coming loss and to say goodbye to their loved one in a special way. Others may respond to anticipatory grief by detaching themselves from the experience or from the dying person in an attempt to avoid the pain.

Santification. Many widowed persons report having ongoing conversations with the deceased, "checking in" with them, and wondering what they would think or do in a particular situation (deVries, 2001). They often dream of the deceased and believe that he or she is watching over the activities of those left behind. Sometimes survivors maintain, at least initially, a type of intimacy with the departed (Troll, 2001). The continuation of strong feelings of attachment to the deceased probably has positive effects in the short-term, but may have negative consequences over time because it can make it difficult to find a new partner who can live up to the image of the deceased (Lopata, 1996).

Grief counselors have noted that sometimes, in their attempts to be accepted and to appear to be *recovered*, survivors focus only on positive memories of the deceased and repress negative memories. This is referred to as **santification.** Repressing the problems one had with a spouse is an incomplete form of grief and can lead to **enshrinement** (excessively building memorials to the person who died). The opposite of enshrinement has been labeled **bedevilement** (James and Friedman, 1998). In the latter type of grieving, the surviving partner focuses only on the bad qualities of the deceased spouse and is unwilling to let go of disappointments and anger. This type of grieving is also incomplete and ineffective. It is difficult to complete the mourning and recovery process without examining and accepting everything about the relationship with the deceased partner (Berardo, 2003).

Social Support to the Bereaved. The extent to which members of the social network provide various types of assistance to the bereaved person is important to the pattern of recovery and adaptation to the loss of the spouse. Available confi-

ContentSELECT

Widow or Widower

dants and access to self-help groups to assist with emotional management can help counter loneliness and promote the survivor's reintegration into society (Dykstra, 1995). The American Association for Retired Persons has produced a number of guides (available in printed form and on the internet) for widowed persons. Community programs that provide education, counseling, and financial services can facilitate the efforts of the widowed and their families to restructure their lives. To be most effective, services and intervention programs must be actively introduced early in the bereavement process, since for survivors this period tends to be the most difficult and can affect later recovery outcomes. It is also important that the programs and services continue to be available to the survivors well beyond the bereavement period. Much of the variation in the response to bereavement comes from personal coping resources. A sense of optimism and a feeling of meaning in life is crucial to effective adaptation to loss. Other factors that influence recovery include self-confidence, self-efficacy, and self-esteem (Berardo, 2002).

Death Stories.   When gerontologist Deborah Kestin van den Hoonaard (1999) asked older women to talk about their experiences as widows, many spontaneously began to tell the story of their husband's death. The death stories typically had three parts: (1) learning that their husbands were dying; (2) taking care of their husbands while coming to terms with the fact of their impending deaths; and (3) experiencing the actual death. Being able to tell the stories seemed to give the women comfort and to help them cope with the transition from wife to widow.

Many women described the exact moment when they realized their husbands were dying. One began to comprehend that something was wrong with her husband when he started to act disoriented on a trip. Another knew that her husband had cancer, but didn't believe that he would die from it. The knowledge of a spouse's impending death can give the couple an opportunity to make the best of the short time left to them and to talk about what will happen to the surviving spouse after the other's death. One woman named Peg shared the following thoughts about the time leading up to her husband's death: "We realized our time was short. So we made the best of it. . . . We did some trips and enjoyed ourselves. And probably had the most serene and loving kind of relationship. . . . it was a time given to us especially." Having advance knowledge about a spouse's death also allows couples to console each other. Martha's husband wanted her to reassure him that she'd be all right after he died. "He used to say, 'I worry about you, how you're going to make out.' And I just said, 'Listen, don't you worry about me, right now our concern is you, keeping you comfortable and content.' And he was very content." As his death got closer, her husband told her that he wanted her to go on with her life:

> About two weeks before he died . . . he woke up and he looked at me, and I was sitting there, and he said, 'Do you want to talk?' I said, 'Sure, I'd love to talk.' So I went over and sat on the edge of his bed beside him, he looked up at me, and he said, 'I want you to go on with your life.' And I said, 'Oh?' 'Yes, I don't want you sitting in the house and moping around. I want you to get out and enjoy yourself.' I said, 'Well, I'll make out fine, dear.' I said, 'Our daughters look after that.' So he went right back to sleep, that was all he could say. (p. 63)

Women who are able to be with their husbands at the point of death often feel privileged to have shared such a special moment with them. Eleanor described her husband's last moments in the following way:

> A very peaceful death for him . . . he wasn't aware of anything . . . . We had gone to bed later on a Friday night . . . we were laying there, and he had his arm under my

The death of a spouse sets in motion a period of bereavement for elderly women.

pillow and his other arm around me . . . And about five minutes before he had . . . said 'I love you so much.' And then he said, 'I've got to move.' And I said, 'Have I got your arm pinched?' . . . And he said, 'No, I'm dizzy.' And that was it. (p. 65)

Those who were not present when their husbands died felt a great deal of distress. Betty, for instance, had been spending night and day in her husband's private hospital room. Her son encouraged her to go home for a night of sleep. She agreed to do so, once she realized that her son would stay by her husband's bed side. Unfortunately, her husband passed away while she was at home. She still felt a great deal of sadness about her decision to go home to sleep when she told the story of her husband's death several years later.

Women who cared for their husbands at home in their dying days talked about the emotional struggle and the sense of the accomplishment they felt. The following story was reported to van den Hoonaard by a woman named Audrey:

And I remember the last week, too, when they brought in the oxygen, and they had this computer thing for the pain medication . . . and I never wanted to be a nurse . . . I said, 'no way'—that wasn't my thing and here all this stuff in here. . . . and [my minister] came in and I said, . . . 'I think I've got to put him in the hospital, you know. I can't handle all this stuff.' And he said, 'No, Audrey, he doesn't want to go to the hospital' . . . and, of course, afterwards I was so thankful that I hadn't weakened. (p. 65)

What role does telling the story of their husbands' last days provide these women in terms of understanding their situation? It helps them make sense of their lives as widows and to hold on to their identities as wives. Becoming a widow means moving into an unwanted and stigmatized social status. Widows find that they have to develop strategies to maintain relationships with their friends, who may drop them when they are no longer part of a couple; with men, who may misinterpret their actions as a sign of interest or availability; and with their children, who may treat them as though they are incapable of taking care of themselves.

Summary

Because of greater longevity, most people today will live a considerable part of their lives as members of three-generation families. The relationships among generations are a major focus of this chapter, along with the marital lives of middle-aged and older couples.

Earlier in this century, young people, and especially young women, were most likely to leave their parental homes only when they married. Today young people leave their parental homes at younger ages and much less frequently to enter marriage. Women tend to leave home at earlier ages than men. The most common living arrangement for young adults, when they first leave home, is with roommates in group quarters. Young adults from families of higher socioeconomic status are likely to leave home at younger ages than those from families of lower socioeconomic status. Parents often use their economic resources to influence when their children leave home. Children leave home earlier when they come from family structures that differ in some way from the normative ideal.

During the twentieth century, there has been a steady increase in the likelihood of young adults returning to live with their parents after having lived away from home. Young men are more likely than young women to return to their parents' homes.

There are problems and disadvantages associated with returning home to live. Problems often stem from a lack of clear expectations on the part of both parents and their children. Sometimes children revert to being dependent on their parents much as they were during adolescence. Some parents may find it disruptive and burdensome to have adult children returning home to live. There are also advantages to children returning home, and research shows that most parents consider it beneficial. Parents can be particularly helpful when children have crises in their lives and need assistance. Parents and adult children get the most satisfaction from living together when they have clear guidelines that minimize conflict.

Whether or not young adult children live with their parents, there is ample evidence that relationships improve when children reach their twenties. Mothers and their adult daughters are likely to have the closest of all parent–adult child relationships.

Middle-aged couples are often described as a generational bridge. They link the two other family generations, often providing help and support for both children and elderly parents. The middle generation also facilitates communication between the younger and older generations.

Women at all generational levels are most likely to be kinkeepers, meaning that they maintain contacts with other family members and display higher levels of affection and intimacy. Because women serve as links between family members, family obligations are stronger through female relatives.

Although some cross-sectional studies have found increases in marital quality in long-term marriages, longitudinal studies have generally found no such increase. The level of love, or expressions of love, are likely to be relatively low among couples who have been married many years. However, long-term married couples report relatively few marital problems and fewer negative sentiments. Long-term married couples are most likely to attribute their marital longevity to friendship, liking, agreement on important issues, and a strong commitment to marriage itself. Love and sex are not considered important factors in the stability of long-term marriages.

Yet, it is clearly a myth that all elderly people lose interest in sex. Studies show that sexual activity decreases as people get beyond age 50, but the decreases are as likely to be due to the lack of a partner and ill health as to a lack of interest. Older people may engage in sexual activity, but it may involve activities other than intercourse.

Retirement from the workforce has not been found to enhance marital quality as some have speculated it might. Marital quality does seem to suffer when a husband retires while his wife continues to work.

The personal and emotional relations between elderly parents and their adult children are overwhelmingly positive. Elderly parents and their children have usually worked out strategies and patterns of interaction that allow them to avoid serious conflict. Very few elderly parents live with their children, but most older people are not isolated or alone. Most have children who live nearby and visit often. When elderly parents require care, it is usually women family members who provide it.

The grandparent–grandchild relationship varies greatly. Some grandparents are very involved in the lives of their grandchildren, while others are more remote and uninvolved. Children are especially likely to receive special benefits from healthy relationships with their grandparents.

Key Terms

Anticipatory grief (p. 363)

Bedevilment (p. 363)

Companionate style of grandparenting (p. 360)

Enshrinement (p. 363)

Generational stake theory (p. 343)

Involved style of grandparenting
   (p. 361)

Launching stage (p. 340)

Modulation of dependency (p. 342)

Mutual mothering (p. 348)

Peerlike mother–daughter
   relationships (p. 348)

Remote-uninvolved style of
   grandparenting (p. 360)

Responsible daughters with
   dependent mothers (p. 348)

Responsible mothers with
   dependent daughters (p. 348)

Role transition events (p. 341)

Sandwich generation (p. 349)

Santification (p. 363)

Review Questions

1. What are the key challenges faced by parents and their children as they go through the transition to adulthood?

2. What are the differences between young adults and their parents in perceptions of their relationships? How does the generational stake theory account for their differences?

3. Describe the changes in ages at which young people leave their parents' homes to live independently? Why have the average ages changed over the twentieth century?

4. What are the factors that are associated with young adult children moving back to live in their parents' homes? What are the advantages and disadvantages of this living situation? What guidelines were given to families in this situation?

5. Describe the quality of the relationship between middle-aged parents and their adult children? What types of relationships between mothers and daughters in this stage have been identified?

6. What are the demands and rewards experienced by family members who are part of the sandwich generation? Describe the benefits and costs of kinkeeping? What feelings of obligation and affection are experienced by women who fill kinkeeping roles?

7. What factors contribute to the success of long-term marriages?

8. How and why does sexual activity change with age?

9. How and why does retirement affect marital satisfaction?

10. What is the quality of the emotional relationships between elderly family members and younger members? What type of aid and assistance is exchanged between the middle and older generations? To what extent are elderly persons in the United States isolated from their children and other family members?

11. To what extent is elder care a female responsibility? What accounts for this pattern?

12. Discuss the two major dimensions of the grandparent–grandchild relationship.

13. Describe the three styles of grandparenting.

14. What values do grandparents wish to pass on to their grandchildren, according to a recent national survey?

15. How many widowed persons are there in the United States? What proportion are over age 65? Why is there a gender difference in the number of widowed persons?

16. How and why is economic well-being associated with a person's adjustment to widowhood?

17. What are the major components of widows' stories about their husbands' deaths? What functions does telling these stories fill for widows?

Critical Thinking Questions

1. To what extent are the stages of individual development determined by biology? To what extent are they shaped by societal forces? What are some of the societal forces that have contributed to the lengthening of adolescence and the postponement of adulthood?

2. Recent changes in federal policies regarding funding to teens who are pregnant require unwed teen mothers to live in their parents' homes. In what ways would this policy benefit teen parents? How might it hurt teen parents? How might this policy change the dynamics of the teen's family?

3. A few decades ago, the elderly were the most disadvantaged group in our society. Today, the elderly are much better off than they were and children have become the most disadvantaged group. Some social commentators have said that children are pitted against the elderly in terms of our nation's priorities. Do you agree or disagree with this statement?

4. Some psychological research has found that men and women's personalities converge as they approach middle and later life. What factors might account for this change?

5. Why is the role of widow so difficult for elderly women in our society and others? Why do some societies treat widows as "second class citizens?"

Online Resources Available for This Chapter

www.ablongman.com/marriageandfamily
- Online Study Guide with Practice Tests
- PowerPoint Chapter Outlines
- Links to Marriage and Family Websites
- ContentSelect Research Database
- Self-Assessment Activities

Further Reading

Books

Bedford, Victoria H., and Blieszner, Rosemary. *Handbook of Aging and the Family.* Westport, CT: Greenwood Publishing Group, 1995. A comprehensive overview of theory and research on family relationships, the contexts of family life, and major turning points in late-life families.

Bengtson, Vern L., Kim, Kyong-Dong, Myers, G., and Eun, Ki-Soo. *Aging in East and West: Families, States, and the Elderly.* New York: Springer, 2000. A comprehensive analysis of recent developments among six Eastern and Western nations concerning population aging and its consequences.

Brubaker, Timothy H. *Families & Aging* (Vision 2010 Series, Volume 4, no. 1). Minneapolis: National Council on Family Relations, 1996. Addresses the impact of divorce, health, housing, ethnic racial diversity, disabilities, economics, and care taking on the elderly and their families.

Burton, Linda. *Families and Aging (Generations and Aging Series).* Amityville, NY: Baywood Publishing Company, 1993. Provides a research perspective on the heterogeneity of later life and offers resources for family members and clinicians who deal with elderly persons.

Logan, John R. and Spitze, Glenna D. *Family Ties: Enduring Relations between Parents and Their Grown Children.* Philadelphia: Temple University Press, 1996. Examines the way relationships between parents and their adult children remain strong in the midst of social change.

Lopata, Helena Z. *Current Widowhood: Myths & Realities (Understanding Families).* Thousand Oaks, CA: Sage Publications, 1996. Explores the myths and assumptions that surround widowhood, looking at the situation of widows in various places and times, and discusses emotional issues, identity, roles, and support systems.

Merrill, Deborah. *Caring for Elderly Parents.* Dover, MA: Auburn House Publishing, 1997. Based on open-ended interviews with adult children and children-in-law, this book documents how people from the working and middle classes manage to provide care for their frail, elderly parents while simultaneously meeting the obligations of their jobs and their immediate families.

Ryff, Carol D. (ed.). *The Parental Experience in Midlife*. John D. and Catherine T. MacArthur Foundation Series on Mental Health and Development. Chicago: University of Chicago Press, 1996. Distinguished scholars from anthropology, demography, economics, psychology, social work, and sociology examine the ways in which the parental experience affects the health, well-being, and development of individuals.

Szinovacz, Maximiliane (ed.). *Handbook on Grandparenthood*. Westport, CT: Greenwood Publishing Company, 1998. Offers critical reviews of historical, cultural, racial, and gender-based variations in grandparenthood; contingencies associated with grandparenthood (e.g., transitions, roles, influence, divorce, surrogate parenting); and interventions available to grandparents.

*Content*SELECT *Articles*

Benight, C., Flores, J., and Tashiro, T. "Bereavement Coping Self-efficacy in Cancer Widows." *Death Studies* 25(97), 2000: 97–125. [Database: Psychology] Understanding that varying coping strategies impact the psychological, physical, and spiritual well-beings of individuals following the death of a spouse, Benight et al. expand upon social cognitive theory to examine *bereavement coping self-efficacy*. BCSE is that self-reflective mechanism by which the bereaved attempts to determine an expected or desired outcome following the death of a spouse. Studying 101 widows of cancer victims, the investigators examined a number of variables, including social support, marital satisfaction, anticipatory bereavement, current life stressors, emotional distress, subjective physical health, and psychological well-being. Benight and his colleagues determined that BCSE was significant in determining emotional distress and psychological and spiritual well-being in the first 12 months following the death of a spouse.

Erickson, M. "Re-visioning the Family Life Cycle Theory and Paradigm in Marriage and Family Therapy." *American Journal of Family Therapy* 26(4), 1998: 341–356. [Database: Psychology] In a cry to critically re-examine the usefulness and utility of the family life cycle in theorizing and family therapy practice, Erickson attempts to articulate the problems inherent with the family life cycle paradigm.

Heywood, E. M. "Custodial Grandparents and Their Grandchildren" *Family Journal* 7(4), 1999: 367–373. [Database: Psychology] Currently nearly one and one half million children in the United States are being cared for and reared by grandparents in the absence of their biological parents. Assuming the children's emotional, social, and financial continuity of care, custodial grandparents place themselves at risk to emotional, social, and financial detriments. The author provides a comprehensive review of the current custodial grandparenting literature and calls for an effective family therapy methodology to best address the complexity of needs with which these families struggle.

Pecchioni, L., and Nussbaum, J. "Mother–Adult Daughter Discussions of Caregiving Prior to Dependency: Exploring Conflicts among European-American Women." *Journal of Family Communication* 1(2), 2001: 133–151. [Database: Psychology] Because daughters often assume a caregiving role for their aging mothers, Pecchioni and Nussbaum examined 36 mother–daughter dyads to determine potential caregiving decisions before the mother became dependent on her daughter. Four interaction patterns were studied: exhibited conflict between mother and daughter; use of control strategies; level of involvement in episodes of discussion [interviews with the researchers]; and regard [positive or negative] for each other. In short, the mothers and daughters in this study indicate a preference for utilizing solution-oriented methods in conflict situations. In turn, these strategies potentially enhance the relational aspects between caregiver [daughter] and care recipient [mother].

Ward, R., and Spitze, G. "Sandwiched Marriages: The Implications of Child and Parent Relations for Marital Quality in Midlife." *Social Forces* 77(2), 1998: 20. [Database: Social Work] Is marital quality impacted by simultaneous (and oftentimes competing) relationships between adult children and aging parents? Ward and Spitze, in a survey study that analyzed the responses of 2,129 married couples ages 40 to 49, sought to discover whether these members of the *sandwich generation* experience a reduction in the quality of marital relations in midlife. The authors conclude that combining generational roles does not appear to be problematic for midlife couples; in fact the sandwiching may actually enhance marital quality.

12

Families and Work

Fixing lunch in her motor coach on Saturday afternoon, Nancy Andretti, 37, doesn't seem worried. Her husband, a veteran NASCAR driver mired in a mediocre season, is off at practice, while Jarett, 8, and Olivia, 6, do crafts at the kitchen table. Renita, their nanny, plays with Amelia, 1.

Nancy grew up just three miles from the Indy 500 racetrack, but she didn't follow racing until she began dating John, a high-school classmate from a famous family of racers (Mario is his uncle; Michael his cousin). Now, after fourteen years of marriage, she leads the nomadic life typical of NASCAR families. More than thirty weekends a year she's piloted in their seven-seat prop plane from her Charlotte, North Carolina, home to distant racetracks. Once there, she joins dozens of other drivers' families in a private infield village of motor homes, which are driven between tracks by full-time drivers. The motor coach itself isn't a hardship: it's a $225,000, forty-two-foot air-conditioned model with a skylight shower and John's signature woven into the leather upholstery. But the schedule is draining. "It just beats you down and wears on you," Nancy says. The upside: many drivers earn millions.

Throughout the afternoon Nancy keeps watch as the kids migrate from Razor scooters to the private playground. She also watches a preliminary race on the motor coach's forty-two-inch liquid plasma TV. When a race car hits the wall and catches fire, Nancy barely glances up. Nasty wrecks are as much a part of racing as the deafening noise. John has been lucky so far. He's broken ribs and required surgery, but avoided serious injury. The Andrettis refuse to dwell on the danger. "You can't do anything about the risks, so I try not to get myself all worked up,"

Key Questions

1 Why are women's jobs valued less highly than men's jobs?

2 What changes in workplace policies and pay schedules will be necessary to close the remaining gender gap in pay in the United States?

3 What is the economic value of household labor? What can be done to increase men's participation in household labor?

4 What is the relationship between women's employment and earnings on the likelihood of divorce?

5 How does parental employment during a child's early years affect the child's later development?

371

says Nancy, who listens to the crew radio so she can hear John's voice if he's in an accident.

As the TV replays the accident, John, 38, comes in from practice. He's lived with the risks not only as a driver, but as a family member, recalling the devastating 1969 crash that forced his father, Aldo, into retirement. He says Jarett and Olivia have some sense of the risks, especially since his teammate Adam Petty's death, though they may not realize it could happen to him. "Why prepare them for something that's going to happen to everyone someday?" he asks. "Do you prepare your kids? Then why should I?"

Instead, they spend time trying to make life on the road as routine as possible. On Friday nights the kids sleep over with other drivers' children. Later they attend a birthday party at Motor Racing Outreach, NASCAR's traveling ministry, whose trailer serves as a drivers' community center. But it's hard to lead a normal life when Dad's a celebrity and Mom's picture is on boxes of Hamburger Helper. . . . Last year, the kids missed nine school days for races—a problem as they move to higher grades. "John wants to do this another ten years," says Nancy. The kids may not.

Source: McGinn, Daniel. "Married to NASCAR: Like the Wives of Cops or Fireman, the Women of the Race-car Circuit Spend Endless Hours Worrying and Praying. How Nancy Andretti Handles the Pressure." *Newsweek,* July 23, 2001, p. 46.

As this true story illustrates, work and family life are closely intertwined, and the pressures of one affect the other. What happens in the home influences what happens at work and what happens at work influences family life. Losing a job, being transferred, or having to work overtime or on the weekends are all likely to affect marriage and family life. Similarly, having a sick child or one who gets into trouble, having a fight with one's intimate partner, or planning a wedding can all interfere with job performance. These are but a few of the many ways in which work and family life can affect each other.

Sometimes work and family life are mutually supportive, but more often they conflict. The needs of families often call for one course of action, while the demands of work call for another. Women, in particular, have difficulty juggling work and family responsibilities because they must consider the needs of their partners, their children, and even their aging parents.

It was, in fact, the dramatic increase in the employment of women, particularly wives and mothers, that led social scientists to study the intersection of work and family. Before the 1970s, most social scientists considered the worlds of employment and family distinctly separate spheres. The world of paid work was the male domain, and family life, the female. Books on marriage and family life paid little attention to employment, occupations, or careers. Today, with the majority of adult women working both inside and outside the home, these topics cannot be ignored.

Employment affects family life in a number of ways. The most obvious is that it provides social and economic resources that can be used for household needs. Because employment is the major, if not the only, source of income for most people, families make sacrifices to meet the demands of employers even if it hurts family relationships. Families relocate to allow a father or mother to take a job with increased pay and status. Some families send teenage children into the labor force to increase the household income. Job requirements affect the *amount* of time workers have to spend with their families and the hours of the day or days of the week they are available. Employment schedules may take workers away from their homes on holidays, for instance, or cause them to be preoccupied with work even when they are at home. Employment also affects workers' attitudes, values, and moods, which may, in turn, influence the way they treat the members of their family. Job stress may leave little energy for a full family life.

Families, of course, also have a major impact on employment patterns and work organizations. First, families socialize each new generation of workers, instilling attitudes and values about work that affect children's occupational choices and job performance. The economic needs of families also act as a major motivator for hard work and occupational success. Finally, family demands influence the conditions under which employees are willing and able to work.

To better understand the ways in which employment and family responsibilities influence each other, let's take a brief look at changes in women's work over the past 200 years. We give particular attention to changes in women's employment patterns throughout the twentieth century. We give careful attention to the gender-based inequities that still exist in the labor force today, including gender labeling of jobs, gender segregation of workers, and a persistent gender gap in pay. We also examine a number of different types of work and family role combinations, including blue-collar couples, the *two-person career*, dual-career couples, and single-parent providers.

Another major focus of this chapter is the friction points between work and family. We also consider the impact of employment on marital power and decision making, marital satisfaction and stability, partners' mental health and well-being, and the impact of mothers' employment on small children. The chapter concludes with a discussion of social policies that are emerging to accommodate the work–family role system.

Work and Family Life in Historical Perspective

Women have always made a significant contribution to their families through their labor. Historically, all members of families contributed directly to household production, whatever form it took—working on the farm, making shoes, or running an inn. But as the predominant manner of subsistence shifted from hunting and gathering, to agriculture, to production of goods, and now to service provision, the nature of women's work has changed. Before the American Revolution, the colonies' economy was based on agriculture. Men were primarily

HAGAR THE HORRIBLE   *Chris Browne*

(*Source:* Reprinted with permission of King Features Syndicate.)

responsible for work in the barn and the fields, while women worked in the home, cooking, cleaning, and caring for children. Women were also the primary manufacturers of goods consumed in daily life. They spun and wove and made lace, soap, candles, and shoes, along with bread and beer. Some women also worked outside the home as innkeepers, shopkeepers, craftspeople, printers, teachers, and landholders. They also provided medical assistance, serving as physicians and midwives and producing medicines, salves, and ointments (Ulrich, 1990). In the southern colonies, slave women worked inside the owner's household as well as their own, and in the fields.

The Impact of Industrialization

The United States began to industrialize after the American Revolution. The first factory was built in New England in 1790. It produced cotton textiles. Women were drawn into the early factories to produce many of the things they had made in their homes. The typical women factory workers at this time were young, single, and relatively well educated. They saw their work in the factories as temporary—only until they married. Factories depended on these young women workers because men were still needed on family farms. Young women's employment was viewed quite favorably by the American public in the early days of industrialization. Alexander Hamilton, then secretary of the treasury, declared both women's and children's employment essential because it made them more useful than they would have been if they hadn't worked outside their homes (Margolis, 2000).

By the beginning of the twentieth century, more than 5 million women and girls over age 10 were in the labor force. The most common type of occupation they held was domestic labor and personal service. A substantial proportion of women worked on farms, and a small group worked in elementary and secondary teaching. Women were also employed in the trade and transportation industries as sales clerks, telegraph and telephone operators, stenographers, secretaries, accountants, and bookkeepers.

World War I (which was fought between 1914 and 1918) accelerated women's entrance into new fields of employment because there was a shortage of male workers due to their service in the armed forces. After the war, however, many women left the labor force, as many state and local governments prohibited wives from taking jobs that could be filled by returning veterans.

When the Great Depression came in 1929, the gains women had made in the labor force during World War I were lost as the few jobs available were given to men. It wasn't until the United States entered World War II in 1941 that women reentered the workforce and did so in dramatically new ways. First, a greater number of women became employed than ever before. Between 1940 and 1946, 5.5 mil-

Around the World

Labor Rights in Indonesia: What Is Menstruation Leave?

To create more solidarity between people in the developed world and Nike workers in Indonesia, U.S. anti-sweatshop activists Jim Keady and Leslie Kretzu adopted the lifestyle, diet, customs, and culture of Indonesian factory workers and lived on $1 a day (the average wages of the workers) during August and September of 2000. Keady and Kretzu did not actually get factory jobs but they interviewed factory workers and published daily reports about what they learned in order to draw attention to the experiences of the workers. The following information is taken from a report written by Kretzu on the issue of menstruation leave, which is guaranteed by Indonesian law.

Indonesian law states that every woman is entitled to two days unpaid menstrual leave per month. Anticipating that some might ask, "How can these women justify taking two days off from work simply because they are menstruating?" I posed the question to several female and male workers, labor organizers, and student activists. The consensus was that the menstrual leave legislation wasn't necessarily drafted for women with office jobs or other positions that are not physically demanding. The two optional menstrual leave days are believed to be aimed at the tens of thousands of factory workers who cannot freely go to the restroom throughout the day, cannot afford pads and pain medication, have mandatory overtime, and work 10- to 15-hour days on a regular basis, sometimes standing for the duration, just to survive.

The procedure to take menstrual leave in Nike's subcontracted factories is plagued with a degree of fear and humiliation that is so severe, most women would rather suffer than take the days off. The reality of the situation is as follows: First, the worker approaches her line chief. If the line chief gives permission, she can approach the foreman. If the foreman gives permission, she can approach the management. After making her way through this management hierarchy, the worker must go to the factory clinic and prove that she is menstruating. She must do this by pulling down her pants and showing blood to the clinic staff. She cannot take the menstrual leave that she is entitled to by law without going through this degrading process. As you can imagine, not many workers ask for the days off. With workers not taking days off, the assembly line is fully staffed, quotas are reached more quickly, and the factory provides for its contractor most efficiently.

The intrusive procedure of proving one is menstruating does not happen every month for every worker, but it does happen. Several of the women workers we interviewed, as well as the organizers we spoke with said it does not happen more frequently because the workers are too scared to even ask to go to the clinic. . . . (Some workers are afraid to take leave because they have to make a production quota and if they don't), the supervisor will get mad. A woman who takes menstruation leave will be hated by her supervisor.

Not only are the female factory workers intimidated in asking for the menstrual leave days they are entitled to, but most women are even afraid to ask to go to the bathroom. There is pressure to meet quotas and fear to not "get on the bad side" of your supervisor. The majority of workers know that simply asking permission to use the bathroom will usually result in their supervisor yelling at them even more. . . .

Union organizers and Indonesian student activists told us that it's not only in Nike factories where these conditions exist but also in factories producing apparel for the Gap, Old Navy, Tommy Hilfiger, Adidas, Fila, Reebok, and Polo, to name a few.

This degrading treatment violates human dignity on many levels. It is a blatant breach of Articles 5, 7, 18, and 23 of the United Nation's Universal Declaration of Human Rights. It is also in violation of the UN's Convention on the Elimination of All Forms of Discrimination against Women.

Source: Clean Clothes Campaign Newsletter (#13), November 2000. Accessed from www.cleanclothes.org/news/newsletter13-indon.htm on May 1, 2002. The Clean Clothes Campaign is an international organization devoted to improving working conditions in the garment and sportswear industry. It began in the Netherlands in 1990 and is now active in ten Western European countries.

lion women (nearly two-fifths of the female population) entered the labor force. Second, married women—even those with dependent children—entered male-dominated occupations. They became welders and shipbuilders, giving rise to the popular image of Rosie the Riveter, who became the symbol of employed women during the war. They worked as switch operators, precision tool makers, crane operators, lumberjacks, drill press operators, and stevedores. Finally, African American women found new employment opportunities beyond domestic work, which had been their typical source of employment in earlier decades. Performing *male* jobs, however, did not increase women's rate of pay. After World War II ended in 1945, there was tremendous pressure on women to return to their *traditional* roles as housewives and mothers.

Homemaker or
Housewife

The Breadwinner–Homemaker System

Historians agree that the so-called traditional family pattern with men as the family breadwinners and women as full-time homemakers emerged in the mid-nineteenth century. The exact date is not easy to pin down, in part because it is tied to the Industrial Revolution, which occurred at different times in different places. Before the Industrial Revolution, most goods were produced in the home or attached workshop, and all family members contributed. Under these conditions, the idea of a breadwinner was meaningless, since virtually every member of the family contributed to the enterprise. But when male workers started working outside their home for wages, the nature of family life and the relationship between spouses changed greatly.

The shift in men's and women's roles was most apparent in the years between 1860 and 1920, during which Americans' views about women and motherhood underwent a profound change. A new cultural role emerged, stressing women's moral duty and responsibility to remain in the home and care for their families. In the **cult of true womanhood,** women were praised and rewarded for taking care of their children and husbands. In return for their saintly efforts, they were to be provided for by husbands who brought home the rewards of their work in business and industry.

This cultural ideal of women in the home was reflected in the emergence of women's and homemakers' magazines in the nineteenth century. These magazines emphasized women's responsibility for maintaining the virtues of home and family life in a world that was harsh and corrupt. Women were also charged with rearing their children so that the next generation would carry on the best qualities of the culture. The slogan that was repeated again and again was "the hand that rocks the cradle shapes the nation."

An implicit feature of the cult of true womanhood was that the home and children served as a kind of community display for the husband's economic success. "The wife became a billboard for her husband's achievement, and the manner in which she dressed, the activities she engaged in, and the kind of home she managed all served to tell the world of her husband's success" (Gordon, 1978, p. 204).

Of course, the other implicit feature of the wife-as-homemaker ideal was that married women had status in the community only through their husbands. The breadwinner–homemaker system put wives in a secondary, dependent, and subordinate role in relation to their husbands.

The earlier system of patriarchy gave men the dominant position in their households just by virtue of being male; the newer cultural ideal added to their dominant position because they were the sole providers for the family. Women had no economic resources of their own and were totally dependent on their husbands' willingness to share their earnings. When husbands did provide for their wives and children, they gained power from doing so.

In the nineteenth century, immigrant women were often employed in "sweat shops" where they made clothing for the rest of society. The same practice prevails today, both in the United States and in less developed societies.

The breadwinner–homemaker system has been breaking down as women have been returning to the labor force, but the cultural ideology supporting the system has persisted. We need only look back to the decade of the 1950s to see this ideology in full force in U.S. society. In that decade, Americans in every social class believed fervently in the ideal of women working in the home and men earning the family's living. This was true although 25 to 30 percent of all married women were employed in the 1950s. Many of those working women, however, did so out of economic necessity, and when they had young children they were often plagued by feelings of guilt, for the prevailing ideology held that they should be in the home.

Throughout the 1990s, remnants of the breadwinner–homemaker system and the ideology that supports it persisted. Even though the majority of women are engaged in paid work and contribute to family income, men are still regarded as the primary providers in many families and are given special consideration and support because of this. But as women make significant contributions to their family economies, especially among blue-collar and working-class families, the ideal of the man as primary breadwinner is being questioned by both women and men (Rubin, 1994). Before discussing this issue further, let's look at the extent of women's participation in paid employment today.

Women at Work Today

*O*ver the past 100 years, the number of women who are employed for pay or seeking paid employment has increased nearly thirteen-fold, from 4 million women in 1890 to over 62.9 million in 2001. Table 12.1 shows this century-long trend. Part of the increase may be accounted for simply by the increase in the population of the United States and by an increase in the overall size of the economy. But Table 12.1 shows that the growth in women's paid labor force participation has more than kept up with the expansion of the economy. In 1890, fewer than one in

TABLE 12.1

U.S. Women in the Labor Force, 1890 to 2001

	1890	1950	1982	1993	2001
Total labor force[a]	23.3[a]	63.9	111.9	128.0	135.1
Total number of women in labor force[a]	4.0[a]	18.4	47.9	58.4	62.9
Women as percentage of labor force	17.2	28.8	42.8	45.8	46.6
Percentage in labor force	17.3	33.9	52.7	57.9	60.7

[a] In millions.

Sources: Data for 1890 and 1950 from Waite, 1981, p. 4. Data for 1982 from *Employment and Earnings,* 1983, p. 8. Data for 1993 from *Employment and Earnings,* 1994, p. 216. Data for 2001 from Bureau of Labor Statistics, 2001.

every five paid workers was a woman. By 2001, almost half were women. Women's paid labor has become a significant component of the U.S. economy. From another point of view, the increased numbers of women in the paid labor force over the past 100 years shows what a typical part of a woman's life paid employment has become.

Of most concern for couples and families is the increase in paid labor force participation among mothers, as Table 12.2 shows. Between 1980 and 2000, the paid labor force participation rates of mothers of school-aged children increased from 64 to 79 percent. The rate for mothers of preschool children increased, as well, from 46.8 to 65.3 percent.

One explanation for the increase in the number of female workers attributes it to changes in the economy. As the U.S. economy grew during the twentieth century and shifted from the manufacture of goods (which had become male dominated) to the provision of services (which is female dominated), the demand for women's labor increased substantially. The supply of *traditional* women workers (young, single women) was not sufficient, which meant a greater call for other women to enter the labor force. The first women added to the labor force in the 1940s, were those whose children were older. But the economy continued to add service sector jobs, and once again the demand for women workers outstripped the supply. The last group of women to join the labor force in large numbers was mothers of young children. This began in the 1950s and gained momentum in the 1960s and 1970s, when 1 million women entered or reentered the labor force each year.

TABLE 12.2

Labor Force Participation Rates of Women by Presence and Age of Children, 1980 to 2000

	1980	1990	2000
Total (all women)	51.1	57.2	60.7
No children under 18	48.1	52.3	54.8
Children 6 to 18	64.3	74.7	79.0
Children under 6	46.8	58.2	65.3

Source: Bureau of Labor Statistics, 2001.

In summary, the continued economic development of the United States—from an agricultural to a goods-producing and, most recently, to a service-providing economy—has increased the demand for female labor. This, along with basic demographic shifts in the supply of women, has caused a considerable increase in female labor force participation since World War II.

Where once women dropped out of the paid labor force when they married, never to return, today women are likely to leave the paid labor force for only short periods of time, if they leave at all. When women's paid labor force participation patterns over the life cycle are graphed, the characteristic U-shape (reflecting high rates in the young adult stages before childbearing, low rates in the childrearing years, and higher rates among women with older children) has all but disappeared. Women no longer automatically leave the labor force on marriage or childbirth.

The work histories of women born during the early years of the baby boom (1946 through 1956) are particularly informative because these women came of age during the late 1960s and 1970s, when dramatic changes were occurring in women's options and life patterns, such as expanding job opportunities for women and increasing marital instability (Gerson, 1987, p. 39). Studies of this generation of women, which includes both Hillary Clinton and Tipper Gore, and perhaps your own mothers, can show us how personal preferences and societal conditions interact to determine the path a particular woman takes through adulthood (Rexroat and Shehan, 1984; Gerson, 1987). Different life pathways develop as the social and economic conditions encountered in adulthood either prevent or help women actualize their childhood aspirations.

Some baby boom women, of course, developed traditional aspirations in childhood. They hoped to devote their time and energies in adulthood to full-time homemaking, fully expecting to marry and raise children. Some of these women were able to actualize their childhood plans, but others encountered unstable relationships with male partners, economic pressures in the household, disappointment with motherhood and full-time homemaking, or unexpected job opportunities that pushed them into the labor force.

Other baby boom women developed nontraditional aspirations for adult life while still in childhood. Even as children they rejected the traditional homemaker role, and once they reached adulthood they sought meaningful employment outside their homes. Some of these, however, encountered hostile circumstances in the workplace that turned them away from employment and back toward the home and the traditional role they had originally rejected.

Four aspects of the societal context, then, are especially important in determining whether a woman's childhood goals are actualized or thwarted in adulthood: (1) a stable relationship with a male partner; (2) economic necessity for employment; (3) job opportunities; and (4) perceived rewards and costs of full-time homemaking (Gerson, 1987).

A stable relationship with a male partner, and the male partner's attitude toward bearing and rearing children, affect the woman's perceptions of her need for economic independence. On the one hand, the amount of income he provides determines whether she enters the labor market out of choice or economic necessity. On the other hand, if the relationship is unstable, the woman may not feel she can depend on her partner. She may decide that she must earn her own income, even pursuing an unsatisfying job if necessary. Pressure from male partners may push some women who are ambivalent about motherhood into having children. In some cases, women delay childbirth as they pursue employment for economic reasons, but discover in the process that they prefer employment to domesticity.

The job opportunities that are available to women also influence the particular pathway a given woman follows. If women who hope to have a nontraditional lifestyle encounter blocked opportunities in the labor market, they may shift their orientations back toward full-time mothering. In contrast, women who plan to work only until their children are born may find that the jobs they formerly regard-ed as "temporary" are so fulfilling, both financially and psychologically, that they are reluctant to leave them. Finally, perceptions of actual rewards and costs of full-time domesticity may change initial orientations. For some women, full-time homemaking and childrearing are more fulfilling than expected. For others, they are less fulfilling. When actual rewards and costs are different from expectations, work–family orientations may shift (Shehan, 1992).

In fact, some data show that the baby boom women who had planned in their early twenties to be housewives at age 35 had greater difficulty fulfilling their plans. Perhaps they had "based their expectations on the labor market experiences of their mother and on the observed behavior of women then in their mid-thirties . . . most of whom would have been home raising families." These women's plans reflected the expected behavior for women at midlife, behavior that was likely to vary with social change (Rexroat and Shehan, 1984).

The unexpected changes in family and economic circumstances that transpired over the 1970s significantly increased women's likelihood of being in the labor force at age 35. Being unmarried and without the economic resources provided by a husband, for instance, increased their labor force participation. Increased educa-tional attainment and extensive employment experience also increased women's likelihood of being in the labor force at age 35. Perhaps women discovered that employment was more rewarding than they had anticipated. Women who wished to be in the labor force at age 35, in contrast, most likely would have attempted to coordinate their employment and childbearing by careful planning (Rexroat and Shehan, 1984).

Members of *generation X* (those born between 1964 and 1975) may take different life pathways than their baby boomer predecessors. A poll of gen X professionals conducted in 2001 by Catalyst shows that their top priorities are establishing a rela-tionship with a significant other and having a loving family. Over three-quarters of the gen Xers in the survey rated these life goals as extremely important. Only one-fifth of the respondents said that earning a great deal of money was extremely important to them. Members of this generation are already finding that work can interfere with personal lives. Three-quarters of those in the poll reported moderate to severe negative spillover from job to personal life. Gen X women appear to be less willing to follow the traditional *male* model of corporate success, which demands single-minded pursuit of career over personal life. One-fifth of the women in the survey said they expected to work part-time at their current place of employment at some time over the next five years, ostensibly to enable them to start a family. Only 2 percent of the gen X men in the survey said they planned to take time off. In this sense, gen X looks similar to their baby boomer predecessors (Catalyst, 2001).

Gender Inequities in Employment

One might conclude, after seeing the tremendous increase in women's labor force participation over the past 100 years, that all barriers to full employment equality for women have been removed. Such a conclusion, however, is premature.

Gender Labeling of Jobs and Gender Segregation of Workers

The employment experiences of women and men differ in many important ways, not the least of which is referred to as **gender labeling.** That is, most jobs are regarded by the public as most appropriate for workers of one sex or the other. An important consequence of the gender labeling of jobs is the **gender segregation** of

TABLE 12.3	

Occupations in Which the Work Force Is at Least 90 Percent Male, 2001

Occupation	Percent Female
Physicists and astronomers	7.7
Air traffic controllers	7.1
Garbage collectors	5.4
Truck drivers	5.3
Mechanics and repairers	4.7
Pest control workers	4.5
Airplane pilots and navigators	3.7
Construction laborers	3.5
Firefighters	2.8
Extractive occupations (e.g., miners)	2.3

Source: U.S. Department of Labor, Women's Bureau web site: www.dol.gov/wb/public/wb-pubs/20/2001/htm

women and men in the workplace. That is, most workers are in jobs in which the majority of their co-workers are people of their own sex. Table 12.3, for instance, presents a list of occupations that are male dominated; meaning that at least 90 percent of the workers are men. Included in this list are a number of jobs that require a great deal of physical strength (such as construction work) or may involve physical danger (such as firefighting), they are sometimes considered inappropriate for women.

Table 12.4 presents a list of *pink-collar* or female-dominated jobs. Many of these involve caring for people who need help (such as the young, the elderly, the sick or

TABLE 12.4	

Occupations in Which the Workforce Is at Least 75 Percent Female, 2001

Occupation	Percent Female
Secretaries	98.4
Receptionists	96.9
Registered nurses	93.1
Hairdressers and cosmetologists	90.4
Nursing aides, attendants, orderlies	90.0
General office clerks	83.7
Elementary teachers	82.5
Cashiers	76.9
Restaurant servers	76.4
Other administrative support workers	76.4

Source: U.S. Department of Labor, Women's Bureau web site: www.dol.gov/wb/public/wb-pubs/20/2001/htm.

While most women workers are employed in pink-collar jobs, such as teaching, nursing, typing, and waiting tables, federal legislation has made it somewhat easier for some women to move into jobs that were once considered appropriate for men only.

infirm, the poor) or in some other way represent an extension of women's traditional work in the home and family (such as housecleaning). Others involve processing paperwork in industry (secretaries and typists) or greeting clients or customers (receptionists, bank tellers, telephone operators). In the popular image, these jobs do not require a great deal of physical strength or expose workers to physical risk or injury. They are *clean* jobs that typically take place indoors. But these portrayals may be more mythical than real. Lifting and carrying babies and children or moving sick patients in hospital beds may require a great deal of strength, as does carrying buckets of water for mopping floors and loads of wet laundry from a washing machine to a dryer or clothesline. Nor can it accurately be said that pink-collar jobs are cleaner than the blue-collar jobs discussed earlier. Changing diapers and soiled sheets, cleaning toilets, and chipping plaque from someone's teeth challenge this image.

It is important to keep in mind that jobs are not inherently male or female, as history shows. For instance, clerical work, which is now female dominated, was at one time a male job. Before office mechanization, clerical work was considered a highly skilled occupation that offered a great deal of upward mobility. Men who started as clerks in small offices could work their way up to manage or even own the business. As offices grew and paperwork proliferated, adding machines and typewriters were introduced and clerical work became female dominated. The status of the job declined, along with its pay and chances for promotion to management. Some observers say that the introduction of adding machines and typewriters reduced the skill level (good penmanship and the ability to add columns of numbers quickly were replaced by machines) and thus justified lower pay, less prestige, and fewer opportunities for advancement. Others argue that when the gender label of the job changed, the salary was reduced.

Not only blue-collar and pink-collar jobs are gender segregated. The professions are also gender-segregated. Some of the highest paying, most prestigious and powerful occupations (such as law and medicine) are considered the *full* professions and are still male dominated, but the representation of women in these professions has increased. In order for women to be proportionately represented, they would have to constitute the same proportion of people employed in these jobs as there are in the labor force as a whole. In 2001, nearly 47 percent of the total workforce was composed of women. Thus, to be proportionately represented in the full professions, women would have to constitute at least 47 percent of the workers in these fields. One profession that approaches proportionate representation of women is college and university teaching. However, the women faculty members are concentrated in the lowest ranks and in the least prestigious institutions. They are more likely to be assistant professors than associate or full professors, and they are more likely to be employed in two-year community colleges than in four-year colleges or universities.

Gender Gap in Pay

One of the consequences of gender labeling is a continuing gap between women's and men's wages. Men who are employed full time, year round, earn considerably more money than women who are employed full time, year round, in all major occupational categories. Table 12.5 provides comparative information on the earnings of women and men from 1951 to 1999. From the highest-ranking occupational categories, such as managerial and professional specialties, through the middle levels of technical, sales, and administrative support, to the female-dominated service occupations and the male-dominated skilled crafts, to laborers in fields and factories, women's earnings are lower than men's.

Women have certainly moved into the workforce in great numbers, but the positions they hold and the rewards they receive are still not equal to those of men. Women generally have lower-status occupations and lower earnings within the same occupations. Such employment disadvantages affect women directly in the workforce and indirectly in their homes and families. The gender gap in pay is one of the major contributors to the **feminization of poverty** (a high proportion of the nation's poor is composed of women) that has developed in the United States. Families headed by women are increasingly likely to live at or near the poverty level even when the mothers are employed full time year round, because lower wages are paid to women.

TABLE 12.5

Women's and Men's Average Earnings, 1951 to 1999

	CURRENT DOLLARS ($)		REAL (1999) DOLLARS ($)		PERCENT WOMEN EARN COMPARED TO MEN
	Women	Men	Women	Men	
1951	2,305	3,605	14,770	23,100	63.9
1961	3,315	5,595	18,471	31,175	59.2
1971	5,593	9,399	23,007	38,664	59.5
1981	12,001	20,260	21,995	37,132	59.2
1991	20,553	29,421	25,140	35,988	69.7
1999	26,324	36,476	26,324	36,476	72.2

Source: U.S. Department of Labor, Women's Bureau, 2000.

Work and Family Types

Researcher Joseph Pleck (1984) was important in outlining the many ways in which employment and family roles affect each other. His outline is still a helpful tool to use in viewing the links between jobs and family life. Pleck identified four distinct roles within each two-parent family: the husband's employment role, the husband's family role (including household labor and child care), the wife's employment role, and the wife's family role. Theoretically, each of these roles may affect and be affected by the other three. Thus, the male employment role may affect the male family role, the female employment role, and the female family role, just as the female family role may affect the other roles.

In reality, though, not every role is equally likely to affect every other role because of **structural buffers,** factors that dampen the impact of some roles on others. Some of the most important structural buffers in the work–family role system are **asymmetrically permeable boundaries** between roles. This term means that the influences between pairs of roles runs in one direction. Thus, the male employment role has a major impact on the male family role, insofar as a man's job is allowed to intrude on his family life, but the male family role is not supposed to affect a man's job performance. For men, the employment role is expected to take priority over domestic labor. The reverse situation exists between the female employment role and domestic labor roles. Among women, family is supposed to take precedence over employment. A second type of structural buffer is **sex segregation.** Tasks are labeled as more appropriate for men or women. Housework and child care are still primarily considered women's work, as are certain pink-collar jobs in the labor market. Thus, even if a woman cannot do all the housework, her husband is less likely to step in to help when these tasks are not considered appropriate for a man.

The links between employment and family life vary tremendously depending on the type of job held by family members (managerial or professional, blue collar, clerical) as well as the characteristics of the family (e.g., how many parents are in the home, how many of the adults in the home are employed). Different types of families can be identified based on the juxtaposition of these two dimensions. In this chapter, we consider **blue-collar couples** in which one or both spouses are employed in blue-collar jobs; the **two-person career,** in which the husband is employed in a professional or managerial job and the wife is not employed but is expected to support and participate in his career; **dual-career couples** in which both spouses are employed in managerial or professional jobs; and **single-parent providers** in which only one parent resides in the home and is primarily responsible for meeting the economic needs of the household. These are not all the possible combinations of occupation and marital status, but they are broad types that allow us to analyze crucial job–family links.

Blue-Collar Couples

Wives in blue-collar families have long had to work outside their homes because of economic necessity, even when they might have preferred to work at home full time. Today the majority of women in the working class are employed. If a blue-collar family has only one earner, almost always the man is employed, while the woman works in the home. Generally this type of family has very traditional gender role expectations.

Blue-collar workers are often dissatisfied with their work. They may change jobs frequently in search of higher wages, better conditions, and higher status.

They also live in constant fear of layoffs or cutbacks in hours because of fluctuations in the economy. One study of working-class families found nearly 15 percent of the men were unemployed at the time of the interviews; another 20 percent had been periodically unemployed (Rubin, 1994).

When only one member of a family works at a blue-collar job, the economic situation of the family is often precarious. Sometimes husbands take on a second job or work overtime to increase family income. This, in turn, reduces the time they have available for family life. Stress on the job may be carried home as fatigue, irritability, or worry. In some cases, men who are dissatisfied with their jobs may demand peace and quiet when with their wives and children, even though wives wish to provide emotional support. Characteristics of blue-collar jobs also influence men's fathering styles. Blue-collar fathers are directive, use physical punishment rather than verbal reasoning, and emphasize conformity and obedience rather than independence and creativity (Schooler, 1996).

Working-class couples in blue-collar jobs face a great many work-related pressures. A typical problem is finding child care or dividing child care duties between wife and husband by working different shifts (Presser, 1994). With relatively low incomes, working-class couples often find the cost of baby-sitters or child care prohibitively high. Sometimes relatives help care for children, at a lower cost, but not in all cases; so couples must make complex arrangements.

> We have a kind of complicated arrangement for the little kids. Two days a week, my mom takes care of them. . . . But she works the rest of the time, so the other days we take them to this woman's house. It's the best we can afford . . . I know they don't get good attention. (Rubin, 1994, p. 93)

After talking to many working-class couples about their difficulties with child care, one researcher concluded, "For most working class families, child care is patched together in ways that leave parents anxious and children in jeopardy" (Rubin, 1994, p. 93).

When wives in working-class households are employed, as most are, their husbands often have ambivalent feelings about it. They may appreciate that their wives are bringing in necessary income and that marital communication and understanding are improving because each understands the problems associated with the other's work. But many working-class husbands cannot completely shake the thought that they have somehow failed in their primary family responsibility when their wives have to work outside their homes. As one husband puts it, "I know she doesn't mind working, but it shouldn't have to be that way. . . . A guy should be able to support his wife and kids" (Rubin, 1994, p. 78).

Working-class wives also have some ambivalent feelings about their work, but their ambivalence is of a different sort. On the one hand, they often say that they hate leaving their children in the care of other people, especially when their children are very young. On the other hand, many working-class wives speak of the satisfaction they feel with their jobs and their contribution to the family income (Rubin, 1994). In the words of one woman, the mother of three children, "I didn't imagine how much I'd enjoy going to work in the morning. I mean, I love my kids and all that, but let's face it, being mom can get pretty stale" (Rubin, 1994, p. 81).

These women often spoke of feeling more in control of their lives since they had started working. One woman, the mother of three teenage children, said: "I couldn't believe what a difference it made when I went to work. . . . I feel like I've got my own life. I never felt like I really ruled my own life before" (Rubin, 1994, p. 82). Yet these women are often reluctant to reveal how fulfilled they are in their jobs, especially to their husbands. One woman, after revealing the pride she feels about her success at work, told the interviewer, "Don't tell him I said that. He'd feel bad if he knew" (Rubin, 1994, p. 82).

ContentSELECT

Working Class

One persistent difficulty for two-earner, working-class families is that the men still feel their wives have the primary responsibility for the home. The men may help with home tasks, such as cooking, cleaning, or caring for children, but often they only do so when their wives ask for help or give them instructions on what to do. Wives must organize and plan the tasks. The wives are sensitive to the inequities of household labor and often resent their unfair share of the load.

For two-earner, working-class families today, there are problems and ambivalence, and yet for some, especially wives, there are also newfound satisfactions. In any case, most blue-collar couples have no choice: Both partners *must* work. The resulting toll on the marriage is an inherent part of economic life.

The Two-Person Career

In most one-earner families, husbands have professional or managerial jobs. Although it might be expected that this group would have greater marital stability and happiness than blue-collar families, it isn't necessarily so. The husband's intense job pressure may more than offset the greater occupational prestige and income. Sociologists make a conceptual distinction between careers and jobs. Careers are extremely involving and demanding. They are a special type of job that requires considerable preparation, lifelong commitment and dedication, and increasing skill and responsibility over the life course.

Because careers are so demanding, individuals with this type of job have little time or energy left over for other pursuits, like cooking, shopping, taking clothes to the dry cleaner, and perhaps even reading to children. Yet most people with careers in our society do not want to forgo a family life in order to advance their careers. Understandably, they want to have it all—career, marriage, and children, along with a clean house, clean clothes, and a well-manicured lawn.

In previous generations, careers were structured on the assumption that the man had a backup person who took care of all his needs so that he was not distracted from his job. As noted above, the *two-person career* refers to the unpaid, but expected, participation of a woman in her husband's all-consuming career (Papanek, 1972).

This type of family arrangement is still often found today. Ministers, executives, politicians, physicians, and military officers often form two-person careers. Wives contribute to their husbands' careers in many ways. They perform the domestic labor or, in the case of very highly paid professionals, they hire and supervise someone else to perform the work. They engage in work-related social functions, which means not only that they attend parties and social events sponsored by their husbands' business associates, but also that they must host such events. Frequently they must act as a stand-in or substitute for their husbands at important public events. The wife of the president of the United States, for instance, may be called on to attend the funeral of a high-ranking official of another country. In some cases, such as men in other elected offices, a wife might step in to perform her husband's job if he becomes seriously ill or dies. Wives often serve as their husbands' most trusted confidantes, providing moral support and advice. Sometimes, especially when a career is just being established, a wife may even perform routine clerical work such as typing, filing, answering telephones, and making appointments.

Even the wives of lower-paid professionals, such as ministers, may be expected to support their husbands' careers rather than have independent careers of their own (Frame and Shehan, 1994). Expectations for ministers' wives include a number of church-related duties. They are expected to attend all services and functions, fill leadership roles in the women's groups, and entertain congregational guests in the parsonage. The woman who marries a minister with no real sense of sharing in his vocation creates a difficult situation for them both, because the ministry is a highly competitive career. Success includes increasing congregational membership, raising money, constructing buildings, and maintaining a favorable image. The cooperation of his wife is essential if the clergyman is to continue to achieve higher-status assignments and salary increases. Her performance of crucial tasks not only frees him from the distractions of daily life, but also provides important services for the church at no added expense (Frame and Shehan, 1994).

Clearly, the woman's role in a two-person career helps the husband immensely and may be a source of pride and achievement for the woman, as well. But, her service pretty much eliminates the possibility of pursuing a job or career of her own. Moreover, when wives remain out of the workforce to devote themselves to maintaining their homes and supporting their husbands' careers, they face special risks if their marriage ends, either through divorce or the death of their spouse. Without the economic support of their husbands, these women often face an abrupt loss of income and a decline in their standard of living. Even among women who have college educations or professional degrees, it may be difficult to find satisfactory employment if they have not been active in the labor force. More than likely, the level of the job and the pay they receive will be far below that of their former husbands. The original assumptions of the two-person career marriage are negated by divorce. Husbands and wives may begin with the idea that theirs is a joint effort, to which both contribute and from which both will eventually benefit, but if the couple divorces, earlier commitments often carry little moral weight. Divorcing husbands continue with the careers they have established, while their ex-wives are left with little to show for their contributions.

Dual-Career Couples

In dual-career families, both spouses require the backup services provided by wives in the traditional two-person career, yet neither the husband nor the wife is available to perform such services for the other. How do men and women who pursue careers survive without a person who can perform the tasks that wives traditionally perform in the two-person career? As you might expect, they experience many challenges as they attempt to balance their careers and their family life.

One of the major problems experienced by dual-career couples is **role overload**, which means they have too many things to do in a given amount of time; too many expectations to fulfill and too many deadlines to meet. Another problem faced by dual-career couples is social disapproval. A generation ago, when dual-career couples were much rarer than they are today, wives with careers did their best to appear to be just like other married women, in an attempt to counteract the criticisms of their curious neighbors, family members, and co-workers. Although the disapproval directed toward professional women, in general, may have all but disappeared in recent years, there still seems to be some public concern directed at women who pursue careers when they have young children. An Oprah Winfrey show that featured secret videotapes of abusive baby-sitters was disrupted by angry audience members who chastised mothers who pursued careers outside their homes when their children were young. This type of reaction from others can cause dual-career couples to experience guilt and anxiety. Men whose female partners have equally challenging and prestigious careers may question their manhood, whereas their wives may worry about their performance of the traditional wife and mother roles.

Because of role overload, along with geographic and social mobility, dual-career couples may have restricted social networks. They may be physically separated from their parents and siblings, and too busy to spend time with friends or neighbors after work or on weekends. They may also avoid socializing with couples who

ContentSELECT

Dual Career or
Dual Earner

hold negative opinions about women with careers and children. Finally, spouses in dual-career couples may have difficulty competing at work with colleagues who have traditional marriages with a backup support person at home.

Single-Parent Providers

A final type of family that must be considered is the single-parent provider. In this situation, a single parent is primarily, if not solely, responsible for fulfilling all the children's emotional and economic needs. These families, which are nearly always headed by women, face severe economic difficulties, often living below the poverty line. The economic difficulties of single mothers arise largely from the fact that the fathers of their children do not provide adequate financial support. Mothers who have never married rarely receive financial support from the fathers, whereas divorced and separated men frequently provide much less than is needed. Even when mothers are employed, their wages are usually low and not adequate to sustain a standard of living equal to what they had before the divorce. In addition, the conflicting demands of employment and family life that exist in dual-provider families are intensified in single-parent families.

In all the different family arrangements we have considered—blue-collar couples, two-person careers, two-career couples, and single-parent providers—work can negatively affect marriage and family life. There are, in fact, particular friction points between work and family that can be identified.

Friction Points between Jobs and Families

*I*t is useful and interesting to think of the interface between jobs and families in terms of friction points, the places at which tension between the two competing sets of responsibilities are felt by family members. There are four major types of friction points: (1) time and schedule problems, (2) employment demands, (3) occupational inequities, and (4) competing social relationships at the workplace.

Time and Schedule Problems

Family members' job times and schedules can cause tension in households in at least two ways. The first occurs when family members work different shifts and thus have little or no time for interacting with each other. In some cases, couples deliberately work different shifts so that they can cover child care themselves, reducing their need for substitute care. But whenever both members of a couple are employed, whether in jobs or in professions, there are likely to be problems associated with work schedules. When married couples have a limited amount of time each day to be with each other and enjoy each other's company, the effect is likely to be harmful to the relationship. When married couples work different shifts or have work demands that are extremely heavy, they cannot give adequate attention to each other. Even their sexual life may suffer as a result. When both members of a couple work, they may not have either the time or the energy for sex. One young married woman, interviewed by Lillian Rubin, said sarcastically, "Sex? . . . Oh yeah, that; I remember now. . . . I guess the worst is when you work different shifts like we do and you get to see each other maybe six minutes a day. There's no time for sex" (Rubin, 1994, pp. 98–99). A husband put it even more bluntly, "Far as I'm concerned, that's one of the things I found out about marriage. You get married, you give up sex" (Rubin, 1994, p. 99).

in the media

When Funerals Are the Family Business

One of the primary characteristics of modern, post-industrial societies is that paid work is usually performed away from the family home. There are notable exceptions, however, and this box focuses on one interesting situation—family-owned and operated funeral homes. The HBO series, *Six Feet Under,* has drawn attention to the "grief management" business by featuring the Fisher family and their business, Fisher & Sons Funeral Home. The Fishers live in suburban Los Angeles. The family patriarch, Nathaniel Fisher, died in the first episode of the series (but he appears in every episode to comment on the comings and goings of his family and their clients). Nathaniel's younger son, David, followed him into the business, while the older son, Nate, left home to pursue his own dreams. After his father's death, Nate, too, became involved in the funeral business. Nathaniel's youngest child, daughter Claire, drives an old lime green hearse to school and experiences the stigma of living in a funeral home.

Family-run businesses have a number of characteristics that can affect family relationships. One of the most obvious is that family members spend most, if not all, of their time together. Tensions may run high simply because of the lack of escape valves. When the family lives in the building that houses the business, the physical boundaries between home and work are blurred. Family members must be prepared to encounter customers or clients in their home during work hours, which may extend into nights and weekends. Like a number of other professionals, funeral directors are on call nearly twenty-four hours a day, seven days a week. In the case of the family-run funeral home, family members must also deal with the public's fear of death and dead bodies and negative stereotypes about undertakers.

In spite of the negative stereotypes, funeral directors score fairly high in terms of public ratings of professional honesty and ethics. A recent Gallup poll found that 36 percent of Americans rated them as high or very high on these dimensions (Bader, 2001). The funeral business can also be financially lucrative. Thomas Lynch, a third-generation funeral director in Milford, Michigan, has written a book about his experiences in the family-owned business. Lynch's own salary is about $70,000 per year, enough to "afford orthodontia but not boarding school for his kids" (Bader, 2001). After covering the many expenses associated with running his business (e.g., maintaining the funeral parlor, paying his employees, and keeping up the hearses) Lynch makes another $50,000 per year in profit.

For more information about this occupation, see *The Undertaking: Life Studies from the Dismal Trade* (by Thomas Lynch), New York: Penguin, 1998.

Source: Bader, Jenny Lyn. "Death Be Not Bad for Ratings." The *New York Times,* June 10, 2001.

Job schedules can also cause family friction when one partner's schedule forces the other to assume the bulk of home and family work. If one partner travels frequently, the other may be forced into *solo parenting.* Or if one partner works during the night and sleeps during the day, he or she may not be able to do housework during the day (Presser, 1994). This forces the other to take on most of the household work, which may cause great resentment and lead to conflict in the relationship.

Employment Demands

The number and type of demands that a job places on a worker may also cause tension in the home. For example, jobs in health care and public safety (such as fire fighting and police work) must be performed on a twenty-four-hour-a-day basis, so

▲ *Some types of work, such as the military, involve frequent separation of employees from their families.*

people who work in these fields must take their turn being *on call*. Being tied to one's workplace through a pager may restrict a person's freedom to go on outings with his or her family.

Certain occupations require moving from one place to another, or for an employee to be separated from her or his family for extended periods of time. Members of the military—men and women, with or without children—are frequently required to be separated from their families, either for military action, peacekeeping, or, as in the case of the Navy, for sea duty.

Along with the military, there are a number of occupations for which geographic mobility is either inherent or highly probable (Daugherty and Kammeyer, 1995). Large corporations and other national organizations frequently ask their managers and executives to relocate as they move up the corporate ladder. Members of the diplomatic corps, much like members of the military, must change duty stations frequently during their careers. The same is true, to a degree, for members of the clergy (Frame and Shehan, 1994). Moving can frequently have negative effects on family relationships. Couples and their children must leave their friends and social groups and develop new ones at their new location. These are disruptive events that may produce tension and stress for couples and families.

Occupational Inequities

Sociologists have long suspected that, at times, spouses who are career oriented might compete with each other. Imbalances in salaries or uneven career advancement favoring their wives may be difficult for men with traditional gender role attitudes to accept.

Another situation that occurs frequently today—one spouse's job requiring a move, which uproots the other from his or her job—can cause tension in the relationship. Recognizing this problem, corporate employers sometimes try to make arrangements with other companies to hire *trailing* spouses. Research has shown that wives are reluctant to take a better job in another location if they think the move will hurt their husbands' career progress. Concerns about their wives' potential problems finding satisfactory jobs in new locations do not seem to discourage men from taking new jobs that offer higher pay (Bielby and Bielby, 1992). This points to the fact that many couples still regard men's jobs as more important than women's. Some couples, when faced with this situation—one spouse is forced to move to another location in order to move up the career ladder—enter into **commuter marriages** in which they live in two separate households. Although commuter marriages may work for a limited period of time, couples almost always see this arrangement as temporary and not very desirable (Rindfuss and Stephen, 1990).

Competing Social Relationships in the Workplace

In many types of employment, socializing with co-workers is an expected part of the job. Sometimes spouses are included in these social activities, but often they are not. Blue-collar male workers often spend time with their co-workers after work, or in the evenings, going bowling or simply having a "night out with the boys." Professional and other high-status employees are more likely to spend time at professional association meetings or other semiofficial functions. Again, spouses may attend, but often they are only marginally involved. The result is that work-related social activities often separate husbands and wives from their spouses and parents from their children.

If work-related social activities lead into a romantic relationship, a different kind of problem exists. Members of the opposite sex frequently come into contact in work settings, and romances do sometimes occur. Even when there is no romantic relationship, a spouse may suspect that there is, and become jealous of a spouse's co-workers. In all cases, romantic involvements with co-workers, real or imagined, can have a devastating effect on a marriage.

Household Labor

Several times in this and earlier chapters, the issue of household labor and child care has arisen. As women have entered the labor force in ever-greater numbers, and as the feminist movement has sensitized women to the inequity of having to do virtually all the household work, the question of who does household work has become increasingly important. For some time now, social scientists have been studying the amount of housework done by women and men and the factors that affect the amount each does (Coltrane, 2000). Much of the research that has been done on the performance of housework fails to take less visible types of responsibilities (e.g., watching children, management of the household, and providing emotional support) into account.

The five most time-consuming and least discretionary household tasks are meal preparation (cooking), shopping for groceries and household supplies, washing dishes and cleaning up after meals, and laundry (which includes washing, ironing, mending, and putting away clothes). While some people enjoy doing this type of work, most men and women say they do not (Coltrane, 1996; DeMaris and Longmore, 1996). Other types of household work (e.g., repairing household goods, yard care, driving family members to and from activities, and paying bill) are more flexible in terms of their scheduling and are less onerous than the routine household tasks listed previously (Coltrane, 1998). Women continue to have primary responsibility for routine tasks—those that must be performed on a regular basis—while men spend most of their housework time in the discretionary tasks—those that don't have to be performed as often and can be scheduled more flexibly. The most recent data available show that married women spend about three times as many hours on the routine tasks as do married men (thirty-two hours versus ten hours per week, respectively). Men, on the other hand, spend almost twice as many hours as women on the discretionary tasks (ten hours versus six hours, respectively).

Most men still do much less housework than women do, with married men creating about as much demand for household labor as they perform. Women's contributions to domestic work have declined over the past decade, but men's contributions have increased at an even slower pace. Women still do most of the routine cooking and cleaning tasks. Men today are less likely to confine their entire contribution to household work to the *outside* tasks, but they still only rarely take full responsibility for a full range of tasks. When men do more of the routine chores, employed women feel that the division of labor is fairer; they are less depressed and report higher levels of marital satisfaction.

As family needs change over the life cycle, the demands for household labor also change. Wives' hours in housework vary tremendously, increasing with the birth of children and remaining high at around 33 hours per week until the children start to leave home. Husbands' average time in housework, however, does not vary much with the expansion and contraction of the family. It hovers around five hours per week.

A similar pattern exists with child care. Women's average time in child care also responds to the ages of children. At all family life cycle stages in which there are children in the home, women's average hours in child care greatly exceed that of men's. When the number of hours on the job are added to time spent in housework and child care, women who are employed full time spend considerably more time working each week than do their husbands. The greatest gap in the total work time of wives and husbands occurs when the oldest child is less than 3 years old. At this stage, women work an extra day (twenty-four hours) each week. This is why some people refer to employed women's work at home as the **second shift** (Hochschild, 1989).

There is some variation in men's time in housework and child care across different social classes and racial or ethnic groups. We have already seen that blue-collar husbands contribute somewhat more to household work than they once did. But they still consider this to be their wives' responsibility. Among the working class, Asian and Latino husbands are still the most reluctant to do work they consider to be "women's work." African American husbands seem to be the most liberated from traditional expectations about household labor. Nearly three-fourths of the African American men in Rubin's study did a substantial amount of cooking, cleaning, and child care, sometimes even more than their wives. It should also be noted that in almost all working-class families the men continued to be responsible for household tasks that have long been considered *men's work*—mowing the lawn, shoveling snow, maintaining cars, cleaning the garage, and doing household repairs (Rubin, 1994).

Is the situation any different in families in which both husbands and wives have higher-status occupations, professional careers instead of jobs? Studies reveal similar patterns of household labor in dual-career couples as have been found in other types of families. Traditional notions about women being primarily responsible for housework, cooking, and child care continue to influence couples even when they have high-status professional careers (Berardo, Shehan, and Leslie, 1987).

Wives with full-time careers spend significantly fewer hours in housework each week than housewives, but they still allocate significantly more hours to

Employed parents often add considerable time to their daily commute when transporting children to and from day care centers.

housework than their husbands. Even women who are university professors or have careers in business are more involved in child care than their husbands and have greater responsibility for seeing that tasks get done. On every child care task except playing with children, and in every chore except household repairs, women are more involved than their husbands. In terms of child care, professional women have primary responsibility for children's physical needs, teaching them basics, getting up during the night, staying home from work to care for a sick child, driving children to and from daycare, and making alternative child care arrangements. They are also more involved in performing the full range of household tasks, such as grocery shopping, cooking, laundry, cleaning, and managing finances.

Even when their husbands contribute to household and child care tasks, professional women, much like working-class women, still have the ultimate responsibility for seeing that these things get done (Biernat and Wortman, 1991). For example, two-career couples are likely to use professional child care services, but the facilities and personnel must be evaluated. This is primarily left to mothers, although fathers may participate and help with the final decision. The task of choosing a safe, trustworthy, and beneficial child care service is a very serious task for mothers and is a primary source of stress and anxiety.

Thus, even if men do substantial amounts of household labor, it is women who typically perform the administrative or executive function. The **executive function** means that women have the ultimate responsibility for home and children, much like an executive in a corporation has ultimate responsibility for the organization. In addition to arranging for child care, women are typically responsible for planning meals, arranging for and supervising household help, keeping track of family members' needs for medical care, and managing children's social calendars. The additional responsibilities can add considerable stress to an already crowded life. In fact, even marriage itself adds many hours per week to a woman's household responsibilities. The executive function is continuous and unrelenting.

Researchers still do not completely understand why men do so little; nor do we know what conditions will increase men's contributions to housework. It appears that the number of hours men and women spend at their paid jobs, along with the relative size of their paychecks, their beliefs about gender and family roles, and their living arrangements influence the allocation of household tasks. Family size, age, life stage, ethnicity, presence and contribution of children, and a number of other factors also enter into the determination of who does what around the house. The most important thing to keep in mind, however, is that "the allocation of domestic labor is embedded in social arrangements that perpetuate class, race, and gender inequities" (Coltrane, 2000, p. 1226). Women, people of color, and those of lower social classes are left to do the most onerous of household tasks, which in turn, may limit their abilities to achieve in higher status positions.

Is the gender inequality in household labor simply a vestige of the past that will be eradicated by the time the next generation comes along? The evidence suggests not. Daughters of mothers who work full time spend more hours per week on housework than sons (Exter, 1991).

Further Effects of Employment on Marriage and Family Life

We have already seen a number of ways in which employment, and especially the employment of women, influences marriage and family life. In the following section, we consider a number of other ways in which employment affects several features of family life and marriage.

Marital Power and Decision Making

Power in intimate relationships is often explained in terms of social exchange theory (see Chapter 2). Individuals who provide highly valued resources to their partners *earn* greater say in decision making that involves both of them. Thus, men's greater power in marriage is a function of their greater contribution of social and economic resources. Wives' employment, according to exchange theory, should increase their power because it increases their contribution of resources relative to their husbands. In fact, studies show that wives' employment does indeed give them more power, especially in working-class marriages where the wife's earnings are so important to family income.

Nevertheless, the balance of power in marriage is far from equal, largely because women's earnings still lag behind their husbands'. Women are viewed as secondary providers whose wages simply supplement their husbands'. Feminist scholars believe that men's power in families is tied to a larger societal system of patriarchy and an ideology of male dominance. Until that ideology weakens, women will continue to have less power in their relationships with men (Moen, 1992, p. 66). In fact, one study shows that when women are the lower earners in a marriage they do more of the housework, as predicted. But in cases in which men are unemployed and are therefore dependent on their wives' incomes, they are even less likely to do housework than other men (Brines, 1994). Perhaps men who are not able to fulfill the traditional provider role are especially reluctant to take on traditional female tasks.

Marital Satisfaction and Stability

Wife and Work

A wife's employment can affect the marital relationship in a number of ways. It can enhance the quality of a relationship by increasing the number of things the partners have in common. The fact that both experience the trials and tribulations of the workforce may make it easier for them to provide comfort and advice to each other, to act as friends and confidantes. Yet employed husbands and wives may also compete with each other, producing tension and conflict in the relationship.

Research conducted in the 1950s showed that couples in which both the husband and wife were employed were less satisfied with their marriages than couples with only the husband employed. But by the late 1960s and early 1970s, this difference had disappeared (Moen, 1992, p. 67). Recent studies show that husbands' and wives' gender role attitudes may be the crucial factor in determining the impact of a wife's employment on marital satisfaction (Rogers and DeBoer, 2001). Husbands who have more egalitarian values are happier with their marriages whether their wives are employed or not. Wives also report higher levels of marital satisfaction when their husbands are supportive and share in child care.

Another important factor in marital satisfaction may be the relative size of the paycheck that wives and husbands bring home. Men who are less successful than their wives may be particularly dissatisfied with their marriage.

About one-fourth of all employed wives in the United States earn as much or more money than their husbands. Various theoretical perspectives make different predictions about the impact of women's greater earnings. Structural functionalism (which holds that gender role specialization and complementarity of husbands' and wives' roles within marriage are the key to marital stability and quality) would predict that marriages in which wives earn more money than their husbands are more likely to end in divorce. There has not been strong or consistent empirical support for this hypothesis (Brennan, Barnett, and Gareis, 2001).

One factor that may complicate the relationship between spouses' earnings and marital satisfaction and stability is the meaning that wives and husbands attach to their relative economic contributions, specifically their identification with the provider role and their gender role beliefs. It is widely believed that the good-provider role is central to men's but not women's self-identity. It follows, then, that men should experience higher subjective rewards than women from their earnings. In addition, gender role beliefs may moderate the impact between earnings and marital role quality. Spouses who have more traditional beliefs may experience lower role quality when wives earn more than their husbands.

Victoria Segunda, executive editor of *Making Bread Magazine* (a financial publication aimed at women), tells of her own ambivalence about earning more money than her husband. When they first married, Victoria's husband Shel encouraged her to quit her job as an editor to pursue her dream of becoming a full-time writer. After ten years, one of her books become a top seller, enabling her to earn more money than her husband. Shel was not at all threatened by her success. In fact, he was really pleased that his investment in her career paid off. Victoria, on the other hand, had some emotional difficulty with the situation. She says "it felt, well, weird, being the primary breadwinner. I wanted my income to be the bonus not the necessity, with Shel hauling in the bigger bucks" (Secunda, www.makingbreadmagazine.com/ features/moneyemotions/salarywar.htm, downloaded on March 11, 2002).

Spouses with more egalitarian beliefs, on the other hand, may not suffer from a decrease in marital quality when traditional gender role expectations are violated by high-earning wives. A recent study provides some support for these hypotheses (Brennan, Barnett, and Gareis, 2001). For husbands who have traditional gender role beliefs, being a good provider and having a dependent wife signifies the importance of his contributions to the marriage and has a positive impact on marital stability. As their wives' earnings approach their own, they may experience a drop in self-esteem and fear that their wives will think less of them. Wives and husbands with less traditional gender role beliefs do not experience a similar drop in marital role quality when women's wages equal or surpass their husbands. It is when husbands increase their child care that employed wives experience an increase in marital role quality.

A question of great interest to social researchers in the past decade concerns the impact of employment on marital stability. As the divorce rate started rising in the United States in the twentieth century, social observers were often quick to blame the rise on women entering the workforce (Greenstein, 1990; Cherlin, 1992). Indeed, the two trends—the increasing number of women employed and the rising divorce rate—have generally been parallel since 1890. But there are exceptions. Between 1945 and 1958, the divorce rate in the United States declined from the post–World War II high while at the same time, women's employment was increasing dramatically. The same pattern continued during the 1980s and into the 1990s. Since the late 1970s, the divorce rate has declined somewhat, while the percentage of married women in the labor force has continued to increase (Greenstein, 1990). Clearly, there must be other explanations for the rising divorce rate than married women's labor force participation patterns.

Other kinds of research on how women's employment affects divorce have produced contradictory findings (White, 1990). One researcher even calls the findings just plain "confusing" (Greenstein, 1990). Some studies have found women's employment is related to a higher likelihood of divorce (Booth, Johnson, and White, 1984; Spitze and South, 1985; Rank, 1987). But other studies have found that some aspects of married women's employment actually reduce divorce (South and Spitze, 1986; Greenstein, 1990).

The usual rationale for linking women's employment to the divorce rate is that women who earn money from their own jobs are less constrained by economic need to remain in unsatisfactory marriages. There is another way to look at the way women's earnings might affect marital stability, however. Women's earnings may improve the family's finances, reduce tensions, and thus increase stability.

Moreover, couples with two incomes may be more reluctant to divorce because they do not want to give up the lifestyle their combined income allows.

Mental Health and Well-Being

As women's participation in the labor force soared in the 1970s and 1980s, a debate ensued about the impact of employment on women's health and well-being. Some researchers proposed that the housewife role doomed women to depression because housework is inherently isolating, restrictive, unskilled, repetitive, devalued, low in status, and thus not very psychologically rewarding. Employment is quite different and may be much more rewarding. However, others argued that housewives are not necessarily depressed, because they derive different meanings from the housewife role (Shehan, Burg, and Rexroat, 1986).

Just as the housewife role can be viewed in either a negative or positive way, employment can also be viewed negatively or positively. The *role strain* perspective holds that employment is detrimental to women's psychological well-being. Combining work and family roles is more stressful for women than it is for men because women take on employment roles over and above their domestic obligations, whereas men are free to concentrate on their paid work (Moen, 1992, p. 47). The *role accumulation* perspective, in contrast, holds that employed women experience higher levels of well-being than those who are exclusively homemakers because they have an additional source of gratification.

It may not be possible to determine the impact of employment on women's psychological well-being unless their own attitudes and their husbands' are taken into account. "Whether women are captives to employment, conflicted about their work and family obligations, coping with these two roles, or committed exclusively to their careers makes an enormous difference on the impact of paid work on their well-being" (Moen, 1992, p. 49). Women who approve of employment and enjoy their jobs are more likely to benefit psychologically from their employment. Women whose husbands help with housework and child care are the most likely to benefit psychologically from employment (Rogers and DeBoer, 2001). The impact of women's employment also depends on the kinds of jobs they hold and on their work conditions. Occupational prestige, absence of physical and psychological pressure, and a degree of challenge and self-direction increase women's well-being.

In recent years, there has also been considerable interest in whether husbands experience psychological distress when their wives are employed. Some researchers hypothesize that husbands experience more depression, anxiety, loss of self-esteem, and other symptoms of poor mental health when their wives are employed. This hypothesis comes from several related views, including the idea that when their wives are employed, husbands have doubts about their own abilities as breadwinners. There is also the view that husbands become psychologically distressed when, as a result of their wives' working, they lose some of their power in the home and have to shoulder more responsibility for household labor. However, other studies show that husbands' well-being improves as wives' income increases, suggesting that any negative effect of wives' employment is due to something other than the loss of status and power as a sole breadwinner. The negative effect of wives' employment on men's psychological well-being is intensified if the men are opposed to their wives' working outside the home. Men who support their wives' employment reported the lowest levels of depression. Possibly, the relationship between wives' employment and husbands' psychological well-being will change as younger men accept and endorse the employment of their wives (Moen, 1992).

HEADline   Parenting and Political Office: The First Pregnant Governor in U.S. History

Can a young mother balance the demands of a growing family with the huge responsibility of running a state of 6 million people? This question has followed Republican Jane Swift since she was chosen to be lieutenant governor of Massachusetts in 1998 by then-governor Paul Celluci. When he left the office in 2001 to become U.S. ambassador to Canada, Swift stepped in as acting governor of Massachusetts—the state's first female acting governor. At the time she became governor, the 36-year-old Swift had a 2-and-a-half-year-old daughter and was pregnant with twins. From the time she became Lieutenant Governor until she announced that she would not run for election in 2002, Swift was watched closely to see how she attempted to combine her career with motherhood. In fact, she was criticized widely for using a State Police helicopter to fly home for Thanksgiving and asking aides to baby-sit her daughter. (She was fined $1,250 for the latter action.) Swift's husband, Charles Hunt, is a contractor who became a stay-at-home dad to take on primary responsibility for their children.

When asked to comment about Swift's situation, House Speaker Thomas Finneran, a Democrat, replied, "I don't think women have been given a fair shake, those women who have entered into politics. There's really a double standard. I think it's a hideously unfair one." He said if Swift were home raising her children and her husband were the governor, "None of you folks would be asking those questions. I don't think they are appropriate questions. She's been elected, she's qualified, she's articulate, she's bright, she's energized by this moment. I don't think it's going to make a difference."

Source: Quoted in LeBlanc. "Jane Swift, Pregnant with Twins, Becomes Massachusetts Governor." *The Nando Times* on-line, April 10, 2001, http://www.nandotimes.com.

The Effects of Mothers' Employment on Small Children

As women entered the workforce in increasing numbers, researchers began to study the effects of maternal employment on children (Hoffman, 1985). Parents and researchers feared that children deprived of the twenty-four-hour-a-day presence of their mothers might turn out badly. Although research suggested that maternal employment did not significantly affect children, many parents and researchers continued to be concerned (Parcel and Menaghan, 1994a, p. 97).

Psychologists and sociologists have continued to study the effects of maternal employment on young children (Desai, Chase-Lansdale, and Michael, 1989; Blau and Grossberg, 1990; Baydar and Brooks-Gunn, 1991; Belsky and Eggebeen, 1991; Vandell and Ramanan, 1992). Some studies have found that young children whose mothers are employed are "less compliant," meaning that the children are less manageable (Belsky and Eggebeen, 1991). Other researchers report that when mothers are employed during the first year of a child's life, cognitive abilities and social development are negatively affected (Baydar and Brooks-Gunn, 1991). And yet other studies show that children with working mothers are no different from other children (Desai, Chase-Lansdale, and Michael, 1989) or that they actually have higher math and reading achievement (Vandell and Ramanan, 1992). In short, the research results on the effects of mothers' employment on children are mixed or contradictory (Parcel and Menaghan, 1994a).

The research may have yielded contradictory data because the initial question was too simplistic. Although maternal employment may influence child outcomes

▲ *Licensed family day care homes are a valuable option for many employed parents.*

(both positively and negatively), so may a great many other things (including father's employment). Two researchers who used a national sample of parents and children to study the effects of "parents' jobs on children's lives" have concluded,

> [T]here is no simple answer to the questions concerning the benefits or dangers of maternal employment. Much depends on the quality of that employment, the demands of partners' occupations, and the demands of other children. It is clear that both mothers' and fathers' work may be more or less helpful to children depending on other resources on which parents must draw and other responsibilities they may shoulder. (Parcel and Menaghan, 1994b, p. 159)

Maternal employment is only one element in an array of occupational and family factors that can influence child development. The nature of the jobs fathers and mothers hold, along with their ability to provide high-quality child care and their psychological and economic resources all play a part in the outcomes for children. Research has simply not proven that the employment of mothers always has negative effects on children's development, even when they are young. Research findings "are incompatible with social policies that discourage maternal employment" (Parcel and Menaghan, 1994a, p. 1003).

Social Policy and Employment

Who is responsible for resolving the dilemmas that emerge from the interface between jobs and families? Historically in our society, the major responsibility has been on workers and their families. They have been forced to adapt to the demands of the workplace. Couples who seek help from marriage and family therapists in balancing their work and family demands are offered a number of solutions: (1) get organized and use their time more efficiently, (2) allocate household responsibilities to children and/or hire household help, (3) modify roles and standards to reduce the pressure originating from the household, (4) reframe the situation in a more positive light, and (5) safeguard physical health and well-being, because illness can throw off a precariously balanced schedule. All these solutions take the structure of work demands for granted and assume that families must bend to meet the workplace. Recently, however, individuals have been asking how government and industry can help reconcile job–family conflicts.

One of the most fundamental changes that must occur in the workplace is for employers to acknowledge that workers have family responsibilities. There are a number of specific ways in which this can be accomplished: Employers can make work schedules more flexible, reduce work demands that negatively affect family life, and offer benefits that directly help workers provide for their family's economic needs.

Flexible Schedules

One option for increasing flexibility in job schedules is flex-time. **Flex-time** eliminates rigid starting and stopping times and allows workers to arrive at work and leave work within a wider range of time as long as they are at work during the designated core hours of the day. Another option is **job sharing** in which two workers split one full-time job. Yet another option is the **four-day work week.** Workers fit a full forty-hour work week into four days rather than five, leaving three-day weekends for their families. Research shows that increased flexibility increases workers' morale and productivity and decreases turnover (the rate at which workers change jobs), absenteeism, and tardiness, all of which translate into bottom-line profits for employers. Communities also benefit insofar as traffic patterns around work sites become less crowded when workers stagger their arrival and departure times.

ContentSELECT

Flexible Work

Reasonable Demands

Two demands of employment that negatively affect families are frequent travel and compulsory relocation. Geographic relocation affects many Americans every year. More than half of these residential changes are job related. Many professions demand frequent relocation. Two of the most notable in this respect are the military and the clergy. United Methodist clergy, for example, relocate once every four years, on the average.

A study of Methodist ministers and their families (Frame and Shehan, 1994) revealed the negative impact of frequent relocation on wives and children. Frequent relocation (1) increases the demand for household labor as families pack and unpack their belongings; (2) disrupts children's friendship networks and requires readjustment to school in a new community; (3) disrupts relationships with professional service providers, such as doctors and dentists; (4) disrupts women's employment patterns, reducing or eliminating an important source of income; (5) increases financial burden due to moving expenses; and (6) disrupts parents' own support networks and produces a feeling of grief and mourning.

As a result of these problems associated with frequent career-related moves, women who were married to Methodist ministers in this study (Frame and Shehan, 1994) had a greater accumulation of stresses, fewer coping resources, more negative feelings about their moves, and significantly poorer mental health and well-being than their husbands. Churches and other employers who require frequent relocation of their employees might consider whether this is necessary, and if they decide it is, they might attempt to make the timing of the moves more compatible with family schedules. They should also provide professional counseling services to help families cope with the disruption associated with moving and assist trailing spouses in finding satisfactory employment in the new community.

Family-Friendly Policies

The federal government and corporate employers have been slow in designing policies that help workers reconcile their employment demands with their family responsibilities. Typically it is only when the problems become so severe that they spill over into the workplace that policies are developed. Employers that depend on a large number of female workers (such as hospitals) have typically been the most concerned with providing family-friendly policies. Their motivation to do this comes from concerns about recruitment, absenteeism, and turnover among women workers. The most common type of assistance they offer is child care.

Many U.S. employers provide some kind of help with child care but only 5 percent provide on-site child care. This is the most beneficial type of assistance that can be provided to employees to help them balance their work and family responsibilities.

Labor shortages may force corporations to respond more directly to easing work–family conflicts among their employees. But there are two limitations on the extent to which the U.S. workforce as a whole will benefit from family-friendly policies. Higher-status workers are more likely than other workers to receive benefits. Most people work for small companies that cannot afford costly policies to accommodate workers' families. To meet the needs of the majority of workers, the federal government must take action (Reskin and Padavic, 1994, p. 160).

The U.S. government has, in fact, provided fewer family-friendly benefits to workers than have many other advanced industrial nations. One reason is that the United States hasn't faced the severe labor shortages, except during war time, that have prompted other nations to attempt to accommodate workers' family needs. During World War II, the federal government did respond to family needs because it needed to encourage women to enter the labor force to fill jobs that had previously been done by men. Over 3,000 daycare centers were established to enable mothers to take jobs outside their homes. When the war ended and men came back to their jobs, the daycare centers were closed and women were encouraged to go back to their homes and children full time.

Many nations require employers to provide family leave for workers to give birth, rear small children, or care for elderly relatives. In the United States, in contrast, there were no federal laws requiring employers to provide such leave until relatively recently. In 1993, President Clinton signed into law the **Family and Medical Leave Act,** which requires employers to provide up to twelve weeks of unpaid leave and job protection after a pregnancy or family emergency. The law covers fathers as well as mothers, and adoptive parents as well as biological ones. However, since it only applies to employers with fifty or more employees, it does not cover most U.S. workers (Reskin and Padavic, 1994).

Some potential negative consequences of family leave policies must be considered, however. Family leave may reinforce the pattern in which child care responsibilities are assigned to women. Because men typically make higher wages than their wives, families with young children may decide it makes more economic sense for mothers rather than fathers to stay home to care for them. In addition, if leave policies are specifically targeted to women, they can discourage companies from hiring women or enable them to justify restricting women to routine jobs where they can be easily replaced. Leave policies may also keep women's wages low to offset the cost of replacing those who are temporarily away from their jobs (Reskin and Padavic, 1994).

Family leave is only one type of family-friendly policy that is being considered in the United States. Others are considered in detail in Chapter 15, which addresses ways in which family problems can be dealt with on the societal and individual level.

Summary

Women have always made significant contributions to their families through their labor. Before industrialization, they worked primarily in the household context. In the early stages of industrialization, women and children were the workers in factories. Later in the nineteenth century, men replaced women in the industrial workplace, and women were charged with taking care of the home and family. This structure is called the breadwinner–homemaker system.

Today women have returned to the workplace in great numbers; nearly 60 percent of all married women are now employed. Over half of all women with children under 18 are employed. Even though women constitute an important part of the workforce, they typically work at certain occupations that are consistent with the traditional tasks of women. Even when women have the same occupations and professions as men, they earn only two-thirds to three-fourths as much as men.

Families can be divided into four employment types: blue-collar couples, the two-person career, dual-career couples, and single-parent providers.

Work and family produce a number of friction points in relationships. Time and schedule conflicts occur when husbands and wives are both working and their jobs give them a limited amount of time together. Employment demands often separate men and women from their families and spouses. Occupational inequities can be troublesome for couples, especially when women earn more, or advance faster in their careers, than their partners. The workplace can also produce social relationships that lead to difficulties between partners.

Household labor, including child care, continues to be done mostly by women. Men increase their proportion of household labor and child care when children get older, but women very often retain the administrative or executive function in all stages of family life.

Employment affects marital power and decision making, generally to the benefit of men, because they earn more at their jobs. Marital satisfaction and stability are also influenced by the employment of women, although the relationship is complex. Women who are employed are likely to have better mental health than women who are not in the labor force, but their mental health can be influenced by their husbands' attitudes toward their employment. The effect of maternal employment on small children has often been studied, and there is no clear evidence showing a negative outcome for children.

Social policies have the potential for resolving the problems of families that are produced by employment. Employers can be especially helpful by allowing flexible schedules, making reasonable demands, and following family-friendly policies.

Key Terms

Asymmetrically permeable boundaries (between/among family roles) (p. 384)
Blue-collar couples (p. 384)
Commuter marriages (p. 390)
Cult of true womanhood (p. 376)
Dual-career couples (p. 384)
Executive function (in the household) (p. 393)

Family and Medical Leave Act (p. 400)
Feminization of poverty (p. 383)
Flex-time (at work) (p. 399)
Four-day, forty-hour work week (p. 399)
Gender labeling of jobs (p. 380)
Gender segregation of workers (p. 380)

Job sharing (p. 399)
Role overload (p. 387)
Second shift (p. 392)
Sex segregation (p. 384)
Single-parent providers (p. 384)
Structural buffers (between/among family roles) (p. 384)
Two-person career (p. 384)

Review Questions

1. Describe women's and men's economic roles in preindustrial America.

2. How did the Industrial Revolution affect women's and men's roles?

3. What is the cult of true womanhood? When and why did it develop? Did it apply to all women equally?

4. Summarize trends in women's employment over the twentieth century. Describe changes in the employment of married women and of mothers over this time period.

5. How and why did World War II affect women's labor force participation patterns?

6. What is meant by gender segregation in the labor force? Identify the causes and consequences of gender segregation.

7. How has the gender gap in pay changed over the past fifty years? What factors contribute to the gap?

8. In what ways do spouses' occupational types (e.g., blue collar or white collar) affect the dynamics of family life?

9. What difficulties do married professional women face in attempting to balance careers with family life?

10. What are the major friction points between jobs and family life?

11. How has the increase in women's employment outside their homes affected the division of household labor?

12. In what ways do employment and income affect marital dynamics (e.g., power, satisfaction, stability) and spouses' health and well-being?

13. What insights does social science research contribute to the continuing debate about the impact of mothers' employment on small children?

Critical Thinking Questions

1. Why does women's work continue to be valued less than men's work? Why do the jobs in which women dominate numerically pay less than jobs that are dominated by men?

2. How likely is it that large numbers of American women will stop working outside their homes and return to full-time homemaking? How would the U.S. economy be affected by a sharp and rapid decrease in the employment of women?

3. In what ways, if any, have technological inventions changed the nature of household work? Are there any ways in which technology could have been used to reduce household labor but wasn't?

4. Some people believe that a primary reason men don't do more housework and child care is because women are resistant to the idea of sharing the work. Do you agree with this statement? Why or why not?

5. In countries where men can get paid leave from their jobs to care for infants, few men do so. Why do you think this might be?

6. In what ways could workplaces be changed to make them more *family-friendly*?

Online Resources Available for This Chapter

www.ablongman.com/marriageandfamily

- **Online Study Guide with Practice Tests**
- **PowerPoint Chapter Outlines**

- **Links to Marriage and Family Websites**
- **ContentSelect Research Database**
- **Self-Assessment Activities**

Further Reading

Books

Barnett, Rosalind, C., and Rivers, Caryl. *She Works/He Works: How Two-Income Families are Happy, Healthy, and Thriving.* Cambridge, MA: Harvard University Press, 1998. Report based on a four year study of 300 middle and working class couples.

Gary, Anita I. *Weaving Work and Motherhood.* Philadelphia: Temple University Press, 1999. Using case studies, this award-winning book examines the meaning of motherhood and work that underlie women's strategies for integrating employment and motherhood.

Hertz, Rosanna, and Marshall, Nancy L. (eds.). *Working Families: The Transformation of the American Home.* Los Angeles: University of California Press, 2001. A collection of essays written by leading scholars both inside and outside academia that presents an updated and integral view of the revolutionary changes in patterns of work and family life occurring today.

Hesse-Biber, Sharlene, and Carter, Gregg Lee. *Working Women in America: Split Dreams.* New York: Oxford, 1999. The book offers a broad perspective on the diversity of women and their work, and suggests we rethink ideas concerning work, family, and gender roles in order to help solve women's work and family life dilemmas.

Hochschild, Arlie. *The Second Shift*. New York: Viking, 1989. An in-depth examination of the ways in which couples allocate household work and create elaborate justifications for women's greater share of the burden.

Hoffman, Lois, and Youngblade, Lise. *Mothers at Work: Effects on Children's Well-Being*. Cambridge: Cambridge University Press, 1999. This important volume examines the effects of the mother's employment on family life, focusing on 448 families in an industrialized city in the Midwest.

Landry, Bart. *Black Working Wives: Pioneers of the American Family Revolution*. Los Angeles: University of California Press, 2000. Using biographical material, historical records, and demographic data, Landry shows how these black pioneers of the dual-career marriage created a paradigm for other women seeking to escape the cult of domesticity and thus foreshadowed the second great family transformation.

Lopata, Helena Znaniecki. *Occupation: Housewife*. Westport, CT: Greenwood Publishing Company, 1971. One of the first sociological studies of housework as an occupation.

Rapoport, Rhona, and Rapoport, Robert. *Dual-Career Families*. New York: Pelican Books, 1971. A pioneering study of challenges faced by couples in which both spouses have demanding careers while raising children.

Stebbins, Leslie F. *Work and Family in America: A Reference Handbook*. Location?: ABC-Clio, 2001. A comprehensive examination of the changing cultures of the workplace, family, and home, including the shifting role of men as they become more involved fathers; trends in daycare and child development; the degree to which dual-career couples share housework; and the relationship between employment and self-esteem.

Williams, Joan. *Unbending Gender: Why Family and Work Conflict and What to Do About It*. Oxford: Oxford University Press, 2001. Outlines a new vision of feminism that calls for workplaces focused on the needs of families and, in divorce cases, recognition of the value of family work and its impact on women's earning power.

Content**SELECT** *Articles*

Albiston, C. "The Rule of Law and the Litigation Process: The Paradox of Losing by Winning." *Law and Society Review* 33(4), 1999: 869–911. **[Database: Sociology]** Albiston, utilizing empirical analysis of judicial opinions that sought to interpret the Family and Medical Leave Act, ably discusses how the litigation process aids in the development of law. This article further explains how judicial opinions potentially impact and influence subsequent interpretations of the law.

Levitan, S. "The Changing Workplace." *Society* 35(2), 1998: 278–287. **[Database: Social Work]** Levitan provides a thorough discussion of the historical nature of work and the labor force. The author purports that the feminization of poverty will only continue to increase if the government does not play an increasing role in the support of and provision to female heads-of-households.

Magnuson, and Norem, S. "Challenges for Higher Education Couples in Commuter Marriages: Insights for Couples and Counselors Who Work with Them." *Family Journal* 7(2), 1999: 125–135. **[Database: Psychology]** The focus of this investigation was on marital relationships of five dual-career couples; specifically, those couples who maintain two separate homes in order to achieve satisfaction in their careers were examined. The commuting couples highlight the challenges to distance marriages as loneliness, added financial costs, and negative reactions from others. Factors contributing to successful "commuting marriages" include increased trust, frequent and regular communication, and increased quality shared time.

Porter, E. "Interdependence, Parenting, and Responsible Citizenship." *Journal of Gender Studies* 10(1), 2001: 5–16. **[Database: Social Work]** What do shared parenting or two-parent families have to offer to children that single parenting does not? The author articulates well her argument that both shared and single parenting may promote the encouragement of family values that aid in a child's moral flourishing. Porter additionally asserts that interdependence is fostered in both family forms, thereby providing meaningful substance to each family member and society as a whole.

Stanworth, C. "A Best Case Scenario? Non-Manual Part-Time Work and Job-Sharing in UK Local Government in the 1990s." *Community, Work, and Family* 2(3), 1999: 295–310. **[Database: Sociology]** Flexible working arrangements allow employees, particularly women, the opportunity to combine the responsibilities of family and home with paid work. In 1998 it was estimated that as many as 56 percent of United Kingdom businesses utilized job-sharing arrangements. In her investigation of attitudes among professional, managerial, and administrative staff, Stanworth found that the job-sharing model was, indeed, desirable among study respondents.

Turkat, I. "Custody Battle Burnout." *American Journal of Family Therapy* 28(3), 2000: 201–216. **[Database: Psychology]** With approximately one million divorces taking place in the US per year, and nearly 100,000 custody battles each year, this present study sought to determine the phenomenology of those participants in custody battles. Specifically, the investigator delineates stressors specific to custody litigation such as adversarial counsel, attorney problems, covert motivations, and loss of privacy. Those psychological response criteria identified in custody battle burnout include the psychological experience of feeling overwhelmed, the exposure to multifaceted and interacting custody litigation stressors, and emotional reactions related to custody litigation.

Separation and Divorce

The following passage is taken from the opening pages of an autobiographical account of a divorce and the emotions that led up to and through the breakdown of the author's marriage. The passage was written by Wendy Swallow, a former staff writer for the Washington Post. *Swallow was married for 12 years. Her book describes the fantasies about divorce she had while still married and the harsh realities she experienced once she and her husband separated.*

1 Are children in high-conflict marriages better off if their parents divorce?

2 In what ways, if any, do men and women adjust to divorce differently?

3 How will divorce rates change over the next twenty years?

4 What impact, if any, has no-fault divorce legislation had on divorce rates in the United States?

5 How have increased rates of labor force participation among married women affected the divorce rates?

As a fantasy, divorce has a lot to recommend it. A good divorce fantasy can feel like an open window in a life otherwise shuttered in on itself. It can comfort a heart stinging from marital strife. It can be intensely private and perfectly controlled, unlike reality, which may be spinning apart. . . .

During the twelve years I was married, I spent many hours fantasizing about divorce. At first it was just a whisper of an idea, held guiltily for a moment and then dismissed, but as the years passed it became something of an obsession. Whenever my marriage made me unhappy, which was often, I escaped in my head into the world of divorce. . . . It was a place where I didn't have to compromise with a difficult spouse. It was a place where I could make my children infinitely happy, a halcyon world of simple pleasures and contented days. I knew it wouldn't be an easy life—money would be tight and I would have to learn how to mow the lawn—but I imagined the inevitable hardships as lessons that would somehow make us all stronger and bind me closer to my two little boys. . . . This fantasizing was the perfect antidote to a marriage that had become a struggle for power over the smallest of choices. . . . Most people, though, will tell you that divorce is a nightmare rather than a fantasy.

Source: Swallow, Wendy. *Breaking Apart: A Memoir of Divorce.* New York: Hyperion, 2001, pp. 11–12.

Nearly everyone who is touched by a separation and divorce finds it painful, disturbing, and saddening. Even husbands and wives who are eager to end their marriages often describe their separation and divorce as one of the most difficult times of their lives. Children of parents who divorce, unless they are very young, are usually distressed by the breakup of their families. Even the parents of divorcing couples suffer along with their children and grandchildren. Couples who have amicable divorces are rare.

This chapter begins with a brief review of the legal and social history of divorce in England and the United States. Several ways of measuring divorce are presented and evaluated before we consider contemporary divorce trends in the United States. Factors associated with divorce lead us to a discussion of the divorce experience. The chapter concludes with a discussion of the effects of divorce on children and various types of child custody arrangements.

Societal Controls on Ending Marriages

The people of all societies seem to value marriage, or some kind of lasting union, between men and women. Once marriages are formed, societies generally put restrictions or impediments on ending the union. The rules for ending marriages differ from society to society and from one historical period to another. In some societies, couples may end their marriages through very simple procedures, such as a husband saying to his wife, "I divorce thee," or a wife placing her husband's possessions outside the front door of their home where he will see them when he returns. During the latter part of the Roman Empire, divorces could be obtained simply by mutual consent of the spouses.

In both England and the United States, divorces were relatively rare until the last half of the nineteenth century, largely because it was difficult to obtain a divorce. Early laws favored husbands, particularly rich ones, as the following consideration of divorce in England shows.

Divorce in English History

The early history of divorce in England is complicated, because both the church and the state were involved. Prior to the seventeenth century, the only official way of ending a marriage in England was to have it annulled by the church (Stone, 1990). If the marriage was judged by church officials to be "spurious" and not a "true" marriage, it could be ended. A spurious marriage might be one, for example, where the husband and wife were too closely related to each other.

Church laws spelled out just how closely a husband and wife could be related, so if a couple could find some witnesses to testify that the rules had been violated, their marriage could be annulled. The church also granted divorces in cases of adultery, desertion, or physical cruelty, but the laws of the church did not allow a **full divorce** (a divorce that allowed remarriage). In these cases, the church only granted a **bed and board divorce** in which the legal obligations of marriage remained but the husband and wife lived separately (Stone, 1990). Not being able to remarry created special difficulties for the rich and titled citizens, because it might keep them from passing their wealth and titles on to legitimate heirs (Menefee, 1981).

A way out of this dilemma was provided after 1690, first for the aristocracy, and later for those who were simply rich, by the parliamentary divorce. A **parliamentary divorce** was full divorce, including the possibility of remarriage, if the House of Lords could be persuaded to pass a private act ending the marriage (Cott, 1983). Getting a private act passed was very expensive and was essentially only available to the rich. In the period between 1697 and 1785, only ninety such private acts were passed by the House of Lords (Stone, 1990). All parliamentary divorces were awarded to husbands, and all were based on grounds that the wives had committed adultery. Adultery by wives was obviously considered a greater threat to marriage than adultery by husbands.

Along with the ways already described for ending English marriages, two other general ways were available before the passage of the divorce law of 1857. Some couples, especially those of the middle and upper middle classes who had moderate wealth and property, entered into private separation agreements.

A **private separation agreement** was somewhat like a modern-day separation agreement in which the husband and wife agree to divide their property and money and keep their finances separate in the future. These agreements also typically required that the husband provide his former wife with a separate maintenance allowance, or **alimony.** Although private separation agreements often allowed the spouses to cohabit with a new mate, they could not remarry.

Couples in the lowest social classes who wished to end their marriages resorted to **desertion** (one of the spouses left home). Since it was most often the husband who left his wife, desertion has been described as "the poor man's divorce" (Stone, 1990, p. 1). Many Englishmen who deserted their wives and families emigrated to America, where they often remarried, even though remarriage was considered bigamy (Gordon, 1978).

There was one other method used by the common people when legal divorce was otherwise impossible: Some men sold their wives. This practice was used in England from the middle of the eighteenth century until the end of the nineteenth (Menefee, 1981). A husband would often lead his wife to the marketplace with a halter or rope, where she would be auctioned off to another man. The symbolism is as clear to us as it was clear to the people of the time: The wife was viewed as part of her husband's property, and if he wished, he could sell her.

Selling of wives was also a public demonstration of the end of the marriage. Although not legal—wife selling violated both church and governmental law—the public nature of the sale did give *self-divorce* a legitimization by the community (Stone, 1990). Often there was a degree of collusion between the divorcing couple and the buyer, since the man who purchased the wife may have been having an adulterous relationship with her.

To summarize, until England made divorce legal in 1857, marriages were ended using a variety of methods, including church annulment of spurious marriages, bed-and-board divorces, parliamentary divorces, private separation agreements, desertion, and the sale of wives.

In England in the nineteenth century, a husband could divorce his wife by taking her to the marketplace and auctioning her off to another man.

The Divorce Act of 1857 allowed women as well as men to file for divorce. The grounds for divorce for women included desertion (after two years) and cruelty by their husbands. Husbands could divorce their wives on the grounds of adultery alone, but that privilege was not granted to wives (Stone, 1990). Thus, the divorce laws continued to favor men, especially with respect to adultery.

Divorce in American History

The first divorce granted in the United States occurred in the Plymouth Colony in 1639. It was granted to James Luxford's wife after she discovered that he had committed bigamy. Luxford was fined a hundred pounds, sentenced to an hour in the stocks on market day, and banished to England. Not all of the colonies in America were as willing to grant divorces as those in New England, however. Southern colonies were more reluctant to terminate marriages. It wasn't until 1803 that the first divorce was granted in Virginia. The unprecedented action was prompted by the discovery that a married white woman had had a relationship with a slave (Feldman, 2000).

Even though divorce was rare in colonial America, the legal availability of divorce and the various grounds for divorce (especially for women) were initiated in the United States sooner than they were in England. Because each state has its own set of laws pertaining to marriage and divorce, change occurred earlier in some states than in others.

The divorce laws in colonial Connecticut were especially liberal. By 1843, Connecticut had added "habitual intemperance" (alcoholism) and "intolerable cruelty" to the grounds for divorce. Connecticut officials even granted a divorce to one woman because her husband was a "freethinker" (atheist) (Gordon, 1978).

During the nineteenth century, many states liberalized their divorce laws. Indiana, in 1824, led the way by adopting a law that included the **omnibus clause,** which added to the customary grounds for divorce "any other cause for which the court shall deem it proper that a divorce should be granted" (Gordon, 1978, p. 286). The omnibus clause opened the gates for any kind of complaint that spouses might have as a basis for requesting a divorce.

National Differences in Access to Divorce

Until recently the constitution of Ireland absolutely prohibited divorce, but in November 1995 a vote by the Irish people made divorce under some circumstances possible. By a very narrow margin (50.3 percent) the voters removed a ban on divorce that had been in place since 1937. The Irish had voted on this issue about ten years earlier and had firmly rejected a constitutional amendment that would have legalized divorce—in 1986, 63 percent of voters opposed the amendment (Barbash, 1995b).

Under the approved constitutional amendment, an Irish couple can be granted a divorce if they have been living apart for four of the previous five years. This very long period of separation makes divorce possible if there is "no reasonable prospect for reconciliation" (Barbash, 1995b, p. A1). Despite the lengthy period of separation required, there are likely to be tens of thousands of Irish divorces when the ban is officially lifted. Many Irish couples have been separated for years, with one or both partners living in "second relationships," but until now they have been unable to divorce and remarry (Barbash, 1995a).

The Catholic Church has waged a vigorous battle against divorce in many European countries, but Ireland was the last holdout. Italy legalized divorce in 1970, Portugal in 1974, and Spain in 1981 (Goode, 1993). Chile continued to debate legal divorce into the opening years of the twenty-first century.

In contrast to the restrictive divorce laws of Ireland, many countries of the world today make divorce relatively easy for their citizens. However, in no country is divorce as easily available as it once was in Russia, where the "postcard" divorce became notorious.

After the Communist revolution in 1917, Russia discarded the old system in which only husbands could get divorces (Moskoff, 1983). The post-revolution Communist regime considered marriage under a patriarchal system a form of slavery for women and concluded that marriage could only be based on free choice and mutual love. Therefore, it initiated a new simplified procedure for obtaining a divorce: Either the husband or wife could at any time request an end of the marriage. If both made the request, the divorce was granted immediately. Even if only one partner requested the divorce, it was granted as soon as matters of alimony, child custody, and other issues could be resolved.

The divorce law of the Soviet Union continued to be revised during the 1920s, finally making divorce so simple it came to be called the postcard divorce. Married people wanting a divorce had only to stop in at a registry office and either orally or in writing indicate that they wished to have a divorce. According to the law, the spouse had to be informed by postcard within three days that the marriage was over (Moskoff, 1983).

Under this system, divorce in the Soviet Union, especially in the cities of Russia, rose to very high levels. Apparently, Soviet officials became concerned about the uses and abuses of this very convenient form of divorce, and in 1936 they began a series of retreats that made divorce increasingly difficult and expensive. By the mid 1940s it had become nearly impossible to get a divorce because of the cumbersome legal procedures. So the country had gone nearly full circle, from extremely easy divorce to nearly impossible (Moskoff, 1983).

Sources: Moskoff, 1983; Goode, 1993; Barbash, 1995a; Barbash, 1995b.

In 1857, another important development in divorce law occurred when a California judge accepted mental cruelty as a legal ground for divorce. His decision was based on the notion that women were sensitive and thus could be harmed just as much by verbal assaults as by physical cruelty. In 1863, the Supreme Court of California ruled that any conduct that caused ill health or bodily pain, even though "operating on the mind only, should be regarded as legal cruelty" (Griswold, 1982, p. 20).

Gradually, from the end of the nineteenth century through the first half of the twentieth, most states in the United States broadened the grounds for divorce. But there was still considerable variation from state to state, which continues today. The Around the World box shows the wide range of divorce laws that exist in various countries of the world, as well.

Measures of Divorce

Many people speak glibly about divorce rates, but often with little understanding of how the numbers are obtained or what they mean. Some measures of divorce are better than others, and some are less meaningful than most people assume. We begin with the best measure, the refined divorce rate. Next we describe the shortcomings of measuring divorce by comparing divorces in a given year to marriages occurring in that same year. Last, we explain why the percentage of marriages ending in divorce is less meaningful than most people assume.

Refined Divorce Rate

One of the most widely used measures of divorce is called the **crude divorce rate.** This simply reports how many divorces occurred for every 1,000 people in the population. Clearly, however, not every person in the population is at risk of being divorced. The most useful measure of divorce comes from comparing the number of divorces in any given year to the number of people who *are* at risk of getting a divorce. The people who are at risk of getting a divorce are obviously the number of married couples in the population. To calculate the **refined divorce rate,** the number of divorces and annulments in a given year is divided by the number of married women in the population. As an example, let's take the figures for the year 1998, when there were 1.1 million divorces and annulments and 59 million married women 15 years of age and older. The number of divorces is first divided by the number of married women, as follows:

$$\frac{1.1 \text{ million}}{59 \text{ million}} = .0186 \times 1,000 = 18.6$$

The resulting decimal fraction is .0186. To get rid of the decimal fraction, we multiply by 1,000. The result is 18.6, which is interpreted in the following way: In 1998 there were almost 19 divorces for every 1,000 married women in the population.

Calculating the rate of divorce this way allows us to compare divorce rates for different size populations. We could, for example, do similar calculations for the United States in earlier years when the population of married couples was much smaller. For example, in 1980 the number of divorces for every 1,000 married women was 22.6—a higher rate than for 1998. In 1960, when the married population was even smaller, this measure of divorce was 9.2, which means that the divorce rate in 1960 was less than half what it was in 1998 (9.2 versus 18.6). Even though the population in 1960 was much smaller (and the population of married couples was also much smaller), we can make the comparison because we are comparing the number of divorces for every 1,000 married couples.

Divorces as a Percentage of Weddings

A measure of divorce that is occasionally used, even though it produces misleading results, compares the number of divorces in a given year to the number of marriages taking place in that same year. For example, in the United States in 1998 there were approximately 2.2 million marriages and 1.1 million divorces (U.S. Bureau of the Census, 2000), so it is easy to see that in that year there were about half as many divorces as marriages. Some people might look at these numbers and conclude that half of all marriages end in divorce, but they would be wrong. The divorces are being compared only to the number of people who marry in any single

TABLE 13.1

Incidence of Marriage and Divorce for Selected Years

Year	Number of Marriages	Number of Divorces	Crude Divorce Rate (per Thousand Population)
1960	1,523,000	393,000	2.2
1965	1,523,000	479,000	2.5
1970	2,159,000	708,000	3.5
1975	2,153,000	1,036,000	4.8
1980	2,390,000	1,189,000	5.2
1985	2,477,000	1,162,000	4.9
1990	2,425,000	1,161,000	4.7
1995	2,355,000	1,184,000	4.5
1996	2,310,000	1,157,000	4.4
1998	2,244,000	1,135,000	4.2
1999	2,318,000	—	4.1

Sources: Adapted from Baca Zinn and Eitzen (2002), p. 381. From U.S. Bureau of the Census, *Statistical Abstract of the United States,* Washington, DC: U.S. Government Printing Office, various years; and "Population Update," *Population Today,* various issues.

year, and these marriages constitute only a small portion of the population at risk for divorce. All married couples, whenever they were married, are at risk of divorce. The numbers needed to calculate this proportion are provided in Table 13.1.

Percentage of All Marriages Ending in Divorce

The most often quoted divorce statistic is the percentage of all marriages that end in divorce. Most often the claim is made that 50 percent of all marriages end in divorce. Although this statistic seems straightforward and meaningful, it does not mean what most people think it does.

To say that 50 percent of all marriages end in divorce does not mean that 50 percent of marriages starting this year will end in divorce. No one can say what will happen in the future; one can only say what has happened to marriages in the past. But what is not usually recognized is how far in the past one must go to make any statement about how many marriages end in divorce.

If we consider, for example, marriages that occurred over the last three years, we can easily see that although some of these marriages already have ended in divorce, it will be many years before we can know how many (and what percentage) will finally end in divorce. If we go back to marriages that occurred ten years ago, we know more about how many of these marriages have ended in divorce, but we do not have a complete record of the number that will end in divorce, because they still have many years to go before they have run their course (either ending in divorce, or the death of one of the spouses).

The farther back in time we go to examine the incidence of divorce, the less confidence we can have that the couples marrying today will have divorce rates that are similar to those in the past. How confident can we feel with predictions about today's marrying couples on the basis of people who were married in the

1970s? Many things have changed in the last thirty years that make couples who marry today different from those of the past. Yet any calculation of the percentage of marriages ending in divorce (of which there are precious few) must necessarily be based on decades-old data.

As a technical matter, the statistical procedures for arriving at estimates of the percentage of marriages ending in divorce are not as simple as one might suppose. For this reason, only a few such studies have been done, and those that have influenced popular perceptions most are based on marriages and divorces that occurred two or more decades ago (Preston and McDonald, 1979; Weed, 1980). More recent statistical analyses indicate that slightly over 40 percent of marriages that occurred *one, two, or more decades ago* will end in divorce (Norton and Miller, 1992; Schoen and Weinick, 1993; Clarke and Wilson, 1994).

Although the percentage of marriages ending in divorce is an appealing statistic, it is not as current or meaningful as most people suppose. Whenever divorce trends or levels are to be discussed, it is best to use rates (the number of divorces relative to the population at risk), as we do in the following discussion of divorce in the United States.

Divorce Rates in the United States

Divorce Rate

There has been an upward trend in divorce in this country for over 100 years. Figure 13.1 shows the long-term trends in divorce in the United States since the 1860s, when divorce statistics were first available. Rates in this graph are based on the number of divorces per 1,000 married women (the refined rate).

The steepest and most persistent increase in divorce started in the early 1960s and continued until about 1980. During this period, the divorce rate more than doubled, with dramatic consequences for the society. Over the last twenty years, the divorce rate has declined slightly but still remains high compared with other countries in the world.

Several other features of the trend in divorce are interesting to note. During the 1930s, there was a substantial dip in the divorce rate that corresponds with the early years of the Great Depression. This suggests that divorces become less frequent during times of economic hardship, and yet by the mid thirties—long before the Depression was over—the divorce rate started increasing again. Moreover, during several economic recessions of the post–World War II period the divorce rates did not go down. Indeed, since 1947 divorce rates have tended to go up during times of economic recession (South, 1985).

A second noticeable feature in the divorce trend as shown in Figure 13.1 is the high peak of divorce after the middle 1940s. This peak corresponds with the end of World War II and probably reflects two major factors: (1) Some married couples separated by the war chose not to return to their prewar married lives, and (2) some marriages that were entered into hastily during the war may have lost some of their original appeal. Since World War II, the effects of subsequent wars have not been consistent. Divorce rates went down after the Korean War and up during and after the Vietnam War (South, 1985).

The modest decline in divorce rates since 1980 may be explained by a number of factors. One contributing factor may be the increase in the average age of marriage, since early marriages are more likely to end in divorce. In the 1980s, when the divorce rates for all other age groups were going down, the divorce rate among married women under age 20 was still increasing (Glick and Lin, 1986).

Divorce in the United States varies considerably by geographic region. The highest divorce rates are found in the West and South, while the lowest are found in the East and Midwest.

Figure 13.1 **Annual Divorce Rates, United States, 1860–1998.** *Divorces per thousand married women aged fifteen and over.*

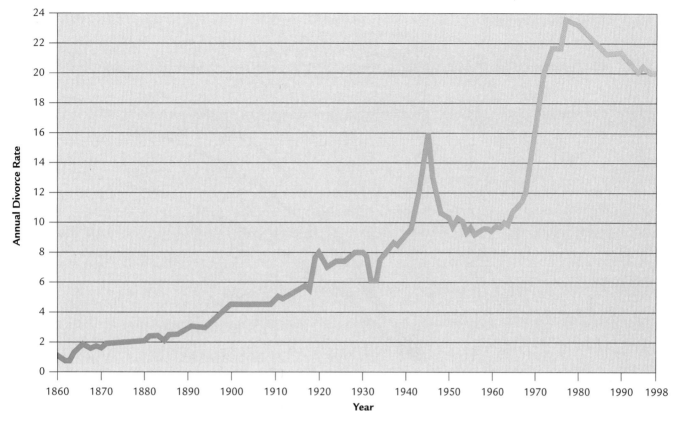

(*Sources:* Baca Zinn and Eitzen, 2002, p. 380. Reprinted from Andres J. Cherlin, *Marriage, Divorce, Remarriage.* Cambridge, MA: Harvard University Press, 1981, p. 22; U.S. Bureau of the Census, *Statistical Abstract of the United States 1984*, 104th ed. Washington, DC: U.S. Government Printing Office, p. 84; Sar A. Levitan, Richard S. Belous, and Frank Gallo, *What's Happening to the American Family?* Rev. ed. Baltimore: John Hopkins University Press, 1988, p. 27; *USA Today*, July 9, 1991, p. 1; and current U.S. Census Bureau documents.)

When Do Marriages End?

After five years, 20 percent of all first marriages have ended, due to separation or divorce. After ten years of marriage this figure rises to 33 percent. If the wife was a teenager when she married, her marriage is much more likely to dissolve within this time period than if she was at least 20 years old when she married. At every anniversary mark, first marriages are more likely to have dissolved if the bride was a teen when she married. Thus, after ten years, nearly half of all marriages to women who were under 18 when they married have dissolved, compared with 40 percent of marriages in which the bride was 18 or 19 at the time she married. Women who were married between the ages of 20 and 24 are less likely to be divorced by the tenth anniversary; and those who were at least 25 at the time they married have the lowest likelihood of divorcing within ten years after marrying. To summarize, the older the age at first marriage, the more likely the relationship is to survive for ten years or more. These trends are presented in Figure 13.2.

The probability that a first marriage will end in separation or divorce also varies by race and ethnicity. African American marriages are more likely to end in separation or divorce than those involving whites, Hispanics, and Asian Americans. After ten years of marriage, 32 percent of the first marriages of white,

Figure 13.2   **Probability of First Marriage Disruption by Duration of Marriage and Wife's Age at Marriage: United States, 1995**

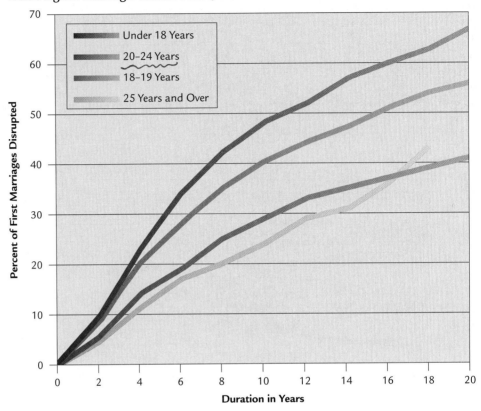

(*Source:* Bramlett and Mosher, 2001, Figure 1, p. 6.)

non-Hispanic women have dissolved as have 34 percent of the first marriages of Hispanic women. In contrast, nearly half of the first marriages of black, non-Hispanic women have dissolved. First marriages of Asian American women dissolve at a considerably slower rate. After ten years, only 20 percent have ended in separation or divorce. These differences are summarized in Figure 13.3. Data come from the 1995 National Survey of Family Growth, cycle 5, which was conducted by the Centers for Disease Control and Prevention (Bramlett and Mosher, 2001).

Factors Associated with Divorce

Researchers have found a number of factors associated with the likelihood of getting a divorce. Most prominent among these are age at marriage, race, socioeconomic status, and religion.

Age at Marriage

All available evidence shows that if a person marries at an early age, the likelihood of divorce is increased. Couples who marry under the age of 18 are more likely to divorce than couples who marry at any later age.

Figure 13.3 **Probability of First Marriage Disruption by Duration of Marriage and Wife's Race and Ethnicity: United States, 1995**

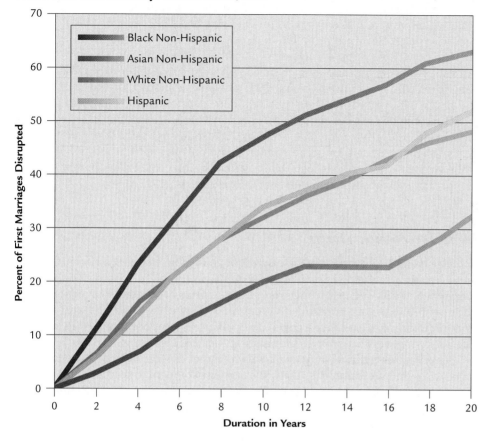

(*Source:* Bramlett and Mosher, 2001, Figure 2, p. 7.)

One possible explanation for the high divorce rate among couples who marry young is that they are poorly prepared for marriage. They do not understand what will be expected of them in marriage, nor do they have the maturity to handle the responsibilities. We discussed readiness for marriage in Chapter 5. A second explanation pertains to choice of partner. Those who marry at an early age may have had only limited dating experience and may not have developed a clear idea of what they value in a partner. They are more likely to see attractive alternatives to the marriages they have entered. Since they are still young, they may perceive a new marriage as preferable to their present marriage (Levinger, 1979). A third explanation is that young couples have fewer barriers to divorce. Many may have married without the approval of their parents; thus they may divorce without their parents opposition. Additionally, they may not have accumulated property together, which means they have fewer reasons to stay together.

A fourth possible explanation for the higher divorce rates of couples who marry young is the greater likelihood of marriage due to premarital pregnancy or childbirth. Having a child before or early in marriage clearly increases the likelihood of divorce. Having a child so early in their relationship gives young married couples less time to make the adjustment to each other or to the demands of married life. It may also limit young parents' educational and occupational opportunities, which may, in turn, increase the financial strains in their marriage (Faust and McKibbin, 1999).

Race

Studies consistently show that African Americans have higher rates of divorce than whites and Latinos (Baca Zinn and Eitzen, 2002; White, 1990). African Americans are also much more likely than white Americans to remain in a separated status. These differences in marital stability are relatively recent (occurring since 1960), however, and reflect the deteriorating economic status of African Americans who live in urban areas. Their greater likelihood of being unemployed and living in poverty contribute to their higher rates of marital disruption.

The combined effects of African American women being less likely to marry, more likely to separate or divorce, and less likely to remarry, lead to a striking statistic: On average, African American women spend only about half the amount of time white women spend in marriage. Marriage has become "just a temporary stage of life" for the average African American woman (Cherlin, 1992, p. 95).

Socioeconomic Status

Marital instability (separation and divorce) is more frequent among people in the lower socioeconomic strata of society than in the higher. People with higher educational levels, higher incomes, and higher-status occupations have lower marital dissolution (separation and divorce) rates (White, 1990; Sassler and Schoen, 1999). Poor families are twice as likely to break up as nonpoor families (Pear, 1993). The effect of poverty is even greater among African Americans.

Lower-status married couples may have higher divorce rates because they face more crises and disruptions in their lives (unemployment, uncertain jobs, welfare dependency). People at higher-status levels, on the other hand, marry later, often waiting to complete a college education, and later marriage is related to lower divorce rates. Higher-status people also have more to lose from divorce, especially in terms of social status. For people in some occupations and professions, such as the ministry and political life, a divorce may be detrimental to careers.

Religion

A national survey conducted in 1999 showed that religion is also related to separation and divorce (Matthews, 1999). Among the major religions in the United States, Protestants as a group have slightly higher divorce rates than Catholics, and Jews have slightly higher rates than Protestants. Among the Protestant denominations, some of the most theologically conservative, such as the Baptists, have relatively high rates of marital dissolution. The reason for this unexpected relationship may be that the lower socioeconomic status of the members of these denominations lead to higher divorce rates.

The Divorce Experience

Marital separation and divorce are very complex experiences. Divorce is not a single act, except perhaps in the strict legal sense—when the divorce is granted by the court. Divorce is multifaceted, often with several processes occurring at the same time. According to one analyst, there are at least six "stations of divorce": "The complexity of divorce arises because at least six things are happening at once. They may come in a different order and with varying intensities, but

In "simple" divorce cases (for example, those with no dependent children or substantial assets), state laws may allow spouses to represent themselves rather than hiring lawyers.

there are at least six different experiences of separation [and divorce]" (Bohannan, 1971, pp. 33–34).

Bohannan labeled these six stations of divorce *emotional, legal, economic, community, psychic,* and *coparental.* We consider each of these stations of divorce separately.

Emotional Divorce

Emotional divorce involves recognizing that the relationship with a spouse is deteriorating and the marriage is ending. This stage may occur years before the final separation and legal dissolution of the marriage. Most people experience the greatest stress during this first stage of the separation and divorce process (Kitson, 1992). Understandably, ending a marriage is very stressful. Individuals must admit they were wrong about their earlier decision to marry. Even couples who have had stormy and difficult marriages often feel a sense of loss, disappointment, and failure as they approach the actual breakup.

Most divorcing couples experience an extreme sense of ambivalence during the emotional divorce. One woman described her ambivalence in vivid terms:

> It was a very sad time. When I was away from him I missed him terribly and wanted to be back together. . . . When I got back with him, I could be back less than 24 hours and I needed to go. . . . And then the same thing would happen. I would go away, I'd miss him . . . I'd want to be near him. It was just on and on. (Hopper, 1993, p. 806)

For many couples, the pain of the emotional divorce is intensified by the fact that one spouse wants to end the marriage, while the other does not. The person who wants to get out of the marriage is usually called the *initiator;* the other spouse is called the *noninitiating partner,* or simply, the *partner* (Vaughn, 1986; Hopper, 1993). The initiator is not necessarily the spouse who files for the legal divorce. Almost all divorcing couples eventually agree on which partner was the initiator. Researchers find relatively few divorcing couples who say that the marriage ended by mutual consent—they almost always assign the initiator role to one spouse and the noninitiating partner role to the other.

The noninitiating partner usually experiences more anger, stress, and pain during the emotional divorce. The initiator may feel guilt, but is better able to maintain an emotional balance during the stresses associated with divorce because he or she has probably been thinking about it for a longer period of time (Vaughn, 1986). The noninitiating partner is often completely unaware of what the initiator has been thinking. Eventually the initiator raises the issue openly with his or her partner. The initiator may broach the issue in different ways, ranging from expressions of dissatisfaction with the marriage to a sudden request for a divorce. This often leaves the noninitiating partner in emotional turmoil or shock.

In the aftermath of the emotional divorce, both partners eventually develop accounts of what happened to the marriage and what brought about the divorce (Weiss, 1975). A **divorce account** is each partner's statement of the important events of the divorce process, explaining what each spouse did and why he or she did it. Hopper's (1993) interviews with divorced couples show that the accounts[1] of the initiator and the noninitiating partner take on customary, nearly stylized, forms.

Initiators almost always emphasize in their accounts that they left their marriages in order to fulfill *individual* needs or ambitions. "Some wanted more emotional closeness, some wanted less; some wanted a more extensive social life outside the marriage, others wanted less; several people wanted more room for personal growth, autonomy, and individual career goals" (Hopper, 1993, p. 807). Noninitiating partners, by contrast, almost always stress why they did not want the marriage to end. Even those noninitiators who were dissatisfied with their marriages generally claim that they did all they could to avoid divorce. They emphasize the importance of commitment to the family and the marriage itself.

The accounts of divorcing spouses also focus on the *reasons* for the divorce. Very frequently the reasons of husbands and wives are very different, even though they seemingly have gone through the same separation and divorce experience (Ponzetti et al., 1992). For example, in one divorce case in which both husband and wife were interviewed, the husband accounted for the divorce by talking about how flirtatious his wife was. The wife, in contrast, said the divorce was caused by her husband's resistance to her efforts to improve herself by returning to college (Weiss, 1975).

But agreement or disagreement in the accounts of a divorce is not the issue. What is important is that in the process of going through the emotional divorce, each spouse must develop an account that makes sense of the fact that the marriage is ending.

Legal Divorce

The term **legal divorce** refers to the process of meeting the state requirements for ending a marriage. We have already seen in this chapter how divorce in the United States evolved through legislation and in the courts. Until the 1960s, the only way a divorce could be obtained in any state was through an **adversary procedure.** An adversary procedure requires one member of a married couple to file a complaint of wrongdoing against the other member, even if both spouses agree they want a divorce.

When the adversary system was the only way to get a divorce, many couples had to exaggerate their complaints, or even commit perjury in order to obtain divorces. Until 1966, for example, adultery was the only ground for divorce in the state of New York, which led some couples to stage adulterous scenes, so that one partner could be "caught in an act of adultery." As a result of such open flouting of the law, there was increasing pressure during the 1960s for reforms in divorce laws.

Oklahoma and Maryland were the first states to adopt what is popularly known as **no-fault divorce** laws (Nakonezny, Shull, and Rodgers, 1995). Such laws

in the media

Divorce Court: TV Judge Settles Conflicts between Former Spouses

In the 1950s, *Divorce Court* was a popular television show that was designed to discourage divorce. The show featured actors such as Alan Alda and Jack Nicholson playing divorcing spouses. *Divorce Court* is back on the air and as popular as it was forty years ago. Mablean Ephriam, an attorney with the LA family courts for more than twenty years, presides over the new version of *Divorce Court.* Ephriam's career began at the Women's Division of the Federal Bureau of Prisons in Terminal Island where she worked as a corrections officer. After putting herself through law

school, Ephriam served as Deputy City Attorney in LA and then became Domestic Violence Coordinator. She went into private practice in 1982.

Ephriam doesn't grant divorces on the show. Participants have already gotten divorced through legal channels when they appear in her court. Ephriam's role is to decide about contested issues, typically money or property. Guests get $500 for appearing on the show. In return, they agree in advance to abide by her rulings. Ephriam believes participants' primary motive for appearing on the show is to

get a chance to tell their side of the story, how they were "done wrong" by their former spouse. In uncontested divorce, hearings are short and spouses may not have the chance to air their grievances. Ephriam also hopes that her show will encourage couples who are still married to try harder to work out their differences; and that it will inspire unmarried people to check out prospective spouses more carefully.

Source: Crary, David. "Real-Life Divorces Find Their Niche in TV Court." *The Detroit News,* February 22, 2000. Detroitnews.com, accessed February 13, 2002.

typically grant divorces on the grounds of irreconcilable differences, irretrievable breakdown, or incompatibility. No-fault divorce removes legal obstacles to divorce and reduces the economic costs. In 1970, California eliminated all types of marital misconduct as grounds for divorce (although the "permanent insanity" of a spouse is still allowed). Today all states have some form of no-fault divorce, although in some states it is still possible to have a fault-based divorce.

Since many states passed no-fault divorce laws in the 1970s, a decade when divorce rates were increasing rapidly, the new laws were often blamed for the increase in divorce rates. Early studies of individual states that had passed no-fault laws did not show significant increases in divorce. However, a more recent study of all fifty states did show that in forty-four states divorces did go up in the years following passage of the no-fault laws (Nakonezny, Shull, and Rodgers, 1995). Although this study does seem to show that more relaxed divorce laws may have contributed to increases in divorce, some additional points should be noted. First, the divorce rate in the United States had started its rapid increase in the 1960s, *before* most states had changed their laws. Second, even though states passed no-fault divorce laws, it was still possible to use the adversary procedure, and many people did. In Ohio, for example, which allowed no-fault law after 1974, two-thirds of divorcing couples still used the adversary system in the middle and late 1970s (Kitson, 1992). Finally, we should also recall that during the 1980s, when no-fault divorce laws were available in virtually all states, the divorce rate actually declined somewhat.

No-fault divorce laws may have reduced the legal aspects of divorce, but they did not eliminate attorneys and the courts from the divorce process. Divorcing couples must divide the economic and material things they have accumulated during their marriages, and if they have children they must reach some agreement about their economic support and custody arrangements. Usually these matters are worked out in a separation agreement, on which both parties must agree before it is filed with the court. The process of working out separation agreements usually requires two attorneys, although some couples try to use only one. As couples try to work out separation agreements, conflicts over the details often erupt. It is not uncommon for couples to fight intensely over things that have nothing to do with the original reasons for the divorce (such as who will get a particular piece of furniture, a pet, or who will get children on special holidays). Even so-called amicable divorces often end up with hostile exchanges over disputed terms of separation agreements.

Some divorcing couples try to avoid these disputes by using mediation. **Mediation** involves a specially trained, neutral person who meets with two contesting individuals, hears their respective claims, and tries to move them toward mutual agreement. Mediators deal with issues about the division of assets, alimony or separate maintenance, custody of the children, and child support payments. Mediation is relatively new, but it is increasingly a part of the legal divorce, and in some states it is now a compulsory part of the divorce process.

The advantage claimed for mediation is that it takes disputes out of the hands of opposing lawyers and gives them to a mediator who is working for the good of both parties. Advocates for mediation claim that when husbands and wives make an agreement through mediation, they abide by it more closely than one imposed on them by the courts (Kitson, 1992).

Others, however, point out that women may be especially vulnerable in the mediation process. Men are likely to be dominant in communication and argument, while women may be reluctant to ask for things for themselves. This gender imbalance can lead to men getting more than their fair share in mediation agreements.

Covenant Marriage

In recent years, policy makers have been struggling to find ways to change existing laws to increase marital stability. The most significant change is embodied in the concept of **covenant marriage.** This new form of legal marriage now exists in three states: Arizona, Arkansas, and Louisiana. Covenant marriage allows couples the option of selecting a more stringent set of legal requirements to govern their marriages and requires the following: (1) some marriage preparation; (2) full disclosure of all information that could reasonably affect the decision to marry; (3) an oath of lifelong commitment to the marriage; (4) acceptance of limited grounds for divorce (e.g., abuse, adultery, addiction, felony imprisonment, and separation for two years); and (5) marriage counseling if problems threaten the marriage. In a representative survey of residents of the three states with covenant marriage, researchers found mixed support for the ideas embodied in the concept. About two-fifths of the respondents expressed strong support for covenant marriage but nearly half had some reservations about specific components. The majority felt that marriage preparation was important and agreed that committing in advance to seeking professional help if problems arose is a good idea. Less support was given to the establishment of long waiting periods before divorce is granted. The researchers who conducted the study concluded that policy efforts designed to strengthen marriage and reduce divorce may be more popular in states with people who have more conservative gender role ideologies and who are religiously active. Additionally, legislation that attempts to implement only specific aspects of covenant marriage (e.g., marriage preparation and marital counseling) may be more readily accepted than legislation that attempts to implement covenant marriage its entirety (Hawkins et al., 2002).

Economic Divorce

Economic divorce consists of dividing the couple's money and property and determining if alimony or spouse maintenance will be awarded. Divorces may be caused by many different factors, but ultimately most divorces come down to eco-

Divorce has become a big business as specialized services emerge to assist divorcing couples complete and file the papers necessary to end their marriages.

nomic issues. Every marriage is an economic partnership, and during divorce the accumulations of that partnership must be divided. Some couples have unpaid debts at the time they divorce, and these too must be settled.

Another economic aspect of divorce pertains to decisions about whether one spouse will continue to support the other after the marital relationship is legally ended (alimony or spouse maintenance). Finally, if couples have minor children, it is necessary to establish the level of child support payments and the extent of other economic obligations for the noncustodial parent. We discuss each of these issues in the next sections.

Divorce, and the ramifications of divorce, are costly. When divorcing couples set up individual households, the costs of housing, utilities, transportation, new household furnishings and appliances, and child care all increase. Incomes often decrease during separation and divorce because of lost days at work and lowered productivity. The economic costs of divorce also include attorneys' fees and perhaps medical, counseling, or psychiatric services for spouses and children.

Although divorce is expensive for all concerned, it is almost always more costly for women than for men. During the last three decades, in the aftermath of changing divorce laws, it became clear that men are likely to bounce back to their predivorce economic levels rather quickly, while women often remain below their predivorce levels. This contributes to the **feminization of poverty,** the high incidence of poverty found in female-headed households.

In one of the earliest studies to demonstrate how divorce affects women economically, Weitzman (1985) concluded that one year after a divorce the economic standard of living for men went up 42 percent, while the economic standard of living for women went down 73 percent. A reanalysis of Weitzman's data indicates that the lowered income level for women may not have been quite as severe—perhaps only a decline of one-third—but it was still substantial (Hoffman and Duncan, 1988). Women who divorce in midlife—the age at which women are most affected by divorce—average a 39 percent loss of income after divorce (Morgan, 1991). These and other studies make it clear that the economic consequences of divorce are much more detrimental for women than for men.

A number of factors contribute to the detrimental economic effects of divorce on women, especially those who have been married for ten years or more and have minor children. The primary factor is that even when married women are

HEADline What Is a Wife's Contribution to Her Marriage Worth, in Monetary Terms?

For over thirty years, Lorna Jorgenson Wendt was a full-time wife, mother, manager of her home, and corporate wife. She was married to Gary Wendt, former CEO of General Electric Capital. In 1995, Gary asked for a divorce. He offered her $10 million—or 10 percent—of their marital assets. The courts offered her $20 million, which she appealed because she felt she deserved $50 million or half of their assets. Her demand to be a 50/50 partner in divorce, as she felt she had been in their marriage, created quite an impact in both the business and legal arenas, prompting an examination of the value contributed to the career success of executives by their wives.

In the United States, nine states have a system of *community property,* which means that property or assets acquired by either husband or wife during the marriage (except for gifts from third parties) belong to the spouses equally. If Lorna Wendt and her former husband had filed for divorce in one of these states rather than in Connecticut (which is not a community property state), Lorna would have received half of the marital estate, which was estimated at $100 million. Most states, however, base property decisions on the principle of *equitable* rather than equal distribution. In these states, judges decide what would be a fair settlement based on the relative value of the contributions made by the spouses as well as their needs after the marriage ends. Often equitable does not mean equal.

In 1998, Lorna founded the Institute for Equality in Marriage, a nonprofit organization designed to help others create and maintain full equality in their marriages. "My case was never about the money," Mrs. Wendt says on the Institute's web site. "It was about someone implying I was a 10 percent participant in my partnership. In reality, I always gave 100 percent, putting my career on hold to raise the children, manage the household and support him in his business endeavors." One of the underlying principles of the Institute is an emphasis on the value of signing prenuptial agreements. When asked in an interview with *Business Week* why she and the Institute believe so strongly in these agreements, Mrs. Wendt replied with the following:

Marriage is the biggest social contract we enter. How can we enter into it without a clear conversation? We have contracts for everything we do—whether it's a business deal or a contract to get your roof redone. The price you pay for no marriage contract means that in the event of a divorce, what assets you get is left to the discretion of a judge. A pre- or post-nuptial agreement is more than [the blueprint] for dividing assets. You're forced to talk about money, equality, and how you define your roles in your marriage, through the guidance of a lawyer. The big question is: Are you and your partner equals? If Gary (her husband) had said to me when we got married, "Your contribution is only worth 10 percent," I hope I would have been smart enough to say, "No, thank you" (to the marriage proposal). We don't think it should be just a legal agreement, but a tool to stimulate an important discussion. There's also a whole self-esteem issue. When you enter into marriage, you have to think about how you feel about yourself. Am I the person who cooks, cleans, and drives the kids, while my husband is the king of the hill? Is a discussion like that going to cause some relationships to fall apart? If so, thank God. At least you know these things before you get married, have kids, then . . . (have) to get divorced (Gutner, 2000).

Sources: Gutner, Toddi. "Lorna Wendt: 'Are You and Your Partner Equals?'" *Business Week* online, December 14, 2000; accessed on May 12, 2002. See also the Institute for Equality in Marriage web site at www.equalityinmarriage.org.

employed, they generally earn less than their husbands. (This was discussed in Chapter 12.) Moreover, a substantial number of women, especially those with small children, are not in the labor force or are employed only part time. As long as these marriages remain intact, the nonemployment, partial employment, and even the lower pay of women may not cause economic difficulties. Since husbands generally earn more than their wives, it may even seem rational for wives to withdraw from the labor force to care for young children (Becker, 1991). But the weakness of this arrangement is all too apparent in the case of divorce. At that point,

wives, especially those who have been out of the labor force for years, are suddenly left without the income that had been provided by their husbands' jobs.

One way for women to retain some of that income is to receive alimony from
their former husbands, and, if they have children, child support as well. However,
the liberalized no-fault divorce laws we discussed earlier, combined with other
laws and court rulings, have reduced the amount and extent of alimony awards
(Weitzman, 1985; Kitson, 1992). The courts now generally hold that alimony is to
be used as backup support only until the divorced person is self-supporting. This
is often referred to as **rehabilitative alimony.** It is not intended to be a guaranteed
income for life. The courts have also made it clear that alimony is not to be viewed
as a punishment for the spouse who must pay it (Weitzman, 1985).

The changing divorce laws have also negatively affected the property settlements women receive in some states, especially through the adoption of community property laws. **Community property laws** say that any earnings and property accumulated during a marriage are owned jointly by the couple. Community
property laws were expected to work to the benefit of wives, especially those who
were not employed. But in California, studies found that women received lower
settlement awards after community property laws went into effect (Weitzman,
1985). Studies in two other states (Washington and Georgia) provide mixed evidence regarding the impact of community property laws. In Washington, but not
in Georgia, women received slightly lower property settlements after the community property laws went into effect (Welsh and Price-Bonham, 1983).

Community property laws also undercompensate women for the contributions they have often made to their husbands' educations, professional degrees,
and career advancements. When marriages stay together until one of the spouses
dies, both partners benefit from the higher wages and benefits that come with professional careers. But when those marriages end in divorce, women who have sacrificed their own potential careers for their husbands' are often left with little to
show for their efforts. The same is true of retirement funds, which are more likely
to be in the husband's name.

Community Divorce

The term **community divorce** refers to changes that occur in relationships with
friends and relatives during and after the divorce. The community divorce is the
most purely social aspect of a divorce. Just as a wedding ceremony is a way of making a public commitment to another person, the community divorce begins when
couples let others know that their marriage is ending. This part of the community
divorce has been called "going public" (Vaughn, 1986, p. 139).

Many husbands and wives have a difficult time admitting to each other, and to
themselves, that the marriage is ending. They are also frequently ambivalent and
uncertain about the action they are taking. In addition, married couples are accustomed to presenting a positive image of their marriage to the outside world. They
often create a façade that disguises their marriage problems, even through the early
stages of a separation. Under these circumstances, it is difficult to announce to family members, friends, or even to children, that the marriage is ending.

Ultimately, however, it is necessary to tell family members and friends about
their marital problems and the likelihood of divorce. When the announcement is
made, family members and even close friends are often shocked and surprised.
Almost everyone at some time or another has said, on learning of a marital separation, "I always thought of them as the perfect couple." Going public might be easier if we had social customs that showed us how it should be done. The announcement of a separation is typically awkward both for the person who makes it and for
the person who hears it. The uncertainty of the situation is revealed by the experi-

ence of one man who, when he told an associate about his impending divorce, was asked, "Do I feel sorry for you or congratulate you?" (Bohannan, 1971, p. 37). Most people respond to the announcement with "Oh, I'm sorry to hear that," which is often what one says on hearing of a death in the family.

After the announcement, friends, family members, and even children often align with one partner or the other. Almost all divorced people report that some friends they had while married are no longer friends. For example, one divorced woman, in response to an interviewer's question, complained bitterly about friends who had dropped her after her divorce. "Friends? . . . They drop you like a hot potato. The exceptions are those real ones you made before marriage, those who are unmarried, and your husband's friends who want to make a pass at you" (Bohannan, 1971, p. 59).

Also, there are no clear social norms about whether or not a divorced person should remain in touch with the parents and siblings of a former spouse. Having children is one factor that influences continued interaction. Grandparents are much more likely to remain in contact with a former daughter-in-law if she has custody of their grandchildren, if she is cooperative and encourages this type of relationship to continue. It may be difficult for a divorced parent to participate in this type of relationship with former in-laws, as the following illustrates:

> The divorce was still very fresh. The air was thick with hate and getting even. I called my daughter long distance one day and asked what the grandchildren were up to. She said they were supposed to attend the circus with their paternal grandparents. "But," she declared, "I'm not letting them go. My ex-husband is insulting on the phone, and whenever I call there and his parents answer, they are cold and nasty. Why should I let them have the pleasure of their grandchildren? They haven't been the least supportive of my situation!" (Cohen, 1994, p. 78)

Custodial grandparents (parents of the divorced parent who has custody of the children) can help ensure that their grandchildren continue to have a relationship with their noncustodial parent's parents, as the following shows:

> When our daughter and grandchildren lived with us, the paternal grandparents, who lived in another state, became more and more distant and removed from the grandchildren's lives. . . . We would dial the phone for the little ones so they could speak to their other grandparents. And we would encourage them to write their other grandparents. And we would help them get started so this would develop into a weekly habit.
>
>   We also told the other grandparents that any time they were near our community, they were welcome to see the grandchildren and could take them for the day. (Cohen, 1994, p. 78)

▪ *Psychic Divorce*

The term **psychic divorce** refers to the process of rebuilding an individual identity and becoming independent of one's former spouse. Gradually, as people go through the emotional, legal, economic, and community divorces, they also move through the psychic divorce. For anyone who has been married any length of time, the marriage relationship is an important part of his or her identity. Thus for many people the psychic divorce is a slow process that can go on long after the legal divorce. A divorced man who still does not buy striped shirts because his former wife did not like them may not yet have accomplished his psychic divorce.

For couples who have little or no contact with each other after the legal proceedings are completed, the psychic divorce is usually accomplished fairly readily. For couples who have minor children, especially when they share custody, the psychic divorce may be especially difficult, if for no other reason than that as parents they continue to come into contact with each other.

■ Coparental Divorce

Nearly two-thirds of all divorcing couples have children under the age of 18 at the time of their divorce, which means that each year over one million children experience the divorce of their parents (Baca Zinn and Eitzen, 2002). These numbers show that as many couples go through the difficult process of divorce, they must also be considering the welfare of their children. The term **coparental divorce** refers to the process of determining custody and visitation rights. For most parents, two questions about children are paramount: (1) How will the children be affected by the divorce? and (2) how shall the custody of minor children be handled?

These two questions have been well researched and are of such importance that they require special attention. We discuss each in the following sections.

The Effects of Divorce on Children

M ost parents, no matter how dissatisfied with their marriages, consider the impact that divorce will have on their children. Indeed, having children decreases the likelihood of divorce. Very young children seem to be particularly effective in reducing divorce. Even the gender of children influences the likelihood of divorce. Parents of sons are less likely to divorce than parents of daughters. Apparently both fathers and mothers are more concerned about the absence of an adult male role model if the child is a male (Faust and McKibben, 1999).

Nonetheless, many parents do divorce, which raises the question of how divorce affects the children. There are two popular beliefs about how divorce affects children. The first, and most common, is that when parents divorce the children are damaged psychologically, leading to various types of negative behavior. The second is that children are not hurt any more by divorce than they would be by living in a home with parents who are constantly fighting. Each of these views has some degree of truth.

There have been numerous studies in the United States alone on the effects of divorce on children (Amato, 2000). Some studies focus on children in their childhood and adolescent years, while others study the long-term effects of divorce— into adulthood. Individual studies have produced varying results. Some studies, especially the qualitative and clinical ones, show widespread negative effects on children at the time of divorce and in the years immediately after (Wallerstein, Lewis, and Blakeslee, 2000). Studies of the long-term effects on children have been less conclusive, although again some have reported long-term negative outcomes. One long-term consequence that has been found is that children whose parents have divorced are themselves more likely to divorce.

The studies show that when parents divorce, their children have lower academic achievement, more behavior problems, difficulties in psychological adjustment, lowered self-esteem, and poorer social relations. However, they also show that the differences between children whose parents divorced and children whose parents did not are not large. These relatively small differences indicate that many children whose parents divorce do not experience negative outcomes, and many children whose parents remain married do. Thus the average difference between the two groups is not great (Amato, 2000).

Some evidence shows that problems of children whose parents divorced may exist *before* their parents divorced (Cherlin et al., 1991). This research calls attention to two points. First, if children manifested problem behavior *before* their parents divorced, it is illogical to claim that the divorce produced the problems. It is even possible that the psychological and behavioral problems of children might contribute to the marital troubles of their parents. The second point, however, is the

ContentSELECT

Children and Divorce

more important one; namely, that other kinds of parental and family behavior are associated with children's problems. Marital discord and a high level of conflict in the home can have just as negative an effect on children as a divorce (Amato, 2002).

A further point to be made about parental conflict is that it does not necessarily end with a divorce. When parents continue a high level of conflict during, and especially after, a divorce, children are likely to have problems. A meta-analysis of twenty-eight studies found that that when parents continued their conflict after the divorce, children were negatively affected (Amato, 1993a).

We may summarize the effects of divorce on children (including adolescents) by making several points: (1) Probably all children whose parents divorce, except perhaps for those who are very young, feel pain and loss when their parents break up; (2) some, but not all, children whose parents divorce display negative outcomes; and (3) parental conflict, whether it occurs in an ongoing marriage, during divorce, or after divorce, is likely to produce negative outcomes in children.

The long-term effects of divorce on children have been relatively harder to determine empirically. Two long-term, and well-respected qualitative studies actually draw different conclusions about the impact of divorce on children. One of the studies, conducted by Judith Wallerstein and her colleagues (Wallerstein, Lewis, and Blakeslee, 2000), followed fifty-nine families over a twenty-five-year period. Family members—both children and their parents—were interviewed five times over this period. Wallerstein and colleagues also obtained comparative data from adults who had grown up in intact families (that is, those not disrupted by divorce). Mavis Hetherington and her colleague (Hetherington and Kelly, 2002) conducted the other study, which followed more than 1,400 families over a twenty-four year period. About half of the families in Hetherington's study were divorced. The data for her studies involved interviews as well as observations in the families' homes. Hetherington's subjects also kept journals of their actions and feelings and completed personality tests. Data were also gathered from parents and peers. Both studies provide extensive data about white middle-class families that broke apart in the early 1970s, just as the divorce rate in the United States was starting its final climb to the high rate it is today.

Both research teams agree that divorce often hurts children, causing anger, anxiety, confusion, behavioral problems, and emotional pain in the first couple of years after the breakup. For some individuals, experiencing a parental divorce can lead to long-term anxiety, insecurity, and a fear of close relationships. They also agree that most children recover, even if it takes many years, and are able to function effectively as adults. Hetherington is more optimistic about children of divorce than is Wallerstein. She acknowledges that while divorce is risky, most children are resilient. Only 20 percent of the children of divorce that she has followed over time are at risk of life-long emotional or behavioral problems, as compared with only 10 percent of children whose parents stayed married. She acknowledges that while this difference in the incidence of problems is as great as the association between smoking and cancer, she still emphasizes the fact that 75 to 80 percent of children of divorced parents are functioning quite well. Hetherington is also optimistic about the increase in the frequency of interaction between divorced fathers' and their children that she has observed over the past thirty years. About one-third of the divorced fathers in her study see their children at least once a week, compared with only one-fourth in the 1970s.

Wallerstein, on the other hand, focuses on the loneliness and anxiety children of divorced parents experience, especially in regard to intimate relationships and commitment. She has found many of them ill-prepared to form adult relationships because they had no good role models while they were growing up. She is also more pessimistic about the involvement of fathers in their children's lives, emphasizing that the majority of men in her study failed to pay for their children's college expenses.

Both Hetherington and Wallerstein have a great deal of support from other social scientists. Their differences are in large part a difference in interpretation. But they are also a function of the different ways in which they conducted their studies. Hetherington's study is generally regarded as the more comprehensive because of its large sample and use of different methods of collecting data. Both, however, focus on white middle-class couples, which is a major limitation.

Some insight into the contrasting findings of Wallerstein's and Hetherington's research may be provided by other recent longitudinal studies. Quite a few have reported that parental divorce is a risk factor for multiple problems in adulthood, including lower socioeconomic status, poor subjective well-being, increased marital problems, and a greater likelihood of seeing one's own marriages end in divorce (see Amato, 1999, for a review of these studies). Possible reasons for these long-term negative effects may be related to the economic hardship produced by parental divorce. Some children of divorce may be unable to attend college, which means that they will have lower occupational attainment and wages in adulthood. Another reason may be associated with the fact that children of divorce may have had no effective adult models to show them how to communicate effectively and resolve interpersonal conflict, which means that they have trouble forming stable, satisfying relationships in adulthood (Amato, 2000).

A meta-analysis of thirty-seven quantitative studies that focused on the long-term effects of divorce also found negative outcomes for the children when they reached adulthood (Amato and Keith, 1991a). Individuals whose parents divorced had poorer psychological health (depression, lower life satisfaction), more family problems (lower marital quality, more divorce), lower educational attainment, lower income and lower occupational prestige, and poorer physical health when they became adults (Amato and Keith, 1991a). The association between parents' divorce and children's problems in adulthood was generally weak, however. Furthermore, some of these relationships between parents' divorce and children's problems in adulthood may be spurious (that is, caused by other factors). For example, children whose parents were of lower socioeconomic status before divorce would themselves be expected to have lower incomes, educational attainments, and occupational prestige. This would be expected because of general patterns in which people tend to have a socioeconomic status in adulthood similar to what they had when growing up.

Two additional points about the effects of divorce on children should be noted: First, more recent studies are less likely to show negative effects on children than earlier studies (Amato, 1993b). This suggests that as divorce became more common in the United States, some of its negative impact on children diminished. Second, although divorce may have some negative effects on children, there are certainly other family characteristics that are equally, or even more, detrimental. These include, as we discussed, marital and family conflict. In addition, there are the pervasive and corrosive effects of poverty, neglect, abuse, and abandonment. These are "the real culprits in children's lives" (Allen, 1993, p. 48).

Child Custody

*D*ivorce ends the marital relationship, but divorced parents continue to have a legally defined relationship with their children. Since divorced parents typically do not live together, the law customarily determines which parent shall have custody of minor children. Historically, in the United States, the courts have usually granted custody of minor children to only one parent. Throughout much of the nineteenth century, in the United States and Great Britain, custody was routinely given to the father. In keeping with the patriarchal family structure of earlier times, the courts assumed that fathers had property rights to their children. Also, since women were not considered legal entities and were themselves seen as dependents, they were considered unqualified to take responsibility for their children (Friedman, 1995).

During the nineteenth century, however, both in the United States and England, ideas about motherhood changed, and the courts began to allow mothers to have custody of their young children, at least for a time. The changing ideas about motherhood were part of what has been called the "cult of true womanhood" or "cult of domesticity" (Stone, 1990). Married women were increasingly remaining in the home, which became the realm of their responsibility. According to this new ideal, women were uniquely suited to giving children the nurturance and moral guidance they needed. With the coming of the Victorian age in the later part of the nineteenth century, a greater emphasis was put on love and nurturing in childrearing, which seemed *instinctively* to be the strong suit of women (Stone, 1990).

American and British law in the nineteenth century took notice of this new view of motherhood and began to give mothers limited custody when very small children were involved. In one divorce case in 1839, "a girl of twenty-one months was awarded to the mother, as 'the most proper person to be entrusted with such a charge, in relation to an infant of this tender age'" (Roman and Haddad, 1978, p. 33). This daughter of "tender age" was awarded to her mother, but when she turned 4 years old, she was returned to her father.

Over the ensuing decades, the doctrine of "tender age" was extended to later and later ages. More and more often, the courts considered the young child to be better off in the custody of the mother. The legal concept of "the best interests of the child" emerged and was used to justify leaving minor children with their mothers. By the 1920s, almost all minor children were being awarded to mothers in the case of divorce (Friedman, 1995).

Divorce and Custody

Types of Custody Today

In the United States today, three types of custody are generally available: sole custody, joint legal custody, and joint physical custody:

- **Sole custody** gives to one parent the rights and responsibilities to provide for the physical, moral, and mental well-being of a child. Under sole custody, the child lives with one parent, but at certain times will visit the noncustodial parent (weekends, summer vacations, holidays).
- **Joint legal custody** gives both parents equal rights to make decisions about the child's welfare, especially on medical, religious, and educational matters, but the child is likely to live with only one parent.
- **Joint physical custody** gives parents equal rights to make decisions about day-to-day child care matters, and typically has the child living similar amounts of time with each parent. The lengths of time depend on the circumstances of the parents, but it is not uncommon for children to stay with one parent during certain days of the week and the other parent on other days of the week. In each residence, the children are likely to have clothes, toys, and other possessions.

In a small number of divorce cases, parents split the custody of their children, with the mother having sole custody of some children and the father sole custody of others—this is called **split custody.** Dividing the children between parents may be done on the basis of gender, age, or other personal considerations, but one common pattern is for mothers to take younger and female children, while fathers take older and male children.

In the United States today, mothers still get sole custody of minor children in the overwhelming majority of cases, but the number has declined from the previously estimated 90 percent to about 85 percent.

Joint physical custody is used most often in high-conflict divorce cases (Maccoby and Mnookin, 1992). This suggests that when married couples have conflict-filled divorces, they are also likely to have conflicts over the children and how they should be raised. Joint physical custody is still used in only a small proportion of divorce cases.

It is not uncommon for divorced parents to make informal changes in the legal custody arrangements (Ganong and Coleman, 1994). Despite the decision of the court, divorced parents may renegotiate between themselves and make changes in the living arrangements of their children. Parents are most likely to make changes in physical custody if the child wishes to live with the other parent (Ganong, Coleman, and Mistina, 1995).

Although some states are passing laws that would make joint custody more common, California, the first state to endorse this arrangement (in 1979) has rescinded a provision of its law giving priority to joint physical custody between the two parents (Hsu, 1996). It is clear from these counter-vailing legislative actions that the issues are far from resolved in the United States.

Good arguments can be made both for and against joint physical custody. Briefly the arguments on both sides can be summarized as follows:

▲ *When divorced fathers have only visitation rights, the children visit his home for short, specified periods of time, such as weekends, certain holidays, and during the summer.*

In Favor of Joint Physical Custody.   When both parents wish to play an active part in the upbringing, education, and general welfare of their children, joint physical custody is fairer than sole custody. It keeps both parents (and especially fathers) more involved in the lives of their children. A related point is that noncustodial parents often take on the limited role of *entertainment parents,* who focus only on providing fun and games for their children instead of taking on a complete range of parental responsibilities (including discipline). If one parent is only an entertainment parent, that is unfair to the custodial parent who must deal with the everyday problems and routine activities of the children.

Against Joint Physical Custody.   The most basic argument against this type of custody is that it may be too difficult for children to have two different homes, between which they are regularly shuttled. Children may have to shift between two home environments where they have different friends, dissimilar eating patterns, and contradictory rules of behavior. In extreme cases, the two parents may have very different philosophies of life and lifestyles. Children under these conditions may be very confused by the contradictory messages they receive from their parents.

Another major argument against joint physical custody is that it requires the two parents to interact much more frequently. The high level of interaction required may not be a problem if the parents are friendly and cooperative, but if the parents are hostile toward each other these encounters are likely to be uncomfortable for the children. Research has shown repeatedly that if children are subjected to hostile and angry parents, it is detrimental to their well-being (Mason, 1999).

The arguments for and against joint custody are not easily resolved by legislation, and yet state legislatures, persuaded by differing arguments, often pass laws that favor one form of custody over the other. The primary consideration should be "the best interests of the child," but that too is not always obvious.

When divorce occurs in a family, it is a distressing experience for everyone, parents and children alike. It is a time of upheaval, when families are literally torn apart. Conflicts and disputes that may previously have been hidden from children suddenly break into the open. It is also a time of great uncertainty, because of the ambivalence that many divorcing people feel about the decision they are making. And, as we have seen, the divorce experience is complex, involving emotions, legal issues, finances, families and friends, and children. In this chapter, we have focused on the nature of divorce and the divorce experience; in the next chapter, we turn to life after divorce.

Summary

The ease or difficulty of ending a marriage has changed over time and differs from one society to another. In England, until well into the nineteenth century, only the wealthiest people could get legal divorces. Common people often simply resorted to desertion, although there was for some time a custom of men selling their wives at auction. In the United States, divorces were also rare until the nineteenth century, when the grounds for granting divorces started to multiply.

The extent of divorce in a society can be measured in a number of different ways, but some ways are better than others. Calculating divorce as a percentage of weddings in a given year is a misleading measure, because divorces come from all existing marriages, not just those occurring in that year. Refined divorce rates are a more meaningful measure because divorces in a year are related to the number of existing marriages. The percentage of marriages ending in divorce is a popular measure, but it is not easy to arrive at and is less meaningful than most people suppose because it must be derived from marriages that took place decades ago.

Divorce rates in the United States have generally increased over the twentieth century, but the greatest increase came during the 1960s and 1970s. Wars and economic depressions have varying effects on divorce rates.

Among the factors associated with divorce, age at marriage is one of the most influential. Those who marry at young ages are less able to perform marriage roles satisfactorily and therefore divorce more often. Race is also a factor related to divorce: African Americans have higher rates than white Americans. People in the lower socioeconomic classes also have higher divorce rates than those in higher statuses. The reason may be that lower-status people marry younger and may face more crises and disruptions in their lives. Religious groups have different divorce rates, but those who have no religion are the most likely to divorce.

Divorce is not a single act, but a process involving several different dimensions. Emotional divorce begins with the recognition that one's marriage may end. Usually one spouse (the initiator) wants the marriage to end, while the other partner does not. In the aftermath of divorce, each partner develops an account of what caused the marriage to end.

The legal divorce involves meeting the government's requirements for ending a marriage. Historically, this was an adversarial process in which one partner filed a complaint against the other. Today in the United States, no-fault divorce is available in all states. Mediation, in which a neutral third party assists couples in reaching a divorce settlement, is used by some people today as a way of reducing legal conflict. Some critics believe, however, that women may be disadvantaged by the mediation process because of gender differences in communication styles.

The term *economic divorce* refers to the division of the economic assets of a marriage. Divorces are generally costly for all parties, but women in contemporary society usually fare less well than men.

The term *community divorce* refers to the changes divorcing couples make in dealing with friends, relatives, and associates. Social customs for ending a marriage are lacking, which adds to the difficulties of divorce. Divorce nearly always causes profound changes in social relationships for both divorcing parties.

The term *psychic divorce* refers to the internal process of regaining individual identity and autonomy after a divorce. For divorcing couples with children, the psychic divorce may be made difficult by the continuing interaction between them in their role as parents.

The term *coparental divorce* refers to determining custody and visitation rights with respect to children. Divorcing parents are often very concerned about how the divorce will affect their children. Although research is plentiful, the answers are still not conclusive. All children whose parents divorce will probably feel some pain and loss; some will have problems, and others will not. There is only a weak relationship between divorce and negative outcomes for children. Children are most likely to have negative outcomes (both short- and long-term) when their parents have conflict-filled divorces, or when parental conflict continues into the postdivorce period. Some studies have found long-term negative effects of parental divorce, but these may be produced by other correlated factors, such as poverty and neglect.

Custody arrangements for children after divorce have changed since the nineteenth century, when fathers were routinely awarded custody of their children. By the 1920s, a reversal of this practice had occurred, and mothers were almost always given custody of minor children. Today the three major forms of custody are sole, joint legal, and joint physical. In the overwhelming majority of cases, mothers still receive sole physical custody, but increasingly joint legal, and somewhat less often, joint physical custody are granted by the courts.

Note

1. Hopper (1993) does not use the term *accounts*, but uses instead the "rhetoric or vocabulary of motives." This latter terminology is part of a larger intellectual and theoretical tradition, which sees the words people use (their vocabulary or rhetoric) to describe their reasons or motives as after-the-fact definitions. These definitions help people explain, to themselves, why they did what they did.

Key Terms

Adversary (divorce) procedure (p. 418)
Alimony/spousal support (p. 407)
Bed and board divorce (p. 407)
Community divorce (p. 423)
Community property laws (p. 423)
Coparental divorce (p. 425)
Covenant marriage (p. 420)
Crude divorce rate (p. 410)
Desertion (p. 407)

Divorce account (p. 418)
Economic divorce (p. 420)
Emotional divorce (p. 417)
Feminization of poverty (p. 421)
Full divorce (p. 407)
Joint legal custody (p. 428)
Joint physical custody (p. 428)
Legal divorce (p. 418)
Mediation (p. 420)
No-fault divorce (p. 418)

Omnibus clause (p. 408)
Parliamentary divorce (p. 407)
Private separation agreement (p. 407)
Psychic divorce (p. 424)
Refined divorce rate (p. 410)
Rehabilitative alimony (p. 423)
Sole custody (p. 428)
Split custody (p. 428)

Review Questions

1. Compare and contrast the various types of statistics that are used in reports about the incidence of divorce.

2. Summarize trends in divorce in the United States since the mid 1800s. Why did the divorce rate change so significantly between 1965 and 1980? How was our society changing at this time?

3. Identify the personal characteristics that are associated with an individual's likelihood of getting divorced.

4. Identify reasons couples give for getting divorced.

5. List and describe the six stations of the divorce process.

6. What factors affect children's adjustment to their parents' divorce?

7. How does parental divorce affect children's own likelihood of divorcing in their adult years? Why does it have this effect?

8. What percentage of divorced women who are supposed to receive child support from the fathers of their children actually receive the payments in full on a regular basis? How does men's failure to pay child support affect the standard of living of their ex-wives and children?

Critical Thinking Questions

1. What are the advantages and disadvantages of the no-fault divorce system relative to the adversarial system? What would be the consequences of making divorce harder to get?

2. What factors might contribute to men's failure to pay child support?

Online Resources Available for This Chapter

www.ablongman.com/marriageandfamily

- Online Study Guide with Practice Tests
- PowerPoint Chapter Outlines

- Links to Marriage and Family Websites
- ContentSelect Research Database
- Self-Assessment Activities

Further Reading

Books

Ahrons, Constance. *The Good Divorce: Keeping Your Family Together When Your Marriage Comes Apart.* New York: Harper Collins, 1994. Based on the author's own research and clinical practice, this book offers advice and explanations to divorced couples for making their binuclear families healthy and happy.

Amato, Paul, and Booth, Alan. *A Generation at Risk: Growing Up in an Era of Family Upheaval.* Cambridge, MA: Harvard University Press, 1997. Based on a fifteen-year study begun in 1980, the book considers parents' socioeconomic resources, their gender roles and relations, and the quality of their marriages. It also examines children's relations with their parents, their social affiliations, and their psychological well-being.

Arendell, Terry. *Fathers & Divorce.* Thousand Oaks, CA: Sage, 1995. Based on interviews with seventy-five divorced fathers, the author examines the masculine discourse of divorce, relationships with former wives, and parenting behaviors.

Cherlin, Andrew. *Marriage, Divorce, Remarriage* (enlarged and revised edition). Cambridge, MA: Harvard University Press, 1992. Examines long-term trends in marital formation and dissolution.

Hetherington, E. Mavis, and Kelly, John. *For Better or For Worse: Divorce Reconsidered.* New York: W. W. Norton & Company, 2002. An analysis of the nature and consequences of divorce based on a twenty-five-year study of 1,400 families.

Kitson, Gay C. *Portrait of Divorce.* New York: Guilford Press, 1992. Data from four studies of marital instability and divorce are presented to provide a comprehensive picture of the divorce process.

Kurz, Demie. *For Richer, For Poorer: Mothers Confront Divorce.* New York: Routledge, 1995. Based on interviews with a random sample of 129 divorced women who talked about the problems they faced.

Wallerstein, Judith, Lewis, Julia, and Blakeslee, Sandra. *The Unexpected Legacy of Divorce.* New York: Hyperion, 2000. An in-depth look at the lives of seven children of divorce who Wallerstein has followed in her twenty-five-year study of the impact of divorce on children.

Weitzman, Lenore. *The Divorce Revolution: The Unexpected Social and Economic Consequences for Women and Children in America.* New York: The Free Press, 1985. The ground-breaking study that called Americans' attention to the dire economic consequence of divorce for women and their children.

*Content*SELECT *Articles*

"The Cost of No-Fault Divorce." *Society* 37(3), 2000: 5. **[Database: Social Work]** Did no-fault divorce legislation lead to measurable increases in divorce rates? A statistical analysis of divorce data from 32 no-fault divorce states indicates that in 25 of the states, divorce rates were higher than projections anticipated. The manuscript thus interprets the empirical findings as evidence that no-fault divorce legislation did, indeed, lead to demonstrable increases in divorce rates. " . . . no-fault laws resulted in a substantial number of divorces that would not have occurred otherwise."

Keoughan, P. "Child Access and Visitation Following Divorce: A Growth Area for Marriage and Family Therapy." *American Journal of Family Therapy* 29(2), 2001: 155–164. **[Database: Psychology]** In an attempt to increase both parental access to children of divorce and the quality of visitations, as well as in an effort to promote and encourage financial support by noncustodial parents, the State of Iowa commissioned the present study. Investigation findings suggest that mediation services prior to, during, and following divorce aid in the improvement to child access and visitation, in addition to the improvement of relational issues.

Neal, J., and Frick-Horbury, D. "The Effects of Parenting Styles and Childhood Attachment Patterns on Intimate Relationships." *Journal of Instructional Psychology* 28(3), 2001: 178–184. **[Database: Psychology]** Authoritative, authoritarian, and permissive parenting styles and childhood attachment patterns were examined to determine how the two variables impact or affect intimate adult relationships. Fifty-six undergraduate respondents were surveyed in areas such as parental caregiving styles, and relationship-with-others and self-relationship qualities. Neal and her colleague discovered that parenting styles do not, contrary to their hypothesis, parallel attachment styles. Study results additionally suggest that parenting styles do not influence one's ability to be intimate with another.

Nock, S., Wright, J., and Sanchez, L. "America's Divorce Problem." *Society* 36(4), 1999: 43–53. **[Database: Social Work]** With vows to love one another until parted by death made by countless couples worldwide, Nock et al. posit that covenant marriage contracts provide couples a legal mechanism by which to publicly and legally affirm their marriage vow intentions. With the premise that marriage is a commitment for life, those couples who choose the covenant marriage option agree to premarital education and counseling. They further agree (prior to the marriage) to seek marriage counseling and make good-faith efforts to resolve marital differences, as well as agree to specific grounds for which they can divorce (i.e., abuse and adultery). Adopted by Louisiana in 1997 in an effort to curb escalating divorce rates, now an additional 20+ states are considering such legislation.

Life after Divorce

14

The Aftermath of Divorce

New Relationships and Remarriage

The following story was given to Professor Sanford Braver by a student enrolled in one of his psychology classes at Arizona State University. Braver included it in the book he wrote about divorced fathers that was based on an eight-year study:

My parents divorced when I was nine. For a while, it wasn't so bad; I just lived in two houses instead of one, and I could never be with both my parents together at the same time. But at least I still had two parents. My dad and I would spend a lot of time playing Monopoly and Risk. And charades—we loved charades.

But things changed a lot about two years later. Dad found a girlfriend, Jennifer, and they started to live together. Dad pretty much stopped seeing me, then just disappeared from my life, like without warning.

I can't tell you what that did to me. I was ten, and I felt the world had collapsed. What had I done wrong? Why did my father stop caring about me? How could he give me up for this woman? I stayed in my room and just cried and cried. I hid under the covers for days. Probably I would have killed myself, if I could have figured out how to do it. It really hurt bad and probably affected me most of the way through high school. I was a loner, and a stoner. I was just a sad, messed-up kid. And it started because I thought I wasn't worthy of my Dad's love.

One day in my senior year in high school, I'm leaving to walk home after my last class, and who should drive by but Jennifer. She asks me to get into her car and go for a frozen yogurt. I have hated this lady almost all my life; she stole my daddy from me! But this time, for some reason, I just wanted to hear her out.

Key Questions

1 How do the quality and stability of remarriages differ from that of intact first marriages?

2 Do the qualities sought in a mate differ for those who are remarrying?

3 What are the legal rights and ethical responsibilities of stepparents?

4 Is there a greater likelihood of sexual and physical abuse in stepfamilies?

435

She tells me that it really *is* sort of her fault that my dad stopped seeing me, but not the way I thought. It was mainly my mom: My mom hated the thought of dad being in love with another woman, and wouldn't let my dad visit me after he started with Jennifer. She says he tried to see me anyway; he even got a lawyer and called the police a few times. But my mom told him she'd never let him see me as long as he was with *her*. She told him she knew there was nothing the police or the courts could really do if she hung tough and she would. So my dad stopped seeing me.

Source: Braver, Sanford L., and O'Connell, Diane. *Divorced Dads: Shattering the Myths.* New York: Jeremy P. Tarcher/Putnam, 1998, pp. 38–39.

*T*he story of Professor Braver's student is not unfamiliar today. Divorce followed by remarriage often leads to families so complicated that they nearly defy description. At a wedding reception, for example, one might hear an introduction like the following: "This is the daughter of my mother's husband's son." It boggles the mind.

Some of the difficulty associated with complex family relationships is that labels do not exist for all the people who are connected to each other through divorce and remarriage. The inadequacy of traditional family terminology is just one of the complications of life after divorce that we consider in this chapter.

The primary concerns of this chapter on life after divorce can be divided into two parts: (1) reordering the lives and relationships of family members, and (2) forming new intimate relationships and families. The first part—reordering lives and family relationships—includes adjusting emotionally and psychologically to divorce, working out new relationships with former spouses, and sustaining or creating relationships with children. The second part—forming new intimate relationships and families after divorce—involves dating, courtship, and often remarriage. The new families created by remarriage require individuals to adapt to expanded family boundaries and new, often ambiguous, family relationships.

The Aftermath of Divorce

"*I*'m trying to put my life back together"; "I'm having to start all over again." These dramatic words are spoken again and again by people in the aftermath of divorce. For many, divorce is a life-changing, if not a life-shattering, experience. At the very least, the postdivorce period is a time of adjustment—adjustments to being unmarried again, to building new relationships with one's children, to establishing new living arrangements, and often, especially for women, adjusting to reduced economic circumstances.

It is difficult to evaluate the impact of divorce because it can have both positive and negative effects on the individuals involved. On the one hand, the majority of people who divorce say that they did the right thing, and even that their lives are better than they were before. On the other hand, many people carry scars from the divorce for many years. Often they continue to be angry at their former spouses, and they demonstrate greater-than-average signs of psychological problems (Wallerstein and Blakeslee, 1990). There is no easy resolution to this paradox, except to say that many people have mixed feelings about their divorces, and some people are better able than others to recover from divorce and move on to new lives.

The impact of divorce on adults and children, is, in fact, one of the most widely studied issues in social science research on families. In the 1990s alone, over 9,000 research articles and dissertations were written on this subject. Because adjustment to divorce is such a complex phenomenon, findings in this huge body of research are often contradictory and thus, inconclusive. In an attempt to organize the findings of the research and to offer explanations for the inconsistencies in it, sociologist Paul Amato, a leading scholar in the study of divorce, developed a conceptual model that can be applied to the study of children as well as adults (2000). This model is represented in Figure 14.1.

Amato refers to his model as the **divorce-stress-adjustment model,** based on the common assumption in the research that divorce is a stressful life transition to which individuals must adjust. There are actually two different perspectives about the ways in which—or the extent to which—individuals adjust. One approach, which Amato refers to as the **crisis model,** assumes that divorce represents a *disturbance* to which most individuals adjust over time. Factors such as personal resources and evaluations of the situation determine the pace with which individuals adjust.

Figure 14.1 **The Divorce-Stress-Adjustment Perspective**

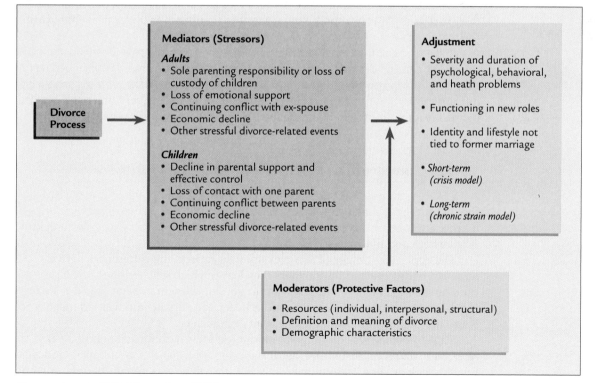

(*Source:* Amato, 2000, Figure 1, p. 1271.)

But after a specific amount of time, the great majority of individuals return to the level of functioning they had before the divorce. The second approach to adjustment, referred to by Amato as the **chronic strain model,** assumes that being divorced involves persistent strains, such as economic hardship, loneliness, and the burden of raising children singlehandedly. The emphasis in this model is that these problems do not go away. Thus, while certain factors such as personal coping resources affect the level of distress that individuals experience, they do not eliminate the stress altogether. The chronic strain model proposes that individuals who have experienced divorce never return to the level of functioning they had before the divorce. Figure 14.1 specifies some of the stressful aspects of divorce as well as the moderating (or protective) factors that may reduce the level and duration of distress individuals experience. Amato concludes, on the basis of his exhaustive review of the research that was conducted in the 1990s, that divorce functions as a short-term crisis for some adults but as a chronic or ongoing source of stressors for others. The same appears to be true for children. Those who suffer long-term negative effects of their parents' divorce are more likely to have experienced economic hardship in childhood (which reduces their educational attainment and occupational status in adulthood) and/or to have been exposed to ineffective parental models of communication and conflict resolution.

We turn now to some specific studies that examine adjustment to divorce.

Effect and Divorce

Evaluating Life after Divorce

When divorced people are interviewed later, after their divorces, whether one, five, or ten years, most say the divorce was the right decision. They are not saying that life now is completely satisfactory; they are simply *affirming* that it was the right decision to have divorced (Wallerstein and Blakeslee, 1990). A person can even have gone through an unwanted divorce and conclude later that it was better to have ended the marriage. For the many others who desperately wanted out of their marriages, it is not surprising if they see their lives as better now than during the marriage.

It seems clear that most people who divorce conclude that they did the right thing. Yet concluding that most divorced people "demonstrated a clear recovery" may be a little too optimistic. Evidence also shows that long after their divorces a significant proportion of people still feel pain and anger deeply, and that psychological distress is found more often among the divorced than among married people.

The Emotional and Psychological Effects of Divorce

Two researchers, after completing a fifteen-year follow-up of divorce, reached the discouraging conclusion that "For many people, the feelings and memories of marital rupture are vivid and fresh ten and fifteen years following the breakup" (Wallerstein and Blakeslee, 1990, p. 28).

The continuing anger of some ex-spouses reflects the differences between the initiators of divorce and the partners they leave, which we described in Chapter 13. Initiators are the ones who most want to get out of the marriage. It is not surprising that when former spouses are studied later, the person who wanted the divorce is usually doing better than the one who opposed it.

This difference was demonstrated in interviews with former spouses ten years after their divorces. In two-thirds of the cases, one partner was happy and relatively free of anxiety and depression, while the other was generally unhappy and suffering from loneliness, anxiety, or depression (Wallerstein and Blakeslee, 1990, pp. 39–40). In only 10 percent of these divorces had *both* the husbands and wives rebuilt happier and fuller lives.

Both age and gender are related to achieving a satisfying life after divorce. Women who divorce when they are younger have a better chance of establishing new and satisfying lives than women who divorce in their forties. Men who divorce in their thirties and forties, especially if they are well established in their occupations or careers, are likely to be happier and more satisfied with their lives than men who divorce in their twenties (Wallerstein and Blakeslee, 1990, p. 41).

Studies based on national samples of adults consistently show that divorced people, on the whole, report the lowest levels of personal happiness (Glenn and Weaver, 1988). The cause-and-effect relationship between divorce and a lower level of happiness is not clear, however. It may be that people who have generally higher levels of personal happiness are less likely to get divorced. Or, of course, divorce may lead to lower levels of personal happiness.

A study of newly married couples compared the psychological well-being of spouses with different divorce histories. For example, wives who had two or more previous divorces were compared with wives who had one, or no, previous divorces. The major difference discovered by this study was that wives who had two or more previous divorces reported "more distress (anxiety, phobias, paranoid ideation, psychoticism, as well as . . . severity of distress) than those in first marriages without a history of divorce and those in remarriages after one divorce" (Kurdek, 1990, p. 706). Husbands who had been divorced two or more times were more likely than other married men to report anxiety. Again, even though husbands and wives with histories of multiple divorce reported lower psychological well-being, that does not mean that divorce *caused* a decline in psychological health. It may simply be that people who divorce more than once have a predisposition to psychological problems.

The same researcher conducted a similar analysis with 6,573 randomly selected adults. The results supported the findings of the newlywed study: Those with two or more divorces reported less happiness and more frequent depression than people with no history of divorce or only one divorce. Furthermore, people who had a history of one divorce reported more frequent depression than those who had never had a divorce (Kurdek, 1991).

This survey supports clinical and qualitative studies showing that divorce has a negative psychological effect on many people. Once again, this connection can be interpreted in two ways. First, individuals with preexisting psychological and emotional problems may be less able to keep their marriages together and thus end up divorced. Or maybe divorce produces or heightens psychological and emotional problems. These alternative interpretations are not necessarily inconsistent; both may contribute to the generally lower emotional and psychological health found among those who divorce.

ContentSELECT

Divorce and
Psychology

Coping with the Role of a Divorced Person

Divorce not only has psychological and emotional effects, it has social consequences as well. The role of *divorced person* often adds to the problems of life after divorce. First, being divorced still carries, for many people, a negative stereotype or a stigma. Also, the role expectations for a divorced person are ambiguous and often limiting; divorced people often feel socially uncomfortable.

Negative Images of Divorced People.   Although the public, as well as important social institutions such as religion and government, generally do not disapprove of divorce as much as they once did, that does not mean that divorced individuals are free of negative images and stereotypes. Many people continue to think of divorce as a sign of failure. Also, many people look for someone to blame when a marriage ends. For these reasons, people may feel ashamed of being divorced (Gerstel, 1987).

Even when divorced people do not view themselves negatively, they often feel that others do. More than one-fourth of a sample of divorced Americans said they had been in social situations in which they felt someone thought less of them because they were divorced (Kitson, 1992). We might suppose that since divorce is much more common than it was forty years ago, the negative views would have diminished, but that does not seem to be true. In a study of women who divorced in the 1940s, a similar percentage said they felt they had been discriminated against by others (Goode, 1956).

Adults who were divorced in the 1980s have been asked about how people treated them after learning about their divorce. The most common response, given by nearly three-fourths of the respondents, was that they were made to feel "less respectable," "dishonest," or "stigmatized." Others felt they were subjected to "moral or religious disapproval" (Kitson, 1992, p. 253).

Many divorced people (about half in one sample) reported that they were reluctant to tell certain people about their impending divorce. Most often they were reluctant to tell their parents or "the family" generally. Even telling friends can be a problem. People going through separation and divorce say they are reluctant to tell their families and friends because they fear disapproval, blame, and other negative reactions.

The negative stigma attached to divorce is intensified when a person is divorced more than once. People who have been divorced twice may say, "I'm going to be very careful about marrying again; I don't want to be a 'three-time loser.'" Newspaper and television stories obviously deem it a newsworthy fact if a person has been married and divorced more than three times. When figure skater Tonya Harding made the news in 1994, her mother was almost always described as a woman who had been married seven times. Very little additional information was provided about her; her multiple marriages seemed to define her sufficiently for the public.

Women often experience a particular negative stereotype when they divorce: They are seen as sexually available. More than half of a sample of divorced people agreed with the statement "Divorced women are constantly sexually propositioned, even by the husbands of their friends" (Kitson, 1992, p. 258). This is a very strong statement, since it specifies that "husbands of friends" are likely to make sexual advances. Many interview studies and personal anecdotes have documented such sexual responses to divorced women. One women described how the husband of a neighbor with whom she had been friendly offered to walk her home after a visit. She described what happened then:

> Maybe I should have known what was going to happen. I turned around at my door to say, "Thank you for walking me home," and it was pawing and grabbing and, "You poor thing, what are you doing for sex? You really must be hurting." And I said, "You goddamn bastard. I'm friends with your wife. Don't you ever, ever, put your hands on me again." (Weiss, 1975, p. 160)

The negative sexual stereotype that is still applied to divorced women is associated with the second social problem of being divorced: the ambiguous and limiting nature of the divorced role.

The Ambiguous and Limiting Nature of the Divorced Role.   Divorced people often feel that they no longer belong, or no longer have a place, in the social world they had when they were part of a couple. More than one-third of divorced people agree with the statement, "One problem of being a divorced person is feeling like

Around the World

The Aftermath of Divorce in India

Divorce in India is different in a number of ways from divorce in the United States, but some outcomes, especially for women, are similar. Considering differences first, India has a much lower level of divorce than the United States, although official statistics for India are misleadingly low. One reason for that is many Indian marriages are not ended by courts, but by councils representing religious castes (Amato, 1994).

As we have seen, in the United States the economic impact of divorce on women is more severe than it is on men. In India, the same is true, but the economic effects on women are much more serious. When a woman in India divorces, she rarely gets any of the property or assets of the marriage, for these are assumed to belong to her husband and his family. Alimony is rare, and child support is inadequate. Many Indian women do not even ask for child support, because they are escaping abusive husbands or they are fearful that their husbands will try to gain custody of their children (Amato, 1994).

Although some stigma is associated with divorce in the United States, divorce is much more stigmatized in India. And the disapproval is much stronger for women than for men. Since women in India are expected to devote themselves to their husbands, and sacrifice their personal needs in favor of husbands, women who divorce are considered to be somehow at fault. Even when the husband's actions are at fault (abuse or adultery), Indian people often assume that it was the wife's behavior that somehow caused her husband to go bad. Divorced men also get more family support, because they frequently have never left the households of their parents and their brothers. Divorced women often return to the homes of parents or siblings, and although they may be temporarily helped they are often viewed as economic burdens and social blemishes on the family (Amato, 1994).

The psychological adjustments to divorce in India are at least as great as they are in the United States. Divorced women in India appear to experience more emotional problems than do men. One study found that two-thirds of divorced and separated mothers reported "depression, thoughts of suicide, and sleep disorders" (Amato, 1994, p. 215). Many divorced Indian women thought of themselves as failures and believed that their lives had ended.

Research on the aftermath of divorce in India, especially as compared with divorce in the United States, reveals similar patterns, even though the cultures and economies of the two countries are very different. However, the divorced women of India do seem to suffer more than American women in the aftermath of marriage dissolution, for three reasons. First, Indian women are almost completely economically dependent on their husbands. Second, the patriarchal family of India provides economic and social security for men after divorce, while women must find a new place to live and a way to survive. Finally, the cultural beliefs of India place more blame on women than on men if a marriage breaks up. Sociologist Paul Amato, who has analyzed the research on the aftermath of divorce in India compared with the United States, offers the following hypothesis: "The greater the inequality between men and women in a given society, the more detrimental the impact of divorce on women" (1994, p. 217).

Source: Amato, 1994.

a 'fifth wheel'" (Kitson, 1992, p. 258). Divorced people often feel their former friends have rejected them for no good reason and are understandably hurt by this behavior. Since this pattern occurs so frequently, one must go beyond the individual characteristics of divorced people and consider the possible social causes.

Divorcing and divorced people are dropped by friends, especially by married friends, for several reasons. First, a divorced person (either male or female) poses a sexual threat (real or imagined) to married couples. Also, the friends of a divorced couple, especially if the divorce is bitter, often feel compelled to chose sides. Thus one spouse remains as a friend, and the other is dropped.

From the perspective of social roles, divorced people no longer fit the standard married person role. Married couples may feel awkward with a separated or divorced friend and not know what to say when many of the usual topics of conversation—kids, family and home—are gone, changed, or too sensitive to discuss.

At the same time that divorced people often feel excluded from the social world of married couples, most are reluctant to join organizations or clubs specifically for the divorced. These clubs are themselves stigmatized—"for losers" or "for people who don't have anybody to turn to." One study found that only 10 percent of divorced individuals joined such organizations (Gerstel, 1987).

There are no well-defined role expectations for those who are divorced, which often leaves the divorced person feeling awkward and uncomfortable. But probably the most ambiguous social role relationship of all for the divorced person is the relationship with one's former spouse.

Husbands and Wives after Divorce

The relationship between two people who have ended their marriage through divorce is complex, confusing, difficult, and varied. The emotional response to a former spouse can range from love to hate.

Emotional Feelings about Former Spouses. Most former spouses have less intense feelings, both positive and negative, toward each other. In a study of divorced couples in California, the vast majority said their former spouses were "neither friend nor foe," although some described their former spouses as their "best friends," and about an equal number said they were "bitter enemies" (Ahrons, 1979, p. 505).

In interviews with people whose marriages had ended about a year earlier, a small percentage of respondents (7 percent) said they still loved their former spouses. Ironically, the same study reported that between 16 and 22 percent believed their *spouses* still had feelings of love toward *them*. Few divorced people (just over 3 percent) say they hate their former spouses. Another 5 percent said they "both hated and loved" their former spouses. A substantial number of divorced people claim they don't feel much of anything about their former spouses, and an equal number "feel sorry" for them.

Continuing to have thoughts about, or longings for, one's former spouse has been called **attachment.** Attachment is not exactly love; it is a psychological response that is expressed by the statement "I can't stop thinking about my wife" (or husband) (Berman, 1985). A number of studies show that continued attachment to one's spouse after divorce is likely to be associated with greater psychological distress (see, for example, Masheter, 1991).

Feelings that spouses have about each other greatly influence their relationship after the divorce. The relationships between former spouses, as we have said, can be especially important for the well-being of their children.

Relationships between Former Spouses. Some couples maintain cordial relationships after divorce, while others are hostile and argumentative. Some couples maintain a high level of contact with each other, while others lose touch with each other completely.

Formerly married couples are most likely to remain in contact when they have children, especially if the children are young. The arrangements for children's visits to the noncustodial parent (or the arrangements between parents with joint physical custody) require at least a minimum of communication. For some couples, however, the communication is much more than minimal. Some divorced couples report that they continue to spend time together beyond what is necessary for the welfare of their children. The continuing relationship between divorced parents, whether the relationship is congenial or not, has led to the concept of binuclear families.

Figure 14.2   **Four Binuclear Family Types**

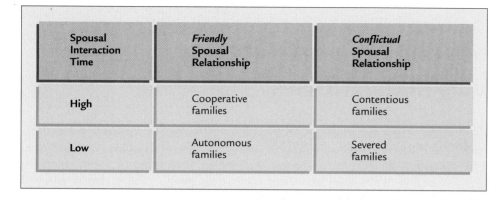

Spousal Interaction Time	*Friendly* Spousal Relationship	*Conflictual* Spousal Relationship
High	Cooperative families	Contentious families
Low	Autonomous families	Severed families

The **binuclear family** is defined as "two interrelated households, maternal and paternal, which form one family system" (Ahrons, 1981, p. 425). Divorce thus splits the original nuclear family into two interrelated households that form one *family system* for the child or children (Ahrons and Rodgers, 1987, p. 42).[1]

Ahrons (1979) describes binuclear families on two dimensions—the level of friendliness (or conflict) between spouses and the amount of time they spend with each other (Figure 14.2).[2] Four types of binuclear families can be identified on the basis of these two dimensions. We call the first type the **cooperative binuclear family** because of the high levels of friendliness and interaction between the former spouses. The second type, called the **autonomous binuclear family,** is characterized by spouses who are friendly, but who keep their interaction at a low level. The third type is the **contentious binuclear family** because the spouses have a conflict-ridden relationship and yet continue to have a high level of interaction. The fourth type is called the **severed binuclear family** because the spouses have a conflict-ridden relationship and a low level of interaction.

The cooperative binuclear family is interesting because it runs counter to the popular image of divorced spouses who continue to be hostile toward each other. In this type of relationship, spouses are often good friends who choose to spend time together with their children, both for enjoyment and the benefit of their children.

An unusual example of the cooperative binuclear family occurs when two divorced partners continue to live in the same household (or close by) after divorce (Ashley, 1994). In one case, a former husband and wife occupied the two sides of a duplex. Their children had specified times for living with each parent, but were encouraged to go freely between their parents' homes.

Some divorced couples actually manage to live in the same house, although they have separate living quarters and lead more-or-less independent personal lives. One woman in such an arrangement admits that she and her former husband had to work it out as they went along. An obvious problem occurs when one or both enter into new relationships. A woman who is in such an arrangement says simply, "We both have dated other people, and we respect each other's privacy" (Ashley, 1994, p. C5).

Very few cooperative binuclear families live in such close proximity, but many talk frequently, either on the phone or in person. They are most likely to discuss matters related to their children, but they also have conversations about other family members (grandparents, siblings), or about personal, economic, and household matters. Cooperative binuclear families may also have occasional meals and outings together for entertainment and enjoyment—especially for their children (Ashley, 1994).

Murderous and Money-Grubbing Stepparents in the Movies

Stepparents, especially stepmothers, have a very negative, and we suspect largely unearned, image in our society. The origin of the negative stereotypes about stepparents isn't clear. But it has been suggested that the image has been perpetuated, if not created, in fairy tales such as *Snow White, Hansel and Gretel*, and *Cinderella*. In these familiars stories, stepmothers poison their stepchildren or convince fathers to abandon them in the woods.

Terrible stepparents are also portrayed in films. Researchers Stephen Claxton Oldfield and Bonnie Butler went to the Internet Movie Database to find summaries of movie plots that involved stepmothers and/or stepfa-thers. They systematically examined the fifty-five plot summaries that included these two key terms. Well over half of the plot summaries portrayed stepparents in negative terms. None presented them in positive terms. About one-fourth of the plots that dealt with stepfathers described them as physically or sexually abusive (e.g., *Freeway*, 1996; *Radio Flyer*, 1992; *P. K. and the Kid*, 1987). Another 15 percent portrayed stepfathers as scheming, bad, and evil (e.g., *Masquerade*, 1988). Nearly 40 percent of the plot summaries that included stepmothers described them as murderous or abusive and about one-fourth portrayed them as money-grubbing.

The social scientists who conducted this study recognize its limitations. They discovered that some films featuring stepparents in central roles were not included in the Internet Movie Database. But they believe their exploratory study provides some insight into the negative portrayal of stepparents in an important cultural media—film. And they believe that conscious attempts could be made by film producers to present more positive portrayals of stepparents in films.

Source: Oldfield, Stephen Claxton, and Butler, Bonnie. "Portrayal of Stepparents in Movie Plot Summaries." *Psychological Reports*, 1999, 82: 879–882. Internet Movie Database web site: http://us.imdb.com.

The second type, the autonomous binuclear family, exists where husband and wife are "neither friend nor foe," but have a civil, respectful relationship with each other. The interactions between parents are relatively infrequent, but they are polite. They often use the telephone to discuss matters relating to their children. When autonomous binuclear families do get together, it is usually for significant events in their children's lives, such as school plays, sporting events, graduations, confirmations, bar or bat mitzvahs, and other ceremonial occasions.

The third type, the contentious binuclear family, is characterized by unresolved conflicts between the parents. Since these couples interact frequently, their children are likely to witness repeated conflict between their parents. The children are also at risk of being used by their parents to hurt or gain advantage over each other. Parents in contentious binuclear families often criticize their former spouses, and they countermand each others' wishes. Parents in contentious binuclear families frequently ask their children for information about the other parent.

Persistent strife between the parents usually also means poor communication, which often leads to problems in coordinating the children's activities. Missed appointments and the resulting inconveniences only add to the strife.

Children who are put in the position of carrying messages between their feuding parents often find the task very difficult (Furstenberg and Cherlin, 1991, p. 40). The hostility that parents feel toward each other is often part of the parent's message that the child is supposed to deliver.

The fourth type is the severed binuclear family. In the severed binuclear family, hostility between the divorced parents persists after the divorce and produces an almost complete absence of communication between them. Often the noncustodial parent (usually the father) leaves the community where his former spouse and children live (Wallerstein and Blakeslee, 1990, chapter 8). Remarriage of one of the spouses (especially noncustodial fathers) usually decreases the contact and increases the hostility between former spouses. Severed binuclear families may have the advantage of keeping hostile former spouses apart, and thus reducing the amount of fighting between them. The children are therefore less often subjected to the unpleasant experience of watching their parents fight. The disadvantage of the severed family is that noncustodial parents often become separated from their children, a topic we discuss in more detail in the following section.

Relations between Divorced Parents and Their Children

The most common custody arrangement following divorce is for children to live with one parent, who has sole custody, while the other parent has visitation rights. Joint physical custody, while still uncommon, is being awarded more often; but even with joint physical custody children still often spend more time with one parent than the other. In 85 percent of the cases where custody is granted to one parent, the mother is favored in the decision (Grall, 2000). The number of fathers who are being granted single custody is growing, however (Meyer and Garasky, 1993).

Child custody arrangements raise several questions about the relations between divorced parents and their children. When mothers have custody, what changes occur in their relationships with their children? What happens to the relationship between fathers and their children when mothers have sole custody? Why do divorced fathers so often fail to make their child support payments? We consider these and other questions in the sections that follow.

ContentSELECT

Divorced Parents
and Children

Custodial Parents and Their Children.   The relationship between children and their parents becomes more intense after a divorce. This is especially true for the custodial parent, but may also be true for the parent who only has visitation rights. Children take on new meaning with the end of a marriage, perhaps because they represent all that is left of the family after the husband–wife relationship has been legally dissolved. Many divorced parents worry that ending the marriage may have harmed their children. Divorced parents may be especially attentive to their children, to assure themselves that the children are all right after the divorce. If the children are doing well, it may seem that the divorce was a tolerable course of action and parental guilt may be reduced (Weiss, 1979a).

Custodial parents often grow much closer to their children, who frequently become their primary sources of support and love. Even very young children are "pressed into becoming advisors, practical helpers, buffers against loneliness and despair, replacements for other adults" (Wallerstein and Kelly, 1980, p. 103). Often the demands of the custodial parent are so great they produce "the overburdened child" (Wallerstein and Blakeslee, 1990, p. 185). The **overburdened child** tries to meet all the parent's needs, whatever they may be—an impossible task.

A child of divorce may try to raise the spirits of a depressed parent, assume more home responsibilities, be a confidant to the parent, give advice, or be an ally in a battle against a former spouse. Robin Moore, for example, was 14 years old when her parents divorced, and through her teenage years she "became her mother's right arm, helping to raise the younger children, and helping to make major decisions, including which house to purchase after the divorce" (Wallerstein and Blakeslee, 1990, p. 95).

Parents who have sole custody of their children after divorce often grow closer to their children and depend on them for love and support.

One feature of a divorced household is that the lines between generations blur, leading to a breakdown of the **parental echelon** (Weiss, 1979a, p. 73). The parental echelon is the parents' level of authority when the marriage is intact. The parental echelon is revealed when parents maintain a solid front when dealing with their children. One aspect of authority structures is that people who are in higher levels cannot side with people who are at lower levels. In a family with both a mother and father, parents generally try to give their first loyalty to each other and, in particular, they do not side with a child in a dispute.

When there is only one parent in a household, the parental echelon loses its meaning. Adults in one-parent homes can make alliances with children without having to be concerned about undercutting the other parent. Indeed, when postdivorce hostility lingers, a parent may make an alliance with a child for the purpose of undercutting the other parent. Whenever there is a breakdown of the parental echelon, especially due to divorce, the parent and child become more equal in rights and responsibilities. This leads to the observation that children who grow up in a home divided by divorce "grow up a little faster."

Children of divorce grow up faster in several ways. First, when children experience the divorce of their parents, they lose much of their innocence about marriage in particular and life in general. As long as a marriage remains intact, children usually give relatively little attention to their parents' relationship. Parents even foster this inattention by not letting their children know what is happening "behind the scenes" of the marriage. But separation and divorce bring problems out into the open. Often the announcement that parents are separating is a complete surprise to their children. As the separation and divorce intensifies, children often see their parents fighting. Or parents, especially when they are upset, may tell the children what has happened to cause the marriage breakup. By the time the divorce is over, children are well aware that married couples do not always live happily ever after.

Children also grow up faster because parents are likely to ask them to take on new household responsibilities. When mothers with custody are employed, they are especially likely to ask their children to take more responsibility, both for themselves and for the household. Since economic resources are often diminished after divorce, children usually become more sensitive to the use of money. Divorced parents often have to be honest with their children about the sacrifices they will have to make in order to make ends meet.

Children who are quite young may be called on to assume nearly adult responsibilities. Some as young as 10 and 11 may be expected to have some of the dinner prepared when their parent comes home from work, or in many cases they simply have to fend for themselves with regard to meals. It is often reported that sons are expected to "fill their father's shoes" when they live with their mothers. This might include doing the heavy work around the yard or house, as well as serving as the authority figure for younger children.

Children of divorce grow up fast because they must face adult realities and responsibilities sooner than most other children. As they grow older, they often express resentment for having been "robbed of their childhood or adolescence," and are angry at their parents for not keeping the family together (Wallerstein and Blakeslee, 1990).

Noncustodial Parents and Child Support.   One of the persistent and most troubling problems associated with noncustodial parents is their failure to make child support payments. Only about 56 percent of divorced parents (that is, 59 percent of mothers and 38 percent of fathers) are awarded child support by the courts. But even when judges order parents to pay child support, they often fail to do so. Figure 14.3 shows the proportion of custodial parents who received full or partial

Figure 14.3   **Custodial Parents Receiving Part or Full Child Support Payments Due: 1993–1997.**

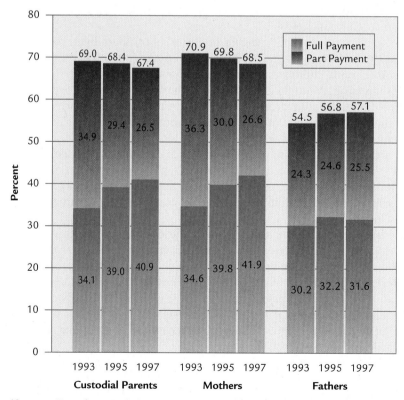

(*Sources:* Data from U.S. Census Bureau, Current Population Survey, April 1994, 1996, and 1998; Grall, 2000, p. 4.)

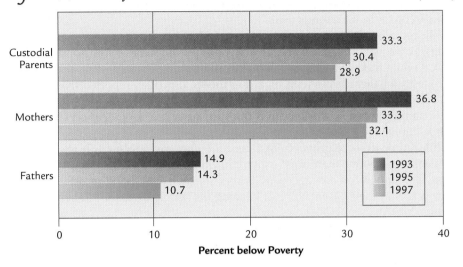

Figure 14.4   **Poverty Status of Custodial Parents: 1993–1997.** *Percent below poverty.*

(*Sources:* Data from U.S. Census Bureau, Current Population Survey, April 1994, 1996, and 1998; Grall, 2000, p. 2.)

support payments in 1993, 1995, and 1997. About 42 percent of custodial mothers and 32 percent of custodial fathers received full payment (Grall, 2000). Certainly the amounts received for child support are almost never adequate for meeting the actual costs associated with providing for a child. The average amount of child support received was $3,600 in 1997, unchanged from 1993 (Grall, 2000). Fathers' failure to pay child support is one of the major reasons for increased poverty among female-headed households.

As Figure 14.4 shows, nearly 33 percent of custodial mothers lived below the poverty level in 1997. The fact that a substantial percentage (more than 40 percent) of divorced women with children are not even *awarded* child support from the courts may be surprising. A number of factors are involved, but one is overriding: economic status (Peterson and Nord, 1990). Children in the least advantaged homes, where the mother has a relatively low educational level and has not had a lawyer representing her in the divorce, are the least likely to receive support from their fathers. Furthermore, mothers with *more* children actually are *less* likely to be awarded child support (Teachman, 1990). Even when child support is received by mothers with lower economic status, the amount of the award is usually lower. It is hardly surprising, then, that divorce contributes greatly to the feminization of poverty in the United States.

When a Census Bureau survey asked women without child support why they were not receiving it, a common answer was that they had not asked for child support (Grall, 2000). Some divorcing women exchange child support for property or monetary settlements. But many women refuse settlement as a way of distancing themselves from their former spouses. Many of these women had husbands who provided poor economic support during the marriage, and they had no reason to expect more after the divorce. Figure 14.5 summarizes reasons given for not having a court award for child support.

Many women, however, wanted child support but did not get it. Often this was because the fathers disappeared and the mothers simply could not locate them to take them to court for child support judgments. Many women, even those in the middle class, did not have the necessary legal assistance and the money to get an agreement through the courts. This echoes the point made earlier that women without legal representation are least likely to be awarded child support.

Figure 14.5 **Reasons No Legal Agreement Established for Custodial Parents: 1998.** *By Percent.*

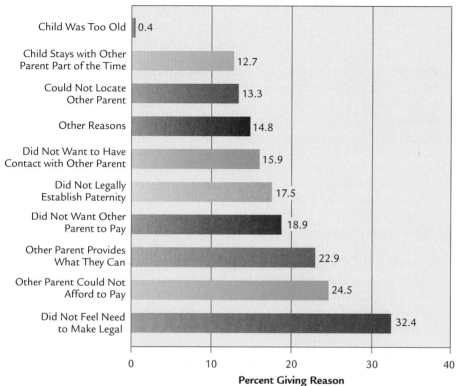

(*Sources:* Data from U.S. Census Bureau, Current Population Survey, April 1998; Grall, 2000, p. 3.)

If a divorced father remarries, his child support payments are likely to diminish, along with the amount of time he spends with his children. Remarriage brings with it new family obligations, perhaps even new children, and these tend to reduce the frequency and amounts of child support payments. Even the remarriages of custodial mothers reduce the economic support divorced fathers provide for their children. When a new husband (and stepfather) enters the home of their children, fathers seem to consider their own economic responsibility diminished.

But the ultimate reason why so many fathers fail to pay child support for their children, according to Furstenberg and Cherlin, is "because they can get away with it" (1991, p. 60). Although in recent years the political, legal, and even moral pressure on fathers to provide economic support for their children has increased, the long-standing public attitude lets fathers off too easily. Many men still see child-rearing as the primary responsibility of mothers, and while many say they intend to meet their parental obligations, their commitment seems to fade as time passes and new familial obligations emerge.

Children and Their Divorced Fathers

Children are likely to have very different relationships with their custodial parent (most often mothers) from their relationships with their noncustodial parent (usually fathers). In the most common arrangement, fathers are the noncustodial parents, with only visitation rights to their children. The role of noncustodial fathers in the lives of their children is not very clear.

HEADline The King of the Deadbeat Dads

Over a period of five years, Jeffrey Nichols moved to three different states in his attempts to avoid making child support payments. When he was finally apprehended by the FBI, he owed his former wife $500,000. Although Jeffrey Nichols's failure to pay child support is far from unusual, the amount of money he owes and the media attention he has received have made him the most notorious deadbeat dad in the nation (Appleson, 1996).

After his arrest, Nichols, a prominent investment banker, did spend four months in prison, and eventually he agreed to pay his former wife $600,000 in back child support.

Nichols is now getting more publicity, because he is challenging the federal law that sent him to prison. The federal law makes it a crime to cross state lines to avoid making child support payments (Appleson, 1996). Nichols is not the first to challenge the law, since it has already been challenged in ten district courts throughout the country, with about half finding it unconstitutional. The law, according to some judges, violates the commerce clause of the Constitution, which allows the free movement of commerce and people across state lines (Appleson, 1996). If the federal law is ultimately ruled unconstitutional, many deadbeat parents will escape prosecution because, as the Jeffrey Nichols case illustrates, moving from one state to another state may allow someone to escape making payments and prosecution for years.

Of course, the federal law only applies to those deadbeat parents who do cross state lines with the intention of avoiding child support payments. If they remain in the same state, only state and local laws apply, and many judges are reluctant to impose jail sentences for the violation of state child support laws (Hall, 1996). Yet other methods of dealing with deadbeat parents, such as automatically deducting funds from paychecks, have not been a sufficient deterrent. In the view of Marilyn Smith, a past president of the National Child Support Enforcement Association, "When you punish the most egregious offenders, it sends a powerful message to others who may be on the fence" (Hall, 1996, p. B1).

In many states, lawmakers have been exploring new ways of compelling parents to pay court-mandated child support. One potentially effective way of forcing people to pay the child support they owe is to revoke licenses they hold. States may revoke driver's licenses, professional or business licenses, and licenses on recreational equipment such as boats, airplanes, snowmobiles, campers, and so on (Turner, 1996). When these resources are threatened, many who owe back payments quickly find the money to pay.

In some jurisdictions, law enforcement officers have started making highly publicized raids on deadbeat parents. Often accompanied by television camera crews, who have been alerted in advance, police make early morning raids at the homes of those who owe child support payments. The glare of negative publicity may also encourage others to keep up with their payments.

Sources: Appleson, 1996; Hall, 1996; Turner, 1996.

Because of the ambiguity of the father's role after divorce, men display a wide variety of responses toward their children. Some divorced fathers continue to be closely involved in the care and supervision of their children; in some cases, fathers actually increase the intensity of their parenting. Others see their children mainly when they come for visits, and then the children are treated primarily as guests. Many noncustodial fathers seem to feel they must entertain their children for their entire visit. Most often fathers have only limited and sporadic contact with their children (Seltzer, 1991b).

It is the ambiguity of the father's role after divorce that may contribute to what is called "the disappearing father" or the "fading father" (Furstenberg and Cherlin, 1991). Although not all divorced fathers disappear from their children's lives after divorce (Meyer and Garasky, 1993), many reduce both their contact and their financial support. There is a widespread tendency for divorced fathers to have less and less contact with their children, especially as children enter adolescence. Many fathers also reduce their financial support, especially if they move away, remarry, and have other children.

> Among the 7.0 million custodial parents due child support payments in 1997, most (84.3 percent) had arrangements with the noncustodial parents for joint child custody or visitation privileges with their children. The 1.1 million custodial parents due support but without joint custody or visitation arrangements had a much lower rate of receiving support, 35.5 percent. The highest rate of receiving at least some child support (83.2 percent) occurred when the noncustodial parent had both joint custody and visitation privileges. (Grall, 2000)

One example of a disappearing father is presented by Wallerstein and Blakeslee (1990, pp. 129–144). Californian Betty Burrelle (a fictitious name) was 33 years old, with three children aged 7, 5, and 3, when her husband Dale decided he wanted out of the marriage. At first Betty opposed the divorce, but eventually she agreed to it, with $1-a-year alimony and $450-a-month child support. Although Dale went on to earn a good income after he moved to New York where he was a hospital administrator, he fell $5,000 behind in child support payments, and the court lowered the amount to $360 per month. Betty and her children now live in New Mexico, which means that Dale, who has remarried, rarely sees his children. Dale claims that during the first year after the divorce he saw his children "a lot," but since his move to New York he sees his children only once a year or so, usually when he is on business trips to the Southwest. The weak relationship of this father with his children is demonstrated by the fact that when he talks about them, he often doesn't use their names, but refers to them as "the older, middle, and younger" child.

▲ Divorced fathers often spend less and less time with their children as time passes, making their interaction with them more difficult.

This father is a somewhat extreme example, but his case reveals several familiar patterns of the disappearing father. The child support he agreed to pay originally, while above average, was far from enough to raise three children. Even so, he fell behind in his payments, and eventually got the courts to lower the amount to $360 per month ($4,320 per year). This father, as is often the case, saw his children fairly often in the first years after divorce, but then less and less often, especially as his job caused him to move farther away. He also remarried and had a new child, which further reduced the time and attention he gave to his older children. Finally, as the children went from childhood to their teenage years, they often had less interest in spending time with their father, preferring to be with their own friends. These are the characteristic patterns of the "disappearing father" (Furstenberg and Harris, 1992).

Statistics from a wide range of studies show that children and noncustodial fathers have relatively low levels of contact. One national survey (Seltzer, 1991b) found that nearly 30 percent of children whose parents had divorced had not seen their fathers during the past year and another (Furstenburg and Cherlin, 1991) found that close to one-half had not visited with their fathers in that time. We may conclude from these studies that between one-third and one-half of children of divorce do not see their fathers in any given year.

Even among those children who *do* see their fathers, the contacts are infrequent and limited. Only one child in six whose parents are divorced sees his or her father at least once a week. When children do see their fathers on a regular basis, their fathers act more like close relatives than parents. They take their children shopping, to dinner, or to movies. Sometimes they play sports with them, but rarely do they help them with homework or school projects.

New Relationships and Remarriage

Most divorced people remarry, and even those who do not, are likely to form some type of intimate relationship after divorce. In this part of the chapter, we explore the dating and remarriage experiences of divorced people. Remarriage typically produces reconstituted or blended families, or as they are more commonly called, stepfamilies. Stepfamilies have special problems, but they also have special strengths as well.

■ Dating and Courtship after Divorce

The return to romantic and intimate involvements after divorce is influenced by a number of factors. First, there is the length of the marriage that has ended. Relatively short-term marriages that end in divorce, especially when there are no children, make dating again relatively easy. But when long-term marriages end in divorce, a return to dating is more difficult. The exceptions, of course, are divorces that were precipitated by a new intimate relationship.

The stressfulness of the marriage that has ended, or of the divorce, may also be a factor in returning to dating. When a person has experienced a tumultuous marriage or a bitter, rancorous divorce, it may be difficult to become involved again with another person.

Generally it is easier for men to begin dating after divorce, especially if the divorce ends a long-term marriage. Women are at a disadvantage in returning to dating after divorce. One reason is the continuing gender bias that makes it difficult for women to initiate dates. Also, the sexual stereotypes that surround divorced women—that they want or need sex—only add to the difficulty of women asking men for dates.

A certain cultural bias also gives men greater latitude in the ages of women they may date. For example, men of middle age may date women who are their age, but they may also date women who are as much as fifteen or twenty years younger than they are. It is relatively rare for women to date men who are substantially younger. Divorced women can date older men, of course, but beyond middle age there are simply fewer men in the population.

In many cases, divorced women have custody of their children, which can also be an impediment to dating and courtship. In addition, their employment can make it difficult for divorced mothers to develop new relationships. One divorced mother with three teenage children reported in an interview that she holds *two* full-time jobs (one as a speech therapist and the other as a night watchman). When asked about her social life, her response was crisp and no-nonsense: "I have no social life. I don't go out" (Wallerstein and Blakeslee, 1990, p. 133). When children are young, they need time and attention, which makes it difficult for the custodial parent to get out and meet potential dating partners. Simply having the children in the home may make entertaining and other social activities more difficult.

Caution and Realism during Courtship.   A common sentiment expressed by divorced people is that their approach to marriage is much more practical and less romantic than it was when they first married. Divorced people often consider their first marriages the result of social pressures or poor judgment, and they are determined not to make the same mistakes again.

The greater practicality of dating and courtship after divorce can be seen in the way couples fully discuss the implications of a potential marriage. One woman, now remarried, said to an interviewer, "Before marrying, we sat down and discussed different things that happen in a marriage. We brought out our views and ideas, and decided that the only way a marriage can work would be to be honest, outspoken, and ready to accept each other's criticism" (Furstenberg and Spanier, 1984, p. 56).

People who have been previously married tend to show their real selves in dating and not just their ideal *dating selves.* In interviews, they often acknowledge that early in a relationship they deliberately present themselves as they really are, not as some idealized image. They are quite willing to let their dating partners see them without their hair made up and in old clothes.

The practicality and realism of dating and courtship after divorce are also found in a willingness to discuss the possibility that the marriage may not work out. They often agree in advance that they will not endure another marriage that has gone bad. In an interview, a divorced woman described her feelings on this point: "I would try my damndest [to make the marriage work] and hope he would try the same way, but if we couldn't work it out then we wouldn't stay together . . . it's a little different from what I thought the first time" (Furstenberg and Spanier, 1984, p. 192).

Remarriage after Divorce

Remarriage has a long history in the United States, but before the twentieth century it almost always occurred because of the death of a spouse, not because of divorce or desertion. In pre-Revolutionary times, in the Plymouth colony, about one-third of all men and one-quarter of all women remarried because of a spouse's death. This pattern continued until the 1920s (Cherlin, 1992). Then the balance shifted, and since that time remarriage has more often followed divorce. Currently over 90 percent of all remarriages follow divorces rather than widowhood (Clarke, 1995b).

Most people who divorce eventually remarry. About three-quarters of divorced men and two-thirds of women remarry after divorce (Cherlin and Furstenberg, 1994). Those who divorce when young are more likely to remarry; this is especially true for women, whose chances for remarriage diminish sharply with age. Women who divorce after age 40 have about a one-in-three chance of remarrying compared with a three-in-five chance for women who divorce before age 30 (Bumpass et al., 1990). Men, in contrast, have a high chance of remarrying, even if they divorce when they are older. The gender difference in remarriage results from both the cultural pattern of men being able to marry younger women, and the demographic fact that there are relatively fewer men than women in the older population.

Remarriage also varies by race and ethnicity. African Americans and Latinos are much less likely to remarry than whites, especially among women (Norton and Miller, 1992).

Recent decades have produced a great many remarried couple households. When there are children in a remarried couple household, they are most likely children of the wife, since mothers most often receive custody of children. There are eight times as many households with biological mothers

▲ *Many remarried couples find that their greater maturity allows them to communicate more effectively and enjoy a satisfying emotional and sexual relationship.*

A daughter receives some last-minute makeup, before she participates in her mother's remarriage ceremony.

and stepfathers as there are households with stepmothers and biological fathers (Cherlin, 1992, p. 86). In only a small number of cases have both the husband and wife brought children to the remarried household.

When one or both partners bring children into a remarriage, the resulting families are called *reconstituted* or *blended families.* However, the more familiar term *stepfamilies* is still often used.

One disadvantage of the word *stepfamily* is that it tends to carry with it some negative connotations. Stepfamilies are seen as beset by problems and filled with friction. Even though this is a stereotype, most serious observers agree that "remarriages . . . are faced with complexity and complications beyond the typical stresses and strains facing any married couple" (Ganong and Coleman, 1989, p. 28). The basis for many of these stresses and strains can be found in the observation that "remarriage is an 'incomplete' institution."

Remarriage as an Incomplete Institution

In first marriages, there is a high degree of understanding about what is expected of husbands, wives, and children in terms of how they relate to one another and how they relate to other kin, such as in-laws and grandparents. But in remarriages, the social norms and social roles are less clear (Kaplan and Hennon, 1992). It is in this sense that remarriage has been called an **incomplete institution** (Cherlin, 1978).

Numerous examples of unclear social norms and inadequate social roles exist in remarried families. Consider the issue of parental control over children's behavior. Generally, the norm in American society is that parents control and provide guidance for their children's behavior. But the role of the stepparent is not clear. Does a stepparent have a right to control the behavior of children who are not his or her own? What rights does a stepparent have to discipline the children of his or her spouse? There are no clear answers for these questions, because the roles of stepparents are not well defined. Remarried couples must work out these issues on their own. This is but one example of the remarried family as an incomplete institution.

There are no clear-cut norms for how a remarried person is expected to relate to a former spouse. Some former partners feel they must show consideration for their former partners, sparing their feelings about the new marriage. Others have no such concerns. A divorced husband named Jim describes how the woman he is marrying (Elaine) finds it difficult to understand his attempts to avoid hurting his former wife Nancy. He says, "Elaine's relationship with her ex-husband is nothing like my relationship with Nancy and she didn't understand my wanting to ease Nancy's pain by not flaunting my new life at her" (Ahrons and Rodgers, 1987, p. 161).

Another sign of remarriage as an incomplete institution can be found in our language. We have no words for a variety of relationships that emerge in remarried households. Even the words we do have carry negative connotations or inappropriate historical legacies. For example, the word *stepparent* was originally applied to a new parent who "steps in" after the death of a parent. The stepparent steps in to fill the role of a dead parent. Today, however, the parent is divorced rather than dead, and living in another household. Moreover, the words *stepmother* and *stepfather* carry some fairly strong negative connotations, as in the "wicked stepmothers" of fairytales. Yet there are no established alternative words for children to use when their parents remarry. In one remarried family, a researcher found that the children of the mother wished to call her new husband *Dad*, but *his* children, who were also living in the home, refused to allow this (Cherlin, 1978). Stepchildren often use the first names of their parent's new spouse, although this may seem inappropriate, especially when children are young.

A number of other relationships also arise from divorce and remarriage for which no appropriate names have emerged. For example, if children live with their divorced mother when their father remarries, there is no term that clearly identifies his new wife. *Stepmother* may be used, but it is not completely appropriate, since the children probably spend very little time in their father's household, except as visitors. American children, at least of a certain age, usually resort to phrases such as "my dad's wife." But even that label is mildly dismissive, since it gives the new wife recognition only with respect to someone else (the father).

The legal system is also inadequate for dealing with many aspects of remarried families (Fine and Fine, 1992). The field of family law has largely developed under the assumption that marriages are first marriages, and the laws have not kept up with the realities of remarriage and stepfamilies.

For instance, the legal rights and responsibilities between stepparents and stepchildren are not clearly defined by either federal or state laws. There are generally no statutes that cover the economic obligations of a stepparent for stepchildren if there is a divorce from the biological parent. Even when the stepparent has been providing the primary economic support for a stepchild, that obligation usually ends with a divorce. Until recently, stepparents were rarely able to gain custody of their stepchildren after a divorce from the natural parent. Some states now have statutes providing that "under some circumstances, a 'fit' nonbiological parent may obtain custody of the child if that is in the child's best interest" (Fine and Fine, 1992, p. 336). Similarly, stepparents are increasingly able to gain visitation rights to see their stepchildren after a divorce if the court holds that visitation is in the best interests of the child.

Inheritance is another legal issue that is complicated by stepfamily relationships. Generally, stepchildren have no legal claim on the estates of deceased stepparents unless they have been specifically named as beneficiaries. When a stepparent dies without having prepared a will, stepchildren have generally been unsuccessful in pressing their claims (Fine and Fine, 1992). Aside from the legal aspects of inheritance, stepparents often face the practical decision of how they are going to distribute their estates to their children. When two remarried parents each have children from previous marriages, and then, in addition, have children

ContentSELECT

Remarriage

together, they face the problem of dividing their estate. Since the children may be of very different ages and have diverse economic circumstances, the parents may find it difficult to agree on how to apportion their estates.

The lack of appropriate words for the members of reconstituted family members, the uncertainties about social roles and norms, and the unresolved legal issues, all attest to the incompleteness of remarriage as an institution. A further complication of reconstituted families arises from the expanded and ambiguous boundaries of stepfamilies.

Expanded and Ambiguous Boundaries of Stepfamilies

Content**SELECT**

Stepfamily or
Stepparent

The boundaries of first-marriage families are well defined. It is easy to identify who is in the family and who is not, and to describe the relationships of family members to each other. The stepfamily, in contrast, usually involves a larger number of people, and there is a lack of clarity about who is and who is not a member of the family. Sociologists Furstenberg and Cherlin (1991) use the term *thin kin* to refer to this new type of extended family; while anthropologist Simpson (1998) refers to the complex relationships as the *unclear* family, an obvious play on the classic term *nuclear* family.

It is certainly true that the more people there are in a family system, the more difficult it is to make decisions about family actions and activities. Consider the simple case of where and when to take a summer vacation. Even in the intact (never divorced) family this can be a difficult decision if both parents are employed and children have various summer activities. Just to find a time when everyone is free at the same time is often difficult. In the remarried family, this decision is greatly complicated, because so many more people are involved. To begin with, the desires and often the legal rights of ex-spouses must be taken into account. If a noncustodial father, for example, has been granted the right to have his children for a month in the summer (a common arrangement), then his schedule must be a part of the planning for a family vacation. If both spouses in a remarriage have children from previous marriages, then the decision making becomes even more complex.

The boundaries of remarried families are also expanded by the addition of extended family members. A remarried couple with children from both previous marriages *and* with children from their present marriage can have four sets of grandparents for their children. All these grandparents might want time with their grandchildren, especially on important holidays. To complicate matters further, any set of grandparents could also be divorced and remarried. In an extreme, though unlikely, case, a particular remarried couple could have as many as eight sets of grandparents to accommodate.

The numerous problems and complications of stepfamilies add special challenges to making remarriage work. We turn next to the quality of remarriages and likelihood of success for remarried couples.

Marital Quality in Remarriages

In a comprehensive review of the research on remarriage conducted in the 1990s, Coleman, Ganong, and Fine (2000) offer a number of insights, including the following. First, they observed that the research findings regarding the differences in marital quality between first marriages and remarriages are mixed. Some studies find no difference, while others report lower levels for remarried couples. Second, they note that findings that are based on observations of spouses' behavior as well as self-report data show that remarried couples are more likely to criticize each other and to express anger and irritation than are first-married couples.

They also report higher levels of tension and disagreement than do first-married couples. Disagreements in remarriages generally center around stepchildren (e.g., disciplines, rules, and distribution of resources). Conflict between spouses may result from arguments between stepparents and stepchildren. In fact, marital quality is lower when both remarried spouses have children from prior relationships.

The Stability of Remarriages

Most studies show that remarriages have a slightly higher chance of ending in divorce than first marriages (Clarke and Wilson, 1994). The likelihood of divorce for the remarried has been estimated at between six to ten percentage points *higher* than the likelihood of divorce for first-married couples (Cherlin, 1992; Clarke and Wilson, 1994).

Several possible reasons have been proposed for the higher divorce rates among remarried couples. The first is suggested by various issues we have already considered: Remarried and stepparent families may encounter more stress and a greater number of potential problems. A second explanation may lie in the personal characteristics of people who divorce and remarry. That is, people who divorce once may have certain psychological or behavioral problems, such as alcoholism and personality disorders, that increase the likelihood of their divorcing again. A third explanation is that people who divorce once are more inclined to end a second marriage if it does not prove to be satisfactory. Having once gone through a divorce, they are more capable of doing it again if they believe the situation requires it. Because of their previous experience, divorced people may be more able to discern when a marriage has unresolvable problems and therefore to move toward ending it. In support of this interpretation, remarried couples who divorce do so sooner than couples in first marriages (Clarke and Wilson, 1994).

A fourth reason why remarried couples may divorce somewhat more often than first-married couples is that the population of first-married couples includes people who are ideologically, religiously, or psychologically unable or unwilling to divorce. Regardless of how dissatisfied they may be with their marriages, these people will not end their marriages by divorce. The remarried population has already demonstrated their willingness to divorce. The two populations—the first-marrieds and the remarrieds—would differ in their levels of divorce for this reason alone, even if none of the other reasons discussed existed.

The Strengths of Remarried Families

Families in general tend to show their greatest strengths in time of difficulty or crisis. Remarried families certainly face special problems, but they often respond strongly and positively to the situations they face. Because remarriages and stepfamilies operate in a realm where the social roles and norms are not clear, the members of these families are often creative. If the language does not provide a ready-made term for all members of the new family, a term is invented. If the norms do not specify exactly what authority a stepparent has over children, families may sit down and discuss what the stepparent's role will be. It may not always be easy for stepfamilies to negotiate the uncharted areas, but it is not impossible if they are willing to discuss and work out the arrangements.

There are reasons to believe that remarried partners are willing to work out new arrangements: They tend to be more honest with each other and at the same time more tolerant (Westoff, 1977). Remarried couples report again and again how in their second marriages they are able to talk about more things with greater candor than in their first marriages. Second marriages are not as closely tied to the unrealistic aspects of romantic courtship. Remarried couples are more likely to present themselves openly and directly, even during the dating and courtship period. One remarried woman described her new openness in the following way: "If we fight, I'm a better fighter now, more verbal. I don't withdraw as much. I'm more direct. If you can talk about a problem, you can resolve it" (Westoff, 1977, p. 131).

Remarried couples are also likely to be more tolerant of their partners and realistic about the everyday aspects of married life. Many report that minor irritations do not bother them as much as in their first marriages. They do not expect married life to be perfect all the time. Couples know they will not please each other in everything they do. A remarried doctor told an interviewer, "I may be getting older, but I'm more tolerant. I'm really happy, so little things don't bother me so much. And you certainly want to make it work. . . . It's a searing experience to break up a marriage. . . . Thank God you have a second chance" (Westoff, 1977, p. 133).

Summary

The majority of people who have divorced say that their lives are better than they were previously, although many still bear the scars of divorce. Generally, the person who wanted the divorce has made a better emotional and psychological adjustment.

Surveys show that divorced people, as a group, are less happy and have more psychological problems than other groups in the population. However, it is not clear whether these characteristics are the *product* or the *cause* of divorce.

Despite the large numbers of divorced people today, negative stereotypes still exist. Divorce is seen by many people as a sign of failure and something about which a person should be ashamed. Divorced women may experience negative stereotypes about their sexual availability. And the divorced role is ambiguous and limiting. Many divorced people feel that they no longer fit in the social world of married people.

The feelings and relationships between divorced husbands and wives are complex, confusing, difficult, and varied. A few love or hate their former spouses, but the feelings of most are less intense. Nearly half either like or feel sorry for their former mates.

The continuing interaction between former spouses, and in particular those who have children, has led to the concept of binuclear families. Binuclear families vary by the level of friendliness (or conflict) between former spouses and by the amount of time they spend in interaction. Variations on these two dimensions produce four types of binuclear families: cooperative, contentious, autonomous, and severed.

The relationship between children and their parents becomes more intense after divorce. Parents continue to be concerned about how the divorce has affected their children. Children of divorce often take on new and heavier responsibilities—they grow up a little faster.

Fathers are usually the noncustodial parents after a divorce, but the role of divorced father has a number of ambiguities. Many become *disappearing dads* or *fading fathers,* having less and less contact with their children. Absent fathers fail to provide economic support for their children, even when they have legal obligations to do so. Failure to pay child support leads to poverty in many single-parent homes.

Dating and courtship after divorce are often stressful, though usually less so for men than women. Most approach remarriage with greater caution and realism than they did their first marriages. Five out of six men and two out of three women remarry after divorce. African Americans are less likely to remarry than whites; and Latinos are least likely to remarry.

Remarried couple households, if there are children from former marriages, are sometimes called *reconstituted* or *blended families,* but the more familiar word is *stepfamilies.* Remarriage has been called an "incomplete institution," meaning that there are no clear-cut norms about the many types of family relationships that form after divorce. Even the names of family members in remarried families are not clearly established. Legal rights and responsibilities among family members are also not clearly defined. Remarried families have expanded and ambiguous family boundaries.

The quality of remarriages is similar to that of first marriages. The exception is that remarried couples have more conflict over childrearing and discipline. Remarriages have a slightly greater likelihood of ending in divorce than first marriages. Part of the reason for this is that some people will not get a divorce for any reason, while divorced people have already demonstrated that they will leave a marriage if it is not satisfactory.

Remarried families have many problems, but they also have certain strengths. They are often more likely to negotiate and improvise when they face family problems. Generally, they are more tolerant when they face the imperfections of other family members.

Notes

1. Our use of the term *binuclear family* conforms to Ahrons's original definition and description. Ahrons and Rodgers (1987) have subsequently expanded the concept to include a wide range of family structures—including never-married and single-parent households (p. 22).

2. The four family types described in Table 14.1 are very similar to the four coparenting patterns derived empirically by Maccoby, Depner, and Mnookin (1990, p. 146).

Key Terms

Attachment (p. 442)

Autonomous binuclear family (p. 443)

Binuclear family (p. 443)

Chronic strain model of adjustment (p. 438)

Contentious binuclear family (p. 443)

Cooperative binuclear family (p. 443)

Crisis model of adjustment (p. 437)

Divorce-stress-adjustment model (p. 437)

Incomplete institution (p. 454)

Overburdened child (p. 445)

Parental echelon (p. 446)

Severed binuclear family (p. 443)

Review Questions

1. Explain the divorce-stress-adjustment model. How do the two subtypes of this model differ in terms of what they predict about adjustment to divorce?

2. How does the selection model explain differences between adults and children who are intact families versus those who have gone through divorce?

3. List and discuss the keys to success in binuclear families.

4. Summarize statistics pertaining to the incidence and timing of remarriage after divorce.

5. Discuss the characteristics of stepfamilies.

6. Summarize recent research pertaining to the happiness and stability of remarriages and stepfamilies.

7. Outline the major differences between stepfamilies and intact nuclear families.

8. Identify the major areas of conflict experienced in stepfamilies.

9. Identify the major strengths of stepfamilies.

Critical Thinking Questions

1. Why do men and women adjust to divorce differently?

2. Why do men and women have different *value* on the remarriage market?

3. How might the characteristics sought in a partner by a divorced person be different from those sought by a never-married person?

4. Why do remarriages have a slightly greater likelihood of divorce than first marriages?

5. In what ways might the children of divorced parents mature more quickly than those from intact families? What could account for these differences?

6. Why have negative stereotypes about stepmothers emerged in our culture? What impact could these stereotypes have on the relationships between women and their stepchildren?

Online Resources Available for This Chapter

www.ablongman.com/marriageandfamily

- Online Study Guide with Practice Tests
- PowerPoint Chapter Outlines
- Links to Marriage and Family Websites
- ContentSelect Research Database
- Self-Assessment Activities

Further Reading

Books

Booth, Alan, and Dunn, Judy (eds.). *Stepfamilies: Who Benefits? Who Does Not?* Hillsdale, NJ: Erlbaum, 1994. Focuses on the ways in which stepfamilies function as organizations for raising children and sources of social support.

Braver, Sanford L., and O'Connell, Diane. *Divorced Dads: Shattering the Myths.* New York: Jeremy P. Thatcher/Putnam, 1998. Unravels six common myths about divorced fathers.

Bray, James H., and Kelly, John. *Stepfamilies: Love, Marriage, and Parenting in the First Decade.* New York: Broadway Books, 1999. A handbook for blended families that offers some substantive advice, based on a ten-year longitudinal study.

Ganong, Larry, and Coleman, Marilyn. *Remarried Family Relationships.* Newbury Park, CA: Sage, 1994. A comprehensive look at remarried families, including the pathways from divorce to remarriage, key relationships in remarried families, and stepparent–stepchild relationships.

Kelley, Patricia. *Developing Healthy Stepfamilies: Twenty Families Tell Their Stories.* New York: Haworth Press, 1995. Provides real-life examples of how well-functioning stepfamilies have coped with the issues of discipline, roles, money management, and family rituals.

Lauer, Robert H., and Lauer, Jeanette C. *Becoming Family : How to Build a Stepfamily That Really Works.* Minneapolis, MN: Augsburg Fortress Publishers, 1999. Drawing on their own experiences, and that of the stepfamilies with whom they have worked, Robert and Jeanette Lauer give realistic, helpful advice on how to deal with the major challenges in stepfamily life.

Levin, Irene, and Sussman, Marvin (eds.). *Stepfamilies: History, Research, and Policy.* New York: Haworth, 1997. A compilation of studies that focus on the factors that promote family cohesiveness and integration.

Mason, Mary Ann, Sugarman, Stephen, and Skolnick, Arlene S. (eds.). *All Our Families: New Policies for a New Century.* New York: Oxford University Press, 2002. Examines the current state of all families and proposes new policies for strengthening those families as we move into the next century.

Pasley, K., and Ihinger-Tallman, M. (eds.). *Stepparenting: Issues in Theory, Research, and Practice.* Westport, CT: Greenwood, 1994. An analysis of research literature on stepparenting and a summary of progress made in research, theory, and practice.

Wright, Janet M. *Lesbian Step Families: An Ethnography of Love* (Haworth Innovations in Feminist Studies). Binghamton, NY: Harrington Park Press, 1998. Explores five lesbian stepfamilies' definitions of the stepparent role and how they accomplish parenting tasks, cope with homophobia, and define and interpret their experiences.

*Content*SELECT *Articles*

Kahn, J., and Meier, S. "Children's Definitions of Family Power and Cohesion Affect Scores on the Family System Test." *American Journal of Family Therapy* 29(2), 2001: 141–155. **[Database: Psychology]** The Family System Test (FAST) is a figure placement tool utilized to measure children's perceptions of power structures and cohesion within family units. A study sample consisting of 151 11-year-olds were asked to describe their familial power structures using the FAST tool. Study findings suggest that respondents' definitions of power and cohesion significantly impacted both perceived family power scores and perceived family cohesion scores.

Putnam, Mary. "What Do I Call My Husband's Ex? Friend." *Newsweek* 139(2), February 18, 2002: 14. **[Database: General Interest]** The author of the article describes her friendly relationship with her husband's ex-wife, Pam. The two women share the responsibility of raising Pam's children and have constructed a respectful relationship to ensure the kids' well-being. In this family's arrangement, vacation plans even include Pam.

Responses to Family Problems
Family Policy and Professional Counseling

15

Family Policies

Marriage and Family Counseling

Margaret Atwood's (1986) book, The Handmaid's Tale, *describes a society of the future—The Republic of Gilead—in which a woman named Offred is one of the handmaids to the Commander.*

At an earlier time of her life, Offred was married to Luke and the two of them had planned for their future—a house and garden, with swings for their children. But now, in the ultra-controlled society of Gilead, she is being forced by the state to live a very different life. Gilead is a totally controlled society, with rules for every aspect of human life.

Offred, as a handmaid of the Commander, is required to have sexual intercourse with him once a month. The objective is for her to become pregnant so that she can contribute a child to the dwindling population of the nation. Offred's only value resides in her ovaries because they have the potential to produce children desperately needed by the Republic of Gilead.

Key Questions

1 Is it possible to eradicate poverty in the United States?

2 Would mandatory premarital counseling for all Americans reduce the divorce rate?

3 How does the United States compare with other nations in regard to family policies?

4 Are changes in family patterns (e.g., births out of marriage, single-parent families, nonmarital cohabitation) a *cause* of societal problems or a *response* to them?

*I*n Margaret Atwood's fictional nation of Gilead *(The Handmaid's Tale)*, dangerously low birth rates led the ruling party to institute a widespread policy that turned fertile women into baby makers. Their rights were sharply curtailed and their freedoms stolen in an attempt to restore the birth rate to a viable level. Their sole function was to conceive and deliver babies.

This fictional account may seem far-fetched but similar situations of near-compulsory pregnancy have actually developed in nations that faced low birth rates. In the 1980s in Romania, for instance, the political leader Nicolae Ceausescu instituted laws that required monthly physical examinations of all fertile women to determine if they were pregnant. Abortions were made illegal, and contraception was difficult to obtain. The intention of the policy was to increase the number of births; the unintended consequence was a sharp increase in maternal deaths due to illegal abortions. In addition, Ceausescu's policy led to many Romanian babies being placed in deplorable orphanages because families were not able to care for the large number of children they were forced to have.

Governments often make sweeping policies designed to change family behavior, especially behavior that is perceived as a problem. Sometimes, as in the fictional Gilead or Ceausescu's Romania, the government wants people to have more children, but more often, in today's world, governments are trying to curtail childbearing. China's one-child policy aims to reduce childbearing because rapid population growth is a threat to the country's future. Leaders fear the food supply will not be sufficient to meet the large population's needs. In the United States in the mid 1990s, Congress passed changes in welfare policies designed to reduce childbearing among unmarried mothers, especially teenagers and those on welfare.

Excessive and out-of-wedlock childbearing are only two of many family behaviors that governments see as problems and therefore subject to governmental intervention policies. Divorce rates, child welfare, nonmarital cohabitation, domestic violence, and unpaid child support payments are other aspects of family life that can be regulated by government policies (Browning and Rodriguez, 2002). In the first part of this chapter, we examine governmental policies that can affect families. We show that such policies can assist, control, or attempt to change families. We also show that many family policy issues are rooted in moral values and political ideologies and thus are controversial.

The first part of this chapter examines family problems on a societal level. Societal level problems also affect the population on a personal or individual level. In the second part, we look at problems within families. When families and their individual members encounter problems, they are likely to seek professional help. Hence, we take a closer look at marital and family therapy and counseling.

Family Policies

*F*amily policy refers to objectives concerning family well-being and the specific measures taken by governmental bodies to achieve them (Aldous and Damon, 1991). All governmental policies affect families in one way or another, even if they didn't intend to do so, or even if their primary purpose was not directly related to changing families. Therefore, we distinguish between policies that were designed to directly impact families and those that were designed for other purposes but that have an impact on family as well.

Direct family policies are aimed explicitly at affecting families (Kammerman and Kahn, 1978). When a government initiates a family planning program, the objective is clear and explicit: to influence the childbearing patterns of couples. A rationale for such a program may be to improve the overall quality of family life or

in the media

Family Politics in the Comics

For more than thirty years, the comic strip *Doonesbury* has commented on a full range of controversial issues related to families and intimate relationships and a wide range of other topics, as well. The strip's creator, Garry Trudeau, is typically regarded as a *left-wing liberal* and has been criticized by conservatives for his "scurrilous charges against Republican candidates and office holders" (Schaefer, 2001). Indeed, when it appeared on October 26, 1970, *Doonesbury* had a decidedly political bent. In its early years, the strip focused on a number of college students—and their friends and associates—who were protesting the war in Viet Nam. In 1975, Trudeau won a Pulitzer Prize for editorial cartooning, the only daily comic strip to ever win the award. Over its thirty-year history, the strip has been canceled, censored, and/or moved from the comics pages to the editorial pages of many newspapers because of its controversial perspective on current events and prominent national figures. There are a few other daily comic strips that could be regarded as political commentaries, but they have a much smaller circulation than *Doonesbury*. *Mallard Fillmore*, a strip with a conservative angle, has been marketed as the anti-*Doonesbury* and has been added by some newspapers in an apparent attempt to give the comic pages some balance.

Liberal Democrats have not been spared criticism in *Doonesbury*. Former President Clinton was chastised on more than one occasion in the strip. One of Clinton's political actions that drew fire from Trudeau pertained to Clinton's failure to veto a bill that would prevent gay marriage. (The strip appears below.) Trudeau's opinion of Clinton's action was voiced in the context of an ongoing story line that involved the character Mark Slackmeyer. Mark first appeared in the strip in the 1970s when he was a campus organizer and political protester. A successful interview with David Cavett led Mark to a career in radio broadcasting. According to his bio on the *Doonesbury* web site, Mark was the only known FM disc jockey to have *outed* himself on the air.

Today, Mark is a disc jockey and co-host of a radio talk show with his life's partner, Chase Talbott, III, an ultraconservative, in contrast to Mark's ultraliberal perspective. Much of the humor of the strips involving these characters derives from their very different political perspectives. After living together for several years, Mark and Chase married in a ceremony on August 7, 1999, on board a plane en route to Pago Pago. They intended to have a lavish wedding attended by their many friends and family. But after Mark's parents objected and the friend they asked to officiate at their wedding backed out due to fear of career repercussions, they flew to Pago Pago for a private ceremony on the beach. But that, too, fell through as the beach was littered with raw sewage, volcanic ash began to fall, and a tidal wave struck the beach. It's a long story. . . .

Sources: Schaefer, David. "When Politics Becomes a Joke," *The American Enterprise* 12, 2000: 14. Also visit the Doonesbury web site at www.doonesbury.com for detailed information about the comic strip's history, characters, and plot line and to participate in opinion surveys.

(*Source:* Doonesbury © G. B. Trudeau 1998. Reprinted with permission of Universal Press Syndicate. All rights reserved.)

China's "one-child" policy is a direct family policy, *aimed at reducing the number of children Chinese families have.*

to hasten economic development in the society, but the action is specifically aimed at reducing the number of children people have.

In another example of direct family policy, both China and India outlawed the centuries-old custom of child marriage. Both countries raised the minimum legal age for marriage so that families could no longer marry off infants and young children, especially their daughters. The objective of these policies may have been to improve the status of women in the society or other reasons, but the effect on marriage and family life was direct.

Policies may also affect families even though their immediate intent may not have been to do so; these are **indirect family policies** (Kammerman and Kahn, 1978). If, for example, a government introduces policies that give women greater opportunities in the workforce, the primary goal is equality in employment. But the same policy may also cause women to delay marriage or to forgo it entirely. In fact, equal opportunity laws in the United States may have contributed to a later age at first marriage among American women. The intended effect was not to change the age at marriage, but that may have been the indirect effect. Many governmental policies and programs have the potential to affect marriage and family life, and often these effects are not anticipated and may not even be detected for some time. Sociologists use the term **latent consequences** to refer to the unintended effects of social policies.

An interesting example of an indirect family policy occurred in Sweden, which had a rapid and surprising increase in its birth rate during the 1980s. The Swedish government, over several previous decades, had passed a series of parental leave policies that allowed women who left the workforce to have children to remain at home (as could their husbands) and receive government payments instead of their salaries or wages. The law provided that a woman could remain out of the workforce for thirty months and that if she had another child within that period, she could continue to receive maternity leave for an additional thirty months. The unintended result of this policy was a rapid increase in the nation's birth rate, as many Swedish couples saw the advantages of having a second child within the thirty-month period (Hoem, 1990).

The Swedish maternity leave policy was initiated largely to improve infant and child care and to ensure that women were not treated unfairly if they left their jobs to bear or care for children. The unanticipated result, however, was an increase in childbearing in Sweden. Because this effect on families was unintended, it is properly called an indirect family policy.

◾ *The Purposes of Family Policy*

Governmental family policies, especially direct policies, *generally do one of three things*—assist, control, or change families—or they do some combination of these (Scanzoni, 1991). The Around the World box identifies some of the major policy issues pertaining to women and families that have been of great concern to the United Nations for over a decade.

Assisting Families. Many government programs, both in the United States and in many other countries, begin with the goal of helping needy families or particular family members. A familiar, and long-standing example of a helping type of family policy in the United States was **Aid to Families with Dependent Children** (AFDC). The underlying objective was to provide all children in the United States with the necessities of life—food, clothing, shelter. The underlying philosophy of AFDC was that it is the responsibility of the government to care for children if parents are unable to do so. As we discuss next, AFDC was discontinued in 1996.

Some countries have programs that give direct financial stipends to families who have children. **Family and child allowances** are cash payments provided by governments to parents based on the presence and number of children. Typically, the payments are made monthly and are the equivalent of 5 to 10 percent of average wages. Currently, eighty-eight countries around the world—excluding the United States—provide child or family allowances. Their purpose in doing so is to share in the costs of rearing children; to equalize the financial burdens carried by those who do and do not have children. In some countries, such as France, the allowances are limited to second and subsequent children. The length of time over which they are awarded may be tied to specific ages or extended until the child completes high school or college (Columbia University's Clearinghouse on International Developments in Child, Youth, and Family Policies, 2002).

The United States spends a much lower percentage of its gross domestic product on child care and family benefits than do France, Germany, Hungary, and Sweden (Hofferth and Deich, 1994). U.S. policies designed to aid families with children generally address those in the lower socioeconomic statuses, whereas European countries provide support and allowances for all children, regardless of their socioeconomic status. In the United States, the closest thing to a federal policy that supports children in all families is the across-the-board tax deduction for each child.

Controlling Families. Although helping families is one major objective of family policy, other policies are designed to control or regulate the behavior of people in families and intimate relationships (Browning and Rodriguez, 2002). Generally, governments justify these regulations as ways of protecting the health or well-being of family members. For example, many cities and states have laws that require medical and school authorities to report injuries that might be the result of child abuse. In Sweden, a policy that forbids parents to use physical punishment has been in place since the 1980s. The Swedish Parliament passed a resolution stating that parents no longer had the right to use corporal punishment on their children; they were no longer allowed to spank, slap, hit, or shake their children.

ContentSELECT

Aid to Families with Dependent Children

Around the World

The United Nations Addresses the Needs of the World's Families

In this chapter, we focus primarily on family policy at the state and federal level within our own country. Family policy, however, can be, and often is, addressed at the global level as well. The United Nations has been at the forefront of efforts designed to improve the status of families, and of individual members within families, for many decades.

The United Nations declared 1994 the International Year of the Family. The main purpose for doing so was to enhance global awareness of family issues and to improve nations' abilities to carry out policies that would tackle family problems. The U.N. secretary-general identified a number of specific efforts that should be undertaken to improve the conditions of families, and of individuals within families:

1. Help families become the medium for forging new values and behaviors consistent with the rights of individual family members, rather than perpetuating attitudes that have worked, at times, to the detriment of society, and *in particular of women* (emphasis added).
2. Protect and strengthen the emotional, financial, and material support provided between members of families, as well as support between related families, including care for infants and children, the elderly, sick, and disabled.
3. Reduce the stress caused by the constant need of individuals in families, especially those comprised of single-parents, to balance work and family responsibilities.
4. Protect families from poverty and the negative effects associated with agrarian change, migration, urbanization, and economic adjustment that often result in the collapse of family functions.
5. Encourage economic self-reliance, particularly by means of income-generating programs among poor and destitute families.
6. Strengthen activities designed to improve nutrition and health, safe water, adequate sanitation, and appropriate shelter, as well as specific health measures, such as vaccination, maternal and child health care and the prevention of accidents and disabili-

ties, *while combating gender discrimination in their provision* (emphasis added).
7. Enhance the ability of families to make informed decisions concerning the spacing and number of children, the means for which should include family life education.
8. Support the role of families in preventing drug and alcohol abuse and in assisting in the early detection, cure, and rehabilitation of addicts.
9. Help families provide an environment supportive of the education of all family members, and *particularly to young women, especially mothers* (emphasis added), who may otherwise have to forego further educational opportunities with a subsequent sacrifice of income.
10. Review and revise laws that relate to the form, structure, organization, membership, function, condition, and status in the community of *all* (emphasis added) forms of families as basic units of society.
11. Prevent all forms of violence within families, including abuse of spouses, children, the elderly and disabled, as well as strengthening families as bases for prevention of delinquency and crime, and the rehabilitation of both victims and offenders.

These statements by the U.N. secretary-general underscore the perspective we have taken throughout this text and are an appropriate way to conclude our discussion of contemporary families. We have argued, much as the U.N. declarations have, that families today take many different forms and that all must be granted legitimacy. We have also consistently called attention to the ways in which gender differentiates individuals' intimate encounters and experiences within families. It is our hope that the statements endorsed by the U.N. pertaining to the establishment of equality for women within families are heeded by all nations of the world as they develop policies to improve the situation of contemporary families. In 2004, the U.N. will celebrate the tenth anniversary of the Year of the Family.

Source: United Nations web site at www.UN.org

Although such acts were not a punishable offense, the purpose of this resolution was to make it clear that children should not be subjected to physical punishment.

Sometimes governments attempt to control family behavior for reasons of morality. Before cohabitation became widely accepted, many city and state governments and government agencies in the United States had policies that penalized unmarried couples who lived together. In the late 1970s, an FBI agent in Washington, D.C., was threatened with dismissal because he was living with a woman to whom he was not married. At about the same time, a woman in Virginia who was a law school graduate was not allowed to take the bar examination in that state because she was cohabiting with a male partner.

Governments frequently have policies that place restrictions on marriage—particularly by defining eligible (or ineligible) mates. Until 1967 many states in the United States prohibited marriages between people of different races. This policy was apparently based on the assumption that it was morally wrong for people of different races to marry and have children. Additionally, most countries, including the United States, have minimum ages at which individuals may marry, and also restrictions on how closely two people may be biologically related to each other if they wish to marry.

Regulatory policies often intervene in the everyday lives of families. Although families are generally granted privacy in their homes, government policy may place limits on what they do there. Government policies have become less and less tolerant of violence and abuse in American families. No longer can parents beat their children to "within an inch of their lives." Children can still be spanked in this country, but if they appear in schools or medical facilities with evidence of excessive punishment or abuse, officials are obligated by law to report the case to the authorities.

▲ As we have seen throughout this text, the U.S. Supreme Court has ruled on many important issues facing families.

Sexual behavior has frequently been the target of governmental controls in the United States. Well into the twentieth century, many states had laws against the sale of contraceptive methods. Until the late 1960s, Connecticut had a law that made it illegal for married couples to possess and use contraceptives. In 1968, the U.S. Supreme Court ruled the law unconstitutional, in a decision referred to as *Griswold* v. *Connecticut*. The Court held that, on the basis of the right to privacy granted by the Fourteenth Amendment, individuals had the right to privacy in decisions concerning personal matters such as the use of birth control methods (Aldous and Dumon, 1990). This constitutional right to privacy was applied again in 1973, when the Supreme Court heard the *Roe* v. *Wade* case and granted Americans the right to terminate a pregnancy by choosing abortion.

Many state laws have also prohibited various forms of sexual acts (sodomy, for example, which includes oral sex). Even married couples were breaking the law if they engaged in these types of sexual acts. The laws against fornication, which are still on the books of many states, prohibit sexual intercourse between two people who are not married. This is the basis on which nonmarital cohabitation is outlawed in many states. Laws against adultery make it illegal for a married person to have sexual relations with someone other than his or her spouse. During the past several decades, many of these laws have been taken off the books or have simply fallen into disuse through nonenforcement.

These are only a few examples of how family life is regulated by government policies. A special case of regulating family life occurs when the government concludes some social trend needs to be changed.

Changing Emerging Family Patterns.   Policies aimed at changing a social trend usually try to restore what is considered a traditional family behavior. One present-day trend that is producing calls for new governmental policies is the increasing percentage of children being born to unmarried women. As we saw in Chapter 9, over one-third of all births in the United States occur to unmarried mothers.

Policymakers at all levels, including the president, have been pushing for policies that might bring the numbers down. In 1996, the U.S. Congress, as part of welfare reform, began to require unmarried teenage mothers to live with their parents in order to receive benefits.

A number of other family trends discussed in this book are viewed with concern in some quarters because they seem to reflect a decline of the traditional family. Political and cultural conservatives, for example, consider the increasing number of employed women a negative development for the traditional family, and they propose policies that might push women out of the workforce and back into the home as full-time homemakers. These conservative observers also believe the loosening of sexual prohibitions over the last thirty years is harmful to family life and advocate policies that would stop, or even reverse, these trends.

Family policy always reflects values, moral views, and ideologies and is frequently controversial. A family policy preferred by one group is likely to be opposed by some other group with different views. In the section that follows, we describe some of the major family policy issues in the United States and the controversies surrounding them.

Contrasting Visions of Families and Governmental Responsibility

Family policy issues produce controversies about what the government should do to assist, control, or change families. Sociologist Nijole Benokraitis identifies four different *camps* or viewpoints about family policies: conservatives, centrists, liberals, and feminists. These perspectives differ on several dimensions—their ideas about the ideal form families should take; the most alarming social issues facing families; the causes of family problems; and the solutions that will achieve, maintain, or restore families to the ideal state. Benokraitis (2000, pp. 14–15) offers the following descriptions of these perspectives:

- **Conservatives** are alarmed that the family is declining and deteriorating morally because of the increased rates of divorce, out-of-wedlock births, and single-parent families.
- **Centrists** feel that many of the family changes reflect decline and deterioration because the massive erosion of fatherhood contributes to the major problems of our time (Popenoe, 1996).
- **Liberals** argue that the family is changing, not deteriorating, because family functions and gender roles have been adapting to economic transformations.
- **Feminists** assert that the family is stronger than ever because many women and men have more options than in the past.

Table 15.1, which is adapted from Benokraitis (2000, pp. 15–17, 19) compares and contrasts the four perspectives in terms of their beliefs about the causes of family changes; the consequences of family changes; and the remedies for addressing family changes. We briefly summarize these perspectives here, once again drawing heavily on Benokraitis's analysis.

TABLE 15.1

"Camps" in the Family Wars: Four Perspectives and Their Beliefs about the Causes, Consequences, and Solutions for Family Problems

	Family Changes Are Due to	Consequences of Family Change	Remedies
Conservative model: The family is declining/ deteriorating	Cultural and moral weakening; Demise of family values; Sexual promiscuity; Generous welfare benefits	Family breakdown; School dropouts; Poverty; Crime; Drug use; Societal violence	Restore religious faith; Reinstitutionalize marriage; Cut welfare payments to unwed mothers and mother-headed families; Stigmatize divorce and out-of-wedlock births; Return full-time mothers to the home
Centrist model: Many aspects of the family are declining/ deteriorating	Selfishness and "me-first" values; Rampant individualism; Parents' failure to nurture their children; Media and parental permissiveness	Children are not developing into responsible adults; Premature sexualization of children; High divorce rates; High out-of-wedlock birth rates; Fathers' absence from the home	Promote self-help programs Provide six months paid leave for intact families following birth or adoption of child; Give two-parent households tax exemptions; Establish paternity at the time of birth and enforce child support payments; Prepare couples for marriage and discourage divorce; Campaign against teen pregnancy
Liberal model: The family is changing, not deteriorating	Economic structure; Changing demographic patterns; Changing family functions and gender roles; Greater acceptance of changing sexual mores	Current economy promotes material poverty among poor and "time" poverty among middle- and working-class families; Job insecurity and deteriorating employment opportunities in many sectors; Growth of two-earner families; Increase of employed mothers; Postponement of marriage	Facilitate women's employment through government-sponsored policies; Provide programs to help women and children become economically secure; Establish more training and job opportunities for low-income workers; Implement universal health insurance; Reform tax law to help dependents and unmarried couples; Intensify child support enforcement
Feminist model: The family is stronger than ever	Women's drive for more equality in many institutions; Changing family definitions, forms, and gender roles; Women's challenging patriarchal systems; Lack of supportive kin, communities, and workplaces	Greater satisfaction in diverse family forms; Greater role flexibility across the life cycle; Divorce often leads to a feminization of poverty; Unfriendly work policies create domestic stress; Outdated family policies reinforce the division of household labor in the home between the sexes as natural or inevitable	Develop more institutional supports for dual-earner and single-parent families; Legislate family-friendly workplace policies; Enforce economic support from absent fathers; Provide quality child care for all families and decent housing in good neighborhoods for poor families; Raise women's wages and salaries to close the gender gap in income; Implement universal health insurance for all families

Source: Adapted from Benokraitis, 2000, pp. 15–17, 19.

Conservative Perspective.   Conservatives place much of the blame for the deterioration of the family institution on shifts in gender roles away from the male breadwinner–female homemaker pattern. When women are employed outside their homes, conservatives argue, they cannot adequately care for or supervise their children. The basic values of our society are not properly transmitted to children. Changes in women's sexual and reproductive behavior—most notably the increasing incidence of sexuality and childbearing outside of marriage—are also problematic, in that they undermine the moral standards of the nation. The overriding objective of the **conservative perspective** is to restore the *traditional* American family, with two biological parents who take responsibility for raising their children with no governmental interference. The best way for families to care for their children is for mothers to stay home and fathers to be sole breadwinners. Once the traditional family is restored, most of the major problems plaguing our society will disappear. The federal government should not provide any kind of support or encouragement for family forms or personal behaviors that run counter to this ideal. Thus, they tend to oppose policies that subsidize single mothers and their children or that extend formal recognition to same-sex couples. They favor policies that restrict divorce.

Centrist Perspective.   Centrists share some but not all basic beliefs with conservatives. The **centrist perspective** suggests that some aspects of the family institution are deteriorating. The cause of this situation is that too much attention in our society is given to individual needs and priorities rather than to family and community needs. Too many adults fail to invest their own personal energy and financial resources into their children and marital relationships. They put their career and other personal goals above family needs. A sense of entitlement (that is, the expectation that others should help them reach their goals) has replaced a sense of duty to others. Because of these misplaced priorities, children and family life suffer. There are high rates of out-of-wedlock birth and divorce, widespread father absence in homes, premature sexual involvement of children, and failure among children to develop into responsible adults. Centrists tend to favor policies that restrict divorce—including those that better prepare couples for marriage, educating them about their duties and responsibilities; that make men more responsible for their children; that allow parents (especially mothers) to stay home with young children; that discourage teen pregnancy; and that generally support traditional two-parent families.

Liberal Perspective.   Liberals, unlike conservatives and centrists, do not believe the family institution has deteriorated. The **liberal perspective** argues that changes in family form are the culmination of long-term changes in family patterns that have developed in response to changes in the economy. While the expansion of the service sector has provided opportunities for women with above average education, the growth of high-tech jobs has led to unemployment or underemployment for many uneducated men. Women's incomes have helped raise many families out of poverty but have led to a time deficit in terms of family life and personal leisure. Lack of jobs among minorities has made marriage unfeasible and has left many families headed by single women living in poverty. Liberals accept a wide range of family forms and do not advocate policies that would restore the traditional, male-dominated nuclear family to prominence. They respect adults' decisions about their living arrangements and believe the government should help the most disadvantaged groups in our society.

Feminist Perspective.   On many issues the **feminist perspective** is identical to the liberal perspective. For instance, both perspectives believe that most family-related problems are the result, not the cause, of a number of significant societal changes. Thus, in order to assist or change family patterns, changes in the broader society are necessary. Many of the changes in families and intimate relationships reflect women's—and some men's—recognition that traditional, male-dominated family forms were unfair. Through employment and economic independence women have gained some ground in their relationships with men, though they still carry the primary burden for domestic labor. And when their marriages end, many women and their children fall into poverty. Feminists advocate institutional support for equitable pay and family-friendly workplace policies along with governmental enforcement of child support orders from noncustodial fathers. Feminist perspectives share some goals and assumptions with the others. For instance, they agree with the conservative perspective that the family is an important institution. Like centrists, they believe that children's needs haven't been given high enough priority in federal policies. And like liberals, they argue that federal policies have often placed corporate priorities above family priorities.

The importance of understanding the key assumptions of each of these perspectives on family policies is that their beliefs are often translated into legislative decisions that affect our daily lives. Liberals, for instance, were successful in pushing the Family and Medical Leave Act through Congress (after a long struggle) and in persuading President Clinton to sign it. Feminists have called national attention to the problem of domestic violence, sexual harassment in the workplace, and the need for more accessible and affordable child care. And, as we discuss, conservatives and centrists were influential in the sweeping welfare reform that occurred in the mid 1990s. They have also been especially effective in encouraging states to encourage or require premarital counseling and to consider instituting covenant marriage. Table 15.2 identifies a number of important family-related policies that were passed during the 1990s. In the next section, we take a closer look at the changes that have taken place in federal aid for poor families.

Changing Governmental Policies for Families: AFDC to TANF

For over sixty years, from 1935 to 1996, the United States had a welfare program for those in need. The program was created and expanded under two presidents, Franklin Roosevelt (in his New Deal program) and Lyndon Johnson (under the War Against Poverty and the Great Society). During the 1960s, President Johnson created the minimum wage, federal aid to education, health and nutrition programs, food stamps, energy assistance, subsidized housing, and Aid to Families with Dependent Children (AFDC) (see Moen and Forest, 1999, pp. 644–647). President Nixon (who was elected in 1968, succeeding Johnson) began to systematically dismantle the existing welfare program. Under President Reagan (elected in 1980), the dismantling of the program was resumed. In 1996, under President Bill Clinton, the fatal blow to the sixty-year program was dealt when the AFDC program was discontinued and welfare assistance to poor families was revamped into the **Temporary Assistance for Needy Families** (TANF) program. The abolishment of AFDC and creation of TANF was the culmination of what many labeled "the Reagan Revolution" (Watts, 1997). To be fair, the welfare system that existed before 1996 was in need of revision. In some ways, it encouraged people to become dependent on government assistance. People who left welfare for jobs lost Medicaid (medical assistance), which was a problem for those whose jobs did not provide medical benefits. Any wages that were earned through work were deducted from welfare payments. In other words, welfare recipients could not supplement their monthly benefit checks with wages without suffering a reduction in

ContentSELECT

Temporary Assistance for Needy Families

TABLE 15.2

Federal Family Policies Enacted during the 1990s (Selected)

Year	Law	Primary Provisions (Selected)
1990	Child Care and Development Block Grant	Provided states with money to improve child care; provided child care tax credits; initiated full-year Head Start programming; expanded the Earned Income Tax Credit and included infants
1992	Child Support Recovery Act	Made it a federal crime to willfully fail to pay child support awarded in another state
1993	Family and Medical Leave Act	Provided twelve weeks of unpaid leave (from jobs) for serious illness or to care for ailing family member
1993	Family Preservation and Support Act	Provided money to develop prevention and intervention programs that would avoid unnecessary out-of-home placements for children
1993	International Parental Kidnapping Crime Act	Established international parental abduction as a felony
1993	Omnibus Budget Reconciliation Act	Expanded Earned Income Tax Credit; addressed court reforms in foster care and adoption cases; mandated states to establish quick paternity procedures
1993	National Child Protection Act	Encouraged criminal background checks on child care providers
1994	Educate America Act	Promoted parental involvement in children's schooling.
1994	Full Faith and Credit for Child Support Orders Act	Required states to enforce child support orders established in other states; required employers to comply with child support orders that require noncustodial children to be included in health coverage
1994	Violence Against Women Act	Increased funding for battered women and established a national domestic violence hotline
1996	Defense of Marriage Act	Defined marriage as a union between one man and one woman, which denied Social Security benefits to same-sex couples; stipulated that no state is required to recognize a same-sex marriage performed in another state
1996	Personal Responsibility and Work Opportunity Reconciliation Act	Ended Aid for Families with Dependent Children and replaced it with Temporary Aid for Needy Families (see detailed discussion in the chapter)
1996	Telecommunications Reform Law	Mandated that new televisions include a V-chip that allows parents to screen out programs they judge inappropriate for their children
1997	Adoption and Safe Family Act	Provided funds for a three-year reauthorization of the Family Preservation and Support Act; promoted adoption and moving children quickly into safe, permanent homes
1998	Deadbeat Parents Act	Made it a felony for anyone who crosses a state line to evade a child support obligation

Source: Adapted from Bogenschneider, 2000, p. 1143.

their benefits, which often were too low to adequately provide for a family. Rather than simply reform the existing system, the U.S. Congress in 1996 passed legislation that replaced it. The new law was called the Personal Responsibility and Work Opportunity Reconciliation Act (Baca Zinn and Eitzen, 2002).

Provisions of the Personal Responsibility and Work Opportunity Reconciliation Act. The welfare reform legislation included a number of major provisions, which are outlined here (Baca Zinn and Eitzen, 2002; see also Blau, Ferber, and Winkler, 2001).

1 Individual states are given a fixed sum of money to distribute to their needy citizens. States have a great deal of flexibility in determining how to allocate the welfare money.

2 Parents who received cash assistance had to go to work within two years.

3 A five-year lifetime limit was placed on receipt of assistance.

4 Unmarried teen parents had to live in their parents' home or in another adult-supervised setting and attend school in order to receive welfare assistance.

5 Federal assistance programs targeted for the poor were cut by $54.5 billion dollars over a six year period. The cuts were distributed in the following way: $27 billion from food stamps; $7 billion from children's share of the Supplemental Security Income program; $3 billion from child nutrition programs (over a six-year period); and $2.5 billion for social services (also over a six-year period).

6 A wide range of benefits were denied to *legal* immigrants. All were cut off from food stamps. Those who entered the country—legally—after 1996 were considered ineligible for federal benefits and state-run programs such as temporary welfare and Medicaid.

7 A cap was placed on the amount of federal money that is given to states. Thus, there can be no adjustments for inflation or population growth. In 2002, the states had less federal money to spend on welfare than they did under the old system.

Short-Term Consequences of Welfare Reform.   On the surface, it appears that the 1996 welfare reform has succeeded in getting 6.6 million people off welfare and into jobs. However, there are some deep, underlying issues that suggest the reform isn't the miracle cure that its proponents had hoped it would be. First, the people who went off welfare early on were those who were most employable, that is, they had some secondary education and job experiences. Those with little education or

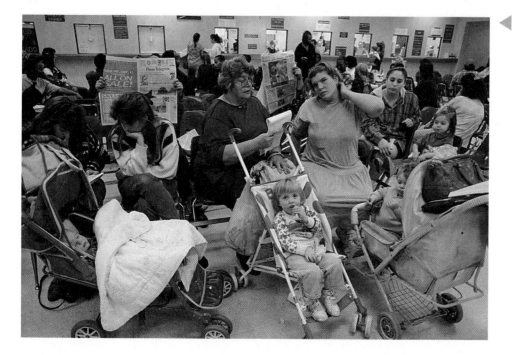

Mothers and children often wait long hours in welfare offices when they apply for Aid to Families with Dependent Children.

experience and few marketable skills, as well as those who are functionally disabled, have more difficulty finding jobs. (The welfare reform legislation includes no provisions for assistance in finding employment.) In 2000, there still were more people on welfare (6.9 million) than had left it. Many of these people will be the most difficult to place in the job market. Another issue that must be considered pertains to the impact of the economic downturn that recently occurred. In 1996, when the reform legislation was passed, the United States was in an economic expansion. New jobs were being created and unemployment was low. In mid 2002, the unemployment rate was rising. This means that many of the less employable persons had lost their jobs. If they had already reached the maximum time limits for welfare, they would have no government assistance to pay rent, utilities, food, and health care. Thus, the long-term impact of the welfare reform efforts of the late 1990s may not be seen for many years.

A third issue to consider when evaluating the impact of the 1996 welfare reform is to keep in mind that the availability of unskilled jobs is restricted to certain types of work in scattered locations. People who want and need to work may not be able to find jobs for which they are qualified. Often the areas of the country with the greatest availability of unskilled jobs are also the areas with the greatest numbers of poor people. In parts of Mississippi, for instance, the poverty rate is 41 percent and the unemployment rate is twice as high as the national average. (The welfare reform legislation did not provide transportation assistance to poor people to travel to jobs. Most of the new jobs are in suburban areas while most welfare recipients live in urban or rural areas.) One study conducted at Mississippi State University in the late 1990s estimated that for every 254 families going on welfare in this part of the state, only one new job was created (Howell, cited in DeParle, 1997). This observation leads to the fourth major issue that must be considered. Not all of the people who have left welfare are working. About 40 percent of those who were forced off welfare have no benefits or wages. Peter Edeleman (2000)—who had been a high ranking official in the Department of Health and Human Services during the Clinton Administration but left his job in protest of the welfare reform legislation—calculated that 2.5 million women left the welfare rolls after the legislation was passed. About 60 percent (or 1.5 million) of them got jobs. The other 40 percent didn't find jobs or get welfare benefits. Thus, about 3 million Americans (roughly 1 million mothers and 2 million children) were forced to deal with the hardships of poverty on their own (Baca Zinn and Eitzen, 2002).

Finally, leaving welfare to work does not guarantee that a family will escape poverty. The jobs that many former welfare recipients find do not pay high enough wages to support a family and may provide few, if any, benefits. After the first year of welfare reform, the income of the poorest 10 percent of female-headed families fell an average of $580 (which was about one-seventh of their income). This is after wages, food stamps, housing subsidies, earned income tax credits, and other benefits were figured into income calculations (Sawyer, 1999). Over 1.25 million people, mostly children, lost Medicaid coverage and became uninsured.

Welfare Reform

Earned Income Tax Credit.   Another federal program designed to assist poor families is called the **Earned Income Tax Credit** (EITC). This was originally established in the mid 1970s to help offset the Social Security payroll tax for low-earner households with children. Over the past twenty-five years, the program has been expanded. In 1990s, the value of the tax credit more than doubled. Also, in 1994, low-income households with no children became eligible for a very small tax credit. The EITC raises income and encourages individuals with low potential wages to seek employment. The government provides a refund if the amount of the tax credit exceeds the taxes that the worker owes. There is strong research evidence to show that the EITC provides a strong incentive for single mothers to enter the paid labor force. On the other hand, married women who are *secondary* earners in their households may be encouraged to leave the labor force because any earnings they received could greatly reduce or even eliminate their earned income tax credit (Blau, Ferber, and Winkler, 2001).

Child Support Enforcement. Governmental assistance in collecting child support payments is another way to help single-parent families. For more than twenty-five years, there have been formal policies aimed at enforcing court-ordered child support among noncustodial parents. The first legislation was enacted in 1975. Additional legislation in 1984 and 1988 further strengthened the law by requiring individual states to adopt numerical guidelines in setting child support awards and allowing them to collect payments from employers who have garnished parents' wages and to allow states to withhold income tax refunds from noncustodial parents who have not made their required child support payments (Blau, Ferber, and Winkler, 2001).

The 1996 welfare reform legislation instituted additional rules that make the establishment of paternity occur faster and easier, added a national registry system for tracking down delinquent parents across state lines, and established new penalties, including revoking parents' professional licenses and seizing their assets. In 1998, another law was passed that further toughened the penalties, including two years in prison for deadbeat dads or moms (Blau, Ferber, and Winkler, 2001).

There has been some concern that the increasing crackdown on parents who do not comply with court-ordered child support may not be flexible enough to deal with the various economic states of parents. Current guidelines are designed for parents who have stable employment and adequate income. Many parents, however, do not have stable employment and have low wages as a result. They may find it very difficult, if not impossible, to pay their court-ordered support in full every month. Some may stop seeing their children because they are not able to provide for them. In 2000, the federal government approved some experimental programs in ten different states that are designed to improve the economic opportunities for young unmarried fathers and encourage them to reconnect with their children (Blau, Ferber, and Winkler, 2001).

Poor Children in the United States. Poverty is still prevalent among young children in our country despite declines since 1993. In fact, the U.S. poverty rate is substantially higher (as much as two to three times higher) than that found in most other major Western industrialized nations. The National Center for Children in Poverty, at Columbia University, periodically releases demographic profiles of low-income children in the United States. In 2002, they reported the following facts about America's children based on U.S. Census data (Song and Lu, 2002a).

Child Support

- Over 11 million children (16 percent) live in poverty. (The federal government set the **poverty line** at an annual income of $13,681 for a family of three in 2000.)
- Twenty-seven million children (37 percent of all children) live at **near-poverty** levels. (Families whose incomes fall below 200 percent of the poverty line are considered to be near-poverty—an annual income of $27,722 or less for a family of three).
- Five million children (6 percent) live in **extreme poverty** (in a family whose annual income is $6,930 or less).
- Children—especially very young children—are more likely to live in poverty than other age group (Figure 15.1).

Poverty rates for very young children (under age 3) vary dramatically by ethnicity and family structure (Song and Lu, 2000b). The rates among African American and Hispanic children are still about three times as high as those among white children (Figure 15.2). In 2000, the poverty rates among African American

Figure 15.1 **Poverty Rates by Age, 1975 to 2000.** *Very young children are more likely to be poor than any other age group.*

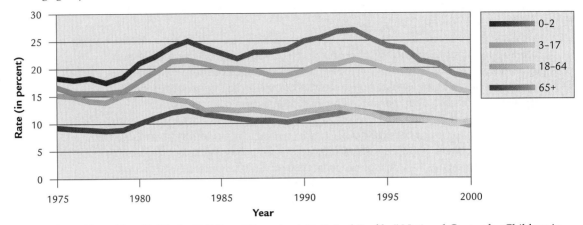

(*Source:* Song, Y., and Lu, H. "Early Childhood Poverty: A Statistical Profile." National Center for Children in Poverty, Columbia University, March, 2002. Web site: cpmcnet.columbia.edu/dept/nccp.)

and Hispanic children were 35 and 30 percent, respectively, while among white children it was 10 percent. Additionally, children who live with single mothers are about five times more likely to be poor than those who live with married parents. Among black children under age 3 who are living with their mothers, over half were poor. Among very young Hispanic children, the rate was slightly lower. But even children who live in two-parent families can live in poverty. This is especially true among Hispanics, for whom about one-quarter of young children living in two-parent homes are poor (Figure 15.3).

In the conclusion to their report, researchers Song and Lu state the following:

> Despite the unprecedented economic boom in the 1990s, there are still 2.1 million children under age 3 living in poverty. Parents' employment does not necessarily guarantee escape from poverty. Among these young children, more are from working families than ever before. The welfare reform of the 1990s has removed much of the safety net of public assistance for poor children. The changing economic envi-

Figure 15.2 **Poverty Rates of Children under Age Three by Race and Ethnicity, 1975 to 2000.** *African American and Hispanic young children are three times more likely to be poor as white children.*

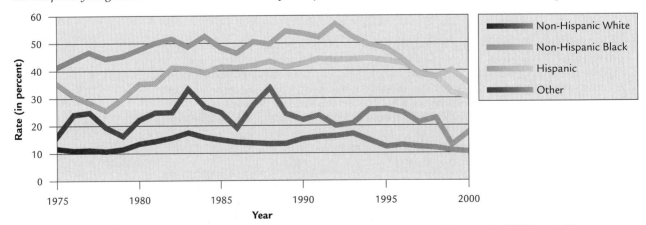

(*Source:* Song, Y., and Lu, H. "Early Childhood Poverty: A Statistical Profile." National Center for Children in Poverty, Columbia University, March, 2002. Web site: cpmcnet.columbia.edu/dept/nccp.)

Figure 15.3   **Poverty Rates by Race and Ethnicity of Children under Age Three Living in Two-Parent and Single-Parent Families, 2000.** *Poor young children are more likely to live in single-mother families, but one-quarter of Hispanic young children in two-parent families live in poverty.*

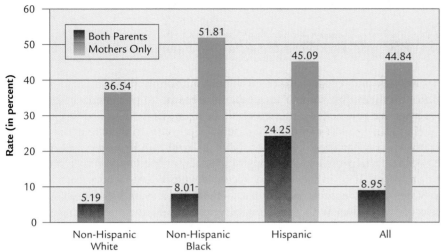

(*Source:* Song, Y., and Lu, H. "Early Childhood Poverty: A Statistical Profile." National Center for Children in Poverty, Columbia University, March, 2002. Web site: cpmcnet.columbia.edu /dept/nccp.)

ronment and increasing unemployment in the current recession pose new challenges for young children in poverty. . . . Other nations with fewer resources than the United States have been able to do a far better job of preventing poverty among their young children. The United States can learn from these nations and from its own dramatic success in reducing the poverty rate for elderly Americans. It is certainly possible to develop and implement strategies to reduce the poverty rate for young children in the United States that would be consistent with American values. (Song and Lu, 2000b, p. 6)

In its 2002 State of Children in America's Union report, the Children's Defense Fund commented on the federal government's proposals for children, including President George W. Bush's budget proposals for 2002 and 2003, which included a tax cut for the nation's wealthiest citizens. Marian Wright Edelman, founder and President of the Children's Defense Fund, notes that "The administration's welfare proposals require poor mothers to work more hours but provide not a single new penny for child care over the next five years. Rather than freezing child care and after-school funding and the number of children in Head Start as the Bush Administration budget proposes, the nation should demand that Congress and the administration freeze and repeal the tax breaks for the wealthiest one percent of Americans instead" (2002). One of the Child Defense Fund's major efforts in 2002 was a proposal that would provide $20 billion in child care funding to assist poor and low-income women to enable them to meet the welfare-to-work mandate. Current federal provisions for child care reach only one in seven eligible children (Children's Defense Fund, 2002).

The family policy issues we have discussed in this chapter and the controversies surrounding them reflect the current social, political, and economic climate of the United States. Family issues are not static, nor is family policy. Family policy is an evolving response to family and societal problems. As we move through the twenty-first century, family issues will undoubtedly change, but family policy objectives will continue to be the same: to assist, control, or change families.

In the remainder of this chapter, we turn our attention to the problems of individuals and families and their efforts to resolve them. Many families and couples today seek help in dealing with their problems by enlisting the services of counselors, therapists, social workers, and other professionals.

Marriage and Family Counseling

All families and couples have problems, although they can usually work through them. But sometimes problems become so persistent or severe that families must turn to outside professionals or agencies for help. In the past, they were likely to turn to kin members or elders, or perhaps to their religious leaders. Many couples still use these resources today, at least as a first step, but more and more people turn to professionals who are specially trained to deal with family and marital problems. It is, in fact, a very recent development—and primarily in the United States and other western countries—that a profession has developed whose sole purpose is to deal with problems between family members (Broderick and Schrader, 1991).

Many couples and families are reluctant, to some degree, to seek outside help. They may see it as a sign of failure, they may fear that they will be stigmatized, or they may simply be embarrassed about revealing their personal lives to an outsider. Each family or couple must make its own decision, based on its reading of the situation, but some guidelines can be offered. Table 15.3, for example, presents a list of questions couples might use in deciding whether or not to see a marriage counselor.

TABLE 15.3

Thirteen Good Reasons to See a Marriage Counselor*

1. We fight a lot.
2. We have trouble communicating; my spouse just doesn't understand.
3. We can't agree on how to raise our child.
4. We need help making a major decision (e.g., whether to have another baby, move, or make a career change).
5. We need help dealing with other family members (e.g., in-laws, stepchildren).
6. We need help dealing with a major crisis (such as illness in the family, birth of a child with special needs, financial loss).
7. We are having conflicts in our sex life.
8. We are drifting apart.
9. I feel suffocated in our marriage.
10. I feel unloved or taken for granted by my spouse.
11. I'm afraid of my spouse.
12. I don't trust my spouse.
13. I'm unhappy being married, but I don't know why.

---

*This checklist by Dr. Evelyn Bassoff, a marriage and family counselor, is for couples who are wondering if they need to seek professional counseling. A couple is instructed to read each of the thirteen statements and decide if it describes their own relationship. Answering yes to one or more of the statements is an indication that professional counseling might be in order.

Source: Campbell, 1993, p. 25.

Seeking Professional Help before Problems Arise

Some engaged and married couples consult marriage or family therapists even before they have problems. This has been called primary prevention (Renick, Blumberg, and Markman, 1992). **Primary prevention** occurs when couples enter programs, even though they have no current severe problems, mainly to acquire resources and abilities that will help them avoid problems in the future (Renick, Blumberg, and Markman, 1992, p. 141).

Premarital counseling is one of the most common examples of primary prevention. In fact, today many states are encouraging it. In anticipation of marriage, and with the aim of improving the quality of their marriages, couples can now enter organized programs that teach them communications skills, problem solving, heightened self-awareness, and ways of enhancing their relationship. Premarital couples who participated in one such program had better marital outcomes, in both the short- and long-term (up to five years), than a control group of couples that did not participate. The participating couples used better communication skills, reported greater satisfaction with their relationships (this was especially true for husbands), had less negative communication, and less physical violence. After five years, the couples who had participated in the program were less likely to be separated or divorced than the control couples (Renick, Blumberg, and Markman, 1992).

Another example of primary prevention is found in a wide range of programs that have been labeled marriage and family enrichment (sometimes the term *enhancement* is substituted for *enrichment*). The term **marriage and family enrichment** refers to "programs designed to strengthen couples or families so as to promote a high degree of present and future family harmony and strength, and hence the long-term psychological, emotional, and social well-being of members" (Guerney and Maxson, 1990, p. 1127).

Most enrichment programs bring a number of couples or families together for a weekend of instruction and interpersonal interaction that is often quite intense. Participants learn ways to enrich their marital or family lives. Some programs are sponsored by religious organizations, while others are secular, conducted by marriage and family specialists.

Although prevention and enrichment programs are quite popular today, the most common form of professional assistance comes *after* a problem has reached an acute or even threatening stage. When couples or families feel they cannot handle a problem by themselves, they often turn to professional therapy of some type. In fact, covenant marriage (as discussed in the previous chapter) requires couples to agree in advance that they will seek professional help if problems arise.

Family and Couple Therapy

In couple and family therapy, the therapist tries to modify basic relationships among members, thereby changing their interactional patterns and reducing problem behavior (Griffin, 1993). The basic assumption is that something is amiss in the way the family members are interacting with one another. The therapist therefore focuses on relationship problems, not on the problems (or pathologies) of particular individuals. Family therapists generally believe in talking to family members or couples together rather than in one-on-one therapeutic sessions, which are characteristic of conventional psychoanalytic or Freudian therapy (Broderick, 1993).

Most families or couples are in therapy only a short time, usually for only ten to twenty sessions. The length of time in therapy seems often to be a function of the therapist's approach rather than the nature of the problem. Some therapists believe that successful therapy must extend over a long period of time (1–2 years), while others are convinced that brief and to-the-point therapy is preferable.

ContentSELECT

Marriage and
Family Therapy

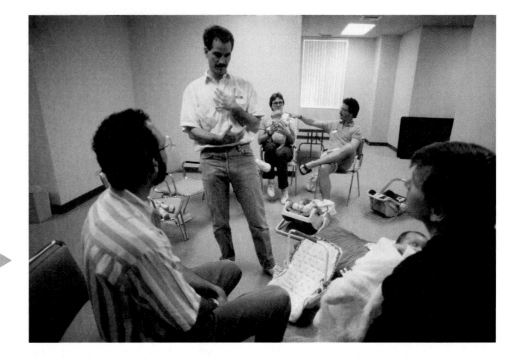

Classes that help couples prepare for important life transitions, such as marriage or the birth of a child, are increasingly being endorsed by state governments as a way to stabilize family life.

The current trend in therapy is called *strategic family therapy* (Piercy and Sprenkle, 1990, p. 1116). **Strategic family therapy** involves a specific and fairly uniform strategy that aims to quickly uncover the source of relationship problems and reduce disruptive behavior in a short time. Strategic family therapy is short-term therapy.

The field of family therapy has many competing approaches and methods. At least fifteen different approaches have been identified, and, as might be expected, there are controversies about which provides the most effective help to families. Although the advocates of particular therapies often claim greater success rates for their method, there is no conclusive independent evidence to prove that any particular method is best (Gurman and Kniskern, 1991; Griffin, 1993).

Effectiveness of Family Therapy

A number of reviews of family therapy have been conducted in recent years. All reviewers agree that family therapy is effective and useful (Piercy and Sprenkle, 1990). They also agree on the following points about the effectiveness of therapy:

1 Marital and family therapies produce beneficial outcomes in about two-thirds of the cases; approximately 61 percent of marital cases and 73 percent of family cases improve during the course of therapy. However, in about 5 to 10 percent of cases, clients *deteriorate* during therapy.

2 When *both* spouses are involved in therapy for marital problems, there is a greater chance of positive outcomes than when only one spouse is treated.

3 Positive results are achieved from marital and family therapy in treatments of relatively short duration (from one to twenty sessions).

4 Family therapy is at least as effective as individual therapy and may be more effective for problems attributed to family conflict. (Piercy and Sprenkle, 1990)

HEADline When Counseling Fails

For over twenty years, the Freeman family lived in Allentown, Pennsylvania. Brenda was a homemaker, and Dennis was a school custodian. They had three sons: teenagers Bryan (17) and David (16) and younger son Erik (11). The Freemans were devout Jehovah's Witnesses, helping to build the new Kingdom Hall the previous year. Members of this religion are known for refusing blood transfusions and for going door-to-door to talk about their beliefs; they are also recognized for welcoming people of different races and ethnic backgrounds into their worship services. One would not expect trouble to come from the children of this couple, but it did (Adams, 1995).

One Monday night at the end of February 1995, Bryan and David, the two older sons, brutally murdered their parents and younger brother. The murder victims were well aware of—and quite fearful of—the troubled minds of Bryan and David. Erik had described his life with his older brothers as a real-life horror story: "You never know when you're going to die." Their father, Dennis, also had feared his teenage sons, sleeping with a baseball bat under his bed in case he needed to protect himself and his wife. And their mother Brenda had reported an earlier incident in which one of her sons stood over her with a hatchet while she begged for her life.

The Freeman parents had tried many different types of professional intervention to deal with their sons' hostile behavior. Two years before the murders, they went to Toughlove International. They sent David and Bryan to several drug and psychological treatment centers, and Brenda called the Pennsylvania Human Relations Commission, a hate group watchdog, for help. About a month before the murders, Brenda called the Anti-Defamation League to set up a meeting with the police. But when the director called her back to set it up, Brenda was already dead at the hands of her sons.

Sometimes even repeated attempts at counseling fail to protect family members from each other. Ann Van Dyke, a civil rights investigator in Pennsylvania, blames this situation, and many like it, on the proliferation of hate groups among teenagers in our country: "Underneath all the phone calls and referrals, the social workers and counselors, is a toxic virus—ancient, mutating, resistant to all interventions" (quoted in Adams, 1995). That virus—hatred—is spreading throughout the country and producing violence against family members as well as strangers. As a result of that hatred, three members of the Freeman family are dead.

Source: Adams, 1995.

When therapy is ineffective, it may be because the therapist has poor relationship skills and attacks sensitive issues early in treatment, or fails to intervene when family conflict occurs in a therapy session. Therapists who do little to structure and guide therapy sessions are also more likely to be ineffective.

A Feminist Critique of Family Therapy

In recent years, some therapists have called attention to the possible sexist bias of traditional family therapy. This led to a feminist critique of family therapy (Piercy and Sprenkle, 1990, p. 1118).

A fundamental principle underlying the feminist critique is that family therapy occurs in the context of a sexist society, a society "that is oppressive to women and invested in maintaining a male-dominated hierarchical structure" (Sirles, 1994, p. 2). Women may thus be blamed for family problems simply because they do not conform to the traditional role expectations for women. Some therapists believe that if women do not accept or follow traditional gender expectations, that in itself is a sufficient explanation for marital or family problems. Feminist critics urge therapists to be more sensitive to the inequities imposed by traditional gender roles and conventional values. They encourage therapists to move couples and families in the direction of healthier, more equitable systems.

The Profession of Marriage and Family Therapy

Sociologists and other social scientists use the term *profession* to refer to a specific kind of occupation. A **profession** is a high-status, knowledge-based occupation that has autonomy and authority over clients.

The field of marriage and family therapy has many of the defining characteristics of a profession. It has a specialized knowledge base drawn from the fields of psychology, sociology, psychiatry, law, biology, and counseling. It has a professional association, the American Association for Marriage and Family Therapy, that accredits training programs, establishes and monitors licensing requirements, and publishes scholarly research in specialized journals.

One function of professional associations is to make sure that the public knows of the profession and the services it offers. There are at least three professional associations that can be contacted for a list of accredited or licensed counselors and therapists in one's local area. These associations and their addresses are

1 The American Psychological Association, 750 First Street NE, Washington, DC 20002. (www.apa.org)

2 The National Association of Social Workers, 750 First Street NE, Suite 700, Washington, DC 20002. (www.naswdc.org)

3 The American Association for Marriage and Family Therapy, 112 South Alfred Street, Alexandria, VA 22314. (www.aamft.org)

The cost of marital and/or family therapy can be covered to some extent by health insurance, but there may be an annual limit on the amount of money that can be paid. If cost is a concern, clients can talk to a therapist about their financial situation to see if the therapist will work on a sliding scale. Some therapists don't charge for the first visit.

Code of Ethics. The field of marriage and family therapy, like most other professions today, has a **code of ethics** to protect clients. This code of ethics begins with an obvious feature of family therapy, namely, that when clinicians become involved in the interpersonal relations of families and couples, they often encounter ethical issues.

The American Association for Marriage and Family Therapy (AAMFT) revised its code of ethics in 2001; this code of ethics is reproduced in Table 15.4. This code is binding on all members of the association. Marriage and family therapists are strongly encouraged to report all alleged unethical behavior of colleagues to appropriate professional associations and state regulatory bodies.

The first rule in the AAMFT ethics code pertains to therapists' responsibilities to their clients. The primary goal of professionals in this field is to advance the welfare of families and individuals. They are to avoid exploiting the trust and dependency of their clients and to forgo forming additional types of relationships with their clients that could impair their professional judgment and increase the risk of exploitation. Sexual intimacy between therapists and clients, for instance, is prohibited.

Another important clause in the code of ethics pertains to the confidentiality of information provided by clients to their therapists. Therapists may not disclose confidences except in the following situations: (1) as mandated by law; (2) to prevent a clear and immediate danger to a person or persons; (3) when the therapist

---

TABLE 15.4

American Association for Marriage and Family Therapy Code of Ethics

1. *Responsibility to Clients.* Marriage and family therapists advance the welfare of families and individuals. They respect the rights of those persons seeking their assistance, and make reasonable efforts to ensure that their services are used appropriately.

2. *Confidentiality.* Marriage and family therapists have unique confidentiality concerns because the client in a therapeutic relationship may be more than one person. Therapists respect and guard confidences of each individual client.

3. *Professional Competence and Integrity.* Marriage and family therapists maintain high standards of professional competence and integrity.

4. *Responsibility to Students, Employees, and Supervisees.* Marriage and family therapists do not exploit the trust and dependency of students, employees, and supervisees.

5. *Responsibility to Research Participants.* Investigators respect the dignity and protect the welfare of participants in research and are aware of federal and state laws and regulations and professional standards governing the conduct of research.

6. *Responsibility to the Profession.* Marriage and family therapists respect the rights and responsibilities of professional colleagues and participate in activities that advance the goals of the profession.

7. *Financial Arrangements.* Marriage and family therapists make financial arrangements with clients, third-party payors, and supervisees that are reasonably understandable and conform to accepted professional practices.

8. *Advertising.* Marriage and family therapists engage in appropriate informational activities, including those that enable laypersons to choose professional services on an informed basis.

Source: Reprinted from the AAMFT Code of Ethics, Copyright © 2001, American Association for Marriage and Family Therapy. Reprinted with permission.

---

is a defendant in a civil, criminal, or disciplinary action arising from therapy; or (4) if there is a waiver previously obtained from the client in writing. Therapists must also obtain written informed consent from clients before videotaping, audiorecording, or permitting third-party observation. They must store and/or dispose of client records in a way that will protect their confidentiality.

Marriage and family therapists must also maintain high standards of professional competence and integrity. They are expected to remain informed of new developments in family therapy knowledge and practice through participating in continuing educational activities. They are not allowed to diagnose, treat, or advise on problems outside their recognized areas of competence. They may only represent themselves as specializing in specific areas of therapy if they have the education and supervisory experience in settings that meet recognized professional standards. They may not use any professional identification (such as business cards, office signs, letterhead, or telephone listings) that include false, fraudulent, misleading, or deceptive claims.

If marriage and family therapists experience personal problems or conflicts that have the potential to impair their work performance or clinical judgment, they must seek appropriate professional assistance. Should they reach a point at which they are no longer competent to practice therapy, their membership in the AAMFT may be revoked and they may be subjected to disciplinary actions.

Codes of ethics, such as the one just presented, sound good, and even somewhat obvious, but they are more difficult to abide by than might be supposed. Consider some of the dilemmas a therapist faces in the following complex (though probably not uncommon) case. Does the therapist advise a wife who is being abused by her husband to file a complaint against him, charging him with physical abuse? Does the therapist reveal to this wife that her husband's affair has not ended, but is still going on? Does the therapist reveal this information to the children? Does the therapist reveal anything about this case to a colleague who is seeing the husband's lover? Of course, the major question is what course of action should this therapist take to "advance the welfare" of this family and all the individuals involved? Does the therapist work to reconcile this couple or help them end their relationship?

In answering these and many similar questions, therapists must be careful not to allow their own values to influence their course of action. Clients are frequently operating under a quite different sets of values, morals, and even religious beliefs from those therapists are using. Therapists must make an effort to understand and give legitimacy to the values of their clients even if those values differ from their own (Odell and Stewart, 1993).

Not only are there ethical dilemmas for therapists, but increasingly there are also potential legal problems. Just as medical practitioners are sued for malpractice, so too can therapists and counselors find themselves in malpractice litigation. Therapists today must often consult their personal attorneys because they are concerned about their own liability should a case come before the courts (Maddock, 1993).

Therapists often face ethical issues in the course of their practices that are not yet covered by the code of ethics. And they face legal issues that are both ambiguous and potentially threatening. Because marital and family therapists are involved daily with families and individuals who are highly stressed and upset and whose lives they are trying to influence, they face complex moral, ethical, and legal issues.

Summary

Governments often make policies that are designed to change family behavior. Some policies are directly aimed at affecting families. Other policies are indirect, because they affect families even though their immediate intent may not have been to do so. Governmental family policies are generally designed to do one of three things: assist, control, or change families.

Family policies reflect values, morals, and ideologies, so controversies about family policy frequently develop. Major controversies exist today about policies relating to children. It is widely recognized that children are not doing well in today's society, but there is disagreement about the causes and about which policies would improve their condition. Many children who live in single-parent homes are living in poverty. A number of policy proposals are aimed at these two conditions. Some critics of the former welfare system claimed that it prompted unmarried women to have children, but the empirical evidence does not generally support that conclusion.

Recent policy debates about work and family have centered on issues of child care and parental or maternity leaves. Political and liberal conservatives have opposing positions on these issues. Feminists have generally supported child care programs, but some feminists have pointed out that such policies may not necessarily lead to gender equality.

When couples and families encounter problems they cannot handle on their own, they are increasingly likely to turn to professional counselors or therapists. Some couples today are consulting marriage or family therapists before they have problems, to learn communications skills, problem solving, heightened self-awareness, and ways of enhancing their relationship. Marriage enrichment programs are designed for couples who wish to improve their relationships.

Family therapy is for couples and families who have problems so severe or persistent that they require professional help. Empirical studies show that most couples and families benefit from therapy, although in a small percentage of cases their situation deteriorates. Therapists generally focus on relationship problems, not on the problems of individual family members. The feminist critique of family therapy has called attention to the way in which some traditional therapy perpetuates inequalities, especially for women.

The profession of marriage and family therapy has grown rapidly, developing a professional association, with accrediting and licensing programs, professional publications, and a code of ethics. Today's therapists face a variety of ethical issues and dilemmas, as well as a growing threat of legal liability.

Key Terms

Aid to Families with Dependent Children (p. 467)

Centrist perspective (p. 472)

Code of ethics (p. 484)

Conservative perspective (p. 472)

Direct family policies (p. 464)

Earned Income Tax Credit (p. 476)

Extreme poverty (p. 477)

Family and child allowances (p. 467)

Family policy (p. 464)

Feminist perspectives (p. 472)

Indirect family policies (p. 466)

Latent consequences (of policies) (p. 466)

Liberal perspective (p. 472)

Marriage and family enrichment (p. 481)

Near poverty (p. 477)

Poverty line (p. 477)

Primary prevention (p. 481)

Profession (p. 484)

Strategic family therapy (p. 482)

Temporary Assistance for Needy Families (p. 473)

Review Questions

1. What is the primary difference between direct and indirect family policies? Provide examples of each type.

2. What are the three primary purposes of family policy? Provide examples of each way in which family policy is used.

3. What were the objectives of the U.N. International Year of the Family?

4. Describe the four *camps* or perspectives about families that influence policy, as outlined by Benokraitis.

5. Summarize the provisions of the welfare reform legislation of 1996. What were the major problems of the welfare system before the reform?

6. How effective has the welfare reform legislation of 1996 been in getting people off welfare and into the work force? In what ways could the data about the numbers of people who've gone off welfare be an inaccurate indicator of the effectiveness of the reform? Briefly discuss the situation in the state of Mississippi in regard to the availability of jobs for people who are leaving welfare.

7. What is the earned income tax credit? When and why was it created?

8. What steps has the federal government taken to enforce child support orders? How did the welfare reform legislation of 1996 add to those efforts? What unanticipated problems might arise as a result of the increased efforts to force parents to pay child support?

9. What income levels are used by the federal government to define poverty, near-poverty, and extreme poverty? According to these definitions, how many children in the United States live in each of these economic situations? How do poverty rates differ by race and ethnicity and by family structure?

10. How has the Children's Defense Fund described the impact of the federal government's welfare reform on children? What major inadequacies has it identified?

11. What skills do couples develop in premarital counseling and marriage enrichment programs? To what extent have these programs been effective?

12. Under what conditions is family therapy most likely to be effective? When it's not effective, what factors might be responsible?

13. What characteristics of the field of marital and family therapy contribute to its status as a profession?

14. What are the basic principles of the American Association of Marriage and Family Therapists's code of ethics? What is the purpose of having a code of ethics?

Critical Thinking Questions

1. What accounts for the fact that different groups of people will examine a set of statistics about American families and draw different implications from them?

2. To what extent is marital and family therapy simply an extension of individual therapy? What can be gained by treating a family as a group rather than as separate individuals?

3. What are the implications for policy of regarding family breakdown as a cause of societal problems rather than as a result of them?

Online Resources Available for This Chapter

www.ablongman.com/marriageandfamily

- Online Study Guide with Practice Tests
- PowerPoint Chapter Outlines

- Links to Marriage and Family Websites
- ContentSelect Research Database
- Self-Assessment Activities

Further Reading

Books

Benokraitis, Nijole V. *Feuds about Families: Conservative, Centrist, Liberal, and Feminist Perspectives.* Upper Saddle River, NJ: Prentice Hall, 2000. This collection of essays and empirical reports presents contrasting viewpoints (i.e., conservative, centrist, liberal, and feminist) about a wide range of contemporary family issues.

Browning, Don S., and Rodriguez, Gloria G. *Reweaving the Social Tapestry: Toward a Public Philosophy and Policy for Families.* New York: W. W. Norton and Company, 2002. Leaders from government, business, labor, law, academia, the media, nonprofit organizations, and a number of faith-based organizations offer recommendations about helping families face the complex challenges of our contemporary world.

Eden, Kathryn, and Lein, Laura. *Making Ends Meet: How Single Mothers Survive Welfare and Low-Wage Work.* New York: Russell Sage Foundation, 1997. An early analysis of the effectiveness of the 1996 welfare reform based on interviews with 400 welfare and low-income single mothers from cities in four different states over a six-year period.

Gill, Richard. *Prosperity Lost: Progress, Ideology, and the Decline of the American Family.* New York: Rowman and Littlefield, 1997. An important book on family issues by a secular conservative.

Lerner, Richard M., Sparks, E.E., and McCubbin, L. D. *Family Diversity and Family Policy: Strengthening Families for America's Children.* Boston: Kluwer, 2000. Describes the various aspects of diversity that characterize contemporary families and discusses their implications for public policy and intervention programs.

Mason, Mary Ann, Skolnick, Arlene, and Sugarman, Stephen. *All Our Families: New Policies for a New Century.* New York: Oxford University Press, 1998. Examines the many types of contemporary families that do not fit the idea of the traditional family, discussing the social and historical context in which these new families have emerged and the challenges to social policy that have arisen along with them.

Popenoe, David, Elshtain, J. B., and Blankenhorn, D. (eds.). *Promises to Keep: Decline and Renewal of Marriage in America.* Lanham, MD: Rowman and Littlefield, 1996. This is the report of the Council on Families in America's 1995 study, "Marriage in America: A Report to the Nation," in which essays by lawyers, theologians, social scientists, policy makers, and activists examine the reasons why the family institution has changed.

Rank, Mark. *Living on the Edge: The Realities of Welfare in America.* New York: Columbia University Press, 1994. Based on a ten-year study of the experiences of families who live on welfare, including their reasons for turning to public assistance, to address stereotypes about poor people in America.

Stacey, Judith. *In the Name of the Family: Rethinking Family Values in the Postmodern Age.* Boston: Beacon Press, 1996. A collection of essays based on studies of diverse types of families meant to illustrate their resilience and flexibility rather than their reflection of the demise of traditional values.

Zimmerman, Shirley L. *Family Policy: Constructed Solutions to Family Problems.* Thousand Oaks, CA: Sage, 2001. A comprehensive overview of the theoretical frameworks underlying family policy and the implications of policies for family well-being.

*Content*SELECT *Articles*

Hagen, J. "Time Limits under Temporary Assistance to Needy Families: A Look at the Welfare Cliff." *Journal of Women & Social Work* 14(3), 1999: 294–315. **[Database: Social Work]** Temporary Assistance to Needy Families (TANF) replaced Aid to Families with Dependent Children (AFDC) in 1996. Hagen aptly discusses the implications of the imposed time limits associated with TANF, including recipient-related issues such as child poverty and child care, and potential barriers to employment, including substance use and abuse, and domestic violence. The author calls for social workers and other helping professionals to make

advocacy for poor women and their children and research a priority.

Hohmann-Marriott, B. "Marriage and Family Therapy Research: Ethical Issues and Guidelines." *American Journal of Marriage and Family Therapy* 29(1), 2001: 1–12. **[Database: Psychology]** The AAMFT has established a code of ethics to insure not only ethical standards in therapeutic practice, but also in the field of marriage and family research. Because marriage and family research participants oftentimes divulge sensitive information and may simultaneously be undergoing therapeutic treatment, researchers must also adhere to the code of ethics. This manuscript highlights the areas of risk assessment, informed consent, confidentiality, and researcher bias, among other guidelines.

Sable, M., Libbus, K., Huneke, D., and Anger, K. "Domestic Violence among AFDC Recipients: Implications for Welfare-to-Work Programs." *Journal of Women & Social Work* 14(2), 1999: 199–217. **[Database: Social Work]** Sable et al. report on the findings of a 1996 study that examined domestic violence among female AFDC recipients in the Midwest. Investigation findings point to over twenty violence-related behaviors from the study participants' partners and/or families, indicating a possible link between domestic violence and the inability to find and keep jobs. The authors further put forward that domestic violence may work against governmental welfare-to-work programs.

Appendix

A

Your Body

*I*n order to have a good understanding of your sexual health, you should be familiar with sexual anatomy. You might find the illustrations on the following page especially useful when reading Appendices B and C of this book, which deal with sexually transmitted diseases and contraception.

The Menstrual Cycle

*I*n a typical twenty-eight-day cycle, day 1 of the menstrual cycle is defined as the first day of menstrual bleeding. *Ovulation* (release of a fertile egg from the ovaries) occurs around day 14, and the lining of the uterus begins to thicken in anticipation of a fertilized egg. The egg slowly descends down the fallopian tubes and reaches the uterus around days 10 to 14. If the egg is not fertilized by a sperm, the lining of the uterus is shed, beginning another menstrual cycle. A woman is most fertile during the period of time immediately before and after ovulation. Women who have fairly regular, twenty-eight-day cycles tend to be most fertile between days 10 and 18 of their cycle.

The average menstrual cycle (the period of time between the start of one bleeding period to the start of the next) is approximately twenty-eight days long; however, individual women vary greatly in terms of the length of their cycle, the duration of bleeding, and the volume of blood lost. For some women, the cycle is only 21 to 25 days. For others it is as long as 30 to 40 days. Some women never have regular bleeding cycles. A woman's period may last from two to seven days, and the blood flow may be light, moderate, or heavy. All of these variations are quite normal, and women should not worry if their cycle is not exactly twenty-eight days long.

Premenstrual Syndrome

The term premenstrual syndrome (PMS) encompasses a wide range of symptoms that occur during the premenstrual period (specifically between ovulation and menstruation). Some of the most common complaints are

- Cramping and abdominal pain
- Mood swings such as depression, irritability, inability to concentrate, and tension
- Breast tenderness
- Fluid retention and mild weight gain (in some women 2 to 5 pounds or more)
- Fatigue or exhaustion
- Headaches
- Food cravings

Source: Appendices A, B, C, and D are adapted from *Sexual Etiquette 101 and More,* which was written by Dr. Robert A. Hatcher, Robert Axelrod, Sarah Cates, Paige J. Levin, and Terrence L. Wade. We wish to thank John M. Stanley, Vice President and Secretary of Bridging the Gap Foundation, Inc. in Dawsonville, Georgia, (706) 265-7435 for granting permission to include this material.

All of the authors of *Sexual Etiquette 101 and More* were participants in the 27th annual summer program in Family Planning and Human Sexuality at Emory University. The program involved undergraduates, graduates, and medical students from the United States and other nations. Students complete research and service projects, work in clinical settings, produce educational materials, and help plan and coordinate conferences while simultaneously acquiring faculty information about family planning and human sexuality through formal and informal lectures and discussions. For applications and further information, write of call the Emory University Family Planning Program, 69 Butler St., S. E., Atlanta, Georgia 30303; phone (404) 616-3709.

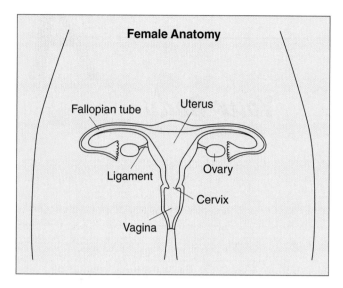

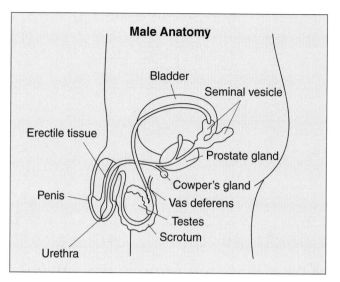

In addition to these symptoms, women with chronic problems such as asthma, epilepsy, or migraine headaches may find that their symptoms are most severe during the premenstrual period. A woman who experiences PMS symptoms so severe that they interfere with her daily life (e.g., keeps her out of school or work) should see a clinician, who may be able to suggest a number of therapeutic remedies.

▪ Menstrual Abnormalities

You should also recognize the signs that indicate your menstrual cycle is not normal. Here are some of the questions you may want to ask yourself. If your answer to one or more of these questions is yes, you may want to consult a clinician.

1. Do you bleed for more than seven days?

2. Has your flow of menstrual blood greatly increased or decreased over the past several cycles? Since beginning or changing birth control methods?

3. Do you soak more than five napkins or tampons a day during your period?

4. Do you regularly have a period more often than every three to six weeks?

5. Are your menstrual cramps so severe that they keep you from doing your daily activities (keep you from going to school or work)?

6. Do you experience severe mood changes (depression, crying, unhappiness, nervousness) or headaches around the time of your period?

7. Do you have spotting of blood (light bleeding) between regular periods?

8. Are you experiencing menstrual cramps or pain that are so bad they cannot be relieved by aspirin, exercise, or some other "home remedy"?

9. Have your periods stopped completely?

10. Do you have fewer than four periods a year?

A good way to check if your menstrual cycle is normal is to ask yourself if your symptoms are so severe that they keep you from going to school or work. If the answer to that question is "yes," then a clinician might be able to help you.

▪ Toxic Shock Syndrome

Toxic shock syndrome (TSS) is a rare but serious illness. It is caused by a bacteria that can infect any part of the body, but is most often associated with the use of tampons. TSS is associated with use of tampons in 99 percent of the cases in menstruating women. Using sanitary pads instead of tampons almost entirely eliminates your risk for TSS, but even if you do use tampons the risk is low.

TSS causes high fever (101° F or higher), vomiting, diarrhea, dizziness, weakness, and a sunburn-like rash. In severe cases it can cause shock, coma, and death. Even though the risk for TSS is low, it is essential that women who use tampons or vaginal barrier methods of birth control (such as diaphragms, cervical caps, contraceptive sponges, and female condoms) learn and recognize the warning signs for TSS. If any of the symptoms of TSS occur while using a tampon or vaginal barrier, remove the object and contact a physician immediately. TSS can be treated if caught early, but can be very serious if left untreated.

Toxic Shock Syndrome Warning Signs
- High fever (101° F or more)
- Vomiting
- Diarrhea
- Dizziness
- Feeling faint or weak
- Muscle aches
- Sunburn-like rash

If you have any of these symptoms while using a tampon or vaginal barrier method, remove the product and see a physician right away. Remember, in severe cases TSS can cause shock and even death.

4 Avoid performance anxiety by being aware of the problem.
5 Focus on sensation rather than thoughts.
6 Use voluntary muscle contractions to increase levels of sexual tension.
7 Try stimulating yourself gently.
8 Consider seeking help.

Other concerns are *dyspareunia* (pain during intercourse) or *vaginismus* (contraction of pelvic muscles during attempted intercourse). Sometimes these concerns are linked to social problems, such as sexual abuse. If this is the case, the concern needs to be solved for each individual woman in a way that meets her needs.

For women with sexual concerns, the following resources may be of some help: *The New Our Bodies Ourselves, The Black Woman's Health Book, Contraceptive Technology,* and *For Yourself: The Fulfillment of Female Sexuality.*

Sexual Concerns of Women

*A*norgasmia, which is a more common concern in women than men, is the inability to have an orgasm. This can take two forms: never having had an orgasm (primary anorgasmia) or the loss of the ability to have an orgasm (secondary anorgasmia).

Reasons for anorgasmia range from cultural values to biological problems. In some cultures, for example, it is frowned on for women to enjoy or be actively interested in sex. Factors such as fatigue, stress, feeling pressured to have intercourse when not ready, or maybe a sexual partner's unawareness of sexual needs could be causing the inability to achieve orgasm. Other common contributing factors include a woman's misinformation or a lack of information regarding the function of her genitalia and a poor body image or self-concept. Also, it may be that a woman has had a sexual trauma, such as rape, which has left her unable to feel pleasure from sex.

Ninety percent of women who experience anorgasmia can be treated by simply learning which sensations are sexually pleasurable for themselves. Here are some suggestions:

1 Become comfortable with your naked body
2 Maintain a comfortable body image.
3 Try to communicate your needs to your partner.

Sexual Concerns of Men

*M*any sexual concerns of men stem from beliefs that sexual interactions are thought of in terms of performance or accomplishment instead of pleasure for both partners.

Impotence, the inability to achieve or sustain an erection, is a common concern of men at some point in their lives, and can be a derivative of either biological problems, drug/alcohol problems, or psychological problems.

Both biological and drug problems might require help from either counselors and/or practitioners. For psychological problems, communicate with your partner and use the first three suggestions given for women who have anorgasmia and/or seek counseling.

Health services at your school may be able to give more detailed descriptions of how to deal with impotence and other problems such as *premature ejaculation* and *ejaculatory delay.*

With time, some men can learn how to control their ejaculation; however, it is completely normal to ejaculate quickly, because you could be very stimulated and excited by intercourse.

Remember that many people experience sexual difficulty at some point in their lives. There is no shame in seeking help or advice. Contact your college health service or your doctor for answers and resources available to you.

Appendix

B

Sexually Transmitted Infections

Protection Against Sexually Transmitted Infections

*T*he term *sexually transmitted infection* (STI) is used to describe over fifty different types of infections that may be passed on from one person to another by sexual contact. Sexual contact includes vaginal and rectal intercourse, oral sex, any sex that results in tissue damage or bleeding, and possibly wet kissing when lips, gums, or other tissues are raw, bleeding, or ulcerated.

STIs are more severe now than they have ever been. Not only are the most common bacterial STIs (that is, chlamydia, gonorrhea) still around, but now we have to worry about the four H-viruses.

These viruses are:

- Human immunodeficiency virus (HIV)
- Herpes simplex virus (HSV)
- Hepatitis B virus (HBV)
- Human papilloma virus (which causes genital warts) (HPV)

Unfortunately, we still have no cure for these viruses.

Because of the dangers associated with these STIs, protecting yourself is of the utmost importance to each person considering having sexual intercourse.

You can protect yourself from STIs in several ways:

- Abstain from all sexual activity involving another person.
- Ask your partner if he or she has ever had any STIs. (Be careful, however; it is well-documented that people who want to proceed with sexual intercourse will lie about past infections, number of partners, and test results.)
- Be sexually intimate with only one person who is only sexually intimate with you, although you never know!

- Don't get involved in any sexual contact without condoms or other barriers that can prevent the transmission of body fluids.

It may be a bit uncomfortable for you to discuss STIs with your partner, but doing so can save your life as well as your partner's.

If you feel you have been exposed to an STI it is very important to get checked out and, if needed, to get treatment as soon as possible.

This next section discusses briefly a few of the more important STIs, typical symptoms, treatments (if available), and consequences if left untreated.

Human Immunodeficiency Virus (the Virus That Leads to AIDS)

*H*uman immunodeficiency virus (HIV) attacks the T-lymphocytes, cells that normally protect people from infection and cancer. An infected person may not have any symptoms at first. Sometimes in the first few days after initial infection, flu-like symptoms appear, and gradually over the years symptoms become severe and the immune system weakens, as acquired immunodeficiency syndrome (AIDS) eventually develops. The average time it takes the HIV virus to become full-blown AIDS is about ten years. Currently, there is no known cure for the HIV virus.

HIV is spread in blood, semen, and vaginal fluids by anal, vaginal, and oral intercourse; by sharing contaminated needles; by the transfusion of contaminated blood; and from a woman to her baby during pregnancy and during breastfeeding. You can't get HIV from day-to-day things like

- Handshakes and hugs
- Bathrooms

- Plates, forks, spoons, and glasses
- Just being in a room with someone who has HIV

Today we know much more about HIV. Anyone who is exposed to bodily fluids that have been infected with the virus may become infected. Presently, the greatest increase in HIV infections is occurring in the heterosexual population. Midway through 2001, the Centers for Disease Control reported there were 466,000 men, women, and children living with HIV/AIDS in the United States. While surveillance data gathered in the 1990s speculated that women would represent nearly half of those infected with the virus by the year 2000, data midway through 2001 indicated that adolescent boys and adult men were infected at a rate 2.5 times more than women. In a one-year period alone (July 2000 to June 2001), men having sex with men contracted the HIV virus at a rate 5.4 times greater than heterosexuals who contracted HIV in the same period did. These data suggest that despite the ever-present risk, sexually active individuals are continuing to practice unsafe sex.

Symptoms

When a person is first infected, he or she may not experience any symptoms. Sometimes people experience flu-like symptoms in the first several days after infection occurs.

HIV infection is apparently not progressive in a small percentage of cases.

Symptoms when they do occur include

- Flu-like symptoms in the days following initial infection (inconsistent)
- Chronic unexplained fatigue (tiredness)
- Unexplained weight loss
- Persistent dermatitis (skin inflammation); other skin conditions
- Persistent diarrhea
- Changes in mental state
- Lung infections

Treatment

No known cure exists for HIV, but a synthetic drug zidovudine (AZT) may help AIDS patients live longer. AZT clearly is effective in decreasing the risk of transmission of HIV from an HIV positive pregnant woman to her baby. An AIDS *cocktail*, a combination of antiviral medications that includes a protease inhibitor, significantly reduces the amount of HIV in the bloodstream. In addition, other therapies are available to help persons

with AIDS treat their opportunistic infections or improve their strength. Sensitive, compassionate support is extremely important.

Chlamydia (cla-MIH-dee-ah)

Every year about 4 million Americans become infected with chlamydia, an infection that is caused by the bacteria *Chlamydia trachomatis*. It is especially prevalent among teenagers and young adults.

Symptoms

May not appear for a long period of time or may never appear in the woman or the man.

In Men. Painful burning sensation while urinating, watery or milky discharge from the penis.

In Women. Abnormal vaginal discharge, irregular vaginal bleeding, pelvic pain accompanied by nausea and fever, painful or frequent urination. Seventy-five percent of women have few or no symptoms.

Treatment

Antibiotics such as doxycycline or azithromycin.

If Untreated. In one million women per year it develops into pelvic inflammatory disease (PID) with scarring of the fallopian tubes, which can lead to the loss of the ability to become pregnant. In men it infects the urethra and may spread to the testicles. The disease is much more symptomatic in men so treatment prevents loss of fertility.

Gonorrhea (gone-o-REE-a)

Gonorrhea is caused by the *Neisseria gonorrhea* bacteria. This bacteria may infect the urethra, bladder, prostate, epididymis, endometrium, fallopian tubes, pharynx, and other body parts. About 800,000 cases of gonorrhea occur every year in the United States.

Symptoms

In Men. Burning sensation during urination, pus-like discharge, fever, painful sex.

In Women. Pain in pelvic area, unusual vaginal bleeding, bleeding after sex, green or yellow-green discharge, swelling or tenderness of the vulva, arthritic pain or pain in the shoulder.

Treatment

Antibiotics such as ceftriaxone or cefixime.

If Untreated. In women it can cause PID, resulting in an ectopic pregnancy or sterility. The longer gonorrhea is left untreated, the greater the chances of permanent damage.

Herpes Simplex (Her-pees Sim-plex)

Herpes is a recurrent virus that remains with a person for life. Two forms of the herpes virus exist: herpes-1 and herpes-2. Although herpes-1 is usually associated with cold sores and fever blisters around the lips, both forms of herpes may be sexually transmitted to the genital regions.

Symptoms

Extremely painful blisters on the vagina, penis, or around the anus; tingling sensation prior to breaking out, and/or fever.

Treatment

No cure—Acyclovir is a drug used both to treat symptoms of the first outbreak and to reduce the number and severity of future occurrences. It is expensive.

If Untreated. Individuals with herpes are subject to recurrent episodes, whether treated or not. The treatments may lessen the pain.

Human Papilloma (pap-e-lo-ma) Virus (HPV)

Every year, 5.5 million Americans are infected with genital HPVs. As many as one out of ten men and women are now infected. Currently, 24 million are affected by HPV.

Symptoms

May not be seen for three months to one year after infection; soft, painless wart-like growths around the anus, vaginal area, penis, or urethra.

Treatment

No cure exists for HPV; the virus remains in your skin for extended periods of time. Visible warts are removed by freezing them off using cryosurgery, using repeated applications of trichloroacetic acid or podofilin to chemically poison them. Interferon, a type of therapy that aids the immune system in targeting the HPV infection, is a newer treatment course. Interferon is a biochemical that is found naturally in the human body's immune system and can be injected directly into the warts. The individual may choose instead to apply Imiquimod, a topical ointment that produces fewer side effects.

If Untreated. HPV may lead to cervical dysplasia, which is a development of abnormal cells or tissues in the cervix, and cervical cancer. HPV may also cause cancer of the penis.

Hepatitis B

Hepatitis B is caused by hepatitis B viris (HBV). No known cure exists for hepatitis B. Between 150,000 and 200,000 new cases of sexually transmitted HBV occur in the United States each year.

Symptoms

Nausea, vomiting, stomach pain, headache, fever, yellow skin (jaundice), dark urine, liver tenderness.

Treatment

Hepatitis B has no cure. A vaccine is available to prevent infection; it comes in a series of three shots.

If Untreated. Hepatitis B can lead to chronic, persistent, active hepatitis, cirrhosis, liver failure, and even death.

Pubic Lice (Crabs)

*P*ubic lice are tiny parasites that look like insects with segmented torsos and claws for clinging to hair. Pubic lice may be spread by contact with infected bedding, clothing, and toilet seats, as well as by intimate and sexual contact.

Symptoms

Lice may cause irritation ranging from slight discomfort to severe itching; nits or adult lice may be seen on pubic hairs.

Treatment

Over-the-counter medications in the form of creams, rinses, or shampoos.

If Untreated. Pubic lice cause no permanent damage, just lots of itching.

Trichomoniasis (trick-oh-mo-NEYE-ah-sis) or "Trich" Infection

*T*richomoniasis is caused by infection of the vagina or the urinary tract by *Trichomonas vaginalis*, a large protozoan organism.

Symptoms

In Men. Urinary tract infection, frequent urination, discharge from penis.

In Women. Vaginal discharge, itching and burning in vaginal-vulva area.

Treatment

Oral antibiotics such as metronidazole. Don't drink alcoholic beverages while taking metronidazole.

If Untreated. Women will have heavy, uncomfortable vaginal discharge and possibly an increased risk of PID.

Syphilis (SIFF-il-is)

*S*yphilis is a bacterial infection caused by *Treponema pallidium*. Syphilis can cause permanent damage if not diagnosed and treated early. About 70,000 persons each year, in the United States, contract syphilis in its early, ulcerative stages.

Symptoms

Vary according to stage of disease.

Early. A painless sore (chancre), skin rash, lymph node enlargement.

Latent. No symptoms, may last for several years.

Treatment

Antibiotics such as penicillin.

If Untreated. Later-stage syphilis: More serious problems such as neurological disorders, dementia, blindness, heart disease, aneurysms, and brain damage. A woman who is infected with syphilis when pregnant can seriously harm her developing baby. So pregnant women should be tested for syphilis *and* use condoms if any risk exists for becoming infected.

Pelvic Inflammatory Disease

*P*elvic inflammatory disease (PID) is caused by untreated bacteria such as chlamydia and gonorrhea. PID leads to 225,000 hospitalizations every year in the United States. About one out of seven women have had treatment for PID. PID is the leading cause of infertility in U.S. women, rendering 150,000 women unable to conceive each year. Women with PID are also at a much greater risk for an ectopic, or tubal, pregnancy due to the scarring of the fallopian tubes.

Symptoms

In Women. Chronic vaginal discharge (sometimes with bad odor), fever, nausea, vomiting, chills, pain in abdomen, pain during intercourse, spotting and pain between menstrual periods or during urination, heavy bleeding, and/or blood clots during menstrual periods, unusually long or painful periods.

Treatment

Combined antibiotics such as ceftriazone and doxycycline; surgery to remove abscessed tissues and/or to repair or remove reproductive organs.

If Untreated.   PID can lead to chronic pain, ectopic pregnancy, and sterility.

Common Questions about Sexually Transmitted Infections

1. **How prevalent is the AIDS virus in the college community?**

   In surveys of colleges and universities, approximately 1 in 500 individuals is HIV positive.

2. **How often should women get pap smears or a pelvic exam? How often should men get checked?**

   Women should get pap smears and pelvic exams annually. Most men are checked prior to college and then when needed for any new symptoms.

3. **Can I have an STI and not have any symptoms?**

   Yes! The greatest danger for sexually active people is that asymptomatic infections can persist for many years. *Chlamydia,* genital warts, and the AIDS virus are among the most hazardous infections. Between 5 and 20 percent of sexually active women are infected with *Chlamydia trachomatis.* Thus, the importance of getting annual pelvic exams and pap smears is stressed. Be aware of your body and the possible symptoms that would alert you to an STI.

4. **Can STIs be spread even though a condom is used?**

   Most STIs are prevented if condoms are used correctly at the time of each and every act of intercourse. Put the condom on carefully so that you don't tear it. Don't use oil-based lubricants such as Vaseline. Remember, the man should not continue thrusting after ejaculation (that is, after he comes). If he does, the condom may slip off into the vagina.

5. **Is it easier for a man or a woman to get an STI?**

   It is far easier for an uninfected woman to become infected by an infected man than for a man to become infected by an infected woman. Sexually transmitted infections are not equal opportunity diseases.

6. **Which STIs can be treated over the counter?**

   Yeast infections, but remember that if a woman has vaginal discharge due to yeast (monilia), she may also have a second infection needing treatment as well.

7. **Which contraceptive methods also protect against STIs?**

   After abstinence, the condom, used consistently and correctly, has the greatest protective effect against STIs. Spermicides have some protective effect, too. If you use a condom and an application of spermicidal foam, cream, jelly, film, or suppository, protection is maximal. Hormonal contraceptives that produce a thick cervical mucus appear to have some protective effect against pelvic infections.

Contraception

Why Contraception?

*E*very woman who engages in vaginal intercourse is at risk of becoming pregnant, and every individual who practices oral, anal, or vaginal intercourse is at potential risk for acquiring STIs. A contraceptive is any technique, method, or device that reduces the risk of a woman becoming pregnant. Some contraceptives also reduce the likelihood of transmission of STIs. Some contraceptives offer noncontraceptive benefits in addition to reducing the risk of pregnancy and STI acquisition. Reduced rates of certain types of cancer and reduction of menstrual bleeding, cramping, and premenstrual syndrome (PMS) in women are just a few of the noncontraceptive benefits of modern contraception.

Every sexually active individual stands to benefit from the consistent and correct use of contraception. Unfortunately, although contraceptives provide many advantages, they are not always easy to use. They can be complicated and messy. They require planning. They may not be with you every time you need them, and even when everything is done exactly as it should be done, no contraceptive (including abstinence) is 100 percent effective. The reason abstinence is *not* 100 percent is because people completely committed to this approach may change their minds, they may be pressured or physically forced to have sex. Many couples find contraception both acceptable and enjoyable. Knowing that you and your partner are protected offers the peace of mind that can make sexual activity more enjoyable.

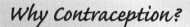 Choosing the Right Contraception

If you have decided to use contraception, you have taken an important step toward sexual responsibility. With so many choices out there, however, trying to choose the right contraceptive can be very intimidating. A method that is not effective for you can lead to an unwanted pregnancy or unwanted diseases. A method that is not safe for you can lead to serious medical consequences. A method that does not fit your personal lifestyle is not likely to be used consistently and correctly. How, then, do you choose? No one can determine which contraceptive is best for you, so you should weigh the advantages and disadvantages of each method as it applies to you and your partner. Regardless of which method you ultimately decide upon, the contraceptive must be safe, effective, and comfortable for both partners involved. A method that is not safe, effective, and comfortable will be used inconsistently or incorrectly.

Making Contraception Work for You

The failure rate for a contraceptive is defined as the likelihood of a woman experiencing a pregnancy in her first full year of use of a single method. The failure rate should not be interpreted as the likelihood of failure every time that contraceptive is used. For example, the failure rate for the perfect user of a condom is 3 percent, meaning that of 100 women who use the condom perfectly for one full year, three will become pregnant. The average couple engages in two acts of sexual intercourse per week, or 104 over the course of a year. The perfect condom user will thus use 104 condoms per year, and 100 perfect users will use 10,400 condoms during that time. Of those 10,400 condoms used, only three uses will result in pregnancy, so the chance of pregnancy occurring when a condom is used is only three failures per 10,400 condoms used, or 0.03 percent. Another way of saying this is that the per-condom failure rate is 0.03 percent, while the failure rate over one year of use is 3 percent of couples using condoms.

A perfect user is someone who uses a given contraceptive correctly every time he or she engages in sexual intercourse. A typical user is anyone who uses that method, which includes both perfect and imperfect users. Typical users are more likely to experience contraceptive failure than a perfect user. Whichever method of contraception you ultimately choose, you must feel comfortable enough with your decision and the method itself to use it perfectly, every time. Consistent, correct, and careful use of contraception often requires cooperation between partners.

Types of Contraception

When considering which contraceptives best meet your needs, you may want to consult the Contraceptive Comfort and Confidence Scale at right. This scale has been designed to help you make an informed choice about your contraceptive. Of course there may be other issues involved that are not included on the Scale; issues that may make your decision more or less difficult. Contraception can be a complex issue, and you may wish to seek out additional information or advice from your school's health clinic, health books, or friends. Keep in mind, however, that all final decisions are yours.

The contraceptives presented in this appendix are arranged in five different groups.

1. *Natural methods* (abstinence, periodic abstinence, withdrawal);
2. *Spermicides* (foams, creams, jellies, suppositories, vaginal contraceptive film);
3. *Barrier methods* (condom, female condom, diaphragm, cervical cap, contraceptive sponge);
4. *Hormonal methods* (birth control pills, Norplant, Depo-Provera, minipills); and
5. *Other methods* (IUDs, sterilization).

Remember that no contraceptive is perfect; there are advantages and disadvantages to each method. You should carefully consider each method and its appropriateness to you and your lifestyle before making a contraceptive decision. Finally, remember that many of these methods are reversible, which means you can change your mind.

Contraceptive Comfort and Confidence Scale

Comfort and confidence in contraceptive methods are essential for successful use. How do you feel about your specific contraceptive options? The questions below will help you discover your attitudes.

Method: _____

Very 1	Somewhat 2	Not at all 3	Don't know ?

- Do I object to this method? ____
- Am I afraid of this method? ____
- Does my partner object to this method? ____
- Will I or my partner be embarrassed by using this method? ____
- Does my religion object to this method? ____
- Will this method interrupt lovemaking? ____
- Will I enjoy intercourse less because of this method? ____
- Does this method cost too much? ____
- Does this method cause health problems? ____
- Have I had problems and/or a pregnancy using this method? ____
- Will this method make my or my partner's menstrual cycle painful or uncomfortable? ____
- Will I have trouble remembering to use this method? ____
- Will I have trouble using this method carefully? ____
- Will I have trouble using this method correctly? ____
- Will I have trouble using this method consistently? ____

"Don't know" answers point to a need for more thinking, more introspection, more cooperation between you and your partner, or more information. "Very" answers may mean the user might not like or be successful with the method. "Somewhat" answers suggest that the user needs to carefully consider whether the method will be suitable since using it will require concerted effort.

Natural Methods

Natural methods of birth control are those that do not use additional devices aside from two consenting partners who work together to protect against pregnancy. These methods include abstinence, withdrawal, and fertility awareness [such as the *rhythm* method and the basal body temperature (BBT) method]. The term *nat-*

ural should not be construed to mean that other birth control is *unnatural*, but simply that natural methods rely on the natural signs and symptoms associated with human sexuality in adults (e.g., impending orgasm in men or indications of a woman's menstrual cycle).

Abstinence

Although there are many contraceptive options for men and women, and although several of those options are very effective when used consistently and correctly, abstinence remains the only potentially 100 percent effective contraceptive. When practiced to avoid pregnancy, abstinence is defined as refraining from penile-vaginal intercourse. When practiced to prevent the transmission of STIs, abstinence means no exchange of body fluids, including blood, semen, and vaginal secretion. Abstinence differs from celibacy in that the former is not necessarily a permanent decision. A man or woman may choose to abstain for days or years, for the duration of a single relationship, or until he or she marries; however, abstinence is only 100 percent effective if it is used 100 percent of the time. Anything less than perfect use—even once—can result in pregnancy or infection.

Abstinence is widely practiced, both in the United States and abroad. In 1988, a national survey found that 49 percent of unmarried men aged 18 to 24 and 71 percent of unmarried women aged 18 to 24 had had either one sexual partner or no sexual partners in the previous year. In other words, more than half of the college age population in the United States appears to have a limited number of sexual partners. Clearly, sexual monogamy and long-term abstinence are still widespread on college campuses.

Effectiveness. When used every time, abstinence is the only potentially 100 percent effective method of contraception. The problem is that people change their minds and couples depending on abstinence do become pregnant.

Cost. Free

Instructions. In theory, abstinence is easy to realize; in practice, however, abstinence can be very difficult to achieve. Certain situations can make it very difficult to resist sexual intercourse. If you choose to abstain, then it is your responsibility to avoid situations where you may feel pressure (self-imposed or otherwise) to engage in sexual intercourse.

1. Decide in advance what you want to do about sex. When you feel clearheaded, sober, and good about yourself, decide which activities you will say "yes" to and which activities you will say "no" to. If you have a partner, discuss your decisions with him or her when you feel close to each other.

2. Identify other sexual practices that you and your partner might enjoy. Abstinence does not mean refraining from all sexual intimacy, only those activities that put one at risk for pregnancy or STIs. People who abstain from intercourse (as well as those who engage in intercourse) may find holding hands, dancing, massaging, kissing, solo masturbation, mutual masturbation, and fantasy as erotic as sexual intercourse. Those abstaining due to concerns about pregnancy may also engage in oral-genital or anal sex, although those abstaining due to STI concerns also need to refrain from those practices. A word of caution is necessary, however: Practicing *outercourse* as a means of sexual intimacy can, and oftentimes does, lead to sexual intercourse.

3. Avoid high-pressure sexual situations. Stay sober, stay aware, stay out of the bedroom.

4. Learn to say "no" and mean it. It is your right and responsibility to say "no," to say it emphatically, and to say it over and over again.

5. Learn to hear "no" and understand that "no" always means just that. You do not have to give a reason for your decision, although you may choose to do so. If you feel threatened or unsafe in any way, leave the scene, or better yet, avoid such situations to begin with. Abstinence is your decision, and you do not have to justify it to anyone.

Advantages

- Always available. Abstinence requires no special materials or devices to work perfectly, only two cooperative partners.
- Highly effective. When used perfectly (that is, 100 percent of the time), abstinence is the single most effective method of birth control.
- Inexpensive.
- 100 percent protection against STIs.
- Can increase self-esteem. Those who choose to abstain may feel a justifiable sense of pride in their decision.
- Can strengthen relationships. A mutual decision to abstain from sexual intercourse can increase the emotional closeness of two partners.

Disadvantages

- Can disrupt relationships. A decision by only one partner to abstain may leave the other partner feeling unwanted, undesirable, or unworthy. Open communication may aid in reducing this unwanted side effect.

■ Difficult to use consistently. Maintaining your decision to abstain can be very challenging in certain high-pressure or passionate situations.

Periodic Abstinence

Periodic abstinence is contraception based on awareness of a woman's pattern of fertility and menstrual cycle. Some methods of periodic abstinence are the rhythm method, the cervical mucus method, and the BBT method. All of these methods identify a woman's fertile and infertile days based on a variety of different symptoms. None of these methods provides protection against STIs.

The most effective method of periodic abstinence is the BBT method, which requires that a woman take her temperature first thing in the morning before getting out of bed. In most women, BBT rises approximately 0.5°F at the time of ovulation. The rise in BBT indicates that a woman has reached the post-ovulatory stage of her menstrual cycle.

Effectiveness. The first-year failure rate for a typical user is 20 percent. The first-year failure rate for a perfect user is 2 percent.

Cost: Free, aside from the cost of purchasing a BBT thermometer.

Instructions
1. Take and record BBT every morning before getting out of bed after at least 3 hours of sleep. Take BBT from the same site (orally, rectally, or vaginally) every morning.
2. There will be a temperature rise between 0.4° and 0.8°F shortly before, during, or right after ovulation.
3. A woman has ovulated when a rise of 0.4° to 0.8°F is sustained for three consecutive days. The exact temperature rise is not important, just the rise over the baseline. BBT will remain elevated until the next period begins.
4. A woman trying to avoid pregnancy can have unprotected intercourse while her BBT is elevated.
5. To avoid pregnancy, a woman must abstain from intercourse or use a back-up method such as condoms during her fertile days (the time after her period but before her BBT rises).

Advantages
■ Readily available. The BBT method does not require any special materials beyond a thermometer.
■ Inexpensive.

■ During infertile days, no back-up method of effective contraception must be used.

Disadvantages
■ No protection against STIs, including HIV.
■ Limited sexual intercourse. During fertile days, abstinence or another method of birth control must be used to avoid unwanted pregnancy. In addition, some of the infertile days overlap with a woman's menstrual bleeding, which some people might find unattractive for intercourse. On the other hand, some individuals find sexual intercourse during menstrual bleeding attractive, because the menstrual blood provides additional vaginal lubrication.
■ High failure rate for populations of typical users. Although better than no method at all, the BBT method has a first-year failure rate of 20 percent for the typical user. Excellent record-keeping helps reduce the failure rate.
■ Necessity for careful record-keeping. To become a perfect user, a woman must take her BBT every morning without fail, before getting out of bed.

Coitus Interruptus (Withdrawal)

Withdrawal means removing the penis from the vagina immediately prior to ejaculation ("coming"). Although simple in theory, withdrawal can be quite difficult to achieve in practice, because it requires that a man pull away just when he wants to thrust more deeply. In addition, during impending orgasm, a man's and a woman's thought processes may become clouded and unclear, inhibiting the ability to practice withdrawal. It is also important to note that withdrawal offers little protection against STIs.

Effectiveness. The first-year failure rate for a typical user is 19 percent. The first-year failure rate for a perfect user is 4 percent.

Cost: Free

Instructions
1. Before inserting his penis into her vagina, the man should wipe the preejaculatory fluid from the tip of his penis. This fluid may contain the bacteria or viruses that cause STIs. This step will *not* prevent the transmission of STIs, but may serve to reduce the risk.
2. Just as a man feels he is ready to ejaculate, he should quickly pull his penis out of her vagina.

3. The man should direct his ejaculation away from the woman's genitals and should avoid any subsequent penile-vaginal contact, even after ejaculation is complete.

4. Keep a back-up method such as post-coital pills ("morning after pills") on hand in case withdrawal is unsuccessful.

Advantages

- Always available
- Requires no extra devices
- Spontaneity. Intercourse is not interrupted to put on a condom, insert a spermicide, etc.

Disadvantages

- No protection against most STDs, including HIV. Even before ejaculation, the penis secretes a small amount of pre-ejaculate, which serves as a lubricant and may contain the viruses and bacteria that cause STDs.
- Minimal control for women. The woman is entirely reliant on the man's ability (and willingness) to pull out when ejaculation seems imminent.
- Interruption. Intercourse is interrupted when the man realizes ejaculation is imminent.
- Difficult to use perfectly, especially for men who cannot control their ejaculation. And even for men who can, withdrawal can be sexually frustrating, as it requires them to pull out when they want to thrust more deeply.

Spermicides

Spermicidal products contain a chemical (usually nonoxynol-9) that kills sperm. Spermicides are available in many different forms, including foams, creams, gels, suppositories, and vaginal contraceptive film (VCF). They may be used effectively alone, or with another method such as condoms or vaginal barrier methods. When used alone or with condoms, the spermicide is inserted into the vagina prior to intercourse. When used with a vaginal barrier method such as a diaphragm or a cervical cap, the spermicide is applied directly to the vaginal barrier. Spermicides have been shown to have a protective effect against several STIs, especially gonorrhea and chlamydia. However, the relationship between spermicide use and HIV risk is less clear, but spermicides are probably somewhat beneficial.

Spermicides are an excellent back-up contraceptive method for many couples. If a woman runs out of birth control pills, condoms, or is late for her Depo-Provera contraceptive injection, she may effectively use spermicides as a temporary means of birth control. Spermicides can also be used after sex as an emergency measure if a condom breaks or a woman notices that a vaginal barrier method is not correctly inserted.

Effectiveness.   When used alone, the first-year failure rate for a typical user is 21 percent. The first-year failure rate for a perfect user is 6 percent. Consistent use is the most important factor in minimizing failure with spermicides. All spermicides are more effective when used with another method such as a condom, diaphragm, or cervical cap. For example, when condoms and spermicide are used together, a perfect user can expect a first-year failure rate of only 0.01 percent, which is as effective as birth control pills used perfectly.

Cost.   The cost of a spermicidal product varies greatly depending on which type is used and how often it is used. The price may range from 35 cents for a single suppository to $12 for a full container of foam. Prices at public health clinics, including college health services, may be lower.

Instructions

1. Store your spermicides in a convenient location that is clean, cool, and dark. Avoid any contact with talcum powder.

2. You should insert the spermicide before intercourse. Foam is effective immediately, but suppositories, cream, gel, jelly, and vaginal contraceptive film require a waiting period between insertion and intercourse. This waiting period is essential for the product to melt and spread inside your vagina. The package instructions that come with your spermicide explain exactly how long you should wait.

3. Wash your hands carefully with soap and water.

4. *Foam.* Shake the foam container vigorously at least twenty times. Then use the nozzle to fill the plastic applicator. Insert the applicator into your vagina as far as it will comfortably go; then push the plunger to release the foam. The spermicide should be deep in your vagina, close to your cervix. You may have intercourse immediately.

   Jelly or cream. Fill the applicator by squeezing the spermicide tube. Insert the applicator into your vagina as far as it will comfortably go; then push the plunger to release the jelly or cream. The spermicide should be deep in your vagina, close to your cervix. You must wait for the product to melt before having intercourse.

   Suppository. Remove the suppository from its wrapping and slide it into your vagina. Push it along the back wall of your vagina as far as you can so that it rests on or near your cervix. You must wait for the product to melt before having intercourse.

Vaginal Contraceptive Film. Be sure your fingers are completely dry. Place one sheet of film on your finger and slide it along the back wall of your vagina as far as you can so the film rests on or near your cervix. You must wait for the product to melt before having intercourse. Some women fold the film over on itself twice and push their finger into the fold as a way to get the film all the way up into the vagina.

5. A dose of spermicide remains effective for one hour, so you may insert the product ahead of time. However, you must use another dose of spermicide with every act of intercourse, even if you have intercourse more than once in a single hour.

6. Leave the spermicide in place for at least six to eight hours after intercourse. Do not douche or rinse your vagina. If you want to douche, you must wait at least six to eight hours.

7. Wash your spermicide inserter after each use with plain soap and water.

8. *Very important:* Read the package instructions for the specific spermicide or barrier contraceptive you are using.

Advantages

- Readily available. Spermicides can be obtained without a prescription at drug stores, pharmacies, and grocery stores, and they can be easily and discreetly carried.

- Woman-controlled. Spermicides can be used by a woman without the need for partner involvement.

- Lubrication. Spermicides can provide lubrication during intercourse, either with or without a condom.

- Emergency contraception. Spermicides can be used as a post-coital contraceptive if it appears that the primary means of birth control (such as a condom) has failed. In this instance, an application of spermicide should be quickly inserted into the vagina. It may have some contraceptive effect. The woman should also see her clinician for emergency contraception pills ("morning after pills").

Disadvantages

- Allergies or irritation. Temporary skin irritation to either the vagina, vulva, or penis is the most common problem associated with spermicide use. Changing to another product may help reduce sensitivity.

- Unpleasant taste. Some couples dislike the taste of spermicides during oral intercourse.

- Messy. Post-coital discharge of the spermicide from the vagina is unpleasant for some couples.

- Insertion difficulty. Some women may have trouble learning to insert spermicide correctly.

Barrier Methods

*B*arrier methods physically prevent the fertilization of a woman's egg by the man's sperm. The most common barrier method among college students is the condom; other barrier methods include vaginal barrier methods such as the diaphragm and contraceptive sponge, and the female condom.

Condom

During the 1980s, as fear and awareness of AIDS increased in the United States, condom use and awareness rose significantly. For women aged 15 to 24 who are at risk of becoming pregnant (that is, sexually active and not trying to become pregnant), the condom is now the second most common method of birth control behind the pill. In addition, many people use condoms to protect themselves or their partners against STIs. People often find latex condoms an attractive contraceptive option because of their proven ability to offer protection against both pregnancy and STIs, including HIV.

A condom is a membrane that is placed on a man's penis before engaging in sexual intercourse. Most condoms in the United States are made of latex, a natural product derived from the inner bark of rubber trees, but a few condoms (about 5 percent) are made from lamb intestines. Latex and lambskin condoms offer similar protection against pregnancy, but differ in that lambskin condoms have tiny pores through which viruses can pass, including the viruses that cause AIDS, hepatitis B, and herpes. Therefore, lambskin condoms are not recommended for protection against viral STIs.

Effectiveness.   The first-year failure rate among typical users is 14 percent. The first-year failure rate for a perfect user is 3 percent.

Cost.   Condoms are among the most inexpensive of contraceptives; the average consumer pays 50 cents per condom. Condom manufacturers, however, often make condoms available to nonprofit family planning facilities, including college health services, at much-reduced rates. In these cases, the price may be as low as 5 to 10 cents per condom, or even as low as 3 cents per condom.

Instructions

1. Place the condom on the erect penis before the penis comes in contact with your partner's mouth, anus, or vagina.

2. Remove the condom from its package, taking care not to tear it with fingernails, teeth, rings, etc. *Do not* pretest the condom for holes by filling it with air or water; every condom is tested prior to distribution.

3. Unroll the condom about 1/2 inch before placing it on the erect penis, and pinch the tip to allow space for semen.

4. Unroll the condom down to the base of the erect penis. The rolled rim should always remain on the outside of the condom. If the rolled rim was on the inside of the condom when the condom was placed on the penis, *do not* simply flip the condom over and use it again. Discard the condom and use a new one, as the preejaculate at the tip of the penis can contain viruses and bacteria.

5. Use adequate lubrication to reduce the chance of condom breakage. For extra lubrication, use water, K-Y jelly, or spermicidal creams, jellies, foams, or suppositories. When using latex condoms, *never* use oil-based products such as cold cream, mineral oil, cooking oil, petroleum jelly (Vaseline), shortening, lotions, massage oil, or baby oil, which will rapidly degrade latex condoms and make them break.

6. Withdrawal should occur soon after ejaculation, while the penis is still erect. During withdrawal, hold the rim of the condom against the base of the penis. This helps keep the condom from slipping off.

7. Condoms should be stored in a cool, dry place away from direct light. Under these conditions, condoms may be used for up to five years past the manufacture date. Condoms may be kept in a wallet or purse for up to one month without losing their integrity.

Advantages

- Proven protection against STIs, including HIV. Latex condoms are the only contraceptive that has been shown to be highly effective in the prevention of STI transmission.

- Accessible and portable. Condoms can be obtained by men or women, without a prescription or medical advice, and from a wide variety of purveyors including drug stores, vending machines, gas stations, family planning clinics, and other sources. In addition, condoms are fairly easily and discreetly carried by men or women.

- Inexpensive.

- Erection enhancement. Many men report that a condom helps maintain an erection longer, extending sexual arousal for both men and women.

- Hygiene. Messy post-coital discharge of semen from the vagina, an annoying aftermath of sex for some couples, is avoided by using condoms.

- Visible proof of protection. Condoms offer immediate, tangible evidence of their effectiveness, as the ejaculate is contained within the condom.

- Can be used as a protective barrier during oral sex. Some individuals cut condoms lengthwise with a pair of scissors, then placing the piece of latex over a woman's vagina when they perform oral sex. Other materials that have been used for similar purposes include dental dams and plastic wrap, although it should be noted that these materials have not been tested with regards to their ability to prevent STI transmission.

Disadvantages

- Reduced sensitivity. Men often comment that the condom reduces sensitivity during intercourse, especially at the head of the penis. Use of textured, ultra-thin, or transparent condoms may help overcome this barrier. Some men have reported that the use of two condoms at once greatly increases friction, sensitivity, and pleasure.

- Interference with erection. Some men may have difficulty maintaining an erection with a condom on. Integrating the placement of the condom on the penis as a routine part of foreplay may help overcome this obstacle.

- Interruption. Often couples object to the interruption of foreplay to put on the condom. Making the condom a part of foreplay can decrease this side effect.

- Decreased pleasure. Some couples enjoy intercourse less if the man's penis is covered.

- Allergy. In rare cases, a man or woman may be allergic or sensitive to latex condoms. Although not effective for the prevention of STIs, lambskin condoms may offer relief from latex sensitivity. Some individuals have reported layering a lambskin condom with a latex condom to compensate for latex sensitivity and still provide STI protection.

- Difficulty with male involvement. In some instances a man will not accept the responsibility for birth control or infection prevention. Unfortunately, some men may even become angry or even violent when their partner demands that a condom be used.

- Condom breakage. Condoms break at a rate of approximately one to two per 100 used, but most condom breaks do not result in pregnancy or disease infection;

factors include whether the break was pre- or post-ejaculatory, where the break occurred (at the tip, base, or shaft of the penis), and the presence of genital ulcers such as warts or lesions. The breakage rate does not appear to be significantly higher for anal intercourse as opposed to vaginal intercourse. Adequate lubrication with a water-based lubricant may help reduce breakage rates with all acts of intercourse. In some instances, women put condoms on more carefully than men.

■ Possible increased HIV risk with spermicidal condoms. One study showed the possibility that the nonoxynol-9 found in many spermicidal condoms can irritate a woman's vaginal canal. This may cause an increased risk of HIV transmission. The results of the study need to be further analyzed, and any condom is much safer than no condom. It may be safest of all, however, to use nonspermicidal lubricated condoms.

Female Condom

The female condom, called Reality, was approved by the FDA in 1993. Reality is a polyurethane sheath that fits inside the vagina. One end anchors the condom against the cervix, while the other end remains outside the vagina after insertion. Reality contains a lubricant and provides full barrier protection of the vagina and part of the vulva.

Effectiveness. The first-year failure rate for typical users is 21 percent. The first-year failure rate for a perfect user is 5 percent.

Cost. One Reality condom costs approximately $2.50, and each condom may be used only once. Prices may be lower in some settings.

Instructions

1. Your condom may be inserted just before intercourse or up to eight hours ahead of time.
2. Wash your hands carefully before inserting the condom.
3. To insert the condom, use the thumb and middle finger of one hand to squeeze the inner ring into a narrow oval for insertion.
4. With your other hand, spread the lips of your vagina. Insert the inner ring and the pouch of Reality into the vaginal opening and with your index finger, push the inner ring with the pouch the rest of the way up into the vagina.
5. The outside ring lies against the outer lips of the vagina when Reality is in place. Any slack will be taken up when the penis enters the vagina.
6. Use a new condom with each act of intercourse.
7. Remove your condom immediately following intercourse, before you stand up. Squeeze and twist the outer ring to keep semen inside the pouch.

Advantages

■ Can be used by latex-allergic individuals.
■ Protection against STIs, including HIV. The female condom lines the vagina completely, providing an effective barrier against STI infection. The female condom is made of polyurethane, a highly tested material used in some medical examination gloves and other sensitive applications. Unless the condom slips out of place or is torn, it should provide very good protection against STIs.
■ Readily available. The female condom is nonprescription and is available in many locations where male condoms are distributed.
■ Sense of control for the woman. If a woman cannot realistically rely on her partner to use condoms, then a female condom is an excellent alternative that prevents pregnancy, inhibits STIs, and places the primary control over birth control in the woman's hands.
■ Can be pre-planned. The female condom can be inserted up to eight hours in advance of intercourse. Some women complain that it occasionally makes a noise when they walk around with a female condom in place.

Disadvantages

■ Cannot be used with a male condom. When used simultaneously, studies have shown that both latex male condoms and polyurethane female condoms tend to rip and tear each other. Thus, using latex male and polyurethane female condoms simultaneously is not recommended.
■ Can slip out of place. The internal rim of the condom, which anchors the condom against the cervix, can be dislodged, thus reducing contraceptive effectiveness.
■ Physically unattractive. Both men and women may find the visible outer ring unappealing.
■ Some women may be uncomfortable with this method. Use of the female condom requires a woman to be very comfortable with her own body.
■ Relatively expensive.

Vaginal Barrier Methods

Vaginal barrier methods include over-the-counter methods, such as the vaginal contraceptive sponge and prescription methods such as the diaphragm and the cervical cap. These methods provide a barrier to the woman's cervix, preventing sperm from reaching the uterus and thus inhibiting fertilization of the egg. They must be inserted in a woman's vagina before intercourse, and they are most often used in conjunction with spermicidal foams or jellies. Studies have shown that vaginal barriers may decrease the likelihood of transmission of some STIs; however, other studies have shown that spermicidal foams or jellies may increase a woman's susceptibility to transmission of the HIV virus.

Women who use vaginal barrier methods or female condoms must be familiar with the symptoms of toxic shock syndrome (see Appendix A). Women are discouraged from leaving these methods in place for more than twenty-four consecutive hours (although it has been suggested that the cervical cap may be left in the vagina for up to forty-eight hours).

Advantages
- Medically safe. These methods have few negative side effects.
- Nonhormonal. Women who are uncomfortable with the thought of altering their "natural" hormonal pattern (as with birth control pills, Norplant, or Depo-Provera) may find these methods attractive.
- Woman-controlled. Women for whom relying on a partner to use condoms is not a realistic option may find the control associated with vaginal barrier methods attractive.
- Intermittent protection. These methods are available for immediate use, no matter how long the interval between acts of intercourse.
- Pre-planning. Any of these methods can be inserted into the vagina well ahead of anticipated sexual intercourse.
- Some STI protection. Studies have shown that these methods decrease the risk for certain STIs, including gonorrhea, chlamydia, and trichomoniasis. Risk for PID and cervical neoplasia related to human papilloma virus infection are substantially reduced in women who use these methods. The data concerning HIV are more ambiguous; some studies have shown that these methods may increase a woman's susceptibility to HIV. More studies need to be done before any conclusions can be made.

Disadvantages
- Increased risk of urinary tract infection, bacterial vaginosis, and vaginal candidiasis.
- Messy. Because of the need to use vaginal barrier methods with spermicides, some women find the post-coital aftermath of semen, vaginal lubrication, and additional spermicide messy and uncomfortable.
- Skin irritation. Some women or their partners may be allergic or sensitive to nonoxynol-9, the active ingredient in many spermicides. Changing to an octoxynol-based spermicide product may help.
- Some women may be uncomfortable with these methods. These methods require a woman to be very comfortable with her own body.
- These methods take time to learn. Correct use of these methods is a skill that must be learned and practiced.
- A woman may need to see a clinician to be fitted.

Diaphragm

The diaphragm is a dome-shaped rubber cap with a flexible rim. It is inserted into the vagina before intercourse, with the dome of the diaphragm covering the cervix. This method should be used with a spermicidal cream or jelly, which is applied to the dome and rim before insertion. The diaphragm, which is available in many different styles and sizes, must be prescribed by a physician.

Effectiveness. The first-year failure rate among typical users is 18 percent. The first-year failure rate among perfect users is 6 percent.

Cost. The diaphragm itself costs approximately $22, and it must be replaced every three years, after pregnancy, or if a significant change in weight occurs. The initial cost of obtaining a diaphragm is higher, because of the need for a doctor office visit. The first-time cost ranges from $50 to $150. The price at public health clinics, such as college health services, may be significantly lower; as low as $10 for the first fitting in some cases.

Instructions
1. The diaphragm may be inserted immediately before intercourse, or up to six hours ahead of time.
2. Wash your hands carefully with soap and water.
3. Squeeze about one teaspoon of spermicidal jelly or cream into the dome and around the rim of the diaphragm.
4. Squeeze the opposite sides of the rim together so that the diaphragm folds. Hold it folded in one hand between your thumb and fingers.
5. Spread the opening of your vagina with your other hand, and insert the folded diaphragm into your vaginal canal. Some women perform this step with one foot propped up, squatting, or lying on their back.
6. Push the diaphragm downward and along the back wall of your vagina as far as it will go. Tuck the

front rim up along the roof of your vagina behind your pubic bone.

7. The diaphragm must remain in place for six hours following the last act of intercourse. If you have intercourse more than once while using a diaphragm, an additional dose of spermicidal cream or jelly is recommended. Do not remove your diaphragm; instead, use the plastic applicator to insert fresh cream or jelly in front of the diaphragm.

8. The diaphragm should not remain in the vagina for more than twenty-four consecutive hours.

9. Before removing your diaphragm, wash your hands with soap and water. Carefully locate the front rim of the diaphragm with your finger. Hook your finger over the rim, then pull the diaphragm down and out.

10. Wash the diaphragm with plain soap and water, then dry it. Check for holes, tears, or cracks in the diaphragm by holding it up to the light.

11. Store the diaphragm in a clean, cool, convenient, and dark location. Do not bring a diaphragm into contact with oil-based products or talcum powder.

Cervical Cap

The cervical cap is a soft rubber cup with a firm round rim. It is used with spermicide and placed against the cervix, creating a seal or suction between the cap and the cervix. The cap protects during multiple acts of intercourse without the need to apply additional spermicide, and it can be left in the vagina for up to forty-eight hours. The cervical cap must be fitted by a clinician and is only available with a prescription.

Effectiveness.   The first-year failure rate for a typical user depends on whether that user has had children. For women who have not had children (nulliparous women) the failure rate is 18 percent. For women who have had children (parous women) the first-year failure rate is 35 percent. For perfect users, the failure rates are 9 percent and 26 percent, respectively, for nulliparous and parous women.

Cost.   The cost of a cervical cap, including the fitting, is very similar to a diaphragm.

Instructions
1. The cap may be inserted immediately before intercourse or up to twenty-four hours ahead of time. Some experts recommend that you allow thirty min-

utes between insertion and intercourse, so that a good suction develops.

2. Wash your hands carefully with soap and water. Fill the dome of the cap 1/3 full with spermicidal cream or jelly.

4. Slide the cap down and back along the vagina and press the rim of the cap around the cervix until it is completely covered.

5. The cap should be left in place for six hours following the final act of intercourse. The cap can be left in the vagina for up to forty-eight hours. Additional acts of intercourse do not require more spermicide.

6. To remove the cap, press on the cap rim until the seal against your cervix is broken, then tilt the cap off the cervix.

7. The cap must be washed and dried carefully after each use.

8. Store the cap in a clean, cool, convenient, and dark location. Avoid contact with oil-based products or talcum powder.

Hormonal Methods

There are a number of hormonal birth control methods available to women in the United States. There are two primary types of hormonal methods: those that involve a combination of hormones such as birth control pills, and those that contain only progestin such as Norplant implants and Depo-Provera injections.

Oral Contraceptives

Birth control pills, or oral contraceptives, can be an excellent method of birth control for women and are the most commonly used method in the United States. In this country, pills are used by 28 percent of women aged 15 to 44 who are at risk of becoming pregnant, and by 16 million women overall. Although in the past there have been concerns regarding the pill's safety for women, the pill is one of the most extensively studied medications ever taken by human beings and is very safe for the vast majority of women. In particular, studies have shown that there is no apparent increase in the risk for breast cancer in women who use pills. In fact, studies have shown that pills offer noncontraceptive benefits to many women. Nevertheless, it remains necessary and important that a woman consult a physician before going on the pill.

Most birth control pills contain two types of hormone: an estrogen and a progestin, each of which contributes to the contraceptive effect. By taking the pill every day at the same time, a steady hormone level is maintained, and a woman's pituitary gland does not produce its normal cyclical pattern of hormones; this prevents ovulation and the woman cannot become pregnant. However, while pills are safe and effective for couples wishing to prevent an unwanted pregnancy, it is important to realize that pills offer no protection against transmission of HIV or other STDs. If either partner is at risk for infection, condoms should still be used with pills.

Effectiveness.   The first-year failure rate in typical users is 3 percent. The first-year failure rate for a perfect user is 0.1 percent.

Cost.   A woman must use thirteen cycles of pills a year for complete protection against pregnancy. At a cost of $20 to $35 per cycle, the annual cost for pills can run between $200 and $300; however, many nonprofit family planning clinics, including college health services, offer pills to women at far lower prices ranging from $3 to $10 per cycle. Many couples find that having the man help with the expense of pills is an excellent way to share the responsibility of family planning.

Instructions for Women Who Take the Pill

1. Pills provide no protection against the transmission of STIs, including HIV. Condom use is highly recommended if either partner is at risk for infection.

2. Choose a back-up method (such as condoms) to use with the first pack of pills. Pills may not completely prevent pregnancy during the first month of use.

3. Begin taking pills the first Sunday that follows the beginning of your menstrual period, or if bleeding begins on a Sunday, start pills that very day. This helps ensure that you are not pregnant when you begin to use the pill.

4. Take one pill at the same time each day until you take every pill in the package. Try to associate taking your pill with something else you do at the same time every day, such as brushing your teeth, since pills work best if taken at the same time every day.

5. Pills come in packs of either twenty-eight or twenty-one pills. The last seven pills of a twenty-eight-day pack are sugar pills, which help you regulate your pill-taking. If you have a twenty-eight-day pack, begin your next pack the very next day. Do not skip any days between packs. If you have a twenty-one-day pack, wait one week after you take your last pill before you start your new pack of pills.

6. If you miss one pill but are less than twelve hours late, take the forgotten pill as soon as you remember. Take your next pill at the regular time, even if that means taking two pills in one day.

7. If you miss one pill and the delay is more than twelve hours, take two pills at once and the next pill at the usual time the following day. You may have some spotting. Use a back-up contraceptive method (such as condoms) for fourteen days in addition to taking your pills.

8. If you miss two pills or more, take two pills at once. After you take those two pills, remove and discard the other forgotten pills. Use a back-up method for fourteen days in addition to taking your pills.

Advantages

- High effectiveness. Even for typical users, the first-year failure rate is only 3 percent, equivalent to perfect use of a condom.

- Beneficial menstrual cycle effects. Pills may decrease menstrual cramps and pain, eliminate midcycle pain, decrease the number of days of bleeding and the amount of blood loss, and reduce premenstrual symptoms such as anxiety, depression, headaches, and fluid retention. Pill use regulates a woman's menstrual cycle, even if it was irregular prior to pill use. Some women consider these to be the most desirable effects of pills, and many women use pills exclusively for their beneficial effects on menstrual pain. Women should not expect to experience all of these benefits, but most women experience some of these positive effects on the menstrual cycle.

- Reversibility. Pills do not cause a long-term loss in fertility.

- Does not interrupt sex.

- Protection against PID. The pill has a protective effect against PID, a major cause of female infertility.

- Protection against ovarian and endometrial cancer. The protective effects of the pill against ovarian and endometrial cancer are especially pronounced in nulliparous women (women who have not had children), and the protective effect of the pill appears to persist long after pills are discontinued.

- Decreased risk for benign breast disease. Pill users are less likely to develop benign (non-cancerous) breast tumors than are women not using the pill.

- Prevention of fibroid tumors and ovarian cysts. Fibroid tumors (the most common tumors in women) and ovarian cysts are both less common in pill users than in nonusers.

- Acne improvement.

Disadvantages

- Pills must be taken daily. When pill use is incorrect or inconsistent, failure rates rise to high levels.

- Expensive. This can be resolved in part by having both partners share the cost.

- Higher risk for smokers. Because both smoking and the estrogen found in birth control pills tend to increase blood clotting, smokers who use pills should pay particularly careful attention to the pill warning signs related to heart attacks and strokes (see following). Better yet, quit smoking.

- Nausea or vomiting. Nausea may occur in the first few cycles of pill use, but tends to lessen or disappear entirely in subsequent cycles.

- Unwanted menstrual cycle changes. While many women experience positive menstrual side effects when using the pill, some women are dissatisfied with missed periods, very scanty bleeding, spotting, or breakthrough bleeding. These changes tend to disappear after several cycles on the pill.

- Weight gain. Usually minor.

- Headaches. Some women experience severe headaches. This is a warning sign for a possible stroke (see following). See your physician immediately. However, headaches gets better in some women who use pills.

- Depression (sometimes severe) and other mood changes may occur in women on pills; however, depression gets better in some women who use pills.

- Decreased libido. Some women experience a decreased interest in sex or a decreased ability to have orgasms.

- Increased risk of chlamydia infection. Because of possible changes in the lining of the cervix, women on the pill may be more susceptible to *Chlamydia trachomatis* infection.

- Danger signs. The following symptoms are important warning signs to a woman using pills. She should see her physician right away.

  A abdominal pain

  C chest pain

  H headaches

  E eye problems such as blurred vision

  S severe leg pain

Progestin-Only Contraceptives

Progestin-only (no estrogen) hormonal methods of birth control come in different packages. Progestin can be delivered orally (Minipills), via injection (Depo-

Provera), or implant (Norplant). These methods have many unique advantages and disadvantages that may make them particularly well suited to some women but not others; for example, progestin-only birth control may be recommended for women whose bodies cannot handle the estrogen present in oral contraceptives. Progestin-only birth control may rely on several mechanisms to prevent pregnancy:

- Inhibition of ovulation.

- Thickening and decreasing the amount of cervical mucus, making it more difficult for sperm to penetrate and reach the egg.

- Creation of a thin, atrophic endometrium.

- Premature luteolysis.

Advantages

- Positive menstrual cycle changes. Scanty or no menstrual bleeding, decreased menstrual cramps and pain (dysmenorrhea), and suppressed midcycle pain, are the most commonly reported positive changes in the menstrual cycle.

- No estrogen. This is advantageous for women who prefer not to have estrogen, or who cannot tolerate estrogen.

- Effective. When used perfectly, progestin-only methods are very effective.

- Decreased risk of endometrial cancer, ovarian cancer, and PID.

- Reduced risk of ectopic pregnancy. Norplant and Depo-Provera, in particular, lower the risk of an ectopic (nonuterine) pregnancy.

Disadvantages

- Negative menstrual cycle disturbances—increased number of days of light bleeding or no menstrual bleeding at all (amenorrhea) are some of the most commonly reported dissatisfactions with progestin-only methods. Rarely, some women experience an increased number of days of heavy bleeding.

- Weight gain. Usually minor, but it can be dramatic. The weight gain is often due to increased appetite.

- Breast tenderness.

- No STI protection. Women at risk of acquiring STIs should continue to use a condom.

Progestin-Only Pills (Minipills)

Minipills are progestin-only contraceptives that must be taken at the same time every day. The minipill contains a very low dose of hormones. Because of this, minipills are slightly less effective than oral contraceptive methods that combine different hormones, so it is even more imperative that women take the minipill regularly and consistently. Some women use condoms with minipills to increase their effectiveness. Minipills provide no protection against STIs.

Effectiveness. The first-year failure rate in typical users is 3 percent. The first-year failure rate for a perfect user is 0.5 percent.

Cost. Prices range from $100 to $300 per year, but may be lower at public health clinics, including college health services.

Instructions
1. Keep a back-up method of birth control (such as condoms) readily available. Because mini-pills contain such a very low dose of hormones, your margin of error is small. If you miss a minipill, use your back-up method until you restart the pills or until your next period.
2. Take one minipill every day until you finish your pill pack. Take the pill at the same time every day to increase its effectiveness. You may want to take the pill after you brush your teeth to help you remember.
3. When you finish a pill pack, start the next pack immediately. Do not skip a day. Never skip a day with minipills.
4. If you miss one minipill, take it as soon as you remember. Also take the next minipill at the regular time, even if that means taking two pills in one day. If you are more than three hours late taking a minipill, use your back-up birth control for the next forty-eight hours.
5. If you miss two or more minipills in a row, immediately start using your back-up birth control. Restart your minipills right away and double up (take twice as many pills as normal) for two days. If your menstrual period does not begin within four to six weeks, see your clinician for a pregnancy test.
6. If you have more than forty-five days without a period at any time while using the minipill, see your clinician for a pregnancy test.

Advantages
- Immediately reversible. Unlike other progestin-only methods, a woman can immediately stop using the minipill.

Disadvantages
- Low margin of error. Because the minipill has such a low dose of progestin, you must be very punctual

about taking your pills. Missing a pill by more than three hours means you must use back-up birth control for the next forty-eight hours.

Norplant

Norplant consists of six silicon capsules that are inserted just under the skin on the inside of a woman's upper arm. Approved by the Federal Drug Administration in November 1990, Norplant is one of the newest and most effective contraceptives available in the United States. It has been extensively studied for almost thirty years, and has been in active use worldwide for eight years. Altogether, more than 1.2 million women have used Norplant for birth control. Norplant is one of the most effective reversible contraceptives available, with only one pregnancy in 1,000 users (0.09 percent) during the first year of use. After five years, the failure rate rises to unacceptably high levels, and the capsules must be removed or replaced. During the first five-year period, the cumulative probability of a pregnancy occurring is less than 2 percent.

Norplant works by releasing a measured amount of a progestin-only hormone each day. Norplant insertion is usually a minor, relatively painless surgical procedure that takes about twenty minutes. Once inserted, Norplant is extremely easy to use and requires no effort from the woman to be effective. It protects against pregnancy within twenty-four hours following insertion, and the woman need not think about contraception again for five years. Norplant does not offer protection against STIs; individuals should continue to use condoms if they feel they are at risk for contracting an STI. Another important consideration with Norplant is the potential difficulty of removal. In addition to the economic cost, the removal surgery can be more complex than insertion, and it can be difficult to find a properly trained clinician.

Effectiveness. The first-year failure rate for both typical and perfect users is 0.09 percent. For a woman who uses Norplant for the full five years, the cumulative five-year failure rate is less than 2 percent (see following); thus Norplant is one of the most effective contraceptive methods available:

Failure Rate for Norplant

First year	0.09 percent
First year, typical condom user	1.20 percent
Cumulative five-year failure rate for Norplant	1.60 percent

Cost. The cost to the patient to have Norplant inserted is between $500 and $700. Over a five-year period, this averages out to about $100 to $140 per year, which compares favorably to other contraceptives such as the pill. It should be noted, however, that approximately 70 percent of Norplant users choose to have their implants removed before the end of five years; this contributes to a decreased cost effectiveness. Removal of the implants varies widely in price from $100 to $1,200.

Instructions. Norplant must be inserted by a physician. The insertion procedure is typically short and often painless. You may feel some discomfort on your arm, but that should disappear quickly.

Advantages

- Very effective long-term contraception. A single decision leads to highly effective contraception that does not depend on any day-to-day responsibility.
- Effective immediately. Norplant is effective within twenty-four hours of insertion.
- Reversible. Following surgical removal of the implants, fertility returns within twenty-four hours.
- Amenorrhea. Amenorrhea, a lack of menstrual bleeding, may be considered an advantage by some women. Over time (usually the first year of use), amenorrhea decreases in Norplant users.

Disadvantages

- Menstrual cycle disturbance. Frequent complaints include an increased number of days of light bleeding and amenorrhea (missed menstrual periods). A few women experience an increased number of days of heavy bleeding, although this is much less common. It is typical for menstrual disturbances to ease after the first few months following Norplant insertion; in the meantime, birth control pills may be prescribed to ease a woman's discomfort.
- Weight gain. Over five years of use, weight gain in Norplant users averages just under five pounds. However, there is no evidence that links this weight gain directly to Norplant.
- Breast tenderness.
- Visibility. In a few women, the implants may be visible under the skin of the upper arm.
- Difficult removal of implants for a small percentage of women. Removal may require two visits to the clinician, and it can be quite costly ($100 to $1,200). It is advisable to find a physician who is trained to remove your implants before undergoing the insertion procedure.

Depo-Provera

Depo-Provera consists of a progestin-only injection that a woman receives from her doctor once every three months. It provides very effective protection against pregnancy. Depo may be convenient for women who do not mind seeing their clinician every three months, and who want a method of birth control that they do not have to think about every day. Depo is a fairly high-dosage birth control method, and it provides no protection against STIs.

Effectiveness. The first-year failure rate in both typical and perfect users is 0.3 percent.

Cost. One injection may cost the patient $35, so the annual cost of Depo will be $140. However, there are the additional economic and convenience costs of transportation and the loss of work necessitated by repeated visits to the clinic, and these factors should be considered when evaluating the annual cost of the injections.

Instructions. Depo-Provera is a physician-administered contraceptive. A woman who uses Depo for contraceptive purposes must visit her doctor once every three months without fail. After one year or more of regular injections, a woman may develop a grace period (of up to two weeks) during which she can be late for her next shot and still not be at high risk of becoming pregnant.

Advantages

- Very private. A partner need not know that a woman is using Depo or "the shot" as it is often called.
- Culturally acceptable. Receiving medication by injection is accepted in some cultures.
- Fewer seizures. Depo decreases the frequency of seizures in women susceptible to them.
- One decision provides long-term contraception.
- Amenorrhea. The incidence of amenorrhea (no menstrual bleeding) increases over time in women using Depo. Some women consider this an advantage.

Disadvantages

- No immediate discontinuation. Unlike many other methods of birth control, Depo-Provera cannot be removed. Uncomfortable side effects disappear with the passage of time, but until the effects of the injection wear off, there is no going back.
- Repeated office visits. Some women find the requirement of receiving injections every three months unacceptable. Injections are not usually very painful.

- Lipid changes. High-density lipoprotein (the "good" lipoproteins in your blood) levels drop in women using Depo-Provera.

Other Methods

*T*here are many other methods of birth control available around the world that have not been discussed in this appendix. We have chosen to focus only on those methods that are most available and widely used by college students in this country. There are two other methods that are widely used in the United States, but that generally are not recommended for college-age couples. These methods are intrauterine devices (IUDs) and sterilization.

Intrauterine Devices (IUDs)

IUDs have been in use in the United States for over forty years. They were very popular with many women until the 1970s, when it was reported that one particular IUD (the Dalkon Shield) was associated with serious pelvic infections. Although the Dalkon Shield was subsequently removed from the U.S. market, overall IUD use in this country dropped precipitously, and negative perceptions of IUDs have continued to plague the contraceptive market. Currently, only two IUDs are approved for use in the United States. By far the more commonly used IUD is the Copper T (CuT 380A), which has been approved by the FDA for ten continuous years of use. Today's IUDs have not been shown to have the serious negative side effects of the Dalkon Shield; nevertheless, public misconceptions about their supposed dangers continue to limit use in this country.

The Copper T IUD consists of a single piece of T-shaped polyethylene, wound with fine copper wire, and a single filament of polyethylene tied to the base of the T-shape. The IUD is inserted into the uterus; and both insertion and removal must be performed by a trained physician. The exact mechanism of action of IUDs is not completely understood. Usually they prevent fertilization by immobilizing sperm or interfering with the migration of sperm from the vagina to the fallopian tubes, thus IUDs usually work by preventing fertilization. Occasionally they work by preventing implantation of a fertilized egg into the lining of the uterus. Rarely they may work by dislodging an implanted blastocyst from the lining of the uterus.

Effectiveness. The Copper T is one of the most effective methods of birth control ever approved by the

FDA. The first-year failure rate is 0.8 percent, while the cumulative seven-year failure rate is only 1.7 percent.

Cost. An IUD costs $150 to $300 at a public family planning clinic. The price includes the physician's insertion fee. Not all college health services provide IUDs.

Instructions. The IUD must be inserted by a trained physician, nurse practitioner, or physician's assistant. Insertion involves dilation (widening) of the cervix and insertion of the IUD with a long pair of forceps. Once inserted, the IUD is a very effective contraceptive, and it is very easy to use. However, IUDs provide no protection against STIs, including HIV.

Advantages

- Highly effective. The CuT 380A is the most effective long-term reversible method of birth control currently available.
- Easy to use. Once inserted, an IUD is a hands off method of birth control.
- Inexpensive. If left in the uterus for ten years, the cost per year of an IUD compares favorably with birth control pills, Norplant, Depo-Provera, and even condoms.
- Nonhormonal. May be attractive to women who have contraindications to either oral contraceptives or progestin-only birth control.
- Reversible. Fertility returns quickly following removal of an IUD.

Disadvantages

- Possibly an increased risk of PID. This is an especially important factor for nulliparous women (women who have not had children) who intend to have children in the future. Because of the higher risk of PID, nulliparous women may not be ideal candidates to receive an IUD. Although they are not necessarily excluded from IUD use, the risks of such a contraceptive need to be honestly assessed with a trained clinician.
- Menstrual problems. Some IUD users may experience increased menstrual pain (dysmenorrhea), but most IUD users experience only a minor increase in blood loss, and no increase in menstrual pain.
- Possibly an increased risk of HIV. Although further study is needed, the IUD may increase uterine bleeding, creating an environment favorable to HIV transmission; however, this risk is not well documented.
- Pregnancy complications. If a woman becomes pregnant while using an IUD, there is a 50 percent chance that the pregnancy will end in a spontaneous abortion if the IUD is left in place. Even if the IUD is removed

early in pregnancy, there remains a 25 percent chance of a spontaneous abortion. Approximately 5 percent of those women who become pregnant with an IUD in place will have an ectopic (nonuterine) pregnancy, a potentially life-threatening condition. It is important to realize that the IUD's superb contraceptive effects make any pregnancy very unlikely—so unlikely, in fact, that the overall rate of having an ectopic pregnancy is actually lower in women with IUDs than in women without.

Sterilization

Sterilization is a surgical procedure that makes a man or woman unable to conceive. In women, the procedure involves blocking the fallopian tubes to prevent the sperm and egg from uniting. In men, the procedure blocks the vas deferens to prevent the passage of sperm into the seminal fluid. Both male and female sterilization are very effective, permanent methods of birth control. Sterilization is the second most common method of birth control in the United States for women aged 15 to 44, and by far the most common method for women aged 30 to 44. Over 40 percent of women aged 35 to 44 who are at risk of pregnancy have undergone female sterilization.

The most prominent characteristic of sterilization is its permanence. Although reversal surgery is sometimes possible, it is very expensive and not always successful. Under varying circumstances, people may view the permanence of sterilization as either an advantage or a disadvantage. For individuals who are absolutely certain that they do not wish to have children in the future, sterilization is a good option. For individuals who are unsure of their future fertility plans, however, sterilization is not recommended. Most college students are not ideal candidates for sterilization because they may want to have children in the future.

If you are considering sterilization, you should realize that sterilization provides no protection against STIs, including HIV. Individuals who have been sterilized still need to take precautions against disease transmission, and quite often that means using condoms. Finally, you should know that young age is one of the highest risk factors associated with regret of the sterilization procedure. Remember, sterilization is a permanent procedure. Once you've started down this road, there is (in most cases) no turning back.

If Contraception Fails

Unintended Pregnancy

Pregnancy. Maybe the condom broke. Maybe the diaphragm was inserted improperly. Maybe no form of contraception was used at all. Maybe a woman was raped. All of these "maybes" can result in pregnancy.

When a woman learns she is pregnant, all sorts of emotions may rush through her. From anger to sadness, happiness to joy, she is caught in a situation she may have tried or hoped to avoid. Everyone reacts to an unplanned pregnancy differently. Before making a decision about what to do, she should look at all of the options available to her.

Options Soon after Sex

If the flaw linked to the contraception used is noticed immediately following the act of intercourse, or if a lack of any contraception has sparked a fear of pregnancy, you can turn to postcoital (after sex) methods. These are usually referred to as "morning after" methods, since women need to get treatment as soon as possible following unprotected intercourse. There are currently three postcoital options:

Postcoital Option 1: Morning After Pills

This method is effective up to seventy-two hours after unprotected sex, making it imperative that you see a clinician as soon as possible. This method is not a form of abortion. A pregnancy is defined as the implantation of an embryo on the uterine wall, which typically occurs ten to fourteen days after fertilization of the egg. Postcoital pills prevent the egg from implanting. They do not, how-

ever, prevent an ectopic pregnancy since that occurs outside of the uterus.

The pills are high-dose birth control pills (hormones) that can be prescribed by a clinician. The short, yet strong burst of hormones provided by the pills interferes with the hormone patterns necessary for a pregnancy to occur. Depending on which birth control pill is prescribed, you will be asked to take either two or four pills as soon as possible after unprotected sex, and then another two or four pills twelve hours later. Call your school's clinic, a physician, Planned Parenthood, or your hospital birth control clinic for these emergency contraceptive pills.

Eating prior to taking the pills will decrease your risk for nausea or vomiting. Of the women who take postcoital pills, 50 to 70 percent experience nausea and 22 percent experience vomiting as side effects. The nausea is usually mild and should stop within a day or so. If you vomit soon after taking the pills, contact your clinician to see if you need to take additional pills, and be aware that there may be other side effects from taking hormones. You should immediately see your clinician if any of the following danger signs (easily remembered by the acronym ACHES) appear in the days following the use of postcoital pills.

A abdominal pain

C chest pain, persistent cough, or shortness of breath

H headaches, dizziness, weakness, or numbness

E eye problems. Blurred or loss of vision

S severe pain in your leg (calf or thigh)

The warning signs are similar for oral contraceptive users because both expose the body to hormonal changes. Unlike the pill, a smoker can use postcoital pills, and side effects from postcoital pills should only be short term. Your menstrual period should resume within the next three weeks; if it doesn't, see your clinician for an exam and pregnancy test.

The widespread availability and use of postcoital pills could annually prevent an estimated 1 million abortions. If the threat of an unwanted pregnancy spurs a woman to action within seventy-two hours after unprotected sex, postcoital pills are an excellent option to take advantage of in terms of privacy, availability, effectiveness, and cost.

Postcoital Option 2: Insertion of Intrauterine Device

A copper IUD may be inserted into the uterus as a postcoital contraceptive for five to seven days following unprotected sex, giving you a little more time than the morning after pill to make a decision. That does not mean, however, to wait until day 7 to call a physician about this option.

The copper IUD, when inserted as a postcoital contraceptive, reduces the chance of a fertilized egg attaching itself to the uterus. It can be left in place as a form of contraception or can be removed after two normal menstrual periods. A postcoital IUD insertion is done after a pelvic exam and is extremely effective, but if you fall into any of the following categories, you may not be considered a safe candidate for the IUD as a postcoital method.

- Women just raped, since they have a high STI risk
- Women in a new relationship, since they have a high STI risk
- Women with multiple partners
- Women with a history of pelvic infection
- Women who have had an ectopic (tubal) pregnancy
- Women who have not had children

A clinician will be able to discuss with you whether the copper IUD is a wise postcoital method for you.

Postcoital Option 3: Wait and See

If your period is late, you may want to have a pregnancy test. Either go to a clinic or get a home pregnancy test, found at pharmacies and grocery stores without a prescription. While the home tests do provide privacy and are fairly easy to use, they are not quite as accurate as some clinic tests. They also cannot be used until after your first missed period. A clinic test can detect the pregnancy hormone (human chorionic gonadotropin) in your blood and urine one week following conception. The earlier a pregnancy is detected, the more time you have to think through your options and make a decision.

Dealing with an Unplanned Pregnancy

*I*f the pregnancy test is positive, more decisions need to be made. Finding someone to talk to may be very important. While a partner, relative, or friend can add emotional comfort, you may also benefit from visiting a clinic and speaking directly with a counselor. If you are hesitant about privacy at your school's clinic, visit a Planned Parenthood clinic, another family planning clinic, or a physician in private practice.

There are several options available. A decision about whether or not to continue the pregnancy to term needs to be made. The final decision to have a child depends on many factors: career and educational goals, financial resources, relationships, religious values, and personal views. While family and friends can help make you aware of your options and act as support, it is the woman herself who must feel comfortable with her decision.

Option 1: Continue the Pregnancy and Care for the Child Yourself

You may decide that while the pregnancy was not planned, you want to keep your child. If your partner does not want you to have the baby, try to envision the long-term reality of raising a child alone. Many women do it, but that does not make it easy. Deciding to have a child may require short-term and long-term lifestyle changes. For example, it is imperative to avoid smoking, alcohol, and drugs because they all can greatly affect the health of a developing fetus. If you decide to have the child, you need to speak with a clinician about prenatal care. This is important throughout all stages of the pregnancy, but especially during the first three month, which is the most vulnerable stage of fetal development.

Option 2: Continue the Pregnancy and Place the Child Up for Adoption or Foster Care

You may decide to continue the pregnancy but are not sure you and your partner are ready to care for a child once it is born. If this is the way you feel, it may be in your and your child's best interest to place your baby up for adoption or foster care. Contact an adoption agency as soon as possible if this is the course of action you plan to take.

Option 3: Abortion

A pregnancy is the implementation of a fertilized egg into the lining of the uterus, and an abortion is the interruption of a pregnancy. There are two types of abortion. A spontaneous abortion or miscarriage occurs when the embryo or fetus dies in the womb and is expelled by the body. An induced abortion occurs when a woman voluntarily decides to terminate her pregnancy. When people refer to abortion, they are usually referring to a medically induced abortion. There are approximately 1.5 million abortions annually in the United States.

While abortion is legal in the United States, states may choose to specify limitations, such as parental consent if you are a minor, a waiting period after first visiting the clinic, etc. Federal law provides access to an abortion up to the 26th week of the pregnancy, although some states have limited the number of weeks to fewer. If a woman wants to have an abortion after the state defined number of weeks, there must be proof of danger to her health or life, or proof that the fetus has severe abnormalities. A call to your local clinic can help you find out what kind of state regulations exist, if any, and abortion providers often have counselors who can help you comply with your state's laws. Do not be discouraged by these regulations if abortion is your choice of action. The United States government has established that abortion is legal.

A note of caution for those opting to terminate their pregnancy. Some clinics pose as abortion clinics but are merely offices run by pro-life groups. Their aim is to lure in and convince pregnant women that choosing abortion is wrong. The decision to have an abortion is often difficult. Having to deal with a false abortion clinic may add significantly to the trauma. Your best bet is to pick a clinic with an established reputation and physicians, nurse practitioners, or other health professionals on staff. Planned Parenthood is an example.

Abortions performed within the first thirteen weeks of pregnancy are safe. In fact, the risk of death for the mother associated with childbirth is about eleven times higher than abortion. An abortion performed after the first thirteen weeks of pregnancy is a more serious procedure and also has higher risks for complications. The most common procedure used is the vacuum curettage method. It is done subsequent to the use of a local anesthetic. Following a pelvic exam, the clinician will slightly dilate the cervix, insert the vacuum curettage, and remove the products of conception. The procedure lasts about fifteen minutes.

Although less than 1 percent of all abortion patients experience a major complication, you should be aware of danger signs following the procedure:

- Fever
- Chills
- Abdominal pain, cramping, or backache
- Tenderness (to pressure) in the abdomen
- Prolonged or heavy bleeding
- Foul vaginal discharge
- Delay of 6 weeks or more in resuming periods

These symptoms are representative of different complications including cervical or uterine trauma, hemorrhaging, infection, and intrauterine blood clots. If you experience any of these symptoms, you should immediately speak with a clinician.

Emotions after having an abortion range from relief to a sense of loss. These feelings combined with physical discomfort may make you want to forget about everything around you. It is still important, however, to follow instructions given by the abortion provider for care after the procedure. This helps prevent the possibility of any medical problems.

As soon as a decision is made to have an abortion, contact a physician or clinic to make plans. The sooner you decide, the safer and less costly the procedure.

Appendix

E

Premarital Agreements

Financial Agreements

For couples who have complicated property holdings, attorneys often advise that they draw up legal documents prior to marriage that specify how property will be disposed of should the couple divorce. An example of such an agreement follows.

PREMARITAL AGREEMENT
[OR ANTENUPTIAL CONTRACT]

This Premarital Agreement is made this ___ day of _____, 19__, between ELMER T. JONES of Centerville, Holmes (the prospective husband); and EUNICE L. GREEN of Wessex, Holmes (the prospective wife); who are also referred to as "the parties."

PREAMBLE

A. Elmer and Eunice plan to marry each other in the near future.

B. Elmer and Eunice both own substantial assets consisting of real and personal property that they wish to retain as separate property.

C. Elmer and Eunice wish to define their financial rights and obligations by this Agreement; and, except as herein stated, each wishes to retain and dispose of his or her separate property, free from any claim of the other by virtue of their contemplated marriage.

D. Elmer and Eunice now wish to fix by this Agreement the rights and claims that will accrue to each of them in the estate and property of the other by reason of this marriage, and to accept the provisions of this Agreement in lieu of, and in full settlement of, all such rights and claims.

[Optional: Both parties have been married previously, and have children by their previous marriages.]

NOW THEREFORE, IN CONSIDERATION of the mutual promises contained herein, and with the intent of being legally bound hereby, Elmer and Eunice agree as follows:

1. ***Full Disclosure.*** Each of the parties has made a full disclosure to the other of his or her financial situation, and the approximate worth of each party. A summary of Elmer's financial statement, prepared by _____, CPA, of Centerville, Holmes, is attached hereto as Schedule A. A summary of Eunice's financial statement, prepared by _____, CPA, of Wessex, Holmes, is attached hereto as Schedule B. [OR: The parties recognize that such schedules represent a reasonable approximation of the assets and liabilities, and were prepared informally without reference to documentation.] The parties further acknowledge that they have had an opportunity to review such summaries prior to the execution of this Agreement.

2. ***Property to Be Separately Owned.*** Each party, during his or her remaining lifetime, shall retain sole ownership of all of his or her respective separate property, and shall have the exclusive right to dispose of such separate property in a manner determined in the sole discretion of such owner thereof, by *inter vivos* or testamentary transfer, as if their forthcoming marriage had never taken place.
   [Note: In lieu of full disclosure, a fair provision may be made from one prospective spouse to the other. But caveat, this is a dangerous alternative, because a court may have to decide what is "fair." Under the Uniform Premarital Agreement Act, full disclosure may be waived by the parties.]

Source: Peter N. Swisher, H. Anthony Miller, and William J. Weston, *Family Law: Cases, Materials and Problems.* New York: Matthew Bender, 1990, pp. 107–112. Reprinted with permission.

Any property, either real or personal, tangible or intangible, acquired by either party before, during, or after the marriage shall be the separate property of that party; and the other party shall make no claim or demand on that separate property.

(a) This separate property includes, but is not limited to, any property acquired by purchase, exchange, gift, or inheritance.

(b) For all purposes of this Agreement the term "separate property" shall mean, with respect to each party hereto, all of that party's right, title, and interest, legal or beneficial, in or to any property, real, personal, or mixed, wherever situated, and regardless of whether now owned or hereafter acquired.

3. *Release of Marital Rights by Elmer.*

(a) Except as specifically provided herein, Elmer waives and releases all rights to any of Eunice's separate property accruing to him, or in which he may be otherwise entitled as Eunice's husband, widower, heir-at-law, next of kin, or distributee; including but not limited to such rights as curtesy or its statutory equivalent; statutory or other allowances to the spouse of a decedent, intestacy distributions, and rights of election to take against Eunice's will.

(b) Also waived and released by Elmer are any property or support rights he may otherwise be entitled to as Eunice's husband based upon the termination of the forthcoming marriage by annulment, divorce, or dissolution of the marriage; except as specifically provided herein.

4. *Release of Marital Rights by Eunice.*

(a) Except as specifically provided herein, Eunice waives and releases all rights to any of Elmer's separate property accruing to her, or in which she may be otherwise entitled as Elmer's wife, widow, heir-in-law, next of kin, or distributee; including but not limited to such rights as dower or its statutory equivalent, statutory or other allowances to the spouse of a decedent, intestacy distributions, and rights of election to take against Elmer's will.

(b) Also waived and released by Eunice are any property or support rights she may otherwise be entitled to as Elmer's wife based upon the termination of the forthcoming marriage by annulment, divorce, or dissolution of the marriage; except as specifically provided herein.

[Note: A monetary award may be given for this release, or no monetary award may be provided, because the marriage itself can be consideration for this mutual release.]

5. *Gifts Not Prohibited.*

(a) No provision of this Agreement shall prohibit either Elmer or Eunice from making a voluntary gift in any amount to his or her respective spouse, and that gift shall become the sole property of the donee spouse.

(b) Such gifts may be lawfully conveyed or transferred during the lifetime of Elmer or Eunice, or by will or otherwise upon death, and neither Elmer nor Eunice intend by this Agreement to limit or restrict in any way the right or power of any party to receive such voluntary transfer or conveyance.

(c) Any such voluntary transfer or conveyance shall be deemed to be a voluntary gift, and shall not be deemed in any way a waiver or abandonment of this Agreement or any part hereof.

6. *Jointly Held Property.* Despite any other provisions of this Agreement to the contrary, the parties may, during marriage, acquire property, or interests in property, in both their names, with or without rights of survivorship. In such an event, the signatures of both parties shall be required to acquire, sell, transfer, convey, pledge, or encumber any such jointly held property. Entry into this arrangement shall not in any way be deemed a waiver of or abandonment of this Agreement or any part hereof. The parties may also establish and contribute to a joint checking account for household expenses on which either party can draw.

7. *Rights of Children.* The parties recognize the possibility that they might have children during the course of their forthcoming marriage, whether natural born or legally adopted. The parties hereby agree that the provisions of this Agreement are not intended to govern or affect the rights of any such children in or to the property of each party hereto; and the parties agree that such property or support for the children shall be governed by applicable law.

8. *Intent of the Parties in the Event of Dissolution, Divorce, or Legal Separation.* The parties contemplate a long and lasting marriage, terminated only by death; and it is the mutual intent of Elmer and Eunice to promote and encourage their marriage through this Agreement.

Nevertheless, the parties are cognizant of the fact that the ratio of marriages to divorces in America has reached a disturbing rate. Therefore, the parties mutually desire to agree upon: (a) the disposition of their property; and (b) the disposition of their support rights; in the event that their marriage, despite their best efforts to promote it, should fail. [Note: For further authority upholding divorce planning in antenuptial agreements, see also *Ivanhoe* v. *Ivanhoe*, 397 So. 2d 410 (Fla. 1981); *Osborne* v. *Os-*

borne, 428 N.E.2d 810 (Mass. 1981); and *Jackson* v. *Jackson*, 626 S.W.2d 630 (Ky. 1982). See also the Uniform Premarital Agreement Act, § 2.01[D] *supra*. Paragraphs 8, 9, and 10 however would not be valid in those jurisdictions that have not yet legally recognized divorce planning provisions in premarital agreements.]

9. ***Payments in Lieu of Spousal Support.*** In the event that the parties' marriage is terminated by dissolution, divorce, or legal separation—regardless of which party has initiated the action, and regardless of the jurisdiction or venue of such action—the parties hereby specifically agree as follows:

(a) Elmer shall not receive any spousal support from Eunice, periodic or lump sum, which otherwise might be available to him in accordance with applicable law.

(b) Eunice shall not receive any spousal support from Elmer, periodic or lump sum, which otherwise might be available to her in accordance with applicable law.

[OR: Limit any spousal support to a certain designated sum of money over a certain designated time period. Tax planning regarding spousal support may also be involved here.]

[OR: Spousal support may be designated in certain specified contingencies.]

(c) In connection with the provisions in this Paragraph 9, each party further acknowledges that he or she:

(i) has fully and fairly advised the other, and been advised by the other, of their respective financial situations;

(ii) has a fair understanding of the financial status of the other as set forth in annexed Schedules A and B, which are made a part of this Agreement;

(iii) considers the proposed payments in limitation of spousal support as fair under the current and probable future circumstances of each party; and

(iv) in sum, considers and believes after full and fair examination of the other's finances and after the advice of independent counsel that each has made a full disclosure to the other, each has a reasonable approximation of the financial situation of the other, and each considers the payments in limitation of spousal support and in lieu of all further obligation to be more than fair. [Alternately, this paragraph may be omitted.]

10. ***Property Division upon Dissolution, Divorce, or Legal Separation*** [Paragraphs in this paragraph, similar to Paragraph 9, may be made to extinguish or limit certain property rights on dissolution, divorce, or legal separation. Alternately, this paragraph may also be omitted.]

11. ***Binding Agreement.*** This Agreement shall be binding upon and inure to the benefit of the parties, their respective heirs, administrators, legal representatives, and assigns except as it affects Paragraph 7 above.

12. ***Further Assurances.*** The parties shall take all steps to make and deliver any documents or other assurances that are reasonably required to give full force to this Agreement.

13. ***Entire Agreement.*** This Agreement contains the entire understanding of the parties, and they shall not be bound by any understandings other than those expressly set forth in this Agreement.

14. ***Subsequent Modification.*** The parties may modify the terms of this Agreement, but any modification shall not be effective unless in writing, signed by both parties, with the same formality as this Agreement.

15. ***Governing Law.*** This Agreement shall be construed and governed according to the laws of the State of Holmes.

16. ***Interpretation.*** No provision in this Agreement is to be interpreted for or against any party because that party or that party's legal representative drafted the provision.

17. ***Paragraph Headings.*** Paragraph titles or headings contained herein are inserted as a matter of convenience only, and for reference, and in no way define or describe the scope of this Agreement or any provision hereof.

18. ***Counterparts.*** This Agreement may be executed in two or more counterparts, each of which shall be an original, but all of which shall constitute one and the same Agreement.

19. ***Sanctions and Penalties.*** Should any party retain legal counsel for the purpose of enforcing this Agreement or preventing the breach of any provision hereof, or for damages for any alleged breach of this Agreement, the prevailing party shall be entitled to be reimbursed by the losing party for all costs and expenses incurred thereby, including, but not limited to, reasonable attorneys' fees and costs for the services rendered to the prevailing party.

20. ***Severability of Provisions.*** If any provision or subprovision of this Agreement shall be deemed by a

court of competent jurisdiction to be invalid, the remainder of this Agreement shall nevertheless remain in full force and effect.

21. ***Advice of Counsel—Prospective Wife.*** Eunice Green hereby declares and acknowledges that she has read and fully understands everything set forth in this Agreement; that she has sought and obtained independent advice from legal counsel of her own selection, and has been fully informed of all legal rights and liabilities with respect hereto; that after such advice and knowledge, she believes this Agreement to be fair, just, and reasonable; and that she signs this Agreement freely and voluntarily.

22. ***Advice of Counsel—Prospective Husband.*** Elmer Jones hereby declares and acknowledges that he has read and fully understands everything set forth in this Agreement; that he has sought and obtained independent advice from legal counsel of his own selection, and has been fully informed of all legal rights and liabilities with respect hereto; that after such advice and knowledge, he believes this Agreement to be fair, just, and reasonable; and that he signs this Agreement freely and voluntarily.

IN WITNESS WHEREOF, the parties have set their hands and seals to this Agreement as of the date first above written.

(SEAL)
ELMER T. JONES
(SEAL)
EUNICE L. GREEN

STATE OF HOLMES
County of Brandeis, to-wit:
This instrument was acknowledged before me this ____ day of ___, 19__ , by ELMER T. JONES.

Notary Public

My commission expires:

STATE OF HOLMES
County of Brandeis, to-wit:
This instrument was acknowledged before me this___ day of ___, 19__ , by EUNICE L. GREEN.

Notary Public

My commission expires:

Covenant Agreement

According to the U.S. Census Bureau, over 957,000 divorces were obtained in the year 2000. In an effort to curb the near 50 percent divorce rate in the United States, at least fifteen different states have adopted some type of marriage preparation/preservation legislation and/or divorce counseling or divorce waiting legisla-tion. One such piece of legislation is the Covenant Marriage Act. This legislation is a declaration of intent between the marital parties that includes an agreement to premarital education, a commitment to the preserva-tion of the marital union (including marital counseling if problems arise), and exclusive grounds for divorce or legal separation. An example of the Louisiana Covenant Marriage Law follows.

LOUISIANA COVENANT MARRIAGE ACT

Contracting a Covenant Marriage

The couple who chooses to enter into a Covenant Marriage agrees to be bound by two serious lim-itations on obtaining a divorce or separation. These limitations, that do not apply to other couples married in Louisiana, are as follows:

1. The couple legally agrees to seek marital counseling if problems develop during the marriage; and
2. The couple can only seek a divorce or legal separation for limited reasons, as explained herein.

Declaration of Intent

In order to enter into a Covenant Marriage, the couple must sign a recitation that provides:

- A marriage is an agreement to live together as husband and wife forever;
- The parties have chosen each other carefully and disclosed to each other "everything which could adversely affect" the decision to marry;
- The parties have received premarital counseling;
- A commitment that if the parties experience marital difficulties they commit to take all reasonable efforts to preserve their marriage, including marital counseling; and
- The couple must also obtain premarital counseling from a priest, minister, rabbi, or similar clergyperson of any religious sect or a marriage counselor.

After discussing the meaning of a Covenant Marriage with a counselor, the couple must also sign, together with an attestation by the counselor, a notarized affidavit to the effect that the counselor has discussed with them:

- The seriousness of a Covenant Marriage;
- The commitment to the marriage is for life;
- The obligation of the couple to seek marital counseling if problems arise in their marriage; and
- The exclusive grounds for divorce or legal separation.

The two documents which comprise the Declaration of Intent—the recitation and the affidavit with attestation—must be presented to the official who issues the marriage license with the couple's application for a marriage license.

Source: www.lafayetteparishclerk.com/covenantmarriage.html

Legal Separation in a Covenant Marriage

In order to obtain a legal separation (which is not a divorce and therefore does not end the marriage), a spouse to a Covenant Marriage must first obtain counseling and then must prove:

- Adultery by the other spouse;
- Commission of a felony by the other spouse and a sentence of imprisonment at hard labor or death;
- Abandonment by the other spouse for one year;
- Physical or sexual abuse of the spouse or of a child of either spouse;
- The spouses have lived separate and apart for two years; or
- Habitual intemperance (for example, alcohol or drug abuse), cruel treatment, or severe ill treatment by the other spouse

Divorce in a Covenant Marriage

A marriage that is not a Covenant Marriage may be ended by divorce more easily than a Covenant Marriage. In a marriage that is not a Covenant Marriage, a spouse may get a divorce for adultery by the other spouse, conviction of a felony by the other spouse and his or her imprisonment at hard labor or death, or by proof that the spouses have lived separate and apart for six months before or after filing for divorce.

In a Covenant Marriage a spouse may get a divorce only after receiving counseling and may only get a divorce for the following reasons:

- Adultery by the other spouse;
- Commission of a felony by the other spouse and sentence of imprisonment at hard labor or death;
- Abandonment by the other spouse for one year;
- Physical or sexual abuse of the spouse or of a child of either spouse;
- The spouses have lived separate and apart for two years; or
- The spouses are judicially or legally separated and have lived separate and apart since the legal separation for:

  (a) One year and six months if there is a minor child or children of the marriage;

  (b) One year if the separation was granted for abuse of a child of either spouse;

  (c) One year in all other cases.

A Note to Presently Married Couples

Couples who are already married may execute a declaration of intent to designate their marriage a Covenant Marriage. They must sign a recitation and an affidavit similar to those described here, after receiving counseling. The counselor must attest to the counseling. This intent to designate their marriage a Covenant Marriage must be filed with the official who issued their marriage license and with whom the marriage certificate of the couple is filed.

If the couple was married outside of Louisiana, a copy of their marriage certificate, with the declaration of intent, shall be filed with the officer who issues marriage licenses in the parish of the couple's domicile.

Resources and Organizations

Adoption

Adoptees' Liberty Movement Association
P.O. Box 85
Denville, NJ 07834
Phone: 973-586-1358
www.almasociety.com

Adoptive Families
42 West 38th St. Suite 901
New York, NY 10018
1-800-372-3300
www.adoptivefamilies.com

The Gladney Center for Adoption
6300 John Ryan Drive
Fort Worth, TX 76132-4122
Phone: 817-922-6088 or 1-800-GLADNEY
www.gladney.org

International Concerns for Children, Inc.
911 Cypress Drive
Boulder, CO 80303-2821
Phone: 303-494-8333
www.iccadopt.org

National Adoption Center
1500 Walnut Street, Suite 701
Philadelphia, PA 19102
Phone: 1-800-862-3678 or 1-800-TO-ADOPT
www.adopt.org

National Adoptive Information Clearinghouse
330 C Street, SW
Washington, DC 20447
Phone: 703-352-3488
www.calig.com/naic

National Council for Adoption
1930 17th Street, NW
Washington, DC 20009-6207
Phone: 202-328-1200
www.ncfa-usa.org

AIDS—See Sexually Transmitted Infections (p. 530)

Alcohol and Drug Abuse

Al-Anon Family Groups
1600 Corporate Landing Parkway
Virginia Beach, VA 23454-5617
Phone: 1-800-356-9996
www.al-anon.alateen.org

Alcoholics Anonymous
475 Riverside Drive, 11th Floor
New York, NY 10115
Phone: 212-870-3400
www.alcoholics-anonymous.org

Cocaine National Treatment and Referral
    Information Service
National Help Line
164 W 74th Street
Manhattan, NY 10023
Phone: 1-800-262-2463
www.ca.org/phones.html

Mothers Against Drunk Driving
P.O. Box 541688
Dallas, TX 75354-1688
Phone: 1-800-438-6233
www.madd.org

National Clearinghouse for Alcohol and
  Drug Information
National Clearinghouse for Drug Abuse
  Information
P.O. Box 2345
Rockville, MD 20847-2345
Phone: 1-800-729-6686
www.health.org

Phoenix House Foundation
164 W. 74th Street
Manhattan, NY 10023
Phone: 212-595-5810
www.phoenixhouse.org

Birth Alternatives

American College of Nurse-Midwives
818 Connecticut Avenue NW, Suite 900
Washington, DC 20006
Phone: 202-728-9860
www.acnm.org

DOULAS of North America (DONA)
P.O. Box 626
Jasper, IN 47547
Phone: 888-788-DONA
www.dona.org

Child Abuse

Childhelp USA® National Headquarters
15757 N. 78th Street
Scottsdale, AZ 85260
Phone: 480-922-8212
Hotline: 1-800-4-A-CHILD (422-4453)
www.childhelpusa.org

Child Welfare League of America
440 First Street NW, Suite 310
Washington, DC 20001-2085
Phone: 202-628-2952
www.cwla.org

Committee for Children
568 First Avenue South, Suite 600
Seattle, WA 98104-2804
Phone: 1-800-634-4449
www.cfchildren.org

Kempe Children's Center
1825 Marion Street
Denver, CO 80218
Phone: 303-864-5252
www.kempecenter.org

National Clearinghouse on Child Abuse and
  Neglect Information
330 C Street SW
Washington, DC 20447
Phone: 1-800-394-3366 or 703-385-7565
www.calib.com/nccanch/

National Committee to Prevent Child Abuse
332 South Michigan Avenue, Suite 1600
Chicago, IL 60604-4357
Phone: 312-663-3520
www.childabuse.org

Parents Anonymous
675 W Foothill Boulevard, Suite 220
Claremont, CA 91711
Phone: 909-621-6184
www.parentsanonymous.org

Parents United International
615 15th Street
Modesto, CA 95354
Phone: 209-572-3446
www.members.tripod.com/~Parents/United
  /Chapters/PU1.htm

Child Custody

National Partnership for Women and Families
Child Custody Project
1875 Connecticut Avenue NW, Suite 710
Washington, DC 20009
Phone: 202-986-2600
www.nationalpartnership.org

Children's Rights

Children's Rights Council
6200 Editors Park Drive, Suite 103
Hyattsville, MD 20782
Phone: 301-559-3120
www.gocrc.com

Child Support

National Child Support Enforcement
  Association
444 North Capital Street, Suite 414
Washington, DC 20001-1512
Phone: 202-624-8180
www.ncsea.org

Death of Children

The Compassionate Friends, Inc.
P.O. Box 3696
Oak Brook, IL 60522-3696
Phone: 1-877-969-0010 or 630-990-0010
www.compassionatefriends.org

American SIDS Institute
2480 Windy Hill Road, Suite 380
Marietta, GA 30067
Phone: 770-612-1030
www.sids.org

SHARE
Pregnancy and Infant Loss Support
St. Joseph Health Center
300 First Capitol Drive
St. Charles, MO 63301-2893
Phone: 1-800-821-6819
www.nationalshareoffice.com

Sudden Infant Death Syndrome Alliance
1314 Bedford Avenue, Suite 210
Baltimore, MD 21208
Phone: 1-800-221-7437
www.sidsalliance.org

Divorce and Remarriage

Association for Conflict Resolution (Academy
  of Family Mediators)
1527 New Hampshire Ave., NW, Third Floor
Washington, DC 20036
Phone: 202-667-9700
www.acresolution.org

Association of Family and Conciliation Courts
6515 Grand Teton Plaza, Suite 210
Madison, WI 53719-1048
Phone: 608-664-3750
www.afccnet.org

Stepfamily Association of America
650 J Street, Suite 205
Lincoln, NE 68508
Phone: 1-800-735-0329
www.saafamilies.org

Domestic Violence

Domestic Violence Hotline
P.O. Box 161810
Austin, TX 78716
Phone: 1-800-799-7233
www.ndvh.org

Family Violence and Sexual Assault Institute
7120 Herman Jared Drive
Fort Worth, TX 76180
Phone: 817-485-2244
www.fvsai.org

The National Coalition Against Domestic
  Violence
P.O. Box 18479
Denver, CO 80218-0749
Phone: 303-839-1852
www.ncadv.org

Pennsylvania Coalition Against Domestic
  Violence and National Resource Center
6400 Flank Drive, Suite 1300
Harrisburg, PA 17112-2778
Phone: 1-800-537-2238
www.pcadv.org

Family Planning

EngenderHealth (formerly known as
  Association for Voluntary Surgical
  Contraception)
440 Ninth Avenue
New York, NY 10001
Phone: 212-561-8000
www.engenderhealth.org

Planned Parenthood Federation of America
Seventh Avenue
New York, NY 10019
Phone: 212-541-7800
www.plannedparenthood.org

Population Connection (formerly known as
  Zero Population Growth)
16th Street NW, Suite 320
Washington, DC 20036
Phone: 202-332-2200
www.populationconnection.org

Family Services

Alan Guttmacher Institute
120 Wall Street, 21st Floor
New York, NY 10005
Phone: 212-248-1111
www.cigi-usa.org

American Family Association
P.O. Box 3206
Tupelo, MS 38803
Phone: 662-844-8888
www.afa.net

Family Service Association of America
W. Lake Park Drive
Milwaukee, WI 53224
Phone: 414-359-1040

National Council on Family Relations
3989 Central Avenue NE, Suite 550
Minneapolis, MN 55421
Phone: 763-781-9331
www.ncfr.org

Family Research Council
801 G Street NW
Washington, DC 2002
Phone: 202-393-2100
www.frc.org

Fertility

American Society for Reproductive Medicine
1209 Montgomery Highway
Birmingham, AL 35216-2809
Phone: 205-978-5000
www.asrm.org

Center for Surrogate Parenting & Egg
  Donation, Inc.
15821 Ventura Blvd., Suite 675
Encino, CA 91436
Phone: 818-788-8288

or
9 State Circle, Suite 302
Annapolis, MD 21401
Phone: 410-990-9860
www.creatingfamilies.com

Eastern Virginia Medical School
Jones Institute for Reproductive Medicine
Colley Avenue
Norfolk, VA 23507
Phone: 804-446-8948
www.jonesinstitute.org

Egg Donation, Inc. (see Center for
  Surrogate Parenting)
www.eggdonor.com

Resolve, Inc.
1310 Broadway
Somerville, MA 02144-1731
Phone: 888-623-0744
www.resolve.org

Gay and Lesbian Resources

Gay and Lesbian Medical Association
459 Fulton Street, Suite 107
San Francisco, CA 94102
Phone: 415-255-4547
www.glma.org

Lambda Legal Defense and Education Fund
6030 Wilshire Boulevard, Suite 200
Los Angeles, CA 90036-3617
Phone: 323-937-2728
www.lambdalegal.org

National Gay and Lesbian Task Force
1700 Kalorama Road NW
Washington, DC 20009-2624
Phone: 202-332-6483
www.ngltf.org

Parents, Families, and Friends of
  Lesbians and Gays
1726 M Street NW, Suite 400
Washington, DC 20036
Phone: 202-467-8180
www.pflag.org

Gender Equality

National Organization for Women
733 15 Street NW, 2nd floor
Washington, DC 20005
Phone: 202-628-8669
www.now.org

Health Information

Alzheimer's Disease and Related Disorders
    Association
919 N. Michigan Avenue
Chicago, IL 60611
Phone: 800-272-3900
www.alz.org

American Cancer Society
Clifton Road NE
Atlanta, GA 30329-4251
Phone: 1-800-ACS-2345

American Dietetic Association
216 W. Jackson Boulevard, Suite 800
Chicago, IL 60606-6995
Phone: 800-877-1600
www.adaf.org

American Institute for Preventative Medicine
30445 Northwestern Highway, Suite 350
Farmington Hills, MI 48334
Phone: 800-345-2476
www.HealthyLife.com

National Cancer Institute
Cancer Information Service
6116 Executive Blvd, MSC8322, Suite 3036
Bethesda, MD 20892-8322
Phone: 1-800-422-6237
www.nci.nih.gov

National Health Information Center
P.O. Box 1133
Washington, DC 20013-1133
Phone: 301-565-4167
www.health.gov/nhic/

Reach to Recovery
W. 56th Street
New York, NY 10019
Phone: 1-800-ACS-2345

Tel-Med, Inc.
24769 Redlands Blvd., Suite L
Loma Linda, CA 92354
Phone: 909-478-0330
www.tel-med.com

Women's Health America
1289 Deming Way
Madison, WI 53717
Phone: 1-800-558-7046
www.womenshealth.com

Infant Care

Healthy Mothers, Healthy Babies Coalition
121 North Washington Street, Suite 300
Alexandria, VA 22314
Phone: 703-836-6110
www.hmhb.org

La Leche League International, Inc.
1400 N. Meacham Road
Schaumburg, IL 60168
Phone: 847-519-7730
www.lalecheleague.org

National Organization of Circumcision
    Information Resource Centers
P.O. Box 2512
San Anselmo, CA 94979
Phone: 415-488-9883
www.nocirc.org

Marriage Enrichment

American Guidance Service
Training in Marriage Enrichment
4201 Woodland Road
Circle Pines, MN 55014
Phone: 800-328-2560
www.agsnet.com

Association for Couples in Marriage
    Enrichment
P.O. Box 10596
Winston-Salem, NC 27108
Phone: 1-800-634-8325
www.bettermarriages.org

Couple Communication Program
Interpersonal Communication Programs, Inc.
South Broadway, Suite 11
Littleton, CO 80122
Phone: 303-794-1764
www.couplecommunication.com

Prevention and Relationship Enhancement
    Program
P.O. Box 102530
Denver, CO 80250-2530
Phone: 1-800-366-0166
www.prepinc.com

Marriage and Family Therapy

American Association for Marriage and
    Family Therapy
112 South Alfred Street
Alexandria, VA 22314
Phone: 703-838-9808
www.aamft.org

National Association of Social Workers
750 1st Street NE
Washington, DC 20002
Phone: 202-408-8600
www.naswdc.org

Mental Illness

National Alliance for the Mentally Ill
Colonial Place Three
2107 Wilson Blvd., Suite 300
Arlington, VA 22201
Phone: 703-524-7600
www.nami.org

Recovery, Inc.
802 N. Dearborn Street
Chicago, IL 60610
Phone: 312-337-5661
www.recovery-inc.com

Missing Children

National Center for Missing and Exploited
    Children
699 Prince Street
Alexandria, VA 22314
Phone: 703-274-3900 or 1-800-THE-LOST
www.missingkids.com

National Network for Youth
1319 F. Street NW, 4th Floor
Washington, DC 20004-1106
Phone: 202-783-7949
www.nn4youth.org

National Runaway Switchboard
3080 N. Lincoln Avenue
Chicago, IL 60657
Phone: 1-800-621-4000
www.nrscrisisline.org

Older People

American Association of Retired Persons
601 E Street NW
Washington, DC 20049
Phone: 1-800-424-3410
www.aarp.org

Children of Aging Parents
Woodbourne Office Campus
1609 Woodbourne Road, Suite 302-A
Levittown, PA 19057
Phone: 1-800-227-7294
www.caps4caregivers.org

Gray Panthers
733 15th Street NW, Suite 437
Washington, DC 20005
Phone: 1-800-280-5362
www.graypanthers.org

National Council on Aging
409 3rd Street SW, Suite 200
Washington, DC 20024
Phone: 202-479-1200
www.ncoa.org

Parenting—see also Single Parents

The Fatherhood Project
7th Avenue, 14th Floor
New York, NY 10001
Phone: 212-465-2044
www.fatherhoodproject.org

National Center for Fathering
P.O. Box 413888
Kansas City, MO 64141
Phone: 1-800-593-DADS
www.fathers.com

Physically and Mentally Challenged

Association for Children and Adults with
Learning Disabilities
4900 Girard Road
Pittsburgh, PA 15227-1444
Phone: 412-881-2253

Learning Disabilities Association of America
4156 Library Road
Pittsburgh, PA 15234
Phone: 412-341-1515
www.ldnatl.org

Mainstream, Inc.
3 Bethesda Metro Center, Suite 830
Bethesda, MD 20814
Phone: 301-654-2400
www.mainstreaminc.org

National Information Center for Children and
Youth with Disabilities
P.O. Box 1492
Washington, DC 20013-1492
Phone: 202-884-8200
www.nichcy.org

Parents Helping Parents
The Family Resource Center
3041 Olcott Street
Santa Clara, CA 95054-3222
Phone: 408-727-5775
www.php.org

Sex Education and Sex Therapy

American Association of Sex Educators,
Counselors, and Therapists (AASECT)
P. O. Box 5488
Richmond, VA 23220-0488
www.aasect.org

Sex Information and Educational Council of
the United States
130 West 42nd Street, Suite 350
New York, NY 10036
Phone: 212-819-9770
www.siecus.org

Sexual Abuse

Incest Survivors Anonymous
World Service Office
Box 17245
Long Beach, CA 90807-7245
www.lafn.org/medical/isa/home.html

National Domestic Violence Hotline
P.O. Box 161810
Austin, TX 78716
Phone: 1-800-799-SAFE (7233)
www.ndvh.org

Sexual Violence Center
2100 Pillsbury Avenue S
Minneapolis, MN 55404
Phone: 612-871-5111
www.sexualviolencecenter.org

Victims of Incest Can Emerge Survivors
P.O. Box 13
Newtonsville, IL 45158
Phone: 1-800-7-VOICE-8
www.voices.action.org

Violence and Traumatic Stress Research Branch
Division of Epidemiology and Services Research
National Institute of Mental Health
Fishers Lane, Room 10C-24
Rockville, MD 20857
Phone: 301-443-3728
www.nimh.nih.gov

Sexually Transmitted Infections

CDC National AIDS Hotline
Phone: 1-800-342-2437
www.cdc.gov/hiv/dhap.htm

American Foundation for the Prevention of
Venereal Disease
Broadway, Suite 638
New York, NY 10003
Phone: 212-759-2069

CDC National Prevention Information Network
P. O. Box 6003
Rockville, MD 20849-6003
Phone: 1-800-458-5231
www.cdcnpin.org

CDC National STD Hotline
P.O. Box 13827
Research Triangle Park, NC 27709
Phone: 1-800-227-8922
www.cdcnpin.org/std/start.htm

Centers for Disease Control
Clifton Road
Mail Stop D25
Atlanta, GA 30333
Phone: 404-639-3286
www.cdc.gov

National Association for People with AIDS
1413 K Street, NW, 7th Floor
Washington, DC 20005-3405
Phone: 202-898-0414
www.napwa.org

National Herpes Hotline
Box 13827
Research Triangle Park, NC 27709-9940
Phone: 919-361-8488
www.ashastd.org/hotlines/herphotline.html

San Francisco AIDS Foundation
995 Market Street, Suite 200
San Francisco, CA 94103
Phone: 1-800-367-AIDS
www.sfaf.org

STD Hotline
American Social Health Association
P.O. Box 13822
RTP, North Carolina 27709
Phone: 1-800-227-8922
www.ashastd.org/index.html

Single Parents

Parents Without Partners
1650 South Dixie Highway, Suite 510
Boca Raton, FL 33432
Phone: 561-391-8833
www.parentswithoutpartners.org

Single Mothers by Choice
31 E 84th Street
P.O. Box 1642
Manhattan, NY 10028
Phone: 212-988-0993
www.mattes.home.pipeline.com

Single Parent Resource Center
200 E. 28th Street
New York, NY 10016
Phone: 212-951-7030
www.singleparentusa.com

Suicide Prevention

The Samaritans
654 Beacon Street, 6th Floor
Boston, MA 02215
Phone: 617-247-0220
www.samaritansofboston.org
www.befrienders.org

Suicide Crisis Center
Phone: 1-800-784-2433
www.suicidehotlines.com

Teenage Pregnancy

Al-Anon/Alateen Family Groups
1600 Corporate Landing Parkway
Virginia Beach, VA 23454-5617
Phone: 1-888-4AL-ANON
www.al-anon.alateen.org

Terminal Illness

Hospice Association of America
228 7th Street SE
Washington, DC 20003
Phone: 202-546-4759
www.nahc.org/HAA/home.html

National Hospice and Palliative Care Organization
1700 Diagonal Rd.
Alexandria, VA 22314
Phone: 703-837-1500
www.nhpco.org

Unintended Pregnancy

AAA Women's Services
6232 Vance Road
Chattanooga, TN 37421
Phone: 423-892-0803
www.aaawomen.org

National Abortion and Reproductive Rights
   Action League
1156 15th Street NW
Washington, DC 20005
Phone: 202-973-3000
www.naral.org

National Right to Life Committee
512 10th Street NW
Washington, DC 20004
Phone: 202-626-8800
www.nrlc.org

Religious Coalition for Reproductive Choice
1025 Vermont Avenue NW, Suite 1130
Washington, DC 20005
Phone: 202-628-7700
www.rcrc.org

Widowhood

Widowed Persons Service
AARP Grief and Loss Page
www.aarp.org/griefandloss

Work and Family

Families and Work Institute
267 Fifth Avenue, Floor 2
New York, NY 10016
Phone: 212-465-2044
www.familiesandwork.org

Glossary

ABC-X model of family stress An explanation of a family's adjustment to a stressful life event in terms of the coping skills and strategies it possesses as well as its perception of how severe the strain from the stressful event will be.

Abortion The expulsion of a fetus or embryo from the uterus.

Accessibility, parental The type of parental involvement that occurs when a parent is in the physical presence of a child but is not interacting directly with that child.

Adoption The act of lawfully assuming the parental rights and responsibilities of another person, usually a child under the age of 18.

Adversary (divorce) procedure A divorce procedure that requires one member of a married couple to file a complaint of wrongdoing against the other member.

Affinal relatives Relatives who are related only by marriage, for example, one's wife's sister.

A-frame relationship A type of relationship in which partners have very weak self-identities and are extremely dependent on each other and on the relationship.

Agape Altruistic love.

Agrarian societies Agricultural societies in which parents or other kin members select marriage mates for their children.

Aid to Families with Dependent Children A U.S. government program discontinued in 1996 which provided aid to needy families or particular family members.

Alimony A financial stipend owed to a divorced person by his or her former spouse. Also referred to as spousal support or spousal maintenance.

Altruistic parenthood A belief that parents are expected to take care of and provide for all of the children they bring into the world.

Ambivalent singles Unmarried persons who are not actively seeking mates but are open to the idea of marriage.

Androcentrism The belief that men are superior to women.

Anticipatory grief The grief experienced prior to the death of a loved one.

Artificial insemination A treatment for infertility in which a high concentration of sperm from a partner or an anonymous donor is injected into the woman's vagina with a syringe.

Asymmetrically permeable boundaries A term meaning that the influences between pairs of work-family roles run in one direction; some work-family roles affect others but not vice versa.

Attachment (post-divorce) Continuing to have thoughts about and longings for one's former spouse.

Attribution conflict A relationship-ending strategy involving an intense argument between partners that becomes the alleged reason for the breakup.

Autonomous binuclear family Divorced spouses maintain a friendly relationship, but a low level of interaction.

Bad dads Men who have little or no contact with their children and provide little or no economic support.

Bed and board divorce In English history, a divorce that allowed the husband and wife to live separately, but the legal obligations of marriage continued.

Bedevilment A form of grief in which one focuses only on the negative memories of a deceased loved one.

Bigamy Having two spouses at one time.

Binuclear family A postdivorce family in which there is a continued interaction between mothers and fathers in the interests of their children.

Biological essentialism Explaining all gender differences in terms of biology.

Bisexuals Persons who are attracted to members of more than one gender.

Blended family (see Reconstituted family)

Blue-collar couple A couple in which one or both partners is employed in a blue-collar job.

Bride price A payment by the groom's family to the bride's family which allows the marriage to take place.

Bundling The custom of engaged or courting couples sleeping together, fully clothed, in the same bed while refraining from any sexual activities.

Centrist perspective (on families) A political and intellectual position about the state of "the" family which attributes decline and deterioration to the decreasing participation of fathers.

Childfree couples Those individuals and couples who voluntarily choose not to have children.

Chronic strain model One perspective of the divorce-stress adjustment model that assumes that being divorced involves persistent strains to which former spouses and their children must adjust.

Clinical samples Research subjects who are selected for study because they are being treated for a specific personal or family problem.

Closed adoption Adoption proceedings in which the original birth certificate is sealed and a new birth certificate is prepared with the adoptive parents' names; prevents the adoptive parents and the birth parents from knowing each other's identities.

Coddling period of childrearing   The dominant cultural view of childhood from the thirteenth through the sixteenth centuries, childhood was viewed as a period of innocence and sweetness.

Code of ethics   A statement of principles or rules members of an organization follows to protect their clients.

Cognitive development theory   An explanation of gender role acquisition emphasizing that once children learn to categorize themselves and others as male or female they are strongly motivated to behave in the gender-appropriate ways of their culture.

Commitment   A component of the triangular theory of love: the decision lovers make about the current and future nature of their relationship.

Common couple violence   Violence in families that is the product of conflicts that sometimes "get out of hand."

Common law marriage   Marriage declared by government to a couple who has lived together for an extended period of time, usually seven years.

Community divorce   Changes that occur in relationships with friends and relatives during and after divorce.

Community property laws   The joint ownership of the earnings and property accumulated during a marriage, divided equally between divorcing spouses.

Commuter marriage   A situation in which each member of a couple lives in a separate household.

Companionate marriages   Marriages in which husbands and wives focus on each other more than on other family members and friends.

Companionate style of grandparenting   A relationship style in which grandparents enjoy and have fun with their grandchildren but have little direct and intimate involvement in the child's life.

Conflict   The disputes or disagreements that result when two or more people are struggling for control over resources.

Conflict-habituated marriage   A union based on built-in antagonisms between husbands and wives.

Conflict Tactics Scale   A list of specific tactics that people use when they have conflicts with a family member, used as a way of measuring family violence.

Consensual union   An intimate relationship in which partners share a home but are not legally married.

Conservative perspective (on families)   A political and intellectual position which holds that the traditional family is deteriorating and in risk of disappearing because of the widespread social changes that have occurred in its form and functions.

Consortium   A legal term used to refer to the services traditionally provided by wives to their husbands.

Constructive communication   Communication that helps to move a relationship in a positive direction, leads to growth and development, helps partners resolve differences, and provides them with emotional support.

Consummate love   According to the triangular theory of love, the type of love that includes all three major components: intimacy, passion, and commitment.

Contentious binuclear family   Divorced spouses who have a conflict-ridden relationship, but a high level of interaction.

Conversational right-of-way   The patterns of turn-taking in conversations which allow only one person to speak at a time.

Cooperative binuclear family   Divorced spouses who maintain high levels of friendship and interaction.

Coparental divorce   The stage of divorce in which custody and visitation rights for children are established.

Correlational method   The type of research in which the researchers describe and explain existing relationships.

Cost escalation   An indirect relationship-ending strategy in which one tries to get his or her partner to end the relationship by making it unrewarding to him or her.

Courtship violence   The use or threat of force or restraint carried out with the intent of causing pain or injury to a dating partner.

Covenant marriage   A recently proposed form of legal marriage that allows couples the option of selecting a more stringent set of legal requirements to govern their marriage.

Crisis model   One perspective of the divorce-stress adjustment model that assumes that divorce represents a temporary disturbance to which most individuals adjust over time.

Cross-cousin marriage   The marriage of two people who have parents who are brother and sister.

Cross-sectional (survey)   Survey data collected at only one point in time.

Crude divorce rate   The measure of divorce that reports how many divorces occurred for every 1,000 people in the population.

Cult of true womanhood   An ideology about women's place in society that developed in the late nineteenth century, emphasizing women's moral duty and responsibility to remain in the home and care for their families.

Cultural press for childbearing   The set of family, religious, ethnic, and economic pressures that encourage people to have children.

Debriefing conversations   Talks in which partners tell each other about the events they experienced while separated during the day.

Decennial census   A census of the population collected every ten years.

Deception in social research   The practice of concealing or lying about the purposes of a study.

De facto marriage   (see **Common law marriage**)

Defense of Marriage Act   A federal law passed in 1996 which stipulates that no state can be forced to recognize a same-sex marriage that was formed in another state.

Dependence   Reliance on another person for continuous support or assistance.

Dependent variable   The outcome of interest in research.

Desertion   Ending a marriage by one of the spouses leaving the marital home.

Destructive communication Communication that puts a greater distance between partners, makes them feel alienated from each other, or causes hurt feelings.

Developmental tasks Major skills that must be learned, or basic needs that must be met in a particular stage.

Direct family policy Government actions aimed explicitly at affecting families.

Direct observation In research studies, the collection of information by the researcher's watching the behavior of the study participants.

Direct sperm injection A treatment for infertility in which sperm are directly injected into eggs under a microscope.

Divorce account Each partner's description of the important events in the relationship, or characteristics of the other partner, that brought about the divorce

Divorce-stress adjustment model A conceptual model based on the common assumption that divorce is a stressful life transition to which individuals must adjust.

Domestic partnership certificate Legal recognition of a cohabiting couple that bestows upon them some legal rights while maintaining the distinction between married and unmarried couples.

Double ABC-X model of family stress An explanation of a family's adjustment to a stressful life event in terms of the coping skills and strategies it possesses as well as its perception of how severe the strain from the stressful event will be, recognizing that families experience a "pile-up" of stresses over time that may affect their ability to cope with new stresses.

Double standard of sexual behavior Traditional rules about sex that give males more sexual freedom than females.

Dowry A financial contribution to a newlywed couple from the bride's parents, typically consisting of household goods, jewelry, or livestock.

Dual-career couple A couple in which both spouses (partners) are employed full-time in high-status professions or managerial positions.

Dysfunctional When institutions and social structures have a detrimental effect on a society.

Earned Income Tax Credit A U.S. government program established in the mid-1970s that provides individuals with a tax refund if the amount of the tax credit exceeds the taxes that the worker owes.

Economic divorce A stage in the divorce process in which the couple's money and property are divided, and alimony payments are established (if necessary).

Economic maturity An individual's ability to support him- or herself and a partner.

Egalitarian beliefs Cultural beliefs that promote equality between women and men.

Emotion work An intense process of evaluating a relationship and then controlling one's feelings about the relationship.

Emotional divorce An early stage of divorce in which there is a recognition that the relationship with a spouse is deteriorating and the marriage is ending.

Emotional maturity An individual's ability to respond appropriately to a full range of situations.

Enculturated lens theory An explanation of the acquisition of gender which proposes that individuals view the world through lenses, or assumptions, especially a belief that males and females are fundamentally different, and males are superior.

Endogamy Rules, norms, social customs, and laws that call for a person to marry someone who is also a member of a group to which he or she belongs (race or religion, for example).

Engagement, parental The amount of time parents spend in one-on-one interaction with a child.

Enshrinement The result of focusing only on the positive memories of a deceased loved one, the term for excessively building emotional memorials to the deceased.

Eros Romantic love.

Ethnographies Data collected by anthropologists about the customs and practices of people in other societies.

Executive function The set of family responsibilities that includes monitoring all members' needs to ensure that they are addressed. Typically a role performed by women.

Exogamy Rules, norms, social customs, or laws that require a person to marry someone who is not a member of his or her own social group.

Experiment A highly controlled method of attempting to demonstrate the existence of a causal relationship between two variables.

Expressive roles Social roles that involve nurturing others and sacrificing one's own needs and ambitions for others.

Extended family Three or more generations sharing a home or living in close proximity.

Extreme poverty The economic condition that results when the annual income of a family of three falls below $6,930.

Fading away An indirect relationship-ending strategy in which both partners know the relationship has ended but do not discuss it.

Fait accompli A relationship-ending strategy in which one person announces to the other that the relationship is over.

Family Any sexual, intimate, or parent-child relationship in which people live together, at least some of the time, with personal commitments to each other, who identify themselves as an intimate group and who are regarded by others as an enduring group, and are economically inter-dependent to some degree.

Family and child allowances Government payments, typically awarded on a monthly basis, to help parents care for dependent children.

Family and Medical Leave Act A federal law requiring employers of fifty or more people to provide male and female employees up to twelve weeks of unpaid leave and job protection after a pregnancy or family emergency.

Family history   Social history devoted to the study of marriage and family life.

Family household   A householder and one or more people living together in the same household who are related to the householder by birth, marriage, or adoption.

Family life-cycle stage   A period of family growth and development that is determined by the presence and age of children, and to a lesser extent, by the age and employment status of parents.

Family of orientation   The family into which an individual is born.

Family of procreation   The family a person forms in adulthood.

Family policies   Government or work-place policies designed to help employees reconcile employment demands with family responsibilities.

Feminist perspective (on families)   A political and intellectual position which holds that contemporary families are stronger and more equitable than in the past because of changing gender roles and expanded options.

Feminization of love   Love defined in a feminized way, that is, in terms of nurturance, sensitivity, and verbal expression of emotions.

Feminization of poverty   The high incidence of poverty found in female-headed households.

Fertility   The childbearing patterns of a population.

Field experiments   Studies conducted under natural, not laboratory, conditions.

Field observation   Researchers making observations in a real, and thus more valid setting, over which they have little or no control of events.

Field of eligibles   The people who are available to be chosen as a partner.

Filtering process   The social process through which ineligible or incompatible individuals are eliminated from further consideration as partners.

Fixed-response question   A type of question used in social research in which respondents are asked to indicate which of a range of possible answers is most applicable to them.

Flex-time   A family-friendly policy in the workplace which allows employees flexibility in the times they arrive at work and the times they leave work to return home.

Flooding   An emotional state that results when a spouse's negativity is so overwhelming that it leaves the other totally overwhelmed and off balance.

Focused time   A type of parent-child interaction in which parents devote their full attention to their children.

Foundlings   Abandoned babies who are found on the street by strangers; common in London in the late nineteenth century; gave rise to the term "foundling homes."

Four-day work week   A workplace policy that allows workers to fit a full forty-hour work week into four days rather than five.

Four horsemen of the apocalypse   Intimate communication, both verbal and nonverbal, that includes criticism, contempt, defensiveness, and/or stonewalling, and which can signal the end of a relationship.

Four-thirds solution   A proposed strategy for balancing work and family in which each parent cuts back their work schedules to two-thirds time and devotes the extra time to their children.

Full divorce   In English history, a divorce that allowed remarriage.

Function   The positive or negative contributions of a structure to a society.

Gender   The bundle of social roles and psychological traits expected of individuals based on their biological sex.

Gender apartheid   A system of gender-based segregation and stratification in which women and girls are stripped of their basic human rights.

Gender identity   A persons conception of him- or herself as either male or female.

Gender labeling of jobs   Identification of jobs as being primarily appropriate for one sex or the other.

Gender polarization   An assumption of Bem's enculturated lenses theory: men and women are viewed as fundamentally different.

Gender role   The behaviors expected of women or men in a given society.

Gender segregation of workers   The separation of female and male workers into different types of jobs.

Gender stereotype   Rigidly held categorical beliefs that certain personality traits are inherently associated with being male or female.

General fertility rate   A statistic that compares the yearly number of births in a society to the number of women of childbearing age in the population.

Generational stake theory   The idea that family members who are at different points in the life cycle may regard their relationships differently.

Gestational surrogacy   A technique in which a woman's eggs are fertilized with her partner's sperm and the fertilized egg is implanted in another woman who will carry it to term.

Good dads   Men who try, at least minimally, to be caring supportive, and active fathers.

Habituation   The gradual development over time of increased familiarity and decreased novelty and stimulation in intimate relationships.

Harsh set-up   Initiating communication with criticism, sarcasm, and/or contempt.

Hawthorne effect   A change in behavior of persons who are being observed or studied simply because they know they are objects of study.

Hermaphrodites   (*see* **Intersexed**)

Heterogamy   Marriages in which the husband and wife belong to different social groups and categories.

Heterosexuals   Persons whose current and primary sexual orientation is toward others of the opposite sex.

H-frame relationship   A type of relationship in which partners have strong self-identities and are extremely independent of each other and of the relationship.

Hidden marriage contract   An unwritten but legally binding set of rights, responsibilities, and obligations of spouses.

Homogamy   Marriages in which the husband and wife have similar social characteristics, such as race or social class.

Homosexuals   Persons whose current and primary sexual orientation is toward others of the same sex and who act on that orientation, or would if they had the opportunity; includes gays and lesbians.

Hooking up   A slang term used to refer to engaging in brief sexual encounters.

Household   A person or group of people who occupy a housing unit.

Householder   The person in whose name a housing unit is either owned, being bought, or rented.

Hymen   Thin mucous membrane at the juncture of the vulva and the vagina.

Hymenotomies   A procedure to enlarge the hymen.

Identification theory   Sigmund Freud's explanation of gender acquisition, emphasizing how children's awareness of genital differences between women and men plays a part in their development as females or males.

Incomplete institution   A term often used to describe remarriage, due to the fact that social norms and roles are less clear for individuals in a remarriage than in an intact first marriage.

Independent variable   The factor that is believed to be the causal agent in a situation.

Indirect family policy   Government actions that affect families even though their immediate intent may not have been to do so.

Infanticide   The murder of a baby.

Infecundity   A precise term for the inability of a man or woman to conceive a child.

Infertility   The inability to become pregnant after twelve months of unprotected intercourse.

Infidelity   Extramarital sexual relations.

Instrumental roles   Traditional male responsibilities in families revolving around wage earning.

Intensive mothering   A prominent cultural view of the mother role that requires women to give top priority to addressing her children's needs.

Intermarriage   Marriage between people of different racial, ethnic, or religious groups.

Interpersonal power   One person's ability to get another person to do what he/she wants that person to do.

Intersexed   Term for an individual whose biological sex is unclear.

Intimacy   A component of the triangular theory of love: the close, connected, and bonded feelings that exist in an intimate relationship.

Intimate partner violence   A wide range of acts used to harm or control, intimidate, or dominate an intimate partner.

In vitro fertilization   A treatment for infertility in which eggs are fertilized outside a woman's body.

Involved style of grandparenting   A relationship style in which grandparents engage directly and intimately in the everyday lives of their grandchildren.

Jealousy   The emotional reaction individuals experience when they believe a relationship of value to them is being threatened in some way.

Job sharing   A workplace policy that allows two workers to split one full-time job.

Joint legal custody   After divorce, both parents are given equal rights to make decisions about the child's welfare, but the child is likely to live primarily with only one.

Joint physical custody   After divorce, both parents are given equal rights to make decisions about their child's welfare, but the child is likely to live primarily with only one, and typically the child lives a similar amount of time with each parent.

Key concepts   Specialized terms that contribute to a theory's unique vocabulary.

Khasegarien   An Iranian business meeting in which a potential marriage is discussed.

Kinderdults   The term for children who are treated simultaneously as both children and adults.

Laboratory observation   Researchers making observations in a laboratory setting. A setting that is highly controlled but may be too artificial.

Latent consequences   The unintended effects of social policies.

Launching stage   The period of family life when the younger generation prepares to make the transition to adulthood by leaving the parental home.

Learned helplessness   A theoretical proposition which holds that when women are confronted with a stressful life event they become depressed rather than take action.

Legal divorce   The stage of divorce that occurs when the state's requirements for ending a marriage are carried out.

Legitimate authority   The right and responsibility to exercise control over others.

Liberal feminism   A feminist view that emphasizes how inequality and oppression of women are based on sexist ideology and ignorance.

Liberal perspective (on family)   A political and intellectual position which holds that changes in contemporary families are not leading to deterioration but are, in fact, increasing their strength and resilience.

Life expectancy   The average number of years a person can expect to live from birth or a given age.

Longitudinal research   Studies that follow people over a period of time, collecting information from them at different times; used to study change in behavior.

Ludus   Game-playing love.

Mania   Possessive love

Marital adjustment   A measure of marital quality that combines questions that reflect feelings *and* questions about interaction, communication, and conflicts.

Marital quality   A generic term that covers how happy, satisfactory, and stable a marriage is.

Marital rape   The use of force, coercion, or violence by husbands in order to have sex with their wives.

Marital scripts   Expectations a person has about what is appropriate behavior for husbands and wives.

Marital stability   Refers to whether a married couple stays together; the marriage does not end by separation, divorce, or other means.

Marital success A term that reflects both marital stability and marital satisfaction/happiness.

Marriage and family enrichment (also called enhancement) Programs designed to strengthen couples or families.

Married couple household A household in which the householder is married and living with his or her spouse.

Mediation (divorce) A specially trained, neutral person meets with two divorcing people, hears their respective claims, and tries to move them toward a mutual agreement.

Metamessages Cultural messages about what traits are valued and which differences between people are significant.

M-frame relationship A relationship in which both partners have high self-esteem and a strong individual identity but still value the connections they have to each other.

Micro-inequities Subtle forms of discrimination that single out, ignore, or discount women and their contributions simply on the basis of gender.

Modeling (imitating) An explanation of gender acquisition through imitation of the behavior of same-sex parents (as well as siblings, teachers, and others).

Modulation of dependency The state of a parent-child relationship in late adolescence or early adulthood in which a child's increasing independence (autonomy) balances his or her continuing emotional attachment to his or her parents.

Monogamy A marriage rule that allows only one marriage partner at a time.

Moralistic period of child rearing The dominant cultural view of childhood from the sixteenth through the eighteenth century, childhood was viewed as a period during which children must be disciplined and prepared for adulthood.

Morbidity Illness patterns in a society.

Multigenerational household A household that consists of the householder and his or her children and grandchildren.

Mutual dependence An advanced stage in the development of love in which partners develop joint routines and consider each other's needs when they make decisions.

Mutual mothering A mother-daughter relationship characterized by a mutual propensity for mothers and daughters to supervise each other's lives.

Near poverty The economic state that results when the annual income of a family of three is no greater than $22,722.

Negative sentiment override A state in which the negative emotions shared by a couple far outnumber the positive emotions.

Negotiated farewell A relationship-ending strategy in which both partners recognize the problems with the relationship and mutually agree to end it.

No-fault divorce Granting of divorce on the grounds of irreconcilable differences, irretrievable breakdown, or incompatibility; the opposite of adversary divorce.

Nonfamily household A household in which a person lives alone or a householder shares his or her home with nonrelatives only.

Nonmarital cohabitation Couples who live together without being married.

Nuclear family A married couple and their children.

Nurture assumption The belief that parents are the most important part of a child's environment.

Observational studies Research in which the researcher gathers data on the behavior of interest by observing it directly.

Omnibus clause Clause added to divorce laws in the nineteenth century which allowed courts to grant divorces in certain circumstances beyond customary grounds.

Open adoption Proceedings in which the biological parents and the adoptive parents are known to each other.

Open-ended question A question to which the respondent is free to give an answer in his or her own words.

Opportunity costs The lost wages, lost promotions, and lost seniority that may come from dropping out of the labor force to have a baby.

Overburdened child After a divorce, a child who tries to meet all of the parent's needs.

Parallel-cousin marriage The marriage between cousins who have parents who are same-sex siblings.

Parental echelon The parents' level of authority in intact marriages.

Parliamentary divorce In English history, a divorce granted by the House of Lords that allowed remarriage.

Participant observation Observations by a researcher who participates in the behavior he or she is observing.

Part-time/limited cohabiting relationship The type of cohabiting relationship that develops without much conscious deliberation or discussion between the partners and often lasts for only a short time.

Passion A component of the triangular theory of love: the psychological and physiological drives that lead to romance, physical attraction, and sexual consummation.

Patriarchal marriage A marriage in which the husband is given absolute authority over his wife.

Patriarchal terrorism Violence, almost exclusively initiated by men, as a way of gaining and maintaining total and absolute control over their female partners.

Patriarchy "Rule of the father"; the nearly universal belief that men have a "natural" right to be in control of their families.

Peerlike relations, mothers and daughters A mother-daughter relationship in which mothers and daughters are close friends.

Peer marriage Relationships that are built on equity (where each partner gives to the relationship in the same proportion that she or he receives) and equality (each partner has equal status and is equally responsible for emotional, economic, and household duties).

Perpetrator (of child abuse) A person who has maltreated a child while in a care-taking relationship to that child.

Personality need fulfillment   The final stage in the development of love relationships in which partners find that they are better able to meet their basic human needs as a result of the emotional exchange and mutual support provided by their partner.

Physical assault   Behaviors that threaten, attempt, or actually inflict physical harm.

Plural marriage   A situation in which a person is married to two or more spouses simultaneously. Another term for polygamy.

Polyandry   A marriage rule that allows females to have more than one husband at one time.

Polygamy   A marriage rule that allows more than one spouse at a time.

Polygyny   A marriage rule that allows males to have more than one wife at one time.

Positive sentiment override   A state in which the positive emotions shared by a couple far outnumber the negative emotions.

POSSLQ   Acronym for persons of opposite sex who share living quarters.

Poverty line   The point on the economic scale at which a family of three has an annual income of $13,681.

Power   The ability to make someone else do what one wants them to do.

Pragma   Practical love.

Premarital cohabitation (same as trial marriage)   A type of cohabiting relationship in which two people who plan to marry, live together until their marriage.

Primary infertility   The inability to conceive among those who have never had children.

Primary prevention   A stage in marriage/family therapy that occurs when couples enter counseling, even though they have no current severe problems, to acquire resources and abilities that will help them avoid problems in the future.

Principle of least interest   A theoretical proposition which holds that when one partner in a relationship is more dependent or involved in the relationship, he or she will have less power.

Private separation agreement   In English history, an agreement between a husband and wife on how to divide their property and money and keep their finances separate in the future.

Profession   A high-status, knowledge-based occupation that has autonomy and authority over clients.

Pronatalism   Dominant societal values that encourage childbearing.

Propinquity (see also Residential propinquity)   Geographic closeness, which is an important factor in the mate selection process.

Pseudo-deescalation   An indirect relationship-ending strategy in which one or both partners state that they want the relationship to be less close or intense, when they actually want the relationship to end.

Psychic divorce   The stage of divorce when an individual identity and independence from one's spouse is established.

Pull factors   Positive aspects of being unmarried that attract an individual to singlehood.

Purdah   An Islamic practice that prohibits a woman from leaving her home except with her husband's permission and only then with her face and body fully covered by loose garments.

Push factors   Negative aspects of being married that cause an individual to reject it in favor of singlehood.

Quasi-experiment   A research method that meets some but not all of the strict standards of a true experiment.

Race defensiveness   A racial socialization strategy that cultivates a dislike for other racial groups among children, but teaches them that is can be useful to imitate the behavior of the dominant racial group.

Race naivete   A racial socialization strategy that downplays the importance of racial issues.

Racial awareness   A racial socialization strategy that teaches children to be proud of their racial group membership.

Racial empowerment   A proactive racial socialization strategy that stresses racial identity and the ability to overcome obstacles in life despite racial barriers.

Racial socialization   The process by which a child learns where he or she fits into the racial context of his or her society.

Radical feminism   A type of feminism that emphasizes how sexual oppression by men leads to the lower status of women.

Random assignment   The process of assigning research subjects to experimental groups without regard to any preexisting characteristics.

Random sampling   A method of choosing research participants which guarantees that every person in the population has an equal change of being selected.

Rape   Any type of sexual activity performed against another person's will, through the use of physical force, threats of force, continual arguments or verbal pressure, use of alcohol and/or drugs, or holding a position of authority over the victim.

Rapport   An initial stage in the development of love, specifically attraction and a feeling of being comfortable with a new partner.

Rapport talk   Debriefing conversations that are viewed by women as a way of strengthening the relationship between partners.

Realistic conflict   Conflict over different interest, values, or goals.

Reciprocity   The unwritten rule of social interaction which holds that when two people (or groups) are in a relationship, the exchanges between them must be of equal or nearly equal value.

Reconstituted family (also blended family and stepfamily)   A remarriage into which one or both partners bring children.

Refined divorce rate   The number of divorces in a year per 1,000 married women.

Rehabilitative alimony   Financial support for a divorced person only until that person is self-supporting.

Relationship maturity   An individual's ability to communicate clearly and effectively with a partner.

Relationship withdrawal   An indirect relationship-ending strategy in which the person desiring to end the relationship spends less and less time with his or her partner.

Reliability (statistical)   Consistency of data.

Remote-uninvolved style of grandparenting   A relationship style in which grandparents have relatively little contact or interaction with their grandchildren.

Repair attempt   Term used to refer to any statement or action an intimate partner takes to prevent the negativity in a conflict from escalating out of control.

Replacement rate   The rate of reproduction needed for a population to maintain its current size, without immigration into a country.

Report talk   Debriefing conversations that are viewed by men primarily as a source of information.

Residential propinquity   The tendency of people to marry someone who lives relatively close to where they live.

Resigned singles   Unmarried persons who want to be married but accept the fact that they will probably never marry because they have not been able to find an acceptable partner.

Resolved singles (*see* **Resigned singles**)

Resources   Any objects, possessions, and services that are valued by members of a society.

Resource theory   An explanation of the balance of power in families based on the members' relative control over valued resources.

Responsibility, parental   The most complete type of parental involvement with a child; involves planning, making decisions, and organizing activities for the child.

Responsible daughters with dependent mothers   A mother-daughter relationship in which daughters have taken on the role of caring for their mothers.

Responsible mothers with dependent daughters   A mother-daughter relationship in which mothers still view themselves as responsible for their daughters.

Role   The behavior generally expected of someone who occupies a particular position in a society or social group.

Role overload   Having too many responsibilities to perform in a limited amount of time.

Role segregation (of marriage)   A pattern of role performance in which wives and husbands perform specialized tasks and engage in few joint activities, especially leisure activities.

Role transition events   Traditional events or occurrences that cultures use to signify movement from one developmental stage to another.

Sandwich generation   The group of middle-aged individuals who may serve as a bridge between their adult children and elderly parents.

Santification   A form of grief in which one focuses only on the positive memories of a deceased loved one.

Scripts   Cognitive schemes used to organize common experiences such as dating and sexual involvement that are usually composed of a set of stereotypical actions.

Secondary infertility   The difficulties some couples face when they try to have additional children.

Second shift   A term coined by sociologist Arlie Hochschild, referring to women's responsibility for performing most, if not all, of the household labor after putting in a full-day's work on a paying job.

Self-concept   A person's thoughts and feelings about him- or herself.

Self-disclosure   The process of revealing one's thoughts and feelings to another person.

Self-image   The evaluation of oneself based on the words of significant others.

Self-report data   In research studies, verbal information provided by study participants.

Self-revelation   A second stage in the development of love in which the partners provide information about themselves.

Serial monogamy   A term sometimes used to emphasize that in societies with high divorce and remarriage levels, people have one spouse following another.

Severed binuclear family   Divorced spouses who have a conflict-ridden relationship and a low level of interaction.

Sex   The biological aspects of anatomy and physiology that are associated with reproduction and used as markers of "maleness" and "femaleness."

Sex (or gender) segregation   (*see* **Gender segregation**)

Sex ratio   The number of men in a population for every 100 women.

Sexual abuse (of children)   Sexual maltreatment of a child by a caretaker who is at least five years older than that child.

Sexual orientation   An enduring emotional, romantic, sexual, and/or affective attraction to individuals of a particular sex/gender.

Sexual revolution   Long-term changes in a culture's dominant sexual attitudes and behaviors.

Sexual scripts   The ideas people have about appropriate sexual partners, sexual activities, and sexual purposes; learned from the culture, interpersonal communication, personal thoughts, desires, and fantasies.

Sibling aggression   Angry behavior by a sibling toward another sibling that is often the result of rivalry

Sibling rivalry   The characterization of brothers and sisters as jealous of each other and contending for the attention of their parents.

Significant others   People who are instrumental in the process through which we learn the meaning of symbols and appropriate ways to behave in our society, and develop a sense of our "self."

Single-parent providers   A household in which an unmarried parent is primarily, if not solely, responsible for fulfilling all of the children's emotional and economic needs.

Social exchange theory   A social theory emphasizing that the motivations for human behavior lie in costs and rewards.

Social history   Historical research devoted primarily to the lives of ordinary people.

Social incompatibility A category of factors characterized by discrepancy in age, educational aspirations, or religious orientations that contribute to the termination of a relationship.

Social institution The patterned, regular way in which a society has organized to meet its basic needs.

Social learning theory An explanation of the acquisition of gender through reinforcement of what is considered gender-appropriate behavior by adults.

Social network influences A category of factors characterized by parental disapproval of the relationship that contribute to the termination of a relationship.

Social status hypothesis A theoretical proposition which explains married women's greater likelihood of being depressed in terms of the limited satisfaction they may find in traditional roles of homemaker and mother.

Social stratification The patterned ways in which privileges and rewards are distributed in a society, resulting in social classes or strata.

Social theory A set of ideas that provides explanations for a broad range of social phenomena.

Socialist feminism A feminist view that emphasizes how inequality and oppression of women are based on the economic structure of society—the social institutions created by those in power.

Socialization The process through which a person learns and generally comes to accept the ways of his or her group or society and acquires a unique character or personality.

Sociobiology A scientific theory that draws on biological principles to explain human behavior.

Sole custody One parent is given the rights and responsibilities to provide for the physical, moral, and mental well-being of the child.

Split custody Custody of the children is split between the parents with the mother having sole custody of some and the father sole custody of others.

Stalking Hostile conduct involving repeated visual or physical proximity, nonconsensual communication, and threats directed at a specific person that cause fear in that person.

State-of-the-relationship talk A relationship-ending strategy in which one person tells the other during a discussion of their perception of the problems with the relationship.

Stepfamilies (*see* Reconstituted families)

Stereotype A rigidly held belief that a category of people has a particular set of personal characteristics.

Sterility A precise term for the inability of a man or woman to conceive a child.

Storge A style of love that emphasizes close friendship above everything else.

Strategic family therapy A specific and fairly uniform strategy that aims to quickly uncover the source of relationship problems and reduce disruptive behavior in a short time.

Structural buffers Factors that dampen the impact of some work-family roles on others.

Structure The regular and patterned activities of a society.

Substitute marriage A type of cohabiting relationship in which couples do not plan to marry but have a lifelong commitment to each other; viewed as a permanent alternative to marriage by the partners.

Surrogate mothering A technique that is used to help an infertile couple become parents, involving the impregnation of a woman who has agreed to carry a baby for the infertile couple.

Survey research A study in which a large number of people are asked to answer questions through questionnaires or interviews.

Swaddling A practice of wrapping an infant tightly in cloths so that it cannot move its arms or legs; believed to calm nervous infants.

Swinging A slang term referring to a couple's consensual and mutual involvement in extra marital sexual relationships with other couples.

Symbols Words, gestures, facial expressions, and objects that have specific meanings for people in a given society.

Systematic collection of data Research carried out according to a strategic plan detailing the number and characteristics of respondents, the way in which respondents will be obtained, and the questions that will be asked (or behaviors observed).

Temporary Assistance for Needy Families A U.S. government program initiated in 1996 which provides aid to needy families or particular family members.

Total fertility rate A statistic that is used to predict the number of births each woman in a population would have if the current fertility patterns continued into the future.

Traditional family A family form in which the husband is employed and the wife is a homemaker.

Transition to parenthood The personal and relational changes that parents experience with the birth of their first child.

Transracial adoption Adoption of a child of one race or ethnic group by adoptive parents who are of another race or ethnic group.

Trial marriage (*see* Premarital cohabitation)

Triangular theory of love A theory that identifies three components of love (passion, intimacy, and commitment), developed by Robert Sternberg.

Two-person career The unpaid, but nonetheless expected participation of a woman in her husband's all-consuming career.

Typology A set of types used to differentiate between or among persons, processes, or objects in order to facilitate scientific study.

Underlying assumptions Those aspects of family life that a theory takes for granted in order to simplify its focus.

Unit of analysis The level at which a theory focuses, that is, whether it attempts to explain individual (micro) or societal (macro) level phenomena.

Vagina A sexual and reproductive organ of the female body located in the pelvic region and composed of multiple layers of muscle tissues.

Validity   Accuracy (of data).

Value maturity   An individual's awareness of and confidence in the goals and ideas he or she holds in highest priority.

Vermont Civil Union Law   Effective July 1, 2000, this law provides same-sex couples in Vermont with many of the traditional benefits and protections of legal marriage.

Vital statistics   Information about birth, death, illness, marriage, divorce, and major life events in a population.

Vulva   The region of the female body that includes the labia majora and minora, the clitoris, and the vaginal opening.

Wet-nursing   The practice of hiring a woman who has recently given birth to breastfeed one's own baby.

Wishful singles   Unmarried persons who hope to marry in the future and are actively trying to find a suitable mate.

References

Abel, Gene G., Becker, Judith, Cunningham-Rathner, Jerry, Mittelman, Mary, and Rouleau, Joanne L. "Multiple Paraphiliac Diagnoses Among Sex Offenders." *Bulletin of the American Academy of Psychiatry and the Law* 16, 1988: 153–168.

Adamec, Christine A. *The Encyclopedia of Adoption.* New York: Facts on File, 1991.

Adams, Jeffrey, and Jones, Warren. "The Concept of Commitment: An Integrative Analysis." *Journal of Personality and Social Psychology* 72(5), 1997: 1177–1196.

Adams, Lorraine. "Too Close for Comfort." *Washington Post,* April 2, 1995, pp. F1, F4, F5.

Adams, S., Kuebli, J., Boyle, P. A., and Fivush, R. "Gender Differences in Parent-Child Conversations About Past Emotions: A Longitudinal Analysis." *Sex Roles* 33, 1995: 309–323.

Ade-Ridder, Linda. "Sexuality and Marital Quality Among Older Married Couples." In Timothy H. Brubaker (ed.), *Family Relationships in Later Life*, pp. 48–67. Newbury Park, CA: Sage, 1990.

Ahrons, Constance R. "The Binuclear Family: Two Households, One Family." *Alternative Life Styles* 2, 1979: 499–515.

Ahrons, Constance R., and Rodgers, Roy H. *Divorced Families: A Multidisciplinary Developmental View.* New York: Norton & Company, 1987.

Alan Guttmacher Institute. "Minors and the Right to Consent to Health Care." *The Guttmacher Report on Public Policy* 3(4), 2001: 4–9.

Aldous, Joan. *Family Careers: Rethinking the Developmental Perspective.* Thousand Oaks, CA: Sage, 1996.

Aldous, Joan, and Dumon, Wilfred. "Family Policy in the 1980s: Controversy and Consensus." *Journal of Marriage and the Family* 52, 1990: 1136–1151.

Allen, Katherine R. "The Dispassionate Discourse of Children's Adjustment to Divorce." *Journal of Marriage and the Family* 55, 1993: 46–49.

Allen, Katherine R. "Reflexivity in Qualitative Analysis: Toward an Understanding of Resiliency among Older Parents with Adult Gay Children." In McCubbin, H. I., Thompson, E. A., Thompson, A. I., and Futrell, J. A. (eds.), *The Dynamics of Resilient Families*, pp. 71–93. Thousand Oaks, CA: Sage Publications, 1999.

Altman, I., and Haythorn, W. W. *Social Penetration: The Development of Interpersonal Relations.* New York: Holt, Rinehart & Winston, 1965.

Alwin, Duane F. "Cohort Replacement and Changes in Parental Socialization Values." *Journal of Marriage and the Family* 52, 1990: 347–360.

Amato, Paul R. "Children's Adjustment to Divorce: Theories, Hypotheses, and Empirical Support." *Journal of Marriage and the Family* 55, 1993a: 23–38.

Amato, Paul R. "Family Structure, Family Process, and Family Ideology." *Journal of Marriage and the Family* 55, 1993b: 50–54.

Amato, Paul R. "The Impact of Divorce on Men and Women in India and the United States." *Journal of Comparative Family Studies* 25, 1994: 207–221.

Amato, Paul R. "Children of Divorced Parents as Young Adults." In E. Mavis Hetherington (ed.), *Coping with Divorce, Single Parenting, and Remarriage: A Risk and Resiliency Perspective*, pp. 147–164. Mahwah, NJ: Erlbaum, 1999.

Amato, Paul R. "The Consequences of Divorce for Adults and Children." *Journal of Marriage and the Family* 62(4), 2000: 1269–1287.

Amato, Paul R., and Keith, Bruce. "Parental Divorce and Adult Well-Being: A Meta-Analysis." *Journal of Marriage and the Family* 53, 1991: 43–58.

American Association for Protection of Children. *Highlights of Official Child Neglect and Abuse Reporting, 1986.* Denver, CO: American Humane Association, 1988.

American Civil Liberties Union. Status of U.S. Sodomy Laws. www.aclu.org/issues 1999.

American Infertility Institute. "Who's Infertile? Us? Interpreting the Red Flags, Flashing Lights, and Other Warning Signs." The American Infertility Institute Fact Sheet. New York: Author, 2001.

American Society for Reproductive Medicine. *Fact Sheet: In vitro Fertilization.* Birmingham, AL: Author, 2001.

Anderson, Stephen A., Russell, Candyce S., and Schumm, Walter R. "Perceived Marital Quality and Family Life-Cycle Categories: A Further Analysis." *Journal of Marriage and the Family* 45, 1983: 127–139.

Angier, Natalie. "Does Testosterone Equal Aggression? Maybe Not." *New York Times,* June 20, 1995, pp. A1, B6.

Applebome, P. "No Room for Children in a World of Little Adults." *New York Times,* May 10, 1998, pp. 1, 3.

Appleson, Gail. "Deadbeat Dad to Challenge Child Support Law." *Reuters North American Wire,* January 30, 1996.

Aquilino, William S. "The Likelihood of Parent–Child Coresidence: Effects of Family Structure and Parental Characteristics." *Journal of Marriage and the Family,* 52, 1990: 405–419.

Aquilino, William S. "Family Structure and Home Leaving: A Further Specification of the Relationship." *Journal of Marriage and the Family* 53, 1991: 999–1010.

Aquilino, William S. "Two Views of One Relationship: Comparing Parents' and Young Adult Children's Reports of the Quality of Intergenerational Relationships." *Journal of Marriage and the Family* 61(4), 1999: 858.

Aquilino, William S., and Supple, Khalil. "Parent–Child Relations and Parent's Satisfaction with Living Arrangements When Adult Children Live at Home." *Journal of Marriage and the Family* 53, 1991: 13–27.

Arendell, Terry. "Conceiving and Investigating Motherhood: The Decade's Scholarship." *Journal of Marriage and the Family* 62(4), 2000: 1192–1207.

Arensberg, C., and Kimball, S. *Family and Community in Ireland.* Cambridge, MA: Harvard University Press, 1940.

Ariès, Phillipe. *Centuries of Childhood: A Social History of Family Life.* New York: Knopf, 1962.

Arnett, Jeffrey. "Young People's Conception of the Transition to Adulthood." *Youth and Society* 29(1), 1997: 3–23.

Aronson, J. "Women's Sense of Responsibility for the Care of Old People: But Who Else Is Going to Do It?" *Gender and Society* 6, 1992: 6–20.

Ashley, Jane. "Apart, Yet Together." *Washington Post*, February 8, 1994, p. C5.

Associated Press. "Boy Seeks Homecoming Queen Run." October 1, 1999.

Atkinson, Maxine P., and Blackwelder, Stephen P. "Fathering in the 20th Century." *Journal of Marriage and the Family* 55, 1993: 975–986.

Avery, Roger, Goldscheider, Frances, and Speare, Alden, Jr. "Feathered Nest/Gilded Cage: Parental Income and Leaving Home in the Transition to Adulthood." *Demography* 29, 1992: 375–388.

Baca Zinn, Maxine, and Eitzen, Stanley. *Diversity in Families* (6th ed.). Boston: Allyn and Bacon, 2002.

Bachu, Amara. "Fertility of American Women: June 1995 (update)." U.S. Bureau of the Census, *Current Population Reports*, Series P-20, no. 499. Washington, DC: U.S. Government Printing Office, 1999.

Ballard-Reisch, D., and Elton, M. "Gender Orientation and the Bem Sex-Role Inventory: A Psychological Construct Revisited." *Sex Roles* 27, 1992: 291–306.

Balswick, Jack. *The Inexpressive Male.* Lexington, MA: Lexington Books, 1986.

Bandura, A. *The Social Foundations of Thought and Action: A Social Cognitive Theory.* Englewood Cliffs, NJ: Prentice Hall, 1986.

Barbash, Fred. "Ireland Debates Allowing Divorce." *Washington Post*, November 16, 1995a, p. A31.

Barbash, Fred. "Irish Vote to Lift Ban on Divorce." *Washington Post*, November, 1995b, pp. A1, A32.

Barich, Rachel, and Bielby, Denise. "Rethinking Marriage: Change and Stability in Expectations, 1967–1994." *Journal of Family Issues* 17(2), 1996: 139–160.

Barnett, Rosalind C., Kibria, Nazli, Baruch, Grace K., and Pleck, Joseph. "Adult Daughter–Parent Relationships and Their Associations with Daughters' Subjective Well-Being and Psychological Stress." *Journal of Marriage and the Family* 53, 1991: 29–42.

Bartholome, Adreanna, Tewksbury, Richard, and Bruzzone, Alex. "I Want a Man: Patterns of Attraction in All-male Personal Ads." *Journal of Men's Studies* 8(3), 2000: 309.

Bartowski, John. *Remaking the Godly Marriage: Gender Negotiation in Evangelical Families.* New Brunswick, NJ: Rutgers University Press, 2001.

Baucom, D. H., and Epstein, N. *Cognitive-Behavioral in Marital Therapy.* New York: Brunner/Mazel, 1990.

Baumrind, Deborah. "Parenting Styles and Adolescent Development." In R. M. Lerner, A. C. Peterson, and J. Brooks-Gunn (eds.), *Encyclopedia of Adolescence*, pp. 746–758. New York: Garland, 1991.

Baxter, L. "Accomplishing Relationship Disengagement." In S. Duck and D. Perlman (eds.), *Understanding Personal Relationships*, pp. 243–265. London: Sage, 1986.

Baydar, Nazli, and Brooks-Gunn, Jeanne. "Effects of Maternal Employment and Child-care Arrangements on Preschoolers' Cognitive and Behavioral Outcomes: Evidence from the Children of the National Longitudinal Survey of Youth." *Developmental Psychology* 27, 1991: 932–945.

Belsky, Jay. "Children and Marriage." In Frank D. Fincham, and Thomas N. Bradbury (eds.), *The Psychology of Marriage: Basic Issues and Applications*, pp. 172–200. New York: Guilford Press, 1990a.

Belsky, Jay. "Parental and Nonparental Child Care and Children's Socioemotional Development: A Decade in Review." *Journal of Marriage and the Family* 52, 1990b: 885–903.

Becker, Gary. *A Treatise on the Family.* Chicago: University of Chicago Press, 1991.

Belsky, Jay, and Eggebeen, David. "Early and Extensive Maternal Employment and Young Children's Socioemotional Development: Children of the National Longitudinal Survey of Youth." *Journal of Marriage and the Family* 53, 1991: 1107–1110.

Belksy, Jay, and Kelly, John. *The Transition to Parenthood: How a First Child Changes a Marriage—Why Some Couples Grow Closer and Others Apart.* New York: Delacorte, 1994.

Belsky, Jay, Lang, Mary E., and Rovine, Michael. "Stability and Change in Marriage Across the Transition to Parenthood: A Second Study." *Journal of Marriage and the Family* 47, 1985: 855–865.

Belsky, Jay, Spanier, Graham B., and Rovine, Michael. "Stability and Change in Marriage Across the Transition to Parenthood." *Journal of Marriage and the Family* 45, 1983: 567–577.

Bem, S. L. *The Lenses of Gender: Transforming the Debate on Sexual Inequality.* New Haven, CT: Yale University Press, 1993.

Bengston, Vern L. "Is the 'Contract Across Generations' Changing? Effects on Population Aging on Obligations and Expectations Across Age Groups." In Vern L. Bengston, and W. Andrew Achenbaum (eds.), *The Changing Contract across Generations*, pp. 3–23. New York: Aldine de Gruyter, 1993.

Benokraitis, Nijole V. *Feuds about Families: Conservative, Centrist, Liberal, and Feminist Perspectives.* Upper Saddle River, NJ: Prentice-Hall, 2000.

Berardo, Donna, Shehan, Constance L., and Leslie, Gerald L. "A Residue of Tradition: Jobs, Careers, and Spouses' Time in Housework." *Journal of Marriage and the Family* 49, 1987: 381–390.

Berardo, Felix. "Widowhood." In James J. Ponzetti (ed.), *International Encyclopedia of Marriage and the Family* (2nd ed.). New York: Macmillan Reference USA, 2002.

Berardo, Felix. "Widowhood: Its Social Implications." In Clifton D. Bryant (ed.), *Handbook of Thanatology: Essays on the Social Study of Death.* Thousand Oaks, CA: Sage. In press.

Berk, Richard A., Campbell, Alec, Klap, Ruth, and Western, Bruce. "The Deterrent Effect of Arrest in Incidents of Domestic Violence: A Bayesian Analysis of Four Field experiments." *American Sociological Review* 57, 1992: 698–708.

Berman, William H. "Continued Attachment after Legal Divorce." *Journal of Family Issues* 6, 1985: 375–392.

Berry, Mary Frances. *The Politics of Parenthood: Child Care, Women's Rights, and the Myth of the Good Mother.* New York: Viking Press, 1993.

Berscheid, E., and Walster, E. "Physical Attractiveness." *Experimental Social Psychology* 7, 1974: 157–215.

Berscheid, Ellen and Reis, Harry T. "Attraction and Close Relationships," pp. 193–281. In Gilbert, D. T., Fiske, S. T., and Lindzey, G. (eds.), *The Handbook of Social Psychology* (4th ed.), Boston: McGraw-Hill, 1998.

Bielby, William, and Bielby, Denise. "I Will Follow Him: Family Ties, Gender-Role Beliefs, and Reluctance to Relocate for a Job." *American Journal of Sociology* 97, 1992: 1241–1268.

Biernat, Monica, and Wortman, Camille B. "Sharing of Home Responsibilities between Professional Employed Women and Their Husbands." *Journal of Personality and Social Psychology* 60, 1991: 844–860.

Biller, Henry B. *Fathers and Families: Paternal Factors in Child Development.* Westport, CT: Auburn House, 1993.

Black, Dan, Gates, Gary, Sanders, Seth, and Taylor, Lowell. "Demographics of the Gay and Lesbian Population in the U.S.: Evidence from Available Systematic Data Sources." *Demography* 37, 2000: 129–150.

Blau, Francine D., and Grossberg, Adam J. "Maternal Labor Supply and Children's Cognitive Development." NBER Working Paper no. 3536. Cambridge, MA: National Bureau of Economic Research, 1990.

Blau, Francine, Ferber, Marianne, and Winkler, Anne. *The Economics of Women, Men, and Work.* Upper Saddle River, NJ: Prentice-Hall, 2001.

Blau, Peter M. *Exchange and Power in Social Life.* New York: Wiley, 1964.

Blood, Robert O., and Wolfe, Donald M. *Husbands and Wives: The Dynamics of Married Living.* New York: Free Press, 1960.

Blumstein, Philip, and Schwartz, Pepper. *American Couples: Money, Work, and Sex.* New York: William Morrow, 1983.

Boeringer, Scott, Shehan, Constance, and Akers, Ronald. "Social Contexts and Social Learning in Sexual Coercion and Aggression: Assessing the Contribution of Fraternity Membership." *Family Relations* 40, 1991: 58–64.

Bohannan, Paul. "The Six Stations of Divorce." In Paul Bohannan (ed.), *Divorce and After*, pp. 33–62. Garden City, NY: Anchor Books, 1971.

Booth, Alan. "Beliefs and Behavior: Does Religion Matter in Today's Marriage?" *Journal of Marriage and the Family* 57(3), 1995: 661–672.

Booth, Alan, and Johnson, David. "Premarital Cohabitation and Marital Success." *Journal of Family Issues* 9, 1988: 255–272.

Booth, Alan, Johnson, D. R., and White, Lynn K. "Women, Outside Employment, and Marital Instability." *American Journal of Sociology* 90, 1984: 567–592.

Bott, Elizabeth. *Family and Social Network.* London: Tavistock, 1957.

Brackett, Kimberly P. "Doing Gender in Everyday Situations: An Examination of Heterosexual Dating." Unpublished doctoral dissertation, University of Florida, Gainesville, 1996.

Bradbury, Thomas N., Fincham, Frank D., and Beach, Steven R. H. "Research on the Nature and Determinants of Marital Satisfaction: A Decade in Review." *Journal of Marriage and the Family* 62(4), 2000: 964–980.

Bramlett, Matthew J., and Mosher, William S. "First Marriage, Dissolution, Divorce, and Remarriage: United States." Advance Data from Vital and Health Statistics, number 323. Hyattsville, MD: National Center for Health Statistics, 2001.

Breathnach, Sarah Ban. "The World According to the Unborn . . . and After." *Washington Post*, January 10, 1983, p. B5.

Brennan, Robert T., Barnett, Rosalind, and Gareis, Karen. "When She Earns More Than He Does: A Longitudinal Study of Dual-Earner Couples." *Journal of Marriage and the Family* 63, 2001: 168–182.

Brewster, K., Cooksey, E., Guilkey, D., and Rindfuss, R. "The Changing Impact of Religion on Sexual and Contraceptive Behavior of Adolescent Women in the United States." *Journal of Marriage and the Family* 60, 1998: 493–504.

Brines, Julie. "Economic Dependency, Gender, and the Division of Labor at Home." *American Journal of Sociology* 100, 1994: 652–688.

Broberg, Anders, Hwang, Carl-Philip, Lamb, Michael, and Ketterlinus, Robert D. "Child Care Effects on Socioemotional and Intellectual Competence in Swedish Preschoolers." In Jeffrey S. Lande, Sandra Scarr, and Nina Gunzenhauser (eds.), *Caring for Children: Challenge to America*, pp. 49–75. Hillsdale, NJ: Erlbaum, 1989.

Broderick, Carlfred. "How to Rewrite Your Marital Script So It Works." *Redbook*, February 1979, pp. 21, 154.

Broderick, Carlfred. *Marriage and the Family*, 3rd ed. Englewood Cliffs, NJ: Prentice Hall, 1989.

Broderick, Carlfred B. *Understanding Family Process: Basics of Family Systems Theory.* Newbury Park, CA: Sage, 1993.

Broderick, Carlfred B., and Schrader, S. "The History of Professional Marriage and Family Therapy." In A. S. Gurman and D. P. Kniskern (eds.), *Handbook of Family Therapy, II*, pp. 3–40. New York: Brunner/Mazel, 1991.

Brody, Elaine. *Women in the Middle: Their Parent-Care Years.* New York: Springer, 1990.

Broman, Clifford L. "Race Differences in Marital Well-Being." *Journal of Marriage and the Family* 55, 1993: 724–732.

Brown, Brett V., Michelsen, Erik, Halle, Tamara, and Moore, Kristin A. "Fathers' Activities with Their Kids." *Child Trends Research Brief* (June). Washington, DC: Child Trends, 2001.

Browning, Don S., and Rodriguez, Gloria. *Reweaving the Social Tapestry: Toward Public Policy for Families.* New York: W. W. Norton, 2002.

Brumberg, Joan Jacobs. *The Body Project: An Intimate History of American Girls.* New York: Random House, 1997.

Brush, Lisa D. "Violent Acts and Injurious Outcomes in Married Couples: Methodological Issues in the National Survey of Families and Households." *Gender and Society* 4: 1990: 56–57.

Bryson, Ken, and Casper, Lynne. "Co-Resident Grandparents and Grandchildren." U.S. Bureau of the Census, *Current Population Reports*, Series P-23, no. 198. Washington, DC: U.S. Government Printing Offfice, 1999.

Buck, Nicholas, and Scott, Jacqueline. "She's Leaving Home: But Why? An Analysis of Young People Leaving the Parental Home." *Journal of Marriage and the Family* 55, 1993: 863–874.

Bumpass, L., and Lu, H. "Trends in Cohabitation and Implications for Children's Family Contexts in the United States." Working Paper no. 98-15. Madison, WI: Center for Demography, University of Wisconsin, 1999.

Bumpass, Larry L., Sweet, James A., and Cherlin, Andrew J. "The Role of Cohabitation in Declining Rates of Marriage." *Journal of Marriage and the Family*, 53, 1991: 913–927.

Bumpass, Larry, Sweet, James, and Cherlin, Andrew. "Changing Patterns of Remarriages." *Journal of Marriage and the Family* 52, 1990: 747–756.

Bureau of Labor Statistics. "Employment Characteristics of Families," Table 5. Available online at www.bls.gov, 2001.

Burgess, Ernest W., and Locke, Harvey J. *The Family: From Institution to Companionship*. New York: American Book Company, 1953.

Burgess, Ernest W., and Wallin, Paul. *Engagement and Marriage*. Philadelphia: Lippincott, 1953.

Burns, Alyson, Mitchell, G., and Obradovich, Stephanie. "Of Sex Roles and Strollers: Female and Male Attention to Toddlers at the Zoo." *Sex Roles* 20, 1989: 309–315.

Burns, John F. "Sex and the Afghan Woman: Islam's Straight Jacket." The *New York Times*, August 29, 1997: p. A4.

Butler, Amy. "Trends in Same-Gender Sexual Partnering, 1988–1998." *The Journal of Sex Research* 37(4), 2000: 333–343.

Buzawa, Eve S., and Buzawa, Carl G. "The Scientific Evidence Is Not Conclusive: Arrest Is No Panacea." In Richard J. Gelles, and Donileen R. Loseke (eds.), *Current Controversies on Family Violence*, pp. 337–356. Newbury Park, CA: Sage, 1993.

Caldwell, M. A., and Peplau, Letitia. "The Balance of Power in Lesbian Relationships." *Sex Roles* 10, 1984: 587–599.

Call, Vaughn, Sprecher, Susan, and Schwartz, Pepper. "The Incidence and Frequency of Marital Sex in a National Sample." *Journal of Marriage and the Family* 57, 1995: 639–652.

Campbell, Angus, Converse, Philip E., and Rodgers, Willard L. *The Quality of American Life: Perceptions, Evaluations, and Satisfactions*. New York: Russell Sage Foundation, 1976.

Cancian, Francesca. "Gender Politics: Love and Power in the Private and Public Sphere." In A. Rossi (ed.), *Gender and the Life Course*, pp. 253–264. New York: Aldine, 1985.

Cancian, Francesca. *Love in America: Gender and Self-Development*. New York: Cambridge University Press, 1987.

Capizzano, Jeffrey, Adams, Gina, and Sonenstein, Feya. "Child Care Arrangements for Children Under Five: Variation Across States." *Assessing the New Federalism Series: National Survey of American Families*, no. B-7. Washington, DC: The Urban Institute, 2000.

Caplan, Lincoln. *An Open Adoption*. New York: Farrar, Straus & Giroux, 1990.

Carr, Deborah, House, James, Neese, Randolph, Wortman, Camille, Sonneja, J., and Kessler, Ronald. *Journal of Gerontology: Social Sciences*, 2001.

Carroll, Joseph. *Majority of Americans Say Roe v. Wade Decision Should Stand*. Princeton, NJ: The Gallup Organization, 2001.

Casper, Lynne M., and Cohen, Phillip N. "How Does POSSLQ Measure Up: Historical Estimates of Cohabitation." *Demography* 37, 2000: 237–245.

Catalyst. *The Next Generation: Today's Professionals, Tomorrow's Leaders*. New York: Catalyst, 2001.

Cate, Rodney, and Lloyd, Sally A. *Courtship*. Newbury Park, CA: Sage, 1992.

Ceci, Stephen J., and Bruck, Maggie. "How Reliable Are Children's Statements? . . . It Depends." *Family Relations* 43, 1994: 255–257.

Chafetz, Janet Saltzman. "The Gender Division of Labor and the Reproduction of Female Disadvantage." In Rae Lesser Blumberg (ed.), *Gender, Family, and Economy: The Triple Overlap*, pp. 74–94. Newbury Park, CA: Sage, 1991.

Chen, Kathy. "Equal Opportunity Isn't a Big Concern for Mosuo Women." *Wall Street Journal*, August 30, 1995.

Cherlin, Andrew J. "Remarriage as an Incomplete Institution." *American Journal of Sociology* 84, 1978: 634–650.

Cherlin, Andrew J. *Marriage, Divorce, Remarriage*, rev. and enlarged ed. Cambridge, MA: Harvard University Press, 1992.

Cherlin, Andrew J., and Furstenberg, Frank F., Jr. *The New American Grandparent: A Place in the Family, a Life Apart*. New York: Basic Books, 1986.

Cherlin, Andrew J., Furstenberg, Frank F., Jr., Chase-Lansdale, P. L., Kiernan, K. E, Robins, P. K., Morrison, D. R., and Teitler, J. O. "Longitudinal Studies of the Effects of Divorce on Children in Great Britain and the United States." *Science* 252, 1991: 1386–1389.

Children's Defense Fund, Child Care and Development Block Grant Reauthorization in 2002. www. cdfactioncouncil.org. 2002

Chodorow, N. *Feminism and Psychoanalytic Theory*. New Haven, CT: Yale University Press, 1990.

Christopher, F. Scott, and Sprecher, Susan. "Sexuality in Marriage, Dating, and Other Relationships: A Decade Review." *Journal of Marriage and the Family* 62, 2000: 999–1017.

Cicirelli, Victor G. "Adult Children and Their Elderly Parents." In Timothy H. Brubaker (ed.). *Family Relationships in Later Life*, pp. 31–46. Beverly Hills, CA: Sage, 1983.

Cicirelli, Victor G. *Family Caregiving: Autonomous and Paternalistic Decision Making*. Newbury Park, CA: Sage, 1992.

Clarke, Sally C. "Advance Report on Final Marriage Statistics, 1989 and 1990" *Monthly Vital Statistics Report* 43 (no. 12, Supplement). Hyattsville, MD: National Center for Health Statistics, 1995b.

Clarke, Sally Cunningham, and Wilson, Barbara Foley. "The Relative Stability of Remarriages: A Cohort Approach Using Vital Statistics." *Family Relations* 43, 1994: 305–310.

Clarke-Stewart, Alison. "Consequences of Child Care for Children's Development." In Alan Booth (ed.), *Child Care in the 1990s: Trends and Consequences*, pp. 63–82. Hillsdale, NJ: Erlbaum, 1992.

Clarke-Stewart, Alison. *Daycare*, rev. ed. Cambridge, MA: Harvard University Press, 1993.

Clark-Nicolas, Patricia, and Gray-Little, Bernadette. "Effect of Economic Resources on Marital Quality in Black Married Couples." *Journal of Marriage and the Family* 53, 1991: 645–655.

Clemetson, Lynette. "Love without Borders: Americans Are Intermarrying Like Never Before, and They're Reshaping Life Couple by Couple." *Newsweek*, September 18, 2000: 62.

Cloud, John. "His Name is Aurora." *Time* September 25, 2000: 90–91.

CNN.com. "Utah Polygamist Sentenced to Five Years." Posted August 24, 2001.

Cobb, S. "Social Support as a Contingency in Psychological Well-Being." *Journal of Health and Social Behavior* 22, 1976: 357–367.

Cohen, Joan Schrager. *Helping Your Grandchildren Through Their Parents' Divorce*. New York: Walker, 1994.

Coker, Ann L., McKeown, Robert E., Sanderson, Maureen, Davis, Keith E., Valois, Robert F., and Huebner, E. Scott. "Severe Dating Violence and Quality of Life Among South Carolina High School Students." *American Journal of Preventive Medicine* 19(4), 2000: 220–227.

Coleman, Marilyn, Ganong, Lawrence, and Fine, Mark. "Reinvestigating Remarriage: Another Decade of Progress." *Journal of Marriage and the Family* 62(4), 2000: 1288–1307.

Collins, Randall. "Conflict Theory and the Advance of Macro-Historical Sociology." In George Ritzer (ed.), *Frontiers of Social Theory*, pp. 68–87. New York: Columbia University Press, 1990.

Coltrane, Scott. *Family Man: Fatherhood, Housework, and Gender Equity*. New York: Oxford University Press, 1996.

Coltrane, Scott. *Gender and Families*. Thousand Oaks, CA: Pine Forge Press, 1998.

Coltrane, Scott. "Research on Household Labor: Modeling and Measuring the Social Embededness of Routine Family Work." *Journal of Marriage and the Family* 62(4), 2000: 1208–1233.

Coltrane, Scott, and Messineo, M. "The Perpetuation of Subtle Prejudice: Race and Gender Imagery in 1990s Television Advertising." *Sex Roles* 42(5/6), 2000: 363–389.

Columbia Encyclopedia. "Bundling." www.bartleby.com/65/bu/bundling.html, 2001. Retrieved on 12/11/01.

Columbia University Clearinghouse on International Developments in Child, Youth, and Family Policies. Comparative Policies and Programs: Family and Child Allowances, 2002. Available on-line at www.childpolicyintl.org/family childallowances.html.

Connors, R. W. "Gender of Infant Differences in Attachment: Associations with Temperament and Caregiving Experiences." Paper presented at the Annual Conference of the British Psychological Society, Oxford, England, 1996.

Conte, Jon R. "Sexual Abuse of Children." In Robert L. Hampton, Thomas P. Gullotta, Gerald R. Adams, Earl H. Potter, III, and Roger P. Weissberg (eds.), *Family Violence: Prevention and Treatment*, pp. 56–85. Newbury Park, CA: Sage, 1993.

Cook, Karen S., O'Brien, Jodi, and Kollock, Peter. "Exchange Theory: A Blueprint for Structure and Process." In George Ritzer (ed.), *Frontiers in Social Theory*, pp. 158–181. New York: Columbia University Press, 1990.

Coontz, Stephanie. *The Way We Really Are*. New York: Basic Books, 1997.

Coontz, Stephanie. *The Way We Never Were: American Families and the Nostalgia Trap*. New York, Basic Books, 2000a.

Coontz, Stephanie. "Historical Perspectives on Family Studies." *Journal of Marriage and the Family* 62(2), 2000b: 283–297.

Corsaro, William A. *The Sociology of Childhood*. Thousand Oaks, CA: Sage, 1997.

Cott, Nancy F. "Divorce and the Changing Status of Women in Eighteenth-Century Massachusetts." In Michael Gordon (ed.), *The American Family in Social-Historical Perspective*, 3rd ed., pp. 347–371. New York: St. Martin's Press, 1983.

Coupland, J. "Discourses of the Commodified Self." *Discourse and Society* 7, 1996: 187–207.

Couturier, Kelly. "Suicide Attempts Fuel Virginity Test Debate." *The Washington Post*, January 27, 1998: p. A18.

Cowan, Carolyn Pape, and Cowan, Philip A. *When Partners Become Parents: The Big Life Change for Couples*. New York: Basic Books, 1992.

Cozby, P. C. "Self-Disclosure: A Literature Review." *Psychological Bulletin* 79, 1973: 73–91.

Crandall, C. S. "Prejudice Against Fat People: Ideology and Self-Interest." *Journal of Personality and Social Psychology* 66, 1994: 882–894.

Crawford, Christine. *Mommie Dearest*. New York: William Morrow, 1978.

Crohan, Susan. "Marital Quality and Conflict Across the Transition to Parenthood: African American and White Couples." *Journal of Marriage and the Family* 58(4), 1996: 933–944.

Crosby, J. F. *Illusion and Disillusion: The Self in Love and Marriage*, 4th ed. Belmont, CA: Wadsworth, 1991.

D'Emilio, John, and Freedman, Estelle B. *Intimate Matters: A History of Sexuality in America*. New York: Harper & Row, 1988.

Darling-Fisher, Cynthia, and Tiedje, Linda Beth. "The Impact of Maternal Employment Characteristics on Fathers' Participation in Child Care." *Family Relations* 39, 1990: 20–26.

Daugherty, Helen Ginn, and Kammeyer, Kenneth C. W. *An Introduction to Population*. New York: Guilford Press, 1995.

DaVanzo, Julie, and Goldscheider, Frances K. "Coming Home Again: Returns to the Parental Home of Young Adults." *Population Studies* 44, 1990: 241–255.

Davidson, Bernard, Balswick, Jack, and Halverson, Charles. "Affective Self-Disclosure and Marital Adjustment: A Test of Equity Theory." *Journal of Marriage and the Family* 45, 1983: 93–102.

Davis, Alan G., and Strong, Philip M. "Working without a Net: The Bachelor and Social Problems." *Sociological Review*, 25, 1977: 109–129.

Davis, Donald. "Portrayals of Women in Prime-Time Network Television: Some Demographic Characteristics." *Sex Roles* 23, 1990: 325–332.

Davis, N. J. "Gender Differences in Masking Negative Emotions: Ability or Motivation?" *Developmental Psychology* 31, 1995: 660–667.

DeLoache, Judy, Cassidy, Deborah, and Carpenter, C. Jan. "The Three Bears Are All Boys: Mothers' Gender Labeling of Neutral Picture Book Characters." *Sex Roles* 17, 1987: 163–179.

DeMaris, Alfred, and Longmore, Monica. "Ideology, Power, and Equity: Testing Competing Explanations for the Perception of Fairness in Household Labor." *Social Forces* 74, 1996: 1043–1071.

deMause, Lloyd (ed.). *The History of Childhood*. New York: Psychohistory Press, 1974.

Demo, David H. "Parent–Child Relations: Assessing Recent Changes." *Journal of Marriage and the Family* 54, 1992: 104–117.

Demo, David H., and Cox, Martha J. "Families with Young Children: A Review of Research in the 1990s." *Journal of Marriage and the Family* 62(4), 2000: 876–895.

Demos, J. *A Little Commonwealth: Family Life in Plymouth Colony*. New York: Oxford University Press, 1970.

Demos, John. *Past, Present and Personal: The Family and the Life Course in American History*. New York: Oxford University Press, 1986.

Denham, S. A., Zoller, D., and Couchoud, E. A. "Socialization of Preschoolers' Emotional Understanding." *Developmental Psychology* 30, 1994: 928–938.

DeParle, Jason. "Welfare Law Weights Heavily on Delta, Where the Jobs Are Few." *New York Times*, October 16, 1997: p. 1A.

Derlega, V., and Chaikin, A. "Privacy and Self-Disclosure in Social Relationships." *Journal of Social Issues* 33, 1977: 102–115.

Desai, Sonalde, Chase-Lansdale, P. Lindsay, and Michael, Robert T. "Mother or Market? Effects of Maternal Employment on the Intellectual Ability of 4 Year Old Children." *Demography* 26, 1989: 545–561.

Desimone, Angie DiFerdinando. "A Bride Discovers that Finding a Groom is the Easy Part: Planning the Wedding—That's the Trouble." *People Magazine* June 3, 1987: 34–39.

DeStefano, Linda, and Colasanto, Diane. "Unlike 1975, Today Most Americans Think Men Have It Better." *Gallup Poll Monthly* (February), 1990: 25–30.

DeVries, Brian. "Grief: Intimacy's Reflection." *Generations*, Summer, 2001: 75–80.

Dobash, R. Emerson, and Dobash, Russell P. *Women, Violence and Social Change*. New York: Routledge, 1992.

Dowling, Claudia. "Miraculous Babies." *Life,* 1993, pp. 75–84.

Downs, W. R., Miller, B. A., Testa, M., and Panek, D. "Long-Term Effects of Parent-to-Child Violence for Women." *Journal of Interpersonal Violence* 7, 1992: 365–382.

Duke, Lynne. "25 Years after Landmark Decision, Still the Rarest of Wedding Bonds." *Washington Post,* June 12, 1992, p. A3.

Dunn, Judy, and Plomin, Robert. *Separate Lives: Why Siblings Are So Different*. New York: Basic Books, 1990.

Durkin, Kevin, and Nugent, Bradley. "Kindergarten Children's Gender-Role Expectations for Television Actors." *Sex Roles* 38(5-6), 1998: 387–403.

Dutton, D., and Aron, A. "Some Evidence of Heightened Sexual Attraction under Conditions of High Anxiety." *Journal of Personality and Social Psychology* 30, 1974: 510–517.

Dykstra, Pearl. "Loneliness Among the Never and Formerly Married: The Importance of Supportive Friendships and a Desire for Independence." *Journal of Gerontology* 50B, 1995: S321–329.

Eagly, Alice H. *Sex Differences in Social Behavior: A Social-Role Interpretation*. Hillsdale, CA: Erlbaum, 1987.

Eakins, Barbara, and Eakins, R. Gene. *Sex Differences in Communication*. Boston: Houghton Mifflin, 1978.

Edelman, Peter. "America's 'Disappeared.'" *Salon.* January 1, 2000: http://salon.com/news/features/2000/01/1/poverty/index.html.

Edens, David. *Marriage: How to Have It the Way You Want It*. Englewood Cliffs, NJ: Prentice Hall, 1982.

Edut, Tali. "Global Woman: Rana Husseini." *HUES*, Summer, 1998: 41.

Edwards, Harry. "Black Muslim and Negro Christian Family Relationships." *Journal of Marriage and the Family* 30, 1968: 605–607.

Egeland, Byron. "A History of Abuse Is a Major Risk Factor for Abusing the Next Generation." In Richard J. Gelles and Donileen R. Loseke (eds.), *Current Controversies on Family Violence*, pp. 197–221. Newbury Park, CA: Sage, 1993.

Egeland, Byron, and Jacobvitz, Deborah. "Intergenerational Continuity of Parental Abuse: Causes and Consequences." Paper presented at the Conference on Biosocial Perspectives in Abuse and Neglect, York, Maine, 1984.

Egeland, Byron, Jacobvitz, Deborah, and Sroufe, L. Alan. "Breaking the Cycle of Abuse." *Child Development* 59, 1988: 1080–1088.

Eggebeen, David, and Uhlenberg, Peter. "Changes in Men's Lives: 1960–1980." *Family Relations* 34, 1985: 251–257.

Ehrensaft, Diane. "The 'Kinderdult:' The New Child Born to Work-Family Conflict." Paper presented at Work and Fam-

ily: Today's Realities, Tomorrow's Visions, conference, Boston, MA, November, 1998.

Ekeh, Peter. *Social Exchange Theory: The Two Traditions*. Cambridge, MA: Harvard University Press, 1974.

Elizabeth, Vivienne. "Cohabitation, Marriage, and the Unruly Consequences of Difference." *Gender and Society* 14(1), 2000: 87–110.

Entwistle, Doris B., and Doering, Susan G. *The First Birth: A Family Turning Point*. Baltimore: Johns Hopkins University Press, 1981.

Erwin, R. J., Gur, R. C., Gur, R. E., Skolnick, B., Mawhinney-Hee, M., and Smailis, J. "Facial Emotion Discrimination: Task Construction and Behavioral Findings in Normal Subjects." *Psychiatry Research* 42, 1992: 231–240.

Espenshade, Thomas J. "Marriage Trends in America: Estimates Implications, and Underlying Causes." *Population and Development Review* 11, 1985: 193–245.

Exter, Thomas. "Everybody Works Hard Except Junior." *American Demographics* 13, 1991: 14.

"Family Health: Viagra, Oral Contraceptives." *MacLeans* 111(25), 1998: 527.

Faust, Kimberly, and McKibbin, Jerome N. "Children and Divorce." In Marvin Sussman, Suzanne Steinmetz, and Gary Peterson (eds.), *Handbook of Marriage and the Family* 2nd ed. New York: Plenum, 1999.

Fausto-Sterling, Anne. *Sexing the Body: Gender Politics and the Construction of Sexuality*. New York: Basic Books, 2000.

Feldman, Ellen. "Till Divorce Do Us Part." *American Heritage* 51(7), 2000: 38–47.

Feldman, Shirley S., and Nash, S. C. "The Transition from Expectancy to Parenthood: Impact of the Firstborn Child on Men and Women." *Sex Roles* 11, 1984: 61–78.

Felson, Richard B. "Aggression and Violence Between Siblings." *Social Psychology Quarterly* 46, 1983: 271–285.

Fields, Jason, and Casper, Lynne. "America's Families and Living Arrangements: March 2000." *Current Population Reports* P20-537. U.S. Census Bureau, Washington, DC, 2001.

Filsinger, Erik E., and Wilson, Margaret R. "Religiosity, Socioeconomic Rewards, and Family Development: Predictors of Marital Adjustment." *Journal of Marriage and the Family* 46, 1984: 663–670.

Fincham, Frank D., Beach, Steven R. H., Moore, Thom, and Diener, Carol. "The Professional Response to Child Sexual Abuse: Whose Interests Are Served?" *Family Relations* 43, 1994: 244–254.

Fincham, Frank, and Bradbury, Thomas N. "Introduction: Psychology and the Study of Marriage." In Frank D. Fincham and Thomas N. Bradbury (eds.), *The Psychology of Marriage,* pp. 1–12. New York: Guilford Press, 1990.

Fine, Mark A., and Fine, David R. "Recent Changes in Laws Affecting Stepfamilies: Suggestions for Legal Reform." *Family Relations* 41, 1992: 334–340.

Finkelhor, David. *Sourcebook on Child Sexual Abuse*. Newbury Park, CA: Sage, 1986.

Finkelhor, David, and Baron, Larry. "High-Risk Children." In David Finkelhor (ed.), *A Sourcebook on Child Sexual Abuse,* pp. 60–88. Newbury Park, CA: Sage, 1986.

Finkelhor, David, and Yllo, Kersti. *License to Rape: Sexual Abuse of Wives*. New York: Free Press, 1985.

Finkelhor, David, with Hotaling, Gerald T., and Yllo, Kersti. *Stopping Family Violence: Research Priorities for the Coming Decade*. Newbury Park, CA: Sage, 1988.

Fischer, J., and Heesacker, M. "Men's and Women's Preferences Regarding Sex-Related and Nurturing Traits in Dating Partners." *Journal of College Student Development* 36(3), 1995: 260–268.

Fischer, Lucy Rose. *Linked Lives: Adult Daughters and Their Mothers*. New York: Harper & Row, 1986.

Fisher-Thompson, D., Sausa, A. D., and Wright, T. F. "Toy Selection for Children: Personality and Toy Request Influences." *Sex Roles* 33, 1995: 239–255.

Fivush, R. "Gender and Emotion in Mother-Child Conversations About the Past." *Journal of Narrative and Life History* 1, 1991: 325–341.

Flynn, Clifton P. "Regional Differences in Attitudes Toward Corporal Punishment." *Journal of Marriage and the Family* 56, 1994: 314–324.

Foley, Lara, and Fraser, James. "A Research Note on Post-Dating Relationships: The Social Embedness of Redefining Romantic Couplings." *Sociological Perspectives* 41(1), 1998: 209–219.

Fouts, G., and Burggraf, K. "Television Situation Comedies: Female Weight, Male Negative Comments, and Audience Reactions." *Sex Roles* 42(9/10), 2000: 925–932.

Fox, Greer Litton, and Murry, Velma McBride. "Gender and Families: Feminist Perspectives and Family Research." *Journal of Marriage and the Family* 62 (4), 2000: 1160–1172.

Frame, Marsha Wiggins, and Shehan, Constance L. "Work and Well-Being in the Two Person Career: Relocation Stress and Coping Among Clergy Husbands and Wives." *Family Relations* 43, 1994: 196–205.

France, David, and Rosenberg, Debra. "The Abortion Pill." *Newsweek* October 9, 2000: 26–30.

Friedman, Debra. *Towards a Structure of Indifference: The Social Origins of Maternal Custody*. New York: Aldine de Gruyter, 1995.

Frieze, Irene Hanson, and Browne, Angela. "Violence in Marriage." In Lloyd Ohlin and Michael Tonry (eds.), *Family Violence*, pp. 163–218. Chicago: University of Chicago Press, 1989.

Fromm, Erich. *The Art of Loving*. New York: Basic Books, 1956.

Furnham, A., and Mak, T. "Sex-role Stereotyping in Television Commercials: A Review and Comparison of Fourteen Studies Done on Five Continents over 25 Years." *Sex Roles* 41(5/6), 1999: 413–437.

Furstenburg, Frank F., Jr. "Industrialization and the American Family: A Look Backward." *American Sociological Review* 31, 1966: 326–337.

Furstenberg, Frank F., Jr., and Spanier, Graham B. *Recycling the Family: Remarriage after Divorce*. Newbury Park, CA: Sage, 1984.

Furstenberg, Frank F., Jr. "The New Extended Family: The Experience of Parents and Children after Remarriage." In Kay Pasley and Marilyn Ihinger-Tallman (eds.), *Remarriage and Stepparenting: Current Research and Theory*, pp. 42–61. New York: Guilford Press, 1987.

Furstenburg, Frank F., Jr. "Good Dads—Bad Dads: Two Faces of Fatherhood." In Andrew J. Cherlin (ed.), *The Changing American Family and Public Policy*, pp. 193–218. Washington, DC: Urban Institute Press, 1988.

Furstenberg, Frank, F., Jr. "The Sociology of Adolescence and Youth in the 1990s: A Critical Commentary." *Journal of Marriage and the Family* 62(4), 2000: 896–910.

Furstenberg, Frank F., Jr., and Cherlin, Andrew J. *Divided Families. What Happens to Children When Parents Part?* Cambridge, MA: Harvard University Press, 1991.

Furstenberg, Frank F., Jr., and Harris, Kathleen Mullan. "The Disappearing American Father? Divorce and the Waning Significance of Biological Parenthood." In Scott J. South and Stewart E. Tolnay (eds.), *The Changing American Family: Sociological and Demographic Perspectives*, pp. 197–223. Boulder, CO: Westview Press, 1992.

Gaelick, Lisa, Bodenhausen, G., and Wyer, Robert S. "Observational Biases in Spouse Interaction: Toward a Cognitive Behavioral Model of Marriage." *Journal of Personality and Social Psychology* 49, 1985: 1246–1265.

Galambos, Nancy L., and Almeida, David M. "Does Parent–Adolescent Conflict Increase in Early Adolescence?" *Journal of Marriage and the Family* 54, 1992: 737–747.

Galinsky, Ellen. *Ask the Children: What America's Children Really Think About WorkingParents*. New York: William Morrow and Company, 1999.

Gallup News Service. "Gallup Poll Analyses: Singles Seek Soul Mate for Marriage." Princeton, NJ: Author, March, 2001.

Gallup, George, and Newport, F. "Virtually All Adults Want Children, But Many of the Reasons Are Intangible." *Gallup Poll Monthly* 297 (June), 1990, pp. 8–22.

Gangestad, S. W. "Sexual Selection and Physical Attractiveness: Implications for Mating Dynamics." *Human Nature* 4, 1993: 205–235.

Ganong, Lawrence H., and Coleman, Marilyn. "Preparing for Remarriage: Anticipating the Issues, Seeking the Solutions." *Family Relations* 38, 1989: 28–33.

Ganong, Lawrence H., and Coleman, Marilyn. *Remarried Family Relationships*. Thousand Oaks, CA: Sage, 1994.

Ganong, Lawrence H., Coleman, Marilyn, and Mistina, Deborah. "Home Is Where They Have to Let You In: Beliefs Regarding Physical Custody Changes of Children Following Divorce." *Journal of Family Issues* 16, 1995: 466–487.

Garbarino, James. "The Incidence and Prevalence of Child Treatment." In Lloyd Ohlin and Michael Tonry (eds.), *Family Violence*, pp. 219–261. Chicago: University of Chicago Press, 1989.

Garza, Joseph M., and Dressel, Paula L. "Sexuality and Later-Life Marriages." In Timothy H. Brubaker (ed.), *Family Relationships in Later Life*, pp. 91–108. Beverly Hills, CA: Sage, 1983.

Gecas, Viktor. "Contexts of Socialization." In Morris Rosenberg and Ralph H. Turner (eds.), *Sociological Perspectives: Social Psychology*, pp. 165–199. New Brunswick, NJ: Transaction Books, 1990.

Gecas, Viktor, and Seff, Monica A. "Families and Adolescents: A Review of the 1980s." *Journal of Marriage and the Family* 52, 1990: 941–958.

Gelles, Richard J. "Methodological Issues in the Study of Family Violence." In Murray A. Straus and Richard J. Gelles (eds.), *Physical Violence in American Families: Risk Factors and Adaptations to Violence in 8,145 Families*, pp. 17–28. New Brunswick, NJ: Transaction Books, 1990.

Gelles, Richard J. "Through a Sociological Lens: Social Structure and Family Violence." In Richard J. Gelles and Donileen R.

Loseke (eds.), *Current Controversies on Family Violence*, pp. 31–46. Newbury Park, CA: Sage, 1993.

Gelles, Richard J., and Conte, Jon R. "Domestic Violence and Sexual Abuse of Children: A Review of Research in the Eighties." *Journal of Marriage and the Family* 52, 1990: 1045–1058.

Gelles, Richard J., and Straus, Murray A. "Determinants of Violence in the Family: Toward a Theoretical Integration." In W. R. Burr, R. Hill, F. I. Nye, and I. Reiss (eds.), *Contemporary Theories about the Family*, pp. 549–581. New York: Free Press, 1979.

Genevie, Lou, and Margolies, Eva. *The Motherhood Report: How Women Feel About Being Mothers*. New York: Macmillan, 1987.

Gerson, Kathleen. "How Women Choose between Employment and Family: A Developmental Perspective." In Naomi Gerstel, and Harriet Engel Gross (eds.), *Families and Work*, pp. 270–288. Philadelphia: Temple University Press, 1987.

Gerstel, Naomi. "Divorce and Stigma." *Social Problems* 34, 1987: 172–186.

Giannarelli, Linda, and Barsimantov, James. "Child Care Expenses of America's Families." *Assessing the New Federalism Series: National Survey of American Families*. Washington, DC: The Urban Institute, 2000.

Gilford, Rosalie. "Contrasts in Marital Satisfaction Throughout Old Age: An Exchange Theory Analysis." *Journal of Gerontology* 39, 1984: 325–333.

Gilford, Rosalie, and Bengston, Vern. "Children and Marital Happiness in Three Generations: Positive and Negative Dimensions." *Journal of Marriage and the Family* 41, 1979: 387–398.

Gilgun, Jane F. "We Shared Something Special: The Moral Discourse of Incest Perpetrators." *Journal of Marriage and the Family* 57, 1995: 265–281.

Glendenning, Frank. "What Is Elder Abuse and Neglect?" In Peter Decalmer, and Frank Glendenning (eds.), *The Mistreatment of Elderly People*, pp. 1–34. Newbury Park, CA: Sage, 1993.

Glenn, Norval. "Quantitative Research on Marital Quality in the 1980s: A Critical Review." *Journal of Marriage and the Family* 52, 1990: 818–831.

Glenn, Norval. "The Recent Trend in Marital Success in the United States." *Journal of Marriage and the Family* 53, 1991: 261–270.

Glenn, Norval. "The Course of Marital Success and Failure in Five American 10-Year Marriage Cohorts." *Journal of Marriage and the Family* 60(3), 1998: 565–577.

Glenn, Norvall, and Marquardt, Elizabeth. *Hooking Up, Hanging Out, and Hoping for Mr. Right: College Women on Dating and Mating Today*. New York: Institute for American Values, 2001.

Glenn, Norval, and Weaver, Charles N. "A Multivariate, Multisurvey Study of Marital Happiness." *Journal of Marriage and the Family* 40, 1978: 269–282.

Glenn, Norval D., and Weaver, Charles N. "Attitudes Toward Premarital, Extramarital, and Homosexual Relations in the 1970s." *Journal of Sex Research* 15, 1979: 108–118.

Glenn, Norval D., and Weaver, Charles N. "The Changing Relationship of Marital Status to Reported Happiness." *Journal of Marriage and the Family* 50, 1988: 317–324.

Glick, Paul, and Lin, Sung-Ling. "Recent Changes in Divorce and Remarriage." *Journal of Marriage and the Family* 48, 1986: 737–747.

Golden, Kristen. "Rana Husseini: A Voice for Justice." *Ms.* July/August, 1998: 36.

Goldscheider, Frances, and Goldscheider, Calvin. *Leaving Home Before Marriage*. Madison: University of Wisconsin Press, 1993a.

Goldscheider, Frances, and Goldscheider, Calvin. "Whose Nest? A Two-Generational View of Leaving Home During the 1980s." *Journal of Marriage and the Family* 55, 1993b: 851–862.

Goldscheider, Frances, and Goldscheider, Calvin. "Leaving and Returning Home in 20th Century America." *Population Bulletin* 48, 1994: 3–35.

Goldscheider, Frances, and LeBourdais, Celine. "The Decline in Age at Leaving Home, 1920–1979." *Sociology and Social Research* 70, 1986: 143–145.

Goldscheider, Frances K., and Goldscheider, Calvin. "The Effects of Childhood Family Structure on Leaving and Returning Home." *Journal of Marriage and the Family* 60, 1998: 745–756.

Goldscheider, Frances K., and Waite, Linda J. *New Families, No Families? The Transformation of the American Home*. Berkeley: University of California Press, 1991.

Goleman, D. *Emotional Intelligence*. New York: Bantam Books, 1996.

Golub, S. *Periods: From Menarche to Menopause*. Newbury Park, CA: Sage, 1992.

Gonzales, M., and Meyers, S. "Your Mother Would Like Me: Self-Presentation in the Personal Ads of Heterosexual and Homosexual Men and Women." *Personality and Social Psychology Bulletin* 19(2), 1993: 131–141.

Goode, William C. *World Changes in Divorce Patterns*. New Haven, CT: Yale University Press, 1993.

Goode, William J. *After Divorce*. New York: Free Press, 1956.

Goodman, Ellen. "See the Family, Know the Man." *Gainesville Sun*, August 6, 1990, p. 8A.

Goodwin, Doris Kearns. *No Ordinary Time: Franklin and Eleanor Roosevelt: The Home Front in World War II*. New York: Simon & Schuster, 1994.

Gordon, Michael. *The American Family: Past, Present and Future*. New York: Random House, 1978.

Gottman, John M. *Marital Interaction: Experimental Interaction*. New York: Academic Press, 1979.

Gottman, John M., and Silver, Nan. *The Seven Principles for Making Marriage Work*. New York: Three Rivers Press, 1999.

Gouldner, Alvin W. "The Norm of Reciprocity." *American Sociological Review* 25, 1960: 161–178.

Grall, Timothy. "Child Support for Custodial Mothers and Fathers." U.S. Bureau of the Census, *Current Population Reports*, Income 1997, Series P-60, no. 212. Washington, DC: U.S. Government Printing Office, 2000.

Grauerholz, Elizabeth, and Pescosolido, Bernice. "Gender Representation in Children's Literature: 1900–1984." *Gender and Society* 3, 1989: 113–125.

Gray, H. M., and Foshee, V. "Adolescent Dating Violence: Differences Between One-Sided and Mutually Violent Profiles." *Journal of Interpersonal Violence* 12(1), 1997: 126–141.

Greenstein, Theodore. "Marital Disruption and the Employment of Married Women." *Journal of Marriage and the Family* 52, 1990: 657–677.

Greil, Arthur. *Not Yet Pregnant: Infertile Couples in Contemporary America.* New Brunswick, NJ: Rutgers University Press, 1991.

Griffin, William A. *Family Therapy: Fundamentals of Theory and Practice.* New York: Brunner/Mazel, 1993.

Griswold, Robert L. *Family and Divorce in California, 1850–1890: Victorian Illusions and Everyday Realities.* Albany: State University of New York Press, 1982.

Griswold, Robert L. *Fatherhood in America: A History.* New York: Basic Books, 1993.

Guerney, Bernard Jr., and Maxson, Pamela. "Marital and Family Enrichment Research: A Decade Review and Look Ahead." *Journal of Marriage and the Family* 52, 1990: 1127–1135.

Gurman, Alan S., and Kniskern, D. P. (eds.). *Handbook of Family Therapy,* Vol. 2. New York: Brunner/Mazel, 1991.

Gwartney-Gibbs, P., and Stockard, J. "Courtship Aggression and Mixed Sex Groups." In M. Pirog-Good and J. Stets (eds.), *Violence in Dating Relationships,* pp. 185–204. New York: Praeger, 1989.

Hagestad, Gunhild O. "Problems and Promises in the Social Psychology of Intergenerational Relations." In Robert W. Fogel, Elaine Hatfield, Sara B. Kiesler, and Ethal Shanas (eds.), *Aging, Stability and Change in the Family,* pp. 11–46. New York: Academic Press, 1981.

Hagestad, Gunhild O. "Parent–Child Relations in Later Life: Trends and Gaps in Past Research." In Jane B. Lancaster, J. Altmann, Alice S. Rossi, and L. R. Sherrod (eds.), *Parenting across the Life Span: Biosocial Dimensions,* pp. 405–434. New York: Aldine de Gruyter, 1987.

Halaby, Jamal J. "In Jordan, the Price of Honor is Women's Blood." Women's eNews, www.womensenews.org/article.cfm. Retrieved on June 11, 2001.

Hall, Charles W. "Deadbeat Dad Gets Rare Jail Time." *Washington Post,* February 7, 1996, p. B1.

Hall, David R., and Zhao, John Z. "Cohabitation and Divorce in Canada: Testing the Selectivity Hypothesis." *Journal of Marriage and the Family* 57, 1995: 421–427.

Hall, Judith. *Nonverbal Sex Differences: Communication Accuracy and Expressive Style.* Baltimore: Johns Hopkins University Press, 1984.

Halle, David. *America's Working Man: Work, Home, and Politics Among Blue-Collar Property Owners.* Chicago: University of Chicago Press, 1984.

Halpern, Diane. *Sex Differences in Cognitive Abilities,* 3rd ed. Mahwah, NJ: Erlbaum Associates, 2000.

Handy, X. "How We Really Feel About Fidelity." *Time,* August 31, 1998: 51–54.

Hareven, Tamara K. "Historical Analysis of the Family." In Marvin B. Sussman, and Suzanne K. Steinmetz (eds.), *Handbook of Marriage and the Family,* pp. 37–57. New York: Plenum Press, 1987.

Harris, Allen C. "Ethnicity as a Determinant of Sex Role Identity: A Replication Study of Item Selection for the Bem Sex Role Inventory." *Sex Roles* 31, 1994: 241–273.

Harris, Judith Rich. *The Nurture Assumption: Why Children Turn Out the Way They Do.* New York: The Free Press, 1998.

Harris, Lis. *Holy Days: The World of a Hasidic Family.* New York: Summit, 1986.

Harris, M. B., Walters, L. C., and Washull, S. "Gender and Ethnic Differences in Obesity-Related Behavior: Attitudes in a College Sample." *Journal of Applied Social Psychology* 21, 1991: 1545–1566.

Harry, J. *Gay Couples.* New York: Praeger, 1984.

Harry, J., and Devall, W. B. *The Social Organization of Gay Males.* New York: Praeger, 1978.

Harry, Joseph. "Gay Male and Lesbian Relationships." In Eleanor Macklin, and Roger Rubin (eds.), *Contemporary Families and Alternative Lifestyles: Handbook on Research and Theory,* pp. 216–234. Beverly Hills, CA: Sage, 1983.

Hasday, Jill E. "Contest and Consent: A Legal History of Marital Rape." *California Law Review* 88(5), 2000: 1373–1486.

Hatala, M. N., and Predhodka J. "Content Analysis of Gay Male and Lesbian Personal Advertisements." *Psychological Reports* 78, 1996: 371–374.

Hatfield, E., and Sprecher, S. *Mirror, Mirror . . . : The Importance of Looks in Everyday Life.* Albany, NY: State University of New York Press, 1995.

Hawkins, A., Nock, S. C., Wilson, J., Sanchez, L., and Wright, J. "Attitudes About Covenant Marriage and Divorce: Policy Implications from a Three State Comparison." *Family Relations* 51(2), 2002: 166–176.

Heaton, Tim B. "Religious Homogamy and Marital Satisfaction Reconsidered." *Journal of Marriage and the Family* 46, 1984: 729–733.

Heaton, Tim B., and Albrecht, Stan, L. "The Changing Pattern of Interracial Marriage." *Social Biology* 43, 1996: 203–217.

Heaton, Tim B., Boyd, Karen D., Jolley, Kennion D., and Miller, Bent C. "Influences of Children's Number, Age, Relatedness, Gender, and Problems on Parental and Marital Relationships." *Family Perspective* 30(2), 1996: 131–159.

Hegelson, V. S. "Masculinity, Men's Roles, and Coronary Heart Disease." In D. Sabo, and D. F. Gordon (eds.), *Men's Health and Illness,* pp. 68–104. Thousand Oaks, CA: Sage, 1995.

Heise, L., Ellsberg, M., and Gottenmoeller, M. "Ending Violence Against Women." *Population Reports,* Series L, no. 11. Baltimore: Johns Hopkins University School of Public Health, Population Information Program, December, 1999.

Hendrick, Susan Singer. "Self-Disclosure and Marital Satisfaction." *Journal of Personality and Social Psychology* 40, 1981: 1150–1159.

Hetherington, E. Mavis, and Kelly, John. *For Better or Worse: Divorce Reconsidered.* New York: W. W. Norton, 2002.

Hickman, S. E., and Muehlenhard, Charlene. "By the Semi-Mystical Appearance of a Condom: How Young Women and Men Communicate Sexual Content in Heterosexual Situations." *The Journal of Sex Research* 36, 1999: 258–272.

Hill, C. T. "Attitudes to Love." In A. Campbell (ed.), *The Opposite Sex,* pp. 152–157. Topsfield, MA: Salem House, 1989.

Hill, C. T., and Rubin, Z. *Families Under Stress.* New York: Harper & Row, 1949.

Hill, C. T., and Rubin, Z. "Social Stresses on the Family." *Social Casework* 39 (January), 1958: 139–150.

Hill, C. T., Rubin, Z., and Peplau, L. A. "Breakups before Marriage: The End of 103 Affairs." *Journal of Social Issues* 32, 1976: 147–168.

Himes, Christine L. "Elderly Americans." *Population Bulletin* 56, 2001: 1–39.

Hochschild, Arlie R. *The Managed Heart: Commercialization of Human Feeling.* Berkeley: University of California Press, 1983.

Hochschild, Arlie, with Machung, Anne. *The Second Shift.* New York: Viking Press, 1989.

Hoem, Jan M. "Social Policy and Recent Fertility Change in Sweden." *Population and Development Review* 16, 1990: 735–748.

Hofferth, Sandra L. "The Demand for and Supply of Child Care in the 1990s." In Alan Booth (ed.), *Child Care in the 1990s: Trends and Consequences*, pp. 3–25. Hillsdale, NJ: Erlbaum, 1992.

Hofferth, Sandra L., and Deich, Sharon Gennis. "Recent U.S. Child Care and Family Legislation in Comparative Perspective." *Journal of Family Issues* 15, 1994: 424–448.

Hoffman, Lois W. "Effects of Maternal Employment on the Two-Parent Family." *American Psychologist* 44, 1985: 15–20.

Hoffman, Saul D., and Duncan, Greg J. "What *Are* the Economic Consequences of Divorce?" *Demography* 25, 1988: 485–497.

Hogan, D., Sun, R., and Cornwell, G. "Cohort Differences, Family Structure, and Adolescent Sexual Activity." Presented at the annual meeting of the American Sociological Association, 1998.

Hollingsworth, L. "Promoting Same-Race Adoption for Children of Color." *Social Work* 43(2), 1998: 104–116.

Holman, Thomas, and Li, Bing Dao. "Premarital Factors Influencing Perceived Readiness for Marriage." *Journal of Family Issues* 18(2), 1997: 124–145.

Homans, George C. *Social Behavior: Its Elementary Forms*, 2nd ed. New York: Harcourt Brace Jovanovich, 1973.

Hopper, Joseph. "The Rhetoric of Motives in Divorce." *Journal of Marriage and the Family* 55, 1993: 801–813.

Horney, K. *Feminine Psychology.* New York: Norton, 1967.

Horowitz, A. V. "Sex Role Expectations, Power, and Psychological Distress." *Sex Roles* 8, 1982: 607–623.

Houseknecht, Sharon K. "Childlessness and Marital Adjustment." *Journal of Marriage and the Family* 41, 1979: 259–265.

Houts, Leslie. "Young Women's Wantedness of First Voluntary Sexual Intercourse." Unpublished manuscript, Gainesville, FL, 2002.

Howe, R. F. "Fertility Doctor Accused of Using His Own Sperm." *Washington Post*, November 20, 1991: pp. A1, A38.

Hsu, Spencer. "Fathers Take Case for Joint Custody to Va. Delegates." *Washington Post,* February 28, 1996: D1, D3.

Huber, Joan. "A Theory of Family, Economy, and Gender." In Rae Lesser Blumberg (ed.), *Gender, Family, and Economy: The Triple Overlap*, pp. 35–51. Newbury Park, CA: Sage, 1991.

Human Rights Commission. "States, Cities, and Counties that Prohibit Discrimination Based on Sexual Orientation in Private Employment." www.hrc.com/issues, 1999.

Humphreys, Laud. *Tearoom Trade: Impersonal Sex in Public Places.* New York: Aldine de Gruyter, 1970.

Hunter, R. S., and Kilstrom, N. "Breaking the Cycle in Abusive Families." *American Journal of Psychiatry* 136, 1979: 1320–1322.

Huston, A., Wartella, E., and Donnerstein, E. *Measuring the Effects of Sexual Content in the Media: A Report to the Kaiser Family Foundation.* Menlo Park, CA: Henry J. Kaiser Family Foundation, 1998.

Hyde, Janet. "How Large Are Gender Differences in Aggression: A Developmental Meta-Analysis." *Developmental Psychology* 20, 1984: 722–736.

Ickes, William. "Traditional Gender Roles: Do They Make, and Then Break, Our Relationships?" *Journal of Social Issues* 49(3), 1993: 71–77.

Ingersoll-Dayton, Barit, Neal, Margaret, and Hammer, Leslie. "Aging Parents Helping Adult Children: The Experiences of the Sandwiched Generation." *Family Relations* 58(3), 2001: 262.

Ingrassia, M. "Boy Meets Girl, Boy Beats Girl." *Newsweek*, December 13, 1993, pp. 66–68.

"The Intermarrying Kind: A Gloomy Study Leads Jews to Fear for Their Future." *Newsweek,* July 22, 1991, pp. 48–49.

Island, David, and Letellier, Patrick. *Men Who Beat the Men Who Love Them.* New York: Harrington Park Press, 1991.

ISLAT. "Reproductive Conceptions: A Symposium on Reproductive Technology." Institute for Law, Science, and Technology, University of Chicago–Kent School of Law, Chicago, 1998.

Jacklin, C. N. "Female and Male: Issues of Gender." *American Psychologist* 44, 1989: 127–133.

Jacoby, Susan. "Great Sex: What's Age Got to Do With It?" *Modern Maturity*, September/October, 1999: 43–49.

Jagger, Elizabeth. "Marketing Molly and Melville: Dating in a Post-Modern, Consumer Society." *Sociology* 35(1), 2001: 39.

James, John, and Friedman, Russell. *The Grief Recovery Handbook.* New York: Harper Collins, 1998.

James, S. E., and Murphy, B. C. "Gay and Lesbian Relationships in a Changing Social Context." In C. J. Patterson, and A. R. D'Augelli (eds.), *Lesbian, Gay, and Bisexual Identities in Families: Psychological Perspectives*, pp. 123–135. New York: Oxford University Press, 1998.

Janus, Samuel S., and Janus, Cynthia L. *The Janus Report on Sexual Behavior.* New York: Wiley, 1993.

Jendrick, Margaret Platt. "Grandparents Who Parent Their Grandchildren: Effects on Lifestyle." *Journal of Marriage and the Family* 55, 1993: 609–621.

Johansson, Sten. "'Implicit' Policy and Fertility During Development." *Population and Development Review* 17, 1991: 377–414.

Johnson, David R., Amoloza, Teodora O., and Booth, Alan. "Stability and Developmental Change in Marital Quality: A Three-Wave Panel Analysis." *Journal of Marriage and the Family* 54: 1992: 582–594.

Johnson, Michael P. "Patriarchal Terrorism and Common Couple Violence: Two Forms of Violence Against Women." *Journal of Marriage and the Family* 57, 1995: 283–294.

Johnson, Michael P., and Ferraro, Kathleen J. "Research on Domestic Violence: Making Distinctions." *Journal of Marriage and the Family* 62(4), 2000: 948–963.

Jones, Lisa, and Finkelhor, David. "The Decline in Child Sexual Abuse Cases." *Juvenile Justice Bulletin*, January, 2001, 1–12.

Jorgensen, S., and Gaudy, J. "Self-Disclosure and Satisfaction in Marriage: The Relation Examined." *Family Relations* 29, 1980: 281–287.

Jourard, Sidney. *The Transparent Self,* 2nd ed. New York: Nostrand, 1971.

Jurgens, J. J., and Powers, B. A. "An Exploratory Study of the Menstrual Euphemisms, Beliefs, and Taboos of Head Start Mothers." In D. L. Taylor, and N. F. Woods (eds.), *Menstruation, Health, and Illness,* pp. 35–40. New York: Hemisphere, 1991.

Kach, Julie A., and McGhee, Paul E. "Adjustment of Early Parenthood: The Role of Accuracy of Preparenthood Experiences." *Journal of Family Issues* 3, 1982: 375–388.

Kahn, Joan R., Kalsbeek, William D., and Hofferth, Sandra L. "National Estimates of Teenage Sexual Activity: Evaluating the Comparability of Three National Surveys." *Demography* 25, 1988: 189–204.

Kaiser, C. *The Gay Metropolis, 1940–1996.* Boston: Houghton Mifflin, 1997.

Kaiser Family Foundation. "Changing Standards: Condom Advertising on American Television." A Special Report of the *Kaiser Daily Health Report,* www.kaisernetwork.org/dailyreports/reproductivehealth, 2001.

Kalmuss, Debra, Davidson, Andrew, and Cushman, Linda. "Parenting Expectations, Experiences, and Adjustment to Parenthood: A Test of the Violated Expectations Framework." *Journal of Marriage and the Family* 54, 1992: 516–526.

Kammerman, Sheila K., and Kahn, Alfred J. *Family Policy: Government and Families in Fourteen Countries.* New York: Columbia University Press, 1978.

Kammeyer, Kenneth C. W., Ritzer, George, and Yetman, Norman R. *Sociology: Experiencing Changing Societies,* 7th ed. Boston, MA: Allyn and Bacon, 1997.

Kanin, E. J., Davidson, K. R., and Scheck, S. R. "A Research Note on Male–Female Differentials in the Experience of Heterosexual Love." *Journal of Sex Research* 6, 1970: 64–72.

Kaplan, Lori, and Hennon, Charles B. "Remarriage Education: The Personal Reflections Program." *Family Relations* 41, 1992: 127–134.

Kaufman, G. "The Portrayal of Men's Family Roles in Television Commercials." *Sex Roles* 41(5/5), 1999: 439–458.

Kaufman, Joan, and Zigler, Edward. "Do Abused Children Become Abusive Parents?" *American Journal of Orthopsychiatry* 57, 1987: 186–192.

Kaufman, Joan, and Zigler, Edward. "The Intergenerational Transmission of Abuse Is Overstated." In Richard J. Gelles and Donileen R. Loseke (eds.), *Current Controversies on Family Violence,* pp. 209–221. Newbury Park, CA: Sage, 1993.

Kempe, C. Henry, Silverman, Frederic N., Steele, Brandt F., Droegemueller, William, and Silver, Henry K. "The Battered Child Syndrome." *Journal of the American Medical Association* 181, 1962: 17–24.

Kenwick, D., Keefe, R., Bryan, A., Barr, A., and Brown, S. "Age Preferences and Mate Choices Among Homosexual and Heterosexual: A Case for Modular Psychological Mechanisms." *Journal of Personality and Social Psychology* 69(6), 1995: 1166–1172.

Kephart, W. "Some Correlates of Romantic Love." *Journal of Marriage and the Family* 29, 1967: 470–474.

Kephart, William M., and Zellner, William W. *Extraordinary Groups,* 5th ed. New York: St. Martin's Press, 1994.

Kerckhoff, A. C., and Davis, K. E. "Value Consensus and Need Complementarity in Mate Selection." *American Sociological Review* 27, 1962: 295–303.

Kerckhoff, Alan C. "The Structure of the Conjugal Relationship in Industrial Society." In Marvin B. Sussman, and Betty E. Cogswell (eds.), *Cross-National Family Research,* pp. 53–69. Leiden, Netherlands: E. J. Brill, 1972.

Kilbourne, Jean. *Deadly Persuasion: Why Women and Girls Must Fight the Addictive Power of Advertising.* New York: Free Press, 1999.

Kimball, Meredith M. "Television and Sex–Role Attitudes." In Tannis M. Williams (ed.), *The Impact of Television: A National Experiment in Three Communities.* Orlando, FL: Academic Press, 1986.

Kinship and Family Organization. New York: Wiley, 1966.

Kirchler, E. "Marital Happiness and Interaction in Everyday Surroundings: A Time-Sample Diary Approach for Couples." *Journal of Social and Personal Relationships* 5, 1988: 375–382.

Kitson, Gay C., with Holmes, William M. *Portrait of Divorce: Adjustment to Marital Breakdown.* New York: Guilford Press, 1992.

Kivett, Vira R. "Racial Comparisons of the Grandmother Role: Implications for Strengthening the Family Support System of Older Black Women." *Family Relations* 42, 1993: 165–172.

Knox, D., Kuluzny, M., and Studivant, L. "Abuse in Dating Relationships Among College Students." *College Student Journal* 33(4), 2000: 505.

Knox, D., Zusman, M. E., Mabon, and Shriver, L. "Jealousy in College Student Relationships." *College Student Journal* 33(1), 1999: 152.

Knox, David Jr. *Marriage: Who? When? Why?* Englewood Cliffs, NJ: Prentice-Hall, 1975.

Koestner, R., and Wheeler, L. "Self-Presentation in Personal Advertisements: The Influence of Implicit Norms of Attraction and Role Expectations." *Journal of Social and Personal Relationships* 5, 1988: 149–160.

Kohn, Melvin. *Class and Conformity: A Study in Values,* 2nd ed., with a reassessment. Homewood, IL: Dorsey Press, 1977.

Koivula, N. "Gender Stereotyping in Televised Media Sport Coverage." *Sex Roles* 41(7/8), 1999: 589–604.

Komarovsky, Mirra. *The Unemployed Man and His Family.* New York: Dryden Press, 1940.

Komter, Aafke. "Hidden Power in Marriage." *Gender and Society,* 3, 1989: 187–216.

Kramarae, Cheris. *Women and Men Speaking.* Rowley, MA: Newbury House, 1981.

Krucoff, C. "The Surrogate Baby Boom." *Washington Post,* January 25, 1983, p. C5.

Kuebli, J., Butler, S. A., and Fivush, R. "Mother-child Talk About Past Emotions: Relations of Maternal Language and Child Gender Over Time." *Cognition and Emotion* 9, 1995: 265–283.

Kurdek, Lawrence A. "Divorce History and Self-reported Psychological Distress in Husbands and Wives." *Journal of Marriage and the Family* 52, 1990: 701–708.

Kurdek, Lawrence A. "The Relations between Reported Well-being and Divorce History, Availability of a Proximate

Adult, and Gender." *Journal of Marriage and the Family* 53, 1991: 71–78.

Kurdek, Lawrence A. "Nature and Prediction of Changes in Marital Quality for First-Time Parent and Nonparent Husbands and Wives." *Journal of Family Psychology* 6, 1993: 255–265.

Kurdek, Lawrence A. "The Nature and Correlates of Relationship Quality in Gay, Lesbian, and Heterosexual Cohabiting Couples: A Test of the Contextual, Investment, and Discrepancy Models." In B. Greene, and G. M. Herek (eds.), *Lesbian and Gay Psychology: Theory, Research, and Clinical Applications*, pp. 133–155. Thousand Oaks, CA: Sage, 1994.

Kurdek, Lawrence A. "Lesbian and Gay Couples." In A. R. D'Augelli, and C. J. Patterson (eds.), *Lesbian, Gay, and Bisexual Identities over the Life Span: Psychological Perspectives*, pp. 243–261. New York: Oxford University Press, 1995.

Lacan, J. *Ecrits: A Selection*. London: Tavistock, 1977.

Lakoff, Robin. *Language and Women's Place*. New York: Knopf, 1975.

Lamb, Michael E. "Introduction: The Emergent American Father." In Michael E. Lamb (ed.), *The Father's Role: Cross-Cultural Perspectives*, pp. 3–25. Hillsdale, NJ: Erlbaum, 1987.

Lance, Larry M. "Gender Differences in Heterosexual Dating: A Content Analysis of Personal Advertisements." *The Journal of Men's Studies* 6(3), 1998: 297–306.

Landale, Nancy S., and Fennelly, Katherine. "Informal Unions among Mainland Puerto Ricans: Cohabitation or an Alternative to Legal Marriage?" *Journal of Marriage and the Family* 54, 1992: 269–280.

Landale, Nancy S., and Forste, Renata. "Patterns of Entry into Cohabitation and Marriage among Mainland Puerto Rican Women." *Demography* 28, 1991: 587–607.

Laner, Mary R., and Ventrone, Nicole A. "Dating Scripts Revisited." *Journal of Family Issues* 21(4), 2000: 488–500.

Laner, Mary R., and Ventrone, Nicole A. "Egalitarian Daters/Traditionalist Dates." *Journal of Family Issues* 19(4), 1998: 468–477.

Laner, R. M. "Courtship Abuse and Aggression: Contextual Aspects." *Sociological Spectrum* 3, 1983: 69–83.

Larson, Jeffry, and Holman, Thomas. "Premarital Predictors of Marital Quality and Stability." *Family Relations* 43(2), 1994: 228–238.

Lauer, Jeanette C., and Lauer, Robert. "Marriages Made to Last." *Psychology Today*, June 1985, pp. 22, 24–26.

Lee, Gary R. "Marital Intimacy among Older Persons: The Spouse as Confidant." *Journal of Family Issues* 9, 1988: 273–284.

Lee, Gary R., and Shehan, Constance L. "Retirement and Marital Satisfaction." *Journal of Gerontology: Social Sciences* 44, 1989b: S226–S230.

Lee, Gary R., Willetts, Marion, and Seccombe, Karen. "Widowhood and Depression: Gender Differences." *Research on Aging* 20(5), 1998: 618–631.

Lee, John Alan. "Three Styles of Loving." *Psychology Today* 8(9), 1974: 46–51.

Lee, Sharon M., and Yamanaka, Keiko. "Patterns of Asian American Intermarriage and Marital Assimilation." *Journal of Comparative Family Studies* 21, 1990: 287–305.

"Legality, Morality, and Abortion." *Gallup Poll Monthly*, no. 354 (March), 1995, 30–31.

Leland, John. "Let's Talk About Sex." *Newsweek* 132(26), 1998: 62.

LeMasters, E. E., and DeFrain, John. *Parents in Contemporary America*. Homewood, IL: Dorsey Press, 1983.

Leslie, L., Huston, T., and Johnson, M. "Parental Reactions to Dating: Do They Really Make a Difference?" *Journal of Marriage and the Family* 48, 1986: 57–66.

Lester, D. "Romantic Attitudes toward Love in Men and Women." *Psychological Reports* 56, 1985: 662.

Levin, Irene, and Trost, Jan. "Understanding the Concept of Family." *Family Relations* 41, 1992: 348–351.

Levinger, George. "A Social Psychological Perspective on Marital Dissolution." In George Levinger and Oliver C. Moles (eds.), *Divorce and Separation: Context, Causes, and Consequences*, pp. 37–60. New York: Basic Books, 1979.

Levinson, David. *Family Violence in Cross-Cultural Perspective*. Newbury Park, CA: Sage, 1989.

Lewis, Robert A. "A Developmental Framework for the Analysis of Premarital Dyadic Formation." *Family Process* 11, 1972: 17–48.

Lewis, Robert A. "A Longitudinal Test of a Developmental Framework for Premarital Dyadic Formation." *Journal of Marriage and the Family* 35, 1973: 16–25.

Lewis, Robert A., and Spanier, Graham B. "Theorizing about the Quality and Stability of Marriage." In Wesley R. Burr, Reuben Hill, F. Ivan Nye, and Ira L. Reiss (eds.), *Contemporary Theories about the Family*, pp. 268–294. New York: Free Press, 1979.

Lin, Ge, and Rogerson, Peter. "Elderly Parents and the Geographic Availability of Their Adult Children." *Research on Aging* 17(3), 1995: 303–331.

Lindahl, K. M., and Malik, N. M. "Marital Conflict, Family Processes, and Boys' Externalizing Behavior in Hispanic American and European American Families." *Journal of Clinical Child Psychology* 28, 1999: 12–24.

Lindholm, Charles, and Lindholm, Cherry. "Marriage as Warfare." *Natural History* 88, 1979: 11–20.

Lloyd, Sally, A. "The Dark Side of Courtship." *Family Relations* 40, 1991: 14–20.

Lloyd, Sally A. *The Dark Side of Courtship: Physical and Sexual Aggression*. Thousand Oaks, CA: Sage, 2000.

Lockheed, M. E. "Reshaping the Social Order: The Case of Gender Segregation." *Sex Roles* 14, 1986: 617–628.

Longman, Phillip J. "The Costs of Children." *U.S. News and World Report* 124(12), 1998: 50–57.

Loomis, Laura Spencer, and Booth, Alan. "Multigenerational Caregiving and Well-Being: The Myth of the Beleaguered Sandwich Generation." *Journal of Family Issues* 16, 1995, 131–148.

Lopata, Helena Z. *Current Widowhood: Myths and Realities*. Thousand Oaks, CA: Sage, 1996.

Lopata, Helena Znaniecki. *Circles and Settings: Role Changes of American Women*. Albany: State University of New York Press, 1994.

Lorber, Judith. "Believing is Seeing: Biology as Ideology." *Gender and Society* 7, 1993: 568–581.

Lye, Diane N., and Biblarz, Timothy J. "The Effects of Attitudes Toward Family Life and Gender Roles on Marital Satisfaction." *Journal of Family Issues* 14, 1993: 157–188.

Maccoby, Eleanor E., and Mnookin, Robert H. *Dividing the Child: Social and Legal Dilemmas of Custody*. Cambridge, MA: Harvard University Press, 1992.

Mackey, R. A., and O'Brien, B. A. "Marital Conflict Management: Gender and Ethnic Differences." *Social Work* 43, 1998: 128–141.

Maddock, James W. "Ecology, Ethics, and Responsibility in Family Therapy." *Family Relations* 42, 1993: 116–123.

"The Main Swain . . ." *People* Magazine, June 3, 1991, pp. 38–41.

Makepeace, J. M. "Gender Differences in Courtship Violence Victimization." *Family Relations* 35, 1986: 383–388.

Malinowski, Bronislaw. *Magic, Science, and Religion and Other Essays*. New York: Anchor Books, 1955. First published in 1925.

Mandelbaum, Paul. "Dowry Deaths in India." *Commonweal* 126, 1999: 18.

Margolis, Maxine L. *True to Her Nature: Changing Advice to American Women*. Prospect Heights, IL: Waveland Press, 2000.

Markens, S. "The Problematic of 'Experience:' A Political and Cultural Critique of PMS." *Gender and Society* 10, 1996: 42–58.

Marriott, Michael. "Living in 'Lockdown.'" *Newsweek*, January 23, 1995: pp. 56–57.

Marsiglio, William. "Contemporary Scholarship on Fatherhood." *Journal of Family Issues* 14, 1993: 484–509.

Marsiglio, William, Amato, Paul, Day, Randal D., and Lamb, Michael. "Scholarship on Fatherhood in the 1990s and Beyond." *Journal of Marriage and the Family* 62(4), 2000: 1173–1191.

Marsiglio, William, and Donnelly, Denise. "Sexual Relations in Later Life: A National Study of Married Persons." *Journal of Gerontology: Social Sciences* 46, 1991: S338–S344.

Martin, Joyce A., Hamilton, Brody E., Ventura, Stephanie J., Menacker, Fay, and Park, Melissa. "Births: Final Data for 2000." *National Vital Statistics Report* 20(5), 2002.

Martin, P., and Hummer, R. "Fraternities and Rape on Campus." *Gender and Society* 3, 1989: 457–473.

Masheter, Carol. "Postdivorce Relationships between Ex-spouses: The Roles of Attachment and Interpersonal Conflict." *Journal of Marriage and the Family* 53, 1991: 103–110.

Mason, Mary Ann. *The Custody Wars*. New York: Basic Books, 1999.

Matthews, Tony. http://3.ns.sympatico.cu/tands.matthews/christdivorce.html. 1999

Mauss, Armand L. "Sociological Perspectives on the Mormon Subculture." In Ralph H. Turner and James F. Short, Jr. (eds.), *Annual Review of Sociology*, Vol. 10, pp. 288–315. Palo Alto, CA: Annual Reviews, Inc., 1984.

McAdoo, Harriette Pipes. "The Village Talks: Racial Socialization of Our Children." In Harriette Pipes McAdoo (ed.), *Black Children: Social, Educational, and Parental Environments*, 2nd ed., pp. 47–55. Thousand Oaks, CA: Sage, 2002.

McCall, Michal M. "Courtship as Social Exchange: Some Historical Comparisons." In Bernard Farber (ed.), *Kinship and Family Organization*, pp. 190–200. New York: John Wiley and Sons, 1966.

McCauley, Ann P., and Geller, Judith S. "Decisions for Norplant Programs." *Population Reports*, Series K, no. 4. Baltimore: Johns Hopkins University Press, 1992.

McCubbin, Hamilton I., and Patterson, Joan M. "The Family Stress Process: The Double ABC-X Model of Adjustment and Adaption." In Hamilton I McCubbin, M. B. Sussman, and Joan M. Patterson (eds.), *Social Stress and the Family:*

Advances and Development in Family Stress Theory and Research, pp. 7–37. New York: Haworth Press, 1983.

McLoyd, Vonnie C., Cauce, Ana Mari, Takeuchi, David, and Wilson, Leon. "Marital Processes and Parental Socialization in Families of Color: A Decade Review of Research." *Journal of Marriage and the Family* 62(4), 2000: 1070–1093.

McNeely, R. L., and Robinson-Simpson, Gloria. "The Truth about Domestic Violence: A Falsely Framed Issue." *Social Work* 32, 1987: 485–490.

Menaghan, E. "Marital Stress and Family Transitions: A Panel Analysis." *Journal of Marriage and the Family* 45, 1983: 371–386.

Menefee, Samuel Pyeatt. *Wives for Sale: An Ethnographic Study of British Popular Divorce*. New York: St. Martin's Press, 1981.

Mernissi, Fatima. *Beyond the Veil: Male–Female Dynamics in Modern Muslim Society*. Bloomington: University of Indiana Press, 1987.

Mernissi, Fatima. *Dreams of Trespass: Tales of a Harem Girlhood*. Reading, MA: Addison-Wesley, 1994.

Meyer, Daniel R., and Garasky, Steven. "Custodial Fathers: Myths, Realities, and Child Support Policy." *Journal of Marriage and the Family* 55, 1993: 73–89.

Milhausen, Robin P., and Herold, Edward. "Does the Double Standard Still Exist? Perceptions of University Women." *Journal of Sex Research* 36(4), 1999: 361–369.

Miller, C. T., Rothblum, E. D., Felicio, D., and Brand, P. "Compensating for Stigma: Obese and Non-Obese Women's Reactions to Being Visible." *Personality and Social Psychology Bulletin* 21, 1995: 1093–1106.

Millman, Marcia. *Warm Hearts and Cold Cash: The Intimate Dynamics of Families and Money*. New York: Free Press, 1991.

Mitchell, K., and Wellings, K. "First Sexual Intercourse: Anticipation and Communication. Interviews with Young People in England." *Journal of Adolescence* 21, 1998: 717–726.

Moen, Phyllis. *Women's Two Roles: A Contemporary Dilemma*. New York: Auburn House, 1992.

Moen, Phyllis, and Forest, Kay B. "Strengthening Families: Policy Issues for the Twenty-First Century." In Marvin Sussman, Suzanne K. Steinmetz, and Gary W. Peterson (eds.), *Handbook of Marriage and the Family*, 2nd ed., pp. 633–663. New York: Plenum, 1999.

Moewe, M. C. "Soccer Dads Wanted Proof Goalie Was Girl." *Tampa Tribune-Times*, October 21, 1990.

Morgan, Leslie A. *After Marriage Ends: Economic Consequences for Midlife Women*. Newbury Park, CA: Sage, 1991.

Morley, R. "Wife-Beating and Modernization: The Case of Papua New Guinea." *Journal of Comparative Studies* 25, 1994: 25–52.

Morse, Jodie. "Gender Bender." *Time* November 9, 1998: 62.

Mosher, William D., and Bachrach, Christine. "Childlessness in the United States: Estimates from the National Survey of Family Growth." *Journal of Family Issues* 3, 1982: 517–543.

Mosher, William D., Williams, Linda B., and Johnson, David P. "Religion and Fertility in the United States: New Patterns." *Demography* 29, 1992: 199–214.

Moskoff, William. "Divorce in the USSR." *Journal of Marriage and the Family* 45, 1983: 419–425.

Mott, Frank L., and Haurin, R. Jean. "Linkage Between Sexual Activity and Alcohol Use Among American Adolescents." *Family Planning Perspectives* 20, 1988: 128–136.

Mueller, Karla, and Yoder, Janice D. "Stigmatization of Non-Normative Family Size." *Sex Roles: A Journal of Research*, December, 1999: 901–914.

Murray, Carolyn Bennett, and Mandara, Jelani. "Racial Identity Development in African American Children: Cognitive and Experiential Antecedents." In Harriette Pipes McAdoo (ed.), *Black Children: Social, Educational, and Parental Environments*, 2nd ed., pp. 73–96. Thousand Oaks, CA: Sage, 2002.

Murry, C. B., Strokes, J. E., and Peacock, M. J. "Racial Socialization of African American Children: A Review." In R. L. Jones (ed.), *African American Children, Youth, and Parenting*, pp. 209–229. Hampton, VA: Cobb & Henry, 1999.

Murry, Velma McBride, and Brody, Gene H. "Self Regulation and Self-Worth of Black Children Reared in Economically Stressed, Rural, Single-Mother Headed Families." *Journal of Family Issues* 51(2), 1999: 112–121.

Murstein, B. I. "Stimulus–Value–Response: A Theory of Marital Choice." *Journal of Marriage and the Family* 32, 1970: 465–481.

Nakonezny, Paul A., Shull, Robert D., and Rodgers, Joseph Lee. "The Effect of No-Fault Divorce Law on the Divorce Rate Across the 50 States and Its Relation to Income, Education, and Religiosity." *Journal of Marriage and the Family* 57, 1995: 477–488.

Nash, Philip Tajitsu. "When Marriage Was Illegal." *Washington Post*, June 14, 1992, p. C5.

National Adoption Information Clearinghouse. *Adoption Statistics: A Brief Overview of the Data*. Washington, DC: Author, 2002.

Neumann, P. J., Gharib, S. D., and Weinstein, M. C. "The Cost of a Successful Delivery with *In Vitro* Fertilization." *New England Journal of Medicine* 331, 1994: 239–243.

Noland, Virginia, and Liller, Karen. "An Exploratory Study of Adolescent Sibling Violence." Published abstract from the 128th Conference of the Public Health Association, Boston, MA, 2000.

Noller, Patricia, and Fitzpatrick, Mary Anne. "Marital Communication in the Eighties." *Journal of Marriage and the Family* 52, 1990: 832–843.

Nolo.com. "Same-Sex Marriages: A History of the Law." See Marriages and Living Together page, Lesbian and Gay Couples at Nolo.com. Available on August 14, 2002.

Norton, Arthur J., and Miller, Louisa F. "Marriage, Divorce, and Remarriage in the 1990s." *Current Population Reports*, Series P-23, no. 180. Washington, DC: U.S. Government Printing Office, 1992.

Nussbaum, J., Pecchioni, L., Robinson, J., and Thompson, T. L. *Communication and Aging*, 2nd ed. Mahwah, NJ: Lawrence Erlbaum, 2000.

O'Leary, K. Daniel. "Through a Psychological Lens: Personality Traits, Personality Disorders, and Levels of Violence." In Richard J. Gelles, and Donileen R. Loseke (eds.), *Current Controversies on Family Violence*, pp. 7–30. Newbury Park, CA: Sage, 1993.

O'Sullivan, L., and Allgeier, E. Rice. "Feigning Sexual Desire: Consenting to Unwanted Sexual Activity in Heterosexual Dating Relationships." *The Journal of Sex Research* 35, 1998: 234–243.

Oakley, Ann. *Becoming a Mother*. New York: Schocken Books, 1980.

Odean, Kathleen. *Great Books for Girls*. New York: Ballantine Trade Paperbacks, 1997.

Odell, Mark, and Stewart, Scott Philip. "Ethical Issues Associated with Client Values Conversion and Therapist Value Agendas in Family Therapy." *Family Relations* 42, 1993: 128–133.

Orenstein, P. *Schoolgirls: Young Women, Self-esteem and the Confidence Gap*. New York: Anchor/Doubleday, 1994.

Ortega, Suzanne, Whitt, Hugh P., and Williams, J. Allen, Jr. "Religious Homogamy and Marital Happiness." *Journal of Family Issues* 9, 1988: 224–239.

Overbye, Dennis. *Einstein in Love: A Scientific Romance*. New York: Viking, 2001.

Pagelow, Mildred Daley. "The Incidence and Prevalence of Criminal Abuse of Other Family Members." In Lloyd Ohlin and Michael Tonry (eds.), *Family Violence*, pp. 263–313. Chicago: University of Chicago Press, 1989.

Palmore, Erdman. *Social Patterns in Normal Aging: Findings from the Duke Longitudinal Study*. Durham, NC: Duke University Press, 1981.

Papanek, Helena. "Men, Women, and Work: Reflections on the Two-Person Career." *American Journal of Sociology* 78, 1972: 852–872.

Parcel, Toby L., and Menaghan, Elizabeth G. "Early Parental Work, Family Social Capital, and Early Childhood Outcomes." *American Journal of Sociology* 99, 1994a: 972–1009.

Parcel, Toby L., and Menaghan, Elizabeth G. *Parents' Jobs and Children's Lives*. New York: Aldine de Gruyter, 1994b.

Parks, M., Stan, C., and Eggert, L. "Romantic Involvement and Social Network Involvement." *Social Psychology Quarterly* 46, 1983: 116–131.

Parsons, Talcott. "The American Family." In Talcott Parsons and Robert Bales (eds.), *Family, Socialization and Interaction Process*, pp. 3–34. New York: Free Press, 1955.

Pate, Antony M., and Hamilton, Edwin E. "Formal and Informal Deterrents to Domestic Violence: The Dade County Spouse Assault Experiment." *American Sociological Review* 57, 1992: 691–697.

Patterson, Charlotte. "Family Relationships of Lesbians and Gay Men." *Journal of Marriage and the Family* 62(4), 2000: 1052–1068.

Pear, Robert. "Poverty is Cited as Divorce Factor." *New York Times*, January 15, 1993: p. A6.

Pearson, Judy C., Turner, Lynn, and Todd-Mancillas, William. *Gender and Communication*, 2nd ed. Dubuque, IA: William C. Brown, 1991.

Peirce, K., and McBride, M. "Aunt Jemima Isn't Keeping Up with the Energizer Bunny: Stereotyping of Animated Spokes-characters in Advertising." *Sex Roles* 40(11/12), 1999: 959–968.

Pence, Elaine, and Paymar, Michael. *Education Groups for Men Who Batter: The Duluth Model*. New York: Springer, 1993.

Peplau, Letitia. "Lesbian and Gay Relationships." In J. C. Gonsiorek, and J. D. Weinrich (eds.), *Homosexuality: Research Implications for Public Policy*, pp. 177–196. Newbury Park, CA: Sage, 1991.

Peplau, L., and Cochran, S. "A Relationship Perspective on Homosexuality." In D. P. McWhirter, S. A. Sanders, and J. Reinisch (eds.), *Homosexuality/Heterosexuality: Concepts of Sexual Orientation*, pp. 321–349. New York: Oxford University Press, 1990.

Peplau, L., Veniegas, R. C., and Campbell. S. "Gay and Lesbian Relationships." *Journal of Social Issues* 40(3), 1996: 31–52.

Peretti, P. O., and Pudowski, B. C. "Influence of Jealousy on Male and Female College Student Daters." *Social Behavior and Personality* 25, 1997: 155–166.

Peterson, J. A., and Payne, B. *Love in the Later Years.* New York: Association Press, 1975.

Peterson, James L., and Nord, Christine Winquist. "The Regular Receipt of Child Support: A Multistep Process." *Journal of Marriage and the Family* 52, 1990: 539–551.

Piercy, Fred P., and Sprenkle, Douglas H. "Marriage and Family Therapy: A Decade Review." *Journal of Marriage and the Family* 52, 1990: 1116–1126.

Pillemer, Karl A., and Finkelhor, David. "The Prevalence of Elder Abuse: A Random Sample Survey." *The Gerontologist* 28, 1988: 51–57.

Pillemer, Karl A., and Moore, D. W. "Abuse of Patients in Nursing Homes: Findings from a Survey of Staff." *The Gerontologist* 29, 1989: 3114–3120.

Pineo, Peter C. "Disenchantment in the Later Years of Marriage." *Journal of Marriage and the Family* 23, 1961: 3–11.

Pines, A. *Romantic Jealousy: Understanding and Conquering the Shadow of Love.* New York: St. Martins, 1992.

Pleck, Joseph. "The Work–Family Role System." In Patricia Voydanoff (ed.), *Work and Family: Changing Roles and Men and Women*, pp. 8–20. Palo Alto, CA: Mayfield, 1984.

Pogrebin, Letty Cottin. *Family Politics: Love and Power on the Intimate Frontier.* New York: McGraw-Hill, 1983.

Pomerleau, Andree, Bolduc, Daniel, Malcuit, Gerard, and Cossette, Louise. "Pink or Blue: Environmental Gender Stereotypes in the First Two Years of Life." *Sex Roles* 22, 1990: 359–367.

Ponzetti, James J., Zvonkovic, Anisa M., Cate, Rodney M., and Huston, Ted L. "Reasons for Divorce: A Comparison Between Former Partners." *Journal of Divorce and Remarriage* 17, 1992: 183–201.

Popenoe, David. *Disturbing the Nest: Family Change and Decline in Modern Society.* New York: Aldine de Gruyter, 1988.

Popenoe, David. "American Family Decline, 1960– 1990: A Review and Appraisal." *Journal of Marriage and the Family* 55, 1993: 527–555.

Popenoe, David. *Life without Father: Compelling New Evidence that Fatherhood and Marriage are Indispensable for the Good of Children and Society.* New York: Martin Kessler Books, 1996.

Powers, W., and Hutchinson, K. "The Measurement of Communication Apprehension in the Marriage Relationship." *Journal of Marriage and the Family* 41, 1979: 89–95.

Presser, Harriet B. "Employment Schedules among Dual-Earner Spouses and the Division of Household Labor by Gender." *American Sociological Review* 59, 1994: 348–364.

Preston, Samuel, and McDonald, John. "The Incidence of Divorce within Cohorts of American Marriages Contracted Since the Civil War." *Demography* 16, 1979: 1–23.

Quadagno, D., Sly, D., Harrison, D., Eberstein, I., and Soler, H. "Ethnic Differences in Sexual Decisions and Sexual Behavior." *Archives of Sexual Behavior* 27, 1998: 57–75.

Raffaelli, Marcela. "Sibling Conflict in Early Adolescence." *Journal of Marriage and the Family* 54, 1992: 652–663.

Rainwater, Lee. *Family Design: Marital Sexuality, Family Size, and Contraception.* Chicago: Aldine, 1965.

Rank, Mank. "The Formation and Dissolution of Marriages in the Welfare Population." *Journal of Marriage and the Family* 49, 1987: 15–20.

Rathbone-McCuan, Eloise. "Elderly Victims of Family Violence and Neglect." *Social Casework: The Journal of Contemporary Social Work* 61, 1980: 296–304.

Regan, P. C. "Sexual Outcasts: The Perceived Impact of Body Weight on Sexuality." *Journal of Applied Social Psychology* 26, 1996: 1803–1815.

Reid, G. M. "Maternal Sex-Stereotyping of Newborns." *Psychological Reports* 75, 1994: 1443–1450.

Reiss, Ira L. "Toward a Sociology of the Heterosexual Love Relationships." *Marriage and Family Living* 22, 1960: 139–145.

Reisser, Paul. "The Painful Hook in 'Hooking Up.'" *Physician: A Web Site of Focus on the Family*, www. family.org/physmag/issues/a0018313.html, 2001. Retrieved on 12/11/01.

Renick, Mari Jo, Blumberg, Susan L., and Markman, Howard J. "The Prevention and Relationship Enhancement Program (PREP): An Empirically Based Preventive Intervention Program for Couples." *Family Relations* 41, 1992: 141–147.

Renzetti, Claire M. *Violent Betrayal: Partner Abuse in Lesbian Relationships.* Newbury Park, CA: Sage, 1992.

Renzetti, Claire, and Curran, Daniel. *Women, Men, and Society: The Sociology of Gender*, 3rd ed. Boston: Allyn & Bacon, 1995.

Reskin, Barbara, and Padavic, Irene. *Women and Men at Work.* Thousand Oaks, CA: Pine Forge Press, 1994.

Resolve. *Resolving Infertility.* Oxford, MD: Quill (Harper Collins), 1999.

Rexroat, Cynthia, and Shehan, Constance L. "Expected versus Actual Work Roles of Women." *American Sociological Review* 49, 1984: 349–358.

Rexroat, Cynthia, and Shehan, Constance L. "The Family Life Cycle and Spouses' Time in Housework." *Journal of Marriage and the Family* 49, 1987: 737–750.

Rheingold, H. L., and Cook, K. V. "The Content of Boys' and Girls' Rooms as an Index of Parents' Behavior." *Child Development* 46, 1975: 445–463.

Rice, F. Phillip. *Intimate Relationships, Marriages, and Families.* Mountain View, CA: Mayfield, 1990.

Riche, Martha Farnsworth. "The Boomerang Age." *American Demographics* 12, 1990: 25–27, 30, 52–53.

Ridley, Carl A., Wilhelm, Mari, and Surra, Catherine A. "Married Couples' Conflict Responses and Marital Quality." *Journal of Social and Personal Relationships* 18(4), 2001: 517–534.

Rindfuss, Ronald R., and Stephen, Elizabeth H. "Marital Noncohabitation: Absence Does Not Make the Heart Grow Fonder." *Journal of Marriage and the Family* 52, 1990: 259–270.

Risman, Barbara. *Gender Vertigo: American Families in Transition.* New Haven: Yale University Press, 1998.

Ritzer, George. *Sociological Theory*, 4th ed. New York: McGraw-Hill, 1996.

Roberto, Karen A. "Grandparent and Grandchild Relationships." In Timothy H. Brubaker (ed.), *Family Relationships in Later Life*, pp. 100–112. Newbury Park, CA: Sage, 1990.

Robinson, Linda C., and Blanton, Priscilla W. "Marital Strengths in Enduring Marriages." *Family Relations* 42, 1993: 38–45.

Rogers, Stacy, and Amato, Paul "A Longitudinal Study of Marital Problems and Subsequent Divorce." *Journal of Marriage and the Family* 59(3), 1997: 612.

Rogers, S., and DeBoer, D. "Changes in Wives' Income and Effects on Marital Happiness, Well-Being, and Risk of Divorce." *Journal of Marriage and the Family* 63(2), 2001: 458–472.

Rollins, Boyd C., and Galligan, R. "The Developing Child and Marital Satisfaction of Parents." In R. M. Lerner and G. B. Spanier (eds.), *Child Influences on Marital and Family Interaction*, pp. 71–105. New York: Academic Press, 1978.

Roman, Mel, and Haddad, William. *The Disposable Parent: The Case for Joint Custody*. New York: Penguin Books, 1978.

Rose, S., and Frieze, I. A. "Young Singles' Contemporary Dating Scripts." *Sex Roles* 28, 1993: 499–509.

Rosenberg, Morris. *Conceiving the Self*. New York: Basic Books, 1979.

Rosenberg, Morris. "The Self-Concept: Social Product and Social Force." In Morris Rosenberg, and Ralph H. Turner (eds.), *Social Psychology: Sociological Perspectives*, new ed., pp. 593–624. New Brunswick, NJ: Transaction, 1990.

Rosenberg, Morris, and Turner, Ralph H. "Introduction to the Transaction Edition." In Morris Rosenberg and Ralph H. Turner (eds.), *Social Psychology: Sociological Perspectives*, new ed., pp. xv–xxiv. New Brunswick, NJ: Transaction, 1990.

Rossi, Alice S. "Intergenerational Relations: Gender, Norms, and Behavior." In Vern L. Bengston, and W. Andrew Achenbaum (eds.), *The Changing Contract Across Generations*, pp. 191–211. New York: Aldine de Gruyter, 1993.

Rossi, Alice S., and Rossi, Peter H. *Of Human Bonding: Parent–Child Relations Across the Life Course*. New York: Aldine de Gruyter, 1990.

Rowe, D. C. *The Limits of Family Influence: Genes, Experience, and Behavior*. New York: Guilford, 1994.

Rubenstein, C. "How Men and Women Love. *Glamour*, April 1986, pp. 282–283, 356, 359, 361.

Rubin, Jeffrey, Provenzano, Frank, and Luria, Zella. "The Eye of the Beholder: Parents' Views on Sex of Newborns." *American Journal of Orthopsychiatry* 44, 1974: 512–519.

Rubin, Lillian. *Worlds of Pain: Life in the Working Class Family*. New York: Basic Books, 1976.

Rubin, Lillian. *Intimate Strangers: Men and Women Together*. New York: Harper & Row, 1983.

Rubin, Lillian B. *Erotic Wars: What Happened to the Sexual Revolution?* New York: Farrar, Straus & Giroux, 1990.

Rubin, Lillian. *Families on the Fault Line: America's Working Class Speaks about the Family, the Economy, and Ethnicity*. New York: Harper Collins, 1994.

Rubin, Zick. *Liking and Loving: An Invitation to Social Psychology*. New York: Holt, Rinehart, and Winson, 1973.

Russo, Francine. "Not by Viagra Alone." *Time* 157(20), 2001: G3.

Russo, Francine. "When Love Is Mixing It Up: More Couples Are Finding Each Other Across Racial Lines—and Finding Acceptance." *Time* 158 (22), 2001, special bonus section on families.

Rymer, Russ. "Annals of Science: A Silent Childhood—I." *The New Yorker*, April 13, 1992a: 41–81.

Rymer, Russ. "Annals of Science: A Silent Childhood—II." *The New Yorker*, April 20, 1992b: 43–77.

Sabatelli, Ronald M. "Measurement Issues in Marital Research: A Review and Critique of Contemporary Survey Instruments." *Journal of Marriage and the Family* 50, 1988: 891–915.

Sabatelli, Ronald, and Shehan, Constance L. "Exchange and Resource Theories." In P. Boss, W. Doherty, R. LaRossa, W. Schumm, and S. Steinmetz (eds.), *Sourcebook of Family Theories and Methods*, pp. 385–411. New York: Plenum Press, 1993.

Sadker, M., and Sadker, D. *Failing at Fairness: How America's Schools Cheat Girls*. New York: Scribners, 1995.

Saluter, Arlene. "Singleness in America." U.S. Bureau of the Census, *Current Population Reports*, Special Studies, Series P-23, no. 162. Washington, DC: U.S. Government Printing Office, 1989.

Saluter, Arlene. "Marital Status and Living Arrangements: March 1990." U.S. Bureau of the Census, *Current Population Reports*, Series P-20, no. 450. Washington, DC: U.S. Government Printing Office, 1991.

Sanchez, Laura, and Thomson, Elizabeth. "Becoming Mothers and Fathers: Parenthood, Gender, and the Division of Labor." *Gender and Society* 11(6), 1997: 747–773.

Sandberg, John F., and Hofferth, Sandra L. "Changes in Children's Time with Parents, 1981–1997." *Demography* 38(3), 2001: 423–436.

Sapiro, Virginia. *Women in American Society*, 2nd ed. Mountain View, CA: Mayfield, 1990.

Sassler, Sharon, and Schoen, Robert. "The Effect of Attitudes and Economic Activity on Marriage." *Journal of Marriage and the Family* 61, 1999: 147–159.

Sawyer, Kathy. "The Poorest Get Poorer." *Washington Post National Weekly Edition*, August 30, 1999: p. 34.

Scanzoni, John. "Balancing the Policy Interests of Children and Adults." In Elaine A. Anderson, and Richard C. Hula (eds.), *The Reconstruction of Family Policy*, pp. 11–22. New York: Greenwood Press, 1991.

Scanzoni, John, Polonko, Karen, Teachman, Jay, and Thompson, Linda. *The Sexual Bond: Rethinking Families and Close Relationships*. Newbury Park, CA: Sage, 1989.

Scanzoni, Letha Dawson, and Scanzoni, John. *Men, Women, and Change: A Sociology of Marriage and the Family*. New York: McGraw-Hill, 1981.

Schappell, Elissa. "Better Off Deb: Scenes from the Biggest Coming-Out Party of the Year." *New York* 31(1), 1998: 13–15.

Schiebinger, Londa. *Has Feminism Changed Science?* Cambridge, MA: Harvard University Press, 1999.

Schneider, F., Gur, R. C., Gur, R. E., and Muenz, L. R. "Standardized Mood Induction with Happy and Sad Facial Expressions." *Psychiatry Research* 51, 1994: 19–31.

Schoen, Robert, and Weinick, Robin M. "The Slowing Metabolism of Marriage: Figures from 1988 U.S. Marital Status Life Tables." *Demography* 30, 1993: 737–746.

Schooler, Carmi. "Cultural and Social Structural Explanations of Cross-National Psychological Differences." *Annual Review of Sociology* 22, 1996: 323–360.

Schulman, Karen. *The High Cost of Child Care Puts Quality Care Out of Reach for Many Families*. Washington, DC: Children's Defense Fund, 2000.

Schwartz, Lori, and Markham, William. "Sex Stereotyping in Children's Toy Advertisements." *Sex Roles* 12, 1985: 157–170.

Schwartz, Mary Ann, and Scott, Barbara Marliene. *Marriages and Families: Diversity and Change*, 3rd ed. Upper Saddle River, NJ: Prentice-Hall, 2000.

Schwartz, Pepper. "Modernizing Marriage." *Psychology Today*, 27, 1994: 54–59, 86.

Seltzer, Judith A. "Relationship between Fathers and Children Who Live Apart: The Father's Role after Separation." *Journal of Marriage and the Family* 53, 1991: 79–101.

Seltzer, Judith A. "Families Formed Outside of Marriage." *Journal of Marriage and the Family* 62(4), 2000: 1247–1268.

Serbin, Lisa, O'Leary, Daniel, Kent, Ronald, and Tonick, Ilene. "A Comparison of Teacher Response to the Preacademic and Problem Behavior of Boys and Girls." *Child Development* 44, 1973: 796–804.

Shapiro, L. "Guns and Dolls." *Newsweek*, May 28, 1990: 57–65.

Shehan, Constance L. "Honesty between Spouses." *Medical Aspects of Human Sexuality* 16, 1982: 66, 70.

Shehan, Constance L. "Wives' Work and Psychological Well-Being: An Extension of Gove's Social Role Theory of Depression." *Sex Roles* 11, 1984: 881–899.

Shehan, Constance L. "Spouse Support and Vietnam Veterans' Adjustment to Post-Traumatic Stress Disorder." *Family Relations* 36, 1987: 55–60.

Shehan, Constance L. "Social Change and Women's Lives: Using a Life Course Framework to Study the Intersection of Work and Family." Paper presented at the annual meeting of the National Council on Family Relations, Orlando, Florida, November 1992.

Shehan, Constance L. "No Longer a Place for Innocence: The Re-Submergence of Childhood in Post-Industrial Societies." In Constance L. Shehan (ed.), *Through the Eyes of the Child: Revisioning Children as Active Agents of Family Life* (vol. 1), pp. 1–17. Stamford, CT: JAI Press, Inc., 1999.

Shehan, Constance L., and Asmussen, Linda. "Gender Roles and Responsibilities in Contemporary Dating Relationships." Paper presented at the annual meeting of the National Council on Family Relations, November 1992.

Shehan, Constance L., Bock, E. Wilbur, and Lee, Gary R. "Religious Heterogamy, Religiosity, and Marital Happiness: The Case of Catholics." *Journal of Marriage and the Family* 52, 1990: 73–79.

Shehan, Constance L., Burg, Mary Ann, and Rexroat, Cynthia. "Depression and the Social Dimensions of the Full-Time Housewife Role." *Sociological Quarterly* 27, 1986: 403–421.

Shehan, Constance L., and Dwyer, Jeffrey W. "Parent–Child Exchanges in the Middle Years: Attachment and Autonomy in the Transition to Adulthood." In Jay Mancini (ed.), *Aging Parents and Adult Children*, pp. 99–116. Lexington, MA: Lexington Books, 1989.

Shehan, Constance L., and Lee, Gary R. "Roles and Power." In John Touliatos, Barry Perlmutter, and Murraya Straus (eds.), *Handbook of Family Measurement Techniques*, 2nd ed., pp. 420–441. Thousand Oaks, CA: Sage, 2001.

Sherman, Lawrence W., and Smith, Douglas A. "Crime, Punishment, and Stake in Conformity: Legal and Informal Control of Domestic Violence." *American Sociological Review* 57, 1992: 680–690.

Sherman, Lawrence W., with Schmidt, Janell D., and Rogan, Dennis P. *Policing Domestic Violence: Experiments and Dilemmas.* New York: Free Press, 1992.

Shorter, Edward. *A History of Women's Bodies.* New York: Basic Books, 1982.

Shostak, Arthur. "Singlehood." In Marvin Sussman and Suzanne Steinmetz (eds.), *Handbook of Marriage and the Family*, pp. 355–367. New York: Plenum Press, 1987.

Sigler, Robert T. *Domestic Violence in Context: An Assessment of Community Attitudes.* Lexington, MA: Lexington Books, 1989.

Signorielli, Nancy, and Bacue, A. "Recognition and Respect: A Content Analysis of Prime-Time Television Characters Across Three Decades." *Sex Roles* 40(7), 1999: 527–544.

Simenauer, Jacqueline, and Carroll, David. *Singles: The New Americans.* New York: New American Library, 1982.

Simons, Ronald L., Johnson, Christine, Beaman, Jay, and Conger, Rand D. "Explaining Women's Double Jeopardy: Factors That Mediate the Association Between Harsh Treatment as a Child and Violence by a Husband." *Journal of Marriage and the Family* 55, 1993: 713–723.

Simpson, Bob. *Changing Families: An Ethnographic Approach to Divorce and Separation.* Oxford, UK: Berg, 1998.

Sirles, Elizabeth Ann. "Teaching Feminist Family Therapy: Practicing What We Preach." *Journal of Feminist Family Therapy* 6, 1994: 1–18.

Skolnick, Arlene. *Embattled Paradise: The American Family in An Age of Uncertainty.* New York: Basic Books, 1991.

Smith, Daniel S. "The Dating of the American Sexual Revolution." In Michael Gordon (ed.), *The American Family in Social Historical Perspective*, 2nd ed. New York: St. Martin's Press, 1978.

Smith, J., Waldorf, V., and Trembath, D. "Single White Male Looking for Thin, Very Attractive . . ." *Sex Roles* 13, 1990: 675–685.

Smith, Tom W. "American Sexual Behavior; Trends, Socio-Demographic Differences, and Risk Behavior." *General Social Survey Topical Report* Number 25. Chicago: National Opinion Research Center, 1998.

Smith, Tom W. *The Emerging 21st Century American Family.* Chicago: National Opinion Research Center, University of Chicago, 1999.

Smock, Pamela. "Cohabiting in the United States: An Appraisal of Themes, Findings, and Implications." *Annual Review of Sociology* 26, 2000: 1–20.

Snell, Andrea, and Fisher, Ann. "More on the Structure of Male Norms: Exploratory and Multiple Sample Confirmatory Samples." *Psychology of Women Quarterly* 22(2), 1998: 136–156.

Snell, William E. Jr., Belk, Sharyn S., Flowers, Amy, and Warren, James. "Women's and Men's Willingness to Self-Disclose to Therapists and Friends: The Moderating Influence of Instrumental, Expressive, Masculine and Feminine Topics." *Sex Roles* 18, 1988: 769–776.

Snell, William E., Jr., Miller, Rowland S., and Belk, Sharyn S. "Development of the Emotional Self-Disclosure Scale." *Sex Roles* 18, 1988: 59–71.

Sobol, J., Nicolopoulus, V., and Lee, J. "Attitudes About Overweight and Dating Among Secondary School Students." *International Journal of Obesity* 19, 1995: 376–386.

Song, Younghwan, and Lu, Hsien-Hen. *Early Childhood Poverty: A Statistical Profile.* Columbia University, New York: National Center for Children in Poverty, 2002a.

Song, Younghwan, and Lu, Hsien-Hen. *Low Income Children in the United States: A Brief Demographic Profile.* Columbia University, New York: National Center for Children in Poverty, 2002b.

South, Scott J. "Economic Conditions and the Divorce Rate: A Time-Series Analysis of the Postwar United States." *Journal of Marriage and the Family* 47, 1985: 31–41.

South, Scott J., and Spitze, Glenna. "Determinants of Divorce over the Marital Life Course." *American Sociological Review* 51, 1986: 583–590.

Spanier, Graham. "Measuring Dyadic Adjustment: New Scales for Assessing the Quality of Marriage and Similar Dyads." *Journal of Marriage and the Family* 42, 1976: 15–27.

Spence, J., and Helmreich, R. *Masculinity and Femininity.* Austin, Texas: University of Texas Press, 1978.

Spielberger, C., and London, P. "Rage Boomerangs." In C. Borg (ed.), *Annual Editions: Health 85/86*, pp. 77–79. Guilford, CT: Dushkin Publishing, 1985.

Spitze, Glenna, and South, Scott J. "Women's Employment, Time Expenditure, and Divorce." *Journal of Family Issues* 6, 1985: 307–329.

Spock, Benjamin, and Rothenberg, Michael. *Dr. Spock's Baby and Child Care*, 4th ed. New York: Pocket Books, 1985.

Sprecher, Susan, Hatfield, Elaine, Cortese, A., Potapova, E., and Levitskaya, A. "Token Resistance to Sexual Intercourse and Consent to Unwanted Sexual Intercourse: College Students' Dating Experiences in Three Countries." *The Journal of Sex Research* 31, 1994: 125–132.

Sprecher, Susan, and Regan, P. C. "College Virgins: How Men and Women Perceive Their Sexual Status." *Journal of Sex Research* 33, 1996: 3–15.

Stacey, Judith. *Brave New Families: Stories of Domestic Upheaval in Late Twentieth Century America.* New York: Basic Books, 1990.

Stacey, Judith. "Good Riddance to 'The Family:' A Response to David Popenoe." *Journal of Marriage and the Family* 55(3), 1993: 545–548.

Stanley, Scott. "Making a Case for Premarital Education." *Family Relations* 50(3), 2001: 272.

Staples, R. "Health Among African American Males." In D. Sabo, and D. F. Gordon (eds.), *Men's Health and Illness*, pp. 121–138. Thousand Oaks, CA: Sage, 1995.

Stark, Rodney, and McEvoy, James, III. "Middle-Class Violence." *Psychology Today*, November 1970: 52–65.

Stein, Peter J. "Singlehood: An Alternative to Marriage." *The Family Coordinator* 24, 1975: 489–503.

Stein, Peter J. "Understanding Single Adulthood." In P. J. Stein (ed.), *Single Life: Unmarried Adults in Social Context.* New York: St. Martin's Press, 1981.

Steinmetz, Suzanne. "Family Violence: Past, Present, and Future." In Marvin B. Sussman, and Suzanne K. Steinmetz (eds.), *Handbook of Marriage and the Family*, pp. 725–766. New York: Plenum Press, 1987.

Steinmetz, Suzanne K., and Straus, Murray A. "The Family as Cradle of Violence." *Society* 10, 1973: 50–58.

Steinmetz, Suzanne K., and Straus, Murray A. (eds.). *Violence in the Family.* New York: Dodd, Mead, 1974.

Stephen, Elizabeth, and Chandra, Anjani. "Use of Infertility Services in the United States, 1995." *Family Planning Perspectives* 32(3), 2000: 132–142.

Sternberg, R. J. "A Triangular Theory of Love." *Psychological Review* 93, 1986: 119–135.

Sternberg, R. J. *The Triangle of Love: Intimacy, Passion, and Commitment.* New York: Basic Books, 1988.

Stetson, Dorothy McBride. *Women's Rights in the U.S.A.: Policy Debates & Gender Roles.* Pacific Grove, CA: Brooks/Cole, 1991.

Stillion, J. M. "Premature Death Among Males." In D. Sabo, and D. F. Gordon (eds.), *Men's Health and Illness*, pp. 46–67. Thousand Oaks, CA: Sage, 1995.

Stone, Lawrence. *Road to Divorce: England 1530–1987.* New York: Oxford University Press, 1990.

Stoneman, Z., Brody, G. H., and MacKinnon, C. E. "Same-Sex and Cross-Sex Siblings: Activity Choices, Roles, Behavior, and Gender Stereotypes." *Sex Roles* 15, 1986: 495–511.

Stout, Martha. *Without Child: A Compassionate Look at Infertility.* Wheaton, IL: Harold Shaw, 1990.

Straus, Murray A. "Victims and Aggressors in Marital Violence." *American Behavioral Scientist* 23, 1980: 681–704.

Straus, Murray A. "Intrafamily Violence and Crime and Violence Outside the Family." In Murray A. Straus and Richard J. Gelles (eds.), *Physical Violence in American Families: Risk Factors and Adaptations to Violence in 8,145 Families*, pp. 431–470. New Brunswick, NJ: Transaction Books, 1990a.

Straus, Murray A. "The National Family Violence Surveys." In Murray A. Straus and Richard J. Gelles (eds.), *Physical Violence in American Families: Risk Factors and Adaptations to Violence in 8,145 Families*, pp. 3–16. New Brunswick, NJ: Transaction Books, 1990b.

Straus, Murray A. "Physical Violence in American Families: Incidence, Rates, Causes, and Trends." In Dean D. Knudsen, and JoAnn L. Miller (eds.), *Abused and Battered: Social and Legal Responses to Family Violence*, pp. 17–34. New York: Aldine de Gruyter, 1991.

Straus, Murray A., and Gelles, Richard J. "Societal Change and Change in Family Violence from 1975 to 1985 as Revealed in Two National Surveys." *Journal of Marriage and the Family* 48, 1986: 465–479.

Straus, Murray A., and Gelles, Richard J. "How Violent Are American Families? Estimates from the National Family Violence Resurvey and Other Studies." In Murray A. Straus, and Richard J. Gelles (eds.), *Physical Violence in American Families: Risk Factors and Adaptations to Violence in 8,145 Families*, pp. 95–112. New Brunswick, NJ: Transaction Books, 1990a.

Straus, Murray A., and Gelles, Richard J. (eds.). *Physical Violence in American Families: Risk Factors and Adaptations to Violence in 8,145 Families.* New Brunswick, NJ: Transaction Books, 1990b.

Straus, Murray A., Gelles, Richard J., and Steinmetz, Suzanne K. *Behind Closed Doors: Violence in the American Family.* New York: Doubleday, 1980.

Straus, Murray A., and Smith, Christine. "Family Patterns and Child Abuse." In Murray A. Straus and Richard J. Gelles (eds.), *Physical Violence in American Families: Risk Factors and Adaptations to Violence in 8,145 Families*, pp. 245–261. New Brunswick, NJ: Transaction Books, 1990.

Straus, Murray A., Hamby, Sherry L., Boney-McCoy, Sue, and Sugarman, David. "The Revised Conflict Tactics Scale (CTS2)." *Journal of Family Issues* 17(3), 1996: 283–316.

Stryker, Sheldon. "Symbolic Interactionism: Themes and Variations." In Morris Rosenberg, and Ralph H. Turner (eds.), *Social Psychology: Sociological Perspectives*, new ed., pp. 1–29. New Brunswick, NJ: Transaction, 1990.

Stull, Donald E., Bowman, Karen, and Smerglia, Virginia. "Women in the Middle: A Myth in the Making?" *Family Relations* 43, 1994: 319–324.

Suitor, J. Jill. "Marital Quality and Satisfaction with the Division of Household Labor across the Family Life Cycle." *Journal of Marriage and the Family* 53, 1991: 221–230.

Suro, Roberto. "Mixed Doubles: Interethnic Marriages and Marketing Strategies." *American Demographics*, November 1999: 56–62.

Swensen, Clifford H., Eskew, Ron W., and Kohlhepp, Karen A. "Stage of Family Life Cycle, Ego Development, and the Marriage Relationship." *Journal of Marriage and the Family* 43, 1981: 841–853.

Symons, D. "Beauty is in the Adaptations of the Beholder: The Evolutionary Psychology of Human Female Sexual Attractiveness." In P. R. Abramson, and S. D. Pinkerton (eds.), *Sexual Nature, Seuxal Culture*, pp. 80–118. Chicago: University of Chicago Press, 1995.

Symons, Donald. *The Evolution of Human Sexuality.* New York: Oxford University Press, 1979.

Szinovacz, Maximiliane, and Harpster, Paula. "Employment Status, Gender Role Attitudes, and Marital Dependence in Later Life." *Journal of Marriage and the Family* 55, 1993: 927–940.

Tanenbaum, Leora. *Slut! Growing Up Female with a Bad Reputation.* New York: Harper Collins, 2000.

Tannen, Deborah. *You Just Don't Understand: Women and Men in Conversations.* New York: William Morrow, 1990.

Tannen, Deborah. *Talking From 9 to 5: How Women's and Men's Conversational Styles Affect Who Gets Heard, Who Gets Credit, and What Gets Done At Work.* New York: William Morrow, 1994.

Tavris, Carol, and Offir, Carole. *The Longest War: Sex Differences in Perspective,* 2d ed. San Diego: Harcourt Brace Jovanovich, 1984.

Teachman, Jay D. "Socioeconomic Resources of Parents and Award of Child Support in the United States: Some Exploratory Models." *Journal of Marriage and the Family* 52, 1990: 689–699.

Teachman, Jay, Tedrow, L., and Crowder, K." The Changing Demography of America's Families." *Journal of Marriage and the Family* 62, 2000: 1234–1246.

Terman, Lewis M. *Journal of Social Psychology* 6, 1935: 143–171.

The Florida Conference. "Marriage Preparation and Preservation Act Becomes Law January 1, 1999." Press release, December 1, 1998. On-line at www.flacathconf.org.

Thompson, C. *Interpersonal Psychoanalysis: The Selected Papers of Clara M. Thompson.* New York: Basic Books, 1964.

Thompson, Sharon. "Putting a Big Thing into a Little Hole: Teenage Girls' Accounts of Sexual Initiation." *Journal of Sex Research,* 27, 1990: 341–361.

Thompson, Victor. *Modern Organization.* New York: Knopf, 1961.

Thorne, Barrie, and Luria, Zella. "Sexuality and Gender in Children's Daily Worlds." *Social Problems* 33, 1986: 176–190.

Thorne, Barrie, and Yalom, Marilyn (eds.). *Rethinking the Family: Some Feminist Questions.* Boston: Northeastern University Press, 1992.

Thornhill, Randy. "Rape in Panorpa Scorpionflies and a General Rape Hypothesis." *Animal Behavior* 28, 1980: 52–59.

Thornton, Arland, Young-DeMarco, Linda, and Goldscheider, Frances. "Leaving the Parental Nest: The Experience of a Young White Cohort in the 1980s." *Journal of Marriage and the Family* 55, 1993: 216–229.

Thun, M. J., Day-Lally, C. A., Calle, E. E., Flanders, W. D., and Heath, C. W. Jr. "Excess Mortality Among Cigarette Smokers: Changes in a 20-year Interval." *American Journal of Public Health* 85, 1995: 1223–1230.

Tinsley, B., and Parke, R. "Grandparents as Support and Socialization Agents." In Michael Lewis (ed.), *Beyond the Dyad,* pp. 161–194. New York: Plenum Press, 1984.

Tjaden, Patricia, and Thoennes, Nancy. *Extent, Nature, and Consequences of Intimate Partner Violence: Findings from the National Violence Against Women Survey.* Washington, DC: National Institute of Justice and Centers for Disease Control and Prevention, 2000.

Troll, Lillian E. "Grandparents: The Family Watchdogs." In Timothy H. Brubaker (ed.), *Family Relationships,* pp. 63–74. Beverly Hills, CA: Sage, 1983.

Troll, Lillian. "When the World Narrows: Intimacy with the Dead." *Generations* 25, 2001: 55–58.

Tucker, M. Belinda, and Mitchell-Kernan, Claudia. "New Trends in Black American Interracial Marriage: The Social Structural Context." *Journal of Marriage and the Family* 52, 1990: 209–218.

Turner, Joseph. "Deadbeat Dads Could Lose 'Fun' Licenses." *Olympia News Tribune,* January 14, 1996, p. A8.

U.S. Bureau of the Census. "Marital Status and Living Arrangements: March 1998 (update)." U.S. Bureau of the Census, Current Population Reports, Series P-20, no. 514. Washington, DC. www.census.gov/prod/99pubs/p.20-514.pdf, 2000.

U.S. Bureau of the Census. *Statistical Abstract of the United States, 1994.* Washington, DC: U.S. Government Printing Office, 1994.

Ulrich, Laurel. *A Midwife's Tale: The Life of Martha Ballard Based on Her Diary, 1785–1812.* New York: Knopf, 1990.

Vaillant, Caroline O., and Vaillant, George E. "Is the U-Shaped Curve of Marital Satisfaction an Illusion? A 40-Year Study of Marriage." *Journal of Marriage and the Family* 55, 1993: 230–239.

Van Ausdale, Debra, and Feagin, Joe R. *The First R: How Children Learn Race and Racism.* Lanham, MD: Rowan and Littlefield, 2001.

Van den Hoonaard, Deborah Kestin. "No Regrets: Widows' Stories about the Last Days of Their Husbands' Lives." *Journal of Aging Studies* 13(1), 1999: 59–72.

Vandell, Deborah, and Ramanan, Janaki. "Effects of Early and Recent Maternal Employment on Children from Low-Income Families." *Child Development* 63, 1992: 938–949.

Vangelisti, Anita L., and Banski, Mary A. "Couples Debriefing Conversations: The Impact of Gender, Occupations, and Demographic Characteristics." *Family Relations* 42, 1993: 149–157.

Vanzetti, Nelly A., Notarius, Clifford, and NeeSmith, David. "Specific and Generalized Expectancies in Marital Interaction." *Journal of Family Psychology* 6, 1992: 171–183.

Vaughn, Diane. *Uncoupling: Turning Points in Intimate Relationships.* New York: Oxford University Press, 1986.

Veevers, Jean. *Childless by Choice.* Toronto: Butterworths, 1980.

Vemer, Elizabeth, Coleman, Marilyn, Ganong, Lawrence H., and Cooper, Harris. "Marital Satisfaction in Remarriage: A Meta-Analysis." *Journal of Marriage and the Family* 51, 1989: 713–725.

Ventura, S. J., Martin, J. A., Curtin, S. C., Matthews, R.J., and Parks, M.M. "Births: Final Data for 1998." National Vital Statistics Report, volume 48, number 3. Hyattsville, MD: National Center for Health Statistics, 2000.

Ventura, Stephanie J., Matthews, T. J., and Hamilton, Brody. "Births to Teenagers in the United States, 1940–2000." *National Vital Statistics Report* 49, no. 10. Washington, DC: National Center for Health Statistics, 2001.

Ventura, Stephanie, and Bachrach, Christine. "Nonmarital Childbearing in the United States, 1940–2000." *National Vital Statistics Report* 48, no. 16. Washington, DC: National Center for Health Statistics, 2000.

Veroff, Joseph, Sutherland, Lynne, Chadiha, Letha, and Ortega, Robert M. "Predicting Marital Quality With Narrative Assessments of Marital Experience." *Journal of Marriage and the Family* 55, 1993: 326–337.

Wagonner, Glen. "The New Grandparents." *Modern Maturity*, March/April, 2001.

Waite, L. "U.S. Women at Work." *Population Bulletin* 36, 1981: 1–43.

Waldron, I. W. "Why Do Women Live Longer than Men?" In P. Conrad and R. Kern (eds.), *The Sociology of Health and Illness*, pp. 34–44. New York: St. Martin's Press, 1986.

Wallace, Peggy. "Utah Polygamist Receives 5 Year Jail Sentence." The Mormon Research Ministry, 2001. www.mrm.org/index.html, 8/24/01.

Wallerstein, Judith S., and Blakeslee, Sandra. *Second Chances: Men, Women, and Children a Decade After Divorce*. New York: Ticknor and Fields, 1990.

Wallerstein, Judith S., and Kelly, Joan B. *Surviving the Breakup: How Children and Parents Cope with Divorce*. New York: Basic Books, 1980.

Wallerstein, Judith, Lewis, Julia, and Blakeslee, Sandy. *The Unexpected Legacy of Divorce*. New York: Hyperion, 2000.

Walster, E., and Walster, G. W. *A New Look at Love*. Reading, MA: Addison-Wesley, 1978.

Walzer, John F. "A Period of Ambivalence: Eighteenth-Century Childhood." In Lloyd deMause (ed.), *The History of Childhood*, pp. 351–382. New York: Psychohistory Press, 1974.

Walzer, Susan. *Thinking about the Baby: Gender and Transitions into Parenthood*. Philadelphia: Temple University Press, 1998.

Ward, Russell A. "Marital Happiness and Household Equity in Later Life." *Journal of Marriage and the Family* 55, 1993: 427–438.

Ward, Russell, Logan, John, and Spitze, Glenna. "The Influence of Parent and Child Needs on Coresidence in Middle and Later Life." *Journal of Marriage and the Family* 54, 1992: 209–221.

Watts, Jeremy. "The End of Work and the End of Welfare." *Contemporary Sociology* 26, 1997: 409–412.

Webster, Stephen W. "Variations in Defining Family Mistreatment: A Community Survey." In Dean D. Knudsen, and JoAnn L. Miller (eds.), *Abused and Battered: Social and Legal Responses to Family Violence*, pp. 49–61. New York: Aldine de Gruyter, 1991.

Weed, James A. "National Estimates of Marriage Dissolution and Survivorship." *Vital and Health Statistics*. Washington, DC: U.S. Government Printing Office, 1980.

Weg, Ruth B. "Sensuality/Sexuality of the Middle Years." In Ski Hunter, and Martin Sundel (eds.), *Midlife Myths: Issues, Findings, and Practice Implications*, pp. 31–50. Newbury Park, CA: Sage, 1989.

Weiner, M. F. "Healthy and Pathological Love—Psychodynamic Views." In K. S. Pope (ed.), *On Love and Loving: Psychological Perspectives on the Nature and Experience of Romantic Love*, pp. 114–132. San Francisco: Jossey-Bass, 1980.

Weiss, Robert L. "Strategic Behavioral Marital Therapy: Toward a Model for Assessment and Intervention." In J. P. Vincent (ed.), *Advances in Family Intervention, Assessment, and Theory*, vol. 1, pp. 229–271. Greenwich, CT: JAI Press, 1980.

Weiss, Robert L., and Heyman, Richard E. "Observation of Marital Interaction." In Frank D. Fincham, and Thomas N. Bradbury (eds.), *The Psychology of Marriage*, pp. 87–117. New York: Guilford Press, 1990.

Weiss, Robert S. *Going It Alone: The Family Life and Social Situation of the Single Parent*. New York: Basic Books, 1979a.

Weiss, Robert S. *Marital Separation*. New York: Basic Books, 1975.

Weisstein, Naomi. "Tired of Arguing about Biological Inferiority?" *Ms.*, November 1982: 41–42, 45–46, 85.

Weitzman, Lenore J. *The Marriage Contract: Spouses, Lovers, and the Law*. New York: Free Press, 1981.

Weitzman, Lenore J. *The Divorce Revolution: The Unexpected Social and Economic Consequences for Women and Children in America*. New York: Free Press, 1985.

Weitzman, Leonore, Eiffler, Deborah, Hokada, Elizabeth, and Ross, Catherine. "Sex Role Socialization in Picture Books for Preschool Children." *American Journal of Sociology* 77, 1972: 1125–1150.

Welsh, Charles I., III, and Price-Bonham, Sharon. "A Decade of No-Fault Divorce Revisited: California, Georgia, and Washington." *Journal of Marriage and the Family* 45, 1983: 411–418.

Westoff, Leslie A. *The Second Time Around: Remarriage in America*. New York: Viking Press, 1977.

Whitbeck, Les B., Hoyt, Danny R., and Huck, Shirley M. " Family Relationship History, Contemporary Parent–Grandparent Relationship Quality, and the Grandparent–Grandchild Relationship." *Journal of Marriage and the Family* 55, 1993: 1025–1035.

White, Lynn K., and Booth, Alan. "Transition to Parenthood and Marital Quality. *Journal of Family Issues* 6, 1985: 435–450.

White, Lynn. "Determinants of Divorce: A Review of Research in the Eighties." *Journal of Marriage and the Family* 52, 1990: 904–913.

Whitehead, Barbara Dafoe, and Popenoe, David. *Gallup Poll Analyses: Singles Seek Soul Mates for Marriage*. Princeton, NJ: Gallup News Service, 1991.

Whitney-Thomas, Jean, and Hanley-Maxwell, Cheryl. "Packing the Parachute: Parents' Experience as Their Children Prepare to Leave High School." *Exceptional Children* 63(1), 1996: 75–88.

Whyte, Martin King. *Dating, Mating, and Marriage*. New York: Aldine de Gruyter, 1995.

Widom, Cathy S. "The Cycle of Violence." *Science* 244 (April 14), 1989a: 160–166.

Widom, Cathy S. "Does Violence Beget Violence? A Critical Examination of the Literature." *Psychological Bulletin* 106, 1989b: 3–28.

"Widow Hopes to Conceive Baby: Dead Husband's Sperm to Be Used." *Gainesville Sun*, Saturday, June 4, 1994, p. 6B.

Wiederman, Michael, and Hurst, Catherine. "Extra-Dyadic Involvement During Dating." *Journal of Personal and Social Relationships* 16(2), 1998: 265–274.

Wilke, Jane R. "Changes in U.S. Men's Attitudes toward the Family Provider Role." *Gender and Society* 7, 1993: 261–179.

Wilke, Michael. "Changing Standards: Condom Advertising on American Television." A Special Report of the *Kaiser Daily Health Report*, www.kaisernetwork.org/dailyreports/repro ductivehealth, 2001.

Willetts, Marion. "Innovative Dyadic Relationships: A Quantitative and Qualitative Analysis." Unpublished Doctoral Dissertation, Gainesville, FL: University of Florida, 1997.

Williams, J. A., Vernon, J. A., Williams, M. C. and Malecha, K. "Sex Role Socialization in Picture Books: An Update." *Social Science Quarterly* 68, 1987: 148–156.

Wilson, Edmund. *On Human Nature.* Cambridge, MA: Harvard University Press, 1978.

Wilson, Edmund. *The Cooledge Effect: An Evolutionary Account of Human Sexuality.* New York: William Morrow, 1982.

Wilson, Margaret R., and Filsinger, Erik E. "Religiosity and Marital Adjustment: Multidimensional Interrelationships." *Journal of Marriage and the Family* 48, 1986: 147–151.

WIN News. "Africa: Forced Marriage of Young Girls Destroys Their Lives." *WIN News* 25(3), 1999: 56.

WIN News. "Uganda: The Facts About the Tradition of Bride Price." *WIN News* 26(1), 2000: 56.

Wolf, Naomi. *Misconceptions: Truth, Lies, and the Unexpected Journey to Motherhood.* New York: Doubleday, 2001.

Wright, R. "Safe, Not Sound: Is the War on Risk Scaring Our Kids to Death?" *Time*, January 25, 1999: 90.

Zimmerman, Don H., and West, Candace. "Sex Roles, Interruptions, and Silences in Conversation." In Barrie Thorne and Nancy Henley (eds.), *Language and Sex: Difference and Dominance,* pp. 105–129. Rowley, MA: Newbury House, 1975.

Name Index

Subject Index

Photo and Text Credits

PHOTO CREDITS

CHAPTER 1: Page xxxii, Mary Kate Denny/PhotoEdit; 6, Frank Siteman/Stock Boston; 7, Bob Daemmrich/The Image Works; 8, Michelle D. Bridwell/PhotoEdit; 9, Cleve Bryant/PhotoEdit; 16, Spencer Grant/PhotoEdit.

CHAPTER 2: Page 28, Michael Newman/PhotoEdit; 31, James Shaffer/PhotoEdit; 37 and 40, Michael Newman/PhotoEdit.

CHAPTER 3: Page 54, John Kuntz/Reuters/Getty Images; 58, Department of Nuclear Medicine, Charing Cross Hospital/Science Photo Library/Photo Researchers; 65, Tony Freeman/PhotoEdit; 69, David Young-Wolff/PhotoEdit; 70, Fotopic International/Index Stock Imagery; 71, Daniel Bosler/Getty Images.

CHAPTER 4: Page 84, Myrleen Ferguson Cate/PhotoEdit; 91, Bettmann/CORBIS; 93, Bob Torrez/Getty Images; 98, Davis Barber/PhotoEdit; 109, Bob Mahoney/The Image Works; 112, Brian Yarvin/Photo Researchers; 118, Richard Hutchings/Photo Researchers.

CHAPTER 5: Page 126, Michael Newman/PhotoEdit; 128, Pace Gregory/Corbis Sygma; 134, AP/Wide World Photos; 137, Robert E. Daemmrich; 149, Alden Pellett/The Image Works; 153, James D. Wilson/Woodfin Camp & Associates.

CHAPTER 6: Page 160, Myrleen Ferguson Cate/PhotoEdit; 166, Robert E. Daemmrich; 169, John Nordell/Index Stock Imagery; 173, Christopher Brown/Stock, Boston; 176, Momatiuk/Eastcott/Woodfin Camp & Associates.

CHAPTER 7: Page 190, Dagmar Fabricius/Stock, Boston; 195, Paul Fusco/Magnum Photos; 203, Robert Harbison; 213, Bob Daemmrich/Stock, Boston; 216, Tom McCarthy/Index Stock Imagery; 226, Brian Yarvin/The Image Works.

CHAPTER 8: Page 232, Lannis Waters/The Palm Beach Post; 239, Benelux Press/Index Stock Imagery; 245, Bill Aron/PhotoEdit; 249, & Wojdyla/Courtesy of Dunebrook; 256, Rhoda Sidney/Stock, Boston.

CHAPTER 9: Page 266, Bushnell/Soifer/Getty Images; 271, Ted Streshinsky/CORBIS; 273, Michael Newman/PhotoEdit; 278, Lorraine Rorke/The Image Works; 279, Jim Daniels/Index Stock Imagery.

CHAPTER 10: Page 300, Myrleen Ferguson Cate/PhotoEdit; 317, Michael Newman/PhotoEdit; 319, Dennis MacDonald/Index Stock Imagery; 325, Pearson Education/PH College; 331, Marilyn Humphries/The Image Works.

CHAPTER 11: Page 338, Bob Daemmrich/The Image Works; 344, Bob Daemmrich/Stock, Boston; 350, Christopher Brown/Stock Boston; 352, Zigy Kaluzny; 358, Jodi Buren/Woodfin Camp & Associates; 362, Michael Newman/PhotoEdit; 365, Myrleen Ferguson Cate/PhotoEdit.

CHAPTER 12: Page 370, Bruce Ayres/Getty Images; 377, Bettmann/CORBIS; 382, A. Ramey/Woodfin Camp & Associates; 390, Bettmann/CORBIS; 392, James Shaffer/PhotoEdit; 398, Mary Kate Denny/PhotoEdit.

CHAPTER 13: Page 404, Michael Siluk/The Image Works; 408, Bettmann/CORBIS; 417, John Neubauer/PhotoEdit; 421, Bob Krist/CORBIS; 429, Erika Stone/Photo Researchers.

CHAPTER 14: Page 434, Michelle D. Bridwell/PhotoEdit; 446, Bob Daemmrich/Stock, Boston; 451, Lori Adamski Peek/Getty Images; 453, Stephanie Rausser/Getty Images; 454, Janice Fullman/Index Stock Imagery.

CHAPTER 15: Page 462, Bob Daemmrich/The Image Works; 466, Bettmann/CORBIS; 469, PhotoDisc/Getty Images; 475, A. Ramey/Woodfin Camp & Associates; 482, Spencer Grant/Photo Researchers.

TEXT CREDIT

Quoted material on page 89: Reprinted by permission of the publisher from *Family and Continuity in Ireland* by Conrad M. Arensberg and Solon T. Kimball, pp. 109, 111. Cambridge Mass: Harvard University Press, Copyright © 1940, 1968 by the President and Fellows of Harvard College.